CASES, PROBLEMS, AND MATERIALS ON

BANKRUPTCY

FOURTH EDITION

BARRY E. ADLER
New York University

DOUGLAS G. BAIRD
University of Chicago

THOMAS H. JACKSON
University of Rochester

New York, New York
Foundation Press
2007

© 1985, 1989, 1990, 1994, 1997, 1999, 2000, 2001 FOUNDATION PRESS
© 2007 By FOUNDATION PRESS
       395 Hudson Street
       New York, NY 10014
       Phone Toll Free 1–877–888–1330
       Fax (212) 367–6799
       foundation–press.com
Printed in the United States of America

ISBN 978–1–58778–757–7

TEXT IS PRINTED ON 10% POST
CONSUMER RECYCLED PAPER

CONTENTS

PREFACE TO THE FOURTH EDITION

There have been two important developments in the world of bankruptcy since publication of the Revised Third Edition. The first is the Bankruptcy Abuse Prevention and Consumer Protection Act of 2005, which imposes a means test on individual debtors in bankruptcy and tinkers with the rules that govern small business debtors. The second development is not new bankruptcy law, but a significant change in bankruptcy practice. In recent years, the secured creditor has increasingly come to dominate the Chapter 11 reorganization process, usurping the traditional role of prebankruptcy management as the debtor in possession. These developments, along with some important recent cases, are the main subjects of the material added in this edition. Nevertheless, bankruptcy remains a domain with coherent principles that unite it. Focusing on these principles should prepare you for whatever you encounter, regardless when or in what form new bankruptcy legislation comes to us.

We owe others a debt of gratitude for help in the preparation of this book. For his tireless research efforts getting this edition into shape for publication, we thank Scott Pearsall. For their help on this or prior editions, we are grateful to Ronald Barliant, Bernie Black, Marcus Cole, Adrian Davis, David Epstein, Bev Farrell, Larry King, Jonathan Levy, Alan Littman, John Loatman, Leslie Keros, Florencia Marotta-Wurgler, Ed Morrison, Nick Patterson, Thomas Plank, Randy Picker, Tom Planck, Eric Posner, Robert Rasmussen, Larry Ribstein, George Royal, Damian Schaible, Alan Schwartz, Alan Resnick, Omer Tene, George Triantis, Steven Walt, Elizabeth Warren, and Jennifer Weidman. We are also grateful for research support from The Sarah Scaife Foundation, The Lynde and Harry Bradley Foundation, and a New York University School of Law summer research fellowship.

B.E.A.
D.G.B
T.H.J.

July 2007

NOTE ON CITATIONS AND CONVENTIONS

Sections of the Bankruptcy Code are cited by section number only, both in our materials and in the opinions. The Bankruptcy Abuse Prevention and Consumer Protection Act of 2005 is called "the 2005 Bankruptcy Act" or simply "the 2005 Act." Unless otherwise indicated, all citations to Article 9 of the Uniform Commercial Code (or "UCC") are to the revised Article 9, which took effect in most states in July 2001. The term "Bankruptcy Code" or "Code" refers to the current code as enacted in 1978 and as amended thereafter. (The law applicable before 1978 is called "the 1898 Act.") The numbering of some Bankruptcy Code sections or subdivisions has changed over time as a result of amendments. When older cases cite provisions that have not relevantly changed, we have indicated the citation to the current version of the Code in brackets. Generally, ellipses are used to indicate deletion of material within a paragraph, while deletion of material through the end of a paragraph or at the beginning, or more, is indicated by three asterisks. Citations and footnotes are omitted without indication. The original footnote numbering in cases is retained.

Part One

DEBT AND THE NEED
FOR BANKRUPTCY LAW

Extensions of credit help both debtor and creditor. Individuals depend on credit to finance their educations, buy their homes, and organize their lives. Business ventures need capital, and often it makes sense for an investor to make a loan rather than participate in the profits and losses as an equity holder. Loans to individuals and firms typically leave everyone better off. The creditors recover their principal with interest. The individual's life is improved, and the firm participates in a vibrant market economy.

The overwhelming majority of loans to individuals and firms are repaid in full. Social norms and other pressures lead many to repay their loans even in the absence of law. Nevertheless, a creditor's willingness to make loans depends in significant measure on that creditor's ability to call upon the state for help if a debtor does not pay what is owed.

Legal rules governing the collection of debts are in the background of every credit transaction. Much turns on how well crafted those rules are. If they are cumbersome and ineffective, creditors will be more reluctant to lend and debtors will find it harder and more expensive to borrow. On the other hand, if these rules allow creditors to behave in a way that is arbitrary and capricious, people as well as firms will be less likely to borrow. Potential creditors, like potential borrowers, will again be worse off.

Creditors have many remedies they can invoke individually. In addition to these tools that each creditor has at its disposal, our legal system also offers creditors as a group a debt collection remedy. This alternative avenue of debt collection comes into play when a bankruptcy petition is filed either by a group of creditors or by the debtor. The procedural and substantive rules of bankruptcy are the subject of this book.

Because bankruptcy law is only one of the two ways that our legal system adjudicates the rights of debtor and creditor, we must understand the other way to put bankruptcy law in its proper perspective. It is to that subject that we turn in our first chapter. We begin with a simple case in which an unpaid supplier calls on non-bankruptcy rules to recover what it is owed. We then ask how a creditor changes its position under nonbankruptcy law when it takes collateral. With these background rules laid out, we turn in the next chapter to an overview of the Bankruptcy Code and the ways in which it tries to cure the deficiencies that exist under nonbankruptcy law.

As we shall see, nonbankruptcy rules suffer from two distinct problems. First, they are premised on individual creditors pursuing their own remedies. When a debtor has many creditors, the actions of each creditor often run counter to what is in the interest of creditors as a group. Bankruptcy law, in the first instance, responds to this collective action problem, a problem akin to the one that exists when individuals, pursuing their own interest, graze too many cattle in a common pasture. Solving this <u>collective action problem</u> gives the Bankruptcy Code much of its complexity.

Individual debt collection remedies also rest on the premise that debtors have sufficient assets to repay what they owe. Problems arise when this premise proves faulty. Debtors often fail to pay their creditors because they do not have assets sufficient to meet their obligations. Legal rules cannot create assets where none exist. One cannot get blood from a stone. Moreover, debt collection rules premised on the existence of such assets have bad (although quite different) effects on both flesh-and-blood borrowers and on corporate debtors.

In the case of individuals, the nonbankruptcy rules of debt collection, if unchecked, can ruin the life of the debtor and the lives of others. Individuals burdened with debt they cannot pay may cease to be productive members of society. Bankruptcy law ensures that creditors can reach whatever assets they could reach outside of bankruptcy and—so long as the debtor has not abused the system—bankruptcy law then extinguishes these debts and allows individual debtors to get on with their lives. Bankruptcy's fresh start for individuals is an insurance policy. As we shall see, the contours of the fresh start (knowing, for example, what sorts of misbehavior constitute abuse) have proved elusive. This insurance policy is one for which everyone pays in the form of <u>higher interest</u> rates and <u>less available credit</u>. The more generous and more available the fresh start for they who receive it, the greater the costs borne by everyone else.

Even though limited liability corporations are radically different from flesh-and-blood individuals, the rules of individual debt collection sometimes brings unnecessary costs and complications in these cases as well, although for different reasons. First there are firms that cannot pay their creditors because they have failed in the marketplace. For these firms, the ordinary rules of debt collection often do not offer a sensible way to shut them and at the same time parcel out assets in a single forum in a way that respects the rights of different investors.

The more important problem arises when a firm could survive as a going concern if the firm had a capital structure that was consistent with its current condition. Individual rules of debt collection prevent a firm from readjusting its capital structure when its creditors are diverse. Bankruptcy gives the investors a way to act collectively. It enables investors to rearrange their rights to the firm and yet still respects the priority the investors enjoy relative to one another under nonbankruptcy law.

I. INDIVIDUAL DEBT COLLECTION OUTSIDE OF BANKRUPTCY

Like legal rules generally, the rules governing debt collection have both a procedural and a substantive component. Procedurally, these rules tell creditors *how* to enforce their claims against their debtor when the debtor cannot or will not voluntarily pay what is owed. Unless a creditor has taken a security interest—that is, unless it has contracted for collateral to secure its loan—a creditor typically has to go to court. If the creditor prevails in the lawsuit and, to use the standard legal parlance, "reduces its claim to judgment," the creditor may then call on the state to seize the debtor's assets and sell them to repay the creditor. Enforcement of the judgment may involve foreclosing on real property, physically seizing personal property, or requiring some third party (such as an employer) to pay part of what it owes the debtor directly to the creditor. The procedures vary from one jurisdiction to another, but their basic contours are the same.

These procedural rules also demarcate the substantive rights of creditors and debtors. For example, a creditor can lay claim only to a percentage of a worker's wages, and a creditor cannot reach certain types of property (such as spendthrift trusts, clothes, or tools of trade). In the case of a general partnership, creditors can look to the assets of individual partners, but in the case of a corporation, creditors can usually reach only the assets of the corporation itself, not the assets of those who own shares of stock in the corporation.

To put individual creditor rights in perspective, one needs a basic understanding of the essential differences among general creditors, lien creditors, and secured creditors. The materials in this chapter provide an overview of the rights and remedies of these creditors.

In reading these materials, two principal questions should be kept in mind. First, what rights does a particular creditor have against a debtor or the debtor's property? This question is fundamentally a two-party issue and, as such, is governed principally by general rules of contract law. Second, what rights does a particular creditor have against other creditors (or other claimants) to the debtor's property? This second issue is generally referred to as the "priority" question. It focuses on how one creditor gains priority over another as to a particular asset of their common debtor. One of the most important questions in bankruptcy is the extent to which these nonbankruptcy priorities should be recognized inside of bankruptcy.

A. THE RIGHTS OF GENERAL CREDITORS

We start by examining the rights and remedies of a garden-variety creditor. The details of the debt collection process vary, but the basic steps are relatively constant across time and place. Although we shall examine a fairly simple transaction, most of the following discussion applies equally to larger and more complex arrangements. Involuntary creditors, such as tort victims, must follow much the same procedures. Perhaps surprisingly, they enjoy no priority over other kinds of creditors.

Supplier sells suits to local clothing stores, requiring its customers to pay within thirty days of delivery. Supplier discovers that one store, Retailer, has not paid for suits delivered more than sixty days before. Supplier sends Retailer another bill. When this tactic fails, Supplier turns to other nonjudicial remedies. Supplier refuses to ship any more suits. It can also plead with Retailer, or, if Supplier is careful, threaten a lawsuit. Supplier can also "discount" its claim (sell at something less than face amount) to a collection agency that will do the same things as Supplier, but perhaps more effectively. (In that case, of course, the inquiry of creditors' remedies simply shifts from Supplier to a third party.) Supplier might also put pressure on Retailer by reporting Retailer's name to a credit bureau.

These remedies are not trivial. Without new inventory, Retailer will lose customers. Supplier's actions may also destroy Retailer's ability to get credit in the future. But these steps do not always lead to payment. Retailer, for example, may claim that Supplier has delivered defective goods or is otherwise in breach of its obligations. More likely, Retailer lacks the money needed to pay Supplier and its other creditors in full. Retailer may play for time by repaying only the creditors it needs to stay in business.

If these alternatives fail (or if Supplier simply chooses not to use them), Supplier must turn to the judicial process. As an unsecured creditor, Supplier is not permitted, without the actual consent of Retailer (or its agent), to take back the suits from Retailer's store or, indeed, to take any other property of Retailer (such as shirts or overcoats of roughly equivalent value). Self-help remedies are not available to unsecured creditors. (Secured creditors have some ability to engage in self-help. We examine these later in this chapter.)

At this point, obtaining the right to reach Retailer's assets is not Supplier's only worry. Supplier also wants to be sure that its right enjoys priority over those of Retailer's other creditors. Priority against other creditors matters whenever a debtor lacks sufficient assets to pay everyone in full. Outside of bankruptcy, obtaining payment is the best way to ensure priority. Supplier, however, can also use the legal process to establish its priority against other unpaid creditors.

At the early stages of its lawsuit, before Supplier has proven its case, Supplier may be able to take advantage of a "prejudgment" or provisional remedy. These take different forms. Supplier, for example, might be able to have a notice filed in the real estate records or in the records in which security interests in personal property are filed. Alternatively, it might be able to have the sheriff seize (or "attach") some of Retailer's physical assets. These provisional remedies ensure that assets will be available to Supplier if it prevails in the litigation. Once these steps are taken, they establish Supplier's priority over Retailer's other creditors.

Prejudgment remedies, however, are not freely available, and a series of Supreme Court cases in the early 1970s placed significant limits on the ability of an unsecured creditor to reach property of its debtor without first providing some sort of notice and holding a hearing before a judicial officer. See North Georgia Finishing, Inc. v. Di-Chem, Inc., 419 U.S. 601 (1975); Mitchell v. W.T. Grant Co., 416 U.S. 600 (1974); Fuentes v. Shevin, 407 U.S. 67 (1972). Supplier is most likely able to use prejudgment remedies if there is some danger that the debtor will abscond with the assets or might otherwise dissipate them over the course of the litigation. To use a prejudgment remedy, Supplier also may have to post a bond to cover any damages Retailer might suffer if Supplier's action later proves unsuccessful.

If no prejudgment remedies are available, Supplier must win its lawsuit both to establish its priority over other creditors and to obtain Retailer's property. If Supplier wins, the court will issue a "judgment." Even if Retailer does not appear, Supplier can still vindicate its claim and receive a default judgment, which is as effective as any other judgment so long as Supplier follows the proper procedures. Debtors most commonly fail to contest actions brought against them in consumer finance transactions.

Judgments normally resemble the following:

It is ordered and adjudged that Plaintiff recover $500 from Defendant and that Plaintiff have execution therefor.

The judgment is then "docketed," which means it is recorded on a "judgment roll." What happens next turns on the kind of property that Retailer owns. The most basic distinction is between land (real property) and other kinds (personal property). There is also an intermediate category called "fixtures." Fixtures are goods such as large pieces of machinery that are bolted to the factory floor. They are so much a part of the building that they are treated as real property, even though they once were personal property and might be again. The transfer of ownership of real property requires more formalities than the transfer of ownership of personal property. To buy land and have rights against the world, one usually must record one's interest in the public records. By contrast, one typically obtains title to personal property simply by taking physical possession of it. (When the property is in possession of a third party, notification to the third party substitutes for physical possession.) These different rules governing the transfer of ownership in turn affect the way in which a creditor reaches these assets after reducing its claim to judgment.

In most states, a judgment alone establishes a lien (called, not surprisingly, a "judgment lien") on a debtor's real property, including fixtures. In many states, the docketing must be in the county where the property is located. Hence, in these jurisdictions, a judgment rendered in one county must be docketed in all other counties in which the debtor has real property in order for the judgment to cover that property. Once a judgment has been entered, however, docketing is a ministerial act (at least within the jurisdiction of the court issuing the judgment).

A judgment lien does not usually give the creditor a right to immediate possession of the debtor's real property. Often, a judgment lien merely encumbers the property in the creditor's favor—it establishes the creditor's place in line and fixes rights against third parties (including buyers and competing creditors). What the lien gives Supplier is a right to go after the property and priority over all those who acquire later liens or who acquire the property after the lien arises. The moment at which Supplier becomes a lien creditor matters tremendously for bankruptcy as well.

Let us now consider how Supplier reaches Retailer's personal property, such as the suits Supplier sold to Retailer, other items of Retailer's inventory, or the equipment in the store. In virtually every jurisdiction, to reach personal property, Supplier would have to do more than simply ensure that its judgment was entered on the docket roll. The docketing of the judgment only gives Supplier the right to obtain a 'writ of execution' from the clerk of the court. A writ of execution is essentially a collection device issued as a matter of course once Supplier has reduced its claim to judgment.

The writ of execution directs the sheriff to seize and sell sufficient property of Retailer to pay the judgment entered in Supplier's favor. When the property is not readily moveable, the sheriff will take other steps to deprive the debtor of the use of the asset and to put others on notice. These steps include disabling a machine by removing a crucial component or by padlocking the warehouse in which goods are stored. These actions constitute a 'levy' on Retailer's property. The priority right of Supplier, its status as a lien creditor, normally dates from the time of levy. In some states, however, once the creditor obtains a levy, priority is dated back to the time the writ of execution was issued or, in other states, to the time the writ was delivered to the sheriff.

Retailer also may have a bank account or a customer that owes it money. Supplier can reach these intangible assets using a procedure known as "garnishment." Using this device, Supplier can force the bank or the customer to pay it instead of paying Retailer.

The next step for real and personal property is a state-supervised sale. Such sales are regulated to protect the debtor and junior creditors. ("Junior" creditors are those who have a priority later in time to the creditor at whose behest the sale is being conducted.) Junior creditors are paid only if the property sells for more than is needed to pay senior creditors in full. In some states, the property must be appraised and cannot be sold for less than a stated percentage of the appraised value, called the "upset" price. This practice is consistent with the modern tendency to expand the debtor-protective devices surrounding the sale. The court that rendered the judgment may undo the sale for sufficient cause, such as fraud, failure to provide the statutorily prescribed notice of the sale to potential buyers, or other procedural irregularity. Insufficient price alone is generally not enough. A very low price, however, may be evidence that the sale was not conducted in a reasonable way.

Any surplus resulting from the sale after the payment of expenses and the judgment under which the property was seized and sold is distributed to any junior creditors or returned to the debtor. Purchasers of the property usually take the property free of the judgment/execution lien. But in some states, a debtor has a statutory right to claim real estate from the purchaser for the sale price, leaving the purchaser with nothing but a return of her money. Such protections for debtors come with a significant downside. The possibility that the sale will be later undone in some cases chills the amount purchasers are willing to bid in all cases.

A number of other factors lower still further the amount realized at such sales relative to the amount that the debtor initially paid for the assets. Used goods usually sell at a sizable discount, and goods seized by the sheriff tend to be used. Moreover, goods sold at a sheriff's sale come without any warranty. And, unlike an entrepreneur whose livelihood depends on profits from sales, the sheriff has no incentive to invest energy in getting the best possible price for the goods. The creditor who forces the sale has an incentive to ensure that the goods are sold for enough to repay the debt, but not to realize any more than this amount. Legal rules try to give those involved the obligation to realize as much as possible, but it is hard to fashion legal rules that make a sheriff or a creditor employ the same skill and enthusiasm they would if selling for their own account.

Supplier should be able to reach all of Retailer's assets if Retailer is a corporation. If Retailer is an individual, however, there will be some kinds of property that are beyond Supplier's reach. Each state has its own list of property on which creditors cannot levy. In Texas and Florida, for example, general creditors cannot reach any of the equity a debtor has in her home. (The debtor's equity is the difference between the value of the house and the amount still owed on the mortgage.) Other states have such "homestead exemptions" but subject them to a dollar cap. Some offer no protection for the homestead at all. Life insurance policies, pension funds, one's tools of trade, clothes, and household furniture are often protected from creditors, although there are usually dollar limits, both in the aggregate and with respect to specific types of collateral. State exemption laws differ dramatically both in the types of property that are covered and in how generous they are.

Federal law also limits the ability of creditors to reach assets. The Consumer Credit Protection Act, for example, limits the extent to which any single creditor may garnish the wages of an individual. See 15 U.S.C. §1673(a) (garnishment of aggregate disposable earnings limited to the lesser of 25 percent or the amount by which the debtor's disposable earnings for a week exceed thirty times the federal minimum hourly wage). In addition, certain types of federal payments, such as Social Security payments, are not subject to legal process and hence are beyond the reach of creditors. See 42 U.S.C. §407(a).

The debtor may no longer have assets sufficient to satisfy the judgment. In many cases, the general creditor will simply be out of luck. There are occasions, however, when the creditor finds that the debtor's assets are now in someone else's hands. Transfers made and obligations incurred with the intent to delay, hinder, or defraud creditors are fraudulent and void as against creditors and have been since 1571. Although written in general terms, the basic transaction at which the statute was first aimed is quite simple. A debtor, hounded by creditors, transfers everything to a friend for a trivial sum. This debtor hopes to shield assets from creditors. When the creditors come to enforce their claims, the debtor will assert that there are no assets on which they can levy. By invoking fraudulent conveyance law, the creditors can pierce through form and go to substance. The transfer is a sham, and the creditors can ignore the transfer and levy on the goods in the friend's hands as if the transfer never took place.

Fraudulent conveyance law has grown beyond its original scope to apply to transactions that are not "fraudulent" in the traditional sense at all. The essence of fraudulent conveyance law can be put simply: Insolvent debtors must receive "fair consideration" or "reasonably equivalent value" for a transfer. An insolvent debtor, one with fewer assets than liabilties, who incurs an obligation and receives too little or nothing in return makes a fraudulent conveyance. The easiest case to imagine is a gift. Large gifts made while in dire financial straits may in fact be motivated as much by a desire to keep assets from creditors as by friendship or affection. So many transactions in which an insolvent debtor gives something away and receives nothing or too little in return are fraudulent that society may be better off voiding all of them, rather than engaging in elaborate case-by-case inquiries. Also, gifts made by an insolvent debtor are gifts of someone else's money. When your assets are large and your debts small, your hands are free. If you are insolvent, however, they are not. When your assets exceed your liabilities, the assets are not really yours.

Corporations do not typically make gifts (save the occasional charitable contribution). Nevertheless, there is a wide variety of corporate transactions that, from the perspective of a creditor, involve a transfer for which the corporation receives nothing or very little in return. Consider an ordinary dividend. Assets flow out of the corporation's coffers, away from the reach of creditors, and the corporation receives nothing in return. Similarly, stock repurchases bring the creditors nothing of value. To be sure, the corporation acquires stock, but stock has no value in the hands of the corporation that issued it.

We can take the simple case of a corporation with a single share-holder. There is no difference between declaring a dividend of $1 million and repurchasing $1 million in stock from the shareholder. In both cases, the shareholder owns the entire corporation after the transactions as before. The only difference is that the shareholder is $1 million richer and the corporation has a correspondingly smaller amount of assets with which to satisfy creditors' claims.

This principle must be qualified in one important respect. When an insolvent debtor pays off a creditor, the creditor is conclusively presumed to give "fair consideration" and "reasonably equivalent value." Such transfers on account of an antecedent debt may affect how assets are distributed among the different creditors, but they do not affect the pool of assets available to the creditors. Creditors as a group are not worse off when one creditor is paid and others are not. A creditor can challenge a payment to another creditor under the fraudulent conveyance laws only if the payment was made with actual fraudulent intent. The rules of individual collection do not concern themselves with protecting one creditor against another. Indeed, as we shall see, bankruptcy law is designed to overcome this deficiency.

The exercises below ask you to work through some of the basic issues in individual debt collection.

EXERCISES

1A(1) Finance Company lends $100,000 to Debtor, who uses it to start a business. The business fails, and Debtor defaults on the loan. Debtor owns a house, but it is subject to a mortgage held by Bank. Debtor owns a late-model car free and clear. Debtor has $10,000 in a checking account and earns $35,000 a year at a new job. In addition, Debtor owns several prints by Matisse, as well as a few pieces of antique furniture inherited from grandparents. What are the problems Finance Company is likely to encounter in trying to recover the money it has lent?

1A(2) Debtor defaults on a $20,000 obligation to Bank, which then sues to collect. After Bank wins and dockets its judgment, Debtor negligently injures Victim, who begins a lawsuit and obtains a prejudgment attachment of Debtor's automobile, which Debtor owns outright at the time. Later Bank levies on the same automobile, and the sheriff conducts a sale that raises $25,000. What should the sheriff do with the money?

B. THE RIGHTS OF SECURED CREDITORS

To this point, we have examined the ways in which a creditor can seize property from an uncooperative debtor and thereby establish its priority to that asset over other creditors. This is not the only means by which a creditor can establish priority. A creditor can also enjoy a priority right by bargaining for it, either when the creditor lends or at any time thereafter. A debtor can grant a creditor a contingent property interest that ripens only if the debtor defaults. Such property interests give the creditor priority over other creditors, if proper notice is given. All such contingent property rights are generically called "security interests." (The term "mortgage" is often used instead of "security interest" when real property is involved.) As with debt collection generally, much turns on whether real or personal property is at stake. In the former case, each state has its own law governing mortgages. With respect to personal property, the governing law is a particular state's enactment of Article 9 of the Uniform Commercial Code.

When first conceived centuries ago, the real estate mortgage took the form of a sale subject to defeasance. The debtor transferred title in (or "mortgaged") the property to the creditor, but could reacquire the land if the loan was repaid. (Because the debtor is making a transfer to the creditor, the "mortgagor" is the debtor and the "mortgagee" is the lender.) Over time, this type of transaction acquired its own peculiar shape, and, like the law governing real estate transactions generally, mortgage law tends to be formal and arcane. Similarly, the procedures the creditor must use to reach the land in the event of default (to "foreclose" on it) are also elaborate and differ from state to state. Nevertheless, once the creditor takes the proper steps and records its interest properly in the real estate records, its priority right as against the world is simply the time of the filing. If the creditor fails to file (or fails to file properly), it loses, except perhaps to those who had notice of its claim. But if the creditor cuts square corners, it prevails even over later buyers of the land.

It is much easier to take a security interest in personal property. The law is considerably simpler and more uniform. But personal property has a dynamic character that land does not. An undeveloped parcel of land is not going anywhere. By contrast, a debtor's inventory turns over constantly and can be moved. Moreover, a sale to a buyer in ordinary course extinguishes a creditor's security interest altogether. The priority rights of creditors who hold personal property as collateral are therefore considerably more complicated. As non-bankruptcy priority rights are of principal concern to us, we shall focus primarily upon security interests in personal property in the rest of this chapter.

If a creditor wants to look to a debtor's tangible assets and enjoy a priority with respect to it over other secured creditors and lien creditors, it must take two steps:

1. The creditor must extend credit and enter into an enforceable security agreement with its debtor in which the debtor gives the creditor the right to take the collateral in the event of default. If the agreement is not in writing, the creditor must take possession of the collateral.

2. In the case of tangible personal property, ownership is inferred from possession. A creditor that wants a priority right in such assets must do something to cure the problem of ostensible ownership, the appearance that the debtor has assets with which to repay debts. A creditor does this by taking possession of the collateral or, more commonly, making a public filing.

These two steps can be taken in either order. When the first step is taken, the secured creditor's security interest has "attached," to use the language of Article 9. When both steps have been taken, the security interest is "perfected."

Before examining issues related to priority rights, it is worth noting that a creditor who takes personal property as collateral has a right that other creditors do not have—the ability to seize assets from a debtor without first going to court (or obtaining the debtor's consent). The importance of this right, however, can be overstated. Article 9 of the Uniform Commercial Code generally allows self-help repossession, as it is called, only if it can be accomplished without a "breach of the peace." As this term has come to be defined, a secured creditor can repossess without the assistance of a court only when the debtor does not *affirmatively* object. A simple trespass is usually a "breach of the peace." A secured creditor may repossess a debtor's car if it is parked in the street but not if it is parked in the garage.

We have already noted that a creditor who takes a mortgage on a debtor's home can reach the home even if a state's homestead law protects the debtor from creditor levy on personal residences. The same rule applies to personal property if the creditor provided the funds that the debtor used to acquire the property in the first place. (Such security interests are known as "purchase money security interests," or "PMSIs.") Under state law, property exempt from execution by unsecured creditors generally is available as collateral for a secured debt. Federal regulations, however, make it an unfair trade practice to take nonpossessory security interests (other than purchase money interests) in household goods. 16 C.F.R. §444.2(a)(4).

The principal advantage of taking a security interest lies in the way it gives the secured creditor the ability to make claims against the debtor's property that take precedence over other creditors' claims. Concern about the problem of ostensible ownership animates Article 9. Article 9 creates a strong policy (respected, we shall see, in bankruptcy) against "secret liens," that is, security interests that purport to give a property interest to a creditor while the debtor appears to the world to own such property.

As with the process by which a general creditor obtains a lien, the important question for consensual security interests is one of timing: *At what time* in the process does a secured creditor gain these priority rights vis-à-vis other creditors? Article 9 generally orders interests according to the time creditors notify the world of their claim. In most cases, creditors can either make a public filing or take physical possession of the collateral. The filing is a simple form called a financing statement. The creditor must identify the type of collateral involved but does not have to set out any of the details of the transaction. The financing statement is intended only to give others notice that a creditor may have a security interest. If they need details, they must look elsewhere.

For most kinds of tangible personal property, Article 9 allows the secured party the choice of notice by filing or possession. Most creditors, however, choose to file. Debtors use most of the equipment and other hard assets they own. A farmer, for example, might grant a security interest in her tractor to obtain a loan, but she needs the tractor to work her farm and produce the crops she will use to pay off the loan. Possession is more common when the assets can be put in the hands of a third party but are available nevertheless when the debtor needs them. The debtor, for example, might keep its inventory in a warehouse next to an air freight service in another city. The creditor's agent can run the warehouse and release collateral to the shipper when a customer has placed an order. Even in such cases, however, filing is so inexpensive that creditors are well advised to file anyway. Among other things, the time of the filing is much easier to ascertain than the time the creditor takes possession.

For some types of collateral, a creditor has only one way of establishing a priority right. Some collateral is intangible, such as accounts receivable, the money that a debtor's customers owe it. Possession of such collateral is simply not possible. Therefore, perfection is possible only through filing. Other collateral may be cash or bearer instruments or some other kind of property that is highly negotiable. Those who acquire such property in good faith are entitled to infer ownership from possession. With respect to these types of collateral, filing is either entirely ineffective or subject to the interests of those who do have possession.

A creditor with a purchase money security interest in consumer goods is relieved of the obligation to possess or file altogether. Its interest is perfected automatically upon attachment. In many cases, such property is exempt from levy and nonpurchase money security interests are not allowed. Hence, the filing would not serve any useful purpose.

We can see the operation of Article 9 readily with an example. Suppose Bank takes an interest in its debtor's drill press to secure a loan. Bank makes an Article 9 filing on July 1, and the debtor signs a proper security agreement on August 1. On August 1, Bank becomes a perfected secured creditor. Bank could have extended credit on August 1 or any earlier time. It does not matter. Every general creditor can become a secured creditor. A creditor need not give its debtor any new value at the time it takes a security interest. The antecedent debt is itself sufficient consideration. The debtor and creditor need only enter into a proper security agreement and make an appropriate filing.

Once Bank's security interest "attaches," it has the right to enforce its security interest against the debtor, quite apart from the July 1 filing. As of August 1, Bank can seize the property in the event of default, provided it can do so without a breach of the peace. (The time of attachment is the only thing that matters. Bank cannot seize collateral earlier, notwithstanding a proper filing, and, as noted, Bank enjoys this right as of August 1 even if it made no filing.) Once it seizes its collateral, Bank must then sell it in a commercially reasonable manner. Bank's property interest is one that entitles it only to realize the value of its loan. If the property is worth more than this amount, the surplus must be returned to the debtor.

In theory, a creditor does not, by taking collateral, gain the ability to penalize the debtor in the event of default. A secured creditor cannot seize property worth more than the loan and either keep it or sell it for more than what it is owed and keep the excess. Nevertheless, we should recognize that, when a creditor has a security interest in consumer goods, the property is likely worth much more to the debtor than to anyone else. Hence, the repossession hurts the debtor more than it benefits the secured creditor. In this context, the collateral is much like a hostage, more valuable to the person to whom it belongs than to the person who holds it. In such cases, repossession may take place, not so much to acquire an asset that can be sold to repay the loan, but to induce the debtor to find money elsewhere or send a signal to other debtors.

no penalty

If the amount realized from the sale of the collateral is less than what Bank is owed, Bank can bring an action against the debtor for the deficiency in the same way any general creditor can. That Bank can pursue such a "deficiency judgment" should come as no surprise. Unless it agreed otherwise (that is, unless Bank made its loan "nonrecourse"), Bank can exercise any rights available to a general creditor. If it chooses, Bank can sue its debtor, reduce its claim to judgment, and have the sheriff seize and sell the collateral, just as it could if Bank had no security interest as well.

deficiency judgment → go after balance

Bank would rarely ignore its rights as a secured creditor. (Cases might arise when the value of the collateral was trivial relative to the debt and to the debtor's other assets.) It is a point that we should remember, however, because of what it tells us if Bank's security interest should prove defective in some way. A lender who tries to become a perfected secured creditor and fails is not worse off than if it had never tried at all. The lender merely remains a general creditor.

Bank can take advantage of its priority right only after its security interest attaches and thereby becomes perfected. But once its security interest is perfected, Bank's priority relates back to July 1, the time that it filed and put others on notice of its interest. (An old version of Article 9 had a different rule in the contest between Bank and creditors who did not have security interests. Under that Article 9, Bank's priority dated from August 1, the time of perfection.) When a secured creditor gives notice to the world by filing a financing statement, its priority is determined by the time of its filing. This priority right extends not only to the machine itself, but also to the identifiable proceeds that the debtor receives in the event that the machine is sold.

Retroactive priority for subsequent perfection of security interest

Associated Revenue also.

When the debtor has insufficient assets to pay its creditors in full, the creditors find themselves in a race to establish their priority rights. Each wants to put a lien on the debtor's assets or, if it has or will have an attached security interest, make an Article 9 filing before others take either step. In the case of real estate, a creditor who fails to file may prevail against later creditors who had actual knowledge of its interest. Article 9, however, makes knowledge largely irrelevant in the case of personal property. If another creditor signed a security interest with the debtor on June 15 but failed to file until August 15, Bank still prevails even if it knew about the competing interest.

Priority rights become more complicated when Bank takes as collateral not only the assets the debtor had on hand at the time it filed, but also assets that the debtor subsequently acquires. The typical example is inventory. By its nature, inventory turns over constantly. A debtor might have $100 of inventory at all times, but the property that constitutes the inventory is constantly changing.

Article 9 allows Bank to assert a security interest in after-acquired property. Let us assume that Bank and the debtor enter into a security agreement on September 1 and Bank makes a proper filing on that date. The collateral is the debtor's inventory, then existing and thereafter acquired.

Bank, of course, loses to a general creditor who levied on the inventory before September 1 or a secured creditor who filed before then. We want to consider the case that arises when a purchase money lender subsequently enters the scene. On October 1, the debtor acquires new goods from Supplier. Supplier retains a purchase money security interest in them. Supplier should prevail. Even though Supplier files after Bank, the debtor would never have acquired the inventory in the first place if Supplier had not been willing to do business with it.

Article 9 allows Supplier to come before Bank, provided Supplier follows the special rules governing "superpriorities" for purchase money lenders. Supplier must file promptly. In the case of inventory, for example, it must file before the debtor *receives possession* of the goods. Moreover, Supplier must notify Bank in writing that it has a purchase money security interest in the inventory.

In this chapter, we have focused on the ways in which creditors can use the legal system to acquire a priority right. As you study this material, however, do not forget the easiest way a creditor can ensure that it will not be left holding the bag. Outside of bankruptcy, if a creditor can persuade the debtor to <u>repay the loan voluntarily</u>, it will ordinarily be able to keep the payments it receives. A general creditor who gets paid in <u>cash</u> will ordinarily prevail over a creditor with a fully perfected security interest in all the debtor's assets.

The fact that nonbankruptcy law permits creditors to retain money collected creates some poor incentives. Such an outcome encourages individual creditors to take assets away from the debtor at exactly the time the debtor's survival may depend on keeping the assets together. The creditors <u>might be</u> better off as a group if each <u>stayed its hand</u>. This collective action problem is emblematic of the kinds of problems bankruptcy law attempts to solve. As we shall see later, once in bankruptcy, creditors may be forced to return payments they received while the debtor was in trouble.

The exercises below help you work through some of the basic features of security interests.

EXERCISES

1B(1) Manufacturer sells a machine to Debtor on January 1. Debtor promises to pay Manufacturer for the machine on February 1. Debtor never pays Manufacturer. On March 1, Bank lends to Debtor and takes a security interest in the machine. On April 1, Bank files a proper financing statement. Manufacturer sues Debtor and reduces its claim to judgment on May 1. Sheriff seizes the machine under a writ of execution on June 1. Who prevails with respect to the machine, Manufacturer or Bank? Would your answer change if Bank never filed its financing statement? Would your answer change if Bank filed only on July 1? If Sheriff sells the machine and the sale proceeds exceed the amount owed to the creditor with priority, what should Sheriff do with the excess? What recourse, if any, does Bank or Finance Company have if not fully repaid? In answering these questions consider UCC §§9-317(a) and 9-615.

1B(2) Debtor bought a drill press from Seller two years ago. Debtor borrowed $50,000 from Bank on an unsecured basis to pay for it. Last year, Debtor borrowed $50,000 from Finance Company, granted it a security interest in the drill press, and signed a written security agreement. Finance Company never files a financing statement. Last month, Bank sued Debtor, but its claim has not been reduced to judgment, and no prejudgment remedies are available to it. Last week Finance Company took possession of the drill press. Who has priority? Would your answer change if Finance Company's security interest were never reduced to writing? In answering these questions consider UCC §§9-201;9-203(b)(3).

1B(3) Bank takes and properly perfects a security interest in Debtor's inventory. Several months later, Debtor defaults on an unsecured loan from Finance Company, as it has on loans from many others. Finance Company threatens to sue, but before it does so, Debtor sells the inventory and uses the proceeds to repay an unsecured loan from Finance Company. Does Bank have any recourse against Finance Company? In answering this question consider UCC §9-332.

II. BANKRUPTCY AS COLLECTIVE DEBT COLLECTION REMEDY

In this chapter we review the ways in which bankruptcy law changes the rights of creditors and debtors. Crucial here is the principle that the Supreme Court announced in Butner v. United States, 440 U.S. 48 (1979): Bankruptcy law respects rights that exist outside of bankruptcy unless a specific bankruptcy provision or policy requires a different rule. Hence, to understand the relationship between bankruptcy law and ordinary rules of debt collection, we need to identify the purposes that bankruptcy serves. We begin with an overview of the policies of bankruptcy. Next we provide an overview of the Bankruptcy Code itself. This discussion establishes the framework used throughout the rest of the book. Finally we describe the bankruptcy forum as the environment in which bankruptcy law operates. Once we complete this look at the bankruptcy forum, we will be ready to discuss the basic rules of bankruptcy in part 2.

A. THE PURPOSES OF BANKRUPTCY AND THE *BUTNER* PRINCIPLE

In chapter 1 we explored the ways in which creditors can individually enforce obligations owed them by their debtor. These rules make the most sense when there is a discrete legal dispute involving the debtor and one creditor. The nonbankruptcy rules of debt collection are not designed to handle the situation that arises when a debtor has too few assets to pay its creditors in full. When this happens, many creditors are likely to pursue the debtor's assets at the same time. Assets are sold off piecemeal, destroying whatever synergy existed between them. Moreover, each creditor must spend increasing resources to beat other creditors to the assets. Bankruptcy law forces diverse creditors to work together and stops the destructive race to assets. Each creditor has the chance to establish both how much it is owed and the priority its claim enjoys without engaging in a destructive and expensive race.

The other policies of bankruptcy focus on the debtor. The ordinary rules of debt collection make no accommodation for individuals who, through bad judgment or bad luck, simply cannot pay their creditors in full. And even if the individual debtors could repay, doing so might cause disruptions in their lives and those of their families that are not commensurate with the benefit to the creditors. Providing debtors relief from these hardships makes credit more costly and less available, but individual borrowers as a group may be better off paying a higher interest rate to be protected from the full consequences of economic misfortune. By limiting the ability of creditors to pursue unlucky individuals, bankruptcy law provides a form of insurance to all borrowers.

The rules of debt collection have a different but also destructive effect on corporate debtors. Some of the corporations that cannot pay their creditors in full nevertheless should survive as going concerns. Nonbankruptcy rules provide no way of permitting this while respecting the rights of the various investors in the firm. Chapter 11 of the Bankruptcy Code solves this problem by providing a process by which a new capital structure is created for the firm that is both consistent with the existing economic conditions and with the rights the creditors and other investors have in the enterprise.

That we use a single piece of federal legislation to address these three separate problems points to both the genius and the sometimes awkward complexity of bankruptcy law. At its inception, bankruptcy law focused only on the first problem, the problem of providing a collective remedy for creditors when ordinary methods of debt collection were unavailing. The word "bankruptcy" derives from statutes of Italian city-states that used the phrase "banca rupta," after a medieval custom of breaking the bench of a banker or tradesman who absconded with his creditors' property. The word was transplanted to England in 1542, when Parliament enacted an "Act Against Such Persons As Do Make Bankrupt," 34 and 35 Henry VIII ch. 4 (1542). The early English bankruptcy statutes were viciously punitive from the perspective of the debtor. They focused on preventing the debtor from hiding assets, and they offered no discharge or other relief.

What the first English statutes governing bankruptcy did was give creditors rights as a group that they did not enjoy on their own. If a debtor committed a specified act of bankruptcy (such as fleeing to parts unknown), creditors could petition the Lord Chancellor to appoint a commission that had the power to gather the debtor's assets together and sell them. The commissioners would then distribute the proceeds "to every of the said creditors a portion, rate and rate like, according to the quantity of his or their debts." 13 Eliz. ch. 7, III (1571). If creditors were not paid in full, "then the said creditor or creditors, and every of them, shall and may have their remedy for the recovery and levying of the residue of their said debts or duties ... in like manner and form as they should and might have had before the making of this act." Id. at X.

Notably, these early English bankruptcy statutes did nothing to help or protect unlucky debtors. Their only purpose was to give creditors another method of collecting debts in addition to those they already had. Moreover, the new remedy was a collective one. Although an individual creditor did not lose the right to sue the debtor at some later time, each creditor had to share the debtor's existing assets with every other creditor. Essential elements of these early English bankruptcy statutes, then, were the sequestration of the debtor's assets and the imposition of restraint on creditors, to ensure that a creditor did not seek repayment in full at the expense of other creditors.

[handwritten margin note: early bankruptcy law: collective remedy for creditors, punitive toward debtor]

Modern bankruptcy law retains these basic elements while addressing the problems that financial distress brings to the debtor. At its core, bankruptcy forces creditors to work together collectively. Cases do arise in which creditors can sit down and work together without legal compulsion; these nonbankruptcy "workouts" are especially likely when the creditors are few and have repeated dealings with one another. But when the creditors are diverse, such cooperation is often not possible. The creditors suffer from a collective action problem. To understand why individual creditors may not be able to resolve this problem without a special legal process, an analogy is helpful.

Imagine a small lake filled with fish. If a single individual owned the lake, that individual would limit fishing in the lake. The owner would contain her desire to consume or sell fish now in order to ensure that sufficient fish were left to reproduce and maintain the population for future years. The story might be quite different if no single person owned the lake. If a group of diverse, self-interested individuals were free to fish, each might try to catch as many fish as possible without considering the future.

Although everyone would benefit if fishing were limited, everyone would also realize that self-imposed limits on fishing would not ensure that a supply of fish would remain. Each individual might well think that, regardless of any restraint she practiced, others would continue to fish. Overfishing (and the destruction of the fish supply) would happen anyway. In the absence of any mechanism for restraining others, no one has an incentive to practice restraint. Self-interest leads the group as a whole to catch too many fish, despite the interest of the group as a whole in preserving the resource for the future.

When a debtor is insolvent and there are not enough assets to satisfy everyone, the creditors are like fishers in a small lake: Their actions collectively can deplete and endanger the common pool. Each creditor has an incentive to act precipitously because if it waits it may not be repaid. General creditors have an incentive to reduce their claims to judgment and levy on the debtor's property. Secured creditors may exercise their rights to repossess collateral. Assets may be sold off for less than if a single individual or entity had controlled their disposition.

When creditors are left to their own devices, their competition for limited assets creates costs quite apart from whether collection threatens a firm as a going concern. Outside of bankruptcy, when creditors anticipate that a debtor may not pay in the ordinary course, they will prepare themselves for a race to the limited pool of assets. Inquiries into the debtor's financial well-being and into the activities of other creditors may intensify. Lawyers and accountants may be hired and instructed to work overtime. This urgent preparation may be expensive for all involved, but from each creditor's perspective, it may be less costly than losing the race to a limited pool of assets.

The situation in which the creditors find themselves is much like an arms race among nations. Money spent on weapons, of debt collection or war, is better spent elsewhere if conflict can be avoided. Bankruptcy law, like a peace treaty, can preempt conflict and prevent waste. Under bankruptcy law, each creditor receives what it could expect to receive outside of bankruptcy, taking account of the possibility that it might have won the race and the possibility that it might have lost. As a group, creditors are better off because they do not have to incur the costs associated with pursuing their individual remedies. Their payoffs are also more certain, something that has value in itself if the creditors are risk averse.

A bankruptcy law can provide a collective remedy to creditors without heeding the welfare of the flesh-and-blood individuals. Indeed, as we have seen, early English bankruptcy law focused only on creditors. The notion of discharge evolved 150 years later, and it came about more to reward cooperation than to assist the unlucky. Parliament first provided for a discharge from debt in bankruptcy in 1705. The Statute of 4 Anne ch. 17 provided that a debtor who conformed to the act and revealed everything would be able to keep 5 percent of whatever assets were gathered together and would be discharged from all prebankruptcy obligations. At the same time, however, the statute also provided that an uncooperative debtor would "suffer as a felon without the benefit of clergy"—an eighteenth-century expression meaning the death penalty. The discharge began as an element of a debt collection device that included capital punishment. The death penalty was the stick; the discharge was the carrot. They formed a package designed to ensure the debtor's cooperation.

Despite these origins, the discharge for individuals has come to be seen as an important independent bankruptcy policy. Lawmakers in this country have always been alert to the problems that debtors suffered when they encountered economic reverses. Early on, each colony instituted some reforms, softening the harsh and unyielding character of English law. Many of the reforms focused specifically on debtors who owed small amounts. Some allowed the debtors the option of indentured servitude instead of prison. Others offered a debtor release from prison and immunity from future arrest if the debtor swore an oath of impoverishment. A few even extinguished the obligation a debtor owed his creditors. Still other new laws protected some kinds of property such as clothes and household goods from creditor execution. These "insolvency laws," as they were known, were part of what the framers had in mind when they gave Congress the power to enact "uniform Laws on the subject of Bankruptcies" in Article I of the Constitution.

Bankruptcy laws, however, did not become a permanent part of our legal system until 1898. Congress passed bankruptcy legislation in 1800, 1841, and 1867. Each of these laws provided for the discharge of debt, but none of them lasted more than a few years. For a long time, relief to debtors came from state law, which primarily served to place certain assets, sometimes including the family homestead, beyond the reach of general creditors.

The 1898 Bankruptcy Act was the first long-lived bankruptcy statute Congress passed. It built on state law that exempted some forms of property from creditor levy, and it embraced the idea that honest individuals who encountered financial misfortune could wipe the slate clean by giving up to their creditors all their nonexempt assets. In return, individuals' debts were discharged and they enjoyed a "fresh start" free from the burden of past obligation. This simple process is now embodied in Chapter 7, the "liquidation" chapter of the current Bankruptcy Code.

Congress later gave individuals the ability to restructure their obligations under what we now know as Chapter 13, the "adjustment" chapter of the current Bankruptcy Code. With an adjustment, individual debtors can keep even their nonexempt assets and instead pay their creditors some of what they owe out of their future income. Creditors receive at least as much as they would have received in Chapter 7, and individuals do not have to give up assets that have more value to them than to anyone else.

In the modern era, the largest asset for most individuals is the ability to earn money in the future. Perhaps for this reason, the Bankruptcy Act of 2005 changed the way in which relief is given to debtors. Under the new provisions, Chapter 7 relief is no longer available to everyone. Instead, the law now channels some relatively high-income individual debtors into Chapter 13 where they must repay at least a portion of what they owe creditors out of their disposable income for a number of years.

In the case of a debtor that is an artificial entity, like a corporation or limited partnership, bankruptcy law—which predates these limited liability enterprises—has a different effect. Ordinary rules of debt collection create a problem peculiar to corporate debtors. A corporation is a legal device that allows different investors to contribute capital to a common business enterprise. The capital structure of the firm establishes the way the firm's earnings are divided among the investors. Insolvent firms cannot survive as going concerns without a new capital structure. By definition, an insolvent firm does not expect to be able to meet its fixed obligations out of its future earnings. One purpose of bankruptcy law is to enable firms to acquire a new capital structure.

To understand the need an insolvent firm has for a new capital structure, we must first understand the crucial distinction between economic and financial distress. A firm may be troubled because it cannot succeed in the marketplace. Competitors produce a better product at a lower cost. This first kind of adversity is called "economic" distress. It exists regardless of a firm's capital structure. The sole owner of a business that attracts no customers will shut it down, even if there are no banks or other creditors in the picture. On the other hand, a firm may be distressed because it cannot generate sufficient revenue to pay its debts. This second kind of trouble is "financial" distress, meaning the firm's income is not enough to pay back what it has borrowed. It is a problem that arises *because* of the firm's capital structure.

Each type of distress can exist without the other. Consider the following example of economic, but not financial, distress. A wealthy entrepreneur opens a restaurant using his own capital. There are no creditors or other investors. This theme restaurant serves British dim sum. It offers plates of cold toast, Beef Wellington, and scones, served by surly waiters. Inspired by a restaurant that successfully tried the same experiment with Italian food, this restaurant is a failure. British food turns out not to have the same following among the young professionals in the neighborhood as does Italian food. No one eats at the restaurant. This restaurant is a firm that has failed. If the restaurant is to succeed, its concept must change, with a new menu and décor. The restaurant's problems have nothing to do with its creditors. It does not even have any. It suffers from economic distress, but not financial distress.

[margin note: economic distress cannot be resolved w/ new capital structure; financial can b]

The opposite is also possible. We can have financial distress without economic distress. A railroad may have cost more to build than anyone expected and thus may find itself unable to pay off the creditors who financed it. Nevertheless, the railroad's assets may best be kept together. That is, the railroad's steel rails and roadbed may well generate more money transporting cargo and passengers than if put to any other use.

A toy manufacturer borrows a large amount to develop and market a toy tied to a movie that flops. The people responsible for this debacle leave the firm. The current managers are the best in the business. Nevertheless, this huge loan and the firm's other obligations exceed the value of the firm itself. This firm, like the railroad, is in financial distress, but not economic distress. The firm is in fine shape with respect to everything it now does, but it cannot pay its debts. Without a new capital structure, it cannot flourish.

A health club might share the same characteristics as the railroad. There are sufficient revenues from member dues to pay the costs of running and maintaining the club, but not enough to pay off all the construction loans. The tennis courts, the pool, the racquetball courts, and the weight machines cannot be put to other purposes. Even though one would not decide to build the health club at all if one could do it all over again, the building, land, and equipment cannot be put to a better use now that the club has already been built. It too suffers from financial distress.

Financial distress exists only if a firm has creditors. If the creditors disappeared, the problem would disappear. With a new capital structure that takes account of existing conditions, the railroad, the toy maker, and the health club would make the best use of their assets

[margin note: Financial distress means creditors]

without the threat that some creditor would come and seize some of them. By contrast, a firm in economic distress suffers regardless of whether it has creditors. Eliminating creditors would not change the fundamental problem the firm faces: The food in the restaurant will still be bad.

These two types of distress often coexist. Many firms face financial distress *because* they are in economic distress. A clothing store cannot pay its creditors because potential customers do not like the fashions it stocks. There can also be a feedback loop between the two forms of distress. The clothing store is insufficiently capitalized and in financial distress. To pay its bills, the store does not fill gaps in its inventory and it does not invest in buying the latest fashions. The store loses customers who no longer find the fashions they want in the sizes they need. The customers shop elsewhere, and the store now encounters economic distress, which in turn aggravates the problem of financial distress.

There is, however, no necessary link between financial and economic distress. *Understanding that financial and economic distress are conceptually distinct from each other is fundamental to understanding Chapter 11 of the Bankruptcy Code.* The legal system can do nothing to solve the problem of economic distress. In a market economy, legal rules cannot direct assets to better uses. Firms must live or die in the marketplace. Laws can do nothing to transform bad restaurants into good ones.

By contrast, legal rules can help firms in financial distress. If creditors started to exercise their individual rights and have the sheriff seize assets such as the steel rails, the railroad would shut down. Bankruptcy can ensure that creditors assert their rights in a way that is consistent with the survival of the firm as a going concern.

Chapter 11 provides an elaborate process that permits the creditors of an insolvent firm to keep the firm intact *if it is economically viable.* In a typical Chapter 11 case, the creditors give up their right to collect their debts from a firm's assets, but receive instead new ownership interests in the firm. The new ownership interests are part of a "reorganized" capital structure that contains less debt. In contrast to the old capital structure, the firm can be expected to meet the fixed obligations of the new one.

To say that firms such as the railroad, the toy maker, or the health club need a new capital structure so that their payment obligations are consistent with the revenues they earn is not to say anything about what should happen to any of the investors. For a corporation, relief from financial distress requires only that the firm's obligations going forward are consistent with its future earnings. The *aggregate* obligations must be scaled back, but doing this tells us nothing about how the firm's earnings should be divided among the old creditors and shareholders. Some rule of division must, of course, be found, but the policy that we are vindicating in providing for a new capital structure does not require any particular division. The policy has *nothing* to do with easing the burdens of any flesh-and-blood individual or ensuring the continued participation in the enterprise of any particular investor.

[margin notes: Ch. 11 Re-org — creditors give up debt collection rights in exchange for equity interest in firm -- if it is economically viable]

The "debtor" in a corporate case is merely the fictitious legal entity created by the corporate charter. No one should care whether it survives or not. We want to ensure that the assets are put to their best use. This question is independent of who owns them or the legal entity in which they reside.

In short, the Bankruptcy Code serves three purposes: (1) saving creditors the costs of a destructive race to the debtor's assets, (2) helping individuals overburdened with debt, and (3) reorganizing the capital structure of firms in financial distress. The second purpose does affect substantive nonbankruptcy rights. In the absence of bankruptcy law, creditors can look to an individual's future earnings. In bankruptcy, they cannot. With this exception, however, bankruptcy law need not change any substantive nonbankruptcy rights. The procedures that one uses to vindicate legal rights must change, but the substantive rights themselves need not.

[margin note: — no individual garnishment in bankruptcy]

This simple observation tells us a great deal about the shape of modern bankruptcy law. It is built on nonbankruptcy law, and it changes nonbankruptcy law only when the purposes of bankruptcy require it. Apart from ensuring flesh-and-blood individuals a fresh start, nothing about the policies of bankruptcy requires a change in substantive nonbankruptcy rights. Therefore, in the absence of a specific bankruptcy provision to the contrary, bankruptcy takes nonbankruptcy rights as it finds them. Only the procedures change, and these change only to solve the particular problems bankruptcy is designed to address. This is known as the *Butner* principle:

> Congress has generally left the determination of property rights in the assets of a bankrupt's estate to state law. Property interests are created and defined by state law. Unless some federal interest requires a different result, there is no reason why such interests should be analyzed differently simply because an interested party is involved in a bankruptcy proceeding.

Butner v. United States, 440 U.S. 48, 55 (1979). Although *Butner* involved a narrow question of North Carolina real estate law under the 1898 Bankruptcy Act, the Supreme Court has continually renewed its adherence to the *Butner* principle. See, e.g., Travelers Casualty & Surety Co. v. Pacific Gas & Electric Co., 127 S. Ct. 1199 (2007); Raleigh v. Illinois Dep't of Revenue, 530 U.S. 15 (2000), excerpted in chapter 5, section B below. The principle applies in almost every bankruptcy case. The most sensible approach to interpreting the Bankruptcy Code is usually one that begins by assuming that Congress intended to vindicate the policy in question with as little disturbance as possible to the nonbankruptcy baseline. To do more, as the Court observed in *Butner*, would treat people differently merely by the happenstance of bankruptcy. It would invite people to seek or avoid the bankruptcy forum for reasons that have nothing to do with the policies bankruptcy law advances.

Butner allows us to draw from a complicated statute a single organizing principle. There are, of course, exceptions, but knowing the outcome under nonbankruptcy law goes a long way toward understanding the problem in bankruptcy. When a litigant seeks an outcome different from the one that would hold outside of bankruptcy, the bankruptcy judge will likely ask the litigant to identify the part of the Bankruptcy Code that compels the departure.

The *Butner* principle explains why the Bankruptcy Code generally leaves the debtor's relationship to the outside world unaltered. For example, the debtor's fresh start is a fresh start merely from the claims of creditors, not from the burdens that everyone bears regardless of whether they have creditors. So, for example, an individual who has lost her license for drunken driving cannot use bankruptcy to have it restored.

Similarly, a firm that needs a new capital structure and is being reorganized in bankruptcy must operate its business under the same set of rules as everyone else. So, for example, an insolvent firm in bankruptcy must comply with applicable environmental laws even if the firm's creditors could achieve a greater return were the debtor permitted to pollute freely. We allow creditors to adjust the rights among themselves but not to enrich themselves at the expense of those who are not creditors.

The exercises that follow ask you to consider the *Butner* principle and its limits.

EXERCISES

2A(1) Debtor is a retail store that files a bankruptcy petition. Efforts to reorganize the firm continue, and its prospects are not clear. During the reorganization process, the state assesses taxes connected entirely with activities of the firm after it filed its bankruptcy petition. If Debtor pays these taxes, it will exhaust all the cash it has on hand and require its immediate liquidation. Can Debtor's representative argue that the Bankruptcy Code, as federal law, preempts state and municipal laws such as this state tax when the laws undermine a debtor's ability to reorganize? In answering this question, consider 28 U.S.C. §959(b). See also Thomas H. Jackson, Bankruptcy, Nonbankruptcy Entitlements, and the Creditors' Bargain, 91 Yale L.J. 857 (1982).

2A(2) Debtor asks Bank for a $10,000 loan to help pay for Debtor's son's wedding reception. Bank notices that Debtor has not worked steadily in recent years and offers the loan at 18 percent interest. Debtor says that he cannot afford the loan at that rate and asks for a lower rate. Debtor promises that in exchange for the lower rate he will pay back the loan no matter what else happens. He even promises that he will not file a bankruptcy petition to discharge the loan. Bank declines on the ground that Debtor's promises are unenforceable. Should they be enforceable? See Barry E. Adler, Ben Polak, and Alan Schwartz, Regulating Consumer Bankruptcy: A Theoretical Inquiry, 29 J. Legal Stud. 585 (2000).

2A(3) Debtor Corporation adopts a corporate charter that binds it to choose between two actions in the event Debtor defaults on any debt it incurs at any time in its existence: either (i) auction all of Debtor's assets together as part of a going concern with the proceeds used to repay creditors and any excess distributed to shareholders; or (ii) cancel Debtor's predefault equity shares and its lowest-priority debt and issue new equity shares to the holders of the canceled debt. Debtor then seeks to borrow based on a promise to creditors that Debtor will never file for bankruptcy. Should such a promise be enforceable? See Douglas G. Baird, The Uneasy Case for Corporate Reorganizations, 15 Journal of Legal Studies 127 (1986); Barry E. Adler, Financial and Political Theories of American Corporate Bankruptcy, 45 Stanford L. Rev. 311 (1993). Consider this exercise again later in connection with Problem 3C-4.

B. A ROAD MAP TO THE BANKRUPTCY CODE

Like other titles of the United States Code, Title 11 is divided into chapters. Chapters 1, 3, and 5 contain provisions that generally apply to all bankruptcy cases. The remaining chapters—all but one odd numbered—set out different procedures for each distinct kind of bankruptcy case. For example, Chapter 7 concerns individual and corporate debtors whose assets are to be liquidated. By contrast, Chapter 11 deals primarily with corporate restructurings.

Chapter 1 provides definitions (§101), tells us which parts of the Code apply to which kinds of cases (§103), and sets out eligibility requirements for each kind of bankruptcy case (§109). Chapter 1 also contains what appears to be a broad grant of power to the bankruptcy judge. Section 105 provides the bankruptcy judge the power to "issue any order, process or judgment that is necessary or appropriate to carry out the provisions" of the Bankruptcy Code. This is not, however, a mandate for bankruptcy judges to do whatever they think just or equitable. The power that a judge enjoys under §105 must derive ultimately from some other provision of the Bankruptcy Code.

The heart of any code lies in its definitional section, and the Bankruptcy Code is no exception. The definitions in §101 are the focal point of many disputes. Section 101 also gives us an introduction to the language of modern bankruptcy practice. It tells us, for example, that the person whom a bankruptcy case concerns is a "debtor." A person or a firm in bankruptcy is no longer called a "bankrupt." Congress amends the Bankruptcy Code about once a year, and amendments often add a definitional provision.

Section 101 defines most, but not all, of the terms that apply throughout the Bankruptcy Code. For example, one of the most important definitions in the Bankruptcy Code is of "notice and a hearing." It resides in §102, which nominally deals with rules of construction. Section 102 defines "after notice and a hearing" in a way that gives less procedural protection than one might otherwise expect. One need give only "such notice as is appropriate in the particular circumstances." Moreover, if no party requests a hearing or if a court finds there is insufficient time to have one, an actual hearing is not necessary.

Section 109 sets out who can take advantage of various chapters of the Bankruptcy Code. Chapter 9, for example, deals with the debts of municipalities, and §109(c) tells us, not surprisingly, that only a municipality may file a Chapter 9 petition. Section 109(c) also tells us that a municipality must be "insolvent" to file a Chapter 9 petition. ("Insolvent," defined in §101(32), generally means total debts in excess of total assets, but for a municipality it means an inability to pay undisputed debts as they come due.) The absence of any mention of insolvency in other parts of §109 creates the negative inference that other debtors need not be insolvent to be eligible for bankruptcy.

Chapter 3 of the Bankruptcy Code deals with case administration. Sections 301 through 308 tell us how a bankruptcy case begins. Sections 321 through 333 set out the rules governing those who administer the bankruptcy estate. These rules require the court to scrutinize, among other things, the hiring of lawyers and other professionals. Attorneys, for example, must file a statement with the court showing how much they will be compensated and the source of the compensation, even if they do not ask for any payment from the debtor. See §329. Moreover, the debtor's attorneys must be disinterested. See §327(a). This disinterestedness requirement complicates the job of any lawyer who wants to continue representing a corporate client after it files a bankruptcy petition. If a firm owes its lawyer anything for services provided prepetition, the lawyer may not be able to represent the firm in the bankruptcy proceeding. By virtue of being owed money, the lawyer is a creditor within the meaning of §101(10), and hence may no longer be disinterested.

Similarly, like any unsecured creditor who collects a debt within ninety days before the filing of a bankruptcy petition, a lawyer who is paid within that period for services already rendered may have to give it back. See §547. This attack may keep the lawyer from being disinterested. A lawyer who represents any of the firm's directors or shareholders personally may not be able to represent the firm in bankruptcy. A lawyer who sits on the firm's board, or who has partners who sit on the board, may also fail this requirement. Court reporters are now filled with cases of lawyers who fail to disclose a conflict, are later disqualified, and then have trouble getting paid for work they have done.

In a Chapter 7 case, the provisions of §321 through §333 must be read in conjunction with §701 through §705. The principal officer in a Chapter 7 case is the bankruptcy trustee. The trustee acts as the representative of the bankruptcy estate and is charged with managing the assets of the debtor and protecting the rights of creditors and others.

The trustee, for example, has the power to bring actions the debtor could have brought outside of bankruptcy.

Similarly, in a case under Chapter 11, the provisions of §321 through §333 must be read in conjunction with §1101 through §1109. For example, in Chapter 11 cases there is typically no trustee. The "debtor in possession" takes on the duties and responsibilities of the trustee. See §1107. Provisions of the Bankruptcy Code that authorize the trustee to take certain actions apply with equal force to the debtor in possession. In the case of a corporation, the old managers of the debtor corporation act as the debtor in possession. Hence, when §363 authorizes the trustee to use, lease, or sell assets of the estate in the ordinary course of business without first obtaining court approval, it is authorizing the old managers to do the same.

Sections 341 through 351 set out a number of basic procedures. One of the crucial moments in the life of a bankruptcy case is the initial meeting of creditors required by §341. In a Chapter 7 case, for example, the creditors elect a trustee during the §341 meeting. They also decide whether to form a creditors committee to monitor the course of the case. See §705(a). The bankruptcy judge is forbidden to attend the §341 meeting. Under the 1898 Bankruptcy Act, bankruptcy judges became closely involved in the administration of the bankruptcy case. Many thought that this involvement prevented them from maintaining the necessary detachment to decide disputes between the parties.

One of the ways in which the Bankruptcy Code insulates the bankruptcy judge from the day-to-day affairs of the debtor is through the U.S. Trustee. The U.S. Trustee is charged with providing administrative oversight of bankruptcy cases and ensuring that they do not languish in bankruptcy court, a likely fate when the stakes are small and no single creditor has the incentive to push things along. (In some jurisdictions, "bankruptcy administrators" are appointed to serve similar functions.)

In recent years, Congress has given the bankruptcy judge more power to keep cases moving, such as by providing in §105 explicit authorization for the judge to hold status conferences.

Because even the simplest bankruptcy cases take time, we need to have rules that keep the creditors from taking matters into their own hands. As time passes, the rest of the world does not stand still. Hence, we also need rules that allow the trustee (and the debtor in possession) to preserve the assets and, in the case of a corporate debtor in reorganization, to run the business. These rules are largely the province of §361 through §366. By far the most important of these sections is §362, which imposes an ("automatic stay") upon all creditors. It requires creditors to cease all debt collection efforts the moment a petition is filed. The automatic stay looms so large that it is easy to forget that the stay is simply a presumption. The court can lift the stay whenever a creditor shows that there is cause or that its interest is not "adequately protected." Moreover, a court has the power under §105 to stay actions that do not come within the scope of §362 so long as it is justified by a policy embraced in some other part of the Bankruptcy Code.

§362 stays

stay: presumed for debt collection, available otherwise

Sections 363 and 364 authorize the trustee (and hence the debtor in possession in Chapter 11 cases) to sell, use, and lease property and to borrow money. When these transactions fall outside the ordinary course of business, however, the Bankruptcy Code requires notice and a hearing and may impose other requirements as well.

A crucial part of any bankruptcy case is identifying the claims that exist against the debtor and the assets the debtor has. Chapter 5 of the Bankruptcy Code tells us how to go about doing this. Sections 501 through 510 focus on claims against the estate. Among other things, this part of the Bankruptcy Code embraces the idea that the general creditors must bear the costs the debtor incurs during the course of the bankruptcy case. After the estate satisfies the special priority for "domestic support obligations" such alimony or child care, if any, the costs of the bankruptcy process are to be paid before the general creditors share what is left. See §§101(14A); 507(a)(2). These "administrative expense claims" include the costs of the bankruptcy proceeding and the expenses of running the business.

costs of bankruptcy come out of general creditors' take

Section 506 addresses the rights of a creditor who has properly perfected a security interest in collateral. "Perfection" is a term of art. To have a perfected interest a creditor ordinarily must take a step to give the world notice of the property claim. A mortgagee typically records its interest in the local real estate records, while a creditor with a security interest in personal property files a financing statement in the secretary of state's office. As we saw in chapter 1, outside of bankruptcy, a creditor with a properly perfected security interest in collateral is entitled to be paid to the extent of the value of the collateral before other creditors.

As a general matter, properly perfected secured creditors beat (or, to use the words lawyers commonly employ, "prime" or "trump") the rights of general creditors in bankruptcy as well (and even beats special priority claims such as those for domestic support or administrative expense). This is a straightforward application of the *Butner* principle. Consistent with that principle, however, the secured creditor takes priority only to the extent of the value of its collateral. Outside of bankruptcy, typically as a matter of contract, a secured creditor can look to collateral to ensure that it is paid not only interest but also the costs of enforcing its claim. Again, bankruptcy provides for the same result. If the collateral is worth more than the amount of the debt (that is, if the creditor is "oversecured"), the creditor has a secured claim equal to the amount of the debt. In addition, §506(b) allows the oversecured creditor to enjoy interest on its claim during bankruptcy and also to be paid any reasonable expenses it incurs if it had a contractual right to security for these expenses up to the amount of oversecurity. (Undersecured creditors do not receive interest or expenses under this provision.)

Section 506 illustrates the way in which the Bankruptcy Code sets out the rights of creditors. To understand what rights a particular creditor enjoys in bankruptcy, one must focus on the claim or claims that creditor has. Under §506(a), if the collateral is worth less than the amount of the debt (that is, if the claim is "undersecured"), the claim is bifurcated. The creditor has a secured claim equal to the value of the collateral and an unsecured claim for the difference. What the creditor receives turns on how each claim is treated.

One must, however, distinguish between the rights that a secured creditor enjoys against the debtor by virtue of its claim and the rights that such a creditor enjoys against particular assets by virtue of its lien—its property interest—in those assets. In a simple Chapter 7 liquidation, the lien that the creditor enjoys is unaffected. It "passes through" bankruptcy.

Assume, for example, that a bank lends a debtor $100,000 and takes a security interest in a piece of real property that an individual debtor owns. A recession hits and the property drops in value and is now worth only $25,000. The debtor files a Chapter 7 petition. Because the debt to the bank exceeds the value of the land, the trustee cannot possibly benefit the general creditors by keeping the property. The trustee may therefore give this property back to the debtor—or "abandon" it, to use the language of §554.

The Bankruptcy Code, §727, provides that the debtor's personal liability to the bank and to all other creditors is discharged. The bank,

[handwritten margin notes: Ch. 7 lien-pass through if trustee abandons it to debtor, Bank can still foreclose]

however, remains free to foreclose on the land once it is in debtor's hands because the lien, if otherwise valid, survives (or "passes through") bankruptcy. Even though the bank had a secured claim of only $25,000 in the debtor's bankruptcy, the bank can enjoy whatever is realized by the sale of the land up to the amount of the loan. This amount could be greater than $25,000 if the land increases in value before the foreclosure sale or if the bankruptcy judge undervalued it. The bank enjoys the benefit of its $100,000 lien, even though its secured claim in bankruptcy against the debtor is for only $25,000. The scope of this principle of lien pass-through, however, is limited because of the special treatment provided for liens in Chapters 11 and 13.

Sections 541 through 562 tell us what assets the estate has. These provisions are all built upon the central idea that we must begin with the set of rights and obligations that exist outside of bankruptcy and then identify specific bankruptcy policies that require departing from the nonbankruptcy baseline. Section 541 establishes the central concept of the "property of the estate." The trustee (or the debtor in possession) is charged with assembling the assets that are available to meet the creditors' claims and then distributing them. These assets are called "property of the estate" and form the "bankruptcy estate."

Section 541 also draws a sharp distinction between individuals and corporations. The future income of individuals does not become property of the estate, while the future income of a corporation does. As we have already noted, drawing this distinction is a crucial feature of bankruptcy's "fresh start" for individual debtors. *[handwritten: → corps don't get a fresh start]*

In many cases, property to which the creditors of a debtor are entitled is property to which a third party lays claim. In these cases, the trustee (or debtor in possession) may have to bring an action to vindicate the creditors' right to the property. If the debtor itself could have brought the cause of action, the cause of action itself is property of the estate under §541. In other cases, the trustee must exercise one of the "avoiding" or "strong-arm" powers. Section 544(a), for example, enables the trustee to set aside unperfected security interests. A creditor who fails to perfect loses its priority in bankruptcy, just as it would lose outside of bankruptcy if any of the debtor's general creditors reduced its claim to judgment and levied on the debtor's assets. *[handwritten margin: §541 trustee should avoid unperfected claims + treat claims as assets of the estate]*

Section 548 allows the trustee to set aside fraudulent conveyances, just as general creditors can outside of bankruptcy. Like its nonbankruptcy counterparts, this enactment of fraudulent conveyance law includes transfers made and obligations incurred for less than reasonably equivalent value while the debtor was insolvent. They also include transfers made and obligations incurred with the intent to hinder, delay, or defraud creditors.

The avoiding powers also allow the trustee to set aside transfers that were made to a creditor on the eve of bankruptcy. This power to avoid such last-minute "preferences" is contained in §547. This departure from nonbankruptcy law reflects the way in which bankruptcy is a collective proceeding that responds to the common pool problem.

The Bankruptcy Code's general provisions in Chapters 1, 3, and 5 are not organized ideally. A number of provisions could well have been placed elsewhere. Section 108, for example, gives the trustee a grace period for taking certain actions. Because the consequences of failing to take action often turn on whether the automatic stay is implicated, this provision is best read in conjunction with §362. Similarly, §554, which addresses the question whether the trustee can abandon an asset of the estate, is best understood in conjunction with §363. Abandoning an asset, however, is simply another kind of use. As we have already noted, the overarching principle of the Bankruptcy Code, reinforced by 28 U.S.C. §959, requires that the trustee act in accordance with applicable nonbankruptcy law.

Section 365 is the Bankruptcy Code provision most conspicuously out of place. Section 365 deals not with the administration of the bankruptcy estate but with executory contracts. Executory contracts are, by their nature, mutual rights and obligations between a debtor and a third party. They are claims against the estate because they give a third party rights against the debtor. They are simultaneously assets of the estate because they give the debtor rights against a third party. Thus they are best seen as combinations of claims and assets. Because both claims and assets fall within the ambit of the Bankruptcy Code's Chapter 5, the section on executory contracts belongs there. The failure to put §365 in the correct place should not, in principle, affect how it is interpreted, but its faulty positioning may have compounded the difficulties lawyers and judges have had in applying it consistently.

The remainder of the Bankruptcy Code is loosely organized around how a case is disposed of once assets are gathered and claims are assigned their priority order under applicable nonbankruptcy law. So, for example, Chapter 7 of the Code provides for a simple liquidation of a bankruptcy estate's assets applied to pay allowed claims es

sentially in order of nonbankruptcy priority but subject to some special bankruptcy rules. These special rules are contained in or referred
to by §726. Also, as noted above, Chapter 7 usually provides for an
individual debtor's discharge of unpaid debts, though there are exceptions if the debtor has misbehaved with respect to her obligations. (A
corporate debtor can be liquidated under Chapter 7, but a corporation
neither receives a discharge nor has any use for one. Once a corporate
debtor's assets are gone, there is nothing left for creditors to go after
later.)

Chapter 7 is properly called the liquidation chapter. But again,
the Bankruptcy Code is not perfectly organized. Not all provisions
relevant to a Chapter 7 case are contained in Chapter 7. For example,
§522 handles the issues that might arise with respect to exempt property, and §523 looks at whether there are any specific obligations of
the debtor, such as taxes or child support obligations, that are not subject to discharge. These provisions by themselves again define the basic contours of the fresh start for the flesh-and-blood individual.

An individual who wishes to retain some otherwise nonexempt
assets, or a relatively affluent individual who is ineligible for Chapter
7 relief because she fails the means test imposed by §707(b), may be
able to use Chapter 13 of the Bankruptcy Code. Under Chapter 13, the
debtor proposes an "adjustment" of her obligations. In a plan of adjustment, a debtor proposes to keep some or all of her property but
promises to repay some or all of her prebankruptcy obligations out of
future income. Each creditor is entitled to receive under the plan at
least as much at it would have received in Chapter 7. Moreover, if a
creditor objects, a court may not confirm a plan unless, in the court's
view, the objecting creditor will be paid in full or the plan exhausts
the debtor's disposable income. Chapter 13 is short, contained entirely
within §§1301-1308 and §§1321-1330.

Chapter 11 is designed primarily for business firms that need to
restructure their debt obligations. (Individuals with large business-
related debts may also find it useful. Subsections 1141(d)(2) and (3)
ensure that individual debtors receive a fresh start similar to the ones
available under Chapters 7 and 13.) In a typical Chapter 11 case, the
debtor in possession has a window of time (presumptively 120 days
up to a maximum of 18 months) to propose a "reorganization plan"
that includes a new capital structure for the firm. After this period of
exclusivity expires, others are free to file plans as well.

Individual creditors cannot be given rights so powerful that each of them has the power to scuttle a reorganization. Chapter 11 strikes a balance between protecting individual creditors and ensuring a process that works in the joint interests of all creditors. Most of the protection a creditor receives comes from its ability to join with similarly situated creditors and vote as a class against the plan. Chapter 11 provides that each claim be placed in a class with similar claims. Each class as a whole votes on whether to approve a plan. Class acceptance requires approval of a majority in number and two-thirds by amount of the claims in the class.

If a class approves the plan, each holder of a claim in that class is bound unless that creditor can show that it would receive more from a Chapter 7 liquidation of the firm than it is receiving under the plan. If a class votes against the plan, however, the court can approve the plan only if it is "fair and equitable" and if it does not "discriminate unfairly." These terms of art require that the *absolute priority* of each claim be respected. Junior classes cannot receive any property on account of their old claims or interests unless senior classes accept the plan or are paid in full. When, for example, a plan provides for some distribution to holders of equity, it can be approved only if each class of claims consents or is paid in full. Moreover, each class is entitled to be treated as well as other classes that enjoy the same priority outside of bankruptcy. When a plan proposes to give one class of unsecured claims 20 cents on the dollar and another 10 cents, it can be approved only if the class that gets 10 cents votes in favor of the plan.

In addition to these principles, two other features of Chapter 11 are worth noting. If a reorganization plan leaves a creditor's rights unaffected, that creditor has no ability to object to the plan. A creditor who possesses the same rights after Chapter 11 as before has nothing to complain about. It is "unimpaired." At least one class of impaired claims, however, has to approve the plan. And if a plan fails to gain the support of even one class of claimholders, one should not believe that the plan in fact advances everyone's interest.

These mechanics, and other requirements, are contained primarily in §§1121-1129. If a plan is confirmed, the old equity interests in, and claims against, the debtor are discharged by §1141. Cancellation of the old claims and interests is an essential part of putting a new capital structure in place. Because the absolute priority ensures that creditors will receive the entire value of the firm or be paid in full, the discharge in Chapter 11 for corporations in no sense offers a "fresh start" to shareholders or anyone else. When a firm is insolvent, the shareholders are not entitled to anything.

[handwritten margin note: Ch.11 allows discharge but not really a fresh start]

These provisions touch on the entire breadth of the Bankruptcy Code. The Bankruptcy Code also contains a special set of rules for municipalities in Chapter 9 and family farmers in Chapter 12. Like the rules for stockbrokers in Chapter 7 and railroads in Chapter 11, their special characteristics are beyond the scope of this book. The special rules governing transnational bankruptcy are set out in Chapter 15 of the Code and are addressed briefly in the last chapter of this book.

In the next part of the book, we study in detail how bankruptcy law coordinates the actions of the creditors and overcomes the collective action problem they face in asserting their claims against an insolvent firm. The third and last part of the book examines in detail how bankruptcy law implements the fresh start for individuals and provides a new capital structure for corporations. Before we turn to these issues, however, we set out briefly in the next section the way in which bankruptcy law tries to create a single forum and the various constraints—constitutional and practical—that prevent this vision from being fully realized. It provides the last piece of background we need before we explore the Bankruptcy Code in detail.

C. THE BANKRUPTCY FORUM

The Bankruptcy Code is designed to enable the debtor's affairs to be sorted out in a single forum. There are, however, a number of constraints that prevent this goal from being fully realized. We review these in this section and then we set out the way in which the bankruptcy courts are organized in the federal judicial system.

The limited jurisdictional reach of the bankruptcy courts constrains the extent to which they can provide a single forum in which to resolve a debtor's problems. The jurisdictional reach of the bankruptcy court is effectively limited to our national boundaries. As our economy becomes increasingly global, however, firms are likely to have assets and creditors in multiple jurisdictions. Another limit stems from several provisions of the United States Constitution. Article III limits what bankruptcy judges can do given that they do not have life tenure. The jury trial right in the Seventh Amendment limits our ability to expedite the resolution of disputes. Finally, the sovereign immunity a state enjoys limits the ability of the bankruptcy court to

[handwritten margin note: bankruptcy judges do not have life tenure]

resolve disputes even when the state is merely asserting its rights as a creditor. We look at each of these problems in turn.

When all the assets of a debtor are located in the United States, we can still realize the goal of having a single forum. Unlike a federal court sitting in a diversity case, the jurisdictional reach of the bankruptcy court is nationwide. Even a creditor who does not have the minimum contacts with California to make it amenable to suit in state court must still file its claim in the bankruptcy court in California if the debtor has chosen to file its petition there. See Harder v. Desert Breezes Master Association, 192 Bankr. 47 (N.D.N.Y. 1996). Indeed, many large bankruptcy cases are now filed in Delaware because 28 U.S.C. §1408 includes domicile as an appropriate venue and many firms are incorporated under Delaware law.

Our economy, however, is increasingly global. A firm may have creditors and assets throughout the world. The law governing transnational bankruptcy is still largely unformed, but we must still resolve these cases in which, as a practical matter, there will be more than one bankruptcy forum. Three distinct sets of problems can be identified:

A. those that arise when an insolvency proceeding is brought against a debtor in another country when many of its assets and creditors are located in this country

B. those that arise when a debtor in this country has assets and creditors located abroad

C. those that arise when a firm has assets and creditors abroad as well as in this country and insolvency proceedings are brought in both.

Chapter 15 of the Bankruptcy Code responds to the first set of problems. A firm's operations are centered in a foreign country, but it has creditors or assets in this country. The creditors may want to vindicate their rights in this country rather than pursue them abroad. A representative from a foreign insolvency proceeding may file an ancillary case under §1515 and ask the bankruptcy judge to enjoin creditors from pursuing their rights in this country. A petition by a foreign representative in a duly initiated foreign proceeding is presumptively valid, as provided by §1516, and this initiates the automatic stay against creditors per §1520. But before the bankruptcy court will step aside in favor of the foreign representative and the foreign proceeding, the court will first consider matters of comity and consider among other factors whether the foreign proceeding will treat holders of all claims fairly. See §§1507; 1522. If the bankruptcy judge is satisfied that the foreign insolvency regime is not repugnant to the Bankruptcy Code and that creditors from this country will not be discriminated against in the distant forum, the rules of that forum will likely govern. Left unsolved, even under new Chapter 15, is the appropriate treatment when the process is fair but the substantive distributional rules depart significantly from those of the Bankruptcy Code.

Large corporations may have assets outside the United States. There is a general presumption against extraterritorial application of U.S. statutes. See EEOC v. Arabian American Oil Co., 499 U.S. 244, 248 (1991). Nevertheless, the bankruptcy estate that §541 creates extends to all of the property of the debtor, wherever located. Hence, notwithstanding the presumption, the automatic stay prevents a U.S. citizen from using the courts in a foreign jurisdiction to exercise control over a debtor whose corporate headquarters is in the United States. See In re Rimsat, Ltd., 98 F.3d 956 (7th Cir. 1996). Similarly, the bankruptcy court can sanction a foreign creditor who pursues the foreign collection of a debt discharged in a bankruptcy in this country in which the foreign creditor actively participated. See In re Simon, 153 F.3d 991 (9th Cir. 1998).

A multinational corporation may have its corporate headquarters in one jurisdiction, the bulk of its assets in another, and its creditors in another still. Hence, when the firm encounters financial distress, creditors (or the debtor itself) may bring an insolvency action in more than one jurisdiction. A parent corporation headquartered in Great Britain uses assets of its U.S. subsidiary to repay a French bank several weeks before entering bankruptcy proceedings in both Great Britain and the United States. The trustee (or other person charged with preserving the bankruptcy estate) seeks to recover the payment to the bank as a voidable preference. The insolvency laws of Great Britain, like those of the United States, limit the ability of creditors to enjoy preferential payments on the eve of bankruptcy. The contours of British law, however, are slightly different, and the trustee has a better chance of success under U.S. law.

In this situation the law must answer two distinct questions: First, it must be decided whether the trustee is free to bring the action in either forum. Second, it must be decided whether the court that hears the action will apply its own law, the law of the other jurisdiction, or a mixture of the two. (The court might, for example, permit the preference action if either jurisdiction's law allowed it or only if both did.)

We return to this question when we study transnational bankruptcies in chapter 13, section B.

Our ability to sort out the affairs of a debtor in a single forum is limited even when we are not dealing with a firm whose activities cross international borders. A debtor might have its assets and creditors in the same city, but we still may not be able to resolve everything in front of the bankruptcy court because of a number of constraints that the U.S. Constitution imposes on the way in which bankruptcy courts do business.

The 1978 Bankruptcy Reform Act entrusted bankruptcy matters to specialized judges. The powers of bankruptcy judges with respect to the disputes before them, however, were much like those of a federal district judge. They could issue writs of execution, conduct jury trials, and hold litigants in contempt. Moreover, the disputes a bankruptcy judge hears are often garden-variety lawsuits that differ from others only in that one of the parties happens to have filed a bankruptcy petition. Much of the work of the bankruptcy judge was that of an ordinary common law judge. For these reasons, the Supreme Court found that bankruptcy judges exercised the "judicial power" within the meaning of Article III of the Constitution. Article III, however, requires those who exercise the judicial power to have life tenure and bankruptcy judges are appointed to 14-year terms. Hence, the Court struck down the procedural provisions of the 1978 Act, and Congress was forced to craft new ones. Northern Pipeline Construction Co. v. Marathon Pipe Line Co., 458 U.S. 50 (1982).

The current rules have their distinctive shape because they give as much control of bankruptcy matters as possible to bankruptcy judges without giving them life tenure. Disappointed litigants have a right to de novo review in the district courts for matters that are not central to the administration of the bankruptcy case, but only appellate review of those matters that are central to the bankruptcy case. There are two rationales for this distinction. The first rests on history and practices that existed at the time the Constitution was drafted. In eighteenth-century England, the Chancellor appointed commissioners to do much of the work of gathering and administering a bankruptcy estate. Because they were not judges, what these commissioners did cannot be considered an exercise of the judicial power within the meaning of Article III. The second rationale rests on an idea imported from administrative law. Because bankruptcy law is entirely created by Congress, adjudication of rights under it (as opposed to deciding matters involving other legal issues) is an adjudication of "public rights" that do not require an Article III judge. See Crowell v. Benson, 285 U.S. 22 (1932).

The Constitution also mandates the use of juries in some disputes that arise in bankruptcy. The Seventh Amendment requires that the right to a jury trial be preserved in federal court for "suits at common law" when the amount in controversy exceeds $20. Many of the questions in a bankruptcy case, including whether a particular person has a claim against the debtor, would be "suits at common law" if brought outside of bankruptcy. It does not follow, however, that all such claims give rise to a right to a jury trial. A bankruptcy court is a court of equity, and it has the right to use "chancery methods" to decide matters that are central to the bankruptcy process. See Barton v. Barbour, 104 U.S. 126, 134 (1881).

We must therefore determine when a suit is so central to the bankruptcy process that it loses its common law character and can be decided without a jury. In Granfinanciera v. Nordberg, 492 U.S. 33 (1989), the Supreme Court found that the jurisdictional rules governing fraudulent conveyance actions in bankruptcy cases were at odds with the Seventh Amendment's jury trial requirement. Under 28 U.S.C. §157(e), if a right to a jury trial exists, the bankruptcy judge may conduct it only if the district judge specially designates her to do it and only if the parties give their express consent.

In resolving the problems that Article III and the Seventh Amendment present, courts often look to the procedural rules under the 1898 Bankruptcy Act. But the 1898 Act needs to be placed in context. In 1867, Congress passed a bankruptcy statute that gave the bankruptcy court jurisdiction over actions the debtor had against third parties. Some of the unhappiness with this law (which was repealed in 1878) was due to the intrusion by federal courts into disputes that had traditionally been the province of state courts. As a result, the jurisdictional provisions of the 1898 Act were crafted much more narrowly, and bankruptcy courts were given only "summary jurisdiction." They were restricted to resolving disputes between parties who consented (actually or constructively) to the jurisdiction of the bankruptcy court or disputes involving property in its actual or constructive control.

Congress abolished this distinction between summary proceedings before the bankruptcy court and plenary proceedings that had to take place elsewhere in 1978. When the new procedures came under constitutional attack, however, Congress looked back and used them as a benchmark. The procedures under the 1898 Act came into being for reasons that had nothing to do with either Article III or the Seventh Amendment, and the distinctions that had grown up around the 1898 Act (a flavor of which is imparted in the ideas of "constructive" control and consent) were elaborate and artificial. Moreover, the Supreme Court never decided whether these procedures passed muster under Article III. The interplay between history and constitutional mandate thus creates much of the intricacy of bankruptcy procedure.

The role of a state as a party in a bankruptcy case also raises jurisdictional issues. A bankruptcy trustee may, for example, seek to recover from a state a voidable preference. Were the state a private party, it would be subject to the decisions of the bankruptcy court. Under the Eleventh Amendment, however, a state is immune from suit in a federal forum unless it waives its sovereign immunity or Congress removes such immunity.

When Congress attempts to abrogate a state's immunity it must, at a minimum, do so expressly. Hoffman v. Connecticut Dept. of Income Maintenance, 492 U.S. 96 (1989). This hurdle is not an issue in bankruptcy because §106(a) of the Bankruptcy Code makes abrogation of the state's immunity explicit. For a time, it was thought, though, that Congress lacked the power to cut back on sovereign immunity under Article I of the Constitution, where its bankruptcy power lies. Seminole Tribe of Florida v. Florida, 517 U.S. 44 (1996). But in Central Virginia Community College v. Katz, 546 U.S. 356 (2006), the Supreme Court held that the Constitution's Article I Bankruptcy Clause empowered Congress to establish actions by a debtor against a State to recover past payments; the Court declined to follow the language in *Seminole Tribe* that would have led to a different holding. Thus, the legitimacy of §106(a) is no longer in doubt.

Generally, then, most of what we shall study plays out in the bankruptcy court and is subject only to appellate review. It is useful to spend some time to see how the rules of procedure bring this about, notwithstanding the limitations that we have discussed.

Federal district courts have original and exclusive jurisdiction over all "cases" under Title 11. 28 U.S.C. §1334. The entire process triggered by the bankruptcy petition is a "case." Hence, this provision provides that a debtor may file its bankruptcy petition only in a federal district court, as opposed to, let us say, a state court. Section 1334 also gives the district courts original (but not exclusive) jurisdiction over all civil "proceedings" arising under Title 11 or arising in or related to "cases" under Title 11. A controversy such as a fraudulent conveyance action that takes place in the course of settling the affairs of a particular debtor is a "proceeding."

Bankruptcy jurisdiction can extend to parties who are neither creditors nor debtors when the dispute is "related to" a case under Title 11. The reach of "related to" jurisdiction has been broadly defined. Courts sometimes seem to ask simply "whether the outcome of the proceeding could conceivably have any effect upon the estate being administered in bankruptcy." In re Salem Mortgage Co., 783 F.2d 626, 634 (6th Cir. 1986). A claim that a creditor has against a guarantor of the debtor that would have no impact on the estate is an example of an action that falls outside the jurisdictional reach of §1334.

Bankruptcy courts are adjuncts of the district courts, and §1334 must be read in conjunction with §157(a) of Title 28. Section 157 allows the district court to "refer" any or all bankruptcy cases to bankruptcy judges. It also provides that the district court may "refer" any or all proceedings arising under the Bankruptcy Code, or arising in or related to a bankruptcy case, to bankruptcy judges. In all district courts this practice is firmly institutionalized. Bankruptcy petitions are, as a practical matter, filed in the bankruptcy courts. The purpose of this circumlocution is to ensure that the dictates of Article III are satisfied. The bankruptcy judge is not acting autonomously and is not exercising the "judicial power," because the bankruptcy judge is merely an adjunct to the district court. Just as a court of equity can appoint a special master, the reasoning goes, the district court can choose to delegate bankruptcy cases to bankruptcy judges.

The idea that the district courts have jurisdiction over bankruptcy cases and proceedings is not entirely a formal fiction. Although everything is routinely referred to the bankruptcy courts, §157(d) gives the district judge the power to withdraw the "reference" in any particular case or proceeding, in whole or in part, for cause. The district court can act either on its own motion or on a timely motion of any party. Although district courts rarely want to hear bankruptcy disputes, they have withdrawn the reference in some important cases.

Withdrawal of the reference is mandatory after a timely motion when "resolution of the proceeding requires consideration of both Title 11 and other laws of the United States regulating organizations or activities affecting interstate commerce." This provision has been read narrowly, as it must be, given that so many disputes in a bankruptcy case involve consideration of federal laws that affect interstate commerce. Courts typically use a "substantial and material" test: With-

low Idraw reference if
subs. + mat. US law
(other)

drawal is mandatory only when the issues presented require a significant interpretation of federal laws, not when what is presented is the straightforward application of federal law to a particular set of facts. A difficult controversy involving the reach of CERCLA or some other equally complex statute is potentially a subject of mandatory withdrawal, but even then, the district court may remand to the bankruptcy court for submission of proposed findings of fact and conclusions of law under §157(c)(1).

The Bankruptcy Code provides that some decisions of the bankruptcy judge over the bankruptcy case are not reviewable by appeal or otherwise. The most important of these may be the decision to dismiss or not to dismiss a case under §305. One needs to bear in mind, however, that the bankruptcy judge, even here, is not completely autonomous because the district court has the power to withdraw the reference.

Once a case is referred to a bankruptcy judge, many decisions are subject only to appellate review by the district court. Section 157 tells us that bankruptcy judges "may hear and determine all cases" referred to them under the Bankruptcy Code, subject to appellate review under 28 U.S.C. §158. "Case" is used in the technical sense here and refers only to the process that begins with the bankruptcy petition. Individual disputes that arise during the debtor's course through bankruptcy are "proceedings." When these proceedings are central to the administration of the case (or, to use the term in Title 28, when they are "core"), the bankruptcy judge is again subject only to appellate review. "Core" proceedings include confirmation of plans, matters concerning the administration of the estate, and the allowance or disallowance of claims against the estate. Section 157(b)(2) contains a list of "core" proceedings, but this list is not by its terms exhaustive.

What remains are "noncore" proceedings. A typical example is a lawsuit that the debtor has against some third party. For these, the bankruptcy judge is subject to de novo review. The bankruptcy judge must submit proposed findings of fact and conclusions of law to the district court. The district court can make a final order only after reviewing de novo those matters to which a party has objected.

Under 28 U.S.C. §158(a), the district courts have appellate review of final judgments, orders, and decrees from the bankruptcy court. The district courts also have jurisdiction to hear appeals from interlocutory orders and decrees. In these cases, however, "leave of the court" is required. It is not clear whether this means parties have to get permission of the bankruptcy judge or the district judge or both.

The courts of appeals have jurisdiction to hear appeals from final decisions, judgments, orders, and decrees under 28 U.S.C. §158(d). Determining what is a "final" judgment for purposes of 28 U.S.C. §158(d) has proven difficult. Assume that there is a final judgment in the bankruptcy court and the district court hears the appeal and remands to the bankruptcy court. Courts are divided on whether an appeal can be taken to the court of appeals. Section 158(d) does not tell us explicitly whether it is sufficient that the bankruptcy judge's decision be final or whether the district court's decision must be final as well. Most courts recognize that a district court's order generally is not final if it remands the dispute to the bankruptcy court, especially if the remand requires the bankruptcy court to make factual findings or exercise its discretion. See In re Koch, 109 F.3d 1285 (8th Cir. 1997).

The uncertainty in the meaning of finality in §158(d) can put lawyers in the awkward position of having to choose between making an appeal of a decision that may prove to be interlocutory or waiving the right altogether if it later proves to have been a final order. Section 158(d)(2) mitigates this problem to some extent. This section allows a court of appeals, in its discretion, to review an interlocutory order, provided the lower court, on its own or at the request of a party (or at the insistence of the parties collectively), certifies the issue of law at question as undecided, of public importance, or of importance to the progress of the case at hand.

The Bankruptcy Rules establish the procedures used in the bankruptcy courts. They do not change the substantive rules of the Bankruptcy Code, but they do affect how the issues are shaped. For example, they distinguish between different types of hearings that take place before the bankruptcy judge. First there are "adversary proceedings," which are conducted under much the same rules as any other civil dispute. Sections of the Federal Rules of Civil Procedure covering such things as pleading, joinder, depositions, interrogatories, and summary judgment have been incorporated into the bankruptcy rules governing adversary proceedings. We learn from Bankruptcy Rule 7001 that adversary proceedings include proceedings to compel someone other than the debtor to deliver property to the trustee, to determine the validity of a lien, to object to a discharge, or to obtain an injunction or equitable relief.

Whenever an actual dispute before the bankruptcy court is not an "adversary proceeding," it is a "contested matter." Among the most common is a motion to lift the automatic stay. The procedures for contested matters are more streamlined and are set out in Bankruptcy Rule 9014. For example, no response is required in a contested matter unless the court orders an answer to a motion. The court, however, has the power to invoke the more elaborate rules for adversary proceedings in contested matters when appropriate.

Bankruptcy courts also have the inherent power under §105 to impose sanctions in order to maintain control of their courtrooms and of their dockets. See In re Volpert, 110 F.3d 494 (7th Cir. 1997); Caldwell v. Unified Capital Corp. (In re Rainbow Magazine), 77 F.3d 278 (9th Cir. 1996). Moreover, Rule 11 of general civil procedure (which sanctions lawyers for frivolous pleadings), or its counterpart under the Bankruptcy Rules, Rule 9011, is available at every stage of bankruptcy litigation. See In re Roete, 936 F.2d 963 (7th Cir. 1991). In addition, §362(h) of the Bankruptcy Code explicitly grants the bankruptcy court the power to award actual and punitive damages to an "individual" injured by any violation of the automatic stay. (Courts, however, are divided on whether "individual" in this context means only flesh-and-blood human beings. Compare In re Chateaugay Corp., 920 F.2d 183 (2d Cir. 1990), and Jove Engineering, Inc. v. IRS, 92 F.3d 1539 (11th Cir. 1996), with In re Atlantic Business & Community Corp., 901 F.2d 325 (3d Cir. 1990).)

With this framework in hand, we can now turn to our study of the Bankruptcy Code and the way it works in practice.

Part Two

THE BANKRUPTCY PROCESS

Mastery of bankruptcy law begins with understanding that the law is in major part a procedure that responds to a collective action problem. Without the bankruptcy process, creditors might attempt to grab assets while debtors might attempt to hide them, even if such actions are not in the collective best interest. To accomplish bankruptcy's objectives, but (as *Butner* dictates) not otherwise distort substantive rights, the law must stay the hands of the creditors, assemble the debtor's assets, and ensure that no one individually or through collusion grabs or removes assets in anticipation of bankruptcy. The law must also ensure that the debtor's postpetition conduct conforms to nonbankruptcy law while the process runs its course.

Bankruptcy's other purposes—providing relief to individuals and reorganizing the capital structure of a firm in financial distress—depend on such a process existing and working effectively, but do not dictate its contours. The best evidence of this is that the Bankruptcy Code's process provisions typically apply to individuals and corporations alike. If implementing such a process had to be done with bankruptcy's substantive purposes in mind, we could not have a process that applied equally to both types of cases and worked effectively with respect to each type. Yet, as we shall see, they do usually work well.

In this part, we group the rules governing the bankruptcy process by the functions they serve. In chapter 3, we look at how a bankruptcy case begins. Here the bankruptcy rules play the role of gatekeeper. They try to keep out those who do not belong in bankruptcy—those whose disputes are unrelated to the problems bankruptcy tries to solve. For example, a family dispute over the administration of a trust fund should not be in bankruptcy court. Bankruptcy's eligibility rules are designed to bar such cases. We also consider which parties can control the moment when the bankruptcy process starts or indeed whether it starts at all. Finally, we consider how bankruptcy courts exercise their discretion to dismiss cases that otherwise meet the Bankruptcy Code's formal requirements.

In chapter 4, we turn to the automatic stay. As we have seen, nonbankruptcy rules of debt collection force each creditor to look out for its own interests. A collective proceeding such as a bankruptcy is inconsistent with such a regime. There must be a rule that supplants individual creditor rights but that does no more than necessary to implement the collective proceeding. The automatic stay ensures that the process can sort out the debtor's problems with creditors, but generally does not otherwise bestow any benefits or impose any costs. Here the hard problems arise because parties sometimes wear multiple hats. Suppose a debtor's factory emits pollution and the state environmental agency fines the debtor before the bankruptcy begins. In this case, the government wears both the hat of a prepetition creditor, as it is owed money, and a postpetition regulator, someone who ensures that the debtor complies with applicable law. Keeping these two roles separate is often difficult.

Once the stay is in place, the primary job of the trustee is to sort out who is owed what and establish what assets the debtor has. (Unless the context suggests otherwise, we follow the language of the Bankruptcy Code and use "trustee" to refer to either a trustee or a debtor in possession.) The trustee must take account of the debtor's liabilities, which give rise to "claims." The process of recognizing and "allowing" claims is the subject of chapter 5. The trustee must also gather assets of the debtor. These become "property of the estate." Chapter 6 explores this process. The basic idea stems again from *Butner*. Painting with broad strokes, and with some exceptions, the bankruptcy estate consists, in the first instance, of whatever rights of the debtor that the creditors could reach outside of bankruptcy, subject to all the limitations applicable outside of bankruptcy.

Sometimes a debtor holds rights that are a liability and an asset at the same time. The debtor is obliged to pay a farmer $10, but the farmer is obliged to give the debtor a bushel of wheat in exchange. The debtor has an obligation to pay for the wheat (a liability) but also a right to receive wheat (an asset). Bankruptcy law treats combined liabilities and assets under the rubric of "executory contracts." We explore these below in chapter 7.

The trustee cannot rest after identifying the obligations and rights of the debtor. Creditors of the debtor sometimes have greater rights against a third party than the debtor. The paradigmatic example arises when a secured creditor fails to record its interest. Under nonbankruptcy law, the secured creditor is still entitled to enforce its rights against the debtor, but not against a general creditor that has reduced its claim to judgment and obtained a lien. We begin chapter 8 with an explanation of how the Bankruptcy Code ensures the same result in bankruptcy for this and related examples, such as when a creditor holds an unperfected statutory lien. Chapter 8 then goes on to show how the Code allows a trustee to recover fraudulent conveyances that a creditor might have recovered outside of bankruptcy. Finally, chapter 8 addresses "preferential" prebankruptcy transfers that the Bankruptcy Code permits the trustee to recover because bankruptcy's collective proceeding cannot work effectively if individual creditors can anticipate bankruptcy and protect themselves at the expense of other creditors.

Bankruptcy proceedings take time, and the rest of the world does not stop while the trustee sorts things out. Chapter 9 below addresses the trustee's powers to manage the estate. These powers are of particular interest when the debtor is a corporation that remains in business. Businesses face many decisions. To operate a business, then, the trustee or (more likely in a Chapter 11 case) the debtor in possession may need to buy and sell assets and borrow. Managing a business is always hard, but there are additional concerns when the business is a debtor in bankruptcy. We want the assets to be managed in a way that maximizes their value, but many decisions are likely to affect each type of investor differently. The decision that is in the interest of all the investors as a group may not be the one that is in the interests of the secured creditor or the old shareholder. We need to take these conflicts into account in the rules that govern the operation of the business inside of bankruptcy.

This survey of the bankruptcy process shows how bankruptcy law attempts to solve the collective action problem. It establishes the backdrop against which the twin substantive policies of debt relief for individuals and financial restructuring for firms play themselves out. As you study the bankruptcy process, bear in mind the *Butner* principle that bankruptcy law takes the nonbankruptcy baseline as a starting point.

III. COMMENCEMENT OF THE CASE

In this chapter we are concerned with whether and under what circumstances a bankruptcy proceeding should take place. We begin with the question of what types of entities should be eligible for bankruptcy. We then look at the mechanics of filing the bankruptcy petition and how malleable these rules are. In particular, we want to know whether parties can take steps before bankruptcy to prevent it from being used, even in circumstances in which the debtor is likely to have problems of the sort bankruptcy is designed to solve. Finally, we look at the discretion a judge has to dismiss cases when the debtor is properly before the court, but under circumstances in which the problems that creditors and their common debtor face might be better resolved elsewhere.

A. ELIGIBILITY IN BANKRUPTCY

Bankruptcy Code §109 focuses on whether a debtor is of a type for whom bankruptcy relief is appropriate. Section 109(a) limits potential debtors under the Bankruptcy Code to a "person"—defined by §101(41) to include individuals, partnerships, and corporations—who "resides or has a domicile, a place of business, or property in the United States," and to municipalities in the United States. Among these terms, "corporation" is further defined by §101(9) to include various entities that behave as a corporation. Beyond this, §109 is type and chapter specific. That is, it describes eligibility by type of debtor for each chapter of the Bankruptcy Code. Understanding §109, like understanding any other provision of the Bankruptcy Code, requires one to see the connection between specific statutory language and the Code's underlying policies.

Chapter 7, the Bankruptcy Code's basic "liquidation" chapter, cannot be used by railroads, domestic or foreign insurance companies, banks, savings banks, savings and loan associations, credit unions, or the like. See §109(b). Railroads are forced into a special set of provisions in Chapter 11, §§1161-1174. Insurance companies, banks, and similar institutions, unlike railroads, are *completely* excluded from being debtors under the Bankruptcy Code. These entities are heavily regulated by special state and federal laws. Hence, the reasoning goes, the rules governing the insolvency of these entities should reflect the same concerns that led to their regulation. In some cases, special insolvency rules for these institutions are well developed, as in the case of banks. But this is not always the case. For instance, while it is true that state laws govern matters such as the liquidation of insurance companies, some of these laws are not developed to any significant extent. Many are skeletal and incomplete, not fleshed out with a developed body of administrative or case law. Indeed, these incomplete state procedures sometimes borrow heavily from the provisions of, and experience under, the Bankruptcy Code. These exclusions have become more problematic as entities have emerged, such as HMOs, that are like insurance companies in many respects but not in others.

Chapter 9 is available only to a "municipality." See §109(c). A municipality is defined by §101(40) as a "political subdivision or public agency or instrumentality of a State." Section 101(52), in turn, provides that "State includes the District of Columbia and Puerto Rico, except for the purposes of defining who may be a debtor under Chapter 9" of the Bankruptcy Code. Implicitly, then, only parts of the fifty United States are eligible for Chapter 9. Municipal bankruptcies have been rare, the notoriety surrounding California's Orange County bankruptcy in the mid 1990s notwithstanding. This is perhaps because ordinarily municipalities can raise taxes to avoid default on their obligations. Nevertheless, many municipalities now have enormous liabilities to their retired workers. These may trigger a series of Chapter 9 bankruptcies over the coming decades.

Chapter 11, the "reorganization" chapter, is available to "any person who may be a debtor under Chapter 7," plus railroads, as noted above, but not a "stockbroker or commodity broker." See §109(d). Note that this definition includes partnerships, even if not a formal legal entity, and individuals, who are thus free to file Chapter 11 petitions. As we have noted, individual debtors rarely find Chapter 11 more attractive than Chapter 7 or Chapter 13 unless the debtor's obligations arise from a failed business venture.

Turning to the special Chapter 11 eligibility terms, stockbrokers and commodity brokers are excluded for the same reason that railroads are included: Chapter 7 has special rules governing the liquidation of stockbrokers and commodity brokers, §§741-753 and §§761-767. These rules govern the treatment of customer accounts and the special problems they raise.

Chapter 13 is available only "to an individual with regular income" (or such an individual and spouse), provided that on the date of the bankruptcy petition the debtor or debtors owe noncontingent, liquidated, unsecured debts of less than $336,900 and noncontingent, liquidated, secured debts of less than $1,010,650. See §109(e). (Note that these limits, like others given throughout this book, change over time.) Chapter 13 discharges a greater number of individual debts than either Chapter 11 or Chapter 7. It is not surprising that Chapter 13 is limited to individuals who earn regular income. The nature of Chapter 13 is for an individual to sacrifice some future income earned through her human capital, which she could shield entirely under Chapter 7, but retain some or all of her nonexempt assets, which would be paid to creditors under Chapter 7. Only an individual has human capital that would be protected under Chapter 7. And unless an individual has regular income, she has little to offer creditors in exchange for nonexempt assets. Individuals who owe more than the dollar caps in Chapter 13 are likely to have business debts and hence must comply with the more elaborate procedures of Chapter 11.

[handwritten margin note: Ch. 13 allows indiv. garnish but retain more non-exempt assets]

In addition to limitations on eligibility based on the type or inherent characteristics of a debtor, there are limitations designed to prevent filings by individuals who are uninformed. Specifically, the 2005 Bankruptcy Act contains provisions that seek to ensure the education of debtors about the law and personal financial management. (The better known provisions of the 2005 Act, which imposes a means test on individual debtors who seek Chapter 7 relief, are discussed later.) Bankruptcy Code §109 now conditions an individual's eligibility as a debtor in bankruptcy on the individual's receipt, within the six months prior to his bankruptcy petition, of credit counseling from an approved, nonprofit agency, if the debtor is capable of receiving such counseling and it is available. Whatever the merits of consumer counseling, Congress' decision to locate a counseling requirement in §109 was a drafting error, because if this provision is literally interpreted, only an individual who has received such counseling is an eligible debtor, assuming that he was able to receive such counseling. Hence, by the terms of the Bankruptcy Code, creditors are now unable to file an involuntary petition against any individual who has not received counseling but might have. While involuntary petitions are rare, this result, cannot have been intended. It remains to be seen how literal courts will be in interpreting this provision. See, e.g., In re Oberle, 2006 WL 3949174 (Bankr. N.D.Cal. 2006).

There are also limitations on frequent filers. Section 109(g) makes an individual debtor ineligible to file a bankruptcy petition under any chapter within 180 days of another bankruptcy case if that case was dismissed because of the debtor's failure to comply with orders of the court. Individual debtors are similarly ineligible if they ask for a dismissal of the case after a creditor requests relief from the automatic stay. This provision penalizes individuals who are not vigilant in pursuing their fresh start.

The exercises below ask you to consider some of these specific eligibility requirements more closely. The case that follows, *Treasure Island Land Trust,* as well as the related notes and problems, explore the more general question of the kind of entity that is eligible for bankruptcy. Only "persons" and "municipalities" are eligible for bankruptcy. The definition of "person" is crafted with this in mind and, while it includes individuals, partnerships, and corporations, it does not include entities such as a simple trust.

An ordinary trust is a way in which a person gives another or others the beneficial interest in assets without at the same time granting the beneficiaries control over the assets. Parents or grandparents, for example, can provide for the education of their children or grandchildren by making gifts in trust. The parents may want to make the gift now rather than wait, but do not yet want their children to have unrestricted use of the income-generating assets. They therefore appoint a trustee (not a bankruptcy trustee) who decides how the assets of the trust—typically stocks and bonds—should be invested and, in accordance with the trust instrument, decides when to use the income or principal for the benefit of the children. These trusts typically do not have creditors because the trustee rarely has the need to borrow money. Such trusts are unlikely ever to have problems that bankruptcy law is designed to solve.

By contrast, a business trust is included in the definition of a corporation in §101(9)(A)(v) and hence is a "person" within the meaning of §101(41) and therefore eligible for bankruptcy. Often called a "Massachusetts" business trust, the business trust is a way of doing business that predates the modern corporation. In the nineteenth century, people would pool their money together and appoint a trustee to manage a joint venture. The business trust did not insulate investors from personal tort liability, but much of the consensual credit was nonrecourse—limited by contract to recovery of the trust assets—and large tort actions against firms were rare during this period. Hence before the rise of the corporation, the business trust was the form of commercial enterprise that most effectively limited the liability of its investors to the amount of capital they contributed. Business trusts serve the same function as corporations and are eligible for bankruptcy for the same reason.

The Bankruptcy Code requires us to draw a line between the simple trust and the business trust. Consider, for example, whether an "Illinois" land trust is more like a simple trust or a business trust from the perspective of bankruptcy. An Illinois land trust is what lawyers call a "dry" trust: The trustee exerts no power over the assets of the trust. All the power lies in the beneficiary. A bank might hold a low-income apartment building in an Illinois land trust for one or more beneficiaries, but the beneficiaries have complete control over the property. (The beneficiaries frequently turn the day-to-day management of the property over to a managing agent, but in this respect they are no different from other real estate investors.) An Illinois land trust converts real property, the apartment building, into personal property, the shares in the trust. This may bring tax benefits and may make property easier to transfer. The most notorious advantage of an Illinois land trust was that it allowed respectable people to own low-income housing on the South Side of Chicago without letting other people know about it. (The trust, rather than the beneficiary, is listed as the owner in the public real estate records.) Whatever the purpose of such a trust, typically the only creditor is a bank that makes a non-recourse secured loan.

Treasure Island Land Trust poses a still harder question. The entity calls itself an Illinois land trust, but in substance was quite different from a typical trust. As you read the case, as well as the related notes and problems, you should ask whether the trust has the attributes that are likely to give rise to the sort of problems that bankruptcy is designed to solve. First, however, the following exercises establish the contours of the overall landscape.

Key Provision: Bankruptcy Code §109

EXERCISES

3A(1) Debtor Corporation runs a full-service medical clinic for a few patients in the eastern United States. The patients pay a fixed fee every year and for that fee Debtor provides all the medical care the patients require. Debtor's expenses are unexpectedly high and Debtor attempts to commence a Chapter 11 bankruptcy case. Is Debtor eligible? Should it be? Would your answer change if Debtor did not run a clinic, but rather served as an intermediary contracting with hundreds of doctors for the provision of care and with thousands of patients for annual fees in exchange for care? Would your answer change if

Debtor were a computer manufacturer who provided warranties to its customers along with the computers sold? See In re Medicare HMO, 998 F.2d 436 (7th Cir. 1993).

3A(2) Debtor is an <u>individual</u> with a <u>regular income</u> who recently lost a high-paying job and now earns only $20,000 per year. Debtor owes <u>$80,000 on unsecured credit-card debt</u>. He has no other obligations. Debtor's only asset of any value <u>is a $70,000 painting</u> he has inherited from his mother. The painting has sentimental value to Debtor, who files a Chapter <u>13 bankruptcy petition</u>, instead of a Chapter <u>7 petition,</u> solely because he wishes to retain the painting. Assuming that the painting is not exempt from collection by creditors, is Debtor eligible for Chapter 13?

3A(3) Debtor was employed through last year, but lost his job five weeks ago. He receives <u>unemployment checks of $850</u> a month. Is Debtor an "individual with regular income" within the meaning of §101(30), and thus able to use Chapter 13?

CASE

IN RE TREASURE ISLAND LAND TRUST

United States Bankruptcy Court, M.D. Florida, 1980
2 Bankr. 332

PROCTOR, BANKRUPTCY JUDGE.

The petition in this cause was filed in the name of Treasure Island Land Trust (the "Trust") on November 28, 1979. On November 30, 1979, R.E. Carrigan, Jr., and Lester E. Larson (the "Movants"), secured creditors, moved to dismiss the petition on the basis that the Trust is <u>not entitled to be a debtor</u> under the Bankruptcy Code. A hearing on the motion was held on January 9, 1980.

The Trust was created by contractual document entitled "Land Trust Agreement," dated March 26, 1971, between the trustee and various named beneficiaries. There have been certain modifications to the contract, but none that change the nature of the agreement or that are otherwise pertinent to the arguments here.

Section 109(a) states that "only a person that resides in the United States, or has a domicile, a place of business, or property in the United States, or a municipality, may be a debtor under this title." Section 109(d) then states that "[o]nly a person that may be a debtor under Chapter 7 of this title, except a stockbroker or a commodity broker, and a railroad may be a debtor under Chapter 11 of this title." [Section 101(41)] defines "person" to include individuals, partnerships, and corporations. [Section 101(9)(A)(v)] defines "corporation" to include business trusts.

Under prior law, §1(8) of the [1898 Act] defined "corporation" substantially the same as [§101(9)] of the Code, with the exception that the new Code includes all business trusts, while §1(8) of the [1898 Act] only included "any business conducted by a trustee or trustees wherein beneficial interest or ownership is evidenced by certificate or other written instrument." This last requirement had been strictly construed by the courts. In eliminating the requirement of written instruments, Congress has presumably made it possible for a broader variety of trusts to obtain relief in the bankruptcy courts. ... It is under such a broader definition that the Trust seeks to qualify as a debtor.

In two excellently written memoranda, the debtor contends that it is a business trust. In their also able briefs, Movants point to the language in the trust instrument specifically stating that the Trust is not a business trust. Debtors invoke the maxim of "substance over form" and urge the Court to look at the true nature of the Trust.

The debtor asserts that it is an "Illinois Land Trust" organized under the laws of Illinois. As a base of argument, it cites [Illinois law] to show that the definition of a land trust under Illinois law is consistent with the general characteristics of a business trust. However, nowhere in the trust instrument is the debtor identified as an "Illinois Land Trust" or does even the word "Illinois" appear. To the contrary, paragraph 19 of the instrument states in its entirety: "FLORIDA LAW GOVERNS CONSTRUCTION: this Agreement shall be construed in accordance with the Laws of the State of Florida." Thus, the law of Illinois is of no weight in the construction of the instrument. "Illinois Land Trust" is a generic label, not a statement of legal existence.

The focus then shifts from the definition of a land trust under Illinois law to the question of whether this particular trust has the characteristics of a business trust.

The basic distinction between business trusts and nonbusiness trusts is that business trusts are created for the purpose of carrying on some kind of business or commercial activity for profit; the object of a nonbusiness trust is to protect and preserve the trust res. The powers granted in a traditional trust are incidental to the principal purpose of holding and conserving particular property, whereas the powers within a business trust are central to its purpose. It is the business trust's similarity to a corporation that permits it to be a debtor in bankruptcy.

The debtor points to, and the Court notes, that the Trust shares several characteristics with a corporation. The Trust was not created by a grant of a settlor, but was formed through the voluntary association of unrelated persons and subscriptions sold through a prospectus. The "beneficial interests" are very much like shares in that they are equal in value, held by a large number of people in varying amounts, and are transferable. However, the interests are not reified in written instruments.

The trust instrument itself rejects any construction of it as a business trust. Paragraph 5 states, in its entirety:

5. OBJECTS AND PURPOSES OF TRUST:

> The objects and purposes of this Trust shall be to hold title to the trust property and to protect and conserve it until its sale or other disposition or liquidation. The TRUSTEE shall not manage or operate the trust property nor undertake any other activity not strictly necessary to the attainment of the objects and purposes stated herein; *nor shall the TRUSTEE transact business of any kind* with respect to the trust property within the meaning of Chapter 609 of the Florida Statutes, or any other law; *nor shall this agreement be deemed to be, or create or evidence the existence of a corporation de facto or de jure, or* a Massachusetts Trust, or any other type of *business trust,* or an association in the nature of a corporation, or a co-partnership or joint venture by or between the TRUSTEE and the BENEFICIARIES, or by or between the BENEFICIARIES.

(Emphasis added.) The debtor urges the Court to look beyond the terminology of the instrument at what it insists are the economic realities of the situation.

In its brief, the debtor claims that the Trust was created to enable the participants to carry on a business and divide the gains and that the Trust in fact operates as a business enterprise. Support for this contention is based on a ruling in the United States District Court for the Middle District of Florida that the Trust's sale of subscriptions to purchasers constitutes a sale of securities under applicable securities law. Sale of securities, debtor asserts, is a clear indicium of a business purpose.

Were there nothing else before it, the Court might find this argument persuasive. However, not only is the debtor unable to point to any business activity in which it was actively engaged, the Court is faced with continuous conduct and assertions to the contrary.

In August, 1979, the trustee of Treasure Island Land Trust filed a motion in the [SEC] case to clarify her position as trustee. The ruling she sought, and which she obtained, was that the collection of assessments was necessary to preserve and protect assets and properties of the Trust. No mention was made of carrying on a business enterprise.

In its schedules and statement of affairs filed in this Chapter 11 proceeding, in response to question 1b, "in what business are you engaged?," the debtor answered, "Purchase of land and holding for resale at a profit." The Court notes that the debtor lists no trade creditors or other debts that customarily result from the conduct of business; the unsecured creditors are principally the accountants and the lawyers.

As the debtor suggests, the Court cannot close its eyes to the economic realities of the situation. The Trust sought, at all costs, to avoid the registration requirements of the securities laws. Now that its form has proven inadequate for its intended purposes, the debtor seeks to abandon it and escape its consequences altogether.

On the one hand, it can be argued that the creators of the trust were free to select the form and language, and that by gambling as to its future construction they assumed whatever risks may ultimately befall them. On the other hand, the debtor might claim that it is being whipsawed, being called a business for securities regulation purposes but not for bankruptcy purposes. Having run afoul of the securities laws, should the debtor be permitted to turn the SEC's arguments to its own advantage? Or should an estoppel theory prevail, binding the debtor to its own representations?

This is an equitable problem which can only be answered by equitable considerations. Equity embraces consistency. It is clear that, in its own view, Treasure Island Land Trust became a business trust on or about November 29, 1979, the day after it filed its petition. It had not registered with the State of Florida as a business trust as required by Florida [law]. The debtor correctly points out that by virtue of the Supremacy Clause of the United States Constitution, Article VI, this failure to register cannot affect its eligibility for relief under the bankruptcy laws. However, it does give a reading of the Trust's intent. The debtor argues that failure to comply with the registration requirement cannot affect the legal existence or nature of the Trust. It draws an analogy to the provisions of Florida foreign corporation law. If a foreign corporation fails to comply with applicable registration requirements, its contracts, deeds, mortgages, security interests, liens or other acts are nonetheless valid. The corporation is only precluded from maintaining an action, suit, or proceeding in a state court until it complies with the statutory requirements. A failure to comply with registration requirements does not, however, deprive a foreign corporation of its existence as a legal entity. If the Court may continue the analogy, much as an unregistered corporation is precluded from the state courts, the existence and validity of the Trust are not here in issue, merely its right to seek relief in the bankruptcy court.

In what might otherwise be a close question, the debtor's course of conduct since its inception causes the Court to refuse to permit the debtor to baldly deny the language of the trust instrument. Treasure Island Land Trust does not qualify as a business trust within the meaning of [§101(9)(A)(v)].

If the trust is not a corporation, the next inquiry is to whether it can otherwise be a debtor. The definition of "person" in [§101(41)] states that "'person' *includes* individual, partnership, and corporation, but does not include governmental unit." (Emphasis added.) Because the definition is nonexclusive, one could argue that a trust might qualify as some other category of debtor.

Under the old Chapter XII of the [1898 Act], debtors eligible for relief were limited to persons other than corporations. Debtors seeking relief under that Chapter thus sought to avoid corporate status. Massachusetts trusts were included in the definition of corporation in §1(8) of the [1898 Act]. The question, then, was whether a simple land trust, not a natural person and not a corporation could otherwise be a "person." * * *

[T]he debtor has been unable to point to, and the Court is unable to find, anything in the legislative history of the Bankruptcy Reform Act that indicates that Congress intended to expand the category of debtors eligible for relief to include simple trusts. Pub. L. 95-598 was entitled the Bankruptcy *Reform* Act. If the plain meaning of the statute does not contradict the old law, and if no intention to alter the Bankruptcy Act can be divined from the legislative materials, this court must assume that there has been no change. Any trust, business or nonbusiness, may be an entity under [§101(15)], but not every entity can be a debtor.* * *

In view of the foregoing discussion, the court shall enter an order granting the motion to dismiss.

NOTES

3A.1. The Treasure Island Land Trust called itself an Illinois land trust perhaps because an ordinary business trust would seem more likely to be subject to securities laws. But the name choice was to no avail. The SEC took the view that Treasure Island Land Trust was engaged in selling securities notwithstanding the labels its developers used when they created it. The SEC took the Treasure Island Land Trust to court and won. To believe that Treasure Island Land Trust was engaged in selling securities, the SEC would have to take the view that Treasure Island Land Trust was a "profit-seeking business venture" and that its developers were selling to investors "a scheme whereby [the beneficiaries] invested [their] money in a common enterprise and were led to expect profits solely from the efforts of the third party or promoter." See Securities & Exchange Commission v. W. J. Howey Co., 328 U.S. 293 (1946). In this light, the bankruptcy court's decision may seem overly formal and wooden, as a "profit-seeking business venture in financial distress" seems an ideal candidate for the bankruptcy process.

3A.2. The *Treasure Island Land Trust* court might have taken a different approach altogether, yet perhaps reached the same conclusion. Rather than ask whether an Illinois land trust is in the abstract a corporation, or in the abstract the sort of entity that could benefit from the bankruptcy process, the court might have asked whether *this* Illinois land trust had a valid reason to be in bankruptcy. The court might have asked, for example, whether the trust had many creditors who threatened a viable business enterprise. Some courts have taken this approach. See, e.g., In re Dolton Lodge Trust No. 35188, 22 Bankr. 918 (Bankr. N.D. Ill. 1982). But this is not the approach that Congress seems to have adopted in §109, as Problems 3A-1 and 3A-2 ask you to consider. Where the characteristics of a specific entity, rather than the type of entity, make it a poor candidate for bankruptcy, the court has other means (including the provisions of §305) to dismiss a properly commenced case. These means are discussed later in this chapter.

PROBLEMS

3A-1. Instead of filing a bankruptcy petition, the owners of an entity like Treasure Island create a new corporation and then transfer all of the entity's assets to that corporation. The corporation at the same time assumes all the liabilities of the entity. Can the newly formed corporation file for bankruptcy? See In re Northwest Recreational Activities, Inc., 4 Bankr. 36 (Bankr. N.D. Ga. 1980).

3A-2. A labor union consisting of freight workers has recently been sued for damages caused during an allegedly illegal strike. The union wants to know if it can file a petition in bankruptcy. Can it? See Highway & City Freight Drivers, Dockmen and Helpers, Local Union No. 600 v. Gordon Transports, Inc., 576 F.2d 1285 (8th Cir.) 439 U.S. 1002 (1978) (case arising under the old Act).

B. FILING THE BANKRUPTCY PETITION

In this section we examine how an eligible debtor's bankruptcy case begins. We look first at the mechanics of commencement, which requires action by the debtor or a creditor. We then look at the less settled question whether parties may agree in advance not to take such action.

Most debtors in bankruptcy enter through the filing of a "voluntary" petition governed by §301 (and by §302 for spousal joint filing). Anyone who may be a debtor under a bankruptcy chapter can "commence" a case by filing under that chapter. The commencement of a voluntary case also serves as an "order for relief," which means, in essence, that a proper voluntary petition without more satisfies the conditions necessary for a court to administer the case. Thus, access to the bankruptcy process is not limited to insolvent debtors or even to those who have borrowed (though a debtor who can pay her bills outside bankruptcy may have little or nothing to gain from bankruptcy). A debtor who wishes to file for bankruptcy must only pay the filing fee, which varies from chapter to chapter. See 28 U.S.C. §1930(a).

An "involuntary" case, governed by §303, is more complicated. Such a case is permitted only in Chapter 7 or 11 against an entity that may be a debtor under that chapter, but not against a farmer or charitable organization. See §303(a). An involuntary case can be commenced by the petition of "three or more entities, each of which is either the holder of a claim" against the debtor or "an indenture trustee representing such a holder," provided that each petitioner holds or represents a claim "not contingent as to liability or the subject of a bona fide dispute as to liability or amount," and provided also that such noncontingent, undisputed claims "aggregate at least $13,475 more than the value of any lien on property of the debtor securing such claims held by the holders of such claims." See §303(b)(1). (An "indenture trustee" is a representative of bondholders who have purchased identical bonds and thus become creditors of the bond issuer.) If there are fewer than twelve "such holders," not counting creditors who are employees and specified others who might have an ulterior motive to keep the debtor out of bankruptcy, any one holder can file an involuntary petition provided that the $13,475 aggregate undersecurity requirement is satisfied. See §303(b)(2). (Statutory amounts are updated periodically according to the provisions of Bankruptcy Code §104.)

If any of these conditions is not initially satisfied, it may be met if the petition is joined by the holder of an unsecured claim that is not contingent. See §303(c). In addition, if the debtor is a partnership, any general partner may file an involuntary petition, as can the bankruptcy trustee of any general partner or the holder of any claim against the debtor if all of the debtor's general partners are themselves in bankruptcy. See §303(b)(3). Finally, an involuntary case can be commenced by the petition of "a foreign representative of the estate in a foreign proceeding concerning" the debtor. See §303(b)(4).

These mechanics may seem arcane. It is important, however, not to miss the forest for the trees. In permitting voluntary bankruptcy petitions, Congress enabled an individual debtor to elect a discharge of obligations, and it permitted any debtor to avoid a potentially costly creditors race to limited assets. Congress permitted involuntary petitions as well because a debtor will not always have an incentive to file for bankruptcy even when the bankruptcy process would preserve the value of a debtor's assets.

Imagine, for example, that an economically failed debtor corporation wastefully continues operation at all its facilities rather than selling off some assets and reinvesting in those that remain. The debtor's managers and equity owners might pursue this strategy in an attempt to retain control and maintain the hope of a turnaround that would enable the debtor to repay all its debts. Despite this hope, the gamble could be a poor one, and the creditors would be left to suffer if the firm continued its wholesale decline. In this situation, the creditors could protect their interest if they could force the debtor into an early bankruptcy process, in which dismissal of the debtor's managers and an efficient disposition of debtor's assets would be possible. An involuntary petition offers creditors an opportunity to protect their interests.

We should also ask why Congress made it so much easier for a debtor to file a voluntary petition than for a creditor or creditors to file an involuntary one. To understand this decision, note first that bankruptcy may result in the whole or partial liquidation of a debtor's assets. If the debtor is a business, such liquidation can mean the loss of jobs and consequent hardship. Thus, limitations on involuntary petitions can be seen in part as an attempt to preserve a going concern for an extended period, even if delay may lead to at least as great a destruction of a business in the long run. Second, a creditor of the debtor may not *merely* be a creditor. The creditor could also be a competitor or could have another reason to force the debtor into an unnecessary bankruptcy.

The Bankruptcy Code goes even further to protect debtors from potentially spurious involuntary petitions. In an involuntary case, unlike a voluntary case, commencement does not constitute an order for relief. After an involuntary petition is filed, the bankruptcy court will issue an order for relief if the petition is not "controverted" by the debtor (or a general partner of the debtor). See §303(h). If the petition is controverted, the court will order relief if the debtor is "generally not paying" debts, other than those subject to a "bona fide dispute," "as such debts become due." See §303(h)(1). The court also will order relief based on a controverted petition in the exceedingly rare event that, within 120 days before the bankruptcy petition, a nonbankruptcy "custodian" has been appointed to administer the debtor's assets. See §303(h)(2). But relief will not be ordered in any other circumstance, and §303(l) (a mislabeled subsection that follows "j") provides that the record of an involuntary petition against an individual will be expunged if a dismissed petition contains false information.

Even if the creditors have much to lose from the debtor's continued operation, creditors can force a debtor into bankruptcy only if the debtor is not current on its obligations. This limitation protects debtors from unscrupulous creditors with ulterior motives, but may at the same time leave creditors unable to stop a debtor from scraping together just enough to pay most current obligations while payment becomes less and less likely on a mountain of unmatured debt.

The exercises below explore the conditions under which a court will order relief for failure to pay debts, and ask you to consider how a creditor can affect those conditions at the time a loan is extended. The case that follows, *Kingston Square Associates*, addresses the question whether a debtor or creditors can effectively pledge not to commence bankruptcy despite insolvency. In the case, a corporate debtor's equity holder who agreed in advance not to instigate a voluntary petition instead persuades three of the debtor's creditors to file an involuntary petition. The related notes and problem then explore measures that debtors or creditors might take to forswear bankruptcy. You should consider why debtors and creditors each might favor such measures.

Key Provisions: Bankruptcy Code §§301; 302; 303

EXERCISES

3B(1) From time to time, Debtor purchases inventory on general credit from Supplier. Bank guarantees Debtor's obligations to Supplier. Debtor has no other creditors. Debtor and Supplier are in a heated, though good faith, dispute over whether Debtor owes Supplier for its last inventory shipment. Supplier and Bank file an involuntary bankruptcy petition against Debtor. Does this petition commence a case against Debtor? Would your answer change if Bank alone filed the initial petition and was later joined in the petition by Supplier?

3B(2) Debtor owes $10,000 to each of twelve creditors. Creditor *A* holds a security interest in Debtor's land, *A*-Acre, worth $15,000. Creditor *B* holds a security interest in Debtor's land, *B*-Acre, worth $6,000. Creditor *C* holds an unsecured claim. Creditors *A*, *B*, and *C* file an involuntary bankruptcy petition against Debtor. Does this petition commence a case against Debtor?

3B(3) Debtor is a corporation that issues a series of bonds (obligations to pay principal and interest in the future). Each bond issue, sold to thousands of investors, is subject to a trust indenture, which vests in the indenture trustee the right to make specified decisions for the bondholders, including the right to file an involuntary bankruptcy petition against Debtor. Debtor has bonds outstanding in Series *A* and in Series *B*. Debtor has no other creditors. The indenture trustee for Series *A* files an involuntary bankruptcy petition against Debtor. Does this petition commence a case against Debtor?

3B(4) Debtor controverts an involuntary bankruptcy petition against it even though it is a few weeks overdue on the payment of a single obligation. Will the court issue an order for relief? What additional information might you find useful?

3B(5) Debtor's warehouse burns along with its entire inventory, which is uninsured. Debtor then misses a small payment on an obligation to Finance Company, one of Debtor's few creditors. Even though Debtor's obligation to Bank is not due for another year, Bank immediately files an involuntary bankruptcy petition against Debtor, who controverts the petition. Will the court issue an order for relief? If the answer is no, how would you advise Bank so that it might avoid a similar situation in the future?

CASE

IN RE KINGSTON SQUARE ASSOCIATES

United States Bankruptcy Court, S.D. New York, 1997
214 Bankr. 713

BROZMAN, CHIEF JUDGE.

Fashion has a role not only in the garment industry but in the legal one as well. One of the newest fashions in commercial real estate financing is so-called "mortgage backed securitization" coupled with the presence of corporate governance provisions known as "bankruptcy remote provisions" designed to make bankruptcy unavailable to a defaulting borrower without the affirmative consent of the mortgagee's designee on the borrower's board of directors.

Here, a group of entities owning apartment complexes was stymied by such provisions from invoking the Chapter 11 process to prevent foreclosure despite the belief of their principal that the properties had value over and above the encumbrances against them. To prevent loss of this claimed value and the potential for reorganization, the debtors' principal paid a law firm to solicit creditors to file involuntary Chapter 11 petitions. Only one trade creditor for each debtor agreed; the other petitioning creditors came from the ranks of the debtors' professionals—attorneys and various consultants. At issue is whether the petitions ought therefore be dismissed as bad faith filings, relief which the mortgagees seek.

By agreement of the parties, the only issue at trial was whether there was collusion mandating dismissal, for it was the mortgagee's contention that, standing alone, collusion in their filing warranted dismissal of these petitions. The parties have not yet tried whether there is any possibility of reorganization. * * *

Each of the eleven debtors (the "Debtors") is or was controlled by Morton L. Ginsberg. The Debtors represent less than one-third of the thirty-eight Ginsberg-controlled entities that were restructured in 1991 or 1993 in transactions financed by The Chase Manhattan Bank, N.A. ("Chase") and REFG Investor Two, Inc. ("REFG") (the "Movants"). All thirty-eight properties, both debtor and nondebtor, are in receivership, with foreclosure proceedings pending against them. In one case, that of Lynnewood Associates, the Movants have foreclosed upon the property. The Debtors did not contest the filing of the involuntary petitions, with the result that orders for relief have been entered in all eleven cases.

Chase and REFG seek the dismissal of the Chapter 11 cases of the eleven Debtors for cause pursuant to §1112(b). The Movants maintain that Ginsberg colluded with the petitioning creditors ("Petitioning Creditors") and their counsel, Pryor, Cashman, Sherman & Flynn ("Pryor Cashman"), to enable each Debtor to improperly avail itself of bankruptcy protection to thwart the Movants' ongoing efforts to foreclose on each of the Debtors' properties. Objections to the dismissal motion have been filed by the Debtors, the Petitioning Creditors, and the limited partners of the Florida Debtors, Lynnewood Associates, and Highland-Montgomery, L.P. * * *

The Debtors became indebted to the Movants pursuant to two loan transactions. In the first, known as MLG I, Chase lent slightly more than $132 million to twenty multi-family entities including the Florida and Metropolitan New York Debtors and took back a mortgage on each property. This transaction closed on August 30, 1991. Chase holds a single blanket mortgage containing cross-collateralization and cross-default provisions for fifteen of the twenty properties. Chase holds individual mortgages on the five remaining properties.

In the second loan transaction, known appropriately enough as MLG II, REFG lent nearly $145 million to eighteen multi-family entities including the Bronx Debtors and took back a mortgage on each property. This transaction closed on February 11, 1993. All eighteen properties are covered by one blanket mortgage with cross-collateralization and cross-default provisions. [The Movants agreed that another entity ("DLJ") would act on their behalf to enforce the mortgages.]

Integral to the MLG I and II transactions was the inclusion in the charters of each corporate Debtor or the corporate general partner of each limited partnership Debtor of a bylaw, commonly referred to as a "bankruptcy remote" or "bankruptcy proof" provision, to prevent the Debtors from seeking voluntary bankruptcy protection without the unanimous consent of the board of directors of each Debtor or of its corporate general partner and the shareholders. Each board originally consisted of Ginsberg and two others, one of whom was his designee and the other of whom was a so-called independent director.

The independent director for each board of directors is Laurence Richardson. ... [Richardson] receives the aggregate amount of $55,000 annually for serving on the various boards of directors created pursuant to DLJ-structured deals.

In 1994, the Movants issued notices of default and commenced foreclosure actions against each property, Debtor and nondebtor. With the consent of each borrower, receivers were installed at all thirty-eight properties. As of mid-1996, the Movants had obtained judgments totaling approximately $370 million and had commenced foreclosure proceedings against each of the thirty-eight properties. * * *

In the almost two years that the receivers have been in place, the Movants have advanced nearly $2 million to pay for repairs, taxes and insurance. No monies have been needed for salaries because the Debtors have no employees.

While no breakdown has been provided as to the number of apartment units for each of the Debtors, the thirty-eight Debtor and nondebtor properties in total aggregate nearly 11,200 units spread over approximately forty-one garden apartment complexes. The only appraisal received into evidence ... valued all the properties at $384 million. If the values contained in the appraisal were found to be correct, equity may exist in the properties. However, the appraisal was admitted for the limited purpose of rebutting the charge that the friendly involuntary petitions were filed in bad faith. As noted at the outset of this decision, the parties agreed in their pretrial order not to treat reorganization prospects initially, as a result of which there is no developed record regarding valuation. * * *

As each director, Kazarnovsky, Ginsberg and Richardson, testified, no meetings were held after the closing of the MLG I and II restructurings until December 16, 1996. At no other time was any meeting ever called, special or regular, to discuss the business activities of the Debtors, the defaults called by the Movants, or the commencement of the foreclosure actions. The directors conducted no business except to approve the $2.4 million loan to the Debtors to provide maintenance for the properties in June 1993. Other than this minor matter, they had little communication with each other, either by telephone or by letter, until this motion was filed. No financial reports were circulated, nor were reports or updates on the legal proceedings distributed either by counsel or by Ginsberg, as president, to the other directors.

The directors testified as to the reasons for such inactivity, even in the face of the foreclosure actions, the installation of receivers and the filing of the involuntary petitions. Both Ginsberg and Kazarnovsky believed that involving Richardson in such meetings would prove fruitless because of their belief that Richardson was simply a pawn of DLJ and would not approve any course of action that would interfere with DLJ's plans. Because both Kazarnovsky and Ginsberg believed that Richardson was DLJ's agent on the board, they purposely ignored him. Significantly, the boards took no action in the face of foreclosure actions being commenced or receivers being installed. Although Ginsberg did retain counsel to contest the foreclosure proceedings in the state courts on behalf of the Debtors, there is no indication that the attorneys ever reported to anyone other than Ginsberg. Richardson learned in 1995 that the properties were being foreclosed, yet he took no action and did not seek any information from anyone as to what was happening although he assumed judgments would be entered against the properties. In any event, he never initiated communication with Ginsberg regarding these events nor did he ask for a directors' meeting.

Richardson's overall testimony at trial was enlightening on a number of topics including his perception of his fiduciary duty as a director, the purpose of the bankruptcy proof provision and his understanding of DLJ's status. Richardson seems not to have taken any interest at all in the properties. He testified that as a director he never reviewed any documents regarding any of the Debtors including rent rolls, judgments, or state court decisions. While apparently unaware of the foreclosure actions against all the properties until 1995, Richardson did acknowledge that he was certainly aware of the status of his directors' fees and made a number of inquiries of DLJ when his fees were in arrears.

According to his testimony, only long after the filing of the involuntary petitions did he become aware that a director has fiduciary duty not only to a corporation's shareholders but to its creditors when the corporation becomes insolvent, Nor did he comprehend his obligations to limited partners in those entities where he was on the board of directors of the corporate general partners. * * *

Finally, Richardson gave his interpretation of what the bankruptcy proof provision was all about. As he read the bylaw, its purpose was to place an "independent" director on the corporate boards of directors to prevent, in the event that Ginsberg filed for personal bankruptcy, Ginsberg's filing from "suck[ing] all of these properties into that proceeding," in order that, as Richardson further explained, "a creditor of Mort Ginsberg would not be able to say that somehow there was a corporate sham and therefore be able to pull these assets in." * * *

The Movants argue that each of the eleven involuntary petitions was filed in bad faith and should be dismissed pursuant to §1112(b). This conclusion is said to be warranted because Ginsberg, acting on behalf of the Debtors, initiated, funded and identified seven friendly creditors to prosecute the involuntary petitions so each Debtor could obtain improper leverage against the Movants by gaining access to the bankruptcy court without violating the bankruptcy restrictions in the bylaws of the various Debtors or their corporate general partners. The Movants point out that the filing of each petition was timed either to stay a scheduled foreclosure sale or to coincide with a particular Debtor's deadline to file an appellate pleading, which resulted, the Movants claim, in the frustration of their attempts to enforce their rights against each property. The Movants dismiss the Debtors' attempts to excuse such behavior by countering that there is no such doctrine as "justifiable collusion."

The Movants have centered their case around the Second Circuit decision, Federal Deposit Ins. Corp. v. Cortez, 96 F.3d 50 (2d Cir. 1996), which held that, in certain circumstances, a collusive filing of a bankruptcy case is a fraud upon the jurisdiction of the Bankruptcy Court and therefore susceptible to immediate dismissal. Because the Movants believe that the Cortez case is controlling, they did not offer initially any evidence regarding any of the Debtors' financial situations, their equity (or lack thereof) in the properties or their ability to reorganize. In other words, the Movants are of the opinion that if I were to find that collusion did occur, under Cortez I am bound to dismiss the cases. As an alternative, the Movants suggest that the facts warrant conversion of the cases to Chapter 7 or appointment of a Chapter 11 trustee. * * *

I agree with the Respondents that a bankruptcy proof provision in a corporate bylaw <u>does not prevent outside creditors from banding together to file an involuntary</u> petition. As they correctly argue, neither the corporate nor partnership documents establish a bar to prevent any party connected with the Debtors from acting on its own to file involuntary petitions. * * *

It is not appropriate for me to rule now on the myriad allegations about Ginsberg's dishonesty, mismanagement and the other horribles alluded to in the various court papers. All I know is that in the face of such behavior, the Debtors and limited partners continued to keep him on as chairman of the board and president of the Debtors, and the Movants accepted his presence without taking any action against him other than to slowly and inexorably close in on each property, notwithstanding that they say they acquired his equity interests and thereby the <u>ability to oust him</u>. In the meantime, the Movants ignore the fact that DLJ acts as lender and shareholder, while dominating the activities of the Debtors to the extent that its board designee, who was supposed to be "independent," <u>abdicated his fiduciary role</u> to the Debtors, creditors and limited partners in favor of the interests of DLJ. * * * *outside party that enforces the mortgages*

While I find that the Respondents (did orchestrate) the filing of these cases, I conclude that their intention was to circumvent the inability of the Debtors to act in the face of the pending foreclosure proceedings by taking some action to preserve value for the Debtors' estates and creditors. I cannot find, as the Movants desire, that the petitions were <u>filed solely to delay or frustrate the Movants' remedies</u> for it is also undisputed that the Petitioning Creditors have introduced at least <u>one third party</u>, and as many as two others, to make proposals to purchase the properties as a <u>package</u>. The Movants may feel bruised because the Respondents outmaneuvered what the Movants thought was an iron-clad provision in the corporate bylaws preventing a bankruptcy filing, but this does not mean that, without more, the petitions must be dismissed.

I have previously held in another context that bad faith will not normally be found where the primary motivation of petitioning creditors was to prevent further <u>dissipation of assets</u> through foreclosure in an attempt to facilitate an orderly workout among all the creditors. The fact that at least one third party has been brought forward early in this proceeding by the Petitioning Creditors certainly helps to establish that their intentions were <u>not simply to stave off foreclosure</u> at the last second and harass the Movants.

here the invol. motivated by belief in workout

Thus, for all of the reasons just explained, I do not conclude that the Movants have proven that these cases were collusively filed.

Section 1112(b) requires consideration of what is in the best interests of creditors and the estates. On the record thus far developed I can draw no conclusion as to whether dismissal is in the parties' best interest. It appears that the only parties who would benefit from dismissal are the Movants, while unsecured creditors and limited partners would be left with nothing if the foreclosures were allowed to continue apace. Accordingly, I find that although the filings of the involuntary petitions were solicited at the behest of Ginsberg, they are an apparent attempt to salvage some value for these estates in the face of the pending foreclosures which would have wiped out the opportunity for anyone other than the Movants to recover anything.

[handwritten margin note: foreclosures might hurt unsecured creditors]

Because I have not found that the Debtors and the Petitioning Creditors acted collusively in filing these cases, I need not reach the merits of the Respondents' position request that I nullify the bylaw provision containing the bankruptcy proof provision as void against public policy. In any event, given that none of the Debtors observed corporate formalities and did not prior to the involuntary filings test the directors' mettle by calling a board of directors' meeting to ascertain whether bankruptcy would be authorized, I do not believe that the issue of validity of the bankruptcy proof provision is properly before me. * * *

The facts presented by these cases are quite troubling. The Debtors and the Petitioning Creditors orchestrated the filing of these involuntary cases to evade what they perceived to be an insurmountable restriction against the Debtors' filing voluntary petitions. The third director has engaged in transparent stalling tactics, the effect of which is to endanger the interests of all parties other than DLJ. Allegations circulate on the periphery that Ginsberg or his subordinates may have acted improperly in managing the properties.

Because of those concerns about Ginsberg and his asserted poor history of performing on a number of other real estate loan transactions, DLJ felt justified in structuring the two loans with Ginsberg to guarantee that it could avoid a bankruptcy filing and move to foreclose on the properties swiftly in case of default regardless of whether the default was based on lack of payment or performance. DLJ thereby put itself in the awkward position of financing the original restructuring transactions, then later assuming obligations toward the creditors and limited partners by acquiring Ginsberg's equity interests, while simultaneously pursuing and enforcing state court judg-ment rights (through the Movants) in order to minimize its loss on the original bonds it repurchased. As a result, DLJ essentially held veto power over the acts the Debtors could take and found itself walking a tightrope between looking out for its own interests and breaching its fiduciary duties. This is too fine a line to comfortably navigate.

[handwritten margin note: R. had CoI]

Moreover, I am also concerned that the properties have been al-lowed to languish at a "mere survival level" while in receivership without the Movants seeking to do anything except let the foreclosure process run its course. The record does not indicate that either DLJ or the Movants are expending much effort to sell the properties or au-thorize the expenditure of any more funds than the barest minimum necessary for upkeep (which could arguably make the properties more saleable). The parties have not agreed to a sale of the properties with a later determination of who is entitled to the proceeds. Of utmost con-cern to me is the fact that no one, the Movants, the Debtors, or the Petitioning Creditors, has even acknowledged the existence of thou-sands of residents living in these buildings, some of which have in-disputably fallen into disrepair. The blame for this sorry state of affairs has to be shared by the Debtors and the Movants. * * *

[handwritten margin note: Units in disrepair in Receivership]

[I] hold that although the Movants have successfully demon-strated that the Debtors and Petitioning Creditors did orchestrate the filing of the eleven involuntary petitions commencing these cases, their behavior is not consonant with what is required by case law for collusion. As a result, the orchestration is not sufficient to warrant the dismissal of the cases without evidence that the Debtors have no chance at rehabilitation. The Movants, if they wish to press their mo-tion, are to obtain a new hearing date to try this issue.

SETTLE ORDER consistent with this decision.

NOTES

3B.1. As a general rule, a debtor cannot waive the right to file for bankruptcy. This rule has been applied not only to individual debtors, for whom such waiver would eliminate the fresh start, but also to cor-porate debtors, whose individual owners are protected by limited li-ability under state corporate law and thus need no relief from the corporation's debt. See, e.g., United States v. Royal Business Funds Corp., 724 F.2d 12 (2d Cir. 1983) (stating, in dicta, that such waivers "generally" were not enforceable, while holding, in the case before it, that a corporation had effectively waived its right to bankruptcy by stipulating that the Small Business Administration would be its receiver).

3B.2. Courts have permitted the functional equivalent of waiver of bankruptcy in some circumstances where the debtor is not an individual. For example, a firm might transfer account receivables— obligations that customers owe the firm—to a special purpose vehicle ("SPV"). Providers of capital to the firm could then purchase interests in the vehicle. The firm might retain a residual interest in the SPV, and perform the vehicle's ministerial functions. But the firm would no longer hold a significant economic interest in the receivables. If the firm were to enter bankruptcy, it might be unlikely that a court would subject the SPV's assets to the firm's bankruptcy, or permit a voluntary petition by the SPV, in violation of an agreement to keep the SPV independent of the firm and out of bankruptcy. The SPV itself might not even be eligible for bankruptcy, as it might be held to be a trust, for example.

Whatever the successes of SPVs, however, one should be wary of drawing broad lessons from them. The described creation of an SPV is, in essence, the sale of receivables. The SPV has no business operation and no employees. Problem 3B asks a question that the court in *Kingston* did not have to address: Can creditors create structures such that, even though the debtor has not technically waived its right to file a bankruptcy petition, no bankruptcy case will ever be commenced?

3B.3. Since *Kingston*, Congress has amended §1112(b), adding detail to the grounds for dismissal or conversion. The changes would not affect the decision in this case, however.

PROBLEM

3B. Debtor Corporation's president owns all the shares of Debtor. The president seeks to have Debtor borrow a substantial sum from Bank, already Debtor's biggest creditor. As conditions of the loan, Debtor adopts anti-bankruptcy provisions in its internal corporate documents and each of Debtor's directors agrees never to have Debtor file a bankruptcy petition. In addition, the president pledges all of her stock as collateral for Bank's loan to Debtor. Despite these conditions, when Debtor defaults on its loan to Bank, Debtor files a voluntary bankruptcy petition. Can Bank enforce the anti-bankruptcy provisions or recover damages from the directors for violation of their "no-filing" agreement? In answering this question, consider the possibility that Bank may wish to liquidate Debtor.

C. DISMISSAL AND ABSTENTION

In the previous section, we explored whether a debtor and creditors could in advance prevent the ultimate commencement of a bankruptcy case even where the debtor ultimately developed problems that bankruptcy law is designed to solve. In this section, we instead consider whether a court on its own motion or a party can have a bankruptcy case dismissed despite proper commencement because the debtor does *not* have problems that bankruptcy law is designed to solve.

[margin handwriting: Sua sponte Court dissmissal]

Debtors—like creditors—have reasons for resorting to bankruptcy other than those motivated by the need to relieve an honest debt burden or reorganize a capital structure. An individual, for example, might run up huge credit card debts for vacations and expensive meals, never intending to repay her obligations but planning all along to file for bankruptcy when the bills come due. In such a circumstance, a bankruptcy court can dismiss a Chapter 7 case for "abuse" and thus deny the debtor a discharge. Dismissal for this sort of abuse is straightforward, and uncontroversial, but what of a debtor who intends to repay when he incurs debts but later, after a change in circumstances, seeks to discharge those debts despite an ability to repay? Congress recently addressed this question.

The 2005 Bankruptcy Act introduces important new limitations on individuals subject primarily to consumer debts who seek to discharge their debts in bankruptcy. According to the newly revised Bankruptcy Code §707(b), a court may dismiss a Chapter 7 case or, with the consent of the debtor, convert the case to Chapter 11 or 13, if the court determines that a grant of relief under Chapter 7 would be an abuse of the bankruptcy process. The court's conversion alternative, as opposed to dismissal, is nominally new, but because the consent of the debtor is required for conversion, this is not an important change. Far more significant are the new grounds on which a court may order dismissal or conversion. If the debtor, or in a joint case, the debtor and her spouse, earn more than the median income, adjusted for family size, in the debtor's home state, then the United States Trustee, the bankruptcy administrator, if any, the bankruptcy trustee, or any party in interest, including a creditor, may move for such dismissal or conversion, or the court may dismiss or convert the case on its own mo-

[margin handwriting: 2005 Act §707(b) → dismissal of Ch. 7 for abuse or conversion to Ch. 11 or 13 w/consent if > median income]

[margin handwriting: Sua sponte or by motion]

tion. Under prior law, a party in interest, such as a creditor, could not make such a motion. If the debtor, or the debtor and her spouse, earn less than such median, the United States Trustee, a bankruptcy administrator, or the court itself may move for dismissal or conversion; as before a creditor may not.

Where §707(b) is invoked, and if the debtor, or the debtor and her spouse, earn more than the applicable median income, the court will determine whether the debtor fails a somewhat Byzantine means test designed to establish whether the debtor can repay, over the next five years, at least some of the obligations she seeks to discharge. Congress' decision to locate the means test within the section devoted to bankruptcy abuse is somewhat misleading. The means test is focused exclusively on the ability to repay debt. If two debtors' incomes, expenses, and household size are the same, the circumstances that brought about the financial distress are irrelevant. The person who incurred sudden medical expenses or lost a job is treated the same as the spendthrift who ran up credit card debt by taking too many vacations. Ability to repay is all that matters. Section 707(b)(2) blocks access to the fresh start for consumers who make more than most and who have enough disposable income to make substantial repayments to their creditors. It provides a hard-and-fast rule that supplements the discretion that the bankruptcy judge enjoys to dismiss abusive filings by those whose debts are primarily consumer debts.

The means test begins with a rough determination of the debtor's monthly income available to pay nonpriority unsecured claims. This determination, in turn, starts with the debtor's current monthly income, then reduces that amount by specified monthly expenses, some deemed and some actual, according to Internal Revenue Service standards, such as for the debtor's (and her dependent's) food, clothing, and health care. Any remainder is then reduced again by what would be the debtor's average monthly payments, for the next five years, on account of secured debts, including any amount that the debtor would have to pay a secured creditor under a Chapter 13 plan for the debtor to retain possession of her primary residence, motor vehicle, or other property necessary for support of the debtor or her dependants. Any remainder is then reduced a final time by 1/60th of the aggregate unsecured claims against the debtor entitled to priority under the Bankruptcy Code.

Abuse is presumed if the amount of the debtor's monthly income, after these deductions, multiplied by 60 is not less than $10,950. With at least this much available monthly income, Congress has decided, a debtor should pay at least some of her nonpriority unsecured claims no matter the aggregate amount of such claims. (Recall that secured and priority unsecured claims are accounted for in the calculation of income available to pay general nonpriority claims.) If the debtor's monthly income, reduced for expenses and for secured and priority unsecured claims under §707(b), multiplied by 60, is between $6,575 and $10,950, then abuse will be presumed unless this amount is less than one fourth of the aggregate, unsecured, nonpriority claims against the debtor. If the debtor's monthly income, so reduced, multiplied by 60, is less than $6,575, then abuse will not be presumed.

Complex formula

If abuse is presumed, as described here, the debtor has an opportunity to rebut the presumption by demonstrating special circumstances, such as a serious medical condition or call to active duty in the military, which might justify additional deductions for expenses or use of a lower than current monthly income for the purposes of the means test. There is moreover, a special exemption from the abuse presumption for a debtor who is a disabled veteran and who incurred her debt primarily while serving on active duty or in homeland defense while not on active duty.

Even if abuse is not presumed—either because the debtor passes the means test or because the debtor, or the debtor and her spouse, earn less than the applicable median income and the means test is thus inapplicable—a court may nonetheless dismiss or convert a Chapter 7 case for abuse if the court determines that the debtor filed the bankruptcy petition in bad faith or that, in the totality of the circumstances, the debtor's financial situation demonstrates abuse. The new language of §707(b) specifically identifies as potentially abusive a debtor's filing a bankruptcy petition in order to reject a personal services contract. Beyond this, however, the provision does not offer guidance as to when a bankruptcy petition not presumed to be abusive becomes so because of bad faith or based on the debtor's financial condition.

court retains ch.7 dismissl conversion power even if debtor doesn't fall above means test

The 2005 Bankruptcy Act also contains a set of procedural and fee shifting rules that have already become controversial. For example, under revised Bankruptcy Code §521, an individual debtor in a Chapter 7 or 13 case has only 45 days from the date of her petition to file a schedule of assets and liabilities as well as other information about the debtor's financial affairs; if the debtor fails to meet this deadline, on motion of a creditor, the court can dismiss the case. Moreover, the same provision requires that a debtor deliver tax returns within 7 days prior to the first creditors' meeting; failure to do so may result in dismissal of the case and denial of discharge. The need to comply with these provisions may make legal representation particularly important for a debtor, yet other provisions of the Act impose strict obligations on legal representatives. Under revised §707(b), the signature of an attorney on a bankruptcy petition, pleading, or written motion now constitutes a certification that the attorney has done a reasonable investigation into the circumstances that gave rise to the petition, pleading, or motion and has determined that each is well grounded in fact and is warranted by law. Further, if the bankruptcy trustee moves to have a case dismissed or converted under §707(b) and the court grants such motion, the court can order the debtor's attorney, if any, to pay the trustee's costs unless the court is satisfied that the attorney formed a belief, based on reasonable investigation, that the debtor was entitled to the relief for which his client petitioned.

These procedural and cost-shifting rules may seem reasonable, and they may be in fact. But as a number of critics have noted, potential liability for a debtor's attorney may well significantly raise the costs of representation. A predictable consequence is that many of the poorest individuals—ironically those who would pass or not be subject to the means test—will be unable to obtain counsel for a bankruptcy petition and, as a practical matter, might therefore be unable to obtain a discharge in bankruptcy even if they are substantively entitled to such relief.

The new means-test provisions are controversial more generally, as well. Supporters of the new provisions argue that debtors who can pay their bills should be forced to do so. After all, the argument goes, a debtor enjoys the use of borrowed money and it might seem that fairness dictates he repay the lender who provided such enjoyment. From the perspective of the debtor and lender at the time of the loan, however, the matter is somewhat more complicated. The terms of a loan contract implicitly include the applicable bankruptcy law. When bankruptcy law liberally permits debtor discharge, one would expect the interest rates on consumer loans to be high as compared to a legal regime that limits discharge. Thus, it is not easy to say to that a debtor behaves unfairly when he seeks a discharge of obligations even if he is able to repay those obligations. Fairness might depend on what the rules the parties anticipated—and incorporated into the interest rate—at the time of the loan. Thus, despite tendentious terminology of the new §707(b) on "abuse," the more liberal discharge rules of the Bankruptcy Code prior to the 2005 Act's means test may have been no more or less fair than the new rules, which may be seen simply as different.

Finally, one might question the efficacy of the 2005 Bankruptcy Act even if one accepts the proposition that a discharge should be unavailable to high-income debtors who can pay much of what they owe. Under prior law, most courts already found that the ability to repay debt was itself grounds for dismissing an individual's Chapter 7 case. See, e.g., Zolg v. Kelly (In re Kelly), 841 F.2d 908, 914-15 (9th Cir. 1988). In this light, the 2005 Act may be seen as a complicated game not worth the candle, one that imposes significant, and perhaps needless, costs borne largely by those whose right to a fresh start is not in doubt, a problem alluded to above.

limited impact on rich, none on poor

Well advised or not, Congress recognized that the means test would channel some debtors ineligible for Chapter 7 into Chapter 13, where they would be required to repay some of their debts with future income. Indeed, this was an objective. A concern arose, however, that a debtor's inability to discharge general obligations in Chapter 7 would leave some debtors stretched too thin to pay domestic support obligations, which are nondischargeable in any case. To encourage debtors to support their former spouses and children if at all possible, the 2005 Act provided for the dismissal of a Chapter 13 case (or conversion to Chapter 7 for an eligible debtor) if a debtor is not current on domestic support obligations. See §1307(c)(11). It is not that a debtor who fails to pay domestic support abuses the bankruptcy process with a Chapter 13 petition; rather payment of support obligations is an entry admission to the Chapter 13 process.

now courts can dismiss or convert Ch. 13 to ch.7 if not current on domestic debts (not dischargeable in ch.7 anyway)

Continuing with an analysis of Chapter 13, a debtor faces dismissal or conversion if he fails to begin specified payments to lessors or secured creditors within 30 days of the commencement of the case. See §§1326(a); 1307(4). These provisions are designed to prevent a debtor from filing a Chapter 13 case as a means to delay an inevitable release of property to lessor or secured lender. In theory, if the debtor truly values retention of the property, and is willing ultimately to pay for this privilege as required, he will be willing to make these initial payments. If he is not so willing, the Chapter 13 case may have an illegitimate purpose.

immediate payment

Dismissal or conversion is relevant not only to individuals but to corporations as well. Just as an individual debtor might attempt to employ the bankruptcy process when she has not satisfied the conditions for relief under that process, a corporate debtor may file for bankruptcy with an ulterior motive. A corporation's managers might, for example, commence a bankruptcy case merely to put off the time that a creditor seizes the assets of the firm, even when there is no hope of saving the firm as a going concern. For cases in which the bankruptcy judge believes that "the best interest of creditors and the debtor" would be ill-served by bankruptcy, §305 grants the bankruptcy court an unreviewable right to dismiss the case, also known as "abstention." Section 1112 gives the court a similar, if redundant, power only in Chapter 11 cases. The Code does not make dismissal under this provision unreviewable.

dismissal/
abstention

The exercises below ask you to consider how abuse might affect an individual or a corporate bankruptcy petition of an insolvent debtor. The first case that follows, *Ross-Tousey*, as well as the related notes and problem, explores the means test for individual debtors and addresses the question of how deemed as opposed to actual expenses are to be handled. The next case, *Colonial Ford*, as well as the related notes and problems, explore the circumstances in which a corporate business debtor with multiple creditors, ostensibly a good candidate for bankruptcy, is subject to an arrangement among its principals that arguably makes bankruptcy unnecessary and dismissal appropriate.

Key Provisions: Bankruptcy Code §§305; 707(b); 1112

EXERCISES

3C(1) Debtor loses her job and decides to go into business for herself. She borrows $100,000 from Bank to start an Internet business. When Debtor applies for the loan, she confides in her brother that the success of the business is a long shot, but she doesn't care much as "it's Bank's money anyway." After the business uses up all $100,000 and fails, Debtor files a petition to commence a Chapter 7 bankruptcy case. Will the court dismiss the case?

3C(2) Debtor completes a medical residency, which paid about $30,000 per year, subject to student loans of $100,000. She lands a job in a prestigious plastic surgery practice and expects to earn on average $750,000 per year over the first ten years of employment there. She defers the job for a year and travels the world, borrowing $50,000 for the adventure. Just before the end of her time off, while driving to the city of the plastic surgery practice, she accidentally runs off the road in a small town. There she falls in love with the local lawyer while she waits for her car to be repaired. She decides to give up her lucrative job and settle in the town, where she will earn about $50,000 per year as a country doctor. This is enough for her comfortably to repay her student loans over time, but the additional $50,000 of ordinary unsecured debt would be a burden. Debtor has no assets (the car was leased) and she files a petition for bankruptcy under Chapter 7. Will the petition be sustained? Would your answer change if Debtor worked as a highly paid plastic surgeon for a year before crashing in the small town and deciding to stay? What additional facts might you need to answer these questions? In answering, please consider, among other provisions, Bankruptcy Code §523(a)(8). Consider this exercise again in connection with Problem 12A-2.

3C(3) Debtor Corporation is a medium-sized manufacturer. Its chief executive officer and sole shareholder has Debtor borrow $100,000 from each of three banks. The CEO lies to each of the banks so that none knows about other loans. Moreover, he fraudulently promises that Debtor's obligations to its trade creditors will never exceed $10,000, even though he gradually increases the debts owed them to $150,000. By the time the CEO is indicted for failing to pay his personal income tax, most of the money that the banks lent Debtor has been siphoned off by the CEO and used to support his lavish life style. Debtor owes the Banks $300,000 and its twenty trade creditors a total of $150,000. Can the CEO file a voluntary petition on behalf of Debtor? Can creditors raise an "unclean hands" defense? Can three of the trade creditors file an involuntary petition against Debtor?

3C(4) Debtor Newspaper, a publicly traded corporation, issues dual-class equity shares: Class A Stock, which can vote, and Class B Stock, which has all the economic attributes of Class A Stock but carries no voting rights. As advertising revenues move from print to electronic news providers, Debtor suffers a financial crisis and files for bankruptcy under Chapter 11. Immediately after the case commences, Rival Newspaper offers to purchase all of Debtor's assets but only if the purchase can be closed quickly and only if Debtor assumes its executory contracts with key employees and suppliers. Manager, who is Debtor's chief executive officer and personally owns all of Debtor's Class A stock, despises Rival's editorial policy, opposes the acquisition, and refuses to have Debtor assume the contracts, preferring, in Manager's words, to "leave scorched earth and rebuild from the ashes than to let Rival touch this newspaper." Debtor's unsecured creditor's committee moves to have the case converted to Chapter 7 or, in the alternative, to have a trustee appointed in the Chapter 11 case. Manager replies that he should be permitted to remain in control as, in his judgment, Debtor's assets are worth more under his control than under the control of anyone else. Who will prevail? In answering this question, consider, among other provisions, §1104(3). Consider this exercise again after reading chapter 13 of this book.

CASES

IN RE ROSS-TOUSEY
United States District Court, E.D. Wisc., 2007
2007 WL 1466647

GRIESBACH, DISTRICT JUDGE.

In this bankruptcy appeal, the United States Trustee appeals a decision of the bankruptcy court denying the Trustee's motion to dismiss the case for abuse, pursuant to §707(b)(1). The Trustee argues that the bankruptcy court erred in allowing the debtors, in calculating their current monthly income, to deduct an "automobile ownership expense" despite the fact that the debtors did not finance their cars and thus had no "ownership expense." …For the reasons set forth below, the judgment of the bankruptcy court will be reversed.

One of the centerpieces of the Bankruptcy Abuse Prevention and Consumer Protection Act of 2005 ("BAPCPA") was the introduction of a means test to distinguish between those debtors who could afford to repay a portion of their debt and those who could not. Under BAPCPA, if the debtor has sufficient disposable income to repay his unsecured creditors at least $166.67 per month ($10,000 over five years), he is steered towards Chapter 13 and must partly repay his debts. §707(b)(2)(A)(i)(II). Chapter 7 relief, which allows for the complete discharge of debt, is now presumptively considered an "abuse" if the debtor is able to pass the means test.

The means test uses an objective formula to determine a debtor's ability to pay. As applicable here, the means test starts with the debtor's current monthly income ("CMI") and reduces that number by certain allowable monthly expenses set forth in §707(b)(2)(A)(ii)-(iv). These include expenses for such things as supporting elderly or ill family members, health insurance, paying for a child's education, and the like. As relevant here, the statute also allows deductions of the broader category of expenses provided in §707(b)(2)(A)(ii)(I):

> The debtor's monthly expenses shall be the debtor's applicable monthly expense amounts specified under the National Standards

and Local Standards, and the debtor's actual monthly expenses for the categories specified as Other Necessary Expenses issued by the Internal Revenue Service for the area in which the debtor resides ... .

The Standards referred to are those used by the IRS to determine a taxpayer's ability to pay delinquent tax. These Standards allow a taxpayer to deduct an operating expense as well as an expense incurred due to the cost of leasing or purchasing a vehicle.

[handwritten: → IRS Stds allow for ownership deduction]

The debtors in this case were both long-term employees of the Mohican North Star Casino. In their Chapter 7 application, they reduced their current monthly income by $358 for "transportation vehicle operation" expenses. They also took deductions of $471 and $332 (nationally standard amounts) for "transportation ownership / lease expenses" for their two cars, even though they owned the cars free and clear and thus did not have any actual monthly expenses associated with car ownership (e.g., leases or loans). With these ownership expenses subtracted from their current monthly income, the debtors "failed" the means test and were allowed relief under Chapter 7.

At its core, the question is whether a debtor who has no "actual" monthly car payments—because he paid cash (or paid off) his car—may nevertheless receive credit for the automobile ownership expense. As all parties to this action have recognized from the outset, the issue presented has produced a split among the many bankruptcy courts that have considered it. See In re Enright, 2007 WL 748432 (Bankr. M.D.N.C., March 6, 2007) (collecting cases). ... The question has also split scholarly commentators. Professor Gary Neustadter argues that the deduction should not be allowed: "a debtor who, at the time of the petition, owns free and clear an older vehicle possibly soon in need of replacement, or a debtor who, at the time of the petition, doesn't own a vehicle but needs to purchase one soon, may not claim any transportation ownership expense as part of the presumed monthly expenses." Gary Neustadter, *2005: A Consumer Bankruptcy Odyssey*, 39 Creighton L. Rev. 225, 295 (2006). In contrast, Bankruptcy Judge Wedoff argues that "since the means test treats the Local Standards not as caps but as fixed allowances, it is more reasonable to permit a debtor to claim the Local Standards ownership expense based on the number of vehicles the debtor owns or leases, rather than on the number for which the debtor makes payments." Eugene R. Wedoff, Means Testing in the New § 707(b), 79 Am. Bankr. L.J. 231, 257-58 (2005). Under this "fixed allowance" view, the ownership expense deduction is allowed simply because the debtor owns a car.

[In the instant case, the] bankruptcy court allowed the deductions based on the rationale set forth in an earlier case before that court, In re Grunert, 353 Bankr. 591, 594 (Bankr. E.D.Wis.2006). That decision, like others allowing similar debtors to take the automobile expense deductibles reads:

> The debtor's monthly expenses shall be the debtor's *applicable* monthly expense amounts specified under the National Standards and Local Standards, and the debtor's *actual* monthly expenses for the categories specified as Other Necessary Expenses issued by the Internal Revenue Service for the area in which the debtor resides ... .

§707(b)(2)(A)(ii)(I) (italics added). *Grunert* and other courts perceive a salient contrast between the statute's use of the terms "actual" and "applicable." As one court put it:

> [T]he use of the word "applicable" in the first clause with regard to some expenses (which include both housing and transportation ownership), and the use of the word "actual" with regard to "Other Necessary Expenses", indicates Congressional intent to distinguish between the two classes of expenses, and to allow debtors to use the deductions found in the Local Standards for the first category. A debtor's actual expenses are only relevant with respect to expenses that fall into the "Other Necessary Expenses" category.

In re Swan, 2007 WL 1146485, (Bankr. N.D.Cal.2007).

These courts reason that because the statute does not require reference to the debtor's "actual" expenses in calculating some monthly expenses, it does not matter whether such expenses are "actually" incurred or not. As Judge Wedoff put it, the auto ownership expenses are fixed allowances without any connection to whether the payments are actually made or not. Eugene R. Wedoff, Means Testing in the New § 707(b), 79 Am. Bankr. L.J. 257-58. Under this line of reasoning, it does not matter that the debtors in this case did not make any car payments—they were allowed the ownership expense deduction simply because they owned two cars.

Although this analysis has been adopted by several courts, I am not persuaded that Congress intended the distinction between "applicable" and "actual" to be so trenchant. It is easy to conclude that the statute's use of the term "actual" means that the expenses so described are to reflect the true (actual) state of the debtor's expenses. It also follows, certainly, that the statute's use of the term "applicable" suggests that the legislature intended it to have a meaning other than "actual." They are not the same. But though it is reasonable to conclude that "actual" and "applicable" have different meanings, that does not mean that Congress, by using two different adjectives, meant that the two terms must have essentially *opposite* meanings.

Instead of viewing "applicable" and "actual" as having virtually opposite meanings, another reading of the statute would allow a debtor to deduct the auto expense listed in the Standards if the debtor actually had an auto expense in the first place. This reading gives meaning to the distinction between "applicable" and "actual" without taking a further step to conclude that "applicable" means "nonexistent" or "fictional." Under this reading, it is true that the debtor's "actual" expense does not control the *amount* of the deduction, but the debtor must still have *some* expense in the first place before the Standard amount becomes "applicable." The term "applicable" merely means, in this context, that when a debtor has an automobile ownership expense, his deduction is not based on that actual expense but on the applicable expenses listed in the Standards. As another court has recently concluded, "[i]f a debtor does not own or lease a vehicle, the ownership expense is not 'applicable' to that debtor." In re Howell, 2007 WL 1237832. Put another way:

> Had Congress intended to indiscriminately allow all expense amounts specified in the National and Local Standards, it would have written 707(b)(2)(A)(ii)(I) to read, "The debtor's monthly expenses shall be the monthly expense amounts specified under the National Standards and Local Standards ... " rather than "The debtor's monthly expenses shall be the debtor's *applicable* monthly expense amounts specified under the National and Local Standards ... ." (Emphasis added).

In re Slusher, 359 Bankr. 290 (Bankr. D. Nev., 2007).

This reading—requiring an "actual" payment to be made before the expense becomes "applicable"—does not improperly equate the two terms, as some courts seem to believe. It merely recognizes that the two terms are applied in different contexts. For some expenses, the statute allows debtors to take their exact (actual) deductions. For other expenses, such as car ownership expenses, the statute's fixed deduction simply treats all debtors who make car payments the same. In other words, the statute allows debtors to itemize certain of their expenses with particularity, but it does not care whether a debtor drives a Mercedes or a Mercury. This reading gives meaning to the important distinction between "applicable" and "actual" without tak-

[handwritten margin note: i.e. deduction is the same regardless of amount— but only gets deducted if some amount was w/drawn]

ing the further, unwarranted, step of concluding that the expense may be applicable even though it does not even exist. * * *

Congress has deemed transportation and car ownership to be among the necessities of life that a debtor is entitled to fund before he must pay back his creditors. Thus, the statute excludes these amounts from the monthly pot of money that the creditors can get their hands on. What's important, therefore, is not *how many* cars a debtor owns, but how many cars he makes *payments* on every month—it is only the *payments* that affect the debtor's ability to repay his creditors. The statute is only concerned about protecting the debtor's ability to continue owning a car, and if the debtor *already* owns the car, the debtor is adequately protected. Section 707(b)(2)(A)(ii)(I) only achieves the statute's goal of protecting debtors' ability to fund the necessities of life when the debtor is actually shouldering a monthly auto expense. When the debtor has no monthly ownership expenses, it makes no sense to deduct an ownership expense to shield it from creditors. * * *

Thus, … in my view the term "applicable" does not simply mean a debtor must only apply the Standard based on the number of cars he owns; he must apply the Standard based on how many cars for which he has monthly ownership *expenses*. The fact that Congress has chosen to standardize the amount allowed for ownership expenses does not mean it also chose to make the Standards into fixed allowances guaranteed to every car owner.

A principal objection to the approach I adopt is that it would lead to unfair or arbitrary results. For example, the individual who makes his forty-eighth and final car payment two months before the cutoff would be penalized for no longer having an auto ownership expense (he could no longer deduct the payment from his CMI), whereas the debtor with only one payment to go would be rewarded because he still had a monthly expense, albeit a fleeting one. Because there is little reason to distinguish between the two debtors in this example, the calculation produces a somewhat unsatisfactory result.

It is also arguably unfair (or at least unwise) to "punish" debtors who chose to drive inexpensive automobiles they own rather than borrow money to purchase more expensive cars. … And, given the limitations of a typical car's lifespan, there is something artificial about considering only *monthly* ownership payments: while the debtor who owns his car free and clear may incur no "monthly" ownership payments, the debtor nevertheless can be expected to incur upkeep and replacement expenses tied to his ongoing ownership of an automobile. * * *

Although these criticisms are well-taken, they do not persuade me that the ownership expense should be allowed when the debtor incurs no such expense. First, though unfairness may sometimes result from the approach I have adopted, it seems unreasonable to expect that the complex and individualized issues involving a debtor's finances are meant to be addressed through an objective and standardized system like the means test. * * *

Moreover, I note that debtors do not have a monopoly on claims of perceived arbitrariness. For instance, if the debtors had their way, they would be allowed the deduction merely because they owned two automobiles, a result their creditors might well find arbitrary. The debtors' situation in this case exemplifies the point. The debtors own a number of cars, including a '69 Chevy truck and an '85 Oldsmobile. One or more of their cars are parked in the debtors' backyard and do not run. These examples prove the point that there is nothing particularly meaningful (as far as the Bankruptcy Code is concerned) about the mere fact that a debtor owns something that happens to qualify as an automobile. In other words, no one would argue that it makes sense to link a debtor's ability to qualify under Chapter 7 to the fact that the debtor happens to have a car rusting away in his backyard. Yet under the debtors' reading of the statute, any of his cars (whether in running condition, parked in the backyard, etc.) would suffice to trigger the ownership expense allowance simply because it is an "automobile" and they "own" it. There is no requirement that the debtors actually need the car in their daily life to drive to work or to the store—in fact, under the debtors' view there is no requirement that the car actually be in working condition. Thus, tying the deduction merely to the number of cars a debtor owns rather than the number he makes *payments* for can lead to arbitrary results not in accordance with the purposes of BAPCPA. Instead, it seems preferable (and less arbitrary) to condition the deduction to ownership *expenses* such as lease or debt payments. Doing so ensures that the car is more likely to be *used* by the debtor in his everyday life, which means that such expenses are exactly the sort of expenses that should trigger an allowance to protect the debtor's continued ownership of the car.

[handwritten annotation:] Court: only a deduction for cars on which debtor makes a payment

IN RE COLONIAL FORD
United States Bankruptcy Court, D. Utah, 1982
24 Bankr. 1014

Mabey, Bankruptcy Judge.

The Bankruptcy Code contains several provisions which promote the private, cooperative, negotiated rebuilding of financially distressed debtors. One of these measures, §305(a)(1), is the subject of inquiry in this case. The facts relevant to this inquiry, briefly summarized, are as follows.

In January 1977, Colonial Ford, Inc. (the debtor) ceased operation as an automobile dealership. Since May 1975, it has been embroiled in litigation with Ford Motor Company, Ford Motor Credit Company, the United States Small Business Administration, and other creditors. This litigation embraces three lawsuits, one of which has journeyed to the Tenth Circuit Court of Appeals and back and resulted in a judgment for $2,897,125 in favor of Ford Credit and against Colonial. Execution on this judgment and liquidation of the former dealership site, which Colonial continues to hold and lease to others, was enjoined by the district court pending resolution of these cases.

In July 1981, Colonial and its creditors settled their differences. The agreement, in essence, accomplished two objectives. First, with the exception of a single cross-claim, it concluded all three lawsuits. Second, creditors reduced their claims and gave Colonial nine months to sell or refinance the dealership site; if this did not occur, a decree of foreclosure would be entered. Creditors, in other words, were willing to take less in exchange for an end to the litigation and swifter realization on their claims.[2]

Colonial was unable to sell or refinance the property and filed a petition under Chapter 11 on March 30, 1982. Ford Credit filed a motion to abstain pursuant to §305(a)(1) on June 1. * * *

---

[2] These reductions, with other concessions, were substantial. Ford Credit, for example, held a judgment for $2,897,125. An injunction barring execution, however, had prevented collection from the fall of 1976 until the settlement in 1981. The settlement reduced the judgment to $1,250,000, provided a moratorium on interest for all but $50,000 of this amount, and postponed foreclosure another nine months. All but three creditors, by default or acquiescence, are dealt with in the settlement. One of these, Ken Rothey, is counsel to and an officer of Colonial. He holds an attorneys lien on the unsettled cross-claim. The others, LeGrande Belnap and Doris Belnap, shareholders of Colonial, have a claim for wages.

Section 305(a)(1) reflects a policy, embodied in several sections of the Code, which favors "workouts": private, negotiated adjustments of creditor-company relations. Congress designed the Code, in large measure, to encourage workouts in the first instance, with refuge in bankruptcy as a last resort. As noted in the legislative history: "Most business arrangements, that is, extensions or compositions (reduction) of debts, occur out-of-court. The out-of-court procedure, sometimes known as a common law composition, is quick and inexpensive. However, it requires near universal agreement of the business's creditors, and is limited in the relief it can provide for an overextended business. When an out-of-court arrangement is inadequate to rehabilitate a business, the bankruptcy laws provide an alternative. An arrangement or reorganization accomplished under the Bankruptcy Act binds nonconsenting creditors, and permits more substantial restructuring of a debtor's finances than does an out-of-court work-out." H.R. Rep. No. 95-595, 95th Cong., 1st Sess. 220 (1977). The reasons for blessing the workout are at least threefold.

First, the workout is expeditious. Debtors and creditors, unbridled by bankruptcy, enjoy a flexibility conducive to speed. By contrast, the "bankruptcy machinery [of] today," may be "a very time-consuming and hydra-headed kind of delaying structure" which "frequently works to the detriment of creditors." Hearings of S. 2266 and H.R. 8200 Before the Subcomm. on Improvements in Judicial Machinery of the Senate Comm. on the Judiciary, 95th Cong., 1st Sess. 599 (1977). Indeed, it has been noted, apropos the settlement in this case, that "delay ... is the most costly element in any bankruptcy proceeding and particularly in a business reorganization. The same amount of money received by the senior creditors four years from now is worth probably less than half of what would be an amount of money received today. In other words, if [a creditor] can anticipate, after this elaborate procedure, [that he] will receive $1 million, then he would be well-advised and usually is anxious to take $500,000 today because it's worth more to him. He has to consider the investment value and the ravages of inflation. This is worth more than the prospect of getting $1 million four years from now." Id. at 490. Many provisions in the Code were fashioned in response to this testimony and as inducements to alacrity in reorganization, including the expansive jurisdiction of the court, the opportunity for creditors to file plans, and modification of the absolute priority rule, to name three. The assist to workouts complements these features of the Code.

Second, workouts are economic Economy, of course, is improved through expedition, as noted above. But the workout is economic because it avoids the superstructure of reorganization trustees, committees, and their professional representatives. These and other costs of administration push junior interests "under water," and because they must be paid at confirmation, diminish prospects for a plan. Moreover, bankruptcy may shipwreck relationships necessary to keep a business afloat. Customers are reluctant to deal with the manufacturer who may not survive to honor the warranty of his product or with the lessor who cannot guarantee the habitability of his premises. The cost of overcoming this reluctance, through marketing campaigns and the like, may be high. Sales will be difficult; prices may be low. Suppliers may dwindle. Costs of credit may increase. "[W]hen word of financial difficulty spreads, the debtor's own debtors often decline to pay as they would have in the ordinary course, suddenly reporting that the dresses were the wrong size, were the wrong color, or were not ordered." Coogan, Broude and Glatt, "Comments on Some Reorganization Provisions of the Pending Bankruptcy Bills," 30 Bus. Law. 1149, 1155 (1975). Likewise, "accounts receivable can deteriorate to an unbelievable extent as soon as word gets around that the debtor is headed for the cemetery." Hearings on H.R. 31 and H.R. 32 Before the Subcomm. on Civil and Constitutional Rights of the House Comm. on the Judiciary, 94th Cong., 1st Sess., Ser. 27, pt. 1, at 483 (1975). These circumstances, among others, handcuff a debtor doing business in Chapter 11.

Third, the workout is sensible. Workouts contemplate, indeed depend upon, participation from all parties in interest, good faith, conciliation, and candor. The alternative is litigation and its bedfellows—bluff, pettifoggery, and strife. Moreover, the parties who are "on-site," and prepared by education or experience, are more able than a judge, ill-equipped in resources and training, to rescue a beleaguered corporation. "The courtroom," after all, "is not a boardroom. The judge is not a business consultant." In re Curlew Valley Associates, 14 Bankr. 506, 511 (Bankr. D. Utah 1981). The problems of insolvency, for the most part, are matters for extra-judicial resolution, calling for "business not legal judgment." Id.

With these advantages in mind, the authors of the Code encouraged workouts in at least two ways.

First, the Code, "[l]ike a 'fleet-in-being' … may be a force towards mutual accommodation," and as such, sets parameters for negotiations preceding a workout. Hearings on H.R. 31 and H.R. 32

Before the Subcomm. on Civil and Constitutional Rights of the House Comm. on the Judiciary, 94th Cong., 1st Sess., Ser. 27, pt. 1, at 396 (1975).* * *

Second, the Code, in several specific respects, contemplates that workouts will be a prelude to, yet consummated in, bankruptcy. ... Indeed, incentives to use "prepackaged plans" are "written all through the new Act." They lead to a "revolving door" in and out of Chapter 11.

Thus, the Code encourages workouts outside, or concluded inside, Chapter 11. Encouragement on both fronts is necessary because dissent from a workout may assume a variety of shapes. Creditors who would otherwise pursue their rights under state law are kept in tow because preferences may be undone following a petition in bankruptcy. Others may be bound, assuming a consensus in number and amount, through confirmation of a plan. What, however, of the maverick who threatens prematurely to disrupt out-of-court negotiations by an involuntary petition, or the party, creditor or debtor, who has "buyer's remorse" and seeks a recapitulation of the settlement in bankruptcy? This form of dissent is the target of §305(a)(1) which provides:

> (a) The Court, after notice and a hearing, may dismiss a case under this title, or may suspend all proceedings in a case under this title, at any time if—

(1) The interests of creditors and the debtor would be better served by such dismissal or suspension. * * *

Colonial questions the applicability of §305(a)(1) in voluntary cases, and whether dismissal, under the circumstances of this case, "better serves" the interests of creditors and the debtor.

Section 305(a)(1) applies in any case, voluntary or involuntary, "under this title." This is consistent with the evolution of the statute, noted above, beginning as a bylaw in §4-208(a), and moving to general applicability in Chapter 3 of the Code. Moreover, this reading is consistent with the policy to encourage workouts. It would be anomalous to protect workouts from involuntary petitions while leaving them vulnerable to voluntary petitions. Creditors would be protected from the renegades in their number who sought involuntarily to commit a debtor to bankruptcy, but they would have no similar check against debtors who compose their debts with the promise that matters will be left out of court and then stage an ambush in Chapter 11.

Section 305(a)(1) permits dismissal where it will "better serve" the interests of creditors and debtors. The statute affords no guidance in defining the "interests" to be considered, nor does it delineate criteria for determining when parties will be better served in or out of bankruptcy. Given the policies underlying §305(a)(1), however, the standards for dismissal may include speed, economy, and freedom from litigation. Other considerations may be fairness, priorities in distribution, capacity for dealing with frauds and preferences, and the importance of a discharge to the debtor. ... Not all of these factors will be involved, nor will they assume equal importance, in every case. Hence, Congress intended the court to exercise considerable discretion in sifting and weighing grounds for dismissal under §305(a)(1).

In this case, the interests of creditors are better served by dismissal. They agreed to a workout because it ended the litigation, and although they compromised their claims, the present value of the amounts to be realized at payout or foreclosure exceeded what they might have gained over time. This was not a workout where debt is rolled over with an eye to recovery, while recognizing the possibility of bankruptcy. Nor was it a workout where a deal was struck prepetition to be confirmed under the auspices of Chapter 11. Here the out-of-court composition was comprehensive, including virtually all creditors and the debtor. It was also final. A business which had lain dormant for years was not to be revived without the elimination of prior debt and the infusion of fresh capital.[15]

Colonial argues that its interests are better served in Chapter 11; otherwise it would not have filed a petition. This argument, however, may be astigmatic for at least two reasons.

First, it ignores the question of who is the debtor for purposes of §305(a)(1). If the case is in Chapter 11, for example, the debtor will be a debtor in possession, and hence the trustee or fiduciary for the estate. The interests of the debtor, under the circumstances, are coincidental with the interests of creditors. Indeed, no debtor is an island, self-existent apart from its creditors who supply the capital, goods, and services necessary to his survival. This idea finds expression, not

---

[15] Indeed, Ford Credit, in reliance upon the settlement, has made payments of $50,000 in attorneys fees to Colonial, and $85,000 in property taxes to its shareholder. Colonial has not offered to refund these monies or otherwise unscramble performance under the agreement.

only in the construct of a debtor in possession, but also at common law where insolvent entities became funds managed in trust for the benefit of creditors. From this standpoint, the interests of creditors receive double weight under §305(a)(1), once from a partisan and again from a fiducial perspective. In any event, the corporate debtor will be a complex of constituencies, including not only creditors but also a board of directors, management, and shareholders. These parties may be divided on some issues; even when united, their views may change from circumstance to circumstance, or from time to time. To say, with Colonial, that the debtor speaks with one voice on all occasions, and that its interests are circumscribed in the management's act of filing a petition, is oversimple.

Second, it overlooks the benefits which debtors in general may derive from out-of-court workouts and which Colonial in particular obtained in this settlement. The choice to settle out of court rather than to file for reorganization, more often than not, will be enlightened. Management eager for asylum in bankruptcy may pause if faced with displacement by a trustee. Shareholders likewise must reckon with the prospect of a creditor's plan, wresting control of the business and eliminating their interest. Moreover, their equity, already thin or nonexistent, may not survive the burden of administrative debt. Debtors, as well as creditors, are familiar with the old saw that a "good" liquidation out of court is better than a "bad" reorganization in Chapter 11. Since the odds are stacked against obtaining confirmation of a plan, and in light of the probability of conversion to Chapter 7, debtors may be well-advised, where their creditors are cooperative, to forego the dislocations and trauma, the depressed markets, the higher cost of money, and other disadvantages of bankruptcy, and work out an arrangement, even if it contemplates an eventual liquidation.

Colonial (or its shareholder, if she is the debtor) garnered these general benefits and two additional bonuses from its settlement. (1) Mrs. Belnap, by paying the SBA, may assume its right of redemption upon foreclosure of the property. This assumption, if exercised, is free and clear of any claim by Colonial or its creditors. This option … might be unavailable to her in Chapter 11. (2) Colonial may have grown weary of the protracted litigation, and realizing that it had reached a point of diminishing returns in court, sought disentanglement from its adversaries through the settlement. Colonial now seeks to keep the benefits of this compact, the reduction in debt, and avoid its burdens, the foreclosure, but this may not be done. An accord, with no satisfaction, releases parties from any duty to honor the compromise, and returns them to the status quo ante. The petition, therefore, may have revived the litigation in district court, with the risks and imponderables which prompted settlement in the first instance. There is no assurance that changing forums and prolonging the fight for another seven years will produce a better bargain for Colonial.

These reasons motivated Colonial to make an agreement with its creditors which composed the debt and provided for sale, refinancing, or foreclosure of the property. The alternative of bankruptcy was available then, as now, and entered the calculus of decisionmaking, but was rejected in favor of the settlement. Colonial asserts, however, that reorganization better serves its interests at present. Attempting to divine the interests of Colonial, given this doublemindedness, is problematical. But even if full credit is given to its present protestations, these do not counterbalance the reasons for avoiding bankruptcy. Even assuming that the protestations and the reasons have equal weight, the policy of encouraging out-of-court workouts, embodied in §305(a)(1), dictates that the interests of Colonial are "better served" by the settlement than by a petition in Chapter 11.

The Code encourages out-of-court workouts. Section 305(a)(1) is one of several instruments useful in achieving this goal. Because an order of dismissal under §305(a)(1) is nonreviewable, the statute should be invoked sparingly. Indeed, §305(a)(1) permits "suspension" as well as dismissal of a case, suggesting the possibility that efforts toward settlement may proceed on more than one front at the same time. Where, however, the workout is comprehensive, and designed to end, not perpetuate, the creditor-company relations, dismissal under §305(a)(1) is appropriate. One "reorganization," under these circumstances, is enough. Section 305(a)(1) precludes an encore, thereby furthering the policies of expedition, economy, and good sense.

NOTES

3C.1. As the court in *Ross-Tousey* points out, the goal of the means test is to determine whether a debtor can afford to pay reasonable ongoing expenses and still afford to repay some of her prepetition debts. With this as an objective, issues of perceived fairness are bound to arise when a debtor's own choices affect what is deemed a reasonable expense for the purposes of the test. As the court's analysis makes clear, a debtor who chooses to own a car and to finance is deemed needier under the means test than one who owns a car outright or does not own a car. This may strike many as perverse. A perhaps better approach would be for Congress to have provided an allowance for auto expense and have that allowance count as a deduction regardless whether the debtor owns a car. That is, perhaps Congress should have taken the approach that *Slusher* (cited in *Ross-Tousey*) understandably concludes Congress declined to adopt. Problem 3C-1 asks you to further consider the question of perverse incentives under the holding of *Ross-Tousey*.

perverse incentives a deductions for means test

3C.2. There is more than one creditor in *Colonial Ford*, but effectively all the creditors have reached an agreement with one another. In that sense, it is much like a one-creditor case. A major purpose of bankruptcy law—resolving conflicts among creditors—is not implicated here, because there are no conflicts among creditors. They all participated in the workout and they all agree that it is in their interest to stay out of bankruptcy. Given that creditors are unanimous on the course of action that is in their interest, it might make sense to treat this case as if the debtor had but a single creditor. In such a case, one might argue that the debtor does not suffer from any of the problems bankruptcy was designed to solve and that dismissal under §305 is therefore appropriate. Courts, however, are likely to resist an approach to the problem that is so straightforward, at least if the debtor is a firm that is still in operation and still has employees. In such a case, the court might fear that the creditors would liquidate the business at cost to the workers. As *Colonial Ford* suggests, however, courts are less likely to be sympathetic to a debtor when the creditors present a united front if there is no active business to save and it seems the debtor is only playing for time to extract a greater concession from the creditors.

3C.3. There is another dimension to the court's decision in *Colonial Ford*. The court concludes: "Colonial now seeks to keep the benefits of this compact, the reduction in debt, and avoid its burdens, the foreclosure, but this may not be done." If the case were decided on the basis that the creditors presented a unified front, perhaps combined with the fact that there were no employee interests at stake, then the agreement of the debtor, or lack thereof, would have been irrelevant to any bankruptcy policy. The united creditors would not destroy value by separating assets more valuable kept together, for instance, the way creditors might in competition. Any emphasis on Colonial's agreement to give up its assets at the workout stage seems misplaced, as such agreement is redundant. Colonial had agreed to give up its assets in the event of default earlier, when it first borrowed. The only issue at the time of the bankruptcy case was whether any bankruptcy policy would be served by <u>continuation of the case. The answer here</u> was no.

3C.4. In a sense, *Colonial Ford* was a simple case, as the creditors' unity and the fact that the corporate debtor had ceased operation *each* made it unlikely that the creditors would destroy value if the case were dismissed. (Even a debtor that goes out of business may have assets more valuable if kept together. It might have a drill press that is more valuable if it can be sold with the custom dies the debtor had designed for it. But this will not ordinarily be an important factor in a dead firm.) Problems 3C-2 to 3C-4 below ask you to face tougher questions with regard to dismissal.

no policy to keep entity whole [handwritten margin note]

PROBLEMS

3C-1. Debtor has regular income but few assets. She owns a five-year-old Saturn sedan (outright) but does not own a home or have any property to which she attaches a personal interest. She has become overextended on her credit cards (expecting a raise that never comes) and contemplates a Chapter 7 bankruptcy petition. Shortly before filing such a petition, Debtor sells her car and replaces it with a five-year-old Nissan, which she purchases on credit. The Saturn and Nissan have roughly the same value. In the state where the debtor lives, the proceeds from the sale of her Saturn qualify as exempt property. Debtor eligibility for Chapter 7 depends on whether she qualifies for a car payment deduction under the §707(b) means test. Does she? Does your answer depend on whether the relevant court adopts the holding of *Ross-Tousey*?

3C-2. Assume the same facts as in *Colonial Ford* except that three of the creditors have second thoughts and bring an involuntary petition against Colonial Ford. Will the compact serve effectively as a waiver of the creditors' right to use the bankruptcy process? Does it matter that the debtor is a corporation rather than an individual?

3C-3. Assume the same facts as in *Colonial Ford* except that three new creditors, all owed small amounts of money, file an involuntary petition. How would the court in *Colonial Ford* apply its analysis to that case? Would it matter that each of the new creditors had a long-standing relationship with the owner of Colonial Ford and filed the petition after lengthy discussions?

3C-4. Firm, a manufacturer, has no substantial debt obligations. Its managers, though wary of ordinary debt, decide to have Firm issue a sort of fixed obligation called "Chameleon Equity shares." Unlike common equity shares, which earn returns that vary generally with the fortune of the firm, Chameleon Equity entitles each holder to a fixed payment that corresponds to principal and interest on a loan. But Chameleon Equity is not like ordinary debt in that the holders do not have a right to collect Firm's assets in the event of default. If Firm defaults, and the default remains uncured for six months, Firm's ordinary equity is automatically transferred to the holders of the Chameleon Equity, and the fixed obligations—principal and interest—due the Chameleon Equity is cancelled. Two months after default on the Chameleon Equity shares, Firm's managers, who also own much of Firm's common equity, file a Chapter 11 bankruptcy petition on Firm's behalf. Should the court dismiss the bankruptcy case? Would your answer change if upon default and lapse of the grace period, Firm were auctioned as a going concern rather than automatically restructured?

Compare Exercise 2A(3). See also Alan Schwartz, Bankruptcy Contracting Reviewed, 109 Yale L.J. 343 (1999); Robert K. Rasmussen, Debtor's Choice: A Menu Approach to Corporate Bankruptcy, 71 Texas Law Review 51 (1992); Lucian A. Bebchuk, A new Approach to Corporate Reorganizations, 101 Harv. L. Rev. 775 (1988); Mark J. Roe, Bankruptcy and Debt: A New Model for Corporate Reorganization, 83 Colum. L. Rev. 527 (1983).

IV. THE AUTOMATIC STAY

For the collective bankruptcy proceeding to be effective, all efforts by creditors to obtain repayment of their debts must stop, regardless of whether the petition is voluntary or involuntary. If such conduct were not restrained, creditors would continue pursuing individual remedies, even though such individual actions run counter to the basic bankruptcy principle that once the proceeding begins, the creditors' interests are best served if they work together. Collective action is accomplished through what is known as the "automatic stay." The stay is designed to prevent a race to a debtor's assets, but not otherwise to alter the relationship between a debtor and society.

Bankruptcy Code §362 stays creditors from bringing actions or enforcing judgments against the debtor when such actions or judgments arise from the debtor's prepetition life. The stay also prevents the attachment of liens on the debtor's assets. More generally, the stay prevents anyone from taking possession of the debtor's property or exercising control over it. When you take your car in to be fixed, for example, the garage has a mechanic's lien on the car securing your obligation to pay. Let us assume that the garage closes its doors forever and files a Chapter 7 petition. By its terms, the automatic stay prevents you from unilaterally seizing the car. In such a case, however, the automatic stay should last no longer than it takes to figure out how much you owe. Parties can always ask to have the stay lifted. The smaller the debtor's property interest, the easier it will be to do this.

The automatic stay provides us with a starting place. When it prevents third parties from reaching property that is not necessary for the debtor's reorganization and in which the debtor has no equity, it is a straightforward matter to go to court and have the stay lifted under §362(d). More detailed discussion of this provision is deferred until chapter 9, section B below. Similarly, if §362 does not prevent someone from taking actions that undermine the bankruptcy process, the trustee can go to court and ask the court to issue a stay under the court's general equitable powers contained in §105(a). Section 105(a) authorizes the court to "issue any order, process, or judgment that is necessary or appropriate to carry out the provisions" of the Bankruptcy Code. This section, however, does not empower courts to issue stays merely because it benefits the debtor. Stays under §105 must be connected with discrete policies of the Bankruptcy Code.

In this chapter, we first examine the way in which the automatic stay limits the actions of creditors. Most obviously, it prevents them from pursuing their nonbankruptcy debt collection remedies. The prohibition extends beyond the creditor's invocation of a formal collection process. It is not always clear which of a creditor's informal actions are permissible and which violate the stay. Hardest are the cases in which the creditor wears multiple hats. For example, a creditor can be a shareholder as well.

The automatic stay also serves to ensure that the debtor's property is not dissipated while its affairs are being sorted out. Hence, the automatic stay affects those who are not themselves creditors. There is a line to draw between protection of a debtor's assets, so that rights can be determined in a single forum, and an extension of the debtor's rights merely because the debtor has filed a bankruptcy petition. Such extension would violate the *Butner* principle. Drawing this line is the second topic of this chapter. In particular, we want to know the extent to which noncreditor third parties with ongoing relations with the debtor can exercise a nonbankruptcy right to terminate the relationship once the petition is filed.

In the last part of this chapter, we focus on the way the stay affects the government when it uses its police and regulatory power. Governmental bodies can bring actions against the debtor notwithstanding the stay to ensure that the debtor plays by the same rules as everyone else. In addition, the automatic stay does not prevent the government, in the exercise of its police and regulatory power, from establishing its rights against the debtor in a nonbankruptcy forum (as opposed to executing on those assets).

A. CREDITOR ACTIONS AND THE AUTOMATIC STAY

Under §362 of the Bankruptcy Code, the filing of a bankruptcy petition operates as a stay of all efforts to sue on or collect a prepetition debt from the debtor or to put a lien on the debtor's property. It is tantamount to an injunction by operation of law rather than by issuance of a court. The stay freezes the debtor's affairs at the moment of the bankruptcy filing. A creditor cannot attempt to collect on a debtor's prepetition obligation whether the attempt is to collect from the debtor's prepetition assets or the debtor's postpetition earnings. A creditor with a prepetition claim must await payment, if any, from the collective bankruptcy process.

The Bankruptcy Code implements this principle with a laundry list of prohibitions in §362(a). The filing of a petition stays the "commencement or continuation" of an action against the debtor, as well as any other "act to collect, assess, or recover" a claim against the debtor, where the action or recovery is to satisfy a prepetition obligation. A filing also stays the "enforcement" of a prepetition judgment and disallows any act to "gain possession of" or "exercise control over" property of the bankruptcy estate, including any act to "create, perfect, or enforce" a security interest or other lien or to "set off any debt" against such property in favor of a prepetition claim. In addition to these general provisions, United States Tax Court cases are specifically made subject to the automatic stay.

As broad as §362(a) is, it has limits. By its own terms, the automatic stay does not apply to actions against third parties or property of third parties. A creditor that is the beneficiary of a letter of credit— a promise by a third party to pay if the debtor does not—can still draw on the letter. Similarly, notwithstanding the automatic stay, creditors generally may pursue guarantors or codefendants of the debtor. In exceptional cases, a court will extend the stay, perhaps through §105, to actions against third parties. Courts take this extraordinary step only when allowing such actions would adversely affect the property of the estate. An example is the case in which the same insurance policy covers the debtor and codefendants. Actions against codefendants could reduce the total obligations of the insurer under the policy. Hence, such action might fall within the stay. But this is the exception rather than the rule. There are other exceptions as well, explicit in §362(b). These are discussed later after we address the heart of the stay and its scope.

In most cases, the application of §362(a) is straightforward. You will not likely see a reported decision in which a general creditor asserts the right to levy on its debtor's property after a bankruptcy petition is filed. Everyone understands that this action is forbidden. Nor will you likely see a decision in which a debtor asserts that the automatic stay bars collection of a postpetition claim from a debtor's postpetition salary. Everyone understands that this action is permitted. Section 362 does most of its work without great controversy.

The exercises below ask you to work through some of the mechanics of §362(a) as it is applied to creditor action. The case (which presents an issue from the bankruptcy of Marvel Entertainment) as well as the related notes and problems center on the question whether a creditor can act in some capacity other than that of a creditor and thus avoid the strictures of the automatic stay.

Key Provision: Bankruptcy Code §362(a)

EXERCISES

4A(1) Debtor sells gaskets that are included in car assembly. Debtor has a contract to supply Manufacturer with 10,000 gaskets, for delivery in four monthly installments of 2,500 gaskets each month. Manufacturer prepays. Debtor makes the first three deliveries in a timely fashion. The fourth delivery is not made. Debtor files a petition in bankruptcy. Manufacturer, who needs the gaskets to meet its production schedule, knows that Debtor in fact has the gaskets in inventory. May Manufacturer take legal action against Debtor to compel delivery of the gaskets it has already paid for? Assume that specific performance would be available under applicable nonbankruptcy law. In answering this question, consider, among other provisions, Bankruptcy Code §101(5).

4A(2) When Bank lends money to Debtor Corporation, it insists that Debtor's chief executive officer, who is also the sole shareholder, co-sign the note of obligation and act as guarantor. In addition, the CEO pledges her house as collateral to support the guarantee. Debtor files a Chapter 11 petition. Can Bank now call on the guarantee? See Celotex Corp. v. Edwards, 514 U.S. 300 (1995).

4A(3) Debtor has a checking account with Bank. The account's balance is $10,000. Debtor has also borrowed $10,000 from Bank. Debtor defaults on the loan. Under nonbankruptcy law, Bank has the right after default to reduce the checking account up to the full amount of the loan. The effect of this right is to give Bank something akin to a security interest in the account. Before Bank exercises this "setoff" right, Debtor files a bankruptcy petition. In response, Bank puts what it calls an "administrative freeze" on the checking account that keeps Debtor from withdrawing any money from the account. Bank insists that it has not exercised its setoff right, but merely preserved that right until a court grants permission to exercise it. Does this action violate the automatic stay? Consider, among other provisions, Bankruptcy Code §§542(b) & 553(a). See also Citizens Bank of Maryland v. Strumpf, 516 U.S. 16 (1995).

4A(4) Some time ago, Debtor injured Bystander in an automobile accident. Bystander has been planning to bring a lawsuit. Yesterday, thirty days before the statute of limitations period expires, Debtor filed a petition in bankruptcy. May Bystander commence a lawsuit, if only to prevent the statute of limitations from running? In answering this question consider, among other provisions, Bankruptcy Code §108(c).

4A(5) Debtor ordered billboards from Advertising Inc. After Advertising produced and displayed the billboards, Debtor filed for bankruptcy without paying for Advertising's services. Advertising promptly puts up new billboards near Debtor's place of business. One of the billboards says: "Debtor is a deadbeat bankrupt." The other says: "These signs will remain up until Deadbeat Debtor pays what he owes." Do these signs violate the automatic stay? Is the First Amendment to the United States Constitution at issue? See Turner Advertising v. National Service Corp., 742 F.2d 859 (5th Cir. 1984).

CASE

OFFICIAL BONDHOLDERS COMMITTEE v. CHASE MANHATTAN BANK

United States District Court, D. Delaware, 1997
209 Bankr. 832

McKELVIE, DISTRICT JUDGE.

* * * The following facts are drawn from the parties' briefs and the record of proceedings below. Approximately 80% of Marvel's common stock is owned or controlled by three holding companies: Marvel Holdings, Inc. ("Marvel Holdings"), Marvel (Parent) Holdings, Inc. ("Marvel (Parent)"), and Marvel III Holdings, Inc. All three holding companies (collectively referred to herein as "the Marvel Holding Companies") are owned by Mr. Ronald O. Perelman. The balance of Marvel's common stock is held by public stockholders (18.84%) and entities owned or controlled by Mr. Perelman (2.35%).

In 1993 and 1994, the Marvel Holding Companies raised $894 million through the issuance of bonds. The bonds were issued pursuant to three separate indentures and were secured by a pledge of approximately 80% of Marvel's stock and by 100% of the stock of Marvel (Parent) and Marvel Holdings. An Indenture Trustee was appointed to act for the bondholders under the indentures. LaSalle is the current indenture trustee.

On December 27, 1996, Marvel and certain of its subsidiaries (collectively referred to herein as "the Debtors") filed separate petitions for relief under Chapter 11 of the United States Bankruptcy Code in the United States Bankruptcy Court for the District of Delaware. The Debtors' cases have been procedurally consolidated and are being jointly administered. On the same day, the Marvel Holding Companies also filed petitions for relief under Chapter 11 in the bankruptcy court. The Marvel Holding Companies' cases have also been procedurally consolidated and are also being jointly administered, although they are being administered separately from the Debtors' cases.

Shortly after the Debtors and the Marvel Holding Companies filed petitions for Chapter 11 relief, the Bondholders Committee was formed in the Marvel Holding Companies' cases to represent parties currently holding the bonds previously issued by the Marvel Holding Companies. After Marvel obtained an order in its case requiring any potential claims against Marvel to be filed within one month of its commencement of bankruptcy proceedings, LaSalle (hereinafter referred to as "the Indenture Trustee") filed several proofs of claims against Marvel on behalf of the bondholders so that they may recover against Marvel in the event Marvel is liable for any wrongdoing with respect to the amounts owed by the Marvel Holding Companies under the indentures.

On January 13, 1997, the Bondholders Committee and the Indenture Trustee moved to lift the automatic stay imposed by the Bankruptcy Code in the Marvel Holding Companies' cases to allow the bondholders and the Indenture Trustee to foreclose on and vote the pledged shares of stock as a result of the Holding Companies' default under the indentures.

On February 26, 1997, after two days of evidentiary hearings, the bankruptcy court entered an order lifting the stay in the Marvel Holding Companies' cases to permit the bondholders and the Indenture Trustee to foreclose on and vote the pledged shares. In lifting the stay, however, the bankruptcy court noted that the issue of whether the automatic stay imposed in the Debtors' cases would be implicated by any subsequent action taken by the bondholders and the Indenture Trustee with respect to the pledged shares was not yet before the court.

On March 19, 1997, the Bondholders Committee and the Indenture Trustee notified the Debtors of the intent of the bondholders and the Indenture Trustee to vote the pledged shares to replace Marvel's board of directors. Subsequently, on March 24, 1997, the Debtors instituted an adversary proceeding in the Debtors' cases by filing a complaint for declaratory and injunctive relief and a motion for a temporary restraining order ("TRO") and a preliminary injunction enjoining the bondholders and the Indenture Trustee from voting the pledged shares to replace Marvel's board of directors. Also on that day, Chase Manhattan Bank, as agent for the senior secured lenders in the Debtors' cases, commenced a similar adversary proceeding in the Debtors cases' wherein it sought substantially the same relief. Both the Debtors and Chase sought injunctive relief pursuant to §§362(a) and 105(a) of the Bankruptcy Code. * * *

The bankruptcy court held that the automatic stay imposed by §362(a)(3) of the Bankruptcy Code prevents the bondholders and the Indenture Trustee from voting the pledged shares to replace Marvel's board of directors unless they first seek and obtain relief from the stay. * * *

It is well settled that the right of shareholders to compel a shareholders' meeting for the purpose of electing a new board of directors subsists during reorganization proceedings. The right of shareholders "to be represented by directors of their choice and thus to control corporate policy is paramount." In re Potter Instrument Co., Inc., 593 F.2d 470, 475 (2d Cir. 1979). Shareholders, moreover, "should have the right to be adequately represented in the conduct of a debtor's affairs, particularly in such an important matter as the reorganization of the debtor." [In re Johns-Manville Corp., 801 F.2d 60, 65 (2d Cir. 1986).] As a result, the election of a new board of directors may be enjoined only under circumstances demonstrating "clear abuse." "Clear abuse" requires a showing that the shareholders' action in seeking to elect a new board of directors "demonstrates a willingness to risk rehabilitation altogether in order to win a larger share for equity." *Johns-Manville*, 801 F.2d at 65. The fact that the shareholders' action may be motivated by a desire to arrogate more bargaining power in the negotiation of a reorganization plan, without more, does not constitute clear abuse.

It follows from these principles that the automatic stay provisions of the Bankruptcy Code are not implicated by the exercise of shareholders' corporate governance rights. Indeed, if it were otherwise, there would be no need to determine whether shareholders' actions evidenced clear abuse. For instance, because the directors of a debtor-in-possession control and manage the debtors' operations, any election of a new board would be considered an attempt to exercise control over the assets of the estate and would thus be barred by §362(a)(3). In each of the cases cited above, however, courts considered only whether shareholders' attempts to elect a new board constituted clear abuse.

Chase suggests that the plain meaning of the language "to exercise control over property of the estate," which was added to §362(a)(3) by Congress in 1984, dictates the application of the automatic stay to an attempt by shareholders to elect a new board of directors. As appellants point out, however, if Congress had intended such a marked departure from well-established law, the legislative history of the 1984 amendment would contain some indication of that intention. * * *

The Debtors rely heavily on two cases in support of the automatic stay. In an oral decision in In re Fairmont Communications Corp., No. 92-B-44861 (Bankr. S.D.N.Y. Mar. 3, 1993), the bankruptcy court applied §362(a)(3) to prevent a creditor and shareholder of the debtor from appointing additional members to the debtor's board of directors pursuant to certain proxies that it had been granted to ensure repayment of its loan to the debtor. In that the automatic stay applied, however, the court noted that it was not "confronted with the conventional case of a shareholder seeking to invoke its corporate governance rights" because the rights the creditor/shareholder sought to exercise "stem[med] from its status as [the debtor's] largest unsecured creditor and [were] implicated only because [its] note [had] not been paid." Tr. at 14.

Similarly, in In re Bicoastal Corp., 1989 Bankr. LEXIS 2046 (Bankr. M.D. Fla. Nov. 21, 1989), the bankruptcy court held that §362(a)(3) prevented a creditor and preferred shareholder of the debtor from exercising its right to elect a majority of the debtor's board of directors that accrued when the debtor failed to timely repay the creditor/preferred shareholder's loan to the debtor. The court observed, however, that by reason of the creditor's dual status as preferred shareholder and creditor, "matters of corporate governing in the orthodox sense" were not implicated and that, if that "were the case, there [was] hardly any doubt that absent some showing of extraordinary circumstances, [the] Court [had] no jurisdictional power to interfere with corporate governance." Id. at 14-15. * * *

The courts in *Fairmont* and *Bicoastal* thus applied the automatic stay provisions of §362(a)(3) in order to prevent creditors of debtors from gaining control of the debtors' estates through the exercise of corporate governance rights. The Debtors argue that here, too, the bondholders are seeking to exercise rights accruing to them as creditors rather than traditional shareholder rights because the shares were pledged as security for the payment of the bonds issued by the Marvel Holding Companies. Appellants, however, did not acquire shareholder rights in Marvel as creditors of Marvel, but rather as creditors of the Marvel Holding Companies. Because the pledged shares were property of the Marvel Holding Companies' estates, appellants were required to seek and, indeed, obtained relief from the automatic stay in the Marvel Holding Companies case that prevented them from exercising control over those shares. The fact that they acquired shareholder rights in Marvel by exercising creditor remedies in the Marvel Holding Companies case is of no moment. * * *

Finally, Chase suggests that Marvel is insolvent and that as a result the automatic stay applies. Chase cites dicta in *Johns-Manville* to the effect that, if a debtor is insolvent, it would probably be inappropriate to permit shareholders to call a meeting because they would no longer have equity in the debtor and thus be real parties-in-interest. Even if that proposition were correct, however, the bankruptcy court has never found that Marvel is insolvent. Accordingly, that issue is not a proper subject of this appeal.

For the reasons stated above, the court concludes that the bankruptcy court erred in holding that §362(a)(3) prevents the bondholders and the Indenture Trustee from voting the pledged shares to replace Marvel's board of directors unless they first seek and obtain relief from the automatic stay. Chase urges the court to sustain the TRO issued by the bankruptcy court on the alternative ground that the bondholders and the Indenture Trustee should be enjoined under §105(a), or at least remand this matter to the bankruptcy court for further consideration of appellees' motions for a TRO under §105(a). The bankruptcy court, however, denied appellees' motions for a TRO under §105(a) on the ground that they failed to show "irreparable harm," as required for injunctive relief under §105(a), and appellees have not appealed that ruling.

NOTES

4A.1. The court in *Marvel* did not give the new shareholders or their board carte blanche to act over the debtor as they saw fit. For example, the new board could not exercise control in a way that would constitute "clear abuse," by showing "a willingness to risk rehabilitation altogether in order to win a larger share for equity." And the board could not act on behalf of the shareholders in their "status" as creditors. These prohibitions are not always easy to apply. The board could not order the removal and payment of the debtor's assets without court permission. (Section 362(a) bars such a blatant step whether taken by a shareholder or a creditor.) But the court offers little guidance as to what other action is forbidden to a shareholder who is also a creditor. Problem 4A-1 asks you to explore how different actions could affect the debtor's reorganization or the debtor's other creditors.

4A.2. In large reorganizations, creditors often assign their claims to others even after the bankruptcy petition starts. Those who specialize in acquiring claims against firms in Chapter 11 often buy multiple classes of claims. As we shall explore in part 3, this trend complicates the reorganization problem because, as here, parties are wearing multiple hats and actions that might be forbidden under one hat are allowed under another. Problems 4A-2 and 4A-3 explore some of the other issues that can arise when creditors serve multiple roles (including that of past creditor and *potential* future creditor). We shall return to this issue again. Firms have an ongoing life while they are being reorganized. The Bank that financed the accounts receivable prepetition is often willing to provide similar financing to the debtor in possession. The trade creditor that sold goods to the debtor before the petition may be the supplier of choice postpetition as well. Chapter 9 explores how the Bankruptcy Code navigates these problems.

PROBLEMS

4A-1. Debtor Corporation is a manufacturer that employs hundreds of workers in a single community. Debtor's assets are worth $10 million as part of Debtor's going concern in its current configuration. But Debtor is debt ridden, subject to secured obligations of $8 million and unsecured obligations of $10 million. Debtor files for bankruptcy under Chapter 11. Shortly thereafter the unsecured creditors buy up the Debtor's equity shares and appoint a new board. The board decides that Debtor is worth $10.5 million if broken up and sold piecemeal. It considers two different actions. The first is to liquidate the firm. The second action considered is to alter Debtor's manufacturing process dramatically and embark on a new business plan that will, before the reorganization concludes, either increase the value of

Debtor's assets to $14 million or reduce that value to $4 million, each with equal probability. Would either action violate the automatic stay?

4A-2. Debtor graduates from law school. While looking for a job (and while uninsured), he is diagnosed with cancer. The cancer goes into remission, but Debtor can't pay the medical bills, let alone his student loans. He files a bankruptcy petition and is now looking for a new job. He asks his law school for a transcript. The law school refuses, citing its general policy not to give any transcript to a student who has defaulted on his loans. Does the law school's refusal constitute a violation of the automatic stay? See In re Merchant, 958 F.2d 738 (6th Cir. 1992).

4A-3. After Debtor files a bankruptcy petition, Creditor writes to Debtor's lawyer. In the letter, Creditor tells the lawyer the amount that the debtor owes, reminds her of Debtor's ability to reaffirm the debt during the bankruptcy process despite the availability of discharge, and offers to extend additional credit after bankruptcy if the debt is reaffirmed. Does the letter violate the automatic stay? In answering this question consider, among other provisions, Bankruptcy Code §524(c). Would your answer change if Creditor sent Debtor a copy of the letter? See In re Duke, 79 F.3d 43 (7th Cir. 1996).

B.   SCOPE OF THE AUTOMATIC STAY

In this section, we explore a second aspect of the automatic stay. The debtor's nonexempt prepetition assets, plus any income derived from those assets, are reserved for the bankruptcy estate to satisfy the prepetition claims. No one—debtor, creditor, or even noncreditor third parties—may reach the assets under the debtor's control without permission of the bankruptcy court. The willingness of the court to allow noncreditor third parties to affect property of the debtor turns, in large part, on the nature and extent of the debtor's property interest under nonbankruptcy law.

Among the most interesting cases are those in which the debtor's interest—in specific property or rights established in an ongoing contractual relationship—is one that a noncreditor third party may terminate unilaterally under nonbankruptcy law. Section 362(a)(3) suggests that a third party may not take back its own property that is in the debtor's possession. The third party, however, will insist that the automatic stay last no longer than is necessary to establish that, given the third party's right to terminate, the debtor has no right to the property. Because the third party is not a creditor, it should not have to become involved with sorting through the debtor's problems with its creditors any more than someone who had never done business with the debtor at all.

Difficulties most commonly arise when the noncreditor third party exercises a termination right for reasons that may or may not be related to the circumstances that led to the filing of the bankruptcy petition. As a noncreditor, the third party is not someone to whom the debtor owes anything. Nevertheless, the third party might be exercising its termination right *because of* the bankruptcy filing. The insurance company may believe that the debtor is a poor risk, but it would never have had cause to reassess its relationship if it had not learned of the bankruptcy filing.

It may be appropriate to keep the third party involved for a second reason. A third party that has an ongoing business relationship with the debtor is different from a stranger that has never had any dealing with the debtor. Many leases are almost indistinguishable from secured transactions. One could argue that because secured creditors are forced to participate in a reorganization after being provided with adequate protection, lessors should be in no different a position. Under this view, anyone with an ongoing relationship with the debtor at the time of the filing should, assuming its interests are adequately protected, be forced to wait until the debtor's problems are sorted out, at least if the third party's action might endanger the debtor's ability to reorganize effectively.

As we shall see in the two cases in this section, as well as in the related notes and problem, neither of these two ideas can be squarely located in the Bankruptcy Code. Nevertheless, both ideas (and especially the first) can be seen as undercurrents in many cases dealing with the relationship between the debtor and third parties. Indeed, in the first case, *Cahokia Downs*, the court seems to limit the third party's ability to take advantage of a unilateral right to terminate because it believes that the exercise is connected to the bankruptcy filing. In the second case, *M.J. & K. Co.*, the court allows the third party to terminate, but only after the court finds that the termination would have been made independent of the bankruptcy filing. In reading both cases, you should examine carefully the provisions of the Bankruptcy Code on which both courts rely. Before turning to the cases, we explore the basic mechanics of §362 in the following problems.

Key Provisions: Bankruptcy Code §§362(a)(3); 541(a)(1)

EXERCISES

4B(1) Customer retrieves her laundry from Cleaner, who filed for bankruptcy the day after Customer dropped off her clothes. Has Customer behaved unlawfully? As a practical matter, does it make any difference if she has?

4B(2) On the first of the month, Hotel Chain delivers to Debtor, which runs a hotel, the following notice: "Pursuant to our agreement as well as state and federal franchise law, your franchise with us is terminated, effective the last day of this month. We have programmed our computer to remove you from our reservation system as of that day." A few days later, Debtor files for bankruptcy. Will cancellation of the franchise at the end of the month violate the automatic stay? See Moody v. Amoco Oil Co., 734 F.2d 1200 (7th Cir. 1984).

4B(3) Debtor rents a computer from Lessor on a five-year lease. After one year, Debtor defaults, and Lessor repossesses the computer. Two weeks after Lessor repossesses the computer, Debtor files a petition in bankruptcy. May Lessor lease the computer to another without first getting relief from the automatic stay?

4B(4) Debtor rents a computer from Lessor on a five-year lease. Debtor fails to make both the March and April payments during the second year of the lease. On April 5, pursuant to a term of the lease, Lessor sends a cancellation notice. Debtor receives the cancellation notice on April 6. On April 10, Debtor files a petition in bankruptcy. May Lessor repossess the computer?

CASES

IN RE CAHOKIA DOWNS, INC.

United States Bankruptcy Court, S.D. Illinois, 1980
5 Bankr. 529

TRAUB, BANKRUPTCY JUDGE.

* * * 1. Cahokia Downs, Inc. is a Delaware Corporation which has operated a race track and owns track facilities on land leased from Cahokia Land Trust.

2. Sportservice, Inc. is the largest creditor of Cahokia Downs and filed an involuntary Chapter 11 on April 2, 1980.

3. Pursuant to the consent of Cahokia Downs, Inc., an order of relief was entered on said petition, and there are at present efforts being made to formulate a plan of arrangement.

4. Sometime in July 1979, Holland America Insurance Company and Cahokia Downs, Inc. entered into a policy of insurance under policy No. FN 013505, being a standard fire policy with a policy period of July 26, 1979 to July 26, 1980, insuring the race track premises.

5. Sayre & Toso, Inc. is the underwriter of said policy.

6. Logger Insurance Agency, Inc., acting as agent of Cahokia Downs, Inc., obtained the policy of insurance and advanced the full premium payment on behalf of Cahokia Downs, Inc. in the amount of $32,309.

7. Cahokia Downs, Inc. is indebted to Logger Insurance Agency for said premium and also to Mark Twain National Bank on a loan agreement for payment of a portion of the policy premium in the approximate amount of $14,000.

8. The race track operated on a seasonal basis, and for a part of each year is completely shut down except for a custodian and certain employees.

9. On April 11, 1980, without prior consent of this Court and after filing of the petition in this matter, the plaintiff, Sayre & Toso, attempted to cancel the policy of insurance on behalf of the plaintiff, Holland America Insurance Company, pursuant to a clause in the contract allowing Holland America Insurance Company to cancel upon thirty days written notice.

10. Sportservice, Inc., the principal creditor, filed a petition for injunctive relief against the cancellation, and, in that matter, this Court held that, while service had not been perfected, the automatic stay was statutory and applied to the cancellation of the insurance. Pursuant to the prior order of this Court, the plaintiffs have now filed this complaint for request to terminate the automatic stay.

11. The primary differences between the status of the insured property in 1979 and the present time are that in approximately October 1979, the Illinois Racing Commission denied racing dates for the Spring and Summer of 1980 to the debtor, and the subsequent filing of this Chapter 11 on April 2, 1980.

[handwritten margin note: cancellation by omission by D-J itself]

12. No attempt was made to cancel the insurance policy because of the cancellation of racing dates until April 11, 1980.

13. The maintenance of insurance on the property is essential for the rehabilitation of the debtor and the protection of the creditors.

[handwritten margin note: insurance → cancellation will impede Ch.11 reorg.]

14. The evidence indicates that the real reason for the attempted cancellation of the insurance was the filing of the bankruptcy proceeding under Chapter 11.

The enactment of the Bankruptcy Code in 1978 greatly enlarged the scope and powers of the Bankruptcy Court. One of the expressed aims of Congress in enacting the Code was to give the Bankruptcy Court sufficient power to enable it to protect the rights of the parties in interest—the debtors and creditors—and, in the case of arrangements, to effect the rehabilitation of the debtor. To that end, Congress enacted [§§105, 362(a), 363(*l*), and 365(a)].

Each of these sections creates very broad powers and is applicable to a debtor under an arrangement as well as the Trustee-in-Bankruptcy. In the instant case, there is no question but that a policy of insurance, especially one in which the premium has been paid, is a valid and binding contract between the insurance company and the insured and would constitute an asset of the bankrupt estate. Furthermore, fire insurance is a necessary protection for both the debtor and its creditors. The cancellation of the insurance would certainly come within the provisions of the automatic stay under §362(a)(3). It is also property which could, within the meaning of §363, be used by the Trustee, and certainly paragraph (*l*) of §363 would be applicable to the cancellation provision in spite of the fact that the provision does not refer to insolvency or the financial condition of the debtor. This is especially true when, as in the instant case, it is quite obvious that the prime reason for the attempted cancellation of the insurance was the bankruptcy.

[handwritten margin note: Court: by K is an asset of the estate]

While the plaintiffs have asserted that their reason for the cancellation of the insurance was the vacancy of the building and the inadequacy of protection, there is, and was, no proof that there was a substantial change in that situation as a result of the bankruptcy. All of the things which the insurance company cited as being indicative of increased risk existed long before the attempted cancellation and the bankruptcy. In fact, a number of them existed and were known to the insurance company at the time of the creation of the original policy. The principal change subsequent to the inception of the policy was the loss of racing dates for the Spring and Summer of 1980, which oc-

[handwritten margin note: pre-textual reasons for cancellation pre-existed]

curred in October. This was many months before the actual filing of the bankruptcy, and consequently was, or should have been, known by the insurance company. In addition, since only a month remains on the insurance policy, should this Court allow the company to cancel its policy, the rebate and the premium would assuredly be minimal and would, accordingly, cause an increased cost to the debtor's estate in obtaining additional insurance. Therefore, even if additional insurance were available, there is no showing that it would be at a lesser price. It is, of course, understood and not contemplated by this Court that the insurance policy should or could be extended beyond its original term.

* * * [T]he new Bankruptcy Code is extremely broad in giving the Bankruptcy Court jurisdiction and broad powers over the contractual relations of a debtor in order to permit the debtor's rehabilitation.

Wherefore, it is ordered that the plaintiffs' petition for termination of the automatic stay be and the same is hereby denied.

IN RE M.J. & K. CO.

United States Bankruptcy Court, S.D. New York, 1993
161 Bankr. 586

GARRITY, JR., BANKRUPTCY JUDGE.

* * * On or about December 16, 1982, [Brooklyn Law School ("BLS")] and the Debtor entered into an agreement (the "Agreement") granting Debtor the exclusive "right, permission, license, and privilege to operate a Law School bookstore for the sale of stationery, casebooks, hornbooks, review books, and bookstore related products, and for no other purpose" at BLS. The Agreement provides that it is to be in full force and effect as of December 16, 1982 "for a period of one year with a three-year contract to follow if Brooklyn Law School is satisfied with the service." On or about December 16, 1982, Debtor began its bookstore operation in space located in the basement of the school building. ... Debtor has operated the bookstore at BLS without interruption since that date. ... BLS and the Debtor agree that since the expiration of the one-year term stated in the Agreement, the parties have made no verbal or written arrangement to extend, renew or otherwise modify the Agreement, or any of its terms or conditions.

The Debtor operates retail bookstores under what it describes as separate license agreements at BLS, The Benjamin N. Cardozo School of Law, Yeshiva University, New York, New York ("Cardozo

Law School") and Touro College Jacob B. Fuschberg Law Center, Touro Law School, Huntington, New York ("Touro Law School"). The merchandise sold by Debtor at the BLS bookstore includes text books and related materials ordered specifically for courses offered at BLS. Given the nature of Debtor's operations, its busiest times of the year are at the beginning and end of each academic semester. The beginning of each academic semester is when Debtor sells the bulk of its text book inventory. At the end of each semester Debtor purchases the text books and related materials it will offer for sale in the following semester. As such, Debtor's book orders are keyed to the BLS curriculum for the next succeeding semester. Although Debtor may be able to estimate its requirements for particular courses which have been previously offered at the law school, it cannot be certain of its inventory needs until BLS supplies it with a list of course offerings, enrollment figures and the required text for each course being offered. As a matter of policy, BLS prohibits faculty members from submitting book orders to the Debtor until the schedule of classes for the next semester is distributed. The schedule for the Spring semester is usually not fixed or published until late in the Fall semester. Estimating text book requirements is particularly problematic for newly offered courses because of the uncertainty over how heavily those courses will be subscribed. Likewise, when previously offered courses are taught by a new professor, or when a new text is published for a particular course, the Debtor cannot be certain of which books to order until it is advised which text will be utilized in the particular course. Debtor's ability to secure book orders is critical to the efficient operation of the law school. If text books are not available at the outset of the semester, teaching plans may be compromised and students will be prejudiced in their efforts to prepare for and participate in class. Because of the uniformity in book assignments among New York metropolitan area law schools, a shortage of books at BLS likely will mean that BLS students will not be able to obtain required texts elsewhere.

On or about September 29, 1993, David G. Trager, as Dean of BLS, received a memorandum from Professor Spencer Weber Waller complaining about Debtor's delay in obtaining the text book for the International Trade Law course he was teaching during the Fall 1993 semester. Dean Trager's undisputed testimony was that Professor Waller's complaint was merely the last in a long series of written and verbal protests from faculty members over Debtor's operation of the bookstore. Shortly thereafter, Dean Trager determined that the school should consider terminating its association with the Debtor and directed appropriate BLS personnel to solicit bids from vendors interested in operating the bookstore. The rationale for Dean Trager's decision was two-fold. First, he reasoned that awarding the bookstore contract to a new vendor would promote efficiency at the law school because the faculty and administration could focus their energies on educating students and not be bothered by issues involving the operation of the bookstore. Second, the action would advance BLS's policy of awarding short-term contracts to service vendors. Under Dean Trager's stewardship the law school has refrained from entering into long-term service contracts in favor of short-term arrangements awarded after competitive bidding. For example, BLS has short-term contracts with its custodial service, as well as the food service that operates the BLS cafeteria. That policy ensures that BLS will receive quality performance at competitive prices. Notwithstanding Debtor's long association with the school, Dean Trager did not believe BLS was bound to retain Debtor service and wanted to explore the school's alternatives.

The Debtor did not formally notify the law school's administration of the filing of its Chapter 11 petition. Dean Trager heard of the event from a faculty member after he received the Waller memorandum. Thereafter he learned that West Publishing Inc., Little, Brown Co. and The Foundation Press, Inc. have refused to ship books and related materials to the Debtor, for ultimate sale to BLS students and faculty, for the Spring 1994 semester, without payment of cash on delivery. He also learned that Debtor is engaged in litigation with Matthew Bender Co., another publisher that supplies law books and related materials to the school. With that information, the Dean became concerned that Debtor would be unable to supply the text books and related materials needed for courses to be taught in the Spring 1994 semester. Accordingly, he determined that the Debtor's operations at the law school should be terminated.

That decision apparently was communicated to Debtor's principal, Mr. Gil Hollander. By letter dated November 5, 1993, Debtor's counsel advised Dean Trager, among other things, that the law school could not interfere with Debtor's operation of its business without first obtaining relief from this Court. That letter also stated that:

> [BLS] and [Debtor] have had mutual contractual obligations extending over 11 years, and which are not up for renewal or termination until December of 1995. The agreement is an executory agreement which [Debtor], as a debtor in possession has a statu-

tory right to reaffirm or reject. We had intended to reaffirm that agreement and we hereby do so.

This letter was the first communication to the law school in which Debtor took the position that it was operating the bookstore pursuant to a long-term contract. * * *

The parties concur that the Agreement gives rise to a license. They differ over the nature of the license, its length and whether cause exists under §362(d)(1) to grant BLS the relief it now seeks. BLS contends that the stay should be modified to permit it to serve the Proposed Notice and remove Debtor from the Premises because the Agreement creates a license in real property which expired on December 15, 1983. The Debtor claims that it has a license to conduct business at BLS that will not expire until December 15, 1995 and that BLS has failed to establish cause for granting it the relief sought herein. * * *

The debtor contends that the rights created under the Agreement give rise to something other than a license in real property, arguing that "[t]he use of the realty, while important, is incidental to what is in effect a guarantee of sales provided the Debtor complies with its agreement." We find no merit to that contention. Nothing in the Agreement guarantees Debtor any level of sales at the bookstore. Moreover, the argument ignores that a license in real property vests the licensee with precisely what Debtor claims to have: exclusive access to a market which the licensee otherwise would not enjoy. * * *

Any right created in Debtor's estate by the Agreement is protected by the automatic stay. The nature and extent of those rights, if any, are fixed by state law. Butner v. U.S., 440 U.S. 48 (1979). The filing of a petition under the Code does not expand those rights. The common law rule is "that a license in real property is revocable at the will of the licensor unless it is coupled with an interest or made irrevocable by the terms of the contract." [In re Yachthaven Restaurant, Inc., 103 Bankr. 62, 78 (Bankr. E.D.N.Y. 1989).] A license created by contract for a definite period expires at the end of that period.

Debtor argues that by permitting it to operate the bookstore beyond the one-year period stated in the Agreement (December 16, 1982 through December 15, 1983), BLS extended it through December 15, 1986, and for successive three-year periods thereafter. That argument ignores that in New York, a contract which by its terms cannot be performed within the year after it was made is unenforceable unless it is in writing. BLS's right to continue the Agreement for three years beyond the stated one-year period is merely an "agreement to agree" which is subject to the Statute of Frauds. The parties concur that the Agreement has not been superseded, amended or extended by another writing. Indeed, there has been no communication among them regarding the terms of the Agreement since shortly after it was executed in 1982. Thus, the Agreement cannot be construed as vesting Debtor with the right to operate the bookstore beyond December 15, 1983.

A license for a fixed period which has lapsed is terminable at will by either party. The only limitation on that right to terminate the license is that the party act in good faith. * * *

[Mr.] Hollander admitted that the Debtor does not have the cash and cannot obtain the necessary credit to purchase the books. He testified that he would infuse the necessary funds into the business personally, and that he had personal credit lines of in excess of $50,000 readily available to him. There is no evidence, however, that those funds will be adequate to ensure that Debtor will be able to obtain the necessary texts.

BLS's good faith in this matter is manifest. Termination of its relationship with Debtor will promote the law school's policy of engaging in short-term service contracts and eliminate the uncertainties presently existing regarding whether Debtor will be able to obtain the text books needed in the Spring semester. Under these facts, and as a licensor at will, it cannot be required to continue its business relationship with Debtor. Accordingly, it is entitled to relief from the automatic stay to serve the Proposed Notice and take appropriate steps to recover possession of the Premises. Based on the foregoing, BLS's motion for relief from the automatic stay is granted. BLS is directed to SETTLE AN ORDER.

NOTES

4B.1. The court in *Cahokia Downs* found it "quite obvious that the prime reason for the attempted cancellation of the insurance was the bankruptcy." But the insurance company, Holland America, is not a creditor. Its premium had been paid. Hence, it does not care whether the racetrack can pay its creditors. It cares only about whether the racetrack is a good insurance risk. The financial distress of the racetrack may be responsible for the higher risks that the insurance company faces. But financial distress might have also led the bookstore to provide poor service in *M.J. & K.* In *Cahokia*, however, the bankruptcy filing itself may have alerted the insurance company to the greater riskiness of the policy. By contrast, in *M.J. & K.*, the court is at pains to suggest that the bankruptcy filing did not itself lead the decision maker to terminate, even though he knew about the bankruptcy and even though the reasons for the termination long predated the bankruptcy filing. The court in *Cahokia* also seems more sensitive to the way in which the termination will affect the debtor's prospects. You should consider whether either of these differences should affect a court's willingness to lift the automatic stay when the party that wants the stay lifted is not owed anything.

4B.2. The general ambition and application of anti-ipso facto provisions such as Bankruptcy Code §363(*l*) is the subject of chapter 6, section B below. For the moment, note that, on its face, §363(*l*) applies only to a clause that is "conditioned on the insolvency or financial condition of the debtor," not on a broad clause such as the one in *Cahokia Downs*, which allows a noncreditor third party to cancel for any reason or no reason at all.

4B.3. Whether or not *Cahokia Downs* was correctly decided or can be reconciled with *M.J. & K.*, it is important to note that neither case even intimated that the stay itself eliminated the nondebtor's termination rights, only that one might need to go to court before exercising such right. The court in *M.J. & K.* lifted the stay and permitted enforcement, while the court *Cahokia Downs* used §363(*l*) to eliminate a termination right. Problem 4B asks you to consider an alternative resolution.

4B.4. The court in *Cahokia Downs* notes that "the maintenance of insurance on the property is essential for the rehabilitation of the debtor and the protection of the creditors." General assertions about the need to promote bankruptcy's policy of rehabilitation, however, prove too much. In reading *Cahokia Downs*, or any other case, one must focus on the issue before the court. In this case, one must ask, not whether the debtor needed insurance, but rather whether Holland America had a right to cancel the insurance contract.

[handwritten margin note: CB: debtors needs not the issue, it's creditors Rights]

PROBLEM

4B. Debtor Corporation, a pen manufacturer, and Retailer are parties to a long-term, long-standing supply contract that is now terminable at will by either party. While the contract is in effect, Debtor is to supply ballpoint pens monthly for $50 a gross. Retailer becomes dissatisfied with Debtor's performance and finds another Supplier that can deliver pens for $45 a gross. Before Retailer can terminate the contract, Debtor files for bankruptcy under Chapter 11. Retailer requests the court's permission to lift the stay so that it may terminate the contract. If the court concludes that Debtor needs income from the contract to stay in business while it reorganizes, what remedy might Retailer demand? Consider this problem again after you read chapters 7 and 9 below.

C. EXCEPTIONS TO THE AUTOMATIC STAY

Section 362(a) is designed largely to prevent creditor collection that bypasses the bankruptcy process. By its terms, however, the provision reaches much else. The §362(a)(1) prohibition on the commencement or continuation of judicial or administrative processes against the debtor and the §362(a)(3) prohibition on any act to obtain property of the estate, for example, would prohibit many ordinary enforcement actions of a police or regulatory nature. Many of the exceptions in §362(b) ensure that §362(a) is not read so broadly as to excuse the debtor from violations of the law. Section 362(b)(1), for example, provides that the automatic stay does not affect the commencement or continuation of a criminal action against the debtor. As a result, a debtor cannot evade a criminal prosecution that might result in a fine by arguing that the action is to recover a claim against the debtor and is thus stayed by §362(a)(1) or that the prosecution seeks possession of property of the estate and is therefore stayed under §362(a)(3).

Section 362(b)(4) sets out the general principle. This provision permits a governmental unit (or an organization acting under the recently established international convention on chemical weapons) to enforce its "police and regulatory power, including the enforcement of a judgment, other than a money judgment." Thus, for example, a debtor cannot argue that the automatic stay insulates it from a costly new workplace regulation, an environmental law, or a new building ordinance.

Consider this point in the following context. Imagine that Debtor runs a plant that emits a minute amount of sulfur dioxide. If Debtor shut down operations and liquidated the firm's assets, Debtor would be worth $100,000. If Debtor can continue running the plant, emitting the sulfur dioxide, it would be worth $150,000—assuming those harmed by the emissions have no effective way of suing Debtor. But the state environmental agency wants Debtor to put a $75,000 scrubber on the plant's smokestack. The state agency threatens a legal action through which an administrative judge will force Debtor to choose between shutdown and installation of the scrubber. Because of §362(b)(4), Debtor cannot ward off the suit by asserting that the agency is "exercis[ing] control over property of the estate" within the meaning of §362(a)(3).

The consequences of the state's action here, and thus of the §362(b) exception that permits it, can be significant. In this illustration, the creditors as a group, of course, would prefer to delay installation of the scrubber as long as possible (again assuming that those harmed by the sulfur dioxide have no effective way of suing Debtor). Enforcing the regulation will likely shut Debtor down, because the creditors, who can block any reorganization, are better off with $100,000 in liquidation proceeds than with the $150,000 going-concern value reduced by the cost of a $75,000 scrubber. This is not a concern of bankruptcy law, however.

Whether a firm should remain intact depends in part on the legal rules that govern it. A legal rule may turn a profitable firm into an unprofitable one. In this case, where scrubbers are required, Debtor's business as a going concern is worth less than if it is liquidated, and for reasons that have nothing to do with the burden of debt. That Debtor might be worth twice as much in a different legal universe is irrelevant for bankruptcy purposes. Consistent with the *Butner* principle, the law here does not reexamine the wisdom of environmental law. The decision to require scrubbers is a choice the legislature has already made, and it has already accepted the possible consequences of fewer firms and cleaner air.

A state's powers to enforce criminal and regulatory law are not the only §362(b) exceptions to the automatic stay. For example, §362(b)(3) permits creditor action to perfect or maintain the perfection of a security interest where the automatic stay would cut short a grace period for such action that exists under state law and that the trustee must honor in bankruptcy. Although this provision is an exception to the automatic stay, it does not permit a creditor to undermine the bankruptcy process through either the removal of assets or an alteration of the priority that would obtain outside of bankruptcy. Chapter 8 below describes the provision more fully in connection with the trustee's powers.

The other §362(b) provisions are not easy to fit within the bankruptcy framework. Some of these provisions seem inapposite, redundant, or unnecessary (because §362(a) would not apply in any case), while others are difficult to reconcile with first principles. Section 362(b)(2) permits, for example, actions for the establishment of paternity or the suspension of a driver's license as well as for alimony, maintenance, or support. Sections 362(b)(6), (7), (17), and (27) permit specified setoffs and settlements in the securities industry. Section 362(b)(8) permits the Secretary of Housing and Urban Development to foreclose on specified mortgages or deeds held by the Secretary. Section 362(b)(9) permits government tax authorities to assess and demand payment of specified tax obligations. Section 362(b)(10) permits a lessor of nonresidential real property to take possession upon lease expiration. Section 362(b)(11) permits specified transactions in negotiable instruments (such as checks). Sections 362(b)(12) and (13) permit specified actions by the Secretaries of Transportation and Commerce, respectively. Sections 362(b)(14), (15), and (16) respectively permit specified actions to accredit, license, and determine the eligibility of educational institutions. Section 362(b)(18) permits creation of a statutory lien for property taxes in specified circumstances.

Added to this list by the 2005 Bankruptcy Act are §362(b)(19), which permits an employer withholds a debtor's wages and contribute them to specified pension plan; §362(b)(20), (21), which permit acts to enforce a lien against a debtor's property when the debtor is not eligible to file a case; §362(b)(22), which, under prescribed conditions and limitations, permits eviction of a debtor tenant pursuant to an order issued prior to the bankruptcy case; §362(b)(23), which, under prescribed conditions and limitations, permits eviction of a debtor tenant who has used illegal drugs on the property or endangered the property; §362(b)(24), which exempts from the stay postpetition transfers expressly permitted elsewhere in the Code; §362(b)(25), which permits a securities self regulatory organization to investigate a debtor or enforce its rules against a debtor (except to collect money); §362(b)(26), which permits a governmental unit to exercise a setoff right with respect to taxes owed for a period prior to the bankruptcy filing; and §362(b)(28), which permits the Secretary of Health and Human Services to exclude a debtor from a federal health care program.

The 2005 Act modified the stay provision in a number of additional ways as well. Most significant in this regard was an attempt to thwart what has been perceived as abusive successive filings by debtors who intend not to seek legitimate bankruptcy relief but simply to delay proper creditor collection efforts. New §362(c)(3) addresses a debtor who files a bankruptcy petition and had a bankruptcy case under Chapters 7, 11, or 13 dismissed within the prior year (other than a case dismissed under the new §707(b) means test and refiled under a different chapter). For such a debtor, the automatic stay will lapse in 30 days after the filing of a petition unless a court extends the stay after notice and hearing. New §362(c)(4) addresses a debtor who had more than one bankruptcy case under Chapters 7, 11, or 13 dismissed within the prior year (again other than a case dismissed under the Chapter 7 means test and refiled under a different chapter). In this case, the stay will not go into effect for any period of time unless the court so orders after notice and hearing. New §362(n) provides that the automatic stay does not apply to the voluntary petition of a small-business debtor if the debtor has another case pending or has had a case confirmed or dismissed in the prior two years unless the court is convinced that the new case will lead to confirmation in a reasonable time and the debtor can prove that the new case resulted from unforeseeable circumstances beyond the debtor's control; this provision applies to subsequent filing either by the debtor or a purchaser of substantially all the debtor's assets.

The exercises below address some exceptions to the automatic stay (including one, in §546, that has a source outside §362). Consider whether the exceptions are consistent with fundamental bankruptcy policy. The two cases that follow explore the relationship between the bankruptcy judge and the government agencies. In the first case, *NextWave*, the court confronts the jurisdictional lines between the bankruptcy court and independent federal agencies. That case arose out of the congressional decision allowing the Federal Communications Commission to auction licenses for the personal communications spectrum. Such an auction, it was hoped, would both raise money for the fisc and allocate the spectrum to those who most valued its use. This dual purpose generates a jurisdictional conflict when a winning bidder defaults on its obligation to pay the purchase price. The second case, *Nicolet*, addresses issues of environmental regulation, and requires you again to consider specifically the police and regulatory power exception of §362(b)(4), including the distinction that provision draws between a "money judgment" and other kinds of judgments.

Key Provisions: Bankruptcy Code §§362(b); 546

EXERCISES

4C(1) Manufacturer sells Debtor a machine on credit and takes a security interest in the machine sold. A day after it is delivered, Bank has the sheriff levy on the machine under state law. The next day, Debtor files for bankruptcy. Less than a week later, Manufacturer files to perfect its interest in the machine. Has Manufacturer violated the automatic stay? See §546(b) and UCC §9-317(e). Consider this exercise again after you read chapter 8 below.

4C(2) Debtor Corporation is a medium-size retailer with numerous trade creditors and a rental agreement with Lessor for Debtor's sales premises. Debtor runs a viable business that recently became subject to a large tort judgment when a delivery driver negligently injured a bystander. Debtor files for bankruptcy under Chapter 11. A month later, its lease expires and the Lessor evicts Debtor, ending any chance of Debtor's continuation as a going concern. Has Lessor violated the automatic stay?

4C(3) Debtor is a lawyer who once had a good practice. Client, however, lost a $10 million judgment. Not only has Client sued for malpractice, but other clients have left. Debtor files a bankruptcy petition. Client then complains to the state bar association, which commences a disciplinary hearing against Debtor. The state supreme court establishes the rules under which the disciplinary process operates and reviews its decisions. The state bar itself, however, is a private organization that is, for example, subject to the antitrust laws. How does the automatic stay affect the disciplinary action? See Wade v. State Bar of Arizona, 948 F.2d 1122 (9th Cir. 1991).

4C(4) Debtor Corporation owns an interest in Bank. After Debtor files for bankruptcy, the Federal Reserve Board begins an administrative proceeding against Debtor. The Fed's allegation is that Debtor improperly influenced Bank and that Bank is thus entitled to damages, which the Fed has the authority to seek on Bank's behalf. The Fed concedes that without court permission neither it nor Bank could collect any judgment while the stay remains in force. But the Fed seeks only the determination of liability. Does the Fed's action violate the automatic stay? See Board of Governors v. MCorp. Financial, Inc., 502 U.S. 32 (1991). See also Robert K. Rasmussen, Bankruptcy and the Administrative State, 42 Hastings Law Review 1567 (1991).

4C(5) Debtor is a power company that seeks to reorganize in Chapter 11. As part of its reorganization plan, Debtor seeks to spin off some of its assets to a third party in violation of applicable state law.

The state objects to the plan and seeks to enjoin confirmation of the plan. May it do so? In answering this question consider, though not directly relevant, §1123(a) and consider this exercise again after reading chapter 13 of this book. See also Pacific Gas & Electric Co. v. California, 350 F.3d 932 (9th Cir. 2003), and compare In re Combustion Engineering, 391 F.3d 190 (3rd Cir. 2004).

CASES

IN RE FEDERAL COMMUNICATIONS COMMISSION

United States Court of Appeals, Second Circuit, 2000
217 F.3d 125

JACOBS, CIRCUIT JUDGE.

* * * In summer 1996, NextWave was the high bidder at FCC auctions for 63 personal communications services ("PCS") spectrum licenses (the "Licenses"). NextWave's winning bids aggregated $4.74 billion. Because NextWave enjoyed the status of a "small business," only ten percent of the amount bid was required to be paid in cash. On February 14, 1997, following some further proceedings to correct NextWave's noncompliance with statutory ownership requirements, the FCC granted the Licenses to NextWave, conditioned upon issuance of a series of promissory notes for the $4.27 billion balance of NextWave's obligations. NextWave promptly executed the notes.

By the time these notes were executed, further auctions had been conducted at which similar licenses had been auctioned at prices significantly lower than NextWave's winning bids. Alarmed that as a result it had bid beyond its capacity to obtain financing, NextWave sought relief from the FCC and the Court of Appeals for the District of Columbia Circuit. Those efforts were unsuccessful. On June 8, 1999, NextWave filed a bankruptcy petition under Chapter 11 and commenced an adversary proceeding against the FCC [in which it disputed the terms under which it acquired the right to use the licenses from the FCC. After losing below, the FCC appealed to this court.] * * *

[In the course of deciding that appeal, we] determined that the purpose of spectrum auctions was chiefly regulatory, not fiscal. [W]e then turned to the FCC's exclusive jurisdiction over regulation of the spectrum. Noting that the FCC's exclusive jurisdiction over licensing matters extended to the conditions placed on licenses, we held that "when the FCC decides which entities are entitled to spectrum licenses under rules and conditions it has promulgated," it is exercising a quintessentially regulatory power. [R]eview of the FCC's regulatory decisions and orders is entrusted solely to the federal courts of appeals and is therefore outside the jurisdiction of the bankruptcy and district courts. * * *

Because "the FCC's auction rules ... have primarily a regulatory purpose," we held that the approach taken by the bankruptcy and district courts—which allowed NextWave to keep PCS licenses under conditions that the FCC considered non-compliant—was "fundamentally mistaken."

We thus held that even where the regulatory conditions imposed on a license take the form of a financial obligation, the bankruptcy and district courts lack jurisdiction to interfere in the FCC's allocation. * * *

On December 16, 1999—after this Court held that the FCC's licensing requirements were not subject to alteration in the bankruptcy court—NextWave filed modifications to its proposed plan of reorganization. Until then, NextWave had been contending that payment of the $4.27 billion still owed was beyond its capacity and that the incurring of the debt was a constructive fraud. But under its proposed modifications to the plan, NextWave would pay in full its overdue obligation to the FCC and undertake to pay the notes as they come due.

On January 11, 2000, NextWave sweetened its offer to the FCC and proposed to pay in a single lump sum the present value of its billions of dollars in notes. The lump-sum payment proposal was new and not part of NextWave's proffered modifications.

The day after NextWave's lump-sum offer, ... the FCC announced the re-auction of the Licenses then held by NextWave. The Public Notice made no mention of the previous licensee, but the FCC's memorandum objecting to the modified reorganization plan explains that the cancellation of the Licenses was occasioned by NextWave's default under the terms of the Licenses. According to the FCC, that default resulted in the "automatic cancellation" of the Licenses. * * *

NextWave moved by order to show cause for an order declaring the Public Notice null and void. The bankruptcy court granted NextWave's motion. * * *

Recognizing that it lacked power to review FCC regulatory actions, the bankruptcy court sought to cast the dispute in non-regulatory terms. ... This misses the point. The FCC need not defend its regulatory calculus in the bankruptcy court; whenever an FCC decision implicates its exclusive power to dictate the terms and conditions of licensure, the decision is regulatory. And if the decision is regulatory, it may not be altered or impeded by any court lacking jurisdiction to review it.

The FCC's decision to re-auction the Licenses previously granted to NextWave is one that implicates the conditions of licensure, in itself a circumstance sufficient to require the bankruptcy court's deference. * * *

In the course of deciding that the FCC's re-auction decision lacked any regulatory purpose, the bankruptcy court was in effect and in fact questioning the FCC's regulatory judgments:

> What regulatory principle or public interest does the FCC invoke to outweigh the investment in these debtors of over $1 billion in debt and equity? What public policy is served by an act of the United States Government which violates basic notions of equity, due process and the Bankruptcy Code? What purpose is served by the FCC's relinquishment of over $4.7 billion for the C Licenses? * * *

Whatever the force of these rhetorical questions, the answers entail regulatory decisions and are outside the jurisdiction of the bankruptcy court. * * *

In short, the FCC made timely payment a regulatory condition; and the bankruptcy court has concluded that such a condition is arbitrary, in the sense that it serves no regulatory purpose that the bankruptcy court is prepared to recognize. However, a regulatory condition is a regulatory condition even if it is arbitrary. It is for the FCC to state its conditions of licensure, and for a court with power to review the FCC's decisions to say if they are arbitrary or valid. * * *

Our mandate required the bankruptcy court to refrain from impeding the regulatory actions of the FCC, in particular, the FCC's enforcement of the payment schedule established by its regulations, orders, and decisions. * * *

The automatic stay has its limits. Here, the applicable limit is set forth in 11 U.S.C. §362(b)(4) .... Undoubtedly, the FCC is a governmental unit that is seeking "to enforce" its "regulatory power."

Nevertheless, the bankruptcy court decided that "§362(b)(4) is not applicable here. The FCC's action is nothing other than a direct attempt to enforce its pecuniary interests." This observation is flatly incompatible with this Court's mandate, as expressed in our earlier opinion. * * *

Even if the bankruptcy court is right on the merits of its arguments against revocation—we have no occasion to express an opinion—it is without power to act on its determination. * * *

We conclude that the bankruptcy court acted in derogation of this Court's mandate and beyond its statutory jurisdiction when it nullified the FCC's Public Notice. The violation of our mandate and the jurisdictional defect are independently sufficient to justify mandamus. * * *

UNITED STATES v. NICOLET, INC.

United States Court of Appeals, Second Circuit, 1988
857 F.2d 202

WEIS, CIRCUIT JUDGE.

* * * Acting under the authority granted it by the Comprehensive Environmental Response, Compensation, and Liability Act, the United States filed this suit in the district court against defendant Nicolet on May 30, 1985. The complaint sought reimbursement of environmental response costs expended and to be expended in the future to clean up an asbestos site in Ambler, Pennsylvania. The Environmental Protection Agency had engaged private contractors to abate the hazard from two waste piles and incurred costs of $1 million. The agency seeks reimbursement of this sum and an additional $300,000 in future remedial costs.

Although at the time of the cleanup, the affected sites were owned by Nicolet, they had been purchased in 1982 from a wholly-owned subsidiary of Turner & Newall. Nicolet joined Turner & Newall as a third-party defendant, seeking indemnification or contribution. The United States then amended its complaint to name Turner & Newall as an original defendant.

Some time later, in July 1987, Nicolet filed for reorganization under Chapter 11 of the Bankruptcy Code. The district court, assuming that the proceedings were subject to the automatic stay provisions of the Code, placed this CERCLA suit in civil suspense. The United States objected to the district court's order and promptly moved for reconsideration. The government argued that its action was a suit by a governmental unit to enforce its police or regulatory power, a proceeding expressly exempt from the automatic stay under §362(b)(4). The district court agreed and directed that the case be transferred from the suspense file to the trial calendar.

* * * Nicolet contends that, because the government seeks to secure a judgment for prepetition expenditures, its suit is simply an attempt to collect money and thus outside the scope of the police power exemption. Turner & Newall asserts that Nicolet is an indispensable party, a status which demands that if the automatic stay is imposed as to Nicolet, proceedings against all other defendants should also be suspended. The government maintains that the case should proceed to trial, emphasizing that—assuming a verdict for the agency—no execution on the judgment would be sought. * * *

The automatic stay provision codified at §362 of the Bankruptcy Code prohibits, inter alia, the commencement or continuation of a judicial or administrative proceeding against the debtor that could have been initiated before the petition was filed, or to recover on a claim that arose prebankruptcy. In addition to providing the debtor with a "breathing spell," the stay is intended to replace an unfair race to the courthouse with an orderly liquidation procedure designed to treat all creditors equally.

Congress recognized, however, that the stay provision was particularly vulnerable to abuse by debtors improperly seeking refuge under the stay in an effort to frustrate necessary governmental functions. To combat the risk that the bankruptcy court would become a sanctuary for environmental wrongdoers, among others, Congress enacted the police and regulatory power exception to the automatic stay.

The two pertinent subsections [now combined in new §362(b)(4)] provide:

362(b) The filing of a [bankruptcy] petition ... does *not* operate as a stay—

(4) under subsection (a)(1) of this section, of the commencement or continuation of an action or proceeding by a governmental unit to enforce such governmental unit's police or regulatory power;

(5) under subsection (a)(2) of this section, of the enforcement of a judgment, other than a money judgment, obtained in an action or proceeding by a governmental unit to enforce such governmental unit's police or regulatory power.

(Emphasis added.) These provisions embody Congress' recognition that enforcement of the environmental protection laws merits a higher priority than the debtor's rights to a "cease fire" or the creditors' rights to an orderly administration of the estate.

The United States concedes that it is not entitled to execute on any judgment it might obtain in these proceedings against Nicolet; §362(b)(5) expressly states that enforcement of a money judgment does not fall within the police and regulatory exception to the automatic stay. But the government contends that the litigation should be permitted to proceed to a trial so that damages, if due, may be fixed. * * *

Nicolet argues that the exemption for regulatory enforcement is intended to apply only to governmental actions seeking prospective relief, and not to suits demanding money damages for past violations. Nicolet maintains that the urgency inherent in cases directing polluters to desist from continuing their illegal activities is absent when a simple monetary judgment is sought. Thus, in appellant's view, any debt owed the United States for cleanup expenditures is materially indistinguishable from that due other creditors who are statutorily precluded from liquidating their claims.

Nicolet's arguments are rational and not at all inconsistent with the statutory text; yet its reasoning is also not compelled by the statute. The stay provisions are sufficiently imprecise that they can be read to intend either of the conflicting results asserted by the parties. Faced with two equally legitimate interpretations of the statutory language, we turn to the law's legislative history for guidance on Congressional intent.

A reading of the legislative history clearly favors the government's position. The Senate and House Committee Reports use identical language in describing the intended effect of the police and regulatory exemption. The reports state that "where a governmental unit is suing a debtor to prevent or stop violation of fraud, environmental protection, consumer protection, safety, or similar police or regulatory laws, *or attempting to fix damages for violation of such a law,* the action or proceeding is not stayed under the automatic stay." S. Rep. No. 989, at 52 (emphasis added); H.R. Rep. No. 595, at 343 (emphasis added). * * *

The Bankruptcy Code does not set out criteria for determining when a regulatory agency is seeking the impermissible "enforcement of a money judgment," but we explained the concept in *Penn Terra.*

There, we wrote that the "paradigm" for such a proceeding is where the plaintiff attempts to seize the debtor's property to satisfy the judgment. "It is this seizure of a defendant-debtor's property, to satisfy the judgment obtained by a plaintiff-creditor, which is proscribed by subsection 362(b)(5)." [Penn Terra Ltd. v. Department of Environmental Resources, 733 F.2d 267, 275 (3d Cir. 1984).]

By simply permitting the government's claim to be reduced to a judgment, no seizure of property takes place. Moreover, that Congress carefully made only enforcement of a money judgment subject to the automatic stay indicates strongly that mere entry of the judgment was not intended to be proscribed. This implication is entirely consistent with the legislative history to which we earlier referred. * * *

Another factor is sometimes added to this calculus. ... The pecuniary purpose test asks whether the governmental proceeding relates principally to the protection of the government's pecuniary interest in the debtor's property, rather than to its public policy interest in the general safety and welfare. In the former situation, the action is not exempt from the stay. Thus, the exemption in §362(b)(4) did not apply to a governmental unit's suit for breach of contract in Corporacion de Servicios Medicos Hospitalarios de Fajardo v. Mora, 805 F.2d 440 (1st Cir. 1986).

In pressing this lawsuit, the United States is not seeking redress for private wrongs or a remedy for a private contract breach. It is not suing in its role as a consuming participant in the national economy, i.e., suing a negligent motorist for damage to a GSA van or a paper-clip manufacturer for a defective order. Rather, the government brought suit against Nicolet in compliance with its explicit mandate under CERCLA "to remove or arrange for the removal of [any] hazardous substance, pollutant, or contaminant." 42 U.S.C. §9604(a). * * *

The recoupment mandate interjects a valuable deterrence element into the CERCLA scheme, ensuring that responsible parties will be held accountable for their environmental misdeeds. These considerations make it plain that the present action falls within the "related to police or regulatory powers" category detailed in *Penn Terra*. We are persuaded that the Environmental Protection Agency is acting in this suit pursuant to its regulatory authority. We find further that it was Congress' intent that proceedings such as this be exempt from the automatic stay up to and including entry of a monetary judgment. Accordingly, the district court did not err in lifting the stay. * * *

The order of the district court will be affirmed.

NOTES

4C.1. The court interprets the jurisdiction of the bankruptcy court narrowly. It then goes on to suggest that agency actions are regulatory even when the agency takes an action (cancellation of a license) only because a debtor failed to make a payment on an obligation. An alternative interpretation of the automatic stay would not attempt to separate an agency from other actors, but would instead distinguish among agency *actions*. The *NextWave* court might have drawn a line between an agency's action as a creditor and an agency's action as a regulator. In other words, the automatic stay would apply under the facts of *NextWave*, but would have no effect on any action that the agency would take regardless of whether the licensee owed the agency any money. For example, the bankruptcy judge would have no power to second-guess the agency's revocation of a license based on nonuse. Problem 4C-1 explores this idea further.

4C.2. Subsequent to the Second Circuit's opinion in *NextWave*, the debtor sought review of the FCC's actions in the D.C. Circuit. In an opinion later affirmed by the Supreme Court, the D.C. Circuit found that the FCC, a government agency, violated Bankruptcy Code §525 when it revoked NextWave's license for failure to pay a debt that was dischargeable in bankruptcy. See FCC v. NextWave, 537 U.S. 293 (2003). Section 525, described more fully below in chapter 11, section C of this book, is an anti-discrimination provision, designed, for example, to prevent a state from depriving a debtor of a driver's license. In *NextWave*, however, the FCC did not seek to revoke the licenses because of some general antipathy toward deadbeats. Rather the FCC acted essentially as a secured creditor that foreclosed on collateral after a default, an activity seemingly beyond the scope of §525. The FCC may have been hoist by its own petard. By insisting that its actions were those of a regulator (and not a creditor), it put itself beyond the reach of §362, but pulled itself within the orbit of §525.

4C.3. Turning to *Nicolet*, everyone agrees that, at the very least, §362(b)(4) requires that a debtor continue to comply with nonbankruptcy laws after it files a bankruptcy petition. The debtor cannot argue that an environmental regulation is stayed on the ground that it is an exercise of "control over property of the estate." In this respect, §362(b)(4) merely implements the *Butner* principle. *Nicolet*, however, holds that §362(b)(4) goes further. Even when all that the state is doing is asserting that the debtor owes money for prepetition violations of regulatory laws, it is entitled to litigate this claim and reduce it to judgment outside the bankruptcy process in the nonbankruptcy forum. The automatic stay prevents the state only from enforcing the money judgment.

but other parties will each litigate right

4C.4. When a prebankruptcy debtor pollutes in violation of state or federal law and damages the environment in a way that would cost money to repair, the government can enforce its regulation in two ways. It can order the debtor to clean up, or it can pay for the cleanup work itself and then seek reimbursement from the debtor. Outside of bankruptcy, there is no functional difference between the two. Indeed, the same cleanup specialists might be hired to do the actual work in either case. And the debtor's other creditors will be deprived of the sum needed for the cleanup in either case. In bankruptcy, however, the government's money judgment may entitle it only to share with others who will seek to collect from the estate, perhaps receiving only a few cents on the dollar. Even as interpreted by *Nicolet*, §362(b)(4) excepts from the stay only an exercise of a regulatory power *other than* enforcement of a money judgment. In bankruptcy, therefore, the government may have an incentive to order a cleanup, and have the estate pay for the work in full, rather than conduct and charge for one.

injunction preferable during bankruptcy

Given the incentives created by *Nicolet*, one might question whether it makes sense to distinguish between a regulatory order and collection of a debt when the debtor's liability arises solely out of prepetition conduct. A more sensible line might be one that excepts from the stay only those actions that the state possesses by virtue of its power to regulate the debtor's postpetition activity. Assertions of a prepetition right would not be treated as an exercise of regulatory power under §362(b)(4) at all. Without the power to enforce a cleanup order postpetition, the government's best option might be to clean up the site quickly while the question of liability is still being litigated. This result could be superior to that of *Nicolet*, where the government may waste time—and risk further damage—in the hope of debtor's compliance. Problem 4C-2 further explores this matter.

4C.5. One should not overstate the importance to the government of a debtor's compliance with an environmental cleanup order. As we shall see below in chapter 9, when a debtor in bankruptcy incurs obligations necessary to comply with applicable law, those obligations are entitled to "administrative expense" priority over the debtor's unsecured prepetition claims. A debtor's CERCLA obligation for future cleanup costs would be entitled to such priority because continued ownership of the contaminated site—wholly apart from any prepetition activity—generates the obligation, which is thus a cost of *present*

→ ongoing environ-ment isn't pre-petition

ownership rather than a past debt. Thus, if a debtor's bankruptcy estate were large enough to pay merely the debtor's administrative expenses, the government could clean up itself and receive full payment even from an insolvent debtor.

4C.6. Ultimately, then, all that may have been at stake in *Nicolet* is the forum in which the EPA's action would be adjudicated in the first instance. In a case in which the EPA is seeking to hold multiple parties responsible, the EPA does not want to pursue Nicolet in a separate forum, nor may it want to pursue Nicolet and others in the bankruptcy forum with that forum's expedited procedures and other rules. In *Nicolet*, the EPA brought its case in federal district court— the same court, though in a different location, that would review any bankruptcy court decision. Forum matters even more when Congress or a state assigns particular disputes to specialized administrative agencies. When specialization is important to accurate decisions, there is a policy that competes with the goal of having all claims against a debtor resolved in a single forum.

This said, however, even if the stay applies to an action, a bankruptcy court may, at its discretion, permit litigation elsewhere. It is not uncommon for a bankruptcy court to lift the stay and allow resolution in another forum where the court believes this other resolution will occur before the bankruptcy case closes. The bankruptcy court can then incorporate the results of the resolution into the bankruptcy case.

PROBLEMS

4C-1. For many years, there were only two taxicabs in Town, each owned by a politically powerful citizen of good standing. A number of years ago, the cab owners persuaded Town to deregulate fares and, as a "safety" measure, to cap the operation of each cab at twelve hours a day. After the measure was passed, practice developed such that only one cab was in service at any time.

Several years later, in part because of widespread complaints about poor taxi service, Town decides to auction off two new taxi medallions, each entitling its holder to operate a cab. (The twelve-hour rule will remain in effect.) To encourage new entrepreneurs and high bids, Town agrees to finance much of the purchase price for each new medallion. Against this background, Firm makes a winning bid of $11,000 for a medallion. Firm uses $1,000 to make a down payment and borrows the $10,000 remainder from Town, to be repaid over time.

Despite Firm's initially optimistic expectations, there is an economic downturn and the demand for cab service declines. As a result, Firm cannot meet its obligations to Town and to Firm's other creditors. Firm files a Chapter 11 bankruptcy petition. Firm is insolvent. It owes $20,000, but the business is worth only $15,000 under current conditions. Nevertheless, Firm would be able to pay off its obligations in full if it could operate its cab service around the clock for the remainder of the bankruptcy case. Firm asks the court to permit its around-the-clock operation. Town opposes such permission and seeks to revoke Firm's medallion. Would such revocation violate the automatic stay? Can the bankruptcy judge authorize Firm's taxicab to operate around the clock? See In re Javens, 107 F.3d 359 (6th Cir. 1997); In re Gull Air, Inc., 890 F.2d 1255 (1st Cir. 1989).

4C-2. Debtor Corporation was once a leading manufacture of hand tools. Debtor's ownership changed about four years ago. At this time, its product line included chain saws, but the new owners determined that competition from abroad made their domestic manufacture unprofitable. Debtor acquired a great deal of debt during this change in ownership, and after a number of reversals and ever more intense foreign competition, it filed for bankruptcy and closed down its operations. Debtor still has substantial assets, and its creditors are likely to be paid a large part of what they are owed. Just before Debtor's bankruptcy petition, the state Consumer Protection Agency won an action against Debtor in state court, where it successfully alleged that the chain saws manufactured under Debtor's old owners were unsafe. The state court ordered Debtor to either add a safety guard itself or pay another vendor to do so. As Debtor no longer has the facilities to repair the saws, it can comply with the order only by paying someone else. Can Agency enforce this order without permission of the bankruptcy court? Would Agency prefer this course to one in which Agency itself added the safety guards and charged Debtor for the work? Would your answer change if state law granted Agency first priority in all of a debtor's assets?

V. CLAIMS AGAINST THE ESTATE

Once a bankruptcy petition is filed and the automatic stay takes effect, all debt collection activity moves to the bankruptcy process. Simply put, this process determines who gets what from the debtor. To answer the question of "who," the Bankruptcy Code has us look to those who hold "claims." A claim, defined in §101(5), is any "right to payment whether or not such right is reduced to judgment, liquidated, unliquidated, fixed, contingent, matured, unmatured, disputed, undisputed, legal, equitable, secured, or unsecured." A claim is also "a right to an equitable remedy for breach of performance if such breach gives rise to" any such "right to payment." So, for example, if a debtor negligently causes a car accident before she files for bankruptcy, the accident victim holds a claim in bankruptcy even if he has not yet initiated a lawsuit against the debtor. Similarly, the holder of an unpaid loan obligation holds a claim even if the loan is not due when the debtor files for bankruptcy. And the holder of a right of specific performance on a contract has a claim if such holder could receive monetary compensation in lieu of performance.

A claim will not necessarily be satisfied, of course. A claim can be thought of as a mere ticket to the bankruptcy process. Once admitted, the holder of the claim must wait to see whether the claim will be "allowed." Section 502 disallows specified types of obligations even though these obligations qualify as claims under §101(5). Only allowed claims are entitled to a share of the debtor's assets. Moreover, if the debtor lacks sufficient assets fully to satisfy all allowed claims, at least some portion of some claims will by necessity remain unpaid at the close of the bankruptcy process. Priority will determine which claims are paid and which go unsatisfied. Thus, a claim is necessary, but not sufficient, for collection from a debtor in bankruptcy.

A. A CLAIM AND WHEN IT ARISES

Determining whether a purported obligation is a claim for the purposes of bankruptcy is often a simple matter. For example, it is clear that a creditor with an unpaid loan, or the government with an unpaid tax bill, has a right to payment that qualifies as a "claim" against a debtor in bankruptcy. Similarly, an injured tort victim with a judgment or a mere cause of action against a debtor has a claim, though one that may be unliquidated—i.e., not reduced to judgment—

and disputed. These obligations are grist for the bankruptcy mill. The exercises below illustrate other straightforward situations. But not all would-be claims are ordinary or straightforward.

The cases, notes, and problems below ask you to consider unusual circumstances. In *Ohio v. Kovacs*, a state government orders a debtor to conduct an environmental cleanup, then seeks to acquire the debtor's assets when the debtor fails to comply with the order. The question is whether the government's power to effectuate the objective of its order in this way constitutes a claim. In *Epstein v. Unsecured Creditors*, a debtor's prebankruptcy negligent behavior will cause accidents long after the bankruptcy case is over. The question is whether the debtor's negligence gives rise to bankruptcy claims even though that negligence does not yet give rise to causes of action under applicable nonbankruptcy law.

In each case, it is important to understand that being found to hold a claim comes with both an upside and a downside. Only those holding claims share in the assets of the estate, but, subject to a few specified exceptions, claims are discharged as well. In the case of an individual or a corporation that reorganizes in Chapter 11, the holder of a claim can no longer look to the debtor for repayment. When one holds an obligation that does not fall within the ambit of a claim, the situation is reversed. One does not share in the distribution of the debtor's assets at the close of the bankruptcy case, but the obligation survives the debtor's bankruptcy and can be asserted against the debtor after bankruptcy. Moreover, under the state law doctrine of "successor liability," the holder of the obligation may be able to bring an action against an entity that has purchased the bulk of a debtor's assets. The notes and problems further explore the linkage between claim definition and discharge.

Key Provisions: Bankruptcy Code §§101(5), (12); 727; 1141

EXERCISES

5A(1) Debtor, an individual, files for bankruptcy, then borrows $10,000 from Bank. On the way home from finalizing this loan transaction, Debtor negligently injures Bystander. Does either Bank or Bystander have claims against Debtor that will be allowed in bankruptcy? Would your answer change if Debtor were a corporation?

5A(2) Debtor sells a house to Buyer during a drought. The house gets fresh water from a local well that is in danger of drying up. Without substantial rainfall over the next two years, any owner of the house will have to allow her lawn and landscaping to wither. The terms of the sale require Debtor to pay Buyer $20,000 if rainfall in the area is not at least twenty inches within two years after the closing on the house. One year after the closing, Debtor files for bankruptcy. Rainfall in the year between closing and the bankruptcy petition was ten inches. Does Buyer have a claim that will be allowed in bankruptcy?

CASES

OHIO v. KOVACS

United States Supreme Court, 1985
469 U.S. 274

JUSTICE WHITE DELIVERED THE OPINION OF THE COURT.

Petitioner State of Ohio obtained an injunction ordering respondent William Kovacs to clean up a hazardous waste site. A receiver was subsequently appointed. Still later, Kovacs filed a petition for bankruptcy. The question before us is whether, in the circumstances present here, Kovacs' obligation under the injunction is a "debt" or "liability on a claim" subject to discharge under the Bankruptcy Code.

I

Kovacs was the chief executive officer and stockholder of Chem-Dyne Corp., which with other business entities operated an industrial and hazardous waste disposal site in Hamilton, Ohio. In 1976, the State sued Kovacs and the business entities in state court for polluting public waters, maintaining a nuisance, and causing fish kills, all in violation of state environmental laws. In 1979, both in his individual capacity and on behalf of Chem-Dyne, Kovacs signed a stipulation and judgment entry settling the lawsuit. Among other things, the stipulation enjoined the defendants from causing further pollution of the air or public waters, forbade bringing additional industrial wastes onto the site, required the defendants to remove specified wastes from the property, and ordered the payment of $75,000 to compensate the State for injury to wildlife.

Kovacs and the other defendants failed to comply with their obligations under the injunction. The State then obtained the appointment in state court of a receiver, who was directed to take possession of all property and other assets of Kovacs and the corporate defendants and to implement the judgment entry by cleaning up the Chem-Dyne site. The receiver took possession of the site but had not completed his tasks when Kovacs filed a personal bankruptcy petition.

Seeking to develop a basis for requiring part of Kovacs' post-bankruptcy income to be applied to the unfinished task of the receivership, the State then filed a motion in state court to discover Kovacs' current income and assets. Kovacs requested that the Bankruptcy Court stay those proceedings, which it did. The State also filed a complaint in the Bankruptcy Court seeking a declaration that Kovacs' obligation under the stipulation and judgment order to clean up the Chem-Dyne site was not dischargeable in bankruptcy because it was not a "debt," a liability on a "claim," within the meaning of the Bankruptcy Code. In addition, the complaint sought an injunction against the bankruptcy trustee to restrain him from pursuing any action to recover assets of Kovacs in the hands of the receiver. The Bankruptcy Court ruled against Ohio, as did the District Court. The Court of Appeals for the Sixth Circuit affirmed, holding that Ohio essentially sought from Kovacs only a monetary payment and that such a required payment was a liability on a claim that was dischargeable under the bankruptcy statute. We granted certiorari to determine the dischargeability of Kovacs' obligation under the affirmative injunction entered against him. * * *

III

Except for the ... kinds of debts saved from discharge §523(a), a discharge in bankruptcy discharges the debtor from all debts that arose before bankruptcy. §727(b). It is not claimed here that Kovacs' obligation under the injunction fell within any of the categories of debts excepted from discharge by §523. Rather, the State submits that the obligation to clean up the Chem-Dyne site is not a debt at all within the meaning of the bankruptcy law.

For bankruptcy purposes, a debt is a liability on a claim. [§101(12)]. A claim is defined by [§101(5)] as follows:

" 'claim' means—

"(A) right to payment, whether or not such right is reduced to judgment, liquidated, unliquidated, fixed, contingent, matured, unmatured, disputed, undisputed, legal, equitable, secured, or un-secured; or

"(B) right to an equitable remedy for breach of performance if such breach gives rise to a right to payment, whether or not such right to an equitable remedy is reduced to judgment, fixed, contingent, matured, unmatured, disputed, undisputed, secured, or unsecured."

The provision at issue here is [§101(5)(B)]. For the purposes of that section, there is little doubt that the State had the right to an equitable remedy under state law and that the right has been reduced to judgment in the form of an injunction ordering the cleanup. The State argues, however, that the injunction it has secured is not a claim against Kovacs for bankruptcy purposes because (1) Kovacs' default was a breach of the statute, not a breach of an ordinary commercial contract which concededly would give rise to a claim; and (2) Kovacs' breach of his obligation under the injunction did not give rise to a right to payment within the meaning of [§101(5)(B)]. We are not persuaded by either submission.

There is no indication in the language of the statute that the right to performance cannot be a claim unless it arises from a contractual arrangement. The State resorted to the courts to enforce its environmental laws against Kovacs and secured a negative order to cease polluting, an affirmative order to clean up the site, and an order to pay a sum of money to recompense the State for damage done to the fish population. Each order was one to remedy an alleged breach of Ohio law; and if Kovacs' obligation to pay $75,000 to the State is a debt dischargeable in bankruptcy, which the State freely concedes, it makes little sense to assert that because the cleanup order was entered to remedy a statutory violation, it cannot likewise constitute a claim for bankruptcy purposes. Furthermore, it is apparent that Congress desired a broad definition of a "claim" and knew how to limit the application of a provision to contracts when it desired to do so. * * *

The courts below also found little substance in the submission that the cleanup obligation did not give rise to a right to payment that renders the order dischargeable under §727. The definition of "claim" in H.R. 8200 as originally drafted would have deemed a right to an equitable remedy for breach of performance a claim even if it did not give rise to a right to payment. The initial Senate definition of claim was narrower, and a compromise version, [§101(5)], was finally adopted. In that version, the key phrases "equitable remedy," "breach of performance," and "right to payment" are not defined. Nor are the differences between the successive versions explained. The legislative history offers only a statement by the sponsors of the Bankruptcy Reform Act with respect to the scope of the provision:

> Section [101(5)(B)] is intended to cause the liquidation or estimation of contingent rights of payment for which there may be an alternative equitable remedy with the result that the equitable remedy will be susceptible to being discharged in bankruptcy. For example, in some States, a judgment for specific performance may be satisfied by an alternative right to payment in the event performance is refused; in that event, the creditor entitled to specific performance would have a "claim" for purposes of a proceeding under title 11.

We think the rulings of the courts below were wholly consistent with the statute and its legislative history, sparse as it is. The Bankruptcy Court ruled as follows:

> There is no suggestion by plaintiff that defendant can render performance under the affirmative obligation other than by the payment of money. We therefore conclude that plaintiff has a claim against defendant within the meaning of [§101(5)], and that defendant owes plaintiff a debt within the meaning of [§101(12)]. Furthermore, we have concluded that that debt is dischargeable.

The District Court affirmed, primarily because it was bound by and saw no error in the Court of Appeals' prior opinion holding that the State was seeking no more than a money judgment as an alternative to requiring Kovacs personally to perform the obligations imposed by the injunction. To hold otherwise, the District Court explained, "would subvert Congress' clear intention to give debtors a fresh start." The Court of Appeals also affirmed, rejecting the State's insistence that it had no right to, and was not attempting to enforce, an alternative right to payment:

> Ohio does not suggest that Kovacs is capable of personally cleaning up the environmental damage he may have caused. Ohio claims there is no alternative right to payment, but when Kovacs failed to perform, state law gave a state receiver total control over all Kovacs' assets. Ohio later used state law to try and discover Kovacs' post-petition income and employment status in an apparent attempt to levy on his future earnings. In reality, the only type of performance in which Ohio is now interested is a money payment to effectuate the Chem-Dyne cleanup ... .

> The impact of its attempt to realize upon Kovacs' income or property cannot be concealed by legerdemain or linguistic gymnastics. Kovacs cannot personally clean up the waste he wrong-

fully released into Ohio waters. He cannot perform the affirmative obligations properly imposed upon him by the State court except by paying money or transferring over his own financial resources. The State of Ohio has acknowledged this by its steadfast pursuit of payment as an alternative to personal performance.

As we understand it, the Court of Appeals held that, in the circumstances, the cleanup duty had been reduced to a monetary obligation.

We do not disturb this judgment. The injunction surely obliged Kovacs to clean up the site. But when he failed to do so, rather than prosecute Kovacs under the environmental laws or bring civil or criminal contempt proceedings, the State secured the appointment of a receiver, who was ordered to take possession of all of Kovacs' nonexempt assets as well as the assets of the corporate defendants and to comply with the injunction entered against Kovacs. As wise as this course may have been, it dispossessed Kovacs, removed his authority over the site, and divested him of assets that might have been used by him to clean up the property. Furthermore, when the bankruptcy trustee sought to recover Kovacs' assets from the receiver, the latter sought an injunction against such action. Although Kovacs had been ordered to "cooperate" with the receiver, he was disabled by the receivership from personally taking charge of and carrying out the removal of wastes from the property. What the receiver wanted from Kovacs after bankruptcy was the money to defray cleanup costs. At oral argument in this Court, the State's counsel conceded that after the receiver was appointed, the only performance sought from Kovacs was the payment of money. Had Kovacs furnished the necessary funds, either before or after bankruptcy, there seems little doubt that the receiver and the State would have been satisfied.

On the facts before it, and with the receiver in control of the site, we cannot fault the Court of Appeals for concluding that the cleanup order had been converted into an obligation to pay money, an obligation that was dischargeable in bankruptcy. * * *

The judgment of the Court of Appeals is affirmed.

EPSTEIN v. OFFICIAL COMMITTEE OF UNSECURED CREDITORS

United States Court of Appeals, Eleventh Circuit, 1995
58 F.3d 1573

BLACK, CIRCUIT JUDGE.

This is an appeal by David G. Epstein, as the Legal Representative for the Piper future claimants (Future Claimants), from the district court's order of June 6, 1994, affirming the order of the bankruptcy court entered on December 6, 1993. The sole issue on appeal is whether the class of Future Claimants, as defined by the bankruptcy court, holds claims against the estate of Piper Aircraft Corporation (Piper), within the meaning of §101(5) of the Bankruptcy Code. After review of the relevant provisions, policies and goals of the Bankruptcy Code and the applicable case law, we hold that the Future Claimants do not have claims as defined by §101(5) and thus affirm the opinion of the district court.

* * * Piper has been manufacturing and distributing general aviation aircraft and spare parts throughout the United States and abroad since 1937. Approximately 50,000 to 60,000 Piper aircraft still are operational in the United States. Although Piper has been a named defendant in several lawsuits based on its manufacture, design, sale, distribution and support of its aircraft and parts, it has never acknowledged that its products are harmful or defective.

On July 1, 1991, Piper filed a voluntary petition under Chapter 11 ... . Piper's plan of reorganization contemplated finding a purchaser of substantially all of its assets or obtaining investments from outside sources, with the proceeds of such transactions serving to fund distributions to creditors. On April 8, 1993, Piper and Pilatus Aircraft Limited signed a letter of intent pursuant to which Pilatus would purchase Piper's assets. The letter of intent required Piper to seek the appointment of a legal representative to represent the interests of future claimants by arranging a set-aside of monies generated by the sale to pay off future product liability claims.

On May 19, 1993, the bankruptcy court appointed Appellant Epstein as the legal representative for the Future Claimants. The Court defined the class of Future Claimants to include:

> All persons, whether known or unknown, born or unborn, who may, after the date of confirmation of Piper's Chapter 11 plan of reorganization, assert a claim or claims for personal injury, prop-

erty damages, wrongful death, damages, contribution and/or indemnification, based in whole or in part upon events occurring or arising after the Confirmation Date, including claims based on the law of product liability, against Piper or its successor arising out of or relating to aircraft or parts manufactured and sold, designed, distributed or supported by Piper prior to the Confirmation Date.

This Order expressly stated that the court was making no finding on whether the Future Claimants could hold claims against Piper under §101(5).

On July 12, 1993, Epstein filed a proof of claim on behalf of the Future Claimants in the approximate amount of $100,000,000. The claim was based on statistical assumptions regarding the number of persons likely to suffer, after the confirmation of a reorganization plan, personal injury or property damage caused by Piper's pre-confirmation manufacture, sale, design, distribution or support of aircraft and spare parts. The Official Committee of Unsecured Creditors (Official Committee), and later Piper, objected to the claim on the ground that the Future Claimants do not hold §101(5) claims against Piper.

[handwritten margin note: speculative amount of damages in the future]

After a hearing on the objection, the bankruptcy court agreed that the Future Claimants did not hold §101(5) claims … . Epstein, as Legal Representative, then appealed from the bankruptcy court's order. On June 6, 1994, the district court affirmed and accepted the decision of the bankruptcy court. Epstein now appeals from the district court's order, challenging in particular its use of the prepetition relationship test to define the scope of a claim under §101(5). * * *

Under the Bankruptcy Code, only parties that hold preconfirmation claims have a legal right to participate in a Chapter 11 bankruptcy case and share in payments pursuant to a Chapter 11 plan. In order to determine if the Future Claimants have such a right to participate, we first must address the statutory definition of the term "claim."

The Bankruptcy Code defines claim as:

(A) right to payment, whether or not such right is reduced to judgment, liquidated, unliquidated, fixed, contingent, matured, unmatured, disputed, undisputed, legal, equitable, secured, or unsecured; or

(B) right to an equitable remedy for breach of performance if such breach gives rise to a right to payment, whether or not such right to an equitable remedy is reduced to judgment, fixed, contingent, matured, unmatured, disputed, undisputed, secured, or unsecured.

The legislative history of the Code suggests that Congress intended to define the term claim very broadly under §101(5), so that "all legal obligations of the debtor, no matter how remote or contingent, will be able to be dealt with in the bankruptcy case." H.R. No. 95-595, 95th Cong., 2d Sess. 309 (1978).

Since the enactment of §101(5), courts have developed several tests to determine whether certain parties hold claims pursuant to that section: the accrued state law claim test,[2] the conduct test, and the prepetition relationship test. The bankruptcy court and district court adopted the prepetition relationship test in determining that the Future Claimants did not hold claims pursuant to §101(5).

Epstein primarily challenges the district court's application of the prepetition relationship test. He argues that the conduct test, which some courts have adopted in mass tort cases, is more consistent with the text, history, and policies of the Code. Under the conduct test, a right to payment arises when the conduct giving rise to the alleged liability occurred. Epstein's position is that any right to payment arising out of the prepetition conduct of Piper, no matter how remote, should be deemed a claim and provided for, pursuant to §101(5), in this case. He argues that the relevant conduct giving rise to the alleged liability was Piper's prepetition manufacture, design, sale and distribution of allegedly defective aircraft. Specifically, he contends that, because Piper performed these acts prepetition, the potential victims, although not yet identifiable, hold claims under §101(5) of the Code.

The Official Committee and Piper dispute the breadth of the definition of claim asserted by Epstein, arguing that the scope of claim cannot extend so far as to include unidentified, and presently unidentifiable, individuals with no discernible prepetition relationship to Piper. Recognizing, as Appellees do, that the conduct test may define claim too broadly in certain circumstances, several courts have recognized "claims" only for those individuals with some type of prepeti-

---

[2] The accrued state law claim theory states that there is no claim for bankruptcy purposes until a claim has accrued under state law. The most notable case adopting this approach is the Third Circuit's decision in In re M. Frenville Co., 744 F.2d 332 (3d Cir. 1984). This test since has been rejected by a majority of courts as imposing too narrow an interpretation on the term claim. See, e.g., Grady v. A.H. Robins Co., 839 F.2d 198, 201 (4th Cir. 1988). We agree with these courts and decline to employ the state law claim theory.

tion relationship with the debtor. The prepetition relationship test, as adopted by the bankruptcy court and district court, requires "some prepetition relationship, such as contact, exposure, impact, or privity, between the debtor's prepetition conduct and the claimant" in order for the claimant to hold a §101(5) claim.

Upon examination of the various theories, we agree with Appellees that the district court utilized the proper test in deciding that the Future Claimants did not hold a claim under §101(5). Epstein's interpretation of "claim" and application of the conduct test would enable anyone to hold a claim against Piper by virtue of their potential future exposure to any aircraft in the existing fleet. Even the conduct test cases, on which Epstein relies, do not compel the result he seeks. In fact, the conduct test cases recognize that focusing solely on prepetition conduct, as Epstein espouses, would stretch the scope of §101(5). Accordingly, the courts applying the conduct test also presume some prepetition relationship between the debtor's conduct and the claimant.

While acknowledging that the district court's test is more consistent with the purposes of the Bankruptcy Code than is the conduct test supported by Epstein, we find that the test as set forth by the district court unnecessarily restricts the class of claimants to those who could be identified prior to the filing of the petition. Those claimants having contact with the debtor's product post-petition but prior to confirmation also could be identified, during the course of the bankruptcy proceeding, as potential victims, who might have claims arising out of debtor's prepetition conduct.

We therefore modify the test used by the district court and adopt what we will call the "*Piper test*" in determining the scope of the term claim under §101(5): an individual has a §101(5) claim against a debtor manufacturer if (i) events occurring before confirmation create a relationship, such as contact, exposure, impact, or privity, between the claimant and the debtor's product; and (ii) the basis for liability is the debtor's prepetition conduct in designing, manufacturing and selling the allegedly defective or dangerous product. The debtor's prepetition conduct gives rise to a claim to be administered in a case only if there is a relationship established before confirmation between an identifiable claimant or group of claimants and that prepetition conduct.

In the instant case, it is clear that the Future Claimants fail the minimum requirements of the *Piper* test. There is no preconfirmation exposure to a specific identifiable defective product or any other pre-confirmation relationship between Piper and the broadly defined class of Future Claimants. As there is no preconfirmation connection established between Piper and the Future Claimants, the Future Claimants do not hold a §101(5) claim arising out of Piper's prepetition design, manufacture, sale, and distribution of allegedly defective aircraft. * * *

NOTES

5A.1. In a portion of *Kovacs* not reproduced above, the Court notes that its opinion does not relieve Kovacs of any duty to comply prospectively with environmental regulation. Therefore, if Kovacs retained contaminated property after his bankruptcy, he might, as we saw above in chapter 4, section C, be subject to a new cleanup order despite the discharge of prebankruptcy liability.

5A.2. Imagine that a Piper aircraft is negligently manufactured prior to Piper's bankruptcy, and a loose chunk of fuselage falls on the head of an infant born after that bankruptcy concludes. It may seem unfair that the infant's rights should be determined by the provisions of Piper's reorganization plan, a plan in which the infant (or any other stranger to the process) could not possibly have had a say. This apparent unfairness may have driven the court in *Epstein* to reject the conduct test for claim definition. But appearances can be deceiving. While the *Piper* test excludes the infant's eventual claim from treatment in the earlier bankruptcy case, and thus permits that future claim to survive discharge, nothing in the bankruptcy process guarantees that Piper will remain in business to pay the infant's claim when the debris finally falls from the sky. Indeed, exclusion of the infant's claim from the Piper bankruptcy may induce current creditors to liquidate the firm rather than reorganize. The bankruptcy court opinion in *Epstein* obliquely addressed this concern, concluding that recognition of the future claims would "hinder, not promote reorganization." But the court offers no explanation for its assertion. In re Piper Aircraft, 162 Bankr. 619 (Bankr. S.D. Fla. 1994).

Bear in mind that it was Epstein, the party speaking on behalf of the future victims, who argued that these victims had claims subject to discharge. The other creditors took the opposite position. Problems 5A-2 and 5A-3 ask you to explore why these parties would take opposing positions.

5A.3. The court discusses the test that other courts have adopted in mass tort cases. Two of the most prominent involved victims of asbestosis. In each case, a company manufactured asbestos before its hazards were widely recognized. Once the dangers of asbestos became known, the company faced potentially enormous liability to current *and future* asbestosis victims. Rather than wait out all potential claims, the company sought to reorganize under Chapter 11 of the Bankruptcy Code. A court that wished to provide for, and then discharge, obligations to future asbestosis victims might simply have held that the debtor's future obligations to such victims are "claims" under one of the tests discussed in *Epstein*. Not all courts addressed the claim determination head on, however. In the well-known Johns-Manville bankruptcy, for example, the court invoked its general equitable powers to fashion relief for future victims and then enjoined future actions. In re Johns-Manville Corp., 68 Bankr. 618, 624-26 (Bankr. S.D.N.Y. 1986). In late 1994, Congress responded with the enactment of §524(g) and (h), which apply retroactively and prospectively to sanction arrangements such as that in *Manville*, but only in asbestos cases.

PROBLEMS

5A-1. Debtor Corporation unlawfully buries containers of toxic chemicals, which begin to leach into the soil. State's environmental protection agency could order Debtor to clean up the site. But State chooses not to risk Debtor noncompliance with any such order and instead cleans up the site itself. Shortly after the cleanup, before State can take any action against Debtor for its cost, Debtor seeks to reorganize under Chapter 11. May State await completion of the bankruptcy process and then seek cleanup costs from the reorganized Debtor? If not, will State necessarily be at a disadvantage by its inability to pursue such a course? Under what conditions would it be so disadvantaged?

5A-2. Debtor Aircraft Corporation manufactures small planes. After years of production, Debtor discovers that a design defect in the engine of its most popular product. This defect can be corrected easily in future production, but cannot be repaired in planes already sold. Debtor calculates that the present value of future liability for this defect is $100 million. At the time of the discovery, Debtor's assets are worth $75 million if held together as part of a going concern. The same assets are worth $50 million if liquidated piecemeal in sales to other aircraft manufacturers. Apart from the future tort obligations, Debtor's aggregate outstanding debt is $50 million, and all of it is unsecured. After Debtor files for bankruptcy, its managers, who have devoted their careers to Debtor, seek to have Debtor's future liability declared a "claim" under §101(5). Debtor's current creditors oppose such characterization.

How might you explain these conflicting positions? If current creditors prevail on this issue, do you think they will support reorganization of Debtor or instead push to have Debtor liquidated? What policies of the Bankruptcy Code are implicated? Assume that state successor-liability doctrine allows product-liability claims to reach manufacturing assets as a unit, but not dismantled components of that unit.

5A-3. Consider the facts of Problem 5A-2, but assume that constitutional guarantees of due process prohibit the discharge of future claims. Is there any reason that current creditors would want to exclude future claims from Debtor's bankruptcy, even assuming that Debtor will reorganize and continue its business? In answering this question, focus on the fact that the $100 million amount of future claims is merely an estimate that may prove too high or too low.

B. ALLOWING AND ESTIMATING CLAIMS

The process of claim satisfaction begins when a creditor, or the debtor on the creditor's behalf, files with the bankruptcy court a "proof of claim" under §501. Once filed, the claim is deemed "allowed" unless a "party in interest" with respect to the claim, usually the debtor, objects to allowance. See §502(a). If a party in interest does object, then the court must decide whether or in what amount to allow the claim. See §502(b), (c). Allowance of a claim recognizes the creditor's right to share in the assets of the estate. At the end of the bankruptcy process a debtor's assets, or interests in those assets, are distributed to holders of allowed claims. Assume that the estate is worth $5,000 and ten creditors file proofs of claim that total $10,000. If all the claims are allowed and enjoy the same priority, each creditor will be paid fifty cents on the dollar. That is, each creditor will be paid half of her allowed claim.

When a debtor objects to a proof of claim, §502(b)(1) provides, in general, that a court is to allow the claim "in lawful currency of the United States as of the date of the filing of the [bankruptcy] petition, ... except to the extent that such claim is unenforceable against the debtor and property of the debtor, under any agreement or applicable law for a reason other than because such claim is contingent or unmatured." This provision embodies simple principles. If an obligation is owed under applicable nonbankruptcy law, a claim is generally allowed. If no obligation is owed, a claim is not generally allowed. If an obligation would be allowed, but for the fact that it has not had time to accrue, a claim is allowed for the unaccrued obligation. So, for example, if the principal on a loan is not due until five years after the filing of the petition, that principal, though unmatured, would nevertheless constitute an allowed claim in the bankruptcy case. In essence, then, the Bankruptcy Code treats a petition for bankruptcy as a notional default on all obligations, which are deemed to be due immediately and are allowed accordingly.

The general rule has exceptions, which are enumerated in §502(b)(2)-(9). By virtue of these provisions, certain claims are disallowed even if they are valid under applicable nonbankruptcy law. For example, a divorced parent's future child support obligations are unmatured claims that are not discharged in bankruptcy. Section 502(b)(5) provides that this kind of unmatured, nondischargeable obligation is not allowed. So long as the debtor can be counted on to meet the obligation in full later, one might argue, there is no reason to give the child a portion of the bankruptcy estate. Also, a claim may be disallowed if a proof of claim is not filed in a timely fashion. See §502(b)(9). This rule rests upon a different rationale: Any process must have deadlines.

Other exceptions are harder to explain. For example, the Bankruptcy Code disallows claims for unmatured interest. See §502(b)(2). Were it not for this prohibition, a creditor might seek allowance not only for principal and matured interest on a loan, but also for the anticipated interest payments it would enjoy. The creditor might have a claim based on anticipated interest payments if the interest rate under the loan agreement was higher than the rate the creditor could earn were the debtor to repay, and the creditor to reinvest principal on the day of the bankruptcy petition. In defense of interest claim disallowance, the legislative history offers an "irrebuttable presumption" that the rate of interest on every obligation is equal to the appropriate discount rate for the obligation. Congress understood that, in reality, a contractual interest rate could differ from the applicable discount (i.e., reinvestment) rate, but this approach simplifies matters and may be justified, given that in the mine-run of cases the claims greatly exceed the debtor's unencumbered assets. The exercises below illustrate the effects of interest-rate variation.

In another deviation from the general rule of claim allowance, the Code places caps on a lessor's and an employee's claim for damages from breach of a real estate lease and an employment contract, respectively. See §502(b)(6), (7). The history of these provisions suggests that damage awards in such cases are hard to measure. But it would seem that imposing a cap would make sense only if damage awards were systematically high. If awards are merely highly variable, a cap leads to an undervaluation of such awards, and a consequent underallowance, in the aggregate.

Also, the 2005 Bankruptcy Act contains a number of provisions designed to assure that consumer debtors receive adequate financial counseling before they file a bankruptcy petition. Related to this effort, new §502(k) provides that the court may reduce by up to 20% the allowed amount of an unsecured, dischargeable consumer debt about which the creditor would not negotiate after an approved credit-counseling agency proposed an alternative repayment schedule on behalf of the debtor.

These exceptions notwithstanding, in most instances, the fundamental principles of claim allowance hold. Even so, basic principles are sometimes difficult to apply. The first two cases below, as well as the related notes and problems, ask you to consider issues raised by the process of claim allowance. The Supreme Court's opinion in *Raleigh* shows how claims in bankruptcy are understood by reference to substantive nonbankruptcy law. *Bittner* presents a court's attempt to estimate the value of a claim that is intractably uncertain at the time of bankruptcy. In the third case below, *Robins*, the court disallows a claim for punitive damages on equitable grounds, even though the court lacks explicit statutory authority to do so.

Key Provisions: Bankruptcy Code §502(b), (c)

EXERCISES

5B(1) Bank loans Debtor $1 million to be repaid in ten annual installments of $100,000, plus accrued interest at the annual rate of 10 percent on the unpaid amount. The first payment comes due at the end of this year. Debtor files a petition in bankruptcy. For what amount should Bank file a claim? Would your answer be different if, between the time of the loan and the time of bankruptcy, market conditions changed so that a similar loan to another borrower would have an interest rate of 5 percent? If you were to draft the relevant provision of the Bankruptcy Code, would you permit the amount of Bank's allowed claim to vary with market conditions? Would your last answer change if most debtors had many debt obligations that bore approximately (though not exactly) the same interest rate?

5B(2) Debtor sells a zero-coupon bond to Bank. A zero-coupon bond, sometimes called an original-issue-discount or OID bond, is an obligation issued at a discount from its face amount to be paid in the future. The purchaser's only compensation for the price of such a bond is the difference between the face amount and the purchase price. That is, the bond promises no periodic payments prior to maturity. The particular bond that Debtor sells Bank promises the holder $1 million in ten years. Bank pays $400,000 for the bond. A year after Debtor issues the bond, Debtor files a petition in bankruptcy. For what amount should Bank file a claim? Does your answer depend on whether market conditions have changed so that Bank would have to pay $600,000 for a similar bond issued by another seller? If you were to draft the relevant provision of the Bankruptcy Code, would you permit the amount of Bank's allowed claim to vary with market conditions?

5B(3) Debtor purchases a computer from Retailer for no cash but promises to pay Retailer $1,000 within two years. The sales contract provides for no reduction in price if Debtor pays early. One year after the purchase, Debtor files a petition in bankruptcy. For what amount should Retailer file a claim? Would your answer depend on how much Retailer would have charged Debtor for an all-cash sale at the time of the purchase?

CASES

RALEIGH v. ILLINOIS DEPARTMENT OF REVENUE

Supreme Court of the United States, 2000
530 U.S. 15

JUSTICE SOUTER DELIVERED THE OPINION OF THE COURT.

The question raised here is who bears the burden of proof on a tax claim in bankruptcy court when the substantive law creating the tax obligation puts the burden on the taxpayer (in this case, the trustee in bankruptcy). * * *

The issue of state tax liability in question had its genesis in the purchase of an airplane by Chandler Enterprises, Inc., a now-defunct Illinois company. William J. Stoecker, for whom petitioner Raleigh is the trustee in bankruptcy, was president of Chandler in 1988, when Chandler entered into a lease-purchase agreement for the plane, moved it to Illinois, and ultimately took title under the agreement.

According to respondent State Department of Revenue, the transaction was subject to the Illinois use tax, a sales-tax substitute imposed on Illinois residents such as Chandler who buy out of State. If the seller does not remit the tax, the buyer must, and, when buying a plane, must file a return and pay the tax within 30 days after the aircraft enters the State. Chandler failed to do this. * * *

Illinois law ... provides that any corporate officer "who has the control, supervision or responsibility of filing returns and making payment of the amount of any ... tax ... who willfully fails to file the return or make the payment ... shall be personally liable for a penalty equal to the total amount of tax unpaid by the [corporation]." The department determines the amount, and its determination is "prima facie evidence of a penalty due," though a Notice of Penalty Liability issued under this provision is open to challenge much like the antecedent Notice of Tax Liability. * * *

The record evidence about Chandler's operations is minimal. ... This evidentiary dearth is not necessarily dispositive, however, due to the provision of Illinois law shifting the burden of proof, both on production and persuasion, to the responsible officer once a Notice of Penalty Liability is issued. * * *

[T]he Court of Appeals held that the burden remained on the trustee, just as it would have been on the taxpayer had the proceedings taken place outside of bankruptcy. * * *

Creditors' entitlements in bankruptcy arise in the first instance from the underlying substantive law creating the debtor's obligation, subject to any qualifying or contrary provisions of the Bankruptcy Code. See Butner v. United States, 440 U.S. 48, 55 (1979). The "basic federal rule" in bankruptcy is that state law governs the substance of claims, Congress having "generally left the determination of property rights in the assets of a bankrupt's estate to state law." Id. at 54. "Unless some federal interest requires a different result, there is no reason why [the state] interests should be analyzed differently simply because an interested party is involved in a bankruptcy proceeding." Id. at 55. In this case, the bankruptcy estate's obligation to the Illinois

Department of Revenue is established by that State's tax code, which puts the burden of proof on the responsible officer of the taxpayer.

The scope of the obligation is the issue here. Do the State's right and the taxpayer's obligation include the burden of proof? Our cases point to an affirmative answer. Given its importance to the outcome of cases, we have long held the burden of proof to be a "substantive" aspect of a claim. That is, the burden of proof is an essential element of the claim itself; one who asserts a claim is entitled to the burden of proof that normally comes with it.

Tax law is no candidate for exception from this general rule, for the very fact that the burden of proof has often been placed on the taxpayer indicates how critical the burden rule is, and reflects several compelling rationales: the vital interest of the government in acquiring its lifeblood, revenue; the taxpayer's readier access to the relevant information; and the importance of encouraging voluntary compliance by giving taxpayers incentives to self-report and to keep adequate records in case of dispute. These are powerful justifications not to be disregarded lightly.

Congress of course may do what it likes with entitlements in bankruptcy, but there is no sign that Congress meant to alter the burdens of production and persuasion on tax claims. The Code in several places, to be sure, establishes particular burdens of proof. But the Code makes no provision for altering the burden on a tax claim, and its silence says that no change was intended.

The trustee looks for an advantage in the very silence of the Code, however, first by arguing that actual, historical practice favored trustees under the Bankruptcy Act of 1898 and various pre-Code revisions up to the current Code's enactment in 1978. He says that courts operating in the days of the Bankruptcy Act, which was silent on the burden to prove the validity of claims, almost uniformly placed the burden on those seeking a share of the bankruptcy estate. Because the Code generally incorporates pre-Code practice in the absence of explicit revision, the argument goes, and because the Code is silent here, we should follow the pre-Code practice even when this would reverse the burden imposed outside bankruptcy. This tradition makes sense, petitioner urges, because in bankruptcy tax authorities are no longer opposed to the original taxpayer, and the choice is no longer merely whether the tax claim is paid but whether other innocent creditors must share the bankruptcy estate with the taxing government.

We, however, find history less availing to the trustee than he says. While some pre-Code cases put the burden of proof on taxing authorities, others put it on the trustee, and still others cannot be fathomed. This state of things is the end of the argument, for without the weight of solid authority on the trustee's side, we cannot treat the Code as predicated on an alteration of the substantive law of obligations once a taxpayer enters bankruptcy.

The trustee makes a different appeal to Code silence ... suggesting that "allowance" of claims is a federal matter. [The] burden-of-proof rule in question here bears only on validity, and "[w]hat claims of creditors are valid and subsisting obligation ... is to be determined by reference to state law." [Vanston Bondholders Protective Comm. v. Green, 329 U.S. 156, 161 (1946).] While it is true that federal law has generally evolved to impose the same procedural requirements for claim submission on tax authorities as on other creditors, nothing in that evolution has touched the underlying laws on the elements sufficient to prove a valid state claim.

Finally, the trustee argues that the Code-mandated priority enjoyed by taxing authorities over other creditors, see §507(a), requires a compensating equality of treatment when it comes to demonstrating validity of claims. But we think his argument distorts the legitimate powers of a bankruptcy court and begs the question about the relevant principle of equality.

Bankruptcy courts do indeed have some equitable powers to adjust rights between creditors. ... But the scope of a bankruptcy court's equitable power must be understood in the light of the principle of bankruptcy law discussed already, that the validity of a claim is generally a function of underlying substantive law. Bankruptcy courts are not authorized in the name of equity to make wholesale substitution of underlying law controlling the validity of creditors' entitlements, but are limited to what the Bankruptcy Code itself provides.

Moreover, even on the assumption that a bankruptcy court were to have a free hand, the case for a rule placing the burden of proof uniformly on all bankruptcy creditors is not self-evidently justified by the trustee's invocation of equality. Certainly the trustee has not shown that equal treatment of all bankruptcy creditors in proving debts is more compelling than equal treatment of comparable creditors in and out of bankruptcy. ... Consider the case when tax litigation is pending at the time the taxpayer files for bankruptcy. The tax litigation will be subject to an automatic stay, but the stay can be lifted by the bankruptcy court for cause, see §362(d)(1) ... . If the bankruptcy court exercises its discretion to lift the stay, the burden of proof will be on the taxpayer in the pre-existing tax litigation, and a tax liability determination will be final. See §505(a)(2)(A). We see no reason that Congress would have intended the burden of proof (and consequent vindication of this trustee's vision of equality) to depend on whether tax authorities have initiated proceedings against a debtor before a bankruptcy filing. Thus, the uncertainty and increased complexity that would be generated by the trustee's position is another reason to stick with the simpler rule, that ... the burden of proof on a tax claim in bankruptcy remains where the substantive tax law puts it.

The judgment of the Court of Appeals is affirmed. * * *

BITTNER v. BORNE CHEMICAL CO.

United States Court of Appeals, Third Circuit, 1982
691 F.2d 134

GIBBONS, CIRCUIT JUDGE.

Stockholders of The Rolfite Company appeal from the judgment of the district court, affirming the decision of the bankruptcy court to assign a zero value to their claims in the reorganization proceedings of Borne Chemical Company, Inc. (Borne) under Chapter 11 of the Bankruptcy Code. [W]e affirm.

I

Prior to filing its voluntary petition under Chapter 11 of the Code, Borne commenced a state court action against Rolfite for the alleged pirating of trade secrets and proprietary information from Borne. The Rolfite Company filed a counterclaim, alleging, inter alia, that Borne had tortiously interfered with a proposed merger between Rolfite and the Quaker Chemical Corporation (Quaker) by unilaterally terminating a contract to manufacture Rolfite products and by bringing its suit. Sometime after Borne filed its Chapter 11 petition, the Rolfite stockholders sought relief from the automatic stay so that the state court proceedings might be continued. Borne then filed a motion to disallow temporarily the Rolfite claims until they were finally liquidated in the state court. The bankruptcy court lifted the automatic stay but also granted Borne's motion to disallow temporarily the claims, extending the time within which such claims could be filed and allowed if they should be eventually liquidated.

Upon denial of their motion to stay the hearing on confirmation of Borne's reorganization plan, the Rolfite stockholders appealed to the district court, which vacated the temporary disallowance order and directed the bankruptcy court to hold an estimation hearing. The parties agreed to establish guidelines for the submission of evidence at the hearing, and, in accordance with this agreement, the bankruptcy court relied on the parties' choice of relevant pleadings and other documents related to the state court litigation, and on briefs and oral argument. After weighing the evidence, the court assigned a zero value to the Rolfite claims and reinstated its earlier order to disallow temporarily the claims until such time as they might be liquidated in the state court, in effect requiring a waiver of discharge of the Rolfite claims from Borne. Upon appeal, the district court affirmed.

II

Section 502(c) of the Code provides:

There shall be estimated for purposes of allowance under this section—

(1) any contingent or unliquidated claim, fixing or liquidation of which, as the case may be, would unduly delay the closing of the case ... .[*]

The Code, the Rules of Bankruptcy Procedure, and the Suggested Interim Bankruptcy Rules, are silent as to the manner in which contingent or unliquidated claims are to be estimated. Despite the lack of express direction on the matter, we are persuaded that Congress intended the procedure to be undertaken initially by the bankruptcy judges, using whatever method is best suited to the particular contingencies at issue. The principal consideration must be an accommodation to the underlying purposes of the Code. It is conceivable that in rare and unusual cases arbitration or even a jury trial on all or some of the issues may be necessary to obtain a reasonably accurate evaluation of the claims ... . Such methods, however, usually will run counter to the efficient administration of the bankrupt's estate and where there is sufficient evidence on which to base a reasonable estimate of the claim, the bankruptcy judge should determine the value. In so doing, the court is bound by the legal rules which may govern the ultimate value of the claim. For example, when the claim is based on an alleged breach of contract, the court must estimate its worth in

---

[*] Reworded slightly in 1984.—EDS.

accordance with accepted contract law.... However, there are no other limitations on the court's authority to evaluate the claim save those general principles which should inform all decisions made pursuant to the Code.

In reviewing the method by which a bankruptcy court has ascertained the value of a claim under §502(c)(1), an appellate court may only reverse if the bankruptcy court has abused its discretion. That standard of review is narrow. The appellate court must defer to the congressional intent to accord wide latitude to the decisions of the tribunal in question. Section 502(c)(1) of the Code embodies Congress' determination that the bankruptcy courts are better equipped to evaluate the evidence supporting a particular claim within the context of a particular bankruptcy proceeding ... .

According to the Rolfite stockholders, the estimate which §502(c)(1) requires is the present value of the probability that appellants will be successful in their state court action. Thus, if the bankruptcy court should determine as of this date that the Rolfite stockholders' case is not supported by a preponderance or 51 percent of the evidence but merely by 40 percent, they apparently would be entitled to have 40 percent of their claims allowed during the reorganization proceedings, subject to modification if and when the claims are liquidated in state court. The Rolfite stockholders contend that instead of estimating their claims in this manner, the bankruptcy court assessed the ultimate merits and, believing that they could not establish their case by a preponderance of the evidence, valued the claims at zero.

We note first that the bankruptcy court did not explicitly draw the distinction that the Rolfite stockholders make. Assuming however that the bankruptcy court did estimate their claims according to their ultimate merits rather than the present value of the probability that they would succeed in their state court action, we cannot find that such a valuation method is an abuse of the discretion conferred by §502(c)(1).

The validity of this estimation must be determined in light of the policy underlying reorganization proceedings. In Chapter 11 of the Code, Congress addressed the complex issues which are raised when a corporation faces mounting financial problems.

> The modern corporation is a complex and multi-faceted entity. Most corporations do not have a significant market share of the lines of business in which they compete. The success, and even the

survival, of a corporation in contemporary markets depends on three elements: First, the ability to attract and hold skilled management; second, the ability to obtain credit; and third, the corporation's ability to project to the public an image of vitality . . .

One cannot overemphasize the advantages of speed and simplicity to both creditors and debtors. Chapter XI allows a debtor to negotiate a plan outside of court and, having reached a settlement with a majority in number and amount of each class of creditors, permits the debtor to bind all unsecured creditors to the terms of the arrangement. From the perspective of creditors, early confirmation of a plan of arrangement: first, generally reduces administrative expenses which have priority over the claims of unsecured creditors; second, permits creditors to receive prompt distributions on their claims with respect to which interest does not accrue after the filing date; and third, increases the ultimate recovery on creditor claims by minimizing the adverse effect on the business which often accompanies efforts to operate an enterprise under the protection of the Bankruptcy Act.

124 Cong. Rec. H11101-H11102 (daily ed. Sept. 28, 1978) (statement of Rep. D. Edwards of California, floor manager for bankruptcy legislation in the House of Representatives). Thus, in order to realize the goals of Chapter 11, a reorganization must be accomplished quickly and efficiently.

If the bankruptcy court estimated the value of the Rolfite stockholders' claims according to the ultimate merits of their state court action, such a valuation method is not inconsistent with the principles which imbue Chapter 11. Those claims are contingent[5] and unliquidated. According to the bankruptcy court's findings of fact, the Rolfite stockholders' chances of ultimately succeeding in the state court action are uncertain at best. Yet, if the court had valued the Rolfite stockholders' claims according to the present probability of success, the Rolfite stockholders might well have acquired a significant, if not controlling, voice in the reorganization proceedings. The interests of those creditors with liquidated claims would have been subject to the Rolfite interests, despite the fact that the state court might ultimately decide against those interests after the reorganization. The bankruptcy court may well have decided that such a situa-

---

[5] The Rolfite stockholders assert that the claims are not contingent since they are not dependent on some future event which may never occur. In as much as the very existence of the claims in the reorganization proceeding is dependent on a favorable decision by the state court, the Rolfite stockholders are clearly mistaken.

tion would at best unduly complicate the reorganization proceedings
and at worst undermine Borne's attempts to rehabilitate its business
and preserve its assets for the benefit of its creditors and employees.
By valuing the ultimate merits of the Rolfite stockholders' claims at
zero, and temporarily disallowing them until the final resolution of the
state action, the bankruptcy court avoided the possibility of a protracted and inequitable reorganization proceeding while ensuring that
Borne will be responsible to pay a dividend on the claims in the event
that the state court decides in the Rolfite stockholders' favor.[8] Such a
solution is consistent with the Chapter 11 concerns of speed and simplicity but does not deprive the Rolfite stockholders of the right to
recover on their contingent claims against Borne.[9]

III

The Rolfite stockholders further contend that, regardless of the
method which the bankruptcy court used to value their claims, the
court based its estimation on incorrect findings of fact. [A]n appellate
court [may] overturn ... findings of fact only when they are clearly
erroneous .... A bankruptcy court may not, however, mask its interpretation of the law as findings of fact. In determining the legal merits
of a case on which claims such as those of the Rolfite stockholders are
based, the bankruptcy court should be guided by the applicable state
law. The determination of such law is of course subject to plenary review ... .

The Rolfite stockholders argue that in assessing the merits of its
state court action for the purpose of evaluating their claims against
Borne, the bankruptcy court erred both in finding the facts and in ap-

---

[8] While the "equitable considerations" referred to by the bankruptcy court
could have properly influenced the method of evaluation of the claims chosen by
the court, they would not have permitted the court to evaluate as zero claims which
in fact have a higher value under the method of evaluation chosen by the bankruptcy
court. But because we find that the bankruptcy court did not err in its evaluation of
the claims, the error, if any, in the court's references to "equitable considerations"
as buttressing its decision would not affect the outcome.

[9] The Rolfite stockholders apparently contend that in barring them from voting
on the reorganization plan, the bankruptcy court deprived them of a property right
without due process of law. Congress has given the bankruptcy courts broad discretion to estimate a claim pursuant to §502(c)(1). As classic economic regulation, the
federal bankruptcy laws need only be supportable on a rational basis to survive substantive due process challenges ... . A bankruptcy court's discretion to treat a contingent, unliquidated claim as did the court here is undoubtedly rationally related to
the legitimate governmental interests expressed in Chapter 11.

plying the law. In reviewing the record according to the standards we have just described, we cannot agree … .

The court's ultimate finding of fact—that the Rolfite stockholders' claims in the reorganization proceeding were worth zero—must also be upheld since it too is not clearly erroneous. The subsidiary findings of the court plainly indicated that the Rolfite counterclaim in the state action lacked legal merit. Faced with only the remote possibility that the state court would find otherwise, the bankruptcy court correctly valued the claims at zero. On the basis of the court's subsidiary findings, such an estimation was consistent both with the claims' present value and with the court's assessment of the ultimate merits. * * *

IN RE A.H. ROBINS CO.

United States District Court, E.D. Virginia, 1988
89 Bankr. 555

MERHIGE, DISTRICT JUDGE.

The matter before the Court addresses the issue as to the propriety of allowing a claim for punitive damages to women who were allegedly injured by the Dalkon Shield intrauterine device ("Dalkon Shield," "IUD") within the context of this Chapter 11 bankruptcy proceeding … .

A.H. Robins Company, Incorporated ("Robins," "the Company," "the Debtor," "Debtor-in-Possession"), a Richmond based corporation that engages in, inter alia, the research, development, manufacture, and marketing of pharmaceuticals and consumer products, acquired the exclusive rights to the Dalkon Shield intrauterine device ("Dalkon Shield," "IUD") from the Dalkon Corporation on June 12, 1970. From that date forward Robins was the sole manufacturer, producer and distributor of the Dalkon Shield in the United States and abroad. Statistics reflect that, from the time Robins acquired the rights to the Shield in June of 1970 until it was removed from the market in June of 1974, approximately 2.2 million were sold. These sales generated gross revenues for the Company in the amount of $11,240,611 and gross profits in the amount of $505,499.

Although the Dalkon Shield was invented and marketed as the newest and safest method of birth control for women, its use resulted in both slight and serious injuries to many of its users as well as inflicting compensable injury to certain individuals related in some degree to a user. In short, what was initially viewed as a safe product became, in some instances, a product of debilitation to many innocent victims. Women who had worn the shield suffered from injuries as slight as discomfort to as serious as pelvic inflammatory disease, ectopic pregnancy, septic abortion and worse. Commencing in 1971, injured parties began to file claims against the Company for both compensatory and punitive damages. By the time Robins filed its petition for relief under Chapter 11, the Company had settled 9,238 claims for approximately $530,000,000. Despite these settlements, Robins, at the time it filed for relief, still faced over five thousand pending cases in state and federal court.

While the litigation against the Company was slow to start, by 1985 an average in excess of seventy (70) cases per week were being filed. These claims against the Company usually sought both compensatory and punitive relief. While the Company was able, to a certain extent, to assess monetarily its compensatory liability, it was unable to estimate the punitive aspect of the claims.

In 1981, in an effort to gain some control over the punitive damages awards, the Company supported certification of a nationwide class action in the United States District Court for the Northern District of California. The District Court, Judge Spencer Williams presiding, granted class certification on the ground that there was a limited fund available to these claimants: claims against the manufacturer exceeded $3 billion and manufacturers assets were presumed to be much less. On appeal, the United States Court of Appeals for the Ninth Circuit vacated Judge Williams' certification, holding that it was erroneous to certify a nationwide class of punitive damages claimants because, amongst other reasons, no effort had been made to make a preliminary fact finding inquiry concerning actual assets, insurance settlement experience and exposure. Nor was any evidence adduced as to the likelihood of Robins being capable or incapable of responding to punitive damages. Additionally, the court concluded that the requirement that a class action be superior to other means of adjudication had not been satisfied.

Having failed to certify a class for punitive damages purposes, Robins was forced to deal with those claims on a case-by-case basis. Prior to its filing for Chapter 11 relief, approximately $13,227,000 in punitive damages were awarded and satisfied as a result of only seven judgments. Notwithstanding these awards, there were over $7,000,000 in punitive damages awarded that were pending appeal when the debtor filed for relief. Robins also had settled, prior to its filing for relief, two awards of punitive damages, in the total amount of $3,438,210.

The Company's punitive damage exposure was staggering. Moreover, it was unpredictable. By the time the Company filed its petition, punitive awards had run from as little as $5 in *Carley v. A.H. Robins Company* to as much as $7,500,000 in *Tetuan v. A.H. Robins Company*. The *Tetuan* award, which was at the time of filing on appeal, had been collateralized prior to Robins filing under Chapter 11 and was, upon affirmance, satisfied.

The Company's liability arising out of these Dalkon Shield claims caused a critical depletion of the Company's operating funds. By June of 1985, the Company's unrestricted funds were estimated to be $5 million. Robins' financial picture had become so bleak that financial institutions were unwilling to lend it money. With only $5 million in unrestricted funds and the inability to secure commercial financing, it appears that Robins had no choice but to file for relief under Chapter 11.

When this issue first arose, the parties disagreed over whether punitive damages should be allowed in this Chapter 11. The Dalkon Shield Claimants Committee ("Claimants Committee") argued that claimants should be able to recover punitive damages from Robins based on the Company's history of egregious conduct. The Committee for Future Tort Claimants ("Futures") argued that, while punitives are allowable, they should, nevertheless, be subordinated to all other general unsecured claims. While these parties have since joined in supporting a consensual plan of reorganization, the Court views their former positions as representative of the relatively few dissenting claimants.

The remaining parties in interest, the Official Committee of Unsecured Creditors ("Unsecured Creditors"), the Official Committee of Equity Security Holders ("Equity Committee") and Robins all argue for the disallowance of punitive damages. The Unsecured Creditors present three alternative positions. First, they argue that §502(b)(1) of the Code proscribes the award of punitive damages because such an award would be contrary to the laws of some states. Second, the Unsecured Creditors argue that the Court has the power to disallow punitive damages under the Court's general equity powers, and, since such an award would preclude a successful reorganization of the Company, they should be disallowed. Finally, the Unsecured Creditors argue that if punitive damages are not disallowed, they should, at a minimum, be subordinated to all other general unsecured claims pursuant to §510(c).

Robins and the Equity Committee argue similar positions. Their view is that prior to Robins' filing for Chapter 11, the Company had satisfied over $13,225,000 in punitive damages awards. Such a substantial expenditure of money, they argue, served any and all remedial purposes which could justify an award of punitive damages. They also argue that any further punitive damages award would preclude a successful reorganization of the Company, and accordingly should be disallowed by the Court under the general equity powers of the Code.

While the Court acknowledges counsels' views regarding the plight of a Company that is exposed to multiple punitive damage verdicts based on the manufacture of one unfortunate product, the Court deems it inappropriate to base its ultimate decision to disallow punitive damages on that rationale alone. Instead, the Court will invoke its equitable power to disallow punitive damages other than the sums allocated "in lieu of punitive damages" as called for in the Debtor's Sixth Amended and Restated Plan of Reorganization.[2] Coupled with this invocation of its equitable powers is the Court's conclusion that there is a firm statutory basis for precluding claims for punitive damages. It is this Court's conclusion that if the Company is to be given an opportunity to reorganize, it cannot be liable for any claim for punitive damages in the traditional sense.

Section 502 provides the statutory framework for the allowance of claims in a Chapter 11 proceeding. Pursuant to §502(a), all claims are deemed "allowed" unless objected to by a party in interest. There are, of course, exceptions to this general rule of allowability, and these exceptions are found in §502(b). In pertinent part, §502(b) provides:

> Except as provided in subsections (e)(2), (f), (g), (h) and (i) of this section, if such objection to a claim is made, the court, after notice and a hearing, shall determine the amount of such claim in lawful currency of the United States as of the date of the filing of the petition, and shall allow such claim in such amount, except to the extent that—

---

[2] Under the Debtor's Sixth Amended and Restated Plan of Reorganization, any funds remaining in the claimants' trust after the compensatory damage claims are satisfied will be distributed proportionally to the claimants in lieu of punitive damages.

(1) such claim is unenforceable against the debtor and property of the debtor, under any agreement or applicable law for a reason other than because such claim is contingent or unmatured.

The Unsecured Creditors argue that §502(b)(1) works to disallow punitive damages in this case. The Unsecured Creditors argue that "any further award of punitive damages with respect to the Dalkon Shield would be contrary to applicable law and hence subject to disallowance, inasmuch as no legitimate purpose can any longer be served by the award of punitive damages." * * *

While the Unsecured Creditors' argument seems plausible on the surface, the Court finds that its position is premised on assumptions which are not properly assumable. The Unsecured Creditors assume that an award for punitive damages has only two purposes: (1) to punish the defendant, and (2) to deter future wrongdoing. Once identifying the two purposes for awarding punitive damages, the Unsecured Creditors argue that these purposes have been served and any further award would only be multitudinous punishment. It is the Unsecured Creditors' position that since the Company had already expended more money in satisfaction of punitive damages awards than it had received from gross receipts of the sale of the Dalkon Shield, and because these staggering awards had driven the company into bankruptcy, the Company had been punished enough. Additionally, they reason that any further award of punitive damages could not deter the Company from any future wrongful conduct, contending that the substantial awards have already served that purpose.

While the premise of the Unsecured Creditors' position follows the majority view for awarding punitive damages, there are still a minority of states that ascribe to a different philosophy. For example, some states award punitive damages for compensatory purposes. Others award punitive damages for the recovery of attorneys fees. While these differences might, at first blush, seem insignificant, they are important in this case due to the state law derivation of each of the bodily injury claims. Thus, while the Unsecured Creditors' application of §502(b)(1) might justify the disallowance of punitive damages in some states, it certainly would not justify disallowance in all states. Moreover, the Unsecured Creditors' position on punitive damage awards is a highly controversial position, and one that has not, to date, been endorsed and upheld by any jurisdiction as a reason for disallowing, or precluding, multiple punitive damages awards against a defendant for the manufacture of one defective product. Numerous law review articles have been written on whether the Eighth Amendment's prohibition against cruel and unusual punishment is violated by successive awards for punitive damages. However, albeit these purely academic discussions, there has been no resolve of the issue.

Accordingly, a request by the Unsecured Creditors that this Court disallow an award of punitive damages because it would be contrary to state law would be an invitation to commit judicial error. The Court will decline the invitation. * * *

While §502 provides the statutory framework for the allowance of a claim, its provisions do not circumscribe the general equity powers of a court exercising bankruptcy jurisdiction. In the past, bankruptcy courts have resorted to their equitable powers to determine whether a claim will be allowable. This practice, while developed within the framework of the Bankruptcy Act, is deeply entrenched in judicial precedent and is relied on by courts today in the interpretation of the provisions of the Bankruptcy Code.

In Pepper v. Litton, 308 U.S. 295 (1939), the United States Supreme Court was faced with the determination of whether a valid state court judgment could be disallowed in a bankruptcy proceeding. The Court held that in passing on an allowance of claims, the court sits as a court of equity. Consequently, the court has far-reaching powers to "sift the circumstances surrounding any claim to see that injustice or unfairness is not done in administration of the bankrupt estate." Pepper v. Litton, 308 U.S. at 308.

The principles of Pepper v. Litton were later relied on by the Court in Heiser v. Woodruff, 327 U.S. 726 (1945). In *Heiser,* the Court once again was faced with a valid state court judgment which was being challenged within the bankruptcy. The Court held that:

> In passing upon and rejecting or allowing the proof of claim in this case, the court of bankruptcy proceeds—not without appropriate regard for rights acquired under state law—under federal statutes which govern the proof and allowance of claims based on judgments. In determining what judgments are provable and what objections may be made to their proof, and in determining the extent to which the inequitable conduct of a claimant in acquiring or asserting his claim in bankruptcy, requires its rejection or its subordination to other claims which, in other respects, are of the same class, the bankruptcy court is defining and applying federal, not state, law.

327 U.S. at 732.

The different principles underlying the determination of a valid state court judgment and the determination of the allowability of a claim in bankruptcy was further explained by the Court in Vanston Bondholders Protective Committee v. Green, 329 U.S. 156 (1946). In *Vanston,* the Court was presented with the issue of whether a claim for interest on interest would be allowable in a reorganization under Chapter X of the Bankruptcy Act. Without deciding whether the interest would have been recoverable in state court, the Supreme Court held the claim in bankruptcy properly disallowable. The Court explained as follows:

> [B]ankruptcy courts must administer and enforce the Bankruptcy Act as interpreted by this Court in accordance with authority granted by Congress to determine how and what claims should be allowed under equitable principles. And we think an allowance of interest on interest under the circumstances shown by this case would not be in accord with the equitable principles governing bankruptcy distributions.

329 U.S. at 162-63. In his concurring opinion in *Vanston,* Justice Frankfurter clarified the courts' power to disallow a claim in stating that:

> [I]n the proper adjustment of the rights of creditors and the desire to rehabilitate the debtor, Congress under its bankruptcy power may authorize its courts to refuse to allow existing debts to be proven. It may do so, for instance, where the recognition of such claims would undermine the fair administration of a debtor's estate.

329 U.S. at 169-70 (Frankfurter, J., concurring).

While the Court acknowledges that these opinions were written in the earlier part of the 1900s when the Bankruptcy Act was the controlling rule of law, the underlying principles of these cases are equally applicable to the present governing law, the Bankruptcy Code. The extraordinary ability of a court to invoke equity as not only a source of remedial relief, but also as a source of judicial power, is as prevalent under the Code as it was under the Act. See §105(a). Accordingly, this Court finds the equitable principles and powers expressed in *Pepper, Heiser,* and *Vanston* to be as applicable to problems arising under the Code, as those which arose under the Act.

Equity provides this Court the power to disallow punitive damages if the Court determines that such an allowance would frustrate the successful reorganization of the Company. It is this Court's finding that punitive damages must be disallowed if Robins is to be given the opportunity provided under Chapter 11 to successfully reorganize and function as a viable entity.

In this case, as in any case, punitive damages cannot be estimated. As Robins stated in its Brief, the award of punitive damages has a wild card characteristic—within six weeks, two separate juries returned punitive damages verdicts against the Company in the divergent amounts of $7.5 million in *Tetuan v. A.H. Robins Company* (May 3, 1985) and $5 in the case styled *Carley v. A.H. Robins Company* (June 12, 1985). This unknown liability would destroy the ability of Robins to reorganize because the impossibility of estimating a liability of the Company renders compliance with numerous provisions of the Bankruptcy Code virtually impossible.

For example, unless confirmation of the plan were to await the liquidation of each and every Dalkon Shield claim, it was necessary for the Court, as it did, to estimate those compensatory claims so that sufficient funds could be allocated in any plan to fully and fairly compensate those to whom the Debtor was legally liable. Indeed, the circumstances of this case were such that a realistic effort to effectuate a sale or a merger at the highest price was extremely doubtful unless and until a prospective principal could be reasonably assured that it could participate in any reorganization with both the knowledge of and its capability of fulfilling its ultimate financial responsibility. The presence of a "wild card" in the form of punitive damages would constitute the death knell of any feasible reorganization plan. See §502(c). In addition, in order for a Chapter 11 plan to be confirmed, the Court must make a determination as to its feasibility, i.e., that confirmation is not likely to be followed by liquidation or the need for further financial reorganization. See §1129(a)(11). Once again, the inability to quantify the potential amount of Robins' liabilities for punitive damages claims would make it virtually impossible for this Court to have determined whether Robins would be capable of meeting its obligations under the plan. It would be similarly difficult for the Court to determine whether the "best interest of the creditors" test of §1129(a)(7) had been met or, in the event any class had rejected the plan, whether the elements of cramdown under §1129(b)(2)(B) could have been satisfied. Given the unquantifiable nature of punitive damage claims, it is also unlikely that a disclosure statement which meets the "adequate information" standard of Section 1125 could have been provided to creditors in order to enable them to vote the now approved plan … .

While it has been argued that, instead of disallowing the claims entirely, the Court should subordinate all punitive damages claims pursuant to §510(c), this Court refuses to follow that option. While subordination may, in some cases, work as a solution to an otherwise inequitable distribution of assets, it would not serve any such purpose in the instant case.

In *Johns-Manville,* the court refused to subordinate punitive damage claims as an alternative solution to complete disallowance ... . While recognizing its statutory authority to subordinate some claims to others, the court concluded that it would be improper to do so in that proceeding. The court reasoned that "whether or not punitive damages are recoverable in bankruptcy, it is well within the authority of this court to disallow a claim for punitive damages, in the circumstances of this case, where allowing such a claim would ill serve the policy of such awards." [In re Johns-Manville Corp., 68 Bankr. 618, 627-28 (Bankr. S.D.N.Y. 1986), aff'd, 78 Bankr. 407 (S.D.N.Y. 1987), aff'd, 843 F.2d 636 (2d Cir. 1988).]

Like *Johns-Manville,* this Court would not be furthering any purpose of an award of punitive damages if it were to subordinate such a claim. Moreover, the problems this Court would face if it were to allow an award of punitive damages, would not be resolved through a subordination. It is the Court's view that subordination would merely postpone what would otherwise be an unfair treatment of claimants. Instead, the plan provides that any remaining funds in the initial trust, after the payment of all eligible compensatory damage claims, will be distributed proportionally in lieu of punitive damages.

Once a thriving, vibrant, and vital corporation, Robins has now, because of its production of the Shield, relegated its Fortune 500 position on Wall Street to debtor-in-possession in a Chapter 11 reorganization in federal court in Richmond, Virginia. The Debtor having now chosen Chapter 11 as a method by which it can satisfy all its debts and thus "start afresh," the Court will not, by sanctioning windfall damages, thwart this realistic goal to reorganize. Disallowance of punitive damages protects those women who have suffered from the Dalkon Shield; absent the looming spectre of punitives, a trust has been established which will, if managed and maintained as contemplated by the Court as expressed in its opinion finding that the Plan was feasible, provide them full and fair compensatory relief. If punitives were allowed, compensation to the women who filed the claims and to other creditors of the debtor would be manifestly jeopardized.

This Court would not be fulfilling its duties in the oversight of this bankruptcy if it were to allow a windfall claim to certain creditors that could jeopardize the full compensation of claims to all others. For these reasons the Court finds it imperative to disallow all punitive damage claims in this bankruptcy.

An appropriate order has issued.

NOTES

5B.1. The *Raleigh* opinion is, by its own terms, a specific application of the *Butner* principle, according to which nonbankruptcy law should determine any question in bankruptcy unless the Bankruptcy Code specifies otherwise or there is some bankruptcy reason to deviate from otherwise applicable law. As the Court notes, there is no particular reason for the burden of proof to be different inside bankruptcy. So even though the Code is silent on the question of burden, the answer is clear.

5B.2. Section 502(c) states that a bankruptcy court may estimate claims "for the purposes of allowance." The estimation may be for substantially more than simple allowance, however. Indeed, if no other determination is later made (and the Bankruptcy Code requires none), the "estimated" claim becomes the basis for payment and discharge. At least that is ordinarily the case. In *Bittner*, the court disallows the Rolfite claims but also "requir[es] a waiver of discharge" of those claims. Despite the disallowance, then, the Rolfite stockholders are free to advance their claims against the reorganized Borne Chemical. If Borne emerges from reorganization with a capital structure such that it was able to satisfy any Rolfite claim, it is hard to imagine a *legitimate* purpose for the Rolfite objection. One might conclude, therefore, that the Rolfite stockholders do not hold legitimate claims, but a desire for undue influence. If this conclusion is correct, the bankruptcy court's combination of disallowance and waiver of discharge neatly dispatches an officious interloper.

5B.3. The Rolfite stockholders argued that the bankruptcy court should estimate their probability of success and discount their claim accordingly. The appellate court, however, took a different view. It held that the bankruptcy court was entitled to assess the merits of the case before it. In other words, an "estimation" is simply a minitrial on the merits, not a probabilistic assessment of the plaintiff's chances. If the process of such estimation is sufficient to be a "notice and hearing" required by Bankruptcy Code §502(b) for a final determination of allowance, then the Rolfite shareholders have had all the process to which they are entitled. So long as it conforms to basic notions of due process, there is much to be said for a bankruptcy process that is simple and swift. Under this view, the court's approach would be justified even if the Rolfite shareholders' claims were discharged. It is a way of meting out rough justice. Those who are likely to fail lose, while those who are likely to prevail win.

The Rolfite shareholders' argument, put in stronger terms, is that an "estimation" is not a minitrial, but rather an abbreviated process that discounts all claims to their expected value. Consider the merits of this approach in addition to whether it is a more literal interpretation of the statutory language. We return to this issue in the problems below.

5B.4. The court in *A.H. Robins* concludes that it "would not be fulfilling its duties in the oversight of this bankruptcy if it were to allow a windfall claim to certain creditors that could jeopardize the full compensation of claims to all others." In *Robins*, however, the reorganization plan proposed a $700 million distribution to shareholders. It is possible, therefore, that disallowance of claims for punitive damages benefited not other creditors, but the shareholders. Because shareholders controlled the firm while it sold the Dalkon Shield, one could argue that the shareholders should have borne the burden of the punitive damages, which are designed to discourage a party's irresponsible behavior.

PROBLEMS

5B-1. Assume the same facts as in Exercise 5A(2), and assume further that Buyer has a claim in bankruptcy. How and in what amount should the court estimate or allow Buyer's claim? In answering this question, it may help to consider how one values an option to purchase a share of stock at a specified date in the future at a specified price. How, if at all, does an estimate or allowance of Buyer's claim differ from the valuation of such an option?

5B-2. Debtor is a hospital that faces a number of malpractice claims over the course of a year. Each gives rise to the same amount in damages, but each involves a different doctor and a different procedure. Each case revolves around its own set of facts, and the facts never become clear until there is a full dress trial. The hospital wins more cases than it loses, but quite a few claims succeed. (Over the past decade, the hospital has lost, on average, 40 percent of the claims filed against it.) After Debtor files for bankruptcy, one hundred patients file malpractice claims. These claims seem indistinguishable from the ordinary malpractice cases usually brought against the hospital. In other words, before the trial takes place and the facts are developed, each patient has about a 40 percent chance of prevailing. If we look at each claim in isolation, we would say that, more likely than not, the patient will lose. But we know that if they all went to trial, the hospital would lose about forty of these cases. How should we estimate each claim for purposes of the bankruptcy? Would your answer be different if all one hundred claims arose from administering the same drug for the same illness?

C. SECURED CLAIMS

Put simply, secured credit is a loan supported by a contingent property interest. Outside of bankruptcy, default on the loan satisfies the contingency and triggers the creditor's right to take the property the debtor has pledged as collateral. The creditor then conducts a foreclosure sale. If the proceeds from the sale are greater than the outstanding loan, the creditor remits the excess. If the proceeds from the sale are less than the outstanding loan, the creditor maintains a claim against the debtor for the deficiency. Section 554 allows the bankruptcy trustee to abandon collateral, thereby permitting a secured creditor to take the assets by foreclosing under state law. The secured creditor may participate in the bankruptcy process for the difference between the amount it realizes on foreclosure and the amount it is owed. Unless the secured creditor agrees otherwise at the time of the loan, that creditor possesses all the rights of an unsecured creditor. Collateral gives a creditor extra rights. Thus, to the extent its collateral falls short of repaying the loan in full, the secured creditor participates in the bankruptcy process as the holder of an unsecured claim.

A trustee may not wish to abandon collateral, however. She may instead intend the debtor to keep the property as part of a reorganization or adjustment of the debtor's obligations. Where the debtor is to retain the collateral, bankruptcy law provides a procedure that substitutes for a foreclosure sale's valuation of property. Section 506(a) of the Code instructs the bankruptcy court to value a creditor's interest in the property and to designate the creditor's claim a "secured claim to the extent of the value of such creditor's interest." Any remaining claim amount is designated an "unsecured claim." The same process separates into secured and unsecured portions any claim held by someone who enjoys a setoff right. In the most common case, the debtor maintains a deposit account at a bank from which it has borrowed money. The bank has the ability under nonbankruptcy law to "set off" against the loan whatever is in the account. The Bankruptcy Code treats the portion of a claim subject to a setoff right as a secured claim and the balance as an unsecured claim. If, for example, the bank had lent the debtor $300 and the debtor has $100 in its account, the Bankruptcy Code gives the bank a secured claim for $100 and an unsecured claim for $200.

Secured claims, so defined, are granted special protection under other provisions of the Code, discussed elsewhere, and unsecured claims, so defined, are treated as ordinary general obligations. In broad strokes, then, the bifurcation process of §506(a) mimics the state law process of foreclosure sale. In either case, the secured creditor is to receive the full value of her collateral and then share in the debtor's other assets to the extent that the collateral's value is less than the creditor's claim.

Though straightforward on its face, this general description of the claim bifurcation process belies its real world complexity. Assume, for now, that collateral valuation and thus bifurcation of an allowed secured claim will occur at the outset of the bankruptcy process, at the same time the claim itself is allowed. A court must decide how to value the collateral. This is not a simple task. The secured creditor will argue for a high valuation (and thus a large share of the reorganized debtor), while the debtor's other creditors, represented by the trustee, will argue for a low valuation. If the judge will not allow the sale of the collateral, she must settle this conflict and estimate the value. But value *to whom*? The debtor? The secured creditor? A hypothetical arm's-length purchaser? After the exercises dispose of easier cases, *Associates Commercial Corp. v. Rash* addresses this issue. *Rash* deals with an individual debtor who files a bankruptcy petition under Chapter 13, but the Code provision in question, §506(a), applies equally in Chapter 11 reorganizations. As the related notes explain, the result in *Rash* has been codified by the 2005 Bankruptcy Act and, in the *Till* decision, there is more recent Supreme Court precedent on the collateral valuation question. But as the related Problem illustrates, it remains important to master the fundamental question addressed by *Rash*.

Key Provision: Bankruptcy Code §506(a)

EXERCISES

5C(1) When Debtor files for bankruptcy it owns GreenAcre, which is worth $100,000 subject to two duly perfected mortgages. Bank's mortgage supports a note on which Debtor owes $75,000. Finance Company's mortgage supports a note on which Debtor owes $50,000. Bank's mortgage has priority. What are the amounts of Bank's and Finance Company's secured and unsecured claims?

5C(2) When Debtor files for bankruptcy, he owes Bank $10,000 and has a savings account at Bank with a balance of $7,000. Under applicable nonbankruptcy law, Bank has a right to set off the savings account against the loan. What are the amounts of Bank's secured and unsecured claims?

5C(3) When Debtor files for Bankruptcy under Chapter 11, she owns WhiteAcre, a parcel of unimproved real estate. The land is subject to a mortgage, which supports an unpaid $100,000 note. A week after Debtor's bankruptcy petition, the court accurately values WhiteAcre at $85,000. Three years later, after Debtor's bankruptcy is converted to Chapter 7 and the estate is liquidated, WhiteAcre has declined in value to $70,000. What is the amount of Bank's secured claim? Consider this question again after you have read chapter 9, section B below.

CASE

ASSOCIATES COMMERCIAL CORP. v. RASH

United States Supreme Court, 1997
520 U.S. 953

JUSTICE GINSBURG DELIVERED THE OPINION OF THE COURT.

We resolve in this case a dispute concerning the proper application of §506(a) of the Bankruptcy Code when a bankrupt debtor has exercised the "cramdown" option for which §1325(a)(5)(B) provides. Specifically, when a debtor, over a secured creditor's objection, seeks to retain and use the creditor's collateral in a Chapter 13 plan, is the value of the collateral to be determined by (1) what the secured creditor could obtain through foreclosure sale of the property (the "foreclosure-value" standard); (2) what the debtor would have to pay for comparable property (the "replacement-value" standard); or (3) the midpoint between these two measurements? We hold that §506(a) directs application of the replacement-value standard.

I

In 1989, respondent Elray Rash purchased for $73,700 a Kenworth tractor truck for use in his freight-hauling business. Rash made a down payment on the truck, agreed to pay the seller the remainder in 60 monthly installments, and pledged the truck as collateral on the unpaid balance. The seller assigned the loan, and its lien on the truck, to petitioner Associates Commercial Corporation (ACC).

In March 1992, Elray and Jean Rash filed a joint petition and a repayment plan under Chapter 13. At the time of the bankruptcy filing, the balance owed to ACC on the truck loan was $41,171. Because it held a valid lien on the truck, ACC was listed in the bankruptcy petition as a creditor holding a secured claim. Under the Code, ACC's claim for the balance owed on the truck was secured only to the extent of the value of the collateral; its claim over and above the value of the truck was unsecured. See §506(a). To qualify for confirmation under Chapter 13, the Rashes' plan had to satisfy the requirements set forth in §1325(a) of the Code. The Rashes' treatment of ACC's secured claim, in particular, is governed by subsection (a)(5). Under this provision, a plan's proposed treatment of secured claims can be confirmed if one of three conditions is satisfied: the secured creditor accepts the plan; the debtor surrenders the property securing the claim to the creditor; or the debtor invokes the so-called "cramdown" power. Under the cramdown option, the debtor is permitted to keep the property over the objection of the creditor; the creditor retains the lien securing the claim, and the debtor is required to provide the creditor with payments, over the life of the plan, that will total the present value of the allowed secured claim, i.e., the present value of the collateral. The value of the allowed secured claim is governed by §506(a).

The Rashes' Chapter 13 plan invoked the cramdown power. It proposed that the Rashes retain the truck for use in the freight-hauling business and pay ACC, over 58 months, an amount equal to the present value of the truck. That value, the Rashes' petition alleged, was $28,500. ACC objected to the plan and asked the Bankruptcy Court to lift the automatic stay so ACC could repossess the truck. ACC also filed a proof of claim alleging that its claim was fully secured in the amount of $41,171. The Rashes filed an objection to ACC's claim.

The Bankruptcy Court held an evidentiary hearing to resolve the dispute over the truck's value. At the hearing, ACC and the Rashes urged different valuation benchmarks. ACC maintained that the proper valuation was the price the Rashes would have to pay to purchase a like vehicle, an amount ACC's expert estimated to be $41,000. The Rashes, however, maintained that the proper valuation was the net amount ACC would realize upon foreclosure and sale of the collateral, an amount their expert estimated to be $31,875. The Bankruptcy Court agreed with the Rashes and fixed the amount of ACC's secured claim at $31,875; that sum, the court found, was the net amount ACC would realize if it exercised its right to repossess and sell the truck. * * * A panel of the Court of Appeals for the Fifth Circuit reversed. In re Rash, 31 F.3d 325 (1994). On rehearing en banc, however, the Fifth Circuit affirmed the District Court, holding that ACC's allowed secured claim was limited to $31,875, the net foreclosure value of the truck. In re Rash, 90 F.3d 1036 (1996). * * *

II

The Bankruptcy Code provision central to the resolution of this case is §506(a), which states:

> An allowed claim of a creditor secured by a lien on property in which the estate has an interest … is a secured claim to the extent of the value of such creditor's interest in the estate's interest in such property, … and is an unsecured claim to the extent that the value of such creditor's interest … is less than the amount of such allowed claim. Such value shall be determined in light of the purpose of the valuation and of the proposed disposition or use of such property … .

§506(a). Over ACC's objection, the Rashes' repayment plan proposed, pursuant to §1325(a)(5)(B), continued use of the property in question, i.e., the truck, in the debtor's trade or business. In such a "cramdown" case, we hold, the value of the property (and thus the amount of the secured claim under §506(a)) is the price a willing buyer in the debtor's trade, business, or situation would pay to obtain like property from a willing seller.

Rejecting this replacement-value standard, and selecting instead the typically lower foreclosure-value standard, the Fifth Circuit trained its attention on the first sentence of §506(a). In particular, the Fifth Circuit relied on these first sentence words: a claim is secured "to the extent of the value of such *creditor's interest* in the estate's interest in such property." See 90 F.3d at 1044 (citing §506(a)) (emphasis added). The Fifth Circuit read this phrase to instruct that the "starting point for the valuation [is] what the creditor could realize if it sold the estate's interest in the property according to the security agreement," namely, through "repossessing and selling the collateral." 90 F.3d at 1044.

We do not find in the … words—"the creditor's interest in the estate's interest in such property"—the foreclosure-value meaning advanced by the Fifth Circuit. Even read in isolation, the phrase imparts no valuation standard: A direction simply to consider the "value of such creditor's interest" does not expressly reveal how that interest is to be valued. Reading the first sentence of §506(a) as a whole, we are satisfied that the phrase the Fifth Circuit considered key is not an instruction to equate a "creditor's interest" with the net value a creditor could realize through a foreclosure sale. The first sentence, in its entirety, tells us that a secured creditor's claim is to be divided into secured and unsecured portions, with the secured portion of the claim limited to the value of the collateral. To separate the secured from the unsecured portion of a claim, a court must compare the creditor's claim to the value of "such property," i.e., the collateral. That comparison is sometimes complicated. A debtor may own only a part interest in the property pledged as collateral, in which case the court will be required to ascertain the "estate's interest" in the collateral. Or, a creditor may hold a junior or subordinate lien, which would require the court to ascertain the creditor's interest in the collateral. The §506(a) phrase referring to the "creditor's interest in the estate's interest in such property" thus recognizes that a court may encounter, and in such instances must evaluate, limited or partial interests in collateral. The full first sentence of §506(a), in short, tells a court what it must evaluate, but it does not say more; it is not enlightening on how to value collateral.

The second sentence of §506(a) does speak to the how question. "Such value," that sentence provides, "shall be determined in light of the purpose of the valuation and of the proposed disposition or use of such property." §506(a). By deriving a foreclosure-value standard from §506(a)'s first sentence, the Fifth Circuit rendered inconsequential the sentence that expressly addresses how "value shall be determined." As we comprehend §506(a), the "proposed disposition or use" of the collateral is of paramount importance to the valuation question. If a secured creditor does not accept a debtor's Chapter 13 plan, the debtor has two options for handling allowed secured claims: surrender the collateral to the creditor; or, under the cramdown option, keep the collateral over the creditor's objection and provide the creditor, over the life of the plan, with the equivalent of the present value of the collateral. The "disposition or use" of the collateral thus turns on the alternative the debtor chooses—in one case the collateral will be surrendered to the creditor, and in the other, the collateral will be retained and used by the debtor. Applying a foreclosure-value standard when the cramdown option is invoked attributes no significance to the different consequences of the debtor's choice to surrender the property or retain it. A replacement-value standard, on the other hand, distinguishes retention from surrender and renders meaningful the key words "disposition or use."

Tying valuation to the actual "disposition or use" of the property points away from a foreclosure-value standard when a Chapter 13 debtor, invoking cramdown power, retains and uses the property. Under that option, foreclosure is averted by the debtor's choice and over the creditor's objection. From the creditor's perspective as well as the debtor's, surrender and retention are not equivalent acts.

When a debtor surrenders the property, a creditor obtains it immediately, and is free to sell it and reinvest the proceeds. We recall here that ACC sought that very advantage. If a debtor keeps the property and continues to use it, the creditor obtains at once neither the property nor its value and is exposed to double risks: The debtor may again default and the property may deteriorate from extended use. Adjustments in the interest rate and secured creditor demands for more "adequate protection," do not fully offset these risks. Of prime significance, the replacement-value standard accurately gauges the debtor's "use" of the property .... The debtor in this case elected to use the collateral to generate an income stream. That actual use, rather than a foreclosure sale that will not take place, is the proper guide under a prescription hinged to the property's "disposition or use."

The Fifth Circuit considered the replacement-value standard disrespectful of state law, which permits the secured creditor to sell the collateral, thereby obtaining its net foreclosure value "and nothing more." See 90 F.3d at 1044. In allowing Chapter 13 debtors to retain and use collateral over the objection of secured creditors, however, the Bankruptcy Code has reshaped debtor and creditor rights in marked departure from state law. The Code's cramdown option displaces a secured creditor's state-law right to obtain immediate foreclosure upon a debtor's default. That change, ordered by federal law, is attended by a direction that courts look to the "proposed disposition or use" of the collateral in determining its value. It no more disrupts state law to make "disposition or use" the guide for valuation than to authorize the rearrangement of rights the cramdown power entails. Nor are we persuaded that the split-the-difference approach adopted by the Seventh Circuit provides the appropriate solution. See In re Hoskins, [102 F.3d 311, 316 (7th Cir. 1996)]. Whatever the attractiveness of a standard that picks the midpoint between foreclosure and replacement values, there is no warrant for it in the Code. Section 506(a) calls for the value the property possesses in light of the "disposition or use" in fact "proposed," not the various dispositions or uses that might have been proposed. The Seventh Circuit rested on the "economics of the situation," In re Hoskins, 102 F.3d at 316, only after concluding that the statute suggests no particular valuation method. We agree with the Seventh Circuit that "a simple rule of valuation is needed" to serve the interests of predictability and uniformity. Id. at 314. We conclude, however, that §506(a) supplies a governing instruction less complex than the Seventh Circuit's "make two valuations, then split the difference" formulation.

In sum, under §506(a), the value of property retained because the debtor has exercised the §1325(a)(5)(B) "cramdown" option is the cost the debtor would incur to obtain a like asset for the same "proposed ... use."[6] * * *

JUSTICE STEVENS, DISSENTING.

Although the meaning of §506(a) is not entirely clear, I think its text points to foreclosure as the proper method of valuation in this case. The first sentence in §506(a) tells courts to determine the value of the "*creditor's* interest in the estate's interest" in the property. This language suggests that the value should be determined from the creditor's perspective, i.e., what the collateral is worth, on the open market, in the creditor's hands, rather than in the hands of another party.

---

[6] Our recognition that the replacement-value standard, not the foreclosure-value standard, governs in cramdown cases leaves to bankruptcy courts, as triers of fact, identification of the best way of ascertaining replacement value on the basis of the evidence presented. Whether replacement value is the equivalent of retail value, wholesale value, or some other value will depend on the type of debtor and the nature of the property. We note, however, that replacement value, in this context, should not include certain items. For example, where the proper measure of the replacement value of a vehicle is its retail value, an adjustment to that value may be necessary: A creditor should not receive portions of the retail price, if any, that reflect the value of items the debtor does not receive when he retains his vehicle, items such as warranties, inventory storage, and reconditioning. Nor should the creditor gain from modifications to the property—e.g., the addition of accessories to a vehicle—to which a creditor's lien would not extend under state law.

The second sentence explains that "such value shall be determined in light of the purpose of the valuation and of the proposed disposition or use of such property." In this context, the "purpose of the valuation" is determined by §1325(a)(5)(B). Commonly known as the Code's "cramdown" provision, this section authorizes the debtor to keep secured property over the creditor's objections in a Chapter 13 reorganization, but, if he elects to do so, directs the debtor to pay the creditor the "value" of the secured claim. The "purpose" of this provision, and hence of the valuation under §506(a), is to put the creditor in the same shoes as if he were able to exercise his lien and foreclose.[*]

It is crucial to keep in mind that §506(a) is a provision that applies throughout the various chapters of the Bankruptcy Code; it is, in other words, a "utility" provision that operates in many different contexts. Even if the words "proposed disposition or use" did not gain special meaning in the cramdown context, this would not render them surplusage because they have operational significance in their many other Code applications. In this context, I also think the foreclosure standard best comports with economic reality. Allowing any more than the foreclosure value simply grants a general windfall to under-secured creditors at the expense of unsecured creditors. Cf. In re Hoskins, 102 F.3d 311, 320 (7th Cir. 1996) (Easterbrook, concurring in judgment). As Judge Easterbrook explained in rejecting the split-the-difference approach as a general rule, a foreclosure-value standard is also consistent with the larger statutory scheme by keeping the respective recoveries of secured and unsecured creditors the same throughout the various bankruptcy chapters.

Accordingly, I respectfully dissent.

---

[*] The Court states that "surrender and retention are not equivalent acts" from the creditor's perspective because he does not receive the property and is exposed to the risk of default and deterioration. I disagree. That the creditor does not receive the property is irrelevant because, as §1325(a)(5)(B)(ii) directs, he receives the present value of his security interest. Present value includes both the underlying value and the time-value of that interest. The time value component similarly vitiates the risk concern. Higher risk uses of money must pay a higher premium to offset the same opportunity cost. In this case, for instance, the creditor was receiving nine percent interest, well over the prevailing rate for an essentially risk-free loan, such as a United States Treasury Bond. Finally, the concern with deterioration is addressed by another provision of the Code, §361, which authorizes the creditor to demand "adequate protection," including increased payments, to offset any derogation of his security interest during a cramdown.

NOTES

5C.1. In essence, the *Rash* Court has to decide whether "value" in §506(a) means value to the debtor or value to the creditor. The tractor truck in *Rash* likely had no subjective value to the debtor, as might a piece of jewelry or an antique that the debtor inherited and then borrowed against when faced with hard times. Hence, the value of collateral to the debtor was simply the debtor's cost of replacement, presumably a retail price. The value of collateral to the creditor is the amount the creditor would receive in a foreclosure sale, presumably a lower, wholesale price. The difference between retail and wholesale price reflects the costs to transfer a product from a wholesaler, such as an auto warehouse, to a consumer, such as the purchaser of a single vehicle. Outside of bankruptcy, the excess of retail over wholesale price would compensate a retailer for such costs, and would not go to the secured creditor.

As a matter of policy, Justice Stevens believes that bankruptcy should not enhance a secured creditor's position. He thus concludes in dissent that the purpose of a §506(a) valuation is "to put the creditor in the same shoes as if he were able to exercise his lien and foreclose." Because the Court, unlike Justice Stevens, feels compelled by the language of the provision to adopt replacement valuation, the Court offers no competing policy justification for its decision. Consider whether such justification exists.

5C.2. The 2005 Bankruptcy Act codifies, and clarifies, the opinion in *Rash*. New §506(a)(2) provides that for a debtor who is an individual in a case under Chapter 7 or 13, the value of a creditor's interest in the estate's interest in personal property shall be determined based on the replacement value of the property as of the date of the filing of the bankruptcy petition without deduction for costs of sale or marketing. The provision goes on, somewhat redundantly, to explain that with respect to property purchased for personal, family, or household purposes, replacement value means the price a retail merchant would charge for property of that kind considering the age and condition of the property at the time the value is determined. Thus, Congress has effectively negated *Rash*'s footnote 6, which suggested that items such as "inventory storage" might be deducted from the valuation. Note, however, that the new language applies narrowly and does not address a corporate debtor or any debtor in Chapter 11 and does not apply to real property.

5C.3. Related to the treatment in *Rash* of a secured creditor's claim is the Supreme Court's decision in Till v. SCS Credit Corp., 541 U.S. 465 (2004). In *Till*, a creditor with a claim secured by the debtor's truck objected to the interest rate it was to be paid under a Chapter 13 plan. In a plurality opinion written by Justice Stevens, the Court began by observing that Bankruptcy Code §1325(a)(5) requires that a plan provide an allowed, secured claim both a continuing lien to secure the claim and a promise of future payments with a present value, as of the date of the plan, not less than the allowed amount of the claim. In this case, because the allowed secured claim was $4,000, the payments promised under the plan would have to be worth an immediate payment of $4,000. The dispute in the case was over the method by which a court should set an interest rate on the $4,000 principal such that the promised payments were worth that amount. All agreed that the higher the prevailing market rate for risk-free funds, the less and the less stable the value of the collateral, and the higher the debtor's risk of nonpayment, the higher the plan's interest rate must be. Disagreement was over how these factors should be incorporated into the plan's interest rate.

There were four competing methods. The "formula rate" approach begins with the prime rate that banks charge their best customers and then allows for an adjustment to reflect the fact that the Chapter 13 debtor may pose a greater risk of nonpayment than prime borrowers. The "presumptive contract rate" approach begins with contract rate on the loan that gave rise to the secured claim, then allows for an adjustment of that rate if at the time of the plan the debtor is either a better or worse credit risk than at the time of the loan. The "coerced loan" approach sets the interest rate that the secured creditor could have earned by foreclosing on the collateral and reinvesting the proceeds on the market in a new loan equivalent to the one under the plan. The "cost of funds" approach sets the interest rate equal to the rate the debtor would have to pay on the market for the loan under the plan.

The plurality held that the "formula rate" approach is the correct one, at least for Chapter 13 cases, reasoning that the "formula rate" is easier to administer than any of the other approaches. Justice Thomas concurred on the grounds that, in his view, §1325(a)(5) does not require the plan to provide a creditor with payments of a present value equal to its secured claim. Justice Scalia, writing for three other justices, dissented arguing that the Code does require that a plan compensate the creditor for the present value of its claim and contending that the formula rate will not accomplish this end. The dissent believed that the presumptive contract rate approach would be as easy to administer and would yield an interest rate that more accurately reflected the debtor's credit worthiness.

The opinion in *Till* is somewhat mysterious. If properly applied, it seems that each of the four approaches would yield *precisely the same* interest rate, as each is designed to yield a promised income stream of exactly the principal amount of the secured claim, $4,000 in the case at hand. Yet the plurality says that "[e]ach of [the three rejected] approaches is complicated, imposes significant evidentiary costs, and aims to make each individual creditor whole rather than to ensure the debtor's payments have the required present value." 541 U.S. at 477. Yet one wonders what the difference is between making a creditor "whole" and ensuring "the required present value."

This gives rise to a second conundrum from the case, which is that the plurality believes the formula rate approach will be simpler to administer. If, as part of the formula rate approach, a court adequately assesses the value and stability of the collateral and the debtor's credit worthiness so that the adjustment to prime can be made properly, it is difficult to imagine how this approach will be easier to administer than the others. The apparent solution to this puzzle is that a court would not engage in the same inquiry under each approach. Indeed, in *Till* itself, all parties seemed to accept that the formula interest rate would be about half of what the other approaches would yield. It is thus difficult to imagine that the inquiry into the conditions of the particular collateral or debtor will be substantial in the formula approach and this perhaps explains both the different outcome from such approach and why the approach may be easier to administer.

There is perhaps a response to these misgivings about the plurality's analysis. The plurality assumes that credit markets are not competitive. Under this assumption, it is possible that the formula rate would be lower than the presumptive contract rate, the coerced loan rate, or the cost of funds rate. That is, one might imagine that a creditor in the open market could extract a surplus from a debtor with an interest rate that would compensate it more than in full for the principal outstanding, and market rate interest might then seem inappropriate. This is, perhaps, what the plurality means in the passage quoted just above, which describes a difference between making the creditor whole and affording the creditor full compensation for its principal.

Even in a noncompetitive capital market, however, one might argue that the interest rate dictated by the Code is the one that allows a creditor to earn a super-competitive return. This may be so because even a monopolist lender, one who can earn, say, 20% on a $4,000 loan to a moderate risk borrower, would not trade $4,000 for the right to receive 10% on the same principal from the same borrower, and it is hard to understand how equal value of principal and income stream can mean anything other than a creditor's indifference between the two. Thus, the plurality may have good policy reasons for its opinion, though perhaps not sound statutory grounds, a point also made in the dissent. For a deeper policy discussion of *Rash* and *Till*, see Alan Schwartz, Valuation of Collateral in *Bankruptcy Law Stories* 103-116, ed. Rasmussen (Foundation Press, 2007).

5C.5. Since the decisions in *Rash* and *Till* the 2005 Bankruptcy Act modified §1325(a)(5), but not in ways that would affect the reasoning of either opinion. The 2005 Act changes to Chapter 13 are discussed below in chapter 12 of this book.

PROBLEM

5C. Bank holds a duly recorded mortgage on Cornerplot, real estate that serves as a retail outlet for Debtor. Insolvent, Debtor files a Chapter 11 bankruptcy petition. At the time of the bankruptcy, Debtor owes Bank $400,000. Bank and Debtor stipulate that if Debtor were forced to sell Cornerplot to someone other than Bank immediately upon filing the bankruptcy petition, Debtor would receive $200,000 for the property and incur negligible sales costs. The parties also agree that if Debtor held the property unencumbered she could, over the course of a few months and at $30,000 expense, find a buyer who places a high value on the location of this parcel and is willing to pay $300,000 for the property. Finally, all agree that the value of Cornerplot to Debtor's continuing business is $400,000. (Debtor would have to spend that much to buy another parcel and customize it to suit Debtor's business.) Debtor intends to retain Cornerplot after a reorganization plan is confirmed. What is the amount of Bank's secured claim?

VI. THE BANKRUPTCY ESTATE

A bankruptcy process requires both fixing the value of the claims of the creditors and assembling the assets available for distribution to these creditors. The addition of each new claim reduces the relative share of every other claimant, while the addition of each new asset increases everyone's share.

The task of determining what assets are available for claimants —identifying "property of the estate"—begins by identifying the property interests of the debtor that become property of the estate. As we shall see below in chapter 8, the trustee possesses "avoiding powers." These enable the trustee to bring into the estate property that the debtor could not enjoy but that its creditors could reach nevertheless. In this chapter, we focus on property that the estate derives through the trustee's ability to assert the rights of the debtor.

A. THE DEBTOR'S INTEREST IN PROPERTY

The assembled assets of the debtor form what is called an "estate." Under Bankruptcy Code §541(a)(1), this estate comprises all "legal or equitable interests of the debtor in property as of the commencement of the case." Thus, if Debtor is a retail store, the inventory, the equipment, and the building itself (assuming that Debtor owns it) are property of the estate. If Debtor leases a building, the bankruptcy estate consists only of Debtor's interest in the building, namely, its right to use the building during the leasehold. The estate also includes all of Debtor's intangible property, including Debtor's accounts receivable, as well as whatever patents, trade secrets, and copyrights Debtor might own. In addition, the estate includes any proceeds or offspring from property of the estate. As a first approximation, then, the estate is simply any right the debtor enjoys that has value in the debtor's hands at the time of the commencement of the case.

There are some important qualifications when the debtor is an individual. The most important asset of many individual debtors is the ability to earn income. An individual debtor's "earnings from services performed" after the commencement of a bankruptcy case are specifically, though implicitly, excluded from the bankruptcy estate. §541(a)(6). Individual debtors, moreover, may exempt from the reach of creditors some assets that do become property of the estate. See

§522. These assets, called "exempt property," typically serve one of two functions: They may enhance the debtor's ability to earn future income or they may otherwise be thought necessary to make a "fresh start" possible. Exempt property often includes the tools of the debtor's trade and the clothes on the debtor's back.

These exclusions apply *only* to individuals. The future income of a corporation, unlike that of a flesh-and-blood individual, is not excluded from the estate. This follows ineluctably from the decision to include all of a corporation's assets as property of the estate. The assets of a firm, tangible or intangible, cannot be property of the estate if the income they generate were not also property of the estate. A corporation's assets have value only to the extent that they will generate income.

Creditors can look to all of a corporation's future earnings. By contrast, they cannot look to any of a flesh-and-blood individual's future income in Chapter 7 and can expect to reach only some of that income in Chapter 13. This difference is fundamental. An individual who leaves bankruptcy with a "fresh start" cannot be meaningfully equated with a corporation that leaves Chapter 11 with a new capital structure. Because the goals advanced in each case are radically different, the rights of creditors to each type of debtor's assets are fundamentally different.

We shall postpone until our review of individual debtors the analysis of difficulties that may arise in separating the flesh-and-blood person's future income from other assets. You should, nevertheless, be aware from now on of the need to accomplish such separation. The basic idea of the rest of §541(a) is easy to state. If we are dealing with a limited liability corporation, the creditors are entitled to whatever the debtor has, including future income. Section 541 lets the trustee sell the debtor's equipment, collect money owed the debtor, and bring the lawsuits the debtor has against third parties for the benefit of the general creditors. The reason is plain enough. The creditors themselves could have reached these assets if the bankruptcy proceeding had never started. They could have resorted to individual methods of debt collection. There is nothing about the bankruptcy process that justifies limiting the trustee's right to reach these assets. Hence they become property of the estate.

We ask whether something is property of the debtor at all, and, if it is, to what extent. Section 541(a)(1) includes as property of the estate "all legal or equitable interests of the debtor in property as of the commencement of the case." That is, the bankruptcy estate includes all interests of a debtor in property, *not* all of the property in which the debtor has an interest,

It is useful to see exactly how §541 handles a relatively easy case. You take your clothes to the dry cleaner and pay in advance. The dry cleaner, much to your surprise, shuts down and files a Chapter 7 bankruptcy petition. The trustee cannot use §541 to assert that your clothes are now property of the dry cleaner's bankruptcy estate and oppose lifting the automatic stay on those grounds. The debtor does not have any right to your clothes that amounts to more than a negligible "interest in property."

Had the dry cleaner not been paid in advance, it might have a mechanic's lien on the clothes that would allow the trustee to keep the clothes until you paid for the cleaning; that is not the issue here, however, since you paid in advance for the dry cleaning. The debtor cannot keep you from taking the clothes back outside of bankruptcy. Hence, nothing of value in the clothes becomes property of the estate under §541(a)(1). The debtor has no right to the clothes, so the creditors have no rights to the clothes. The debtor's rights define the outer limits of what the trustee can claim under §541(a)(1). If the debtor holds interests in property, then the estate includes those interests, but not more. The debtor's property rights do not increase by happenstance of bankruptcy.

There are, of course, harder cases as well. Consider, for example, an insurance policy. The insurance policy itself belongs to the debtor and is property of the estate. The debtor, however, may not be entitled to the proceeds of the policy outside of bankruptcy. The policy, for example, may provide that the insurance company's obligation runs to the victim of an accident, not to the debtor. If the debtor has no ability to reach these proceeds under nonbankruptcy law, bankruptcy law will not give the debtor this ability. Hence, the proceeds of the insurance are not property of the estate. The victim of the accident, in addition to being a general creditor, may be entitled to pursue the insurance company during or after bankruptcy and to keep the proceeds of the policy rather than sharing them with the other creditors of the debtor.

Another way to conceive of property of the estate under §541 is to imagine that the estate includes property in which the debtor has an interest, but subject to all limitations that are applicable outside of bankruptcy. So, for example, one might say that the insurance policy is property of the estate. But if so, one would hasten to add that the estate's interest in the policy is subject to the limitation that any proceeds from the policy are the beneficiary's property.

This idea rests at the foundation of bankruptcy law and was definitively set out in Chicago Board of Trade v. Johnson, 264 U.S. 1 (1924). In that case, a man named Henderson owned a seat—i.e., a right to do business—on the Chicago Board of Trade. Under the rules of the Board of Trade, members could sell their seats only if they first repaid anything they owed to other members of the Board. Henderson entered bankruptcy with many debts, including debts to members of the Board of Trade. The Supreme Court held that the seat was property of the estate, but that the creditors in bankruptcy could enjoy only what the debtor owned. Because the debtor could not sell the seat without first paying off the other members of the Board, the general creditors could not enjoy the seat free of this encumbrance, either. Hence, the seat came into the estate, but it came subject to the claims of the other members of the Board of Trade. They would be paid first from the proceeds should the bankruptcy trustee decide to sell it.

The principle established by *Chicago Board of Trade*, and codified in §541(a)(1), can be seen as a variant of the *Butner* principle. Bankruptcy law honors nonbankruptcy rights except to the extent that bankruptcy policies require otherwise. The bankruptcy goals of an individual's fresh start or a business recapitalization do not, in the first instance, require that the estate include a greater interest in property than that of the debtor. Section 541(a)(1) has a limited scope accordingly.

Section 541(a), however, creates only the core of the bankruptcy estate. The trustee has the ability to bring additional assets into the estate. The inquiry under §541 is the first of two. Before one can conclude that property is not property of the bankruptcy estate, one also needs to ask whether the property could become property of the estate, not by virtue of the rights of the debtor, but rather by virtue of the trustee's "avoidance" powers.

Property of the debtor subject to an attached, but unperfected, security interest illustrates the point. The property comes into the estate under §541(a)(1) subject to the security interest. Even though it is unperfected, the secured creditor's interest in the collateral is superior to the debtor's. Section 544(a), however, grants the trustee the rights of a hypothetical lien creditor, the same rights that the unsecured creditors—the bankruptcy estate's beneficiaries—might enjoy but for the bankruptcy petition and the automatic stay. Thus, a trustee can avoid and recover for the estate an unperfected security interest in the debtor's property. In other words, the trustee can eliminate the secured creditor's interest in the property because, under applicable nonbankruptcy law, a creditor that reduced its claim to judgment and levied on the property could take it free from such interest.

As we shall see, the avoiding powers are crafted to expand the pool of assets available to the creditors, while at the same time honoring the *Butner* principle. Return to the example of the clothes you leave at the dry cleaner in bankruptcy. As we would expect, the trustee lacks the power to keep the estate using the avoiding powers. Outside of bankruptcy, a levying creditor of the dry cleaner cannot reach the clothes. Because the clothes are beyond the reach of creditors outside of bankruptcy, they do not become property of the estate inside. We examine in chapter 8 below the trustee's §544(a) "strong-arm" power, along with other avoidance powers the trustee may use to enhance the basic bankruptcy estate. For now, understand that, in the main, the avoiding powers translate individual creditor rights to the bankruptcy forum and, in the process, may bring additional property into the bankruptcy estate. See §541(a)(3) or (4).

Section 541(a) contains additional miscellaneous provisions for other augmentations of the bankruptcy estate. Section 541(a)(2) brings into the estate specified interests of the debtor or the debtor's spouse in community property, a provision designed to prevent evasion by one spouse who keeps property in the name of the other. Section 541(a)(5) brings into the estate specified property acquired by an individual debtor within half a year of the bankruptcy petition and on account of another's death or a settlement between the debtor and the debtor's spouse. Section 541(a)(6) brings into the estate property generated by other property of the estate. Section 541(c)(1), the subject of section B below, brings property into the estate notwithstanding limitations on the debtor's interest triggered by the debtor's bankruptcy, insolvency, or weak financial condition.

There are statutory exclusions to property of the estate. Most reside in the express provisions of §541(b). Some of these are straightforward, if arguably unnecessary to state, such as the exclusion of the debtor's power to act on behalf of a third party or of a debtor lessee's interest in an expired nonresidential lease. Other express exclusions are the result of concessions to special interests, such as the exclusion of specified oil and gas interests and, added by the 2005 Bankruptcy Act, the exclusion of specified funds placed in an education individual retirement account or used to purchase tuition credit at least a year before the bankruptcy petition. The 2005 Act also excludes from the estate, for example, tangible personal property in the possession of a licensed lender and pledged to such lender on a nonrecourse basis. In addition to the §541(b) exclusions, §541(c)(2) effectively keeps out of the estate a debtor's beneficial interest in a so-called spendthrift trust, created to prevent alienation by the beneficiary.

Our primary focus here is on the first of the trustee's estate building tools, §541(a)(1). The exercises below ask you to work through some mechanics of §541(a), mainly of §541(a)(1). The cases below, *Begier* and *LTV*, as well as the related notes and problems, further explore how courts follow the §541(a)(1) mandate to separate interests of the debtor from interests of others.

In *Begier*, the debtor was required to withhold wages owed employees and place them in a segregated trust account before turning them over to the IRS. The debtor failed to maintain such account and used money from a general account instead just before it filed a bankruptcy petition. As we shall see in chapter 8, section D below, such a payment is a voidable preference under Bankruptcy Code §547 and can be recovered by the trustee, but only if the source of the payment is property that belongs to the debtor. The beneficial interest another holds in a trust is not property of the debtor and hence does not become property of the estate. See §541(d). The IRS argues that it can retain the payment, despite the preference rules, because the money in the general account was still held by the debtor in trust. The Internal Revenue Code provides for a constructive if not actual trust of all funds "collected or withheld" by the debtor. The question before the Court, then, is whether funds never segregated by a debtor can be characterized as subject to a constructive trust. The case therefore raises the more general question of how bankruptcy law responds when nonbankruptcy law treats property in the possession of a debtor as held in "constructive" trust for the benefit of others. "Constructive" trusts most often arise when people act fraudulently, and those who perpetrate frauds are not strangers to bankruptcy court.

In *LTV*, the debtor steel corporation created special subsidiary with a single purpose, to facilitate what has become known as structured finance. In a typical structured finance arrangement, the debtor transfers to a subsidiary the debtor's inventory or receivables, then has the subsidiary borrow, on a secured basis, from a bank that becomes the subsidiary's only creditor. The debtor has the subsidiary distribute to the debtor the loan proceeds, which the debtor uses in its operations. The transaction, structured as a sale, is designed to be "bankruptcy remote." That is, the lender is able to realize on the inventory and receivables even in the event that the debtor files for bankruptcy. The automatic stay does not apply, as the inventory no longer belongs to the debtor—at least if the transaction is deemed a true sale—and the subsidiary never files for bankruptcy. *LTV* raises the question of whether bankruptcy law should upset such structures.

Key Provision: Bankruptcy Code §541(a)

EXERCISES

6A(1) Debtor owns a half-interest in an oil well that is Debtor's sole source of income. Debtor files for bankruptcy. Does the well become property of the estate?

6A(2) Debtor attended medical school, graduated, and set up practice. Debtor has both a medical degree and a license to practice medicine. When Debtor was divorced, the divorce court held that the medical degree and license to practice were "property" and subject to "equitable distribution" in the divorce. The divorce court concluded that the license and medical degree had a "current value" of $300,000. The court awarded Debtor's spouse 20 percent of this amount, payable in semiannual installments over the next six years. Debtor files for bankruptcy. Are Debtor's medical degree and license to practice property of the estate under §541? Consider this exercise again after you have read chapters 10 and 11 below.

6A(3) Debtor's husband of twenty years dies in January. Under the will that he wrote fifteen years before, he leaves everything he has to his mother and nothing to his wife. Under state law, Debtor may, if she files the appropriate document within six months of her husband's death, elect to take one-third of his estate, notwithstanding the will. Debtor files a bankruptcy petition in April. Should the trustee be able to compel Debtor to exercise her right to a share of her husband's estate?

CASES

BEGIER v. INTERNAL REVENUE SERVICE

Supreme Court of the United States, 1990
496 U.S. 53

JUSTICE MARSHALL DELIVERED THE OPINION OF THE COURT.

This case presents the question whether a trustee in bankruptcy
may "avoid" (i.e., recover) from the Internal Revenue Service payments of certain withholding and excise taxes that the debtor made
before it filed for bankruptcy. We hold that the funds paid here were
not the property of the debtor prior to payment; instead, they were
held in trust by the debtor for the IRS. We accordingly conclude that
the trustee may not recover the funds.

American International Airways, Inc., was a commercial airline.
As an employer, AIA was required to withhold federal income taxes
and to collect Federal Insurance Contributions Act taxes from its employees' wages. 26 U.S.C. §3402(a) (income taxes); §3102(a) (FICA
taxes). As an airline, it was required to collect excise taxes from its
customers for payment to the IRS. §4291. Because the amount of
these taxes is "held to be a special fund in trust for the United States,"
§7501, they are often called "trust-fund taxes." By early 1984, AIA
had fallen behind in its payments of its trust-fund taxes to the Government. In February of that year, the IRS ordered AIA to deposit all
trust-fund taxes it collected thereafter into a separate bank account.
AIA established the account, but did not deposit funds sufficient to
cover the entire amount of its trust-fund tax obligations. It nonetheless
remained current on these obligations through June 1984, paying the
IRS $695,000 from the separate bank account and $946,434 from its
general operating funds. AIA and the IRS agreed that all of these
payments would be allocated to specific trust-fund tax obligations.

On July 19, 1984, AIA petitioned for relief from its creditors under Chapter 11 of the Bankruptcy Code .... AIA unsuccessfully operated as a debtor in possession for three months. Accordingly, on
September 19, the Bankruptcy Court appointed petitioner Harry P.
Begier trustee and converted the case to a Chapter 7 liquidation .... .
Among the powers of a Chapter 7 trustee is the power under §547(b)
to avoid certain payments made by the debtor that would "enabl[e] a
creditor to receive payment of a greater percentage of his claim
against the debtor than he would have received if the transfer had not
been made and he had participated in the distribution of the assets of

the bankrupt estate." H.R. Rep. No. 95-595, p. 177 (1977). Seeking to exercise his avoidance power, Begier filed an adversary action against the Government to recover the entire amount that AIA had paid the IRS for trust-fund taxes during the 90 days before the bankruptcy filing.

The Bankruptcy Court found for the Government in part and for the trustee in part .... It refused to permit the trustee to recover any of the money AIA had paid out of the separate account on the theory that AIA had held that money in trust for the IRS .... It allowed the trustee to avoid most of the payments that AIA had made out of its general accounts, however, holding that "only where a tax trust fund is actually established by the debtor and the taxing authority is able to trace funds segregated by the debtor in a trust account established for the purpose of paying the taxes in question would we conclude that such funds are not property of the debtor's estate." ... The District Court affirmed. ... On appeal by the Government, the Third Circuit reversed, holding that *any* prepetition payment of trust-fund taxes is a payment of funds that are not the debtor's property and that such a payment is therefore not an avoidable preference. * * *

We affirm.

Equality of distribution among creditors is a central policy of the Bankruptcy Code. According to that policy, creditors of equal priority should receive pro rata shares of the debtor's property. See, e.g., §726(b) .... Section 547(b) furthers this policy by permitting a trustee in bankruptcy to avoid certain preferential payments made before the debtor files for bankruptcy. This mechanism prevents the debtor from favoring one creditor over others by transferring property shortly before filing for bankruptcy. Of course, if the debtor transfers property that would not have been available for distribution to his creditors in a bankruptcy proceeding, the policy behind the avoidance power is not implicated. The reach of §547(b)'s avoidance power is therefore limited to transfers of "property of the debtor."

The Bankruptcy Code does not define "property of the debtor." Because the purpose of the avoidance provision is to preserve the property includable within the bankruptcy estate—the property available for distribution to creditors—"property of the debtor" subject to the preferential transfer provision is best understood as that property that would have been part of the estate had it not been transferred before the commencement of bankruptcy proceedings. For guidance, then, we must turn to §541, which delineates the scope of "property of the estate" and serves as the postpetition analog to §547(b)'s "property of the debtor."

Section 541(a)(1) provides that the "property of the estate" includes "all legal or equitable interests of the debtor in property as of the commencement of the case." Section 541(d) provides:

> Property in which the debtor holds, as of the commencement of the case, only legal title and not an equitable interest ... becomes property of the estate under subsection (a) of this section only to the extent of the debtor's legal title to such property, but not to the extent of any equitable interest in such property that the debtor does not hold.

Because the debtor does not own an equitable interest in property he holds in trust for another, that interest is not "property of the estate." Nor is such an equitable interest "property of the debtor" for purposes of §547(b). As the parties agree, then, the issue in this case is whether the money AIA transferred from its general operating accounts to the IRS was property that AIA had held in trust for the IRS.

We begin with the language of 26 U.S.C. §7501, the Internal Revenue Code's trust-fund tax provision: "Whenever any person is required to collect or withhold any internal revenue tax from any other person and to pay over such tax to the United States, the amount of tax so collected or withheld shall be held to be a special fund in trust for the United States." The statutory trust extends, then, only to "the amount of tax so collected or withheld." Begier argues that a trust-fund tax is not "collected or withheld" until specific funds are either sent to the IRS with the relevant return or placed in a segregated fund. AIA neither put the funds paid from its general operating accounts in a separate account nor paid them to the IRS before the beginning of the preference period. Begier therefore contends that no trust was ever created with respect to those funds and that the funds paid to the IRS were therefore property of the debtor.

We disagree. The Internal Revenue Code directs "every person receiving any payment for facilities or services" subject to excise taxes to "collect the amount of the tax from the person making such payment." §4291. It also requires that an employer "collec[t]" FICA taxes from its employees "by deducting the amount of the tax from the wages *as and when paid*." §3102(a) (emphasis added). Both provisions make clear that the act of "collecting" occurs at the time of payment—the recipient's payment for the service in the case of excise taxes and the employer's payment of wages in the case of FICA taxes.

The mere fact that AIA neither placed the taxes it collected in a segregated fund nor paid them to the IRS does not somehow mean that AIA never collected the taxes in the first place.

The same analysis applies to taxes the Internal Revenue Code requires that employers "withhold." Section 3402(a)(1) requires that "every employer making payment of wages shall deduct and withhold *upon such wages* [the employee's federal income tax]." (Emphasis added.) Withholding thus occurs at the time of payment to the employee of his net wages. S. Rep. No. 95-1106, p. 33 (1978) ("[A]ssume that a debtor owes an employee $100 for salary on which there is required withholding of $20. If the debtor paid the employee $80, there has been $20 withheld. If, instead, the debtor paid the employee $85, there has been withholding of $15 (which is not property of the debtor's estate in bankruptcy).") ... The common meaning of "withholding" supports our interpretation. See Webster's Third New International Dictionary 2627 (1981) (defining "withholding" to mean "the act or procedure of deducting a tax payment from income *at the source*") (emphasis added).

Our reading of §7501 is reinforced by §7512, which permits the IRS, upon proper notice, to require a taxpayer who has failed timely "to collect, truthfully account for, or pay over [trust-fund taxes]," or who has failed timely "to make deposits, payments, or returns of such tax," §7512(a)(1), to "deposit such amount in a separate account in a bank [and] keep the amount of such taxes in such account until payment over to the United States," §7512(b). If we were to read §7501 to mandate segregation as a prerequisite to the creation of the trust, §7512's requirement that funds be segregated in special and limited circumstances would become superfluous. Moreover, petitioner's suggestion that we read a segregation requirement into §7501 would mean that an employer could avoid the creation of a trust simply by refusing to segregate. Nothing in §7501 indicates, however, that Congress wanted the IRS to be protected only insofar as dictated by the debtor's whim. We conclude, therefore, that AIA created a trust within the meaning of §7501 at the moment the relevant payments (from customers to AIA for excise taxes and from AIA to its employees for FICA and income taxes) were made.

Our holding that a trust for the benefit of the IRS existed is not alone sufficient to answer the question presented by this case: whether the *particular dollars* that AIA paid to the IRS from its general operating accounts were "property of the debtor." Only if those particular funds were held in trust for the IRS do they escape characterization as "property of the debtor." All §7501 reveals is that AIA at one point created a trust for the IRS; that section provides no rule by which we can decide whether the assets AIA used to pay the IRS were assets belonging to that trust.

In the absence of specific statutory guidance on how we are to determine whether the assets transferred to the IRS were trust property, we might naturally begin with the common-law rules that have been created to answer such questions about other varieties of trusts. Unfortunately, such rules are of limited utility in the context of the trust created by §7501. Under common-law principles, a trust is created *in property*; a trust therefore does not come into existence until the settlor identifies an ascertainable interest in property to be the trust res ... . A §7501 trust is radically different from the common-law paradigm, however. That provision states that "the *amount* of [trust-fund] tax ... collected or withheld shall be held to be a special fund in trust for the United States." (Emphasis added.) Unlike a common-law trust, in which the settlor sets aside particular *property* as the trust res, §7501 creates a trust in an abstract "amount"—a dollar *figure* not tied to any particular assets—rather than in the actual dollars withheld. Common-law tracing rules, designed for a system in which particular property is identified as the trust res, are thus unhelpful in this special context.

Federal law delineating the nature of the relationship between the §7501 trust and preferential transfer rules is limited. The only case in which we have explored that topic at any length is United States v. Randall, 401 U.S. 513 (1971), a case dealing with a postpetition transfer of property to discharge trust-fund tax obligations that the debtor had accrued prepetition. There, a court had ordered a debtor in possession to maintain a separate account for its withheld federal income and FICA taxes, but the debtor did not comply. When the debtor was subsequently adjudicated a bankrupt, the United States sought to recover from the debtor's general assets the amount of withheld taxes ahead of the expenses of the bankruptcy proceeding. The Government argued that the debtor held the amount of taxes due in trust for the IRS and that this amount could be traced to the funds the debtor had in its accounts when the bankruptcy petition was filed. The trustee maintained that no trust had been created because the debtor had not segregated the funds. The Court declined directly to address either of these contentions ... . Rather, the Court simply refused to permit the IRS to recover the taxes ahead of administrative expenses, stating that "the statutory policy of subordinating taxes to costs and expenses of administration would not be served by creating or enforcing trusts which eat up an estate, leaving little or nothing for creditors and court officers whose goods and services created the assets." * * *

In 1978, Congress fundamentally restructured bankruptcy law by passing the new Bankruptcy Code. Among the changes Congress decided to make was a modification of the rule this Court had enunciated in *Randall* under the old Bankruptcy Act. The Senate bill attacked *Randall* directly, providing in §541 that trust-fund taxes withheld or collected prior to the filing of the bankruptcy petition were not "property of the estate." See S. Rep. No. 95-1106, p. 33 (1978). ("These amounts will not be property of the estate regardless of whether such amounts have been segregated from other assets of the debtor by way of a special account, fund, or otherwise, or are deemed to be a special fund in trust pursuant to provisions of applicable tax law.") The House bill did not deal explicitly with the problem of trust-fund taxes, but the House Report stated that "property of the estate" would not include property held in trust for another ... . Congress was unable to hold a conference, so the Senate and House floor managers met to reach compromises on the differences between the two bills. See 124 Cong. Rec. 32392 (1978) (remarks of Rep. Edwards) ... . The compromise reached with respect to the relevant portion of §541, which applies to postpetition transfers, was embodied in the eventually-enacted House amendment and explicitly provided that "in the case of property held in trust, the property of the estate includes the legal title, but not the beneficial interest in the property." 124 Cong. Rec., at 32417 (remarks of Rep. Edwards). Compare id., at 32363 (text of House amendment). Accordingly, the Senate language specifying that withheld or collected trust-fund taxes are not part of the bankruptcy estate was deleted as "unnecessary since property of the estate does not include the beneficial interest in property held by the debtor as a trustee. Under [§7051], the amounts of withheld taxes are held to be a special fund in trust for the United States." Id., at 32417 (remarks of Rep. Edwards).

Representative Edwards discussed the effects of the House language on the rule established by *Randall*, indicating that the House amendment would supplant that rule:

> [A] serious problem exists where "trust fund taxes" withheld from others are held to be property of the estate where the withheld amounts are commingled with other assets of the debtor. The courts should permit the use of reasonable assumptions under which the Internal Revenue Service, and other tax authorities, can

demonstrate that amounts of withheld taxes are still in the possession of the debtor at the commencement of the case.

Ibid.

The context of Representative Edwards' comment makes plain that he was discussing whether a *post*petition payment of trust-fund taxes involved "property of the estate." This focus is not surprising given that *Randall*, the case Congress was addressing, involved a postpetition demand for payment by the IRS. But Representative Edwards' discussion also applies to the question whether a *pre*petition payment is made from "property of the debtor." We have explained that "property of the debtor" is that property that would have been part of the estate had it not been transferred before the commencement of bankruptcy proceedings ... . The same "reasonable assumptions" therefore apply in both contexts.

The strict rule of *Randall* thus did not survive the adoption of the new Bankruptcy Code. But by requiring the IRS to "demonstrate that amounts of withheld taxes are still in the possession of the debtor at the commencement of the case [i.e., at the filing of the petition]," 124 Cong. Rec., at 32417 (remarks of Rep. Edwards), Congress expected that the IRS would have to show *some* connection between the §7501 trust and the assets sought to be applied to a debtor's trust-fund tax obligations ... . The question in this case is how extensive the required nexus must be. The Bankruptcy Code provides no explicit answer, and Representative Edwards' admonition that courts should "permit the use of reasonable assumptions" does not add much. The House Report does, however, give sufficient guidance regarding those assumptions to permit us to conclude that the nexus requirement is satisfied here. That Report states:

> A payment of withholding taxes constitutes a payment of money held in trust under Internal Revenue Code §7501(a), and thus will not be a preference because the beneficiary of the trust, the taxing authority, is in a separate class with respect to those taxes, if they have been properly held for payment, as they will have been if the debtor is able to make the payments.

H.R. Rep. No. 95-595, supra, at 373.

Under a literal reading of the above passage, the bankruptcy trustee could not avoid *any* voluntary prepetition payment of trust-fund taxes, regardless of the source of the funds. As the House Report expressly states, the limitation that the funds must "have been properly held for payment" is satisfied "if the debtor is able to make the payments." The debtor's act of voluntarily paying its trust-fund tax obligation therefore is alone sufficient to establish the required nexus between the "amount" held in trust and the funds paid.

We adopt this literal reading. In the absence of any suggestion in the Bankruptcy Code about what tracing rules to apply, we are relegated to the legislative history. The courts are directed to apply "reasonable assumptions" to govern the tracing of funds, and the House Report identifies one such assumption to be that any voluntary prepetition payment of trust-fund taxes out of the debtor's assets is not a transfer of the debtor's property. Nothing in the Bankruptcy Code or its legislative history casts doubt on the reasonableness of that assumption. Other rules might be reasonable, too, but the only evidence we have suggests that Congress preferred this one. We see no reason to disregard that evidence.

We hold that AIA's payments of trust-fund taxes to the IRS from its general accounts were not transfers of "property of the debtor," but were instead transfers of property held in trust for the Government pursuant to §7501. Such payments therefore cannot be avoided as preferences. The judgment of the Court of Appeals is affirmed.

JUSTICE SCALIA, concurring in the judgment.

Representative Edwards, the House floor manager for the bill that enacted the Bankruptcy Code, said on the floor that "[t]he courts should permit the use of reasonable assumptions" regarding the tracing of tax trust funds ... . We do not know that anyone except the presiding officer was present to hear Representative Edwards. Indeed, we do not know for sure that Representative Edwards' words were even uttered on the floor rather than inserted into the Congressional Record afterwards. If Representative Edwards did speak these words, and if there were others present, they must have been surprised to hear him talking about the tracing of 26 U.S.C. §7501 tax trust funds, inasmuch as the bill under consideration did not relate to the Internal Revenue Code but the Bankruptcy Code, and contained no provision even mentioning trust-fund taxes. Only the Senate bill, and not the House proposal, had mentioned trust-fund taxes—and even the former had said nothing whatever about the *tracing* of tax trust funds ... . Only the Senate Committee Report on the *unenacted* provision of the Senate bill had discussed that subject ... .

Nonetheless, on the basis of Representative Edwards' statement today's opinion concludes that "[t]he courts are *directed*" (presumably it means directed by the entire Congress, and not just Representative Edwards) "to apply 'reasonable assumptions' to govern the tracing of funds." ... (emphasis added). I do not agree. Congress conveys its directions in the Statutes at Large, not in excerpts from the Congressional Record, much less in excerpts from the Congressional Record that do not clarify the text of any pending legislative proposal.

Even in the absence of direction to do so, however, I certainly think we should apply reasonable assumptions to govern the tracing of funds. Unfortunately, that still does not answer the question before us here. One "traces" a fund only after one identifies the fund in the first place. The problem here is not "following the res" of the tax trust, but identifying the res to begin with. Seeking to come to grips with this point, the Court once again resorts to legislative history, this time even farther afield. It relies upon the House Report on what later became §547, which says:

> A payment of withholding taxes constitutes a payment of money held in trust under Internal Revenue Code §7501(a), and thus will not be a preference because the beneficiary of the trust, the taxing authority, is in a separate class with respect to those taxes, if they have been properly held for payment, as they will have been if the debtor is able to make the payments.

H.R. Rep. No. 95-595, p. 373 (1977).

The Court decides this case by "adopting" "a literal reading" of the above language ... . I think it both demeaning and unproductive for us to ponder whether to adopt literal or not-so-literal readings of Committee Reports, as though they were controlling statutory text. Moreover, even applying the lax legislative-history standards of recent years, this Committee Report should not be considered relevant. If a welfare bill conditioned benefits upon a certain maximum level of "income," courts might well (regrettably) regard as authoritative the Committee Report's statement that "income" means "income as computed under the Internal Revenue Code"; but surely they would not regard as authoritative its statement that a particular class of receipt *constitutes* income under the Internal Revenue Code. Authoritativeness on the latter sort of point is what the Court accepts here. The proposed (and ultimately enacted) provision of law to which this Committee Report pertained was the general provision of the Bankruptcy Code setting forth the five conditions for a voidable preference ... . The Committee Report's discussion of withholding taxes paid during the preference period presumably clarifies the meaning of the phrase "property of the debtor" in this text. If that is authoritative concerning the construction and effect of §7501, imagine what other laws concerning "property of the debtor" could also have been enacted through discussion in this Committee Report. The matter seems to me plainly too far beyond the immediate focus of the legislation to be deemed resolved by the accompanying Committee Report. It was certainly thoughtful of whoever drafted the report to try to clear up the issue of what kind of an estate, legal or equitable, the debtor possesses in trust-fund taxes that are paid, but that discussion is a kind of legislative-history "rider" that even the most ardent devotees of legislative history should ignore.

If the Court had applied to the text of the statute the standard tools of legal reasoning, instead of scouring the legislative history for some scrap that is on point (and therefore ipso facto relevant, no matter how unlikely a source of congressional reliance or attention), it would have reached the same result it does today, as follows: Section 7501 obviously intends to give the United States the advantages of a trust beneficiary with respect to collected and withheld taxes. Unfortunately, it does not always succeed in doing so. A trust without a res can no more be created by legislative decree than can a pink rock-candy mountain. In the nature of things no trust exists until a res is identified. Ordinarily the res is identified by the settlor of the trust; in the case of §7501 it is initially identified (if at all) by the statute, subject (as I shall discuss) to later reidentification by the taxpayer. Where the taxes subject to the trust-fund provision of §7501 are *collected* taxes, the statute plainly identifies the res: it is the collections. There may be difficulty in tracing them, but there is no doubt that they exist. Where, however, the taxes subject to the trust-fund provision are *withheld* taxes, the statute provides no clear identification. When I pay a worker $90 there is no clearly identifiable locus of the $10 in withheld taxes that I do *not* pay him. Indeed, if my total assets at the time of the payment are $90 there is no conceivable locus.

We may have to grapple at some later date with the question whether the lack of immediate identification means that no trust arises, or rather that §7501 creates some hitherto unheard-of floating trust in an unidentified portion of the taxpayer's current or later-acquired assets. We do not have to reach that question today, because even though identification was not made by the statute immediately, it *was* made by the taxpayer when it wrote a check upon a portion of a designated fund to the Government. (It is clear from the statutory scheme that the taxpayer has the power to identify which portion of its assets constitutes the trust fund; indeed, 26 U.S.C. §7512 permits the government to compel such identification where it has not been made.) Even if no trust existed before that check was written, it is clear that a trust existed then. See 1 W. Fratcher, Scott on Trusts §26.5 (4th ed. 1987) (promise to create trust becomes effective when settlor transfers or otherwise designates res as trust property).

The designation here, however, occurred within the 90-day preference period. Ordinarily, the debtor's alienation of his equitable interest by declaring a trust would constitute a preference. It seems to me, however, that one must at least give this effect to §7501's clearly expressed but sometimes ineffectual intent to create an *immediate* trust: if and when the trust res is identified from otherwise unencumbered assets, the trust should be deemed to have been in existence from the time of the collection or withholding. Thus, the designation of res does not constitute a preference, and the funds paid were not part of the debtor's estate.

For these reasons, I concur in the judgment of the Court.

IN RE LTV STEEL COMPANY, INC.

United States Bankruptcy Court, N.D. Ohio, 2001
274 Bankr. 278

BODOH, BANKRUPTCY JUDGE

* * * Debtor is one of the largest manufacturers of wholly-integrated steel products in the United States. Debtor mainly produces flat rolled steel products, hot and cold rolled sheet metal, mechanical and structural tubular products, and bimetallic wire. Debtor currently employs approximately 17,500 people in various capacities, and Debtor is also responsible for providing medical coverage and other benefits to approximately 100,000 retirees and their dependents. Debtor and 48 of its subsidiaries filed voluntary petitions for relief under Chapter 11 of Title 11, United States Code, on December 29, 2000. These cases are jointly administered.

* * * [T]he current controversy stems from a series of financial transactions that Debtor executed after its previous reorganization. The transactions in question are known as asset-backed securitization or structured financing ("ABS"), and are generally designed to permit a debtor to borrow funds at a reduced cost in exchange for a lender securing the loan with assets that are transferred from the borrower to another entity. By structuring the transactions in this manner, the lender hopes to ensure that its collateral will be excluded from the

borrower's bankruptcy estate in the event that the borrower files a bankruptcy petition.

Abbey National is a large financial institution located in the United Kingdom. Debtor and Abbey National entered into an ABS transaction in October 1994. To effectuate this agreement, Debtor created a wholly-owned subsidiary known as LTV Sales Finance Co. ("Sales Finance"). Debtor then entered into an agreement with Sales Finance which purports to sell all of Debtor's right and interest in its accounts receivables ("receivables") to Sales Finance on a continuing basis. Abbey National then agreed to loan Two Hundred Seventy Million Dollars ($270,000,000.00) to Sales Finance in exchange for Sales Finance granting Abbey National a security interest in the receivables. * * *

[Sales Finance is not] a debtor in this proceeding. Nevertheless, Debtor filed a motion with the Court on December 29, 2000 seeking an interim order permitting it to use cash collateral. This cash collateral consisted of the receivables ... that are ostensibly owned by Sales Finance ... [as well as inventory ostensibly owned by another special purpose subsidiary]. Debtors stated to the Court that it would be forced to shut it doors and cease operations if it did not receive authorization to use this cash collateral. A hearing was held on Debtor's cash collateral motion on December 29, 2000 as part of the first day hearings. [Interim authorization was granted, with Abbey National to receive as substitute collateral newly generated inventory and receivables.] * * *

Abbey National argues that the interim cash collateral order should be modified because ... there is no basis for the Court to determine that the receivables which are Abbey National's collateral are property of Debtor's estate .... * * *

Section 541(a) of the Bankruptcy Code provides that upon the filing of a bankruptcy petition an estate is created consisting of "all legal or equitable interests of the debtor in property as of the commencement of the case." The estate created by the filing of a Chapter 11 petition is very broad, and property may be included in Debtor's estate even if Debtor does not have a possessory interest in that property.

Abbey National contends that the interim order is flawed because, on its face, the transaction between Debtor and Sales Finance is characterized as a true sale. Therefore, Abbey National argues, since Debtor sold its interests in the receivables to Sales Finance, Debtor no longer has an interest in the receivables and they are not property of the estate. * * *

[T]here seems to be an element of sophistry to suggest that Debtor does not retain at least an equitable interest in the property that is subject to the interim order. Debtor's business requires it to purchase, melt, mold and cast various metal products. To suggest that Debtor lacks some ownership interest in products that it creates with its own labor, as well as the proceeds to be derived from that labor, is difficult to accept. Accordingly, the Court concludes that Debtor has at least some equitable interest in the inventory and receivables, and that this interest is property of the Debtor's estate. This equitable interest is sufficient to support the entry of the interim cash collateral order.

Finally, it is readily apparent that granting Abbey National relief from the interim cash collateral order would be highly inequitable. The Court is satisfied that the entry of the interim order was necessary to enable Debtor to keep its doors open and continue to meet its obligations to its employees, retirees, customers and creditors. Allowing Abbey National to modify the order would allow Abbey National to enforce its state law rights as a secured lender to look to the collateral in satisfaction of this debt. This circumstance would put an immediate end to Debtor's business, would put thousands of people out of work, would deprive 100,000 retirees of needed medical benefits, and would have more far reaching economic effects on the geographic areas where Debtor does business. However, maintaining the current status quo permits Debtor to remain in business while it searches for substitute financing, and adequately protects and preserves Abbey National's rights. The equities of this situation highly favor Debtor. As a result, the Court declines to exercise its discretion to modify the interim order … . * * *

NOTES

6A.1. Keep in mind that *Begier* does not address the trustee's avoiding powers. These powers, the subject of chapter 8 below, sometimes allow the trustee to reach assets that the debtor itself could not enjoy. Hence, even after one concludes that assets are held in constructive trust and do not come into the estate under §541(a)(1), one must ask whether the trustee can reach them nevertheless through the exercise of one of the avoiding powers. In *Begier*, for example, the trustee could have avoided the IRS's beneficial interest in the trust funds had the trust imposed by the Internal Revenue Code been a "statutory lien" that attached under proscribed conditions. See §545, described below in chapter 8, section B.

6A.2. The battle in *Begier* is one between creditors. This is not always the case when the issue is whether to include property in the estate. In Patterson v. Shumate, 504 U.S. 753 (1992), for example, the Court decided that an individual debtor's inalienable interest in a pension plan was excluded from the bankruptcy estate under §541(c)(2). The upshot was that the debtor, rather than any creditor, ultimately would enjoy that interest. In effect, then, exclusion from the bankruptcy estate there operated to exempt property. Consider *Patterson* later in this book when you work through Problem 11B-2.

6A3. In an unexcerpted portion of *LTV*, Abbey National argued that the substitute collateral it was granted for the prepetition receivables was inadequate to protect its interest. On this basis, the bank asked to have the stay lifted if it applied at all. See chapter 5, section C of this book. The court judged the substitute collateral as adequate and thus declined to lift the stay. The very purpose of structured finance is to prevent just this result, where the court substitutes its judgment for that of the creditor. It is telling, moreover, that the court in *LTV* relied in part on what it called the "equities of the situation." One might wonder whether Abbey National would be as quick to lend on favorable terms when the next debtor pledges to keep collateral out of any bankruptcy proceeding, and one might wonder too whether that debtor would have a chance to open its doors (or keep them open) in the first place. Whatever one thinks about the substantive outcome of *LTV*, however, the court is validly concerned that the formality of structured finance not give a secured creditor greater rights than it would have under ordinary circumstances. That is, one might well argue that the economics of secured lending rather than the corporate structure of the debtor and its affiliates should determine whether collateral is property of the estate.

6A4. In reading *LTV*, note the connection to the *Chase Manhattan Bank* (*Marvel Comics*) case, which appears in chapter 4, section A of the book. In *Marvel Comics*, the court warned that ex ante contractual arrangements between debtor and third parties would not be permitted to interfere with the rehabilitation of the debtor. *LTV* echoes this concern. This said, the conflict between debtor in possession and a secured creditor may occur less frequently now, given the increasing incidence of secured creditor control of the bankruptcy process, discussed below in chapter 13 of the book.

6A5. In a sense, the court in *LTV* performed a substantive consolidation of the debtor and its subsidiary. Substantive consolidation is discussed in chapter 10, section B below.

PROBLEMS

6A-1. Debtor creates a sham business and lures investors with a promise of a $150 return within a month in exchange for each $100 investment. For several months, the number of participants increases by more that 50 percent each month. As a result, Debtor is able to pay off the old investors from what it receives from new investors and still support an extravagant life-style. Eventually, however, the pool of new investors dries up. When Debtor's scheme is about to be uncovered, Debtor takes the $100,000 she had just received from a thousand new participants, puts it in a suitcase, and heads for the airport, where she is arrested.

Debtor becomes subject to an involuntary bankruptcy proceeding. The $100,000 in proceeds from the last participants are Debtor's sole assets. The trustee cannot trace any funds that might have been paid to investors in previous months. The applicable law of Debtor's state provides that "one who commits fraud is deemed to hold any proceeds of fraudulent activity in trust for the victims of such activity." How should the trustee distribute the $100,000 in the trustee's possession?

(These facts are loosely based on those in Cunningham v. Brown, 265 U.S. 1 (1924). The name of the debtor in that case, Charles Ponzi, became synonymous with this method of separating the greedy and the gullible from their money.)

6A-2. Debtor Corporation manufactures and distributes paper used by photo shops to create prints from film negatives. In need of a capital infusion, Debtor sells all of its manufacturing equipment to Newco, Inc., which obtains the purchase price for the equipment through a secured loan from Bank. Newco then forms a partnership with Debtor, under the terms of which Debtor and Newco are to divide evenly the net revenues from paper production; the partnership is terminable at will by either Debtor or Newco. After a period of success, the partnership founders financially when digital photography replaces film at an unexpectedly high rate of speed. Owner, the sole shareholder of Debtor and of Newco, dissolves the partnership and has Debtor file for bankruptcy under Chapter 11. Owner asks Bank to finance Debtor's continued manufacture of photographic paper, but on a smaller scale in accord with a business model that focuses exclusively on the market for prints from disposable cameras, which Owner believes will contain film for some time to come. Bank agrees and proposes that after it forecloses on Newco's equipment it will lease the equipment to Debtor on agreed terms. Debtor's creditors object to this plan. They seek to have a trustee replace Owner at the helm of Debtor and to have the court block Bank's foreclosure on Newco's equipment. What result? In addition to Bankruptcy Code §541(a), consider §1104, discussed in chapter 13 below.

B.   IPSO FACTO MODIFICATIONS

The Bankruptcy Code §541(a) provides that the bankruptcy estate includes all "interests of the debtor in property" as of the commencement of the case. When a debtor enjoys a leasehold interest in Black-Acre, only the lease comes into bankruptcy. It is harder, however, to translate a property interest to the bankruptcy forum when the debtor's rights are limited in a way that implicates the bankruptcy process itself. Section 541(c)(1) provides, in general, that:

> [A]n interest of the debtor in property becomes property of the estate ... notwithstanding any provision in an agreement, transfer instrument, or applicable nonbankruptcy law—
>
> (A) that restricts or conditions transfer of such interest by the debtor; or
>
> (B) that is conditioned on the insolvency or financial condition of the debtor, on the commencement of a [bankruptcy] case, or on the appointment of or taking possession by a trustee ... or custodian before such commencement, and that effects or gives an option to effect a forfeiture, modification, or termination of the debtor's interest in property.

Section 541(c)(1)(A)'s mandate that restrictions on transfer be ignored ensures that a contractual or applicable nonbankruptcy law restriction on transfer cannot prevent a transfer from the debtor to the debtor's bankruptcy estate. The subsection does *not* itself make it possible for the trustee to transfer an asset *from* the estate to a third party in the face of an otherwise valid transfer restriction. This provision makes certain that the bankruptcy mechanism itself does not alter nonbankruptcy rights.

One can view §541(c)(1)(B), commonly known as an "anti-ipso-facto-clause" provision, in much the same light. This provision applies where, but for the provision, bankruptcy, insolvency, or financial distress short of insolvency would "ipso facto" modify—including through forfeiture or termination—a debtor's interest in property. Imagine, for example, that a debtor agrees in advance with some creditors to cede the debtor's entire interest in selected property if the debtor commences a bankruptcy case or becomes insolvent. If such an agreement were enforceable, the selected assets would not become part of the bankruptcy estate, but would instead go directly to the favored individual creditors. The agreement would thus allow the individual creditors to evade bankruptcy's collective process. Consequently, Congress drafted §541(c)(1)(B) effectively to disallow any modification of a debtor's interest in property if such modification applies not generally, but only when bankruptcy or another process for the distribution of a debtor's assets occurs or seems imminent. An ipso facto modification of a debtor's interest is invalid regardless of whether applicable nonbankruptcy law merely enforces a clause in the contract or operates independently.

We read about a related provision in chapter 4 above. Recall that in *Cahokia Downs* the court ruled that Bankruptcy Code §363(*l*) invalidated a bankruptcy-motivated attempt to terminate an insurance policy. As we shall see in chapter 7 below, §365 contains similar provisions for clauses in executory contracts.

The prohibition of ipso facto clauses does not *necessarily* honor nonbankruptcy rights, however. It is one thing to say that an ipso facto clause cannot remove property from the bankruptcy process; it is quite another to say that the rights contained in those clauses are unenforceable. Section 541(c)(1) certainly says the former. It may also say the latter.

To understand this distinction, consider a variation on *In re M.J. & K.*, a principal case in chapter 4. Law School grants Bookseller a five-year "Exclusive Right" to operate on Law School's premises. The agreement provides, however, that this right is not transferable and is terminable at the option of Law School in the event of Bookseller's bankruptcy or insolvency. Two years later, Bookseller becomes insolvent and files a Chapter 11 petition.

The bankruptcy petition does not by itself deprive Bookseller of the exclusive right to sell books at Law School. One might characterize what happens at the commencement of the case as a transfer of assets to the bankruptcy estate. Section 541(c)(1)(A) ensures that the assets do become part of the estate notwithstanding the no-transfer clause. This provision is sensible. The "transfer" of assets is merely a formality required by the bankruptcy process; Bookseller has not transferred the Exclusive Right to *another* business and thus the bankruptcy has not affected Law School's substantive rights under the no-transfer provision.

Matters become somewhat more difficult when Law School asks the bankruptcy court for permission to enforce its termination option. Law School concedes that Bookseller's Exclusive Right becomes property of the estate notwithstanding the termination option. Law School argues, however, that this simply subjects the right to the automatic stay. Law School raises *Chicago Board of Trade* and contends that the Exclusive Right comes into the bankruptcy estate subject to all applicable nonbankruptcy limitations, including Law School's termination option. Law School argues further that failure to honor its termination option would force Law School to risk what may be poor performance from an insolvent vendor. The bankruptcy process itself might alleviate some of the pressures on Bookseller. But Law School fears that insolvency is both a financial failure and a signal of economic failure. Law School reserved the option to terminate based on this signal and accepted a lower price for the Exclusive Right as a consequence. Just as a perfected secured creditor retains a security interest in collateral even though the collateral comes into the bankruptcy estate, Law School asserts that its termination option survives inclusion of the Exclusive Right in the bankruptcy estate.

Confronted with these arguments, a bankruptcy court would have to decide whether, for the purposes of §541(c)(1), inclusion of an interest "notwithstanding" an ipso facto termination right means inclusion of the interest *in derogation of* that right. A court might be inclined to answer this question in the affirmative, and eliminate the termination option, if Law School learned of Bookseller's insolvency from initiation of the bankruptcy process itself, perhaps through a public notice of the petition. That is, a court that wished to follow the *Butner* principle, and honor nonbankruptcy entitlements, need not permit bankruptcy to trigger the enforcement of those entitlements. If, however, Law School could make a plausible case that it learned or would have learned of Bookseller's insolvency regardless of the bankruptcy process, adherence to *Butner* seems to require survival of the termination option.

This does not mean that the court must lift the stay and permit immediate termination. The court might instead require that Bookseller set aside assets to which Law School would have recourse in the event that Bookseller's performance became unacceptable. This set-aside would be similar to protection that a secured creditor might seek for collateral under §362(d), described below in chapter 9, section B. Such a result would give effect both to §541(c)(1)(B) and to the general principle that bankruptcy law not upset substantive non-bankruptcy rights.

Whatever the merits of this position, however, courts do not separate the right immediately to enforce an ipso facto clause from the right ultimately to benefit from that clause. Instead, courts reach all-or-nothing decisions. Either a clause is a violation of the ipso facto prohibition and is wholly nullified, or it is not a violation and the property it affects never comes into the estate.

Keep these issues in mind as you consider the materials below. The case, *In re Allen*, introduces another wrinkle as well. In that case, the debtor is a motor carrier that is no longer in business but has claims against its customers based on undercharges from past services. The debtor is subject to the Negotiated Rates Act (NRA), which disallows undercharge claims by carriers that have ceased operations. Thus, the condition of forfeiture is not bankruptcy, insolvency, or weak financial condition, but is arguably a proxy for one of these conditions. The court must decide whether §541(c)(1)(B) prohibits the NRA's disallowance of the undercharges. The NRA is a federal, not a state, law. But note also that §541(c)(1)(B) operates with respect to all "applicable nonbankruptcy law." And, for the relevant discussion in these cases, the court assumes that Congress did not intend the NRA to supersede the Bankruptcy Code.

Key Provision: Bankruptcy Code §541(c)(1)

EXERCISES

6B(1) After Debtor defaults on a secured obligation to Bank, Bank repossesses Debtor's car, as permitted by the security agreement and UCC §9-609. Debtor then agrees that Bank can keep the car in satisfaction of Debtor's obligation. Shortly thereafter, Debtor files for bankruptcy. Does the car become property of the estate on the ground that Bank's ownership of the car is the result of a forfeiture triggered by the default, which is an aspect of Debtor's financial condition?

6B(2) Two entrepreneurs form a corporation and each holds half the stock. Each has the right to buy out the other's shares for a nominal price on either the death or bankruptcy of the other. One shareholder, Debtor, becomes insolvent and soon thereafter files for bankruptcy under Chapter 7. At the time of the bankruptcy, Debtor owed many obligations but held no valuable asset other than the shares. To whom will the shares ultimately belong? Would your answer change if the purchase option vested automatically in one shareholder at the moment the other became insolvent? In answering these questions, make any reasonable assumption about whether Debtor's co-shareholder could exercise the purchase option against a general creditor with a valid lien on the shares. Consider also Bankruptcy Code §365 and return to this exercise after reading this book's next chapter.

CASE

IN RE L. LOU ALLEN

United States Bankruptcy Court, N.D. Illinois, 1994
183 Bankr. 519

COAR, BANKRUPTCY JUDGE.

* * * The Plaintiff, L. Lou Allen, trustee on behalf of the bankruptcy estate of TSC Express Co. ("Trustee"), seeks to recover freight charges for transportation services provided to the Defendant, Krueger Ringier, Inc. ("KRI"). * * *

On May 14, 1991, TSC filed its petition for bankruptcy under Chapter 7 of the Bankruptcy Code. Prior to filing for bankruptcy, TSC operated as a motor common carrier trucking company, authorized to and actually doing business in interstate commerce pursuant to [the Interstate Commerce Act,] and the rules and regulations of the [Interstate Commerce] Commission. In addition, TSC operated as an intrastate trucking company pursuant to Georgia law.

During the period between May 16, 1988 and September 15, 1989, TSC, as a motor common carrier, transported certain goods and/or merchandise from and to various locations of KRI. After delivering the products to KRI, TSC billed KRI for its services at the rate agreed upon by the two parties. Shortly thereafter, KRI paid these invoices in full. But, TSC never filed a copy of the negotiated price agreement with the Commission, in contravention to 49 U.S.C. §10764. Subsequently, TSC ceased transporting property and filed its petition for bankruptcy relief.

The Trustee, with the prior approval of the bankruptcy court, contracted for an audit of all TSC freight bills for the three years prior to bankruptcy in order to determine the difference between the rates filed by TSC with the Commission [referred to as a tariff] and the rates that TSC had negotiated and billed KRI. (In numerous prior cases with similar facts, this difference has been referred to as the "undercharge.") Based on the audit results, the Trustee billed KRI $12,299 for undercharges. KRI has refused to pay, and the Trustee now seeks to recover the undercharges, pre-judgment interest of $2,939, and any other costs. * * *

In late 1993, the President signed the Negotiated Rates Act ("NRA"). The NRA [§2] provides in relevant part:

(e) Alternative Procedure for Resolving Disputes—

(1) General Rule—[I]t shall be an unreasonable practice for a motor carrier of property ... to attempt to charge or to charge for a transportation service ... the difference between the applicable rate that is lawfully in effect pursuant to a tariff ... and the negotiated rate for such transportation service if the carrier or freight forwarder is no longer transporting property. * * *

[The Trustee argues] that the NRA nullifies §541(c)(1). The relevant portion of §541 states:

(c)(1) [A]n interest of the debtor in property becomes property of the estate ... notwithstanding any provision in an agreement, transfer instrument, or applicable nonbankruptcy law—

(B) that is conditioned on the insolvency or financial condition of the debtor ... and that effects or gives an option to effect a forfeiture, modification, or termination of the debtor's interest in property.

While the right to recover freight bills constitutes an interest in property within the realm of §541, the NRA does not effect a forfeiture of that interest under §541(c)(1)(B). * * *

[T]he NRA does not conflict with §541 as it is not triggered by the financial condition of the debtor, an essential and necessary requirement of §541(c)(1)(B). The NRA applies when a carrier is no longer transporting property ... . This criteri[on] is separate and distinct from a requirement that depends on the financial status of the debtor. The essential distinction is that the forces of the marketplace and the incentive to maintain good business relations will restrain operating carriers from making unfounded or tenuous undercharge claims, but there is no such check on nonoperating carriers.

The financial condition of the debtor is only one reason why a motor carrier may cease transporting property. The NRA would apply in various other circumstances, including when a conglomerate decides to leave the motor common carrier industry or when the owner of a company decides to retire and close up shop. On the other hand, the NRA would not apply to a motor common carrier in bankruptcy and still transporting property. The NRA does not contain the phrase "financial condition" or any similar phrase. Although the NRA is applicable nonbankruptcy law, it is not conditioned on the financial condition of the debtor. Therefore, the NRA does not violate §541(c)(1)(B).

NOTES

6B.1. The court in *Allen* decided that the customers' rights under the NRA were not conditioned on a prohibited factor and thus TRC had no claim to undercharges. The court did not even address the possibility that TRC's bankruptcy estate might include a right to collect undercharges, though one subject to the customers' substantive rights under the NRA. Had the court found that the NRA violated §541(c)(1), the customers would have had *no* rights under the NRA. The court did not treat §541(c)(1) as merely a provision to prevent a contractual or legislative opt out of the bankruptcy process. Instead, the court applied §541(c)(1) as a provision that, if applicable at all, can substantively alter nonbankruptcy entitlements. The problems below ask you to explore further the wisdom of this all-or-nothing approach.

6B.2. One might argue that a motor carrier that "no longer transports property" for the purposes of the NRA is a carrier with an altered "financial condition," for the purposes of §541(c)(1). When a carrier no longer receives revenues, its financial condition is changed. The *Allen* court argued that "financial condition" cannot be read so broadly. In the view of the *Allen* court, cessation of operations would be an illegitimate basis for forfeiture only if cessation were necessarily the *result of* a change in financial condition. Because even a financially sound carrier can choose to liquidate its shipping business, the court concluded, forfeiture based on cessation of operations is not the equivalent of the prohibited forfeiture based on "financial condition."

Put another way, the *Allen* court believed that §541(c)(1) prohibits modification of a debtor's interest in property only if that modification would be triggered by a crisis such as bankruptcy, the appointment of a receiver, or the debtor's *weak* financial condition. Under the NRA, cessation of operations triggers forfeiture of a debtor's claims whether the debtor is in weak or strong financial condition. It is thus applicable even in the absence of financial or economic distress. Hence, the NRA does not run afoul of the Bankruptcy Code.

A different interpretation is possible, however. Though some financially sound carriers will cease operations, it seems likely that most carriers who do so will have failed economically. And many of these failed carriers will be financially burdened by debt, often to the point of insolvency. Exceptional cases aside, then, the NRA may be seen as an indirect attempt to accomplish what, in the courts' view, is forbidden by the Bankruptcy Code, modification of a debtor's property rights based on the debtor's financial crisis.

PROBLEMS

6B-1. Debtor Corporation is a distributor of audio equipment. Debtor borrows $1 million from Bank and agrees to repay Bank with interest in one year. The loan agreement between the parties contains the following provision: "If at any time prior to repayment Debtor ceases to become an audio equipment distributor, all interests in all of Debtor's property vests in Bank." Bank duly files an ordinary financing statement that lists Debtor's mainframe computer and distribution software as collateral. Shortly after the loan is made, before the loan is repaid, Debtor suspends its business operations and files a Chapter 11 bankruptcy petition. Debtor uses the time in reorganization to restructure its debt obligations to Bank as well as others and to retool as a medical supplier. Debtor's one marketable asset is the distribution software, which it can easily adapt for a new business if it can stay in operation and thus retain its key employees, who as a team created the software. At the time of the bankruptcy petition, the software is worth something more than $1.5 million. Is the software part of Debtor's bankruptcy estate? Would your answer change if Debtor's forfeiture were triggered not by a cessation of operations but by an inability to pay debts as they became due? In either case, should Bank have a smaller interest in the software than it would were it an ordinary secured creditor?

6B-2. Co-builder and Debtor are construction contractors and partners in a project to build a shopping mall. The partnership agreement provides, among other terms, that "inasmuch as Co-builder and Debtor would each be fully liable for any damages that might result from their failure to complete the mall on time, each herewith contributes $10,000 to a joint project fund, the complete interest in which will vest in one should the other default on any obligation." Each contributes to the fund as the agreement provides. Shortly after work begins, however, Debtor fails to pay its subcontractors for work completed. The subcontractors, in turn, refuse to continue on the project, and work is delayed. As a result, Co-builder seeks to withdraw and retain all $20,000 from the joint fund, as it is entitled to do under applicable nonbankruptcy law. Before Co-builder can withdraw the money, however, Debtor files a petition in bankruptcy. Does the joint fund become property of Debtor's bankruptcy estate? If so, to what extent? If the fund does become property of the estate, does Co-builder have a claim against Debtor for Co-builder's interest in the fund? If Co-builder does have such a claim, is that claim secured or unsecured? Assuming that the fund does, to some extent, become property of the estate, how might Co-builder and Debtor have structured this arrangement so that Co-builder would have been able to keep all $20,000 away from the bankruptcy process?

6B-3. For a debtor that is attempting to reorganize under Chapter 11, what is the fundamental difference between Bank's interest in Problem 6B-1 and Co-builder's interest in Problem 6B-2? Which interest more closely resembles the shippers' rights under the NRA as described in *Allen*?

VII. EXECUTORY CONTRACTS

In the previous chapters, we have distinguished between claims against the estate on the one hand and assets of the estate on the other. A tort action that a third party has against the debtor is a claim, for example, while a tort action that the debtor has against someone else is an asset. In this chapter, we look at something that is an asset and a liability simultaneously. When a contract is executory, the debtor is obliged to a party and that party is obliged to the debtor. Neither party has completed material performance under the contract. Otherwise the contract would simply be a liability of the party that remained to perform and an asset of the other party.

We can think of an executory contract as a fusion of both a liability and an asset. We can also readily sort such contracts into two types: those in which the value of debtor's asset is greater than the associated liability, and those in which the liability exceeds the value of the asset. In other words, an executory contract of a debtor can be either a *net* asset or a *net* liability.

It is useful to see this idea at work in a simple case. Refinery promises to deliver a barrel of oil next week and Debtor promises to pay $50 for that oil at that time. This is an executory contract: Refinery is obliged to deliver oil and Debtor is obliged to pay for it. From Debtor's perspective, whether the contract is good or bad turns on the price of oil. If the market price of oil rises and now sells for $60, the executory contract is a net asset. If the price falls to $40, the contract is a net liability.

The Bankruptcy Code §365 governs executory contracts and unexpired leases to which a debtor is a party. Section §365, in the main, ensures that bankruptcy law honors the nonbankruptcy rights of both the debtor and the nondebtor party. Before we explore some of the difficult issues that have arisen under §365, we should note that the provision works well in our simple case.

If the market price of oil has risen and the executory contract is a net asset for Debtor, the trustee can have the bankruptcy estate spend $50 and get something in return that is worth $60 (the oil). This is a good deal, and the trustee should be able to take advantage of it, just as the trustee can bring all other assets of Debtor into the estate under §541. Refinery has a losing deal, but it would have been a losing deal even if no bankruptcy petition had been filed. There is nothing about bankruptcy that should let Refinery off the hook.

Section 365 ensures this result. The formal process by which the trustee takes advantage of the favorable contract (and lives up to the debtor's obligations under the contract) is called "assumption." When the trustee assumes the contract and brings it into the bankruptcy estate, the estate enjoys all the benefits of the contract, but bears all of its burdens as well. The trustee cannot get the oil without parting with the $50. As under §541(c), the trustee under §365 can bring this asset into the estate even if the contract forbids the assignment of the contract or relieves Refinery of its obligation in the event of Debtor's insolvency.

Section 365 parallels what we have seen before when the executory contract is a net liability as well. Let us say that the price of oil falls and the market price of a barrel is now only $40. This executory contract is a net liability. Debtor has promised to pay $50 for something that is worth only $40. But Refiner's legal right outside of bankruptcy in the event of breach is merely an action for damages, the right to sue for the differential between the market price and the contract price. In this respect, Refiner is in the same position as a creditor whom Debtor has not paid. To ensure that Refiner is treated no better and no worse than other creditors, the trustee has the right to breach the contract. The breach transforms Debtor's promise to deliver oil into a claim for money damages and thus puts Refiner on the same footing as the general creditors. This power to transform net liability contracts into a damage claim by breach is, in the language of the Bankruptcy Code, the ability to "reject" an executory contract.

This, as a rough approximation, tells you what is at stake in §365. In this chapter, we explore a number of issues. But we should begin with a note of caution: Section 365 is one of the least satisfactory provisions of the Bankruptcy Code. In its operation, there are departures from basic principles that are hard to fathom. Some of them arise from the application of rules designed for simple contracts, such as one involving the sale of a barrel of oil, to much more complicated transactions. Other odd results come from the fact that §365 applies the same rules to an individual and corporate debtor, though the debtor's circumstances can be significantly different. We begin by examining the contours of the executory contract. We then focus on the issues of assumption and rejection respectively.

A. EXECUTORY CONTRACTS DEFINED

Neither "executory contract" nor "unexpired lease" is defined by the Bankruptcy Code. While the latter term has presented few, if any, interpretive problems, the same cannot be said of the former. The definition of executory contract given here—material performance required by both sides—is associated with the scholar Vern Countryman. Most courts adopt the Countryman definition, but some do not.

Several courts have suggested that where the only performance remaining by the debtor is the payment of money, there can be no executory contract even if the other side's performance is not completed either. See, for example, Lubrizol Enterprises v. Richmond Metal Finishers, 756 F.2d 1043 (4th Cir. 1985). These courts rely on a statement from the legislative history that an obligation on a note is not usually an executory contract. But this reliance seems misplaced, as the statement was not of a general proposition. Close examination of the statement reveals an assumption that the obligee on the note had no duties left to perform. The statement's disqualification of the note as an executory contract may have had nothing to do with the remaining one-sided obligation being to pay money and everything to do with the remaining obligation being one-sided.

Reliance on an isolated statement from legislative history, moreover, is not the only way in which courts stray from the Countryman definition. One judge, for example, decided that a contract was not executory because characterization of the contract as executory would not have benefited the estate. See In re Booth, 19 Bankr. 53 (Bankr. D. Utah 1982).

At the heart of each case that rejects the Countryman definition of executory contracts is a dispute over the nature of the bankruptcy rights and bankruptcy obligations associated with such a contract. A bankruptcy court may be called on to determine whether or how a debtor can assume a contract that is a net asset or reject a contract that is a net liability. And a court may be asked to determine when a debtor must exercise any option it may have with respect to a contract. A debtor or nondebtor party's support of or opposition to characterization of a contract as executory depends on these determinations. The case, *Energy Enterprises*, and notes below illustrate this proposition. We begin with some exercises that review the mechanics of §365.

Key Provision: Bankruptcy Code §365

EXERCISES

7A(1) Buyer agrees to purchase oil from Seller in six months for $50 per barrel. After four months, Seller files a petition for bankruptcy. Is the oil-purchase agreement an executory contract for the purposes of Bankruptcy Code §365? Would your answer change if Buyer, rather than Seller, entered bankruptcy? Does your answer depend on whether, at the time of bankruptcy, the price of oil is greater or less than $50 per barrel?

7A(2) Bank lends Debtor $1 million to be repaid with interest in a year. Four months later, Debtor files a petition for bankruptcy. Is the loan agreement an executory contract for the purposes of §365?

7A(3) Retailer prepays Accountant for work to be done in the future. Before the work is complete, Retailer files a petition in bankruptcy. Is the agreement between Retailer and Accountant an executory contract for the purposes of §365?

7A(4) Retailer leases a building from Landlord for a period of one year. Before the lease is up, Retailer files a petition in bankruptcy. Is the lease subject to §365? Would your answer change if Landlord, rather than Retailer, entered bankruptcy? Would your answer change if Retailer leased not a building from Landlord, but equipment for Retailer's shop?

CASE

ENERGY ENTERPRISES CORP. v. UNITED STATES

United States Court of Appeals, Third Circuit, 1995
50 F.3d 233

SCIRICA, CIRCUIT JUDGE.

* * * In this bankruptcy matter, we must decide whether certain terms in a class action settlement agreement constitute an executory contract under §365. The Internal Revenue Service contended the settlement agreement was not an executory contract. Both the bankruptcy court and the district court agreed with the IRS, and the class members appealed. We will affirm.

I

The facts are undisputed. Columbia Gas System, Incorporated, its subsidiary, Columbia Gas Transmission Corporation (TCO), and their affiliates comprise a natural gas system which explores, produces, purchases, stores, transmits, and distributes natural gas. TCO is Columbia Gas System's principal gas purchaser from producers in the Southwest, Midcontinent, and Appalachia and operates extensive underground storage facilities.

On July 26, 1985, Enterprise Energy Corporation and two other companies filed a class action against TCO in the United States District Court for the Southern District of Ohio. The district court certified as a class the producers of natural gas in the Appalachian region who were parties to gas purchase contracts with TCO. The class comprised 2,163 member producers who held 852 gas purchase contracts. TCO had invoked a price reduction under a cost recovery clause which formed the basis of their complaint.

The gas purchase contracts set the price for each unit of natural gas delivered to TCO at the maximum price permitted under the Natural Gas Policy Act of 1978 during the month of delivery. The class members alleged that TCO breached their gas purchase contracts by paying less than the maximum price after it invoked the cost recovery clause.

For five years there was extensive discovery. As trial loomed, the parties entered into a Stipulation of Proposed Class Action Settlement ("settlement agreement"), which the district court approved on June 18, 1991. * * *

The settlement agreement required TCO to deposit $30 million into an escrow account "in settlement of, and as a full and complete discharge and release of TCO, for all of [the class members'] claims arising on or before January 1991." TCO was to pay $15 million into escrow by March 21, 1991, and the other $15 million by March 23, 1992. This schedule was apparently set for TCO's convenience; TCO's duty to make the second payment was not contingent on the class members' performance of any of their obligations. TCO paid the first $15 million on time but then filed for bankruptcy.

Under the settlement agreement, class members were entitled to receive their share of the escrow monies only after they executed a release of claims and a supplemental contract. The settlement agreement stated "payments to individual Class Members out of the escrowed amounts will be contingent upon receipt by [TCO] of a duly executed release of all such Claims and a duly executed contract supplement. ... " While each class member had to execute a release to get payment from the escrow fund, the claims each held against TCO were to be extinguished (and they in fact were ...) by the court order accepting the settlement agreement.

The supplemental contracts were designed to implement amendments and clarifications of pricing and other terms concerning future gas deliveries to TCO. The settlement agreement established the terms of these contracts, including increasing the price TCO would pay to the class members. Because many class members relied on TCO as the principal purchaser of their gas, the supplemental contracts were important to them. * * *

By July 31, 1991, the class members involved in forty-one of the purchase contracts had completed the execution of the release and supplemental contracts and were entitled to their share of the escrow monies. But on that day, thirteen days after the settlement agreement had become final, TCO filed a voluntary Chapter 11 petition in bankruptcy in Delaware. On February 20, 1992, the class members filed a motion to compel TCO to assume or reject the settlement agreement under §365. TCO and the class members had agreed that TCO would assume the settlement agreement and jointly filed a proposed order.

After notice of the proposed order was sent to the proper parties, the United States filed an objection on behalf of the Internal Revenue Service, one of TCO's creditors. Finding the settlement agreement was not executory within the meaning of §365, the bankruptcy court upheld the objection and denied the class members' motion.

The class members appealed to the United States District Court for the District of Delaware. The district court held that the settlement agreement was a contract, but affirmed the bankruptcy court on the grounds the contract was not executory for purposes of §365. Therefore TCO did not have the option of assuming or rejecting the settlement agreement. This appeal followed. * * *

III

In this appeal, we must decide whether the settlement agreement was a contract, and if so, whether it was executory so that TCO could elect to assume or reject it under §365. * * *

At the outset, we should ask whether this settlement agreement would be considered a contract had there been no bankruptcy. Generally, application of the Bankruptcy Code does not change the attributes of a given legal relationship. *Butner v. United States,* 440 U.S. 48, 99 (1979). Thus, if the settlement agreement should be considered a contract under relevant nonbankruptcy law, it will be a contract in bankruptcy "[u]nless some federal interest requires a different result. ... " *Id.* at 55.

Although settlement agreements may be judicially approved, they share many characteristics of voluntary contracts and are construed according to traditional precepts of contract construction. In a non-bankruptcy context, we have treated a settlement agreement as a contract.

We see nothing special in this bankruptcy that counsels a different approach. The core of this settlement agreement was consensual obligations. ... What is especially significant in this case is that there remains an agreement that the debtor can breach which could give rise to a claim against it. [We] consider this settlement agreement as a contract for purposes of §365. * * *

IV

The heart of this dispute is whether the settlement agreement was executory on July 31, 1991, when TCO filed its bankruptcy petition. The term "executory contract" is not defined in the Bankruptcy Code, and the phrase does not indicate its intended scope.

The legislative history of §365 suggests a broad reading of "executory." Congressional reports stated "[t]hough there is no precise definition of what contracts are executory, it generally includes contracts on which performance remains due to some extent on both sides." H.R. Rep. No. 595, 95th Cong., 1st Sess. 347 (1977).

Most courts have agreed that the definition suggested by the legislative history would cut too broadly, "since it is the rare agreement that does not involve unperformed obligations on either side." *Mitchell v. Streets,* 882 F.2d 233, 235 (7th Cir. 1989). As one commentator observed, "[a]ll contracts to a greater or less extent are executory. When they cease to be so, they cease to be contracts." Vern Countryman, *Executory Contracts in Bankruptcy: Part I,* 57 Minn. L. Rev. 439, 450 (1973).

The language and legislative history of §365 having proved unavailing, courts and commentators sought to analyze the purpose of §365 in order to formulate a definition of "executory contract." Executory contracts in bankruptcy are best recognized as a combination of assets and liabilities to the bankruptcy estate; the performance the nonbankrupt owes the debtor constitutes an asset, and the performance the debtor owes the nonbankrupt is a liability. See Thomas H. Jackson, The Logic and Limits of Bankruptcy Law 106-107 (1986). The debtor (or trustee that has stepped into the debtor's shoes) may elect to assume an executory contract, in which case §365 mandates that the debtor accept the liability with the asset and fully perform his end of the bargain. §365(b).

The debtor will assume an executory contract when the package of assets and liabilities is a net asset to the estate. When it is not the debtor will (or ought to) reject the contract. §365(a). Because assumption acts as a renewed acceptance of the terms of the executory bargain, the Bankruptcy Code provides that the cost of performing the debtor's obligations is an administrative expense of the estate, which will be paid [ahead of general obligations] out of the assets of the estate.[8] §507(a)[(2)].

Through the mechanism of assumption, §365 allows the debtor to continue doing business with others who might otherwise be reluctant to do so because of the bankruptcy filing.

Rejection, which is appropriate when a contract is a liability to the bankrupt, is equivalent to a nonbankruptcy breach. §365(g). Rejection leaves the nonbankrupt with a claim against the estate just as would a breach in the nonbankruptcy context, and unless the nonbankrupt's claim is somehow secured, he will be a general unsecured creditor of the estate. Accordingly, if the debtor is insolvent, the nonbankrupt's claim for breach will not be paid in full. An appropriate rejection in bankruptcy will thus benefit the creditors as a whole at the expense of the nonbankrupt. See Thomas H. Jackson, The Logic and Limits of Bankruptcy Law 108 (1986).

In cases where the nonbankrupt party has fully performed, it makes no sense to talk about assumption or rejection. At that point only a liability exists for the debtor—a simple claim held by the nonbankrupt against the estate—and "[t]he estate has whatever benefit it can obtain from the other party's performance and the trustee's rejec-

---

[8] In In re Taylor, 913 F.2d 102, 106-107 (3d Cir. 1990), we stated: [T]he "assume or reject" dichotomy means simply that if the trustee wishes to obtain for the estate the future benefits of the executory portion of the contract, the trustee must also assume the burdens of that contract, as an expense of bankruptcy administration (i.e., having priority over all pre-bankruptcy claims of creditors).

tion would neither add to nor detract from the creditor's claim or the estate's liability." Countryman, supra, at 451. Rejection is meaningless in this context, and assumption would be of no benefit to the estate, serving only to convert the nonbankrupt's claim into a first priority expense of the estate at the expense of the other creditors.

Likewise, if the debtor has fully performed, the performance owed by the nonbankrupt is an asset of the bankruptcy estate and should be analyzed as such, not as an executory contract. Jackson, supra, at 107. Rejection of the contract at this point is no different from abandonment of property of the estate, an action taken only when the property is "burdensome to the estate or ... is of inconsequential value and benefit to the estate." §554(a).

These considerations led us to adopt, as have many courts of appeals, the following definition of executory contract for purposes of §365: "[An executory contract is] a contract under which the obligation of both the bankrupt and the other party to the contract are so far unperformed that the failure of either to complete performance would constitute a material breach excusing performance of the other." Sharon Steel Corp. v. National Fuel Gas Distrib. Corp., 872 F.2d 36, 39 (3d Cir. 1989).

Def.
Executory
Contract

Thus, unless both parties have unperformed obligations that would constitute a material breach if not performed, the contract is not executory under §365. When it is the nonbankrupt party who has substantially performed so that its failure to complete performance would not constitute a material breach excusing performance of the debtor,[10] the nonbankrupt party is "relegated to the position of a general creditor of the bankrupt estate." Marcus & Millichap Inc. v. Munple, Ltd., 868 F.2d 1129, 1130 (9th Cir. 1989). The time for testing whether there are material unperformed obligations on both sides is when the bankruptcy petition is filed.

In this case, the settlement agreement was created by the parties in a federal court in Ohio, and Ohio law would therefore normally ap-

---

[10] In order to determine whether failure to perform the remaining obligations would constitute a material breach, we need to consider contract principles under the relevant nonbankruptcy law. In Hall v. Perry (In re Cochise College Park, Inc.), 703 F.2d 1339, 1348 n.4 (9th Cir. 1983), the court noted "a bankruptcy court should determine whether one of the parties' failure to perform its remaining obligations would give rise to a 'material breach' excusing performance by [the] other party under the contract law applicable to the contract."

ply. However, the parties do not indicate any particular law as governing either the issue of material breach or the construction of the settlement agreement. ... Accordingly, like the parties and the district court, we will construe the issue of what would constitute a material breach under general contract principles. * * *

As we have noted, at stake is the relative priority of the claims of the IRS and the class members to TCO's assets in bankruptcy. If the contract is executory, TCO would assume it, and the $15 million TCO still owes would become an administrative expense of the estate. As an administrative expense, the class members' claims would fall into the category afforded ... payment priority [ahead of general obligations]. §507(a)[(2)]. If the contract is not executory, the class members would have a general unsecured claim and would have lowest payment priority, and would be paid after the IRS's claim, which is seventh in priority regardless of the outcome of this dispute. §507(a)[(8)].

A

The contract was clearly executory on TCO's side when it filed for bankruptcy, a point both parties appear to accept. It had not paid the second $15 million into escrow, nor had it completed the administrative work necessary to authorize distribution of the escrow monies to those class members who had signed and executed releases and supplemental contracts. While the administrative details TCO still had to perform are arguably non-material (an issue we need not reach), the $15 million payment is unquestionably a material obligation, and TCO's failure to make the second payment certainly would constitute a material breach.

B

The materiality of the class members' unperformed obligations is a closer question. As we have noted, the obligations on both sides must be so far unperformed so that failure of either to complete performance would constitute a material breach excusing performance of the other. The class members had unperformed duties under the settlement agreement. Only 41 of the 852 contracts had been processed when TCO filed for bankruptcy, and the class members responsible for the remaining 811 contracts still had to execute releases and supplemental contracts in order to receive their shares of the escrow fund. It must be the contention of the class members that these obligations are sufficiently material that failure to perform would constitute a material breach of the agreement by the class members. * * *

[W]e turn first to an analysis of the releases and then to the contract supplements. If a class member declined to execute a release, the settlement agreement provides that TCO retains that class member's portion of the $30 million. But the class member's cause of action against TCO on the gas purchase contract would not be revived. All such claims were extinguished when the district court's order became final on July 18, 1991.

The language of the settlement agreement makes clear the parties intended to make execution of the releases a condition of payment rather than a duty: "[P]ayments to individual Class Members out of the escrowed amounts will be contingent upon receipt by [TCO] of a duly executed release ... . If the amount allocated to a particular contract by Class Counsel ... is not finally distributed to that particular contract, then such Distributable Amount ... shall be returned to [TCO]."

The parties specified that the class members' claims would be extinguished (as they in fact were) by the court order accepting the settlement agreement. Thus, the releases served no more than the administrative purpose of a condition to the class members' ability to get payment from the escrow fund. * * *

The consequence of a class member's failure to execute a release supports this textual analysis. A class member who failed to execute a release would not get its share of the settlement fund, but TCO would still get the benefit of the class member's inability to sustain a cause of action. As the district court observed, "the parties seem to agree that if this case involved a simple exchange of money for execution of a release of all claims, there would be no question that the contract would not be executory." Nor would any class member's failure absolve TCO from its duty to place the second $15 million into escrow, a duty which was to ripen on March 23, 1992, without regard to the actions of any class member. No failure on the part of the class members to execute a release under the settlement agreement could have created a material breach of the contract. Rather, the releases were a condition for each member to get its share of the settlement money.

The settlement agreement also required each class member to complete a supplemental contract for future gas sales to TCO. * * * There is no indication that the supplemental contracts were designed to do more than take the terms of the global settlement agreement created by the class and TCO and apply them specifically to each class member. As such they were functionally ministerial duties; they did not, nor were they supposed to, alter the relationship forged by the settlement agreement. The terms of the supplemental contracts were expressly stated in the settlement agreement itself and were designed to be implemented with it. This demonstrates the supplemental contracts were intended to confirm, not to create, the new purchasing arrangement between TCO and the class members.

We agree with the district court that "executing the contract supplements will be little more than a perfunctory act utilizing preapproved terms and conditions. ... An individual class member's failure to execute the supplemental contract would not constitute a material breach of the settlement agreement but rather would be the failure of a condition that would relieve TCO's obligation to pay that member its portion of the escrow monies.

Further, TCO cannot really be concerned with whether a given class member executes a supplemental contract, as the main terms governing the future purchases were embodied in the settlement agreement itself. The supplemental contracts were more important to the class members (the obligors) than to TCO (the obligee). Class counsel made clear before the district court that the supplemental contracts were important to the class members. The supplemental contracts required TCO to pay higher prices than under the old contracts and thus benefited the class, and the class even concedes the primary benefit of the contract supplements inured to the class members. Without more, it was unlikely that the parties intended that failure to execute them would be a breach by the class members. * * * [N]ot every contract that appears executory because it has not been completely performed is executory for purposes of §365. * * *

C

An examination of the purpose of §365 leads to the same result. The only functional difference between assumption and rejection in this case, were the contract to be considered executory, is that assumption would give the class a higher priority to the unpaid $15 million. In return TCO would gain nothing of value: the releases add no rights to the estate not already given by the district court's order, and the supplements provide only a marginal benefit to TCO. The Ohio District Court's order bound the class as a whole. Once the order became final and unappealable, all the class members were bound by it. Accordingly, the class members' failure to complete the tasks required for them to receive their money could not breach the agreement between the class and TCO, but could only serve as the failure of conditions precedent to their right to settlement monies. Assumption would not add assets to the bankruptcy estate. The agreement is not an executory contract for purposes of §365. * * *

NOTES

7A.1. In *Energy Enterprises*, TCO, through its management as debtor in possession, would have assumed the settlement agreement because it preferred its suppliers to the IRS. General sentiment about the IRS notwithstanding, such preference is not a valid reason to assume an executory contract. The court did not have to squarely address the assumption attempt because it found that the settlement was not executory. As we shall see, however, assumption requires court approval, which this court might well have withheld had the request come up.

7A.2. The court explains that assumption of an executory contract gives rise to an administrative expense—i.e., high priority—for the debtor's obligations under the contract. The debtor cannot demand the full benefits of an executory contract without fully satisfying the obligations. Put another way, bankruptcy law honors the implicit right to setoff within any executory contract. This and other issues of administrative expense priority are described below in chapter 9, as is the concept of abandonment, also mentioned by the court in *Energy Enterprises*.

B.   ASSUMPTION

An executory contract or unexpired lease that is favorable to the debtor is a net asset. The bankruptcy trustee should be able to preserve such an asset for the estate just as she can preserve any other asset of the debtor. Preservation of a net-asset contract or lease is called "assumption" and is explicitly permitted by §365(a), subject to court approval, if assumption is timely under §365(d) and complies with other specified requirements such as the cure of defaults as provided by §365(b).

The "cure" requirement may seem straightforward, but consider the fact that some breaches are by their nature incurable. A literal interpretation of the "cure" requirement could deprive a debtor of an opportunity to assume even if the debtor could pay damages for the breach and still profit from the contract. For example, in In re Claremont Acquisitions, Corp., 113 F.3d 1029 (9th Cir. 1997), a franchise agreement was subject to termination unless the debtor-franchisee continuously operated the franchise business, an auto dealership. By the time of the debtor's bankruptcy petition, the debtor had already failed to operate the business, and of course the debtor could not go back in time to remedy this breach of continuity. The court in *Claremont* held that despite the impossibility of cure, the failure of cure meant that the debtor could not assume the agreement. The 2005 Bankruptcy Act partially addressed this situation with new §365(b)(1)(A), which permits a trustee or debtor to assume in such a case, but only where the agreement in question is real-property lease (ironically, unlike in *Claremont* itself). The provision also appears to add (in extraordinarily dense language) that if the lease thus assumed is of nonresidential real property, the trustee (or debtor-in-possession) must cure the breach to the extent possible—to begin operation of a lapsed business, e.g., where the breach is of a continuity requirement—and must compensate the lessor for pecuniary damages from the breach.

The case of impossible cure aside, that the trustee can assume an executory contract or lease, but only if done in a timely fashion after the cure of any default, is to be expected from a process that gathers assets as subject to others' interests in those assets. Section 365(c), however, places an odd limitation on the kinds of contracts that may be assumed:

> The trustee may not assume ... any executory contract ... whether or not such contract ... prohibits or restricts assignment of rights or delegation of duties, if ... applicable law excuses a party, other than the debtor, to such contract ... from accepting performance from or rendering performance to an entity other than the debtor or the debtor in possession.

This limitation is puzzling. The trustee must be able to assert control over the debtor's assets and ensure that the creditors can enjoy whatever assets they could enjoy outside of bankruptcy. It is not clear why the debtor's ability to assume a contract should turn on whether the debtor could delegate its performance under the contract to a third party. Section 365(c) prevents some valuable contracts from being enjoyed by creditors without the blessing of the other party to the contract, but it is not apparent why this should be so.

We may be able to understand §365(c) by first focusing on the way it works in the case of the flesh-and-blood individual. In that case, its operation appears at first blush sensible. This provision is one of the few places in the Bankruptcy Code in which we encounter problems from treating individuals and firms in financial distress in the same way.

With respect to individuals in Chapter 7, §365(c) might seem to be part of the fresh start. Consider an opera singer who has a contract to sing with an opera house next year. Now slightly past his prime, the singer cannot now bargain for a new contract that would be as favorable. The opera singer is deeply in debt and files a Chapter 7 petition. The opera singer wants to be able to sing at the opera house and enjoy the promised fee. The opera company would like to cancel the engagement. The creditors of the opera singer want to be able reach the lucrative fee to recover some of what they are owed.

As a matter of first principle, the singer should be able to take advantage of the contract as it is part of his future earnings and therefore his fresh start. The creditors should not be able to reach the fee for the same reason. *Butner* tells us that the opera house should not be excused from an unfavorable contract by the happenstance of the singer's financial problems. In the absence of §365(a), one might reach just this result. Section 541(a)(6) may exclude the fee from the estate. It represents "earnings from services performed by an individual debtor after the commencement of the case."

Section 365(c) might have been intended to ensure this same outcome despite §365(a). The trustee cannot assume such a personal services contract, a contract that the opera singer could not have assigned to anyone outside of bankruptcy.

This reading, however, generates a problem. Once one assumes that the singer's deal with the opera company is an executory contract that falls within the ambit of §365, the apparent sense of §365(c) begins to unravel. The inability of the trustee to assume the contract means that it is rejected and §365(g) deems rejection a breach of the contract. This would generate the odd result that the singer's bankruptcy filing released the opera house from an unfavorable contract. This outcome is hard to defend on the basis of bankruptcy policy. A court might rule that the singer's contract with the opera house is personal to him, thus not subject to the trustee's assumption or rejection. See, e.g., In re Carrere, 64 Bankr. 156 (Bankr. C.D. Cal. 1986). In this event, however, the language in §365(c) applies only in cases in which there is a corporate debtor, and hence this rationale for the section is unavailable.

Let us consider an analogous set of facts involving a corporate debtor. A traveling opera signs a contract with a summer festival to mount several performances. After several months of bad reviews and indifferent productions, the opera company files for bankruptcy. The summer festival would prefer to book another act or at least renegotiate its contract with this company. By contrast, the opera company pins its hopes of reorganization upon its appearance at this summer festival. Hence, the trustee wants to assume this contract in bankruptcy. Under nonbankruptcy law, the trustee would have no ability to assign its contract to appear at the festival to another opera company. Section 365(c)(1), however, seems to establish a hypothetical test: The trustee may not *assume* an executory contract over the nondebtor's objection if applicable law would bar *assignment* to a hypothetical third party. The limitation applies even when the trustee has no intention of assigning the contract in question to any such third party. Taken literally, §365(c)(1) bars assumption in this case because applicable state law excuses the summer festival "from accepting performance from ... an entity other than the debtor or debtor in possession. ... " The summer festival, like the opera house in the case of the singer, enjoys a windfall by happenstance of bankruptcy. This outcome is again hard to square with bankruptcy policy.

A comparison of these two hypotheticals illustrates the consequences of the "may not assume" language in §365(c)(1). Congress intended the language to protect individual debtors from forced labor for the benefit of creditors. The provision saves individuals from an aggressive trustee. The same language, however, when applied to a corporate debtor, deprives the bankruptcy estate of a valuable asset. When the debtor is a corporation, preventing assumption leaves no individual with a right to perform on her own as part of a fresh start. Instead the unintended beneficiary is the nondebtor party to the contract. It receives a windfall when it is released from its obligations.

To make §365 consistent with §541(c) and the *Butner* principle, it would have to take on a radically different form. It might need to exclude contracts for future services by individual debtors from its reach altogether. Moreover, it would need to allow the trustee to assume every contract of a corporate debtor, while still prohibiting assignment whenever state law either relieved third parties from accepting performance from nondebtors or enforced contractual provisions prohibiting assignment.

A second problem arises in those cases in which the trustee can assume the contract under §365. Section 365(f)(1) allows the trustee to assign a contract notwithstanding a provision in the contract that prohibits assignment or one in applicable law. Once the trustee assigns a contract, the assignee alone is liable for breach, even though under state law the assignor remains liable unless released by the other party. See §365(k). The cases below attempt to reconcile §365(c) and (f). Much of the difficulty arises because, unlike §541, §365 links assumption and assignment. The effect is to define assumption too narrowly and assignment too broadly. It limits the ability of the trustee of the corporate debtor to bring valuable contracts into the estate even when nothing about the operations of the debtor has changed that would release the third party under nonbankruptcy law. At the same time, it expands the trustee's ability to assign contracts relative to the nonbankruptcy baseline.

When the trustee assumes a contract that is in default, he must cure defaults or provide adequate assurance of cure, including compensation for injury, and provide adequate assurance of future performance. The trustee must also give adequate assurances of performance whenever the contract is assigned, regardless of whether there has been a default. We saw in the last chapter that ipso facto clauses are generally disregarded in bankruptcy. For this reason, defaults under ipso facto clauses need not be cured. As we would expect, §365(e) and (f)(3) contain a prohibition on such clauses parallel to the one we saw in §541(c).

The exercises below illustrate the basic functions of Bankruptcy Code §365(b), (d), and (f). The cases that follow, *Perlman* and *Institut Pasteur*, as well as the related notes and problems demonstrate how the link between assumption and assignment in §365(c) has been a source of much difficulty and disagreement.

Key Provisions: Bankruptcy Code §365(a)-(f)

EXERCISES

7B(1) Debtor Corporation files a voluntary petition for bankruptcy. Six weeks later, the bankruptcy trustee seeks to have Debtor assume an executory contract with Supplier. There has been no default on the contract. Should the court permit this assumption over Supplier's objection? Does your answer depend on whether the bankruptcy case is under Chapter 7 as opposed to Chapter 11? Might your answer change if Debtor attempted to assume not an ordinary executory contract but a commercial real estate lease between Debtor and a landlord?

7B(2) Debtor is a retailer that enters bankruptcy after severe cash shortages cause Debtor to default on numerous obligations. Despite its general failure to pay, Debtor has not defaulted on its still executory contract with Supplier. Debtor seeks to assume this contract. Supplier objects, claiming that it feels insecure about Debtor's ability to perform in the future. Must Debtor provide adequate assurance of future performance before Debtor can assume? Would your answer change if Supplier had a right to demand such assurance under the Uniform Commercial Code, §2-609? Would your answer change if Debtor had missed a payment on the contract with Supplier? Would your answer change if Debtor wants not only to assume the contract with Supplier but also to assign Debtor's rights and obligations under the contract?

7B(3) Debtor is a wholesaler with two important executory contracts. One is an agreement that permits Debtor to purchase inventory from Manufacturer on credit. The second contract is an agreement to sell inventory to Retailer on credit. (The distribution contracts with other retailers have expired.) Each contract contains a termination-in-the-event-of-insolvency clause as well as a nonassignment clause. After Debtor files for bankruptcy the trustee wishes to assume and assign each contract. May the trustee do so? Could the trustee have merely assumed each contract? Note that § 365(c)(2) limits a debtor's ability to assume a contract for the extensions of credit. You should read it before answering these questions. See In re Thomas B. Hamilton Co., 969 F.2d 1013 (11th Cir. 1992)

7B(4) Debtor rents commercial space in Landlord's shopping center. The unexpired lease provides that the leased premises must be used only as a sporting goods store and prohibits assignment by the lessee. After filing a bankruptcy petition, Debtor seeks to assume the lease and assign it to a restaurant in a weaker financial condition than that of Debtor at the time Debtor entered the lease. Can Landlord prevent this assumption and assignment? Would your answer change if Debtor sought to assume and assign not an unexpired lease, but a similarly drafted executory contract for space in a publisher's multi-retailer mail-order catalogue? Would your answer change if the limitation on the leased premises related not to the use of the premises but to the height and hair color of the lessee? In answering these questions consider, among other provisions, §365(b)(3).

7B(5) Country Club hosts social events and offers dining facilities, tennis courts, a swimming pool, and a golf course. Members must pay an annual fee to continue their memberships. There is a waiting list for general memberships. Among club members, there is also a waiting list for golf privileges. Debtor, who has a club membership with golf privileges, files a Chapter 7 bankruptcy petition. Will Debtor be able to enjoy the membership after his bankruptcy case closes? Or can the trustee assume and assign Debtor's membership with its golf privileges to a nonmember or to a member who is on the waiting list for golf privileges? See Rieser v. Dayton Country Club Co., 972 F.2d 689 (6th Cir. 1992).

7B(6) Debtor is multi-billion dollar national retailer that files for bankruptcy under Chapter 11. Almost immediately upon filing, Debtor's largest creditors oust the prepetition managers and put in place a skilled turnaround team. New management's most important task is to determine which of Debtor's 500 outlets should be continued and which should be abandoned, a process that will take a minimum of one year to do properly. In many locations, Debtor holds leases on its retail space that are below market, but only if the location can support a retailer in that space. Thus, the decision whether to assume or reject the leases must be made on a case-by-case basis. What dilemma does Debtor's management face? In answering this question, in addition to the provisions of §365, consider §503(b)(7) and return to this exercise after reading chapter 9, section D below, which describes administrative expense priorities.

CASES

PERLMAN v. CATAPULT ENTERTAINMENT, INC.

United States Court of Appeals, Ninth Circuit, 1999
165 F.3d 747

FLETCHER, CIRCUIT JUDGE.

Appellant Stephen Perlman ("Perlman") licensed certain patents to appellee Catapult Entertainment, Inc. ("Catapult"). He now seeks to bar Catapult, which has since become a Chapter 11 debtor in possession, from assuming the patent licenses as part of its reorganization plan. * * *

Catapult, a California corporation, was formed in 1994 to create an online gaming network for 16-bit console videogames. That same year, Catapult entered into two license agreements with Perlman, wherein Perlman granted to Catapult the right to exploit certain relevant technologies, including patents and patent applications.

In October 1996, Catapult filed for reorganization under Chapter 11 of the Bankruptcy Code. Shortly before the filing of the bankruptcy petition, Catapult entered into a merger agreement with Mpath Interactive, Inc. ("Mpath"). This agreement contemplated the filing of the bankruptcy petition, followed by a reorganization via a "reverse triangular merger" involving Mpath, MPCAT Acquisition Corporation ("MPCAT"), and Catapult. Under the terms of the merger agreement, MPCAT (a wholly-owned subsidiary of Mpath created for this transaction) would merge into Catapult, leaving Catapult as the surviving entity. When the dust cleared, Catapult's creditors and equity holders would have received approximately $14 million in cash, notes, and securities; Catapult, in turn, would have become a wholly-owned subsidiary of Mpath. The relevant third party creditors and equity holders accepted Catapult's reorganization plan by the majorities required by the Bankruptcy Code.

On October 24, 1996, as part of the reorganization plan, Catapult filed a motion with the bankruptcy court seeking to assume some 140 executory contracts and leases, including the Perlman licenses. * * *

Section 365 of the Bankruptcy Code gives a trustee in bankruptcy (or, in a Chapter 11 case, the debtor in possession) the authority to assume, assign, or reject the executory contracts and unexpired leases of the debtor, notwithstanding any contrary provisions appearing in such contracts or leases. This extraordinary authority, however, is not absolute. Section 365(c)(1) provides that, notwithstanding the general policy set out in §365(a):

> (c) The trustee may not assume or assign any executory contract or unexpired lease of the debtor, whether or not such contract or lease prohibits or restricts assignment of rights or delegation of duties, if

> (1)(A) applicable law excuses a party, other than the debtor, to such contract or lease from accepting performance from or rendering performance to an entity other than the debtor or the debtor in possession, whether or not such contract or lease prohibits or restricts assignment of rights or delegation of duties; and

> (B) such party does not consent to such assumption or assignment ... .

Our task, simply put, is to apply this statutory language to the facts at hand and determine whether it prohibits Catapult, as the debtor in possession, from assuming the Perlman licenses without Perlman's consent.[1]

While simply put, our task is not so easily resolved; the proper interpretation of §365(c)(1) has been the subject of considerable disagreement among courts and commentators. On one side are those who adhere to the plain statutory language, which establishes a so-called "hypothetical test" to govern the assumption of executory contracts. On the other side are those that forsake the statutory language in favor of an "actual test" that, in their view, better accomplishes the intent of Congress. * * *

We begin, as we must, with the statutory language. [T]he statute by its terms bars a debtor in possession from assuming an executory contract without the nondebtor's consent where applicable law precludes assignment of the contract to a third party. The literal language of §365(c)(1) is thus said to establish a "hypothetical test": a debtor in possession may not assume an executory contract over the nondebtor's objection if applicable law would bar assignment to a hypothetical third party, even where the debtor in possession has no intention of assigning the contract in question to any such third party.

Before applying the statutory language to the case at hand, we first resolve a number of preliminary issues that are either not disputed by the parties, or are so clearly established as to deserve no more than passing reference. First, we follow the lead of the parties in assuming that the Perlman licenses are executory agreements within the meaning of §365. Second, it is well-established that §365(c)'s use of the term "trustee" includes Chapter 11 debtors in possession. Third, our precedents make it clear that federal patent law constitutes "applicable law" within the meaning of §365(c), and that nonexclusive patent licenses are "personal and assignable only with the consent of the licensor." Everex Systems, Inc. v. Cadtrak Corp., 89 F.3d 673, 680 (9th Cir. 1996).

---

[1] Perlman also contends that, even if Catapult were entitled to assume the Perlman licenses, §365(c)(1) also prohibits the assignment of the Perlman licenses to Mpath, accomplished by Catapult here through the contemplated Catapult-MPCAT-Mpath reverse triangular merger. Because we conclude that §365(c)(1) bars Catapult from assuming the Perlman licenses, we express no opinion regarding whether the merger transaction contemplated by Catapult would have resulted in a prohibited "assignment" within the meaning of §365(c)(1).

When we have cleared away these preliminary matters, application of the statute to the facts of this case becomes relatively straightforward:

> (c) *Catapult* may not assume … *the Perlman licenses*, … if
>
> (1)(A) *federal patent law* excuses *Perlman* from accepting performance from or rendering performance to an entity other than *Catapult* … ; and
>
> (B) *Perlman* does not consent to such assumption … .

§365(c) (substitutions in italics). Since federal patent law makes nonexclusive patent licenses personal and nondelegable, §365(c)(1)(A) is satisfied. Perlman has withheld his consent, thus satisfying §365(c)(1)(B). Accordingly, the plain language of §365(c)(1) bars Catapult from assuming the Perlman licenses.

Catapult urges us to abandon the literal language of §365(c)(1) in favor of an alternative approach, reasoning that Congress did not intend to bar debtors in possession from assuming their own contracts where no assignment is contemplated. In Catapult's view, §365(c)(1) should be interpreted as embodying an "actual test": the statute bars assumption by the debtor in possession only where the reorganization in question results in the nondebtor actually having to accept performance from a third party. Under this reading of §365(c), the debtor in possession would be permitted to assume any executory contract, so long as no assignment was contemplated. Put another way, Catapult suggests that, as to a debtor in possession, §365(c)(1) should be read to prohibit assumption and assignment, rather than assumption or assignment.

Catapult has marshalled considerable authority to support this reading. The arguments supporting Catapult's position can be divided into three categories: (1) the literal reading creates inconsistencies within §365; (2) the literal reading is incompatible with the legislative history; and (3) the literal reading flies in the face of sound bankruptcy policy. Nonetheless, we find that none of these considerations justifies departing from the plain language of §365(c)(1).

Catapult first argues that a literal reading of §365(c)(1) sets the statute at war with itself and its neighboring provisions. Deviation from the plain language, contends Catapult, is necessary if internal consistency is to be achieved. We agree with Catapult that a court should interpret a statute, if possible, so as to minimize discord among related provisions. * * *

Catapult, for example, singles out the interaction between §365(c)(1) and §365(f)(1) as a statutory trouble spot. Subsection (f)(1) provides that executory contracts, once assumed, may be assigned notwithstanding any contrary provisions contained in the contract or applicable law:

> (f)(1) Except as provided in subsection (c) of this section, notwithstanding a provision in an executory contract or unexpired lease of the debtor, *or in applicable law,* that prohibits, restricts, or conditions the assignment of such contract or lease, the trustee may assign such contract or lease under paragraph (2) of this subsection ... .

(emphasis added).

The potential conflict between subsections (c)(1) and (f)(1) arises from their respective treatments of "applicable law." The plain language of subsection (c)(1) bars assumption (absent consent) whenever "applicable law" would bar assignment. Subsection (f)(1) states that, *contrary provisions in applicable law notwithstanding,* executory contracts may be assigned. Since assumption is a necessary prerequisite to assignment under §365, a literal reading of subsection (c)(1) appears to render subsection (f)(1) superfluous. * * *

Subsection (c)(1), however, states a carefully crafted exception to the broad rule—where applicable law does not merely recite a general ban on assignment, but instead more specifically "excuses a party ... from accepting performance from or rendering performance to an entity" different from the one with which the party originally contracted, the applicable law prevails over subsection (f)(1). In other words, in determining whether an "applicable law" stands or falls under §365(f)(1), a court must ask why the "applicable law" prohibits assignment. Only if the law prohibits assignment on the rationale that the identity of the contracting party is material to the agreement will subsection (c)(1) rescue it. We agree with the Sixth and Eleventh Circuits that a literal reading of subsection (c)(1) does not inevitably set it at odds with subsection (f)(1).

Catapult next focuses on the internal structure of §365(c)(1) itself. According to Catapult, the literal approach to subsection (c)(1) renders the phrase "or the debtor in possession" contained in §365(c)(1)(A) superfluous. In the words of one bankruptcy court, "[i]f the directive of §365(c)(1) is to prohibit assumption whenever applicable law excuses performance relative to any entity other than the debtor, why add the words 'or debtor in possession?' The [hypothetical] test renders this phrase surplusage." In re Hartec [Enters., Inc., 117 Bankr. 865, 871-72 (Bankr. W.D. Tex. 1990).]

A close reading of §365(c)(1), however, dispels this notion. By its terms, subsection (c)(1) addresses two conceptually distinct events: assumption and assignment. The plain language of the provision makes it clear that each of these events is contingent on the non-debtor's separate consent. Consequently, where a nondebtor consents to the assumption of an executory contract, subsection (c)(1) will have to be applied a second time if the debtor in possession wishes to assign the contract in question. On that second application, the relevant question would be whether "applicable law excuses a party from accepting performance from or rendering performance to an entity other than ... *the debtor in possession.*" §365(c)(1)(A) (emphasis added). Consequently, the phrase "debtor in possession," far from being rendered superfluous by a literal reading of subsection (c)(1), dovetails neatly with the disjunctive language that opens subsection (c)(1): "The trustee may not assume *or* assign. ... " 11 U.S.C. §365(c) (emphasis added). * * *

We conclude that the claimed inconsistencies are not actual and that the plain language of §365(c)(1) compels the result Perlman urges: Catapult may not assume the Perlman licenses over Perlman's objection. Catapult has not demonstrated that, in according the words of subsection (c)(1) their plain meaning, we do violence to subsection (c)(1) or the provisions that accompany it.

Catapult next urges that legislative history requires disregard of the plain language of §365(c)(1). First off, because we discern no ambiguity in the plain statutory language, we need not resort to legislative history.

We will depart from this rule, if at all, only where the legislative history clearly indicates that Congress meant something other than what it said. Here, the legislative history unearthed by Catapult falls far short of this mark. The legislative history behind §365(c) was exhaustively analyzed by the bankruptcy court in [In re Cardinal Industries, 116 Bankr. 964, 978-80 (Bankr. S.D. Ohio 1990)]. Its discussion makes it clear that there exists no contemporaneous legislative history regarding the current formulation of subsection (c)(1). Catapult, however, argues that the language as ultimately enacted in 1984 had its genesis in a 1980 House amendment to an earlier Senate technical corrections bill. In explaining the amendment, the report stated:

This amendment makes it clear that the prohibition against a trustee's power to assume an executory contract does not apply where it is the debtor that is in possession and the performance to be given or received under a personal service contract will be the same as if no petition had been filed because of the personal service nature of the contract.

However, since the report relates to a different proposed bill, predates enactment of §365(c)(1) by several years, and expresses at most the thoughts of only one committee in the House, we are not inclined to view it as the sort of clear indication of contrary intent that would overcome the unambiguous language of subsection (c)(1). Catapult makes the appealing argument that … there are policy reasons to prefer the "actual test." That may be so, but Congress is the policy maker, not the courts.

Policy arguments cannot displace the plain language of the statute; that the plain language of §365(c)(1) may be bad policy does not justify a judicial rewrite. And a rewrite is precisely what the actual test requires. The statute expressly provides that a debtor in possession "may not assume *or* assign" an executory contract where applicable law bars assignment and the nondebtor objects. §365(c)(1) (emphasis added). The actual test effectively engrafts a narrow exception onto §365(c)(1) for debtors in possession, providing that, as to them, the statute only prohibits assumption and assignment, as opposed to assumption or assignment.

Because the statute speaks clearly, and its plain language does not produce a patently absurd result or contravene any clear legislative history, we must "hold Congress to its words." [Brooker v. Desert Hosp. Corp., 947 F.2d 412, 414 (9th Cir. 1991).] Accordingly, we hold that, where applicable nonbankruptcy law makes an executory contract nonassignable because the identity of the nondebtor party is material, a debtor in possession may not assume the contract absent consent of the nondebtor party. A straightforward application of §365(c)(1) to the circumstances of this case precludes Catapult from assuming the Perlman licenses over Perlman's objection. Consequently, the bankruptcy court erred when it approved Catapult's motion to assume the Perlman licenses, and the district court erred in affirming the bankruptcy court.

INSTITUT PASTEUR v. CAMBRIDGE BIOTECH CORP.

United States Court of Appeals, First Circuit, 1997
104 F.3d 489

CYR, CIRCUIT JUDGE.

* * * CBC manufactures and sells retroviral diagnostic tests for detecting the human immunodeficiency virus (HIV) associated with AIDS. Its HIV diagnostics division annually generates approximately $14 million in revenues. Institut Pasteur, a nonprofit French foundation engaged in AIDS-related research and development, owns various patented procedures for diagnosing HIV Virus Type 2 ("HIV2 procedures"). Pasteur Sanofi Diagnostics holds the exclusive right to use and sublicense Institut Pasteur's patents.

In October 1989, CBC and Pasteur entered into mutual cross-license agreements, whereby each acquired a nonexclusive perpetual license to use some of the technology patented or licensed by the other. Specifically, CBC acquired the right to incorporate Pasteur's HIV2 procedures into any diagnostic kits sold by CBC in the United States, Canada, Mexico, Australia, New Zealand and elsewhere.

Each cross-license broadly prohibits the licensee from assigning or sublicensing to others. Nevertheless, either Pasteur or CBC was authorized to "extend to its Affiliated Companies the benefits of this Agreement so that such party shall remain responsible with regard [to] all [license] obligations." "Affiliated Company" is defined as "an organization which controls or is controlled by a party or an organization which is under common control with a party."

CBC filed its Chapter 11 petition on July 7, 1994, and thereafter continued to operate its retroviral diagnostic testing business as debtor-in-possession. Its reorganization plan proposed that CBC assume both cross-licenses, continue to operate its retroviral diagnostics division utilizing Pasteur's patented HIV2 procedures, and sell all CBC stock to a subsidiary of bioMerieux, a giant French biotechnology corporation and Pasteur's direct competitor in international biotechnology sales. Pasteur previously had licensed bioMerieux to use its HIV2 procedures, but the earlier license related to a single product manufactured by bioMerieux (i.e., bioMerieux's VIDAS automated immunoassay test system), and applied only to VIDAS sales in markets other than the United States, Canada, Mexico, Australia, and New Zealand, markets expressly encompassed within the CBC cross-licenses.

Not surprisingly, in due course Pasteur objected to the Plan. Citing Bankruptcy Code §365(c), it contended that the proposed sale of CBC's stock to bioMerieux amounted to CBC's assumption of the patent cross-licenses and their de facto "assignment" to a third party in contravention of the presumption of nonassignability ordained by the federal common law of patents, as well as the explicit nonassignability provision contained in the cross-licenses. Isabelle Bressac, Pasteur's licensing director, attested that Pasteur would not have granted its competitor, bioMerieux, or a subsidiary, a patent license under the terms allowed CBC. * * *

Pasteur argues that the CBC Plan effects a de facto assignment of its two cross-licenses to bioMerieux, contrary to Bankruptcy Code §365(c)(1) which provides as follows:

> The trustee [viz., CBC] may not assume or assign any executory contract ... , whether or not such contract ... prohibits or restricts assignment of rights or delegation of duties, if—

> (1)(A) applicable law excuses a party[ ] other than the debtor[ ] [viz., Pasteur] to such contract ... from accepting performance from or rendering performance to an entity other than the debtor or the debtor in possession, whether or not such contract ... prohibits or restricts assumption or assignment; and

> (B) such party [viz., Pasteur] does not consent to such assumption or assignment ... .

Pasteur argues that in order to encourage optimum product innovation the federal common law of patents presumes that patent licensees, such as CBC, may not sublicense to third parties absent the patent holder's consent. This federal common law rule of presumptive nonassignability thus qualifies as an "applicable law," within the meaning of §365(c)(1)(A), which precludes Pasteur from being compelled to accept performance from any entity other than CBC—e.g., bioMerieux's subsidiary—and therefore prevents CBC from either assuming or assigning these cross-licenses. Further, says Pasteur, even assuming that section 365(c) might allow a debtor simply to assume the cross-licenses without a subsequent assignment to a third party, CBC formally structured this Plan transaction as an assumption by the debtor-in-possession, whereas in substance it was an assignment of the cross-licenses to bioMerieux, a complete stranger to the original cross-licensing agreements.

These contentions are foreclosed by our decision in Summit Inv. & Dev. Corp. v. Leroux (In re Leroux), 69 F.3d 608 (1st Cir. 1995), which analyzed and interpreted companion Bankruptcy Code §365(c) and (e) and their relevant legislative history. As in the present case, in *Leroux* we were urged to interpret §365(c) and (e) as mandating a "hypothetical test." Under such an approach, the Chapter 11 debtor would lose its option to assume the contract, even though it never intended to assign the contract to another entity, if either the particular executory contract or the applicable nonbankruptcy law purported to terminate the contract automatically upon the filing of the Chapter 11 petition or to preclude its assignment to an entity not a party to the contract. Id. at 612.

We rejected the proposed hypothetical test in *Leroux*, holding instead that §365(c) and (e) contemplate a case-by-case inquiry into whether the nondebtor party (viz., Pasteur) *actually* was being "forced to accept performance under its executory contract from someone other than the debtor party with whom it originally contracted." Id. Where the particular transaction envisions that the debtor-in-possession would assume and continue to perform under an executory contract, the bankruptcy court cannot simply presume as a matter of law that the debtor-in-possession is a legal entity *materially* distinct from the prepetition debtor with whom the nondebtor party (viz., Pasteur) contracted. Id. at 613-14 (citing H.R. Rep. No. 1195, 96th Cong., 2d Sess. §27(b) (1980); NLRB v. Bildisco & Bildisco, 465 U.S. 513, 528 (1984)). Rather, "sensitive to the rights of the nondebtor party (viz., Pasteur)," the bankruptcy court must focus on the performance actually to be rendered by the debtor-in-possession with a view to ensuring that the nondebtor party (viz., Pasteur) will receive "the full benefit of [its] bargain." Id. at 612-13 (citing S. Rep. No. 989, 95th Cong., 2d Sess. 59 (1978)).

Given the pragmatic "actual performance" test adopted in *Leroux*, the ultimate findings of fact and conclusions of law made by the bankruptcy court below did not constitute error. CBC simply does not occupy the same position as the debtor in [Everex Systems v. Cadtrack Corp. (In re CFLC, Inc.), 89 F.3d 673 (9th Cir. 1996)], upon which Pasteur relies most heavily. The Plan in *CFLC, Inc.* unmistakably provided for an outright assignment of the debtor's patent license to an entirely different corporation with which the patent holder Cadtrak Corporation had never contracted. By contrast, CBC all along has conducted, and proposes to continue, its retroviral diagnostic enterprise as the same corporate entity which functioned prepetition, while utilizing Pasteur's HIV2 procedures in that same prepetition endeavor.

Pasteur nonetheless insists that the reorganized CBC is different than the prepetition entity, not due merely to its Chapter 11 filing but because it is now *owned by* a different legal entity than before—namely, bioMerieux's subsidiary *qua* CBC shareholder. Pasteur's contention finds no support, however, either in Massachusetts law or in the cross-license provisions it negotiated.

Stock sales are not mergers whereby outright title and ownership of the licensee-corporation's assets (including its patent licenses) pass to the acquiring corporation. Rather, as a corporation, CBC "is a legal entity distinct from its shareholders." Seagram Distillers Co. v. Alcoholic Beverages Control Comm'n, 401 Mass. 713, 519 N.E.2d 276, 281 (1988). Absent compelling grounds for disregarding its corporate form, therefore, CBC's separate legal identity, and its ownership of the patent cross-licenses, survive without interruption notwithstanding repeated and even drastic changes in its ownership.

Furthermore, Pasteur's position finds no support in the negotiated terms of its cross-licenses. As the patent holder—and given CBC's corporate form and the governing Massachusetts law—Pasteur was free to negotiate restrictions on CBC's continuing rights under the cross-licenses based on changes in its stock ownership or corporate control.[11] Nevertheless, these cross-licenses contain no provision either limiting or terminating CBC's rights in the event its stock ownership were to change hands. The generic nonassignability provisions found in these cross-licenses plainly do not address the circumstance presented here. Rather, these nonassignability provisions simply beg the essential question, which is whether bioMerieux's subsidiary, by virtue of its acquisition of CBC stock, terminated *CBC's* rights under the cross-licenses. Interpreted as Pasteur proposes, CBC's own rights under the cross-licenses would terminate with any change in the identity of any CBC stockholder.

Other cross-license provisions directly undercut Pasteur's interpretation as well. These cross-licenses explicitly authorize CBC to share its license rights with any "affiliated company," which on its face presumably encompasses a parent corporation such as bioMerieux's subsidiary. Yet more importantly, CBC insisted upon a

---

[11] Notwithstanding Pasteur's reliance on the important policy goals animating the federal common law of patents, the product-innovation theme promoted under patent law may well be accommodated by allowing patent holders to control sublicensing *through negotiated contract restrictions*.

provision which would afford it the unilateral right to terminate any sublicense Pasteur might extend to a company called Genetic Systems "if control of Genetic Systems shall ... be acquired, directly or indirectly, by any person or group of connected persons or company not having such control at the date hereof, by reconstruction, amalgamation, acquisition of shares or assets or otherwise." Taken together, these provisions persuade us that Pasteur foresaw, or reasonably should have foreseen, that CBC might undergo changes of stock ownership which would not alter its corporate legal identity, but nonetheless chose not to condition the continued viability of its cross-licenses accordingly.[12]

NOTES

7B.1. The *Perlman* court addressed federal patent law at the center of both that case and *Institut Pasteur*. The court said: "[O]ur precedents make it clear that federal patent law constitutes 'applicable law' within the meaning of §365(c), and that nonexclusive patent licenses are 'personal and assignable only with the consent of the licensor.' " The court relied on *Everex Systems*, which found that patent licenses must be nonassignable because the patent holder would otherwise lose control of her patent and with it much of the incentive to innovate that undergirds federal intellectual property law. As the *Everex Systems* court put it, without the restriction on assignment, "every licensee would become a potential competitor with the licensor-patent holder in the market for licenses under the patents." 89 F.3d at 679. Patents would be worth less and investment in discovery would become less profitable. It becomes essential under federal pat-

---

[12] Lastly, Pasteur misplaces reliance upon In re Alltech Plastics, Inc., 5 U.S.P.Q.2d 1806 (Bankr. W.D. Tenn. 1987). . . . Following the conversion of its original Chapter 11 reorganization case to a Chapter 7 liquidation, Alltech discontinued all operations and discharged its employees. Before the debtor once again converted to Chapter 11, its trustee liquidated virtually all its assets, except for its patent license. Noting that plan confirmation is a fact-intensive, equity-based inquiry, the bankruptcy court characterized the sale of Alltech's stock to Fluoropak Container Corporation as a de facto assignment of the patent license to a noncontracting party. It so held because *unlike CBC*, Alltech had ceased to exist except as a "shell." The bankruptcy court specifically observed that the "attempted innovative rebirth of a corporate shell is not analogous to a sale of stock by an active corporation," id. at 1810-11, and that "the present case is distinguished from one where the reorganizing debtor, operating continuously and in good standing with its licensor, seeks to approve the sale of its stock [to a third party]," id. at 1812. . . .

ent law, then, that the patent holder be able to restrict assignment of a license.

7B.2. The court in *Perlman* tries to reconcile §365(c)(1) and §365(f)(1). The court says that, "in determining whether an 'applicable law' stands or falls under §365(f)(1), a court must ask why the 'applicable law' prohibits assignment. Only if the law prohibits assignment on the rationale that the identity of the contracting party is material to the agreement will subsection (c)(1) rescue it." This reasoning is difficult to fathom. *Every* prohibition on assignment is based "on the rationale that the identity of the contracting party is material to the agreement" if there is any rationale at all. This is tautological, as prohibitions on assignment affect nothing other than the identity of the contracting party.

There is another way to reconcile the two subsections. Section 365(c) prevents the trustee from assuming any contract if state law provides explicitly that such contracts cannot be assigned. This kind of a state law is to be distinguished from the more general state law that would simply enforce an agreement prohibiting assignment. Despite §365(c), the trustee may assume contracts that contain clauses prohibiting assignment, even if nonbankruptcy law would enforce such clauses. Section 365(f) goes on to provide that the trustee can assign such contracts, notwithstanding a clause prohibiting assignment. See In re Pioneer Ford Sales, 729 F.2d 27 (1st Cir. 1984) (Breyer, J.).

7B.3. State contract law ordinarily allows parties to specify in their contracts whether their duties can be delegated to others. The typical provision merely provides a presumption for the courts to apply in the face of silence. By overriding what the parties provide in their contract, but nevertheless respecting applicable nonbankruptcy law, §365(c) converts a nonbankruptcy law presumption into a mandatory term. Like the failure to recognize the difference between assumption and assignment, the failure to recognize the difference between mandatory rules and off-the-rack default terms introduces anomalies. It might have made more sense for the trustee to honor any restrictions applicable under nonbankruptcy law, including restrictions applicable merely because the law would enforce explicit contractual terms. The problems below explore some of the difficulties that arise under current law.

7B.4. *Pasteur* shows that the concept of assignment may become elusive when there is a corporate debtor. The ownership of a corporation can change even though the obligations under the contract continue to remain with the same entity. The court in *Pasteur* implies that a third party can limit such a corporate control transaction through contract. Such clauses, however, are functionally identical to contractual limitations on assignment, limitations that §365(f)(1) strikes down.

PROBLEMS

7B-1. Contractor, a debtor in bankruptcy, seeks to assume and assign an executory contract with the United States. The contract, which is for the production of a naval vessel, includes a clause that "prohibits assignment by Contractor." Consider whether Contractor can proceed as it desires in each of the following circumstances:

(i) applicable law permits the United States to reject assignment of a defense contract even if the contract itself explicitly permits assignment;

(ii) applicable law permits the United States to reject assignment of a defense contract unless the contract itself explicitly allows assignment;

(iii) applicable law permits the United States to reject assignment of a defense contract only if the contract itself explicitly prohibits assignment.

7B-2. Auto Dealer and Parts Distributor each sell Manufacturer's products. Each is subject to an ongoing franchise agreement with Manufacturer. Each agreement prohibits the assignment of rights to receive Manufacturer's product without prior approval of Manufacturer, which, according to each agreement, "can be withheld for any reason or no reason." In the state where both Auto Dealer and Parts Distributor operate, there is a special law that permits automobile dealerships to assign their interests subject to the franchisor's approval, which "may not be unreasonably withheld." This law is mandatory. That is, it cannot be altered by contract. There is no similar law for parts distributors. The state generally permits assignment of franchises, but enforces contractual restrictions on assignment. Auto Dealer and Parts Distributor each file for bankruptcy. Can the trustee assume or assign either franchise agreement? Assume, for the sake of illustration, that no federal franchise law applies.

7B-3. Debtor and two others are general partners in a limited real estate partnership—one in which general partners have unlimited liability and plenary management rights while limited partners have limited liability and limited or no management rights. Under state partnership law, a general partner ceases to be a general partner upon filing a bankruptcy petition unless the partnership agreement provides otherwise. The partnership agreement in this case converts a general partner's interest into a limited partnership interest upon the filing of a bankruptcy petition and divests the partner in bankruptcy of the contract right to participate in the partnership management. Debtor files a Chapter 11 petition. Can Debtor continue as a general partner? Can Debtor make someone else a general partner? If Debtor can continue as a general partner but not make someone else a general partner, can Debtor establish a committee of Debtor's creditors and promise to vote on partnership matters as the committee directs? In answering these questions, consider, among other provisions, §365(e)(1) and (2). See also Summit Investment & Development Corp. v. Leroux, 69 F.3d 608 (1st Cir. 1995); In re Antonelli, 148 Bankr. 443 (D. Maryland 1992).

7B-4. City and Debtor Corporation enter into a franchise agreement. Under this agreement, Debtor enjoys the exclusive right to erect, maintain, and operate a cable television system. The grant is enacted into law as a municipal ordinance. It provides that "the rights and privileges herein granted not be assignable." After two years, amid complaints of poor service and with many fewer subscribers than had been projected, Debtor files a Chapter 11 bankruptcy petition. Both City and Debtor agree that the franchise agreement is an executory contract. Debtor's reorganization plan proposes that Debtor assume the contract with City and then sell all shares in the reorganized company to Debtor's competitor. Should the court confirm this plan? See In re James Cable Partners, 27 F.3d 534 (11th Cir. 1994).

C. REJECTION

The Bankruptcy Code §365(a) provides in general that "the trustee, subject to the court's approval, may ... reject any executory contract or unexpired lease of the debtor." The general rule is that rejection of an executory contract or unexpired lease of the debtor "constitutes a breach of such contract or lease ... immediately before the date of the filing of the [debtor's bankruptcy] petition." §365(g). A claim arising from such rejection and breach will be allowed or disallowed "the same as if such claim had arisen before the date of the filing of the petition." §502(g). See In re Enron Corp., 330 Bankr. 387

(Bankr. S.D.N.Y. 2005) (adopts literal interpretation to allow date of petition, rather than date of rejection, damages when different). These provisions together ensure that nondebtors have (essentially) the same rights in bankruptcy as they do outside.

Rejection is a decision by the trustee not to assume a contract. It is not a special power to terminate or rescind debtor's obligations. When an executory contract is rejected:

(1) the estate is no longer under any obligation to perform;

(2) the estate is no longer entitled to receive the benefits of the contract;

(3) the rejection is a breach of the contract creating an un-secured prepetition claim for the nondebtor party; and

(4) this "claim" (and nothing else) is dischargeable in the bankruptcy proceeding.

Imagine that a debtor files a bankruptcy petition while it is obligated to build a house for a landowner in exchange for $100,000 to be paid at the end of the job. Assume that it would cost the debtor more than $100,000 to build the house, and another builder could construct it for $120,000. The court would then give the debtor permission to reject the contract. Such rejection would result in the debtor's breach of the contract. Under nonbankruptcy law, this breach would give rise to damages of $20,000. Under §§365(g) and 502(g), then, the landowner would have an allowed general claim of $20,000 and it would share in the bankruptcy estate with other allowed general claims.

Not all cases of rejection are this simple. For instance, it may not be clear at bankruptcy's outset whether the debtor will benefit more from assumption than from rejection of a contract. While the trustee decides whether to assume or reject, the nondebtor party may have an obligation to perform immediately. As we will see below in chapter 9, any such performance will likely entitle the party to a high priority "administrative" claim against the debtor in exchange, even if the contract is ultimately rejected. Moreover, under §365(d), the party may request an accelerated assumption or rejection decision. Neither of these guarantees payment, however.

Even when the trustee's rejection decision to reject is early and unequivocal, difficult problems can arise. Under applicable nonbank-ruptcy law, the victim of a contract breach sometimes enjoys rights that extend beyond a claim for money damages. In such cases, a bankruptcy court must decide whether "rejection" under §365 alters those rights. Much of the difficulty in reconciling the case law on the rejection of executory contracts stems from the failure of some courts to distinguish between the power of rejection on the one hand and the consequences that flow from rejection on the other. After the exercises below explore the basics, the first two cases, *Leasing Services Corp.* and *In re Register*, ask you to consider this distinction. The third case, *Northwest Airlines*, explores the special circumstance of collective bargaining agreements. The notes and problems that follow the cases address related themes.

Key Provisions: Bankruptcy Code §§365; 502(g); 1113

EXERCISES

7C(1) Debtor Corporation is a construction subcontractor who agrees to build an observation deck for Contractor for $100,000. As it turns out, Debtor miscalculated the costs of construction, which now will cost it $150,000. But Debtor does not discover this until just before Contractor must begin construction of the deck. To replace Debtor at the last minute would cost Contractor $175,000. Debtor, deeply insolvent, files for bankruptcy and Debtor's managers, as debtor in possession, must decide whether to assume or reject the contract. What would Debtor's creditors prefer? Are Contractor and Debtor jointly better off if Debtor does the work? What might Contractor offer Debtor to avoid rejection? Would any of your answers change if Debtor's cost of construction were $200,000 rather than $150,000?

7C(2) Debtor is a retailer. It leases its store and maintains its inventory through a long-term sales contract with Supplier. Debtor has missed payments on both agreements. Debtor files for bankruptcy. Under the lease, the lessor of Debtor's store is required to renovate the premises. Debtor's supplier is due to make a large shipment. Must either the lessor or supplier fulfill these obligations before Debtor assumes the lease or contract? In answering this question consider, among other provisions, §365(b)(4). Consider this question again after you have read chapter 9, section D below and learn how the Bankruptcy Code gives priority to administrative expenses.

LEASING SERVICES CORP. v.
FIRST TENNESSEE BANK

United States Court of Appeals, Sixth Circuit, 1987
826 F.2d 434

KEITH, CIRCUIT JUDGE.

Appellant-cross appellee First Tennessee Bank National Association ("Bank") appeals the district court's grant of summary judgment in favor of appellee-cross appellant Leasing Services Corporation ("LSC"). In its ruling, the court held that LSC was the holder of a security interest, senior to the Bank's own security interest, in the collateral of Metler Crane and Rigging Co. ("Metler"). The court reasoned that the rejection by the trustee-in-bankruptcy of unexpired portions of certain lease agreements between Metler and a third party did not alter the relative priorities between the secured creditors of Metler. * * * For the reasons set forth below, we affirm the judgment of the Honorable Thomas G. Hull.

I

On October 23, 1980, Chatham Machinery, Inc. leased two cranes to Metler. The leases were assigned to LSC. The amounts due under the leases were secured by a security interest in Metler's inventory, goods, equipment and machinery. LSC perfected its security interest by filing the appropriate UCC-1 financing statements.

After LSC had perfected its security interest, the Bank made several loans to Metler and obtained a security interest in the same collateral. The Bank perfected its security interest by filing the appropriate financing statements.

On December 11, 1984, Metler was placed into involuntary bankruptcy pursuant to Chapter 7 of the Bankruptcy Code. Metler surrendered all of its equipment and machinery, except the two cranes, to the Bank. Pursuant to an order in the bankruptcy proceedings, the Bank sold this collateral and realized $443,895 from the sale. The trustee-in-bankruptcy later abandoned these assets, thereby leaving the parties to sort out their claims to these funds. Also, the trustee-in-bankruptcy did not assume Metler's obligation under the lease agreements and was deemed to have rejected these contracts. LSC therefore reclaimed possession of the cranes and sold them, establishing a deficiency balance in the amount of $81,493.

On July 8, 1985, LSC made a demand upon the Bank for payment of $81,493, plus interest and attorney fees. LSC asserted that Metler was indebted to LSC in that amount under the leases, and that LSC had a security interest in the proceeds realized from the sale of Metler's collateral that was superior to that of the Bank. The Bank refused to pay LSC.

On October 1, 1985, LSC filed suit against the Bank seeking $81,493, plus interest from April 11, 1985, and attorney fees. LSC claimed that the Bank, by refusing to recognize LSC's prior lien, had converted to its own use funds which LSC was entitled to receive. The Bank answered LSC's complaint by denying that LSC possessed a superior security interest. * * *

On March 4, 1986, the district court granted summary judgment in favor of LSC, holding that LSC's security interest was superior to that of the Bank. * * *

II

On appeal, the Bank initially argues that the district court erred in holding that LSC possessed the superior security interest. It contends that the lease agreements between Metler and LSC (the assignee) were executory contracts, or unexpired leases. The Bank further contends that pursuant to §365(d)(1), the rejection of the lease agreements by the trustee operated as a matter of law as a rejection of all covenants contained in the leases, including the grant of the security interest. Thus, the Bank argues that the rejection of the leases constituted a breach of the executory and nonexecutory portions of the contracts, leaving LSC in the position of an unsecured creditor.

LSC argues that while rejection of a lease obligation does have the effect of a breach of the contract, it does not affect the creditor's secured status. We agree.

Section 365 provides that a debtor-in-possession or a trustee may assume or reject any executory contract or unexpired lease of the debtor. Rejection denies the right of the contracting creditor to require the bankrupt estate to specifically perform the then executory portions of the contract. Rejection also limits the creditor's claim to damages for breach of contract.

The statutory purpose of Section 365 of the Bankruptcy Code is to enable the trustee to assume those executory obligations which are beneficial to the estate while rejecting those which are onerous or burdensome to perform. * * *

Thus, rejection or assumption of an executory contract determines only the status of the creditor's claim, i.e., whether it is merely a prepetition obligation of the debtor or is entitled to priority as an expense of administration of the estate. The extent to which a claim is secured is wholly unaffected. * * *

The Bank strenuously argues that the trustee's rejection of the contracts extended to nonexecutory as well as executory portions of the agreement. As a result, it argues that LSC was divested of its security interest. The law, however, does not support the Bank's position. In [Jenson v. Continental Financial Corp., 591 F.2d 477 (8th Cir. 1979),] the Eighth Circuit held that a security agreement securing debtor's obligations under a rejected class action settlement agreement was nonexecutory and therefore valid. The security agreement had been given to secure debtor's obligations under either the settlement or under any judgment subsequently obtained if the settlement failed. The court found that the settlement agreement entered into by the parties was an executory contract subject to rejection by the trustee. However, the security agreement was found to be nonexecutory and was not subject to rejection by the trustee. *Jenson,* 591 F.2d at 482. The court stated:

> The consideration given for the security interest was forbearance on the part of the plaintiffs from pressing for the immediate appointment of a receiver for the defendants. This consideration was performed in full by the plaintiffs and the bankrupts have had the full benefit thereof. As such, the trustees have no power to reject the security agreement as executory under Section 70b.

Similarly, in the present case, the security interest granted to LSC to secure Metler's obligation under the leases was fully vested. The consideration for the grant of the security interest was the lessor agreeing to lease the cranes to Metler and LSC agreeing to take an assignment of the leases. Thus, the security interest was nonexecutory and therefore not subject to the rejection power of the trustee. * * *

Applicable state law mandates that the first creditor to perfect a security interest has priority status. In the present case, LSC was the first to perfect its interest. Thus, the district court was correct in stating that an acceptance of the Bank's argument "would be to advance the Bank's later-perfected security interest above LSC's prior lien, negating the priority provisions set forth in Article 9 of the Uniform Commercial Code." * * *

Accordingly, for the reasons set forth above, we affirm the Honorable Thomas G. Hull's grant of summary judgment in favor of LSC. * * *

IN RE REGISTER

United States Bankruptcy Court, M.D. Tennessee, 1989
95 Bankr. 73

PAINE, CHIEF BANKRUPTCY JUDGE.

The issue presented is whether a covenant-not-to-compete contained in a franchise agreement is still enforceable after the debtors-Retailers rejected the executory franchise agreement. The plaintiff, Silk Plants, Etc. Franchise Systems, Inc., is seeking to enjoin the debtors from operating a business in apparent violation of the covenant-not-to-compete. * * *

On March 8, 1986, the Registers executed a franchise agreement with the plaintiff granting the Registers a franchise to operate a Silk Plants, Etc. specialty retail store offering artificial flowers, plants and related items. Under part of the franchise agreement the debtors covenanted not to engage in any capacity in a business offering to sell or selling merchandise or products similar to those sold in the Silk Plants, Etc. Systems business for a period of two years after the termination of the franchise agreement. The covenant-not-to-compete was also limited to business activities within a ten-mile radius of the Register's Silk Plants, Etc. store.

On March 15, 1988, the Registers filed their Chapter 13 bankruptcy petition. On May 18, 1988, the Registers rejected the franchise agreement through an agreed order with Silk Plants, Etc. Since then the Registers have operated a business very similar to their former Silk Plants, Etc. franchise. The plaintiffs then filed this adversary proceeding to enjoin the Registers from operating that store arguing that such activities violated the covenant-not-to-compete contained in the original franchise agreement.

Debtors in a bankruptcy proceeding may accept or reject executory contracts. The primary purposes behind allowing debtors to reject executory contracts are (1) to relieve the estate from burdensome obligations while the debtor is trying to recover financially, and (2) to effect a breach of contract allowing the injured party to file a claim. * * *

Both of these goals are furthered by permitting debtors to reject covenants-not-to-compete with the rest of the executory contract. In fact, equitably enforcing such clauses in contracts that have been rejected would directly frustrate the purposes of relieving debtors from burdens that would hinder rehabilitation. For these reasons the debtor should be able to reject the covenant-not-to-compete along with the rest of the executory contract; Silk Plants, Etc. should then be able to file a claim for the injury resulting from that breach of contract under §502(g) of the Bankruptcy Code. * * * This is also consistent with the general rule that executory contracts must be accepted or rejected as a whole. * * * The franchise agreement here clearly is an executory contract and as such may be rejected as it was in this case.

Silk Plants, Etc., however, argues that the covenant-not-to-compete was not executory and so cannot be rejected. According to Silk Plants, the covenant was severable from the executory parts of this contract and was based on a separate consideration which Silk Plants, Etc. had fully provided. This separate consideration according to Silk Plants, Etc. was the provision of training and information at the beginning of the franchise relationship. Silk Plants argues that it fully performed its portion of this severable agreement when it provided the promised training and information to the debtors.

The franchise agreement, when taken as a whole, however, shows that the debtors and Silk Plants Etc. contemplated that the covenant-not-to-compete would only be enforceable if Silk Plants performed on the entire franchise agreement, not just the sections requiring it to provide special training to the debtors. If Silk Plants had rejected the contract in a bankruptcy proceeding or had otherwise breached the franchising agreement the debtors clearly would not have had to honor the covenant-not-to-compete.

Silk Plants' reliance on Leasing Service Corp. v. First Tennessee Bank, N.A., 826 F.2d 434 (6th Cir. 1987) is misplaced. The question there was whether the granting and perfecting of a security interest was severable from the rest of a lease. A security interest is far different from a covenant-not-to-compete. Once perfected the security interest is a present interest in property; it establishes the priority of the holder of the security interest; and the existence of the security interest is not dependent on the holders' performance of the rest of the contract. For example, in *Leasing Service Corp.* if the lessor had breached, it would have been liable to the tenant for damages. If the lessor had some valid claim against the tenant, however, the security interest would have been available to satisfy that claim regardless of the lessor's breach. Here, however, the Franchisor's ability to enforce the covenant-not-to-compete is totally dependent on his faithful performance of the entire agreement. Thus the covenant-not-to-compete is not severable from the rest of the executory contract.

Silk Plants, Etc. next argues that a covenant-not-to-compete is enforced by an injunction and other equitable relief and not by a suit for money damages. Therefore the breach of this covenant does not give rise to a claim as defined by [§101(5)]. Silk Plants, Etc.'s right to equitable relief then should not be affected by the bankruptcy.

In support of this claim Silk Plants, Etc. cites In re Noco, Inc., 76 Bankr. 839 (Bankr. N.D. Fla. 1987) and In re Carrere, 64 Bankr. 156 (Bankr. C.D. Cal. 1986). Both of these cases may be distinguished from the instant case because in both cases the filing of bankruptcy had elements of bad faith. The bankruptcies seemed to have been filed solely for the purpose of avoiding the covenants-not-to-compete. Such is not the case here. In addition in *In re Noco,* the court specifically found that the contract was not executory. * * *

To the extent that these cases support Silk Plants, Etc.'s position, this court declines to follow them. For purposes of [§101(5)], the principle issue is whether this court is capable of reducing the injury that Silk Plant incurs as a result of the breach of this covenant to a dollar amount. If it can, then Silk Plants has a claim under [§101(5)] and §502(g). * * * Although state courts have ruled that they cannot put a value on the injury incurred for breach of these covenants this Court believes that it can. As the court in [In re] Norquist [43 Bankr. 224 (Bankr. E.D. Wash. 1984)] noted, "The equitable configuration of this court may very well permit a just determination and treatment of [a breach of a covenant-not-to-compete] which would not be accomplished under the rigid application of evidentiary rules in state court." *Norquist,* 43 Bankr. at 231. This approach furthers the underlying goals of §365 by relieving the debtor completely of the burden of this executory contract and by granting the creditor a claim for the injury incurred.

The court holds that the covenant-not-to-compete terminated when the contract was rejected and that Silk Plants may file a claim for breach of the entire franchise agreement, including the covenant-not-to-compete, under §502(g).

NORTHWEST AIRLINES CORP. V. ASSOCIATION OF FLIGHT ATTENDANTS-CWA.

United States Court of Appeals, Second Circuit, 2007
483 F.3d 160

WALKER, CIRCUIT JUDGE.

This dispute between the Association of Flight Attendants ("AFA") and Northwest Airlines ("Northwest") is situated in a peculiar corner of our law more evocative of an Eero Saarinen interior of creative angularity than the classical constructions of Cardozo and Holmes. Northwest, under the protection of Chapter 11 of the Bankruptcy Code and with the bankruptcy court's imprimatur, has rejected the collective-bargaining agreement that until recently governed its relationship with the AFA and imposed new terms and conditions of employment upon its flight attendants. The AFA does not wish to accede to these terms and conditions of employment and threatens a work stoppage unless Northwest agrees to terms and conditions that are more favorable to the flight attendants.

The District Court for the Southern District of New York (Victor Marrero, *Judge*) issued a preliminary injunction precluding the AFA and its members from engaging in any form of work stoppage. It held that any such work stoppage would cause irreparable harm and, at this juncture, violate the Railway Labor Act. On this basis, the district court concluded that the Norris-LaGuardia Act did not deprive it of jurisdiction to issue the injunction.

We agree [and] hold that the Railway Labor Act forbids an immediate strike when a bankruptcy court approves a debtor-carrier's rejection of a collective-bargaining agreement that is subject to the Railway Labor Act and permits it to impose new terms, and the propriety of that approval is not on appeal.

Background

In December 2004, Northwest, one of the nation's largest air carriers, began negotiating changes to the collective-bargaining agreement ("CBA") governing its relationship with its flight attendants, who were then represented by the AFA's predecessor, the Professional Flight Attendants Association ("PFAA"). Since April 2005, these negotiations have been conducted under the auspices of the National Mediation Board ("NMB"), which is authorized by the Railway Labor Act to mediate disputes between carriers and their employees.

In September 2005, Northwest filed for protection under Chapter 11 of the Bankruptcy Code. Northwest's plan for reorganization required that its employees make significant concessions. Most of the unions that represent groups of Northwest employees have since negotiated new agreements.

Unable to reach an accommodation with its flight attendants, on November 7, 2005, Northwest sought bankruptcy court approval of certain interim modifications to the relevant CBA under 11 U.S.C. §1113. On November 16, the bankruptcy court granted Northwest the requested relief. Nevertheless, the parties continued to negotiate in the hope of reaching a new mutually satisfactory agreement. On March 1, 2006, the PFAA leadership tentatively agreed to a new CBA (the "March 1 Agreement"); the membership, however, rejected the agreement by a margin of four-to-one.

In addition to seeking interim relief from its CBA, Northwest sought in September 2005 to obtain permanent relief from its CBA pursuant to §1113. After the flight attendants rejected the March 1 Agreement, Northwest reiterated this request, and, this time, the bankruptcy court granted Northwest's motion to reject its CBA. The bankruptcy court explained:

> [t]he Court would do the flight attendants and the Debtors' thousands of other employees no favor if it refused to grant the Debtors' §1113 relief, and the Debtors joined the ranks of the many other airlines that have liquidated as a consequence of a Chapter 11 filing.

In re Nw. Airlines Corp., 346 Bankr. 307, 330 (Bankr. S.D.N.Y. 2006) Along with this relief, the bankruptcy court permitted Northwest to impose the terms of the March 1 Agreement upon the flight attendants. Neither party appealed this decision.

The bankruptcy court conditioned its decision on Northwest's agreement to negotiate for an additional two weeks before it would allow the March 1 Agreement to take effect. Negotiations ensued, this time with the Association of Flight Attendants ("AFA"), which the flight attendants had elected as their new representative on July 7, 2006. On July 17, Northwest and the AFA reached another tentative agreement; again, however, on July 31, the flight attendants rejected the proposed agreement, this time by the narrower margin of 55-45%.

Northwest then imposed the March 1 Agreement. The AFA responded by notifying Northwest of its intent to disrupt Northwest's service by using a tactic suitably named CHAOS ("Create Havoc

Around Our System"), which entails mass walkouts for limited periods of time and pinpoint walkouts at certain airports or gates.

Northwest moved to enjoin the strike. Bankruptcy Judge Gropper denied the motion on the basis that Northwest's rejection of the CBA and imposition of the March 1 Agreement amounted to a "unilateral action in changing the status quo that in turn frees the employees to take job action." 346 Bankr. At 344. On appeal, the district court reversed and granted the preliminary injunction. Judge Marrero held that Northwest had not unilaterally changed the status quo and that the union remained bound by the status quo provisions of the RLA, which forbid the exercise of self-help pending the exhaustion of various mechanisms to resolve disputes, including NMB mediation. The AFA and intervenor Air Line Pilots Association filed a timely appeal.

Discussion

The AFA appeals entry of a preliminary injunction. We review the district court's judgment for abuse of discretion, although our review of its application of the law is de novo. We inquire whether Northwest has shown, first, irreparable injury, and, second, either (a) likelihood of success on the merits, or (b) sufficiently serious questions going to the merits and a balance of hardships decidedly tipped in [its] favor.

This appeal turns on Northwest's likelihood of success on the merits, any assessment of which, in turn, requires us to interpret and heed three different statutory schemes: Section 1113 of Chapter 11 of the Bankruptcy Code; the Railway Labor Act of 1926 ("RLA"), 45 U.S.C. § 151 *et seq.;* and the Norris LaGuardia Act of 1932 ("NLGA"), 29 U.S.C. § 101 *et seq.*

Section 1113(a) provides that a carrier subject to the RLA may "reject a collective bargaining agreement" if the bankruptcy court determines (among other things) that "the balance of the equities clearly favors rejection of such agreement" and that rejection is "necessary to permit the reorganization." However, to make such a determination, the bankruptcy court must specifically find that (1) the carrier has "ma[de] a proposal" to its employees "which provides for those necessary modifications in the employee benefits and protections that are necessary to permit the reorganization," (2) the carrier has provided its employees "with such relevant information as is necessary to evaluate the proposal," and (3) the "authorized representative of the employees has refused to accept such proposal *without good cause.*" §1113(b)(1), (c) (emphasis added). Moreover, §1113 also explicitly precludes carriers from "terminat[ing] or alter[ing] any provisions of a collective bargaining agreement prior to compliance with the provisions" of §1113.

Congress passed §1113 in response to the Supreme Court's decision in NLRB v. Bildisco & Bildisco, 465 U.S. 513 (1984). In *Bildisco,* the Court held (1) that a debtor did not violate the National Labor Relations Act ("NLRA") by "unilaterally changing the terms of the [CBA]" after filing for bankruptcy, 465 U.S. at 519, and (2) that the "Bankruptcy Court should permit rejection of a[CBA] ... that burdens the estate ... [if] after careful scrutiny, the equities balance in favor of rejecting the labor contract," *id.* Section 1113, by precluding a debtor from unilaterally changing the terms of its CBA without court approval upon entering bankruptcy, overturned the Supreme Court's first holding, while leaving the second (more or less) intact.

The NLGA deprives federal courts of jurisdiction to issue "any restraining order or temporary or permanent injunction in a case involving or growing out of a labor dispute, except in a strict conformity with the provisions of this chapter." 29 U.S.C. § 101. While this jurisdiction-stripping provision generally admits of only limited exception, the Supreme Court has held that the NLGA does not preclude courts from enforcing the mandates of the RLA. Even so, however, a party seeking an injunction under the NLGA must have clean hands:

> No restraining order or injunctive relief shall be granted to any complainant who has failed to comply with any obligation imposed by law which is involved in the labor dispute in question, or who has failed to make every reasonable effort to settle such dispute either by negotiation or with the aid of any available governmental machinery of mediation or voluntary arbitration.

29 U.S.C. § 108.

The RLA "abhors a contractual vacuum." Air Line Pilots Ass'n, Int'l v. UAL Corp., 897 F.2d 1394, 1398 (7th Cir.1990). Accordingly, a collective-bargaining agreement between a carrier subject to the RLA and its employees or their union (we use the two terms interchangeably) hardly ever expires. Rather, once a CBA becomes "amendable," the carrier and the union are bound by statute to embark upon an "almost interminable" re-negotiation process. Detroit & Toledo Shore Line R.R. Co. v. United Transp. Union, 396 U.S. 142, 149 (1969). During the pendency of this re-negotiation process, the RLA "obligate[s] [the parties] to maintain the status quo." Consol. Rail Corp. v. Ry. Labor Executives' Ass'n, 491 U.S. 299, 302 (1989).

The term "status quo," found throughout the case law, appears nowhere in the RLA. Several of the RLA's provisions require that parties to a CBA governed by the RLA maintain objective working conditions during the pendency of any dispute arising under (or during the re-negotiation of) their CBA. The Supreme Court has described the function of these status quo provisions as follows:

> The [RLA]'s status quo requirement is central to its design. Its immediate effect is to prevent the union from striking and management from doing anything that would justify a strike. In the long run, delaying the time when the parties can resort to self-help provides time for tempers to cool, helps create an atmosphere in which rational bargaining can occur, and permits the forces of public opinion to be mobilized in favor of a settlement without a strike or a lockout."

Shore Line, 396 U.S. at 150. Only after the parties have fully exhausted the dispute resolution and re-negotiation processes does a CBA expire, freeing the parties from their contractual obligations and the RLA's rules governing the preservation of the status quo.

While the status quo provisions are integral to the RLA, ... [c]ritical to this case, ... the RLA also imposes a separate duty, which is [distinct from] the RLA's status quo provisions: carriers and unions must "exert every reasonable effort to make [agreements] ... and to settle all disputes," 45 U.S.C. § 152 (First), even when the rules governing the RLA's status quo are not in effect. As the Supreme Court has explained, "[t]he statute does not undertake to compel agreement between the employer and employees, but it does command those preliminary steps without which no agreement can be reached. It at least requires the employer to meet and confer with the authorized representative of its employees, to listen to their complaints, to make reasonable effort [sic] to compose differences-in short, to enter into a negotiation for the settlement of labor disputes ... Virginian Ry. Co. v. Sys. Fed'n No. 40, 300 U.S. 515, 548 (1937)

We conclude that, in light of Northwest's court-authorized rejection of its CBA under §1113, the Norris-LaGuardia Act does not bar the district court's preliminary injunction because the union's proposed strike would violate this separate duty under Section 2 (First) to "exert every reasonable effort to make [agreements] ... and to settle all disputes." 45 U.S.C. § 152 (First). The union concedes that it has an ongoing duty to negotiate under Section 2 (First), but, nevertheless, argues that it is "free to strike" because Northwest "unilaterally alter[ed] the contractual 'status quo.' " Appellant's Br. at 15. [T]this argument fails because Section 2 (First) operates independently of the RLA's status quo provisions ... . Moreover, the AFA fails to recognize the unique effect on the status quo of a debtor's rejection of a CBA pursuant to §1113. * * *

[W]e reach three conclusions: (1) Northwest's rejection of its CBA after obtaining court authorization to do so under §1113 abrogated (without breaching) the existing collective-bargaining agreement between the AFA and Northwest, which thereafter ceased to exist; (2) Northwest's abrogation of the CBA necessarily terminated the status quo created by that agreement, after which termination both the RLA's explicit status quo provisions and the implicit status quo requirement of Section 2 (First) ceased to apply; but (3) the AFA's proposed strike would, at present, violate the union's independent duty under the RLA to "exert every reasonable effort to make ... [an] agreement," 45 U.S.C. § 152 (First), and thus may be enjoined.* * *

[We do not dispute that a] union would be free to strike following contract rejection under §365. See, e.g., Truck Drivers Local 807 v. Carey Transp. Inc., 816 F.2d 82, 93 (2d Cir.1987). However, substantial differences between §1113 and §365 justify a different understanding of the consequences of invoking the former. Congress passed §1113 in response to the Supreme Court's holding that a debtor did not violate the NLRA by unilaterally changing the terms and conditions of employment detailed in a CBA after entering bankruptcy. Congress sought to ensure that carriers could not avoid their agreements with their employees immediately upon entering bankruptcy, cf. §1113(e) (authorizing interim changes under limited circumstances); rather, it made contract avoidance possible only after a debtor procured court permission. But under §365, if a debtor rejects an executory contract, [breach is deemed to occur immediately prior to the bankruptcy petition]. Rejection under §365 thus leads to a legal fiction at odds with the text of (and impetus behind) §1113. Consistent with Congress's purpose, we are obligated to construe the statutory scheme to distinguish the legal consequences of rejection under §365—including our suggestion that employees aggrieved by the rejection may strike—from the legal consequences of rejection under §1113.

In cases governed by the NLRA, we have also hinted that a union is free to strike, even following contract rejection under *§1113*. See, e.g., In re Royal Composing Room, Inc., 62 Bankr.403, 405 (Bankr.S.D.N.Y.1986), *aff'd* 848 F.2d 345 (2d Cir.1988). But a union's right to strike under the NLRA depends upon the terms of the

CBA to which it is a party (for instance, the existence or continued viability, or lack thereof, of a contractual "no-strike clause"). *See* 29 U.S.C. § 163. If successful procurement of a §1113 order permits an employer to *abrogate* a CBA, it follows that a union subject to the NLRA would become free to strike consistent with *In re Royal Composing Room* precisely because it would no longer be bound by any contractual no-strike clause to which it might at one point have agreed. At the same time, however, a union subject to the RLA would still be under an obligation first to "exert every reasonable effort to make [agreements] ... and to settle all disputes" pursuant to Section 2 (First), notwithstanding the non-viability of any contractual no-strike clause. * * *

[T]he AFA argues that Northwest has not made "every reasonable effort to settle" this dispute, see 29 U.S.C. § 108, and thus lacks the requisite "clean hands" to secure an injunction under the NLRA. However, only if a carrier "has failed to take the steps required of it by the Railway Labor Act ... [do we forbid it] injunctive relief against the strike of its employees." Rutland Ry. Corp. v. Bhd. of Locomotive Eng'rs, 307 F.2d 21, 41 (2d Cir.1962). But ... Northwest has, to this point, fulfilled its duties under Section 2 (First). Moreover, because it abrogated the existing CBA under authority of a §1113 court order, Northwest did not violate either the RLA's explicit status quo provisions or the implicit status quo requirement of Section 2 (First). We have no indication in the record that Northwest is unwilling to return to the NMB, and indeed would expect it to do so. Nor has it sought to short-circuit the RLA's procedures in any other way.

Conclusion

Although this is a complicated case, one feature is simple enough to describe: Northwest's flight attendants have proven intransigent in the face of Northwest's manifest need to reorganize. On that basis, we conclude that the AFA has violated Section 2 (First) of the RLA and affirm the preliminary injunction.

NOTES

7C.1. The court in *Register* distinguished the *Leasing Services* case on the ground that, under applicable nonbankruptcy law, the security interest in *Leasing Services* was a vested "present interest in property," while the covenant not to compete in *Register* was contingent on future performance by Silk Plants. It is not clear, however, why this distinction should matter. In neither case was it the holder of the contractual right in question who breached the agreement. In each case, it was instead the debtor who breached through rejection.

We might gain some purchase on the issues in *Register* by returning to first principles. Rejection is nothing more than a decision to breach the executory contract. It does not grant the trustee the power to rescind the contract or repudiate the estate's obligations. Hence, one must ask what would have happened, absent bankruptcy, had the debtor breached the contract. Outside bankruptcy, it was beyond the Registers' power to rid themselves of the covenant not to compete. Silk Plants could have enforced it by asking a court to enjoin them. The court might have concluded that such a covenant survives bankruptcy, as nothing in the right to "reject" an executory contract under §365 expressly expands a debtor's ability to escape obligations it cannot escape outside of bankruptcy.

One might argue that the Registers needed to be released from the covenant not to compete in order to enjoy the fresh start to which they are entitled. Given that §365 applies equally to corporations as well as to individuals, however, it may not make sense to look toward it to answer this question. Rather, one might want to focus upon §541(a)(6) and the related question whether liens and other encumbrances on an individual's future earnings should survive bankruptcy. We return to this question in chapter 11 below.

7C.2. In Lubrizol Enterprises v. Richmond Metal Finishers, 756 F.2d 1043 (4th Cir. 1985), a debtor rejected a contract that granted a licensee the right to use the debtor's intellectual property. Even though applicable nonbankruptcy law would have permitted the licensee to use the property, the debtor's repudiation of the contract notwithstanding, the court ruled that rejection in bankruptcy deprived the licensee of that right and left the licensee with a mere claim for damages. Congress reacted to this case with the adoption of Bankruptcy Code §365(n), which permits a licensee of intellectual property to retain its rights despite rejection of an executory contract. Congress had previously granted similar dispensation to lessees of real property, under §365(h), and to purchasers of an interest in real property, under §365(i).

Ironically, such protection of certain nondebtor classes supports the holding of cases such as *Register*. The need to except technology licensees, as well as lessees and purchasers of real property, suggests by negative implication that rejection has these effects in the case of other kinds of executory contracts and leases. Indeed, the very adoption of §365 itself may fairly be interpreted as a congressional attempt to displace the protections of nonbankruptcy law, which would define the consequences of breach in the absence of a special provision in the Bankruptcy Code. It is not clear, however, what principle here supports deviation from the rules of otherwise applicable law.

7C.3. It is important to be clear about what is at stake in these cases. To illustrate, assume that in *Register*, Silk Plants will suffer a $10,000 loss if the Registers compete in violation of their covenant. Now consider the consequences of alternative holdings. If the covenant survives bankruptcy, despite rejection of the franchise agreement, the covenant will be specifically enforced in state court, and Silk Plants will not suffer any loss. If the bankruptcy court instead permits competition, as the court did in *Register*, Silk Plants will be left with a general claim of $10,000. Assuming that the Registers are insolvent, Silk Plants ultimately will collect only part of that claim. Enforcement of a covenant not to compete against an insolvent debtor is superior to a general claim against that debtor.

7C.4. The 2005 Bankruptcy Act revises Bankruptcy Code §707(b), which provides the circumstances under which a court will dismiss or convert a Chapter 7 bankruptcy petition for abuse of the bankruptcy process. Section 707(b)(3)(B) now expressly gives as an example of potential abuse a debtor's attempt to reject a personal services contract. That Congress perceived a need for this provision may be read by courts to endorse the holding of cases such as *In re Register*. Such a reading would be ironic given the apparent desire of Congress to prevent the results of such cases. To be sure, where §707(b) means that a debtor's bankruptcy case will be dismissed, a debtor will be unable to rid herself in bankruptcy of a covenant not to compete. But for a case in which the debtor is deemed to have a legitimate reason for Chapter 7 debt relief, independent of the debtor's desire to reject a personal services contract, the rejection of a related covenant might be a byproduct.

7C.5. *Northwest Airlines* provides a good account of §1113 and its history as well as of the special politics embedded in the Railway Labor Act. Beyond this background, though, on the issue of a union's right to strike, the case can be reduced to a simple observation: Although the Bankruptcy Code §1113 does not grant a court the power to enjoin a strike, neither does it *remove* such power if provided by another source.

7C.6. When a court invokes §1113 and modifies a collective bargaining agreement, one might have thought that the affected union or workers would, at the very least be entitled to a prepetition claim for damages under §365(g). The court in *Northwest Airlines* suggests otherwise, however. Other courts are in accord. In United Food and Commercial Workers Union, Local 328 v. Almac's Inc., 90 F.3d 1 (10th Cir. 1996), for example, the bankruptcy court permitted interim changes because it believed the debtor's business would not survive the unaltered agreement. The union then claimed damages from the changes, which the union characterized as a rejection of the collective bargaining agreement. The court, however, ruled that a "change" is not a "rejection," and disallowed the claim even though the changes would have been a breach under nonbankruptcy law.

Whatever rights §1113 grants the debtor to avoid the specific performance of a collective bargaining agreement, that provision says nothing about a union's claim for damages in the event of modification. The *United Food Workers* court assumed that alteration of the collective bargaining agreement was necessary for the debtor profitably to survive. If the court was correct, then the creditors as a group benefited from such alteration just as the creditors as a group benefit whenever the bankruptcy process prevents piecemeal liquidation through individual creditor action. A group benefit from bankruptcy is not a reason for an ordinary creditor who loses its collection right to lose its *claim* as well. It is not clear why a union as a party to a "changed" executory contract should lose its claim.

7C.7. One might question further whether the conditions for modification or rejection of a collective bargaining agreement can *ever* be satisfied (though all parties in *Northwest Airlines* assumed that they could). This question is explored below in Problem 7C-3.

PROBLEMS

7C-1. Company enters into a service agreement with Contractor. According to the agreement, for one year, Contractor is to maintain Company's equipment at sites scattered throughout Company's home county. In exchange, for the course of the contract, Company is to pay Contractor $10,000 per month and is to provide Contractor with use of a Company car worth $20,000. With more than six months remaining on the contract, and while in possession of the car, Contractor files a petition in bankruptcy. The trustee rejects the service agreement. Is Company entitled to the car or merely to a $20,000 claim against Contractor's estate?

7C-2. Buyer and Seller enter a contract pursuant to which Buyer is to purchase a Picasso for $1 million. Before the date of transfer, Seller files a petition in bankruptcy and Seller's trustee rejects the sales contract. Can Buyer demand specific performance of the contract despite the putative rejection? Should Buyer be able to demand specific performance? Consider this problem again after you study the trustee's avoidance powers in the next chapter.

7C-3. Debtor files a bankruptcy petition under Chapter 11 while subject to a collective bargaining agreement that would pay unionized workers somewhat more than $100 million per year for the next ten years. At the time of the petition, the market rate for similar labor is $50 million. Debtor's projected annual gross revenues over the period of the collective bargaining agreement are $200 million, an estimated $70 million of which would be required to pay operating expenses other than payments to unionized workers, $30 million of which would be required to satisfy prebankruptcy liens on Debtor's assets. Prompted by Debtor's general creditors, Debtor moves to modify the collective bargaining agreement. Should the motion granted? If so, what form should the modification take? Would your answers change if the collective bargaining agreement would pay unionized workers something less than $100 million per year?

VIII. THE AVOIDING POWERS

A bankruptcy trustee is invested with more than just the debtor's rights at the time the debtor files for bankruptcy. The trustee also possesses a set of powers known as the "avoiding powers." Some of the avoiding powers merely allow the trustee to do what a creditor could have done under applicable nonbankruptcy law. The trustee's ability to assert the rights of a hypothetical lien creditor, for example, ensures that the trustee has powers similar to those creditors have outside of bankruptcy when they pursue their legal rights. Other avoiding powers implement specific bankruptcy policies. Section 547, for example, gives the trustee the ability to recover assets that creditors grabbed on the eve of bankruptcy. This power to avoid "preferences" ensures that the bankruptcy process can in fact overcome the collective action problem that arises when an insolvent debtor has multiple creditors. Other avoiding powers give the trustee powers analogous, but not identical, to those that creditors have outside of bankruptcy. For example, the trustee has the right to avoid fraudulent conveyances under §548 that parallel the powers creditors enjoy outside of bankruptcy.

A. THE TRUSTEE'S STRONG-ARM POWER

The Bankruptcy Code grants the trustee the right to step into the shoes of other people, hypothetical and actual. Section 544(a) allows the trustee to act as a hypothetical lien creditor and, in the case of real property, as a hypothetical purchaser. Section 544(b) allows the trustee to avoid and recover for the estate a debtor's transfers that an actual creditor could have avoided. Keep in mind that a trustee may take advantage of each of these powers in turn, gathering property for the estate as she goes.

1) ASSERTING RIGHTS OF HYPOTHETICAL CREDITORS AND PURCHASERS

The Bankruptcy Code §544(a) allows the trustee to take certain actions that a creditor or purchaser could take under applicable non-bankruptcy law. Specifically, this subsection states:

> The trustee shall have, as of the commencement of the case, and
> without regard to any knowledge of the trustee or of any creditor,
> the rights and powers of, or may avoid any transfer of property of

the debtor or any obligation incurred by the debtor that is voidable by—

(1) a creditor that extends credit to the debtor at the time of the commencement of the case, and that obtains, at such time and with respect to such credit, a judicial lien on all property on which a creditor on a simple contract could have obtained such a judicial lien, whether or not such a creditor exists;

(2) a creditor that extends credit to the debtor at the time of the commencement of the case, and obtains, at such time and with respect to such credit, an execution against the debtor that is returned unsatisfied at such time, whether or not such a creditor exists; or

(3) a bona fide purchaser of real property, other than fixtures, from the debtor, against whom applicable law permits such transfer to be perfected, that obtains the status of a bona fide purchaser and has perfected such transfer at the time of the commencement of the case, whether or not such a purchaser exists.

Section 544(a)(1), known as the "strong-arm" power, is probably the most commonly used avoiding power. This provision, in essence, makes the trustee an ideal, hypothetical lien creditor at the time of the debtor's bankruptcy: "Ideal," because no actual knowledge is imputed that might, under nonbankruptcy law, defeat an action; "hypothetical," because the trustee can act whether or not there is a real judgment creditor who could exercise rights or powers or avoid a transfer.

In a typical application of §544(a)(1), the trustee attacks a security interest held against the debtor's property but unperfected at the time of bankruptcy. (A creditor with a security interest in the debtor's equipment may have neglected to file a financing statement as Article 9 requires or may have filed in the wrong location.) In this case, the trustee can assert the rights of one who lent money to the debtor at the commencement of the case and, upon default, reduced her claim to judgment and obtained a lien on the equipment. The security interest would have been enforceable against the debtor, and the collateral would still be subject to it when brought into the estate under §541(a). But a lien creditor could have taken the equipment and sold it to satisfy its claim notwithstanding the unperfected security interest. Hence, §544(a) empowers the trustee to avoid the security interest. The equipment becomes part of the bankruptcy estate by virtue of this power, and the general creditors as a group can look to it to satisfy their claims.

The unperfected secured creditor becomes a mere general creditor. The creditor's *claim* against the debtor is valid after the operation of §544 if it was valid before. A creditor with an allowed claim who loses its security interest to the trustee shares in the equipment along with all the other general creditors. Secured creditors who lose their security interests are still creditors, unless they agreed to make their loans nonrecourse. *— nonrecourse unperfected could lose entire value of claim*

Section 544(a)(1) allows the trustee to defeat other claims to the debtor's assets as well. For example, under state real property law a seller's judgment creditor typically acquires rights superior to those of a purchaser if the judgment creditor establishes a lien on the property (and thus perfects her interest) before the purchaser records. The purchaser of a car who fails to record her name on the certificate of title is also at risk. Whenever a lien creditor could have prevailed outside of bankruptcy, the trustee prevails inside. *↳ so trustee could trump P purchaser if lien creditor would outside of § by law*

The trustee's powers as hypothetical lien creditor track substantive nonbankruptcy entitlements. Outside of bankruptcy, each general creditor has the ability on default to obtain a judgment and then establish a lien on a debtor's property. When a bankruptcy petition is filed, the automatic stay prevents any creditor from putting a lien on the asset, just as it prevents the secured creditor from perfecting its interest. When a bankruptcy petition is filed, it is unclear whether a holder of an unperfected interest in property would have perfected before a creditor established a lien. And, assuming that *a* creditor would have established a lien prior to the holder's perfection, it is unclear *which* creditor would have done so. The effect of the bankruptcy filing is to call off the race among creditors and to treat them all the same. An interest unperfected at the time of the debtor's bankruptcy becomes part of the estate and is thus shared by all creditors *including* the original holder of the interest that has been avoided. (The secured creditor shares because it already enjoys the rights of a general creditor, quite apart from its security interest; a bona fide purchaser of property recovered by a trustee holds an allowed claim against the debtor for the value of that property.)

The remainder of §544(a) rests on a similar rationale. In some jurisdictions, a simple judgment creditor must execute on the judgment in order to win the race against the unperfected secured creditor. Hence, §544(a)(2) allows the trustee to play the role of a creditor who has already made this attempt. Section 544(a)(3) addresses a similar issue. In some jurisdictions, a lien creditor cannot defeat even an unrecorded interest in real property. In such jurisdictions, a creditor who wants to establish priority over an unrecorded interest in real property must execute on and acquire the property in satisfaction of her debt, or have the property sold, in accord with state law. Once the acquirer records her ownership, the unrecorded interest in the property becomes subordinate to the new owner's interest and, if the property has been sold, the unrecorded interest becomes subordinate to the creditor's interest in the sale proceeds as well. The automatic stay generally prevents the creditor from starting down this road to claim satisfaction. Section 544(a)(3) allows the trustee to play the role of a creditor who has completed the process against real property.

[margin note: → to displace unrecorded interest]

Situations can arise in which a secured creditor can prevail against a lien creditor even when the lien came into being before the secured creditor filed. A manufacturer sells inventory to a retailer and retains an interest in the inventory to secure payment of the purchase price. Under Article 9, this kind of secured creditor (commonly called a purchase money lender) prevails against lien creditors, provided it files its financing statement within twenty days of the time the debtor takes possession of the goods. See UCC §9-317(e). (The prior version of Article 9 provided a ten-day window.) Section 546(b)(1) addresses the situation that arises when bankruptcy intervenes after the debtor has the goods, but before the secured creditor has filed. It again preserves the result outside of bankruptcy. It provides that the rights and powers of the trustee under specified avoidance provisions, including §544, "are subject to any generally applicable law that permits perfection of an interest in property to be effective against" one who acquires rights earlier. Section 362(b)(3) provides further that the secured creditor can file without violating the automatic stay.

[margin note: So purchase money lender can trump lien creditor (incl. trustee) (can avoid SI's) even if filed below]

Section 546 contains other provisions that cut back on the trustee's §544(a) powers. The trustee must act within a time limit, which varies by circumstance as specified in §546(a). There are also a few limited, special-case exemptions. These protect a seller's interest in the reclamation of goods sold (including fish or grain) and protect margin, settlement, or swap transactions in the securities industry. See §546(c)-(g).

Once the trustee applies §544(a), and there is no applicable exception, the process is complete if the trustee has established a superior interest in the debtor's own property, such as when the trustee defeats an unperfected security interest. In this case, because the debtor's property is already included in the bankruptcy estate, subordination of that interest is all the trustee requires. There is nothing more to recover. If, however, the trustee has established a superior interest in property previously transferred by the debtor, such as real estate sold to a purchaser who has not recorded her interest, the trustee must affirmatively recover the property.

Section 550(a)(1) allows the trustee to recover the avoided transfer or its value from "the initial transferee" or "the entity for whose benefit" the transfer was made. Sections 550(a)(2) and (b) also permit recovery from subsequent transferees down the line until we reach a transferee in the chain who takes the property for value and without knowledge that the initial transfer was voidable. The trustee may not recover from that transferee or any subsequent good faith transferee of the property whether or not the subsequent transferee gives value. Despite multiple potential sources, §550(d) limits the trustee to a single recovery. And §550(e) provides that, in the event a transfer is avoided, any transferee retains a lien for the costs of her improvements to the property, if any, limited by the value of those improvements. Section 551, in turn, preserves for the benefit of the estate any transfer avoided by the trustee. Sections 550 and 551 may make explicit what is implicit in the rights and powers the trustee enjoys under §544(a). These sections, however, also apply to the trustee's other avoiding powers, where the power to recover the property is less clear-cut.

The exercises below ask you to work through some of the §544(a) mechanics. The case that follows, *Kors, Inc. v. Howard Bank*, along with the related notes and problems, ask you to consider the intersection among the trustee's hypothetical status under §544, the preservation of avoided transfers under §551, and recovery of those transfers under §550. A problem also explores the issue of circular priority that can arise when the trustee defeats one of multiple competing interests in property.

Key Provisions: Bankruptcy Code §§544; 550; 551

EXERCISES

8A(1) Debtor grants Bank a security interest in two parcels of real estate, BlackAcre and WhiteAcre. Bank records a mortgage that includes only BlackAcre. After Debtor files for bankruptcy, Bank asserts its state-law right to take possession of WhiteAcre and thus perfect its interest despite the defect in the recorded mortgage. Can the bankruptcy trustee take WhiteAcre free from Bank's security interest?

In answering this question consider, among other provisions, Bankruptcy Code §546(b)(2).

8A(2) Debtor sells WhiteAcre to Abel, who fails to record his ownership interest. Later, Abel sells WhiteAcre to Baker, who immediately records her interest. Shortly thereafter, Debtor files for bankruptcy. Can the trustee recover WhiteAcre or its value? From Abel? From Baker?

8A(3) Swindler defrauds Customers out of $1 million. Under state law, any assets Swindler has are held in equitable trust for victims such as Customers. In addition to the $1 million fraud claim, Swindler owes Bank $5 million. Swindler has assets of less then $1 million when he files for bankruptcy. Can the trustee bring Swindler's assets into the estate? In answering this question, consider, among other provisions, Bankruptcy Code §541(d). See also Belisle v. Plunkett, 877 F.2d 512 (7th Cir. 1989).

CASE

KORS, INC. v. HOWARD BANK

United States Court of Appeals, Second Circuit, 1987
819 F.2d 19

PIERCE, CIRCUIT JUDGE.

David D. Robinson, trustee for the bankrupt corporation, Kors, Inc. ("Kors"), appeals from a judgment of the United States District Court for the District of Vermont ordering the proceeds of a sale of the debtor's machinery to be paid in accordance with a subordination agreement among the Rutland Industrial Development Corporation ("RIDC"), the Small Business Investment Corporation of Vermont, Inc. ("SBIC"), and the Howard Bank ("Bank"). Appellant contends that, under §§544 and 551, the trustee may avoid a subordination agreement for the benefit of the estate. We disagree.

Background

We summarize only the facts believed necessary to an understanding of the issues on appeal. In 1977, Kors entered into negotiations with SBIC, RIDC and the Bank to obtain financing for the operation of a plastics manufacturing business. RIDC, a nonprofit local development corporation, agreed to lease equipment to Kors. The

Bank agreed to loan funds to Kors and RIDC to purchase the equipment and SBIC agreed to lend Kors working capital.

On July 12, 1978, RIDC, Kors, and the Bank executed a security agreement ("Security Agreement"), wherein RIDC proposed the purchase of new equipment and machinery from Rietenhauser USA Sales Corp. ("Rextrusion") which RIDC would lease to Kors.[1] For this purpose, the Bank loaned $1,510,000 to RIDC and Kors as joint debtors. The collateral for the Security Agreement was described as the equipment and machinery to be purchased from Rextrusion by RIDC including "all additions, accessories and substitutions thereto, and all proceeds of their disposition." The Security Agreement required that Kors and RIDC "not permit any other security interest to attach to the Collateral," but acknowledged a subordinate security interest of SBIC, described below, in a loan to Kors of $400,000. On July 13, 1978, the Bank, as secured party, filed financing statements with the Rutland City Clerk and the Vermont Secretary of State, signed only by RIDC, as the debtor, but not by Kors.

Earlier, on June 19, 1978, SBIC loaned working capital in the amount of $400,000[2] to Kors pursuant to a loan and security agreement ("Loan and Security Agreement"), wherein Kors agreed to secure its indebtedness to SBIC through its accounts receivable, inventory and all of Kors "machinery, equipment and tangible property of every kind and nature now and hereafter acquired, including all such property as may be leased to [Kors] by Rutland Industrial Development Corporation." However, also contained in this Loan and Security Agreement, which RIDC agreed to execute, was a clause in

---

[1] Pursuant to a lease agreement ("Lease Agreement") dated June 19, 1978, RIDC leased this machinery to Kors for a period of ten years and granted Kors the option to purchase the leased equipment at the end of the term for a nominal charge. The Lease Agreement was subject and subordinate to the Security Agreement given to the Howard Bank by RIDC and Kors for the principal amount of $1,510,000. No financing statement was filed by RIDC with respect to the Lease Agreement.

Although RIDC was to hold legal title to the leasehold, Kors was to be the equitable or beneficial owner. Kors negotiated the purchase of the Rextrusion machinery and the Rextrusion machinery was delivered directly to Kors under documents of sale listing Kors as buyer. The bankruptcy court found that the lease was a capital lease intended to have effect as a security rather than an operating lease. Further, the bankruptcy court found that Kors was the owner of the collateral.

[2] Additional funds were loaned to Kors by SBIC on November 26, 1979, March 10, 1980, and August 1, 1980. The total amount loaned to Kors by SBIC is $1,000,000.

which SBIC and RIDC agreed to subordinate their respective interests to the Howard Bank, or any other lender financing the purchase by Kors of additional machinery and equipment. Specifically, SBIC and RIDC agreed to be "subject and subordinate to the effect given to any prior security interests therein required to be given to the Howard Bank ... and to subordinate its security interests to any other Lender as may hereinafter finance the purchase by [Kors] of additional machinery and equipment." Apparently, this clause was included to encourage banks to lend Kors funds to promote its production capacity.

SBIC filed financing statements for the $400,000 loan to Kors on July 19, 1978. SBIC's financing statements were "subject however to the effect given a previous security interest granted to the Howard Bank."[3] Thus, both the Security Agreement among RIDC, Kors and the Bank, and the Loan and Security Agreement among RIDC, SBIC and Kors identify an obligation by SBIC and RIDC to subordinate their security interests to the Bank's security interest.

Kors filed a voluntary bankruptcy petition on November 24, 1980 under Chapter 11 of the Code, which was converted to a Chapter 7 liquidation proceeding on August 14, 1981. The appellant, David D. Robinson, was appointed trustee and on April 22, 1982, with the consent of the parties and pursuant to a court order, the trustee sold all of Kors' equipment for a total of $1,100,000.

The bankruptcy court determined, inter alia, that the Bank did not properly perfect its security interest in any collateral; that the trustee, pursuant to §544 of the Code, preserved the unperfected security interest for the benefit of the estate; and that the estate was subrogated to the Bank's rights under its subordination agreement with SBIC for the benefit of all the creditors of the estate. On appeal to the district court, the latter reversed so much of the bankruptcy court determination as held that the trustee stood in the position of the Bank with respect to the subordination agreement, and ruled instead that the proceeds of the sale should be distributed in accordance with the subordination agreement. In all other respects, the judgment of the bankruptcy court was affirmed by the district court.

---

[3] In late 1979, the Bank filed additional financing statements, signed only by RIDC, for additional loans of $176,000 and $750,000. On December 20, 1979, SBIC filed and signed a statement of subordination with regard to the $750,000 loan wherein RIDC was listed as the debtor. Thus, both the financing statement and the subordination statement filed by SBIC acknowledged that SBIC's security interest was subordinate to the Bank's.

On appeal to this court, appellant urges that the rights and powers of the trustee under §§544 and 551 are superior to the rights of parties to a subordination agreement. Appellee argues that §510(a) of the Code requires that the subordination agreement be enforced among the parties.

We affirm the judgment of the district court for the reasons stated below.

Discussion

The issue we must decide herein is whether, pursuant to §§544 and 551 of the Code, the trustee in bankruptcy can obtain rights under a subordination agreement that is authorized by §510(a) of the Code. Resolution of this issue requires us to examine how these three sections of the Code interact, if at all.

Section 544(a) of the Code, the "strong-arm" clause, enables the trustee in bankruptcy to act as a hypothetical lien creditor as of the day the bankruptcy case is filed .... Pursuant to this section, the trustee in bankruptcy can avoid unperfected liens on property belonging to the bankruptcy estate. * * *

Once the trustee has assumed the status of a hypothetical lien creditor under §544(a)(1), state law is used to determine what the lien creditor's priorities and rights are .... Hence, the bankruptcy court and the district court examined Vermont law to determine what rights the trustee had as a hypothetical lien creditor under §544(a)(1).

The bankruptcy court found, and the district court agreed, that under Vermont law the Howard Bank failed to perfect its security interest in the Kors equipment. Under Article 9 of the Vermont Uniform Commercial Code, a security interest may be perfected by filing a financing statement signed by the debtor. The failure to identify and obtain the signature of a debtor on a financing statement is fatal to the perfection of the security interest. As owner of the collateral, Kors was the debtor whose signature was necessary on the financing statement for perfection .... Thus, at the commencement of the bankruptcy case, the Bank had an unperfected security interest in Kors' collateral.

Since Vermont law gives a lien creditor rights superior to those of the holder of an unperfected security interest, the trustee, pursuant to §544(a)(1) of the Code, had rights superior to those of the Bank on the date of the bankruptcy filing. * * *

Section 551 of the Code automatically preserves for the benefit of the estate any interest avoided under §544. ... Applying §551 the bankruptcy court preserved the Bank's unperfected interest for the benefit of the estate. However, the bankruptcy court also held that the Bank's interest in the separate subordination agreement among RIDC, SBIC and the Bank was preserved for the benefit of the estate, putting the trustee in the Bank's shoes with respect to the subordination agreement as well as the Security Agreement. The district court reversed this determination, reasoning that the subordination agreement is not a part of the Bank's unperfected security interest and is not itself a security interest, and therefore the trustee's powers under §544(a)(1) and §551 do not extend to the Bank's rights under the subordination agreement.

We agree with the district court that the trustee's subrogation powers under §544(a)(1) and §551 do not extend to a subordination agreement protected by §510(a). While §544(a)(1) enables the trustee in bankruptcy to step into the shoes of a hypothetical lien creditor to avoid unperfected liens in the debtor's property, he may, pursuant to §551, preserve only those rights which existed against the bankrupt. Thus, equipped with lien creditor status under §544(a)(1) and subrogation power under §551, the trustee may preserve those rights and powers that a lien creditor would have against the bankrupt under Vermont law. However, §510(a) enables creditors to subordinate their priorities by agreement if permitted to do so by nonbankruptcy law. In this case, the applicable nonbankruptcy law is 9-316 [revised as current UCC §9-339] of the Vermont Uniform Commercial Code which states:

> Nothing in this article prevents subordination by agreement by any
> . person entitled to priority.

Such subordination agreements are uniformly upheld by the courts. * * *

In this case the trustee sold the equipment owned by Kors for $1,100,000. Sections 544(a)(1) and 551 put the trustee in the shoes of the Bank with respect to the Bank's unperfected security interest in the proceeds of Kors equipment and machinery. Hence, the trustee properly preserved the Bank's lien in the proceeds of the sale of Kors equipment which was financed by the Bank. It was improper, however, for the trustee to be subrogated to the Bank's rights with respect to the subordination agreement among RIDC, SBIC, and the Bank. Under Vermont law, subordination agreements will be enforced only between those parties entitled to priority who enter such an agreement. Thus under Vermont law, the trustee would not accede to the benefits of the subordination agreement because Kors was not a part of that agreement. Moreover, the trustee was vested only with the rights the Bank had against Kors. The Bank's rights against Kors existed pursuant to the Security Agreement for the Rextrusion equipment. The Bank's subordination rights existed against SBIC and RIDC, not Kors. Hence, since the Bank had no rights as against Kors with respect to the subordination agreement, the trustee was not vested with any of the Bank's rights in that agreement.

At the same time, the Bank's rights with respect to its unperfected security interest on Kors' collateral were separate and distinct from its rights under the subordination agreement among the lenders. Therefore, the trustee, acting under §544(a)(1) and §551 obtained only those rights and powers derived from the unperfected security interest against Kors in the collateral and did not acquire the rights of the Bank under the subordination agreement. Consequently, the bankruptcy court should have enforced the subordination agreement according to the terms of the parties to that agreement. * * *

We therefore affirm the judgment of the district court.

NOTES

8A.1. In a sense, *Kors* is a simple case. Section 544(a) grants the trustee all the "rights and powers" of a hypothetical lien creditor. In Vermont, as in other states, these rights and powers include the ability to take property free from the encumbrance of an unperfected security interest. Thus, the trustee's interest in the Kors' collateral was superior to and unaffected by Bank's unperfected interest. No lien creditor at the time of the Kors bankruptcy, however, could trump the *perfected* security interests of SBIC or RIDC, so those interests survive attack under §544(a). The order of priority, then, is SBIC or RIDC, the trustee, then Bank. This is ultimately a victory for Bank, which benefits from a side deal, the subordination agreement, whereby SBIC and RIDC agree to give Bank whatever value they receive from the Kors' collateral. In sum, under state law, no lien creditor could claim an interest in the subordination agreement or its proceeds, so neither can the trustee.

The doctrinal complication of *Kors* stems from the references, in §§544(a) and 551, to the avoidance of transfers. The court treats a lien creditor's superior interest in collateral as an "avoidance" of an unperfected, and thus inferior, interest. The court then applies §551 and "preserve[s]" the interest "for the benefit of the estate." That is, as the court interprets the Code, the trustee does not merely hold an interest superior to Bank's unperfected security interest, as would a lien creditor; the trustee holds the security interest itself. This interpretation raises the question whether that interest includes Bank's rights under the subordination agreement. The court concludes sensibly that the trustee is not entitled to those rights, but §551 obscures matters, rather than reinforcing the core idea that the trustee's strong-arm power merely allows the trustee to exercise the rights and powers that the creditors would have enjoyed outside of bankruptcy.

8A.2. It might seem that §551 is largely unnecessary, as §550 also applies broadly and permits the trustee to recover an avoided transfer or its value. Section 551, however, may address a priority circularity problem that can sometimes arise under facts similar to those in *Kors*. Problem 8A-1 illustrates such a circularity problem and asks you to consider whether §551 is indeed a solution. Problem 8A-2 explores whether §551 creates a conflict with the explicit or implicit limitations of §550.

PROBLEMS

8A-1. Debtor grants Bank a mortgage on GreenAcre. Bank neglects to record that mortgage. Debtor later grants Finance Company a mortgage on GreenAcre. Finance Company records its mortgage, though it knows of Bank's earlier interest. (In the relevant jurisdiction, even an unrecorded mortgage is effective against later mortgages that are taken with knowledge of the earlier interest.) Soon thereafter, Debtor files for bankruptcy. What interest in GreenAcre has priority?

8A-2. Debtor finances his new car with a $20,000 secured loan from Bank. Because of Bank's own administrative error, Bank does not record its security interest and allows Debtor to obtain a clean certificate of title, one that does not list any security interest. Debtor later sells the car to Buyer, who has no idea that Bank has an interest. Debtor spends the sale proceeds on a vacation, then files for bankruptcy. Trustee asserts a claim for $20,000 against the car in the hands of Buyer. Will Trustee prevail?

2) ASSERTING RIGHTS OF ACTUAL CREDITORS

Bankruptcy Code §544(b)(1) allows the trustee to "avoid any transfer of an interest of the debtor in property or any obligation incurred by the debtor that is voidable under applicable law by a creditor holding an unsecured claim." An essential difference between §544(b) and §544(a) is the distinction between actual and hypothetical. Under §544(b), the trustee takes on the role of an actual creditor, to whom the debtor incurred an obligation before bankruptcy, while under §544(a) the trustee takes on the role of a hypothetical creditor who makes a loan at the time of bankruptcy.

In most cases, any right of an actual unsecured creditor is also a right of the hypothetical creditor created by §544(a). So, in most instances, the trustee's §544(b) powers are superfluous. The exceptional case is one in which, under applicable nonbankruptcy law, an existing creditor can challenge a transaction, but a creditor who arrives on the scene after a transaction has taken place cannot.

Imagine, for example, that a creditor lends a debtor a sum of money that the debtor uses to purchase equipment. Assume that later, when the debtor becomes insolvent, the debtor gives or sells all his equipment to a friend for less than fair market value. As to the lender, the gift or sale is a fraudulent transfer (also known as a "fraudulent conveyance") because, under state law, an insolvent debtor cannot favor others with assets that might have been used to pay creditors. See, e.g., Uniform Fraudulent Transfer Act ("UFTA") §5. The transfer might not be fraudulent as to a subsequent creditor. (This distinction in fraudulent conveyance law is based on the notion that a subsequent creditor can take the debtor's lack of assets into account at the time of the loan.) Compare UFTA §4. Thus, it is possible that, under state law, the pretransfer lender can collect the equipment in the hands of the purchaser, though a posttransfer creditor could not. In this case, when the debtor enters bankruptcy, the trustee cannot recover the property using the powers of a hypothetical lien creditor that lent at the time of the petition. Section 544(b) brings into the estate property that creditors could have reached outside of bankruptcy but that the hypothetical lien creditor test of §544(a) fails to reach.

While the existence of an actual creditor who might have set aside a transfer is essential, the amount that the actual creditor is owed does not put a ceiling on the amount that the trustee can recover. Moreover, any recovery goes to the estate, where it is enjoyed by all the creditors. It does not go to the creditor who could have brought the action under nonbankruptcy law. These twin ideas—that the trustee has the power to avoid the *entire* transfer and that the avoided transfer is enjoyed by *everyone*—were set out in Moore v. Bay, 284 U.S. 4 (1931). In the one of the exercises, we ask whether this result makes sense.

Fraudulent conveyances—and the related bulk transfers, governed by Article 6 of the Uniform Commercial Code—dominate the case law surrounding §544(b). The exercises below, which illustrate these transactions, ask you to consider primarily the *extent* of avoidance under §544(b) and require you to focus on *whom* such avoidance benefits. Analysis of fraudulent conveyance law as part of the Bankruptcy Code, including a discussion of special protection for certain gifts to charitable organizations—with such protection made applicable to a trustee's state-law actions by §544(b)(2)—is deferred until section C below. As you will see, that analysis looks at the overlap between §544(b) and §548, a section that provides the trustee with her own set of fraudulent conveyance powers.

The case that follows, *Ozark Restaurant Equipment*, as well as the related notes and problem further explore the nature of a trustee's §544(b) avoiding powers. The case considers a veil-piercing action, where a creditor of the debtor, not the debtor itself, has a claim against the controlling shareholders of a debtor for the shareholders' misbehavior.

Key Provisions: Bankruptcy Code §§544; 550; 551

EXERCISES

8A(4) At a time that Debtor owes a total of $100,000 in general claims, Debtor sells all of his inventory in bulk to Wholesaler for $75,000. Wholesaler does not provide notice of the sale to Debtor's creditors. Debtor then absconds with the cash before creditors realize that the inventory is gone. After the Debtor vanishes, the creditors file an involuntary bankruptcy petition. How much, if any, of the asset transfer can the trustee avoid and recover? On behalf of whom? In answering this question, consider, among other provisions, UCC Revised Article 6, §6-107. Would your answer change if Wholesaler paid only $10,000 for the inventory, worth $75,000, but duly notified Debtor's creditors?

8A(5) Debtor borrows $10,000 from Abel on a general obligation, then gives all of his assets, worth $50,000, to his cousin. In subsequent months, Debtor borrows, then spends, another $200,000. A little more than a year after the borrowing stops, Debtor files for bankruptcy. Assuming that Debtor's transfer to his cousin is avoidable as a fraudulent conveyance under state law, how much, if any, of the asset transfer can the trustee avoid and recover, and on behalf of whom?

CASE

IN RE OZARK RESTAURANT EQUIPMENT CO.

United States Court of Appeals, Eighth Circuit, 1987
816 F.2d 1222

MAGILL, CIRCUIT JUDGE.

The sole issue in this appeal is whether a Chapter 7 bankruptcy trustee has standing to assert, on behalf of the debtor corporation's creditors, an alter ego action against the principals of the corporation. The district court held in the negative. For the reasons discussed below, we affirm.

I. Background

In September of 1980, Bruce Anderson and Elmer Dale Yancey purchased Ozark Restaurant Equipment Co., Inc. ("Ozark") of Springdale, Arkansas, the debtor in this case. Both were 50% shareholders and directors of the corporation; Yancey was also an officer. In addition to owning Ozark stock, Anderson owned 50% or more of the stock in a number of other companies with which Ozark did business. On August 24, 1982, after an abysmal performance, Ozark filed for relief under Chapter 7 of the Bankruptcy Code.

In October of 1982, the Chapter 7 trustee of Ozark filed three adversary proceedings which were subsequently consolidated for trial before the bankruptcy court. The first proceeding was an alter ego action, which was brought solely by the trustee on behalf of all of Ozark's creditors[3] against the following defendant-principals of Ozark: Anderson; Yancey; Kenneth Eads, director and president of Ozark; Robert Whiteley, a business consultant hired by Anderson to

---

[3] At oral argument, the trustee, in response to a question from this court, stated that the creditors were asked to join in the action, but that none of them wished to do so.

help with Ozark's finances; and Anderson Cajun's Wharf, Inc. The trustee alleged, inter alia, that because of the defendant-principals' abuses of the corporation, the corporate veil should be pierced and the individuals should be held personally liable for Ozark's debts. ... On March 21, 1984, the bankruptcy court ordered judgment in favor of the trustee ... .[4] All defendants except Eads appealed the judgment.

On May 22, 1986, the district court issued an order ... reversing the court's judgment in the alter ego action. Regarding the alter ego claim, the court, relying heavily on Caplin v. Marine Midland Grace Trust Co., 406 U.S. 416 (1972), determined that a Chapter 7 trustee has no standing on his own to bring an alter ego action on behalf of the debtor corporation's creditors ... . Ozark's trustee subsequently appealed, arguing that a Chapter 7 trustee does have standing to bring an alter ego claim on behalf of the debtor corporation's creditors.

II. Discussion

Although acknowledging that the district court had the right to raise the standing question, the trustee argues that the court's holding was incorrect as a matter of law. The trustee maintains that a Chapter 7 trustee has standing to assert an alter ego claim on behalf of the unsecured creditors of the debtor corporation based on three different areas of the Bankruptcy Code: (1) §544; (2) §704 and §541; and (3) §105 and general equitable principles running throughout the Code. We begin by addressing the trustee's second argument.

A. §§704 and 541

Section 704 of the Code outlines the duties of a Chapter 7 trustee and requires the trustee to "collect and reduce to money the *property of the estate* for which the trustee serves ... ." Section 541 defines "property of the estate" and for our purposes, the relevant subsection

---

[4] [A]s to the alter ego claim, the court found that Ozark was a mere instrumentality of the principals, and thus "pierced the corporate veil," holding the four individuals jointly and severally liable for $136,653 or the amount of unsecured debt listed in the bankruptcy petition. The court pierced the veil based on its numerous findings of corporate abuse, including grossly inadequate capitalization; heightened fiduciary obligations of Yancey and Anderson as sole shareholders; Ozark's never having made a profit, and its net worth plummeting from negative $1,400 in 1980 to negative $146,000 in 1982; Anderson-related companies profiting from Ozark because of, among other things, low sale mark-ups and no interest on accounts payable; failure to keep adequate books and records; distribution of false financial statements; failure to pay taxes; and, the failure to hold regular meetings of the shareholders and directors.

is 541(a)(1), which defines property of the estate as "all legal or equitable interests of the debtor in property as of the commencement of the case." In arguing that §704 permits a Chapter 7 trustee to pursue an alter ego theory cause of action to pierce the corporate veil on behalf of the creditors of the debtor corporation, the trustee failed to acknowledge the key limiting language in §541(a)(1)—property of the estate comprises only "legal and equitable interests *of the debtor.*" Upon further examination of §704 and §541 and the nature of the alter ego action, it becomes apparent that the trustee's standing argument based on these two sections must fail. * * *

First, it is clear that causes of action belonging to the *debtor* at the commencement of the case are included within the definition of property of the estate .... Any of these actions that are unresolved at the time of filing then pass to the trustee as representative of the estate, who has the responsibility under [§704(a)(1)] of asserting them whenever necessary for collection or preservation of the estate .... For example, these sections give the trustee authority to bring an action for damages on behalf of a debtor corporation against corporate principals for alleged misconduct, mismanagement, or breach of fiduciary duty, because these claims could have been asserted by the debtor corporation, or by its stockholders in a derivative action .... Accordingly, whenever a cause of action "belongs" to the debtor corporation, the trustee has the authority to pursue it in bankruptcy proceedings.

Where, however, "the applicable state law makes such obligations or liabilities run to the corporate creditors personally, rather than to the corporation, such rights of action are not assets of the estate under §541(a) that are enforceable by the trustee [under §704(a)(1)]." 4 Collier on Bankruptcy, ¶541.10[8], at 541-69 to 541-70. ... In this respect, we recognize that "[g]enerally, the corporate veil is never pierced for the benefit of the corporation or its stockholders[.]" 18 Am. Jur. 2d Corporations §46 (1985) ... but see 1 Fletcher Cyclopedia on the Law of Private Corporations §41, at 388 (1983) (hereinafter "Fletcher Cyclopedia"). This general statement of the law is followed in Arkansas, where the courts have held that "[a] corporate entity is to be disregarded only if the corporate structure is illegally or fraudulently abused *to the detriment of a third person.*" Thomas v. Southside Contractors, Inc., 260 Ark. 694, 543 S.W.2d 917, 919 (1976) (emphasis added). Thus, the obligations and liabilities of an action to pierce the corporate veil in Arkansas do not run to the corporation, but to third parties, e.g., creditors of the corporation.

Further, although an action to pierce the corporate veil may be brought under a number of different theories, the "alter ego doctrine" of piercing the corporate veil

> fastens liability on the individual who uses a corporation merely as an instrumentality to conduct his own personal business, *and such liability arises from fraud or injustice perpetrated not on the corporation but on third persons dealing with the corporation. The corporate form may be disregarded only where equity requires the action to assist a third party.* Accordingly, a sole shareholder may not choose to ignore the corporate entity when it suits his convenience.

1 Fletcher Cyclopedia, supra, §41.10, at 397 (emphasis added).

Because the corporate entity will be disregarded under Arkansas law only if it has been abused to the detriment of a third person, and because the nature of the alter ego theory of piercing the corporate veil makes it one personal to the corporate creditors rather than the corporation itself, it is axiomatic that the claim does not become property of the estate under §541(a)(1), nor is it enforceable by the trustee under [§704(a)(1)]. Accordingly, we conclude that the trustee here does not have standing under these sections to bring an alter ego action on behalf of Ozark's creditors.[7]

B. §544

The trustee's principal argument in this case is based on §544 of the Code. The trustee maintains that §544(a), the "strong-arm clause," enables the trustee to pursue an alter ego action in his creditor's capacity, because that section gives the trustee the rights and powers of a creditor who could have obtained a judicial lien, whether or not such a creditor exists. Additionally, the trustee maintains that §544(b), which allows a trustee to avoid certain transfers of the debtor that are voidable under applicable law by a creditor holding an unsecured claim also gives the trustee standing to pursue an alter ego action for the benefit of all creditors.

Admittedly, a trustee's rights and powers under §544 are extensive. We do not believe, however, that they encompass the ability to litigate claims, such as the instant alter ego cause of action, on behalf

---

[7] It is possible that some states permit the corporation or its stockholders to assert an alter ego cause of action to pierce the corporate veil, and thus, that a bankruptcy trustee would be able to enforce the claim on behalf of the debtor corporation under §541 and §704. * * *

of the debtor corporation's creditors. A careful reading of Caplin v. Marine Midland Grace Trust Co., 406 U.S. 416 (1972), supports this conclusion, as recognized by the district court.

In *Caplin*, the Supreme Court held that a reorganization trustee lacked standing under the old Bankruptcy Act to assert, on behalf of the bankrupt corporation's creditors (debenture holders), claims of misconduct against a third party (the indenture trustee). Having recognized that the Bankruptcy Act itself contained no provisions authorizing the trustee to so act, the Court proceeded to analyze the issue in terms of "the nature of [reorganization] proceedings, the role of the trustee in reorganization, and the way in which standing to sue on behalf of debenture holders would affect or change that role." Id. at 422. After discussing these criteria, the Court determined that three reasons militated against allowing the trustee to have standing.

First, the Court found that nowhere in the statutory reorganization scheme was there any suggestion that the trustee should "assume the responsibility of suing third parties on behalf of debenture holders." Id. at 428. The Court noted that under [1898 Act §167(3)], the trustee had a duty to investigate potential causes of action of the estate, but that nothing in that section enabled the trustee to collect money not owed to the estate. Further, the Court noted that [1898 Act §70] (the relevant parts of which are now embodied in §541 and §544) did not give the trustee this authority, but rather, "[the trustee's] task is simply to 'collect and reduce to money the property of the estates for which [he serves].'" Id. at 428-29 (quoting [1898 Act] §47(a)(1), now [§704(a)(1)]). Second, the Court noted that the bankrupt corporation had no claim against the indenture trustee, and that at the most, the trustee's claims of misconduct involved a situation where the corporation and the indenture trustee were in pari delicto. The Court thus expressed concern over whether the indenture trustee would be subrogated to the claims of the creditors. Third, the Court was concerned that "a suit by [the trustee] on behalf of debenture holders may be inconsistent with any independent actions that they might bring themselves." Id. at 431-32. The Court noted that the trustee's action would not preempt suits by the individual creditors, and that such suits would be likely because it would be "extremely doubtful that the trustee and all debenture holders would agree on the amount of damages to seek, or even on the theory on which to sue." Id. at 432. Relatedly, the Court expressed concern over who would be bound by the settlement obtained by the trustee.

Although the Court concluded that the above reasons required a finding against the trustee, the Court expressly invited Congress to decide differently:

> Congress might well decide that reorganizations have not fared badly in the 34 years since [the reorganization chapter] was enacted and that the status quo is preferable to inviting new problems by making changes in the system. Or, Congress could determine that the trustee in a reorganization was so well situated for bringing suits against indenture trustees that he should be permitted to do so. In this event, Congress might also determine that the trustee's action was exclusive, or that it should be brought as a class action on behalf of debenture holders, or perhaps even that the debenture holders should have the option of suing on their own or having the trustee sue on their behalf. Any number of alternatives are available. Congress would also be able to answer questions regarding subrogation or timing of law suits before these questions arise in the context of litigation. Whatever the decision, it is one that only Congress can make.

Id. at 434-35. Congress, however, declined to accept the invitation.

In 1978, six years after *Caplin* was decided, Congress overhauled the bankruptcy laws when it enacted the Bankruptcy Code. As part of the revision, Congress consolidated [1898 Act §70c and §70e] into §544(a) and (b) of the Code, respectively, which apply to both reorganization and liquidation trustees. Although §544 clarified and expanded the trustee's role with respect to creditors, in no way was it changed to authorize the trustee to bring suits on behalf of the estate's creditors against third parties. In fact, the legislative history suggests just the opposite.

As originally proposed by the House, §544 was to contain a subsection (c), which was intended to overrule *Caplin*.[9] It is extremely

---

[9] Subsection (c) would have provided as follows:

(c)(1) The trustee may enforce any cause of action that a creditor, a class of creditors, an equity security holder, or a class of equity security holders has against any person, if—

(A) the trustee could not recover against such person on such cause of action other than under this subsection;

(B) recovery by the trustee for the benefit of such creditor or equity security holder or the members of such class will reduce the claim or interest of such creditor or equity security holder or of such members, as the case may be, against or in the estate;

noteworthy, however, that this provision was deleted before promulgation of the final version of §544. Because subsection (c), as a part of §544, would have applied to both reorganization and liquidation trustees, and because Congress refused to enact subsection (c), we believe Congress' message is clear—no trustee, whether a reorganization trustee as in *Caplin* or a liquidation trustee as in the present case, has power under §544 of the Code to assert general causes of action, such as the alter ego claim, on behalf of the bankrupt estate's creditors. Further, although we believe congressional intent is clear and is thus determinative of the issue, because *Caplin* is still good law and is the only Supreme Court case to address the standing question, albeit in a reorganization setting, we feel obliged to address how the Court's concerns in that case apply to the case at bar.

First, just as there was nothing in the statutory reorganization scheme of the [1898 Act] authorizing the trustee to collect money not owed to the estate, similarly, there is nothing in §544 or the liquidation framework of the Code authorizing a Chapter 7 trustee to collect money not owed to the estate. Rather, the Chapter 7 trustee's sole relevant duty regarding collection of money is under [§704(a)(1)], and is geared to §541(a)(1), requiring the trustee to collect and reduce to money, among other things, the legal and equitable interests of the debtor. See §§[704(a)(1)], 541(a)(1). As already discussed, see Part

---

(C) there is a reasonable likelihood that recovery against such person will not create an allowable claim in favor of such person against the estate; and

(D) enforcement of such cause of action is in the best interest of the estate.

    (2) If the trustee brings an action on such cause of action—

(A) the court, after notice and a hearing, may stay the commencement or continuation of any other action on such cause of action; and

(B) the clerk shall give notice to all creditors or equity security holders that could have brought an action on such cause of action if the trustee had not done so.

    (3) A judgment in any such action brought by the trustee binds all creditors or equity security holders that could have brought an action on such cause of action. Any recovery by the trustee, less any expense incurred by the trustee in effecting such recovery, shall be for the benefit only of such creditors or equity security holders.

H.R. 8200, 95th Cong., 1st Sess. 416-17 (1977). * * *

A, supra, and as recognized by the district court, the alter ego action fails to meet this ontological test.

Moreover, contrary to the trustee's suggestion, we do not believe that §544 in its present form grants the trustee this right. First, as discussed above, in declining to explicitly authorize such standing in the wake of *Caplin*, it is difficult to ascertain how congressional intent could be stronger. Second, to argue that §544 in its present form grants the trustee this power is, we believe, to misconstrue the section's intended application. Although §544(a) and (b) are admittedly broader than their predecessors, the substantive changes do not in any way suggest that the trustee was given the additional power to bring general causes of action on behalf of the estate's creditors. In this vein, we note that §544(a) and (b) are flavored with the notion of the trustee having the power to avoid "transfers" of the debtor, as were its predecessors, sections 70c and e of the Act .... An alter ego action, however, does not entail invalidating of a transfer of interest, but instead imputes the obligations of one party to another regardless of any "transfers."

In summary, nowhere in §544(a) or (b),[12] nor in other relevant provisions of the Code is there any suggestion that the trustee has been given the authority to collect money not owed to the estate.

Second, although there are no in pari delicto or subrogation concerns in this case, the third concern of *Caplin*—the trustee's suit would not preempt similar suits by other creditors of the corporation—is equally applicable to this case. If the trustee in the instant case was allowed to pursue and recover on the alter ego cause of action on behalf of Ozark's creditors, there obviously would be questions as to which creditors were bound by the settlement.[13] This is because the trustee is not the real party in interest, and thus does not

---

[12] Section 544(b) will generally come into play under three scenarios: (1) where a trustee cannot avoid a fraudulent conveyance under §548 because of the permitted period of recovery, and thus has to resort to recovery under the applicable state fraudulent conveyance act; (2) where a trustee wants to recover under the applicable state bulk sales statute; or (3) where there has been an illegal payment of corporate dividends or purchases of stock and the local law allows an unsecured creditor to bring the action. In fact, we have found no authority suggesting that a creditor's alter ego claim may be asserted under this subsection.

[13] We note that if Congress had enacted the proposed version of subsection (c) of §544, this problem would have been solved. See note 9 supra, especially proposed subsection (c)(3).

have the power to bind the creditors to any judgment reached in the litigation.

In conclusion, based on congressional intent, as evidenced by the failure to expressly give the trustee standing to bring creditors' causes of action, and based on the concerns in *Caplin*, two of which directly apply to this case, we hold that the Chapter 7 trustee in this case does not have standing under §544 to bring an alter ego cause of action on behalf of the debtor corporation's creditors.

C. §105 and Equitable Principles

It is true that §105 allows a bankruptcy court to apply equitable principles that are necessary or appropriate in a particular case to carry out the provisions of the Code. These powers, however, do not include the ability to award equitable relief where the party asserting the cause of action for such relief does not have standing under any other section of the Code ... . Because no provision of the Code gives the trustee in this case standing to assert the alter ego claim, any equitable relief must be denied. Although this result may seem harsh in light of the bankruptcy court's clear findings that the corporate structure was abused, an opposite result would contradict the Code's directives.

III. Conclusion

Because the Code does not give the Chapter 7 trustee in this case standing to bring an alter ego action on behalf of the debtor corporation's creditors, the district court's order is affirmed.

NOTES

8A.3. Although the court does not say so, the trustee in *Ozark Restaurant Equipment* might have a substantive problem with an alter ego action under §544(a) even if the court were willing to entertain such an action. An alter ego, or veil-piercing, case often depends on the relationship between the corporate debtor's principals and the creditor plaintiff. As the court notes in the first part of its discussion, these cases are akin to fraud actions. The trustee, as a hypothetical creditor, may not be able to assert the specific allegations needed to prevail in such an action.

One can argue that the trustee should nevertheless prevail in a veil-piercing action under §544(b). This provision allows the trustee to "avoid any transfer of an interest of the debtor in property" that any actual "creditor holding an unsecured claim" could avoid. One might characterize a veil-piercing, or alter ego, action as one that seeks to recover from shareholders assets that should belong to a debtor corporation and should thus be available to the debtor's creditors. So characterized, this diversion of assets that should be in corporate solution might be deemed a "transfer" of corporate assets.

There would be a danger, however, for the law to adopt too expansive a view of "transfer" for the purposes of §544(b). A line of argument premised only upon whether an action is available to a creditor (and not whether it involves an actual transfer of assets by the debtor) proves too much. There has to be some link between the action that a creditor has and the creditor's relationship with the debtor. Otherwise, nothing would prevent the trustee of a corporate debtor from asserting the right of a creditor of the debtor to contest that creditor's own mother's will. No one would seriously argue that the bankruptcy trustee could pursue the creditor's rights to his mother's estate, as that estate has no connection to the debtor or the bankruptcy case.

8A.4. Despite the outcome, the trustee's argument in *Ozark Restaurant Equipment* is stronger than a mere plea for a literal reading of §544(b). The trustee wants to pursue not just any rights of creditors, but rights that creditors have by virtue of their claims against the debtor. Indeed, one might wonder why the alleged malfeasance of the debtor's principals—presumably for looting the company—did not give rise to a claim by the debtor against them. Such a claim would unquestionably belong to the trustee, who might bar the claim of individual creditors as derivative. See, e.g., In re Fox, 305 Bankr. 912 (BAP, 10th Cir. 2004). Recovery of assets that should have belonged to the debtor, and should thus have been available to the creditors, seems an appropriate role for the trustee, who is charged with representation of the creditors' interests. One might argue, therefore, that the *Ozark Restaurant Equipment* court relies on an arbitrary formality when it denies the trustee's §544(b) action because the rights in question belong to the creditors personally rather than to the estate of which the creditors are beneficiaries. The distinction the court draws, however, may be more than formal. To understand why, consider the court's footnote 13 and Problem 8A-3.

PROBLEM

8A-3. Debtor Corporation keeps sloppy books that do not adequately distinguish corporate assets from those of Debtor's sole shareholder, Principal. Acquaintance is an affluent but unsophisticated member of Principal's country club. Over lunch, after a quick review of Debtor's records, Principal convinces Acquaintance to lend Debtor $50,000 on an unsecured basis. Shortly thereafter, Debtor applies for a loan from Bank. Dissatisfied with Debtor's corporate records, Bank inquires further and discovers that although Principal possesses substantial wealth, Debtor's assets consist only of the $50,000 borrowed from Acquaintance. Bank nevertheless agrees to lend Debtor $200,000. Although the loan is unsecured and not guaranteed, it carries a high interest rate. Debtor's subsequent business ventures are unsuccessful. Debtor pays no more than interest on its loans and files for bankruptcy with assets of only $25,000. Over the objection of Acquaintance, the trustee seeks to bring a veil-piercing claim against Principal. Will the trustee succeed?

B. STATUTORY LIENS

A statutory lien is a lien that arises "solely by force of a statute," rather than by agreement or levy of a judgment creditor. See §101(53). State law, for example, commonly gives a "mechanic's lien" on a building or other structure to a contractor who supplies labor or materials on credit. Section 545 sets out the avoiding powers that establish the relative rights of those holding such liens and the general creditors as a group. There are two benchmarks, both of which we have seen before.

Section 545(1) permits the trustee to avoid a statutory lien that is triggered by commencement of a bankruptcy case, the debtor's insolvency, or other events closely correlated with these. This prohibition against ipso facto clauses is analogous to the ones we have seen in §541(c) when we examined property of the estate and in §365(e) and (f) when we examined executory contracts. The ipso facto prohibition, however, serves a different purpose. Instead of limiting the ability of private parties to contract on the filing of a bankruptcy petition, it limits nonbankruptcy laws that have the same effect.

The logic of this prohibition seems straightforward. Bankruptcy law respects nonbankruptcy rights, but a priority right that applies only in bankruptcy, or only under conditions where a debtor is virtually certain to be in bankruptcy, seems not to be a generally applicable nonbankruptcy right, but rather a bankruptcy rule under a different name. Bankruptcy laws lose their coherence if such state-created rules are given full effect. On closer analysis, however, one discovers that all priorities, generally applicable or triggered by financial failure, matter only when the debtor is insolvent and virtually certain to be in bankruptcy. By definition, solvent debtors are capable of paying *all* their obligations of whatever priority. Priority matters only when there is not enough to go around. There is a puzzle, then, both that states would adopt priority rules that were explicitly tied to insolvency and that Congress objects to these priorities but not to others.

Section 545(2) permits the trustee to avoid a statutory lien to the extent that such lien "is not perfected or enforceable at the time of the commencement of the case against a bona fide purchaser" who purchases at that time. This makes the trustee a hypothetical purchaser of property, real or personal. The provision is analogous to §544(a)(3), which makes the trustee a hypothetical purchaser of real property. If state law grants priority in property or sale proceeds to the first who executes, then the trustee's victory over a statutory lien merely reflects the possibility that a general creditor would have won the race but for bankruptcy. This is the same argument made on behalf of §544(a)(3). If, however, state law would apply the proceeds of any sale first to a statutory lien even as the law released the property itself from the lien, then §545(2) alters, rather than honors, nonbankruptcy priority.

The exercises below ask you to work through some of the §545 mechanics. The case, *In re Walter*, along with the subsequent notes ask you to consider a statutory lien that provides its own definition of a purchaser who can defeat the lien. The issue is whether a hypothetical "bona fide purchaser" under §545 can be interpreted to possess traits that meet the lien-statute definition. As the notes that follow the case explain, §545(2) has been amended since the decision in the case. The problem that follows asks you to explore the issue in context of the amendment.

Key Provision: Bankruptcy Code §545

EXERCISES

8B(1) Jeweler repairs Debtor's watch but Debtor cannot afford to pay for the repairs. Debtor agrees to let Jeweler hold the watch until

Debtor can come up with the money. Later, Debtor files for bankruptcy. Under applicable state law, in any insolvency proceeding, a repairer has a first priority claim in repaired goods for the costs of repair. Can the trustee avoid Jeweler's interest in the watch?

8B(2) Plumber is an independent contractor who routinely works for Debtor. The ordinary practice is for Debtor to pay Plumber in advance for work that Plumber is to perform. Recently, however, Debtor has become insolvent and cash-starved. Because of Debtor's weak financial condition, Plumber agrees to alter the usual arrangement and work on credit. Debtor owes Plumber $50,000 for work on a house when Debtor files for bankruptcy. Under applicable state statute, Plumber has a mechanic's lien on the house. Can the trustee avoid that lien?

8B(3) Seller supplies Debtor specially designed stained glass on credit. Before the glass becomes a fixture in Debtor's construction project, Debtor signs a financing statement that Seller duly records as a fixture filing against the glass. A month later, just before Debtor files for bankruptcy, Debtor sells the building in which the glass is installed. The purchaser does not check for a fixture filing and is unaware of Seller's lien. State statute provides Seller with an automatic mechanic's lien on the glass. Under state law, however, a mechanic's lien is not generally effective against a bona fide purchaser. Can the trustee avoid Seller's interest in the glass? In answering this question consider, among other provisions, Bankruptcy Code §546(c).

8B(4) Debtor acquires a unique gold necklace from Collector. The terms of the exchange are that Debtor will use her best efforts to sell the necklace, and if she succeeds, will pay Collector all proceeds from the sale up to $100,000. Unbeknownst to Collector, Debtor is a criminal who intends to sell the necklace quickly, probably for less than $100,000, and abscond with the money. Before Debtor can execute her plan, however, she is arrested for similar past activity. Under applicable state statute, those who perpetuate frauds hold the products of fraud in constructive trust for their victims. Nevertheless, state courts have interpreted the statute such that bona fide purchasers from such individuals take free of victims' claims. Debtor files for bankruptcy. Can the trustee avoid Collector's interest in the necklace? In answering this question consider, among other provisions, Bankruptcy Code §101(37).

8B(5) Tenant fails to pay rent. Under state common law, Landlord possesses a lien on Tenant's possessions located in the leased apartment. After Tenant files for bankruptcy, can the trustee avoid this lien?

IN RE WALTER

United States Court of Appeals, Sixth Circuit, 1995
45 F.3d 1023

MILBURN, CIRCUIT JUDGE.

The defendant-trustee, John J. Hunter, appeals the district court's order reversing a decision of the bankruptcy court and holding that the trustee could not avoid the statutory liens of the plaintiff-Internal Revenue Service (the "IRS"). The sole issue on appeal is whether the district court properly determined that the trustee could not, under §545(2), avoid the statutory liens of the IRS on debtors' motor vehicle pursuant to the Internal Revenue Code §6323(b)(2). For the reasons that follow, we affirm.

I

On October 19, 1989, the debtors, Elmer and Dorla Walter, filed a petition for reorganization under Chapter 11 of the Bankruptcy Code in the United States Bankruptcy Court for the Northern District of Ohio. At the time of the filing, debtors owned a 1986 Kenworth Tractor, which is the motor vehicle at issue in this case. Debtors listed the IRS as a creditor having claims for federal taxes. As of the petition filing date, debtors' assessed tax liabilities relating to the filed notices of tax liens totaled $389,395, including interest and penalties. On February 7, 1990, the IRS filed a proof of claim listing the nearly $390,000 as secured claims against debtors. The IRS also listed unsecured priority claims and unsecured general claims totaling $2,595.

On June 5, 1990, on debtors' motion, the bankruptcy court converted debtors' reorganization case to a liquidation case under Chapter 7 of the Bankruptcy Code. At that time, the bankruptcy court appointed John J. Hunter as trustee. In July 1990, the trustee took possession of the motor vehicle at issue, a 1986 Kenworth Tractor, which had been in debtors' possession when they filed their petition. Pursuant to a notice of intent to sell, on October 4, 1990, the trustee sold the motor vehicle for $24,000, free and clear of all liens.

After the sale, the trustee filed an objection to the IRS' proof of claim. The trustee asserted that because he occupied the position of a bona fide purchaser of the motor vehicle, the tax liens on the proceeds from the sale of the motor vehicle could be avoided and that the IRS' secured claims should be treated as unsecured priority claims. On April 14, 1992, the bankruptcy court entered an order sustaining the trustee's objection to the IRS' secured claims. It found that the IRS properly filed its notices of tax liens, but concluded that the tax liens could be avoided under §545(2) of the Bankruptcy Code because the tax liens did not extend to the motor vehicle under Internal Revenue Code §6323(b)(2). On June 10, 1992, the bankruptcy court entered an order that disposed of the trustee's remaining objections and allowed the IRS an unsecured priority claim of $823, and an unsecured general claim of $391,218, of which $389,395 was formerly secured by the federal tax liens.

[T]he district court reversed the bankruptcy court. It held that the tax liens could not be avoided under §545(2) and that the proceeds of the sale of the motor vehicle were subject to the liens. It reasoned that while the trustee is given the status of a hypothetical bona fide purchaser, the trustee in this case failed to acquire possession of the motor vehicle before acquiring notice of the tax liens.

This timely appeal by the trustee followed.

II

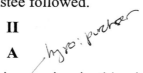

A

* * * This is a case of first impression in this circuit which involves the collision of §545(2) and Internal Revenue Code §6323(b)(2). Because of the complexity of the relationship between these two statutory provisions, we shall begin by setting forth the general legal principles involved in this case.

Section 545 of the Bankruptcy Code dictates when a trustee can avoid statutory liens. The relevant part of that section provides:

> The trustee may avoid the fixing of a statutory lien on property of the debtor to the extent that such lien—
>
> (2) is not perfected or enforceable at the time of the commencement of the case against a bona fide purchaser that purchases such property at the time of the commencement of the case, whether or not such a purchaser exists.

Pursuant to this section, a trustee may step into the shoes of a hypothetical bona fide purchaser and claim the same defenses to statutory liens on a debtor's property as would a bona fide purchaser. A trustee acquires that right as of the commencement of the case, which is the date of filing the bankruptcy petition.

Upon filing a petition under Chapter 11, a debtor obtains the title of "debtor-in-possession." §1101(1). A debtor-in-possession has virtually all of the rights and powers of a bankruptcy trustee, including the power to avoid statutory liens under §545(2). §1107(a). Because a trustee stands in the shoes of a hypothetical bona fide purchaser, it follows that a debtor-in-possession enjoys the same protections as would a bona fide purchaser at the time of the commencement of the case.

A federal tax lien under Internal Revenue Code §6321 is a statutory lien subject to avoidance. A federal tax lien on all property of a delinquent taxpayer arises at the time the tax liability of the taxpayer is assessed. 26 U.S.C. §§6321, 6322. Generally, a federal tax lien is made valid against third parties by filing a notice of federal tax lien. However, it may not be valid against specified third parties under certain circumstances. Section 6323(b)(2) of the Internal Revenue Code in relevant part provides:

> Even though notice of a lien imposed by §6321 has been filed, such lien shall not be valid [w]ith respect to a motor vehicle (as defined in subsection (h)(3)), as against a purchaser of such motor vehicle, if—
>
> (A) at the time of the purchase such purchaser did not have actual notice or knowledge of the existence of such lien, and
>
> (B) before the purchaser obtains such notice or knowledge, he has acquired possession of such motor vehicle and has not thereafter relinquished possession of such motor vehicle to the seller or his agent.

Having set forth the general legal principles involved in this case, we now turn to the specific issue on appeal.

B

* * * In this case, the petition was originally filed under Chapter 11 on October 19, 1989. The case was converted to a liquidation case under Chapter 7 of the Bankruptcy Code on June 5, 1990. Because the conversion relates back to the original filing on October 19, 1989, [see §348,] the trustee steps into the shoes of a hypothetical bona fide

purchaser as of that date. It follows that the trustee may avoid the federal tax liens if a hypothetical bona fide purchaser who obtained the motor vehicle on October 19, 1989, could avoid the federal tax liens.

C

The trustee [argues] that the district court erred in its application of §6323 of the Internal Revenue Code. Specifically, the trustee argues that the district court erred in concluding that the trustee could not take advantage of the protections of Internal Revenue Code §6323(b)(2) because the trustee did not have possession of the motor vehicle before he received notice of the lien when he was appointed to administer the Chapter 7 estate. The trustee states (and the IRS agrees) that it is irrelevant whether the trustee had possession of the motor vehicle because the strength of the lien is tested against a hypothetical bona fide purchaser. The trustee reasons that because debtors had possession of the motor vehicle when they filed the original Chapter 11 petition, the trustee may now avoid the lien. * * *

Whether a bona fide purchaser may avoid a statutory lien is a matter that is left to state or federal lien law. Thus, where a statutory lien is created by state law, state law governs in determining whether the lien can be avoided by a bona fide purchaser, and the characteristics of a bona fide purchaser will also be determined by state law. Where a statutory lien is created by federal law, however, federal law governs in determining whether the lien may be avoided by a bona fide purchaser, and the characteristics of a bona fide purchaser will also be determined by federal law.

The statutory liens in this case are federal tax liens created pursuant to Internal Revenue Code §6321, and they are generally valid against third parties once notices of federal tax liens have been filed. See 26 U.S.C. §6323(a). However, §6323(b) of the Internal Revenue Code affords protection for certain interests even though notice has been properly filed. The trustee in this case claims he is protected by Internal Revenue Code §6323(b)(2), which protects a purchaser of a motor vehicle if before the purchaser received actual notice or knowledge of the lien, he acquired possession of the motor vehicle. The applicability of that provision to the trustee in this case raises two distinct issues.

The first issue is whether the trustee may claim protection under Internal Revenue Code §6323 in the first instance. Internal Revenue Code §6323(b) affords protection only for a "purchaser," which is defined as "a person who, for adequate and full consideration in money or money's worth, acquires an interest (other than a lien or security interest) in property which is valid under local law against subsequent purchasers without actual notice." 26 U.S.C. §6323(h)(6). Because a trustee may stand in the shoes of a bona fide purchaser for purposes of §545(2), the issue becomes whether a bona fide purchaser meets the definition of a purchaser. Although the term "bona fide purchaser" is not defined in the Bankruptcy Code, it is generally understood to mean "[o]ne who has purchased property for value without notice of any defects in the title of the seller." Black's Law Dictionary 177 (6th ed. 1990). Thus, "value" is a much lower standard than "adequate and full consideration in money or money's worth." Because a bona fide purchaser is not necessarily a purchaser for purposes of Internal Revenue Code §6323(b)(2), it follows that a trustee standing in the shoes of a hypothetical bona fide purchaser does not fall within the protection of this statute.[7]

The second issue is whether the trustee, who stands in the shoes of a hypothetical bona fide purchaser, meets the possession and no actual notice or knowledge requirements of Internal Revenue Code §6323(b)(2). As stated above, the purchaser must have possession to have priority over a federal tax lien.

Numerous courts have addressed this issue by determining whether the Bankruptcy Code grants a hypothetical bona fide purchaser "hypothetical possession" over the property upon the filing of the petition, and they have not reached consistent results. One group of cases holds that the Bankruptcy Code does not grant hypothetical possession to a hypothetical bona fide purchaser. Another group of cases, however, holds to the contrary.

In In re Tape City, U.S.A., Inc., 677 F.2d 401 (5th Cir. 1982) (per curiam), the Fifth Circuit examined whether §545(2) allowed a debtor-in-possession to avoid Louisiana vendor's privilege, which is a statutory lien that has no formal perfection requirements. In *Tape*

---

[7] This conclusion is not inconsistent with the rationale of Internal Revenue Code §6323. The purpose of this so-called superpriority statute is to encourage the alienability of certain enumerated assets without threats of tax liability and to protect bona fide purchasers who obtained the assets without knowledge of the tax lien. . . . As to the protection rationale, because the trustee is not actually giving value for the asset, he need not be afforded the same protection as a true bona fide purchaser. Thus, because the rationale of Internal Revenue Code §6323 would not be advanced by extending the term purchaser to include a trustee, we conclude that a trustee is not protected by this statute.

City, the debtor filed bankruptcy under Chapter 11 and remained in possession of its property. The vendor, which had sold merchandise to the debtor, claimed that its vendor's privilege constituted a secured claim and demanded adequate protection of its interests in the merchandise. Under Louisiana law, a vendor of movable property which has not been paid has a vendor's privilege on the price of such property. Louisiana law allows a bona fide purchaser to avoid the privilege if there has been both transfer of title and physical delivery of the property to the bona fide purchaser. ... In applying the bona fide purchaser test, the court refused to assume that the debtor had parted with possession: "Even if [the debtor-in-possession] is considered a trustee who, under the legal fiction of the [Bankruptcy] Code, takes as a bona fide purchaser, we cannot accept [the debtor-in-possession's] argument that the mere filing of bankruptcy petition somehow transfers physical possession of the goods." Id. at 403-404. * * *

Tape City relied on In re Trahan, 283 F. Supp. 620, 626 (W.D. La.), aff'd, 402 F.2d 796 (5th Cir. 1968) (per curiam), which was decided under §67(c)(1)(B) of the Bankruptcy Act, the predecessor to Bankruptcy Code §545(2). In *Trahan*, the district court concluded that while §67(c) of the Bankruptcy Act gave the trustee the status of a bona fide purchaser, it did not give him physical possession of the property. "Possession by the original vendee is a requisite for protection of the seller and the enforcement of his vendor's privilege under Louisiana law." Id. Therefore, the district court held that absent such possession, the trustee could not avoid the vendor's privilege. Id. The Fifth Circuit affirmed based on the opinion of the district court. * * *

However, the *Trahan/Tape City* line of cases is not without criticism. The First Circuit disapproved of *Trahan* in In re J.R. Nieves & Co., 446 F.2d 188 (1st Cir. 1971). *Nieves* involved a vendor's privilege created under an article of the Puerto Rican Civil Code that was similar to the Louisiana Civil Code article at issue in *Tape City*. Under the article, a bona fide purchaser must take possession of the merchandise to defeat a seller's lien. The court stated, "In our view, when Congress spoke of the 'rights' of a hypothetical purchaser, it contemplated a full-blooded, not an anemic, purchaser." Id. at 192. Thus, it concluded that a characteristic of a hypothetical bona fide purchaser was possession of the merchandise and held that the trustee, as a hypothetical bona fide purchaser, could avoid the seller's lien. However, the "full-blooded" bona fide purchaser which the court was referring to was based on its state law definition of bona fide purchaser. Therefore, the First Circuit's broad definition of bona fide purchaser is limited to liens created under Puerto Rican law. * * *

In each of these cases, the court resolved the question of whether the lien could be avoided by a bona fide purchaser by looking at the law controlling the validity of the lien. We agree with, and shall follow the approach of the courts in these cases.

* * * [A] hypothetical bona fide purchaser could not avoid the federal tax liens because possession of the motor vehicle was in debtors and that possession cannot be imputed to a hypothetical bona fide purchaser .... Bankruptcy Code §545(2) makes clear that the trustee may only avoid a statutory lien that a bona fide purchaser could. Thus, where a bona fide purchaser is without the power to avoid a lien because the controlling law requires something more than mere bona fide purchaser status for protection, the trustee also is without power to avoid the lien. To state it as have many courts before us, the Bankruptcy Code does not grant hypothetical possession to a hypothetical bona fide purchaser.

III

For the reasons stated, the judgment of the district court is affirmed.

NOTES

8B.1. The *Walter* court stresses that it will resolve "the question of whether the lien could be avoided by a bona fide purchaser by looking at the law controlling the validity of the lien." It is not clear what this means exactly. The structure of §545(2) is to grant the trustee certain hypothetical characteristics and then use applicable lien law to determine what rights the trustee garners from such characteristics. No one disputes this. The debate is over *what* characteristics the term "bona fide purchaser" should include. Compare Note 8A.1. Lien law is not even *apposite* to this question, much less dispositive. Similarly puzzling is the court's view, expressed in footnote 7, that "because the trustee is not actually giving value for the asset, he need not be afforded the same protection as a true bona fide purchaser." Congress well understood that there are relevant differences between a trustee's actual position and that of a bona fide purchaser. This is precisely why §545(2) grants the former the characteristics of the latter.

The relevant question at the time of the *Walter* opinion was not what nonbankruptcy lien law provides, but rather what reach Congress intended for the trustee. On one hand, one might wonder why Congress would have wanted the trustee to lose priority because a bona fide purchaser does not *necessarily* pay full value or take possession. Such a result would rest heavily on a highly technical point. It may seem more plausible that Congress envisioned a "full-blooded, not an anemic, purchaser," as stated by the court in *Nieves*, cited in *Walter*. On the other hand, the Internal Revenue Code is a *federal* statute, and it would be odd for Congress to enact an explicit priority scheme in a tax statute only to have that scheme routinely undermined in its own Bankruptcy Code.

8B.2. Some doubt about Congressional intent has been dispelled since *Walter* was decided. The 2005 Bankruptcy Act amended §545(2) to except from the trustee's lien avoidance powers "any case in which a purchaser is a purchaser described in section 6323 of the Internal Revenue Code of 1986, or in any other similar provision of State or local law." This codifies the holding of *Walter* on its facts, but one might wonder about the reach of "any other similar provision of State or local law." Consider Problem 8B.

8B.3. The *Walter* problem does not arise under §544(a)(3). There Congress granted the trustee not merely the rights of a "bona fide purchaser" of real estate, but specifically the rights of such a purchaser who has a "perfected" interest.

PROBLEM

8B. Seller has a state statutory lien in liquor supplied on credit to Debtor. The lien is valid against all except "lawful bona fide purchasers of liquor inventory." A month after Seller's delivery, Debtor files for bankruptcy. Can the trustee avoid Seller's lien?

C. FRAUDULENT CONVEYANCES

The interests of a debtor can vary widely from those of the debtor's creditors. A debtor and her creditors may enjoy cooperative interactions when a loan is made and while times remain good. But once full repayment becomes improbable, either because the debtor cannot or will not make good on her obligations, the relationship between debtor and creditor can become adversarial. Inasmuch as the debtor controls the means of repayment, conflict can spell trouble for creditors.

Even when a creditor turns to the basic state debt-collection process, it may prove insufficient. If an individual debtor, or the manager of a corporate debtor, is dishonest, he may transfer assets to an accomplice so that the debtor appears to have no assets with which to repay creditors. Fraudulent conveyance law ensures that a creditor can reach fraudulently transferred property, at least if the transferee was an accomplice to the fraud. Modern fraudulent conveyance statutes can be found in the Uniform Fraudulent Conveyance Act (UFCA) and the Uniform Fraudulent Transfer Act (UFTA), which have served as models for state law.

Traditional fraudulent conveyance law reaches even beyond the scenario in which the debtor transfers property to a willing accomplice. Sometimes a dishonest debtor will exchange easily discoverable property, such as equipment, for easily consumed or concealed property, such as cash. If the debtor is successful in consuming or concealing the proceeds of such a transfer, the debtor's creditors can look to the debtor's transferee for collection even if the transferee was an innocent player in debtor's scheme. There is a caveat, however. If the person who receives a fraudulent transfer is herself a bona fide purchaser of the property transferred, she is entitled to retain the value she paid the debtor for the property. If she paid less than fair value, but in good faith, she may have to part with the property, but she can demand a return of what she paid.

As we discussed in chapter 1, fraudulent conveyance law goes further still. Despite the term *fraudulent* conveyance or transfer, the law applies even when the debtor is honest, or at least not demonstrably dishonest. The law embodies a general principle that a debtor cannot make a gift to others of property that could otherwise satisfy unpaid debt obligations. Imagine that an insolvent debtor decides that his sister should have his car. The debtor can transfer title to his sister, but his creditors can use fraudulent conveyance law to avoid the transfer and recover the car. It does not matter whether the debtor intended to recover the car later from his sister or even whether the debtor knew that he was insolvent and thus unable to pay his debts in full. If the debtor in fact had an illicit motive, then his fraud would be "actual." But fraudulent conveyance law would deem the transaction a "constructive" fraud even if the debtor had the best intentions toward his creditors but was merely generous to his sister.

A constructive fraudulent conveyance, moreover, is not limited to outright gifts by an insolvent debtor. If a debtor formally sells property, but for less than fair value, the transfer is constructively fraudulent regardless of the debtor's intent. A bona fide purchaser of the debtor's property will be protected to the extent of the amount she paid, as in the case of a transfer that is part of an actual fraud. But even an honest transferee will have to part with the benefit of her bargain in this situation. A constructive fraud can occur, in addition, even when the debtor is not technically insolvent at the time of the transfer. Fraudulent conveyance law applies when the transfer itself renders the debtor insolvent. Moreover, it applies as well when a transfer leaves a business debtor, though solvent, with unreasonably small capital.

All that has been said about property transferred by the debtor applies as well to obligations incurred by the debtor. Imagine, for example, that an insolvent debtor, rather than give a car to his sister, promises to pay for a car his sister hopes to buy from someone else. The sister might be able to invoke general principles of promissory estoppel and enforce this promise. But the debtor's creditors could nonetheless avoid this promise as a fraudulent conveyance. Were this promise enforceable against the insolvent brother, the sister, as a mere recipient of a gratuity, would compete for the debtor's assets with creditors who lent money in the past. For this reason, when a debtor incurs an obligation, that obligation is subject to the same scrutiny, and under the same rules, as a transfer of property.

These are the basic principles of fraudulent conveyance law. The principles can apply to a bankruptcy case in one of two ways. As we have seen, §544(b) permits the trustee, on behalf of the estate, to avoid any transfer that an unsecured creditor could have avoided under applicable nonbankruptcy law but for the automatic stay. See section A above. Thus, if a debtor's general creditor could avoid a fraudulent conveyance under state law, the trustee can avoid that transfer under the Bankruptcy Code. Second, §548 provides independent substantive grounds for the trustee to avoid a fraudulent conveyance made within two years before the debtor's bankruptcy petition regardless of the rights any unsecured creditor may have.

Although there are some small differences among state fraudulent conveyance laws, and between state laws and the provisions of §548, the substantive law in each instance is essentially the same, as summarized above. For example, UFCA §7 provides that "every conveyance made and every obligation incurred with actual intent ... to hinder, delay, or defraud ... is fraudulent as to both present and future creditors." Section 548(a)(1)(A) uses virtually the same language to address a transfer that was actually fraudulent.

Similarly, under UFTA §5, a transfer or obligation incurred for less than "a reasonably equivalent value" is constructively fraudulent if the debtor "was insolvent at [the time of the transfer or obligation] or became insolvent as a result ... ." Section 548(a)(1)(B) again uses essentially the same language. And "insolvency" is defined in each case as total assets less than total liabilities. See UFTA §2; Bankruptcy Code §101(32).

UFTA §4 deems a transfer or obligation incurred as constructively fraudulent if the exchange is for less than a reasonably equivalent value and the debtor either is engaged in business or a transaction with assets of a value "unreasonably small" in relation to the business or transaction, or the debtor "reasonably should have believed that he would incur debts beyond his ability to repay." (The same provision proscribes, though redundantly, a sort of actual fraud where at the time of a transfer for less than equivalent value the debtor "intended to incur, or believed" he would incur obligations beyond his ability to repay.) Once more, the Bankruptcy Code, in §548(a)(1)(B), uses much of the same language to reach essentially the same results. (Although §548(a)(1)(B) does not deem a transfer fraudulent if a debtor merely "should have believed" that he would incur unpayable debts, as a practical matter, almost any debtor who "should" but does not actually hold such a belief will be engaged in a business with "unreasonably small" capital assets.)

In the application of these provisions, moreover, "value" exchanged, in turn, is defined by both UFTA §3 and §548(d)(2) to include the transfer of property and the satisfaction of or provision of security for an antecedent obligation of the debtor but to exclude certain "unperformed promises" of support for the debtor or others.

Once a debtor files for bankruptcy, state fraudulent conveyance law (available to the trustee because of §544(b)) and the fraudulent conveyance provisions of §548 usually lead to the same outcome. There are circumstances in which only one avenue is available to the trustee. The trustee must rely on state fraudulent conveyance law, for example, when the transfer occurs more than one year before the filing of the petition. Because of the one-year window in §548, a fraudulent conveyance attack is available, if at all, only under state law. There are circumstances too when state fraudulent conveyance law will be unavailable. The trustee can use state fraudulent conveyance law only if an actual creditor exists who can invoke it. Section 548 contains no such limitation. For example, it is possible that the state law gave the action only to creditors who extended credit before the fraudulent conveyance and that no such creditors exist. Such cases arise rarely. The best justification for §548 is that it saves the trustee from sorting through the conflict of law question that might arise if the debtor's assets and creditors were spread across many jurisdictions.

There is one way, however, in which §548 is more limited than traditional fraudulent conveyance law and in which the Bankruptcy Code cuts back on the reach of state fraudulent conveyance law in bankruptcy. After some cases in which the trustee had brought fraudulent conveyance actions against religious institutions, Congress added §548(a)(2) to the Bankruptcy Code. It provides:

> A transfer of a charitable contribution to a qualified religious or charitable entity or organization shall not be considered to be a transfer covered under paragraph (1)(B) in any case in which—
>
> (A) the amount of that contribution does not exceed 15 percent of the gross annual income of the debtor for the year in which the transfer of the contribution is made; or
>
> (B) the contribution made by a debtor exceeded the percentage amount of gross annual income specified in subparagraph (A), if the transfer was consistent with the practices of the debtor in making charitable contributions.

Because of the constraints of the First Amendment, the new provision applies to qualified charitable contributions generally—defined in §548(d)(3) by reference to tax law—and not just religious organizations. This provision has a counterpart in §544(b)(2), which prohibits the trustee from avoiding a transfer "that is not covered under §548(a)(1)(B), by reason of §548(a)(2)."

Section 548 contains some other special rules. For example, a conveyance by an insolvent partnership to one of its general partners within a year before the partnership's bankruptcy is avoidable regardless of intent or consideration exchanged. See §548(b). This provision is of limited significance inasmuch as typically a general partner is personally liable for the partnership's debts in any case. Also in §548 are special rules applicable to the securities industry, where "value" received in exchange for a transfer can sometimes be difficult to determine. See §§546(e)-(g) and 548(d)(2), (e).

A particularly interesting special fraudulent conveyance provision was added to the Code by the 2005 Bankruptcy Act. New §548(a)(1)(B)(ii)(IV) adds to the definition of constructive fraud a transfer made, or debt incurred, in exchange for less than a reasonably equivalent value, made to or for the benefit of an insider under an employment contract and not in the ordinary course of business. This provision is meaningful only when the debtor is solvent at the time of the transfer, or the transfer would be deemed fraudulent even without the new definition. This provision, therefore, may be seen not merely as a creditor-protection provision, the traditional role of fraudulent conveyance law, but as an attempt by Congress to supplement, or override, state corporate law that might leave the debtor itself no recourse against the transferee.

Once the trustee avoids a fraudulent transfer under either §544(b) or §548, the property transferred is preserved for the estate under §551. The trustee can then recover the avoided transfer under §550, which applies broadly to transfers avoided by the trustee. Section 550(e) provides that, in the event a transfer is avoided, any transferee retains a lien for the costs of her improvements to the property, if any, limited by the value of those improvements. This lien supplements any lien a transferee holds under §548(c) by virtue of a good-faith payment for the property transferred.

The exercises below ask you to work through some of the fraudulent conveyance mechanics. The three cases that follow, *BFP*, *Moody*, and *Manhattan Investment Fund*, as well as the related notes and problems, require you to go beyond mechanics and consider the policies underlying fraudulent conveyance law.

BFP is a case about the meaning of "reasonably equivalent value" in the context of a real estate foreclosure, where the challenged transfer is not voluntary. Every illustration above involves a voluntary transfer by an insolvent debtor, not an involuntary transfer, or debt collection, which is treated elsewhere in the Bankruptcy Code. See §547, discussed below in this chapter. Fraudulent conveyance law, however, applies to involuntary transfers as well. See UFTA §12; Bankruptcy Code §101(54). *BFP* explores the rationale for application of fraudulent conveyance law to involuntary transfers.

Moody interprets, among other provisions, the meaning of "unreasonably small capital" under UFCA §5 and, indirectly, under Bankruptcy Code §548(a)(2)(B)(ii). The context is a leveraged buyout, and in at least one of the transfers challenged it is undisputed that the transferee parted with reasonably equivalent value in exchange for the property transferred. In each case, the recipient of a challenged transfer attempts to distinguish the debtor's ultimate loss on what was at the outset a fair bargain from a transaction that cannot at its inception work in the debtor's favor. Keep this theme in mind as you work through the material.

Manhattan Investment Company addresses the definition of "good faith" for the purposes of §548(c). The context is one of a stock broker's liability for its participation in securities fraud. Special provisions related to stock brokers are also addressed.

Key Provisions: Bankruptcy Code §§548; 550; 551

EXERCISES

8C(1) Debtor uses borrowed funds to purchase equipment and supplies for her house-painting business. After a time, Debtor realizes that she will not be able to make much money in the business. Debtor plans to leave town and evade her creditors' collection efforts. The only assets Debtor has of value are her truck, in which she will travel, and a compressor, which is too cumbersome to move and store easily. Debtor enters into a heated negotiation with Purchaser, who ultimately buys the compressor for $15,000. Debtor leaves town the next day. Six months later Debtor's creditors file an involuntary bankruptcy petition against her. Can the trustee recover the compressor from Purchaser? Does the value of the compressor at the time of sale or at the time of bankruptcy matter? Would your answer change if Purchaser purchased the compressor on credit and planned to pay Debtor later at her new address? Would your answer change if Purchaser were a close friend of Debtor's and the negotiations amicable? Would your answer change if the bankruptcy petition were sixteen rather than six months after the sale of the compressor?

8C(2) Debtor Corporation is a bicycle retailer in desperate need of cash. Debtor holds a clearance sale of all its merchandise, which it liquidates for three-fourths of the usual price. Debtor also sells its repair equipment to a competitor for less than half of what this equipment usually fetches in the market. Debtor then closes its doors for a month, and reopens as a flower shop. This was all to no avail. Debtor files for bankruptcy six months later. Can the trustee recover the merchandise or equipment?

8C(3) Debtor is a movie producer who earns about $1 million per year, but is deeply in debt because his last three movies have flopped. Just before the release of his latest film, Debtor donates a sculpture worth $200,000 to his church. This was Debtor's first charitable contribution. Within a year of Debtor's contribution, his new movie fails as well and Debtor files for bankruptcy. From whom, if anyone, can the trustee seek recovery? Would your answer change if the donation was in cash instead of a sculpture? When answering these questions, consider, among other provisions, Bankruptcy Code §548(d)(3).

8C(4) Six months before Debtor files for bankruptcy, Bank collects all $10,000 outstanding on an unsecured loan. At the moment before this collection, Debtor's assets were worth $20,000 while Debtor's liabilities totaled $100,000. Can the trustee recover the collection as a fraudulent conveyance? Would it matter whether the collection was voluntary or involuntary?

1) REASONABLY EQUIVALENT VALUE

The case below, *BFP*, as well as the notes and problem that follow ask you to ponder what is meant by "reasonably equivalent value" in the context of an involuntary transfer. Specifically, the case addresses foreclosure on a debtor's real property. (The case involves a "deed of trust." Under California law, a security interest in land can be taken with this device. As you will see in the case, the deed of trust functions in much the same way as a conventional real estate mortgage.) There are two transfers to consider. The first is the debtor's initial grant of a security interest. The second is the debtor's ultimate surrender of the property pursuant to that security interest. Each transfer is relevant, though only the latter is challenged.

CASE

BFP v. RESOLUTION TRUST CORP.

United States Supreme Court, 1993
511 U.S. 531

JUSTICE SCALIA DELIVERED THE OPINION OF THE COURT.

This case presents the question whether the consideration received from a noncollusive, real estate mortgage foreclosure sale conducted in conformance with applicable state law conclusively satisfies the Bankruptcy Code's requirement that transfers of property by insolvent debtors within one year prior to the filing of a bankruptcy petition be in exchange for "a reasonably equivalent value." [§548(a)(1)(B)].

I

Petitioner BFP is a partnership, formed by Wayne and Marlene Pedersen and Russell Barton in 1987, for the purpose of buying a home in Newport Beach, California, from Sheldon and Ann Foreman. Petitioner took title subject to a first deed of trust in favor of Imperial Savings Association (Imperial)[1] to secure payment of a loan of $356,250 made to the Pedersens in connection with petitioner's acquisition of the home. Petitioner granted a second deed of trust to the Foremans as security for a $200,000 promissory note. Subsequently, Imperial, whose loan was not being serviced, entered a notice of default under the first deed of trust and scheduled a properly noticed foreclosure sale. The foreclosure proceedings were temporarily delayed by the filing of an involuntary bankruptcy petition on behalf of petitioner. After the dismissal of that petition in June 1989, Imperial's foreclosure proceeding was completed at a foreclosure sale on July 12, 1989. The home was purchased by respondent Paul Osborne for $433,000.

In October 1989, petitioner filed for bankruptcy under Chapter 11. Acting as a debtor in possession, petitioner filed a complaint in Bankruptcy Court seeking to set aside the conveyance of the home to respondent Osborne on the grounds that the foreclosure sale constituted a fraudulent transfer under §548. Petitioner alleged that the home was actually worth over $725,000 at the time of the sale to Osborne. Acting on separate motions, the Bankruptcy Court dismissed the complaint as to the private respondents and granted summary judgment in favor of Imperial. The Bankruptcy Court found, inter alia, that the foreclosure sale had been conducted in compliance with California law and was neither collusive nor fraudulent. In an unpublished opinion, the District Court affirmed the Bankruptcy Court's granting of the private respondents' motion to dismiss. A divided bankruptcy appellate panel affirmed the Bankruptcy Court's entry of summary judgment for Imperial .... [T]he panel majority held that a "non-collusive and regularly conducted nonjudicial foreclosure sale ... cannot be challenged as a fraudulent conveyance because the consideration received in such a sale establishes 'reasonably equivalent value' as a matter of law."

---

[1] Respondent Resolution Trust Corporation (RTC) acts in this case as receiver of Imperial Federal Savings Association (Imperial Federal), which was organized pursuant to a June 22, 1990, order of the Director of the Office of Thrift Supervision, and into which RTC transferred certain assets and liabilities of Imperial. * * *

Petitioner sought review of both decisions in the Court of Appeals for the Ninth Circuit, which consolidated the appeals. The Court of Appeals affirmed. BFP filed a petition for certiorari, which we granted.

II

Section 548 of the Bankruptcy Code sets forth the powers of a trustee in bankruptcy (or, in a Chapter 11 case, a debtor in possession) to avoid fraudulent transfers. It permits to be set aside not only transfers infected by actual fraud but certain other transfers as well—so-called constructively fraudulent transfers. The constructive fraud provision at issue in this case applies to transfers by insolvent debtors. It permits avoidance if the trustee can establish (1) that the debtor had an interest in property; (2) that a transfer of that interest occurred within one year of the filing of the bankruptcy petition; (3) that the debtor was insolvent at the time of the transfer or became insolvent as a result thereof; and (4) that the debtor received "less than a reasonably equivalent value in exchange for such transfer." [§548(a)(1)(B)]. It is the last of these four elements that presents the issue in the case before us.

Section 548 applies to any "transfer," which includes "foreclosure of the debtor's equity of redemption." Bankruptcy Code §101(54). Of the three critical terms "reasonably equivalent value," only the last is defined: "value" means, for purposes of §548, "property, or satisfaction or securing of a ... debt of the debtor," §548(d)(2)(A). The question presented here, therefore, is whether the amount of debt (to the first and second lienholders) satisfied at the foreclosure sale (viz., a total of $433,000) is "reasonably equivalent" to the worth of the real estate conveyed. The Courts of Appeals have divided on the meaning of those undefined terms. In Durrett v. Washington Nat. Ins. Co., 621 F.2d 201 (5th Cir. 1980), the Fifth Circuit, interpreting a provision of the old Bankruptcy Act analogous to [§548(a)(1)(b)], held that a foreclosure sale that yielded 57% of the property's fair market value could be set aside, and indicated in dicta that any such sale for less than 70% of fair market value should be invalidated. This "*Durrett* rule" has continued to be applied by some courts under §548 of the new Bankruptcy Code. See In re Littleton, 888 F.2d 90, 92, n.5 (11th Cir. 1989). In In re Bundles, 856 F.2d 815, 820 (7th Cir. 1988), the Seventh Circuit rejected the *Durrett* rule in favor of a case-by-case, "all facts and circumstances" approach to the question of reasonably equivalent value, with a rebuttable presumption that the foreclosure sale price is sufficient to withstand attack under [§548(a)(1)(b)]. In this case the Ninth Circuit adopted the position ... that the consideration received at a noncollusive, regularly conducted real estate foreclosure sale constitutes a reasonably equivalent value under [§548(a)(1)(B)]. The Court of Appeals acknowledged that it "necessarily part[ed] from the positions taken by the Fifth Circuit in *Durrett* ... and the Seventh Circuit in *Bundles*." 974 F.2d, at 1148.

In contrast to the approach adopted by the Ninth Circuit in the present case, both *Durrett* and *Bundles* refer to fair market value as the benchmark against which determination of reasonably equivalent value is to be measured. In the context of an otherwise lawful mortgage foreclosure sale of real estate, such reference is in our opinion not consistent with the text of the Bankruptcy Code. The term "fair market value," though it is a well-established concept, does not appear in §548. In contrast, §522, dealing with a debtor's exemptions, specifically provides that, for purposes of that section, "'value' means fair market value as of the date of the filing of the petition." ... Section 548, on the other hand, seemingly goes out of its way to avoid that standard term. It might readily have said "received less than fair market value in exchange for such transfer or obligation," or perhaps "less than a reasonable equivalent of fair market value." Instead, it used the (as far as we are aware) entirely novel phrase "reasonably equivalent value." "[I]t is generally presumed that Congress acts intentionally and purposely when it includes particular language in one section of a statute but omits it in another," Chicago v. Environmental Defense Fund, 511 U.S. 328, 338 (1994), and that presumption is even stronger when the omission entails the replacement of standard legal terminology with a neologism. One must suspect the language means that fair market value cannot—or at least cannot always—be the benchmark.

That suspicion becomes a certitude when one considers that market value, as it is commonly understood, has no applicability in the forced-sale context; indeed, it is the very antithesis of forced-sale value. "The market value of ... a piece of property is the price which it might be expected to bring if offered for sale in a fair market; not the price which might be obtained on a sale at public auction or a sale forced by the necessities of the owner, but such a price as would be fixed by negotiation and mutual agreement, after ample time to find a purchaser, as between a vendor who is willing (but not compelled) to sell and a purchaser who desires to buy but is not compelled to take the particular ... piece of property." Black's Law Dictionary 971 (6th ed. 1990). In short, "fair market value" presumes market conditions that, by definition, simply do not obtain in the context of a forced sale.

Neither petitioner, petitioner's amici, nor any federal court adopting the *Durrett* or the *Bundles* analysis has come to grips with this glaring discrepancy between the factors relevant to an appraisal of a property's market value, on the one hand, and the strictures of the foreclosure process on the other. Market value cannot be the criterion of equivalence in the foreclosure-sale context. The language of [§548(a)(1)(B)] ("received less than a reasonably equivalent value in exchange") requires judicial inquiry into whether the foreclosed property was sold for a price that approximated its worth at the time of sale. An appraiser's reconstruction of "fair market value" could show what similar property would be worth if it did not have to be sold within the time and manner strictures of state-prescribed foreclosure. But property that must be sold within those strictures is simply worth less. No one would pay as much to own such property as he would pay to own real estate that could be sold at leisure and pursuant to normal marketing techniques. And it is no more realistic to ignore that characteristic of the property (the fact that state foreclosure law permits the mortgagee to sell it at forced sale) than it is to ignore other price-affecting characteristics (such as the fact that state zoning law permits the owner of the neighboring lot to open a gas station). Absent a clear statutory requirement to the contrary, we must assume the validity of this state-law regulatory background and take due account of its effect. "The existence and force and function of established institutions of local government are always in the consciousness of lawmakers and, while their weight may vary, they may never be completely overlooked in the task of interpretation." Davies Warehouse Co. v. Bowles, 321 U.S. 144 (1944).

There is another artificially constructed criterion we might look to instead of "fair market price." One might judge there to be such a thing as a "reasonable" or "fair" forced-sale price. Such a conviction must lie behind the *Bundles* inquiry into whether the state foreclosure proceedings "were calculated ... to return to the debtor-mortgagor his equity in the property." 856 F.2d at 824. And perhaps that is what the courts that follow the *Durrett* rule have in mind when they select 70 percent of fair market value as the outer limit of "reasonably equivalent value" for forecloseable property (we have no idea where else such an arbitrary percentage could have come from). The problem is that such judgments represent policy determinations that the Bankruptcy Code gives us no apparent authority to make. How closely the price received in a forced sale is likely to approximate fair market value depends upon the terms of the forced sale—how quickly it may be made, what sort of public notice must be given, etc. But the terms for foreclosure sale are not standard. They vary considerably from State to State, depending upon, among other things, how the particular State values the divergent interests of debtor and creditor. To specify a federal "reasonable" foreclosure-sale price is to extend federal bankruptcy law well beyond the traditional field of fraudulent transfers, into realms of policy where it has not ventured before. * * *

Fraudulent transfer law and foreclosure law enjoyed over 400 years of peaceful coexistence in Anglo-American jurisprudence until the Fifth Circuit's unprecedented 1980 decision in *Durrett*. To our knowledge no prior decision had ever applied the "grossly inadequate price" badge of fraud under fraudulent transfer law to set aside a foreclosure sale. To say that the "reasonably equivalent value" language in the fraudulent transfer provision of the Bankruptcy Code requires a foreclosure sale to yield a certain minimum price beyond what state foreclosure law requires, is to say, in essence, that the Code has adopted *Durrett* or *Bundles*. Surely Congress has the power pursuant to its constitutional grant of authority over bankruptcy, U.S. Const., Art. I, §8, cl. 4, to disrupt the ancient harmony that foreclosure law and fraudulent conveyance law, those two pillars of debtor-creditor jurisprudence, have heretofore enjoyed. But absent clearer textual guidance than the phrase "reasonably equivalent value"—a phrase entirely compatible with pre-existing practice—we will not presume such a radical departure.[7] * * *

---

[7] We are unpersuaded by petitioner's argument that the 1984 amendments to the Bankruptcy Code codified the *Durrett* rule. Those amendments expanded the definition of "transfer" to include "foreclosure of the debtor's equity of redemption," §101(54), and added the words "voluntarily or involuntarily" as modifiers of the term "transfer" in §548(a). The first of these provisions establishes that foreclosure sales fall within the general definition of "transfers" that may be avoided under several statutory provisions, including (but not limited to) §548. See §522(h) (transfers of exempt property), §544 (transfers voidable under state law), §547 (preferential transfers), §549 (postpetition transfers). The second of them establishes that a transfer may be avoided as fraudulent even if it was against the debtor's will. See In re Madrid, 725 F.2d 1197, 1199 (9th Cir. 1984) (preamendment decision holding that a foreclosure sale is not a "transfer" under §548). Neither of these consequences has any bearing upon the meaning of "reasonably equivalent value" in the context of a foreclosure sale.

[T]he States have created diverse networks of judicially and legislatively crafted rules governing the foreclosure process, to achieve what each of them considers the proper balance between the needs of lenders and borrowers. * * * It is beyond question that an essential state interest is at issue here: We have said that "the general welfare of society is involved in the security of the titles to real estate" and the power to ensure that security "inheres in the very nature of [state] government." American Land Co. v. Zeiss, 219 U.S. 47, 60 (1911). Nor is there any doubt that the interpretation urged by petitioner would have a profound effect upon that interest: The title of every piece of realty purchased at foreclosure would be under a federally created cloud. (Already, title insurers have reacted to the *Durrett* rule by including specially crafted exceptions from coverage in many policies issued for properties purchased at foreclosure sales. To displace traditional state regulation in such a manner, the federal statutory purpose must be "clear and manifest," English v. General Elec. Co., 496 U.S. 72, 79 (1990). Otherwise, the Bankruptcy Code will be construed to adopt, rather than to displace, pre-existing state law. See Butner v. United States, 440 U.S. 48, 54-55 (1979).

For the reasons described, we decline to read the phrase "reasonably equivalent value" in [§548(a)(1)(B)] to mean, in its application to mortgage foreclosure sales, either "fair market value" or "fair foreclosure price" (whether calculated as a percentage of fair market value or otherwise). We deem, as the law has always deemed, that a fair and proper price, or a "reasonably equivalent value," for foreclosed property, is the price in fact received at the foreclosure sale, so long as all the requirements of the State's foreclosure law have been complied with.

This conclusion does not render [§548(a)(1)(B)] superfluous, since the "reasonably equivalent value" criterion will continue to have independent meaning (ordinarily a meaning similar to fair market value) outside the foreclosure context. Indeed, [§548(a)(1)(B)] will even continue to be an exclusive means of invalidating some foreclosure sales. Although collusive foreclosure sales are likely subject to attack under §548(a)(1)[(A)], which authorizes the trustee to avoid

---

Nor does our reading render these amendments "superfluous". . . . Prior to 1984, it was at least open to question whether §548 could be used to invalidate even a collusive foreclosure sale. It is no superfluity for Congress to clarify what had been at best unclear, which is what it did here by making the provision apply to involuntary as well as voluntary transfers and by including foreclosures within the definition of "transfer."

transfers "made ... with actual intent to hinder, delay, or defraud" creditors, that provision may not reach foreclosure sales that, while not intentionally fraudulent, nevertheless fail to comply with all governing state laws. * * *

For the foregoing reasons, the judgment of the Court of Appeals for the Ninth Circuit is affirmed.

NOTES

8C.1. The Court's opinion in *BFP* was over a vigorous dissent by Justice Souter, not reproduced here. Justice Souter did not believe that "Congress intended a peppercorn paid at a noncollusive and procedurally regular foreclosure sale to be treated as the 'reasonabl[e] equivalent' of the value of a California beachfront estate." But the Court did not find that a peppercorn could be equivalent to the value of the estate. It found only that the peppercorn could be equivalent to the value of the *debtor's interest* in the estate. That is, the Court found, explicitly, that the debtor's interest in the property was subject to a foreclosure process just as that interest would be subject to a zoning ordinance. Bankruptcy law, the Court concluded, should not diminish the mortgagee's interest in the property, albeit an interest heightened by the foreclosure process, any more than bankruptcy law should diminish the neighbor's interest in the enforcement of a zoning restriction. This result is an application of the *Butner* principle, as the Court notes.

Put another way, the holding of *BFP* rests on an assumption that ex ante the debtor's transfer of a mortgage interest in its property subject to California's forced-sale rules is a transfer for reasonably equivalent value. That is, if a debtor subjects its property to forced-sale rules as part of the fair exchange for money borrowed, it is hardly a fraudulent conveyance for a creditor later to receive performance on its bargain. Thus a debtor's unsecured creditors, on notice of the recorded transfer or able to anticipate such a transfer, should have no ground to object. The Court concluded that the Bankruptcy Code's fraudulent conveyance provisions should not be used to upset a state's attempt "to achieve what [it] considers the proper balance between the needs of lenders and borrowers." Problem 8C-1 asks you to consider how far a court might go in honoring such a balance.

8C.2. Although the Court's holding is supported by fundamental bankruptcy policy, one might wonder, as did the dissent in *BFP*, why

Congress explicitly applied fraudulent conveyance law to "<u>voluntary</u>
<u>or involuntary</u>" transfers. See §548(a) (emphasis added). After all,
argued the dissent, it would have been meaningless for Congress to
decide that §548 covers involuntary transfers and then define "reasonably equivalent value" such that <u>no involuntary transfer could ever</u>
<u>be fraudulent.</u> The Court responds, in footnote 7, that the inclusion of
involuntary transfers in §548 may merely be an attempt to clarify application to (collusive foreclosures) Perhaps so, but if this was Congress' goal it might more directly have applied §548 to "voluntary *or*
collusive involuntary" transfers. The Court tries a different tack as
well, noting that an <u>involuntary transfer</u> may run afoul of the fraudulent conveyance laws if, for example, a <u>foreclosure sale</u> "fail[s] to
<u>comply with all governing state laws</u>" and thus yields a sale price less
than "reasonably equivalent value," measured by the hypothetical sale
price that compliance would have garnered. If, however, a foreclosure
sale that failed to comply with state law were <u>invalid</u> under state law,
the trustee could simply retain the mortgaged property through §541,
without need of §548.

PROBLEM

8C-1. Bank holds a mortgage on Debtor's real estate, WhiteAcre,
in a jurisdiction that permits a creditor to take and retain collateral in
satisfaction of a defaulted secured obligation regardless of the value
of the collateral or outstanding amount of the obligation. Less than a
year prior to Debtor's filing of a bankruptcy petition, while the Debtor
is deeply insolvent, Debtor defaults on a scheduled payment of its
$500,000 obligation to Bank. As it is entitled to do under applicable
state law, Bank uses the default to take title to WhiteAcre, which an
owner could, with minimal effort, sell for at least $1 million. Can
Debtor's bankruptcy trustee avoid the transfer of WhiteAcre as a
fraudulent conveyance?

2) UNREASONABLY SMALL CAPITAL

The case below, *Moody*, is primarily about the meaning of "unreasonably small capital" as that term appears in UFCA §5 and Bankruptcy Code §548(a)(2)(B)(ii). The context is a leveraged buyout
(commonly called an "LBO"). In order to understand the case, and the
significance of the court's holding, it is necessary first to understand
how an LBO works.

A leveraged buyout is a corporate control transaction in which new investors acquire a modest equity stake in a firm while the firm itself takes on significant new debt and uses this new debt to repurchase the equity held by the old shareholders. After this transaction, the firm has a new owner and a much higher debt-to-equity ratio. There is a *buyout*, because the equity of the firm has changed hands. The buyout is *leveraged* because the firm now carries a much higher debt burden.

Let us look at a simple case. Firm has a number of general creditors and ten shareholders, each with an equal share of Firm. Firm also has, at fair saleable value, $3 million in assets and $2 million in unsecured debt. Entrepreneur buys the shares of one of the ten shareholders for $100,000. Firm borrows $900,000 from Bank and gives Bank a security interest in all its assets. Firm uses this money to buy back the shares of the other nine shareholders for $900,000. At the end of the day, Firm is much more highly leveraged. Firm has greater debt, but the same assets. Instead of being a $3 million firm with $2 million in debt, it is a $3 million firm with $2.9 million in debt. The old shareholders have cash. Entrepreneur enjoys all the profits that the ten shareholders used to share among themselves and has risked only $100,000. More than this amount is at risk, of course, but that risk falls on the unsecured creditors.

The old shareholders, Entrepreneur, and Bank all participate in the LBO voluntarily. The old unsecured creditors, however, are taken along for the ride, and the interest rate on their obligations, which may have been set without contemplation of the LBO, is now woefully low. If Firm succeeds, all creditors, including the unsecured creditors, will be paid and Entrepreneur will get rich. If the fortunes of Firm sag only a little, however, Firm may not be able to meet its loan obligations. Bank has a secured loan. Hence, it will be paid. As soon as Firm's value falls below $2.9 million, however, the old unsecured creditors suffer the entire loss unless they have a legal remedy. The unsecured creditors' legal remedy, if one exists, will take the form of a fraudulent conveyance attack, often brought by a trustee in bankruptcy after an LBO fails. To succeed the trustee must show both that the LBO transactions depleted the firm of assets in exchange for less than "reasonably equivalent value" and that the transactions left the firm insolvent or with "unreasonably small capital."

In a fraudulent conveyance action that follows an LBO, the trustee has three potential targets: the purchaser, the old shareholders, and the lender who finances the transaction. Often it is the lender, typi-

[margin handwriting: purposes]

cally a bank with a security interest in all the debtor's assets, that is the trustee's prime target. The purchaser and shareholders may well lack the resources to make good on the unsecured creditors' losses or may be too dispersed to locate and sue, or both. It would seem, however, that the trustee would have difficulty bringing the action against the lender, as the lender exchanged cold hard cash for debtor's promise to pay and the security interest supporting the promise. But we reach these issues only if the transaction left the debtor with "unreasonably small capital." The constructive fraud provisions of fraudulent conveyance law are unavailable when the debtor is well capitalized.

[margin handwriting: the debtor has capital → must prove actual fraud]

Although *Moody* does not break down the transactions of an LBO to analyze individual actions against the various defendants, you should keep these individual actions in mind as you read. The notes and problem after the case ask you to consider whether the trustee should have to meet different hurdles in reaching the lender rather than the other potential targets.

CASE

MOODY v. SECURITY PACIFIC BUSINESS CREDIT INC.

United States Court of Appeals, Third Circuit, 1992
971 F.2d 1056

SCIRICA, CIRCUIT JUDGE.

This bankruptcy case requires us to address, once again, the application of the fraudulent conveyance laws to a failed leveraged buyout. In United States v. Tabor Court Realty Corp., 803 F.2d 1288, 1297 (3d Cir. 1986), we established that the Pennsylvania Uniform Fraudulent Conveyance Act (UFCA) extends to leveraged buyouts. This case raises several questions about the application of this Act to the failed leveraged buyout of Jeannette Corporation.

On July 31, 1981, a group of investors acquired Jeannette in a leveraged buyout. Less than a year and a half later, Jeannette, which had been profitable for many years, was forced into bankruptcy. The bankruptcy trustee brought this action to set aside the advances made and obligations incurred in connection with the acquisition. The trustee alleges that the leveraged buyout constitutes a fraudulent conveyance under the UFCA and is voidable under the Bankruptcy Code.

After a bench trial, the district court entered judgment for defendants. We will affirm.

I

A

Founded in 1898, Jeannette Corporation manufactured and sold glass, ceramic, china, plastic, and candle houseware products in the United States and Canada. For many years, Jeannette was a profitable enterprise. From 1965 to 1978, its annual net sales grew on a consolidated basis from $9.6 million to $61.7 million and its annual gross profit margin ranged from 18% to 32.9%. In each of those years, Jeannette earned a net profit. From 1975 to 1977, Jeannette's sales increased annually by 16%. Its consolidated pre-tax profit was $3.4 million in 1977 and $6.1 million in 1978.

In 1978, the Coca-Cola Bottling Company of New York, Inc. acquired Jeannette for $39.6 million. Shortly thereafter, Coca-Cola … invested $6 million in Jeannette for capital expenditures, and $5 million for maintenance and repair of its physical plant.

At first, Jeannette was not as profitable under Coca-Cola's ownership. … However, Jeannette's performance rebounded in 1980. Net sales increased by $9 million and the company's gross profit margin doubled. * * *

B

In late 1979, Coca-Cola decided to sell Jeannette and focus attention on its core bottling business. In June 1981, John P. Brogan expressed an interest in acquiring Jeannette. Brogan was affiliated with a small group of investors in the business of acquiring companies through leveraged buyouts, the hallmark feature of which is the exchange of equity for debt. On July 22, 1981, Coca-Cola agreed to sell Jeannette for $12.1 million on condition that Brogan complete the transaction by the end of the month.

Brogan contacted Security Pacific Business Credit Inc., a lending group that had financed one of his prior acquisitions, about obtaining financing. He submitted one year of monthly projections, based in large part on Jeannette's 80-page business plan for 1981, which showed that Jeannette would have sufficient working capital under the proposed financing arrangement in the year following the acquisition. Before agreeing to finance the transaction, however, Security Pacific undertook its own investigation of Jeannette.

Security Pacific assigned this task to credit analyst Stephen Ngan. Based on his discussions with Jeannette personnel and a review of the company's financial records, Ngan made his own set of projections. He concluded that Jeannette would earn a pretax profit of $800,000 after interest expenses in its first year of operation, and recommended that Security Pacific finance the acquisition. He thought Jeannette was a "well-established" company with "a good track record for growth and earnings."

After reviewing Ngan's recommendation, together with ... a 55-page report on Jeannette prepared by another bank, Security Pacific decided to finance the acquisition. At that point, Coca-Cola formally approved the sale of Jeannette to J. Corp., which had been incorporated for the purpose of acquiring Jeannette.

C

The acquisition of Jeannette was consummated on July 31, 1981. J. Corp. purchased Jeannette with funds from a $15.5 million line of credit Security Pacific extended Jeannette secured by first lien security interests on all Jeannette's assets. J. Corp. never repaid Jeannette any portion of, or executed a promissory note for, the amount ($11.7 million) Security Pacific initially forwarded to J. Corp. on behalf of Jeannette to finance the acquisition. Other than new management, the only benefit Jeannette received was access to credit from Security Pacific.[3]

---

[3] The transaction comprised the following steps, which were deemed by the parties to have taken place at once: (1) J. Corp. entered into an agreement with Coca-Cola and KNY Development Corporation, a wholly owned subsidiary of Coca-Cola, to purchase all outstanding stock of Jeannette; (2) J. Corp. obtained a $12.1 million unsecured loan from Security Pacific and executed a demand note therefor; (3) these funds were transferred from Security Pacific to Coca-Cola to fund the purchase of Jeannette stock, which was transferred from KNY Development to J. Corp.; (4) upon acquisition of the stock, J. Corp. appointed a new board of directors for Jeannette and named Brogan chairman; (5) Jeannette entered into a $15.5 million revolving credit arrangement with Security Pacific, in exchange for which it granted Security Pacific first lien security interests in all its assets; (6) on behalf of Jeannette, Brogan directed Security Pacific to remit $11.7 million from the revolving credit facility to J. Corp., which was used to repay all but $400,000 of the demand note to Security Pacific; and (7) Jeannette and Security Pacific entered into a "lock box" agreement, whereby Jeannette's accounts receivable would be forwarded to the Mellon Bank and credited against the outstanding balance on Jeannette's line of credit.

As with most leveraged buyouts, the acquisition left Jeannette's assets fully encumbered by the security interests held by Security Pacific. Jeannette could not dispose of its assets, except in the ordinary course of business, without the consent of Security Pacific, and was prohibited from granting security interests to anyone else. As a result, Jeannette's sole source of working capital after the transaction was its line of credit with Security Pacific. * * *

D

Jeannette operated as a going concern from the latter half of 1981 into 1982. ... Although Jeannette's performance initially tracked expectations, its financial condition deteriorated steadily in 1982. Jeannette experienced a shrinking domestic glassware market, a marked increase in foreign competition, dramatic price slashing and inventory dumping by its domestic competitors, and a continued nationwide recession. * * *

* * * On October 4, 1982, an involuntary bankruptcy petition was filed under Chapter 7 of the Bankruptcy Code. Jeannette's trade creditors filed $2.5 million in proof of claims, over 90% for goods or services provided after June 1982, none for goods or services supplied before the leveraged buyout.

In November 1982, Jeannette sold the assets of its Brookpark division for $1.1 million in cash and notes and the assumption of $62,000 of liabilities. Jeannette's Royal China subsidiary was placed in bankruptcy in 1983, and, a year later, its operating assets were sold for $4.2 million and the assumption of liabilities. Finally, in September 1983, Jeannette's remaining assets were auctioned off for $2.15 million.

E

On September 22, 1983, plaintiff James Moody, the trustee of the bankruptcy estate of Jeannette, filed this action in federal district court against defendants Security Pacific, Coca-Cola, ... J. Corp., ... Brogan, and other individuals. He alleges that the leveraged buyout constitutes a fraudulent conveyance under the UFCA [as adopted in Pennsylvania] and is voidable under §544(b).[5] After a bench trial, the

------

[5] Section 544(b) of the Bankruptcy Code provides that "[t]he trustee may avoid any transfer of an interest of the debtor in property or any obligation incurred by the debtor that is voidable under *applicable law* by a creditor holding an unsecured claim. . . ." §544(b) (emphasis added). The "applicable law" here is the

district court made findings of fact and conclusions of law and entered judgment for defendants.

According to the district court, the leveraged buyout was not intentionally fraudulent because it was "abundantly clear" that defendants expected the transaction to succeed and hoped to profit from it. Likewise, although the leveraged buyout was made for less than fair consideration to Jeannette, the district court held that it was not constructively fraudulent.

Because the leveraged buyout was made for less than fair consideration, the district court placed on defendants the burden of proving solvency by clear and convincing evidence. The court, however, concluded that defendants met this burden. Jeannette was not rendered insolvent in the "bankruptcy sense" because the "present fair salable value" of Jeannette's assets immediately after the leveraged buyout exceeded total liabilities by at least $1-2 million. In making this determination, the district court valued assets on a going concern basis.

Nor was Jeannette rendered insolvent in the "equity sense" [an inability to pay debts when due] or left with an unreasonably small capital. Based on the parties' projections, which it found "reasonable and prudent when made," and the availability on Jeannette's line of credit with Security Pacific, the district court found that Jeannette was not left with an unreasonably small capital after the acquisition.

UFCA, and it is clear that there is an unsecured creditor into whose shoes plaintiff trustee may step.

Plaintiff also alleges that the leveraged buyout is voidable under the fraudulent conveyance provisions of the Bankruptcy Code, and that certain defendants engaged in an unlawful dividend and/or distribution of Jeannette's assets under the Pennsylvania Business Corporations Law. After concluding that the transaction did not constitute a fraudulent conveyance under the UFCA, however, the district court summarily rejected these claims. It reasoned that, because the fraudulent conveyance provisions of the Bankruptcy Code are modeled after and typically interpreted in conjunction with those of the UFCA, it follows that if the leveraged buyout is not fraudulent under the UFCA, it is not fraudulent under §548 of the Bankruptcy Code. . . . Likewise, if Jeannette was not rendered insolvent by the leveraged buyout, no unlawful dividend and/or distribution of assets could have occurred under §§1701 and 1702 of the Pennsylvania Business Corporations Law because those provisions proscribe transfers of shares and dividends made by insolvents.

We agree with the district court's analysis of plaintiff's federal bankruptcy and unlawful dividend and/or distribution of assets claims. Accordingly, because we conclude that the leveraged buyout does not constitute a fraudulent conveyance under the UFCA, we do not address these claims.

Rather than a lack of capital, the district court attributed Jeannette's demise to intense foreign and domestic competition, a continued recession, and, to a lesser degree, mismanagement, which led to a drastic decline in sales beginning in early 1982.

After entry of judgment, plaintiff moved for final judgment, which the district court granted. This appeal followed. * * *

III

A

The UFCA proscribes both intentional and constructive fraud. Under the Act's intentional fraud provisions, any conveyance made or obligation incurred either without fair consideration by one who "intends" or "believes" that he will incur debts beyond his ability to pay as they mature," or with an "actual intent ... to hinder, delay, or defraud ... creditors" is fraudulent. Actual intent to defraud may be inferred from the circumstances surrounding a transfer.

The UFCA's constructive fraud provisions operate without regard to intent. Under §4, any conveyance made or obligation incurred "by a person who is or will be thereby rendered insolvent" is fraudulent if it is made or incurred for less than fair consideration. Insolvency has two components under Pennsylvania law: insolvency in the "bankruptcy sense" (a deficit net worth immediately after the conveyance), and insolvency in the "equity sense" (an inability to pay debts as they mature). Fair consideration requires a "good faith" exchange of "a fair equivalent."

Under §5, any conveyance made or obligation incurred by a person engaged in "a business or transaction" is fraudulent if it is made or incurred without fair consideration and leaves that person with an "unreasonably small capital." The relationship between "insolvency" under §4 of the UFCA and "unreasonably small capital" under §5 is not clear. However, as we discuss below, the better view would seem to be that "unreasonably small capital" denotes a financial condition short of equitable insolvency. The UFCA's constructive fraud provisions furnish a standard of causation that attempts to link the challenged conveyance with the debtor's bankruptcy.

At first, the applicability of the UFCA's fraudulent conveyance provisions to leveraged buyouts was a matter of some dispute. However, we think it settled, as a general matter at least, that the fraudulent conveyance provisions of the UFCA extend to leveraged buyouts, and defendants do not contest their applicability here. * * *

With these general principles in mind, we turn now to an analysis of the leveraged buyout of Jeannette under the constructive and then intentional fraud provisions of the UFCA.

B

1

According to the district court, the leveraged buyout was without fair consideration to Jeannette because, in exchange for granting Security Pacific security interests in all its assets and undertaking an $11.7 million demand obligation at 3 1/4 percent above prime, all Jeannette received was new management and access to credit. Defendants do not challenge this finding, and we accept it for purposes of our analysis here. * * *

2

We turn now to the thrust of plaintiff's attack, the district court's solvency and adequacy of capital analyses. As we have discussed, under §4 of the UFCA a conveyance is fraudulent if it is made without fair consideration and renders the transferor insolvent. "A person is insolvent when the present, fair, salable value of his assets is less than the amount that will be required to pay his probable liability on his existing debts as they become absolute and matured." The Pennsylvania Supreme Court has interpreted this provision as requiring solvency in both the "bankruptcy" and "equity" sense. Insolvency is determined "as of the time of the conveyance." Angier v. Worrell, 31 A.2d 87, 89 (1943).

The district court valued Jeannette's assets on a going concern basis and found that immediately after the leveraged buyout the present fair salable value of Jeannette's total assets was at least $26.2 to $27.2 million. ... It then found that the company's total liabilities were $25.2 million. Thus, the district court concluded that Jeannette was solvent in the bankruptcy sense "by at least $1 to 2 million and most probably by more ...."

At trial, plaintiff argued that Jeannette was rendered insolvent in the bankruptcy sense because the present fair salable value of Jeannette's total assets could not have exceeded the $12.1 million J. Corp. paid for Jeannette's stock. The district court rejected this argument and undertook its own valuation of Jeannette's assets. We find no error here. Although purchase price may be highly probative of a company's value immediately after a leveraged buyout, it is not the only evidence. The parties here viewed the $12.1 million purchase

price as a "significant bargain," made possible by Coca-Cola's decision to focus attention on its bottling business and Brogan's ability to
close the deal quickly.

Plaintiff argues that valuation on a going concern basis fails to
give effect to "present" in the UFCA's "present fair salable value"
language, and the district court should have calculated the amount the
company would have received had it attempted to liquidate ... on the
date of the acquisition or immediately thereafter. We disagree. Where
bankruptcy is not "clearly imminent" on the date of the challenged
conveyance, the weight of authority holds that assets should be valued
on a going concern basis. * * *

Accordingly, we conclude that the district court did not err in
finding that Jeannette was solvent in the bankruptcy sense after the
leveraged buyout.

3

Next, we look at whether the leveraged buyout either rendered
Jeannette insolvent in the equity sense or left it with an unreasonably
small capital. Although it recognized that these issues were "conceptually distinct," the district court considered them together. Plaintiff
contends this was improper because "unreasonably small capital" denotes a financial condition short of equitable insolvency.

As we have discussed, under §5 of the UFCA any conveyance
made or obligation incurred by a person engaged in "a business or
transaction" is fraudulent if it is made or incurred without fair consideration and leaves that person with an "unreasonably small capital."
Unlike "insolvency," "unreasonably small capital" is not defined by
the UFCA. This has engendered confusion over the relationship between these concepts: some courts have equated a finding of equitable
insolvency with that of unreasonably small capital, whereas others
have said that unreasonably small capital encompasses financial difficulties short of equitable insolvency.

We believe the better view is that unreasonably small capital denotes a financial condition short of equitable insolvency. * * *

[W]e think it telling that having adopted §4 of the UFCA, which
proscribes conveyances made without fair consideration that render
the debtor "insolvent," the drafters saw fit to add §5, which proscribes
conveyances made without fair consideration that leave the debtor
with an "unreasonably small capital." If the drafters viewed these

concepts interchangeably, one would expect them to have employed the same language.

Finally, whereas §4 covers conveyances by persons generally, §5 covers conveyances by "persons in business." In the business setting, "capital" is a term of art. As a general matter, it refers to "[a]ccumulated goods, possessions, and assets, used for the production of profits and wealth." Black's Law Dictionary 189 (5th ed. 1979). Viewed in this light, an "unreasonably small capital" would refer to the inability to generate sufficient profits to sustain operations. Because an inability to generate enough cash flow to sustain operations must precede an inability to pay obligations as they become due, unreasonably small capital would seem to encompass financial difficulties short of equitable solvency.

In any event, we do not think the district court erred in considering whether the leveraged buyout left Jeannette with an unreasonably small capital in conjunction with whether it rendered the company equitably insolvent. These distinct but related concepts furnish a standard of causation which looks for a link between the challenged conveyance and the debtor's insolvency. * * *

4

In undertaking its adequacy of capital analysis, the district court focused on the reasonableness of the parties' projections, but also considered the availability on Jeannette's line of credit with Security Pacific. It found the parties' projections reasonable and, based on the availability of credit as well as the company's historical cash flow needs, determined that Jeannette was not left with an unreasonably small capital under the circumstances. Rather than a lack of capital, the district court attributed Jeannette's demise to the "substantial drop in orders and sales that began in 1982," which it attributed in turn to increased foreign and domestic competition and the continued recession. * * *

Because a leveraged buyout may fail for reasons other than the structure of the transaction itself, we think the determination whether a leveraged buyout leaves a target corporation with an unreasonably small capital requires ... careful inquiry. At least from the viewpoint of the unsecured creditor, leveraged buyouts present great potential for abuse. As we noted in [Mellon Bank v. Metro Communications, Inc., 945 F.2d 635, 646 (3d Cir. 1991)], "[a]n LBO may be attractive to the buyer, seller, and lender because the structure of the transaction ... allow[s] all parties to shift most of the risk of loss to other creditors ... ."[27] Therefore, we believe failed leveraged buyouts merit close scrutiny under the fraudulent conveyance laws.

The [analysis in Credit Managers Ass'n v. Federal Co., 629 F. Supp. 175 (C.D. Cal. 1985)] appears to strike a proper balance. It holds participants in leveraged buyout responsible under §5 of the UFCA when it is reasonably foreseeable that an acquisition will fail, but at the same time takes into account that "businesses fail for all sorts of reasons, and that fraudulent [conveyance] laws are not a panacea for all such failures." [Markell, Toward True and Plain Dealing: A Theory of Fraudulent Transfers Involving Unreasonably Small Capital, 21 Ind. L. Rev. 469, 506 (1988).] Therefore, we hold the test for unreasonably small capital is reasonable foreseeability. Under this analysis, [t]he critical question is whether the parties' projections were reasonable.

5

Because projections tend to be optimistic, their reasonableness must be tested by an objective standard anchored in the company's actual performance. * * *

In hindsight it is clear that the figures employed by Brogan and Ngan were not entirely on the mark. ... However, Ngan's sales projection was based on expected price increases and new product lines and still was $15 million less than that contained in Jeannette's own 1981 business plan. ... Jeannette's actual performance after the acquisition supports the district court's finding that the parties' projections were reasonable. As we have noted, in the five months following the acquisition, Jeannette had a positive cash flow and realized $6 million in gross profits. Of the $2.5 million in proof of claims filed by trade creditors, over 90% were for goods or services provided Jeannette after June 1982; none were for goods or services provided prior to July 31, 1981.

This is not to say that Jeannette did not experience grave financial problems in the wake of the leveraged buyout. ... Less than a year after the acquisition, the company began shutting down opera-

---

[27] We recognize that certain voluntary creditors may be able to protect themselves against leveraged buyouts through loan agreements. However, not all creditors have the bargaining power to obtain such contractual protection and most [*sic*] creditors are involuntary. See *Tabor Court Realty Corp.*, 803 F.2d at 1297 n.2.

tions at its Jeannette Glass division and selling off its subsidiaries. By October 1982, it had gone into bankruptcy.

The district court properly found that Jeannette's failure was caused by a dramatic drop in sales due to increased foreign and domestic competition, rather than a lack of capital. Plaintiff plausibly contends that defendants should have anticipated some of these problems and incorporated a margin for error. But we cannot say the district court erred in finding that the drastic decline in sales was unforeseeable as of the date of the leveraged buyout. Therefore, we conclude that the district court properly determined that the leveraged buyout did not leave Jeannette with an unreasonably small capital.

Because we assume the notion of unreasonably small capital denotes a financial condition short of equitable insolvency, it follows that the transaction did not render Jeannette equitably insolvent either. And because the leveraged buyout neither left Jeannette with an unreasonably small capital nor rendered it equitably insolvent, we agree with the district court that the acquisition does not constitute a fraudulent conveyance under either §§4 or 5 of the UFCA.

C

All that remains to be decided is whether the district court properly determined that the leveraged buyout did not violate the UFCA's intentional fraud provisions. As we have discussed, a conveyance is intentionally fraudulent if it is made either without fair consideration by one who "intends or believes that he will incur debts beyond his ability to pay as they mature" or with an "actual intent ... to hinder, delay, or defraud either present or future creditors." * * *

The district court found that "defendants did not know or believe that Jeannette's creditors could not be paid, and did not intend to hinder, defraud, or delay creditors." This conclusion followed from the absence of any direct evidence of fraud, as well as defendants' profit motives, the parties' awareness of the transaction's leveraged nature, and Jeannette's operation as a going concern for at least five months following the acquisition.

Plaintiff apparently concedes that there is no direct evidence that defendants intended to defraud Jeannette's creditors. However, he asserts that the district court erred in failing to consider the "well-established principle" that "parties are held to have intended the natural consequences of their acts." Applying this principle, plaintiff reasons that because the leveraged buyout had the foreseeable "effect" of hindering and delaying creditors of Jeannette, it follows that defendants intended to defraud them. We cannot agree.

In *Tabor Court Realty Corp.*, [803 F.2d 1288 (3d Cir. 1986)], we relied in part on the principle that "a party is deemed to have intended the natural consequences of his acts" in upholding the district court's finding of intentional fraud. 803 F.2d at 1305. The facts of that case, however, are more egregious than those here. The target corporation in *Tabor* was "clearly on the brink of insolvency" at the time of the challenged leveraged buyout. [United States v. Gleneagles Inv. Co., 565 F. Supp. 556, 581 (M.D. Pa. 1983).] Thus, the leveraged buyout was not only voidable under the intentional fraud provisions of the UFCA, but also under the Act's constructive fraud provisions.

By contrast, Jeannette was not on the brink of insolvency at the time of the leveraged buyout, and the acquisition was not constructively fraudulent. Therefore, even assuming participants in leveraged buyouts may be held accountable under the intentional fraud provisions of the UFCA for the natural consequences of their actions, we do not believe Jeannette's insolvency was a natural consequence of the leveraged buyout. We conclude, then, that the district court properly held that the leveraged buyout was not intentionally fraudulent.

IV

In sum, we will affirm the district court's conclusions that the leveraged buyout does not constitute a fraudulent conveyance under either the constructive or intentional fraud provisions of the UFCA. * * *

NOTES

8C.3. The court in *Moody* starts its constructive fraud analysis with the observation that "the leveraged buyout was without fair consideration to Jeannette because, in exchange for granting Security Pacific security interests in all its assets and undertaking an $11.7 million demand obligation at 3 1/4 percent above prime, all Jeannette received was new management and access to credit." This is a muddy conclusion, because it is not clear what the court means when it refers to "the leveraged buyout." In fact, the "leveraged buyout" consisted of seven transactions listed by the court in footnote 3.

After the LBO, Jeannette did not have anything to show for its obligation to Security Pacific. Jeannette transferred the money it borrowed to J. Corp., its parent company (owned by Brogan), so that J.

Corp. could pay its own debt to Security Pacific. In essence, Jeannette borrowed money and paid out the proceeds as a dividend. As we discussed in chapter 1, dividends are transfers a corporation makes without receiving reasonably equivalent value in return. Hence, a dividend can be challenged under fraudulent conveyance law if it leaves the corporate debtor insolvent or with unreasonably small capital. But the fraudulent conveyance action would ordinarily lie against the shareholder that received the dividend. Security Pacific can defend against a fraudulent conveyance action by pointing out that the security interest it has in Jeannette's assets was received in exchange for the money it gave to Jeannette. Jeanette did use the loan to make a dividend, but the way in which a borrower uses a loan should not make one creditor liable to other creditors.

The suspect transfer is the obligation and security interest issued by Jeannette to Security Pacific. When we pass over form and look at substance, Security Pacific did not pay anything to *Jeannette*. The court implicitly adopts a "conduit" theory. In other words, for the purposes of fraudulent conveyance law, no loan proceeds have been paid to the target of an LBO—here Jeannette—if with those proceeds, as an integrated part of the LBO, the target repurchases shares or provides financing to one who does.

Because Security Pacific's funds did not come to rest in Jeannette, it is treated as if it had not made the loan to Jeannette at all. Security Pacific is treated as if it gave money to J. Corp. and Jeannette obliged itself to pay Security Pacific without itself receiving anything in return. Thus, had the court found that Jeannette possessed unreasonably small capital, Security Pacific could not have claimed that it paid reasonably equivalent value for the security interest Jeannette had transferred to it *or for the underlying obligation to repay the loan.* If, in substance, Security Pacific gave nothing to Jeannette, it should not be entitled to share in any of its assets.

8C.4. Even without the conduit theory, had the court found that Jeannette possessed unreasonably small capital, the trustee might have prevailed against both Coca-Cola and J. Corp. (and perhaps as well against Brogan as the owner and arguably the alter ego of J. Corp.). From an ex ante perspective, the transaction as a whole benefited both Coca-Cola and J. Corp. It may be *relatively* straightforward to see how Coca-Cola benefited. In exchange for its Jeannette shares the bottler received cash in excess of the pre-LBO value of those shares. J. Corp.'s ex ante benefit is harder to measure, particularly given how things turned out. But J. Corp. paid Jeannette only a small amount for the shares. If things had turned out differently, it might have earned an extraordinarily large return that would have more than offset the risk that it would be wiped out if, as it happened, things went poorly.

Unlike Security Pacific, Coca-Cola and J. Corp were actual recipients of property for less than fair consideration. J. Corp., however, is a corporate shell created for the LBO. It has no assets to reach. The dividend it received from Jeannette has long since left it. Any action against J. Corp. can benefit the trustee only if the trustee can pierce the corporate veil and reach J. Corp.'s shareholders. These concepts are not easy. Problem 8C-2 uses an illustration of a simple LBO with manageable numbers to help you examine the potential winners and losers in such a transaction.

8C.5. Ultimately, the court in *Moody* found no fraudulent conveyance. As a comparison, imagine, for example, that the sole shareholder of a small pizza parlor has the business sell its brick ovens and purchase sushi refrigerators instead. The shareholder may reason that the sushi business is more risky, but potentially more rewarding. She is willing to take the risk, in part, because some of the losses will be borne by the restaurant's creditors, who lent expecting steady returns from pizza. It is likely that no court would find the sale of the pizza ovens a fraudulent conveyance. There was a transaction that increased the creditors' risk. Had the creditors wanted to assure themselves that the restaurant continued in the pizza business, they could have included in their loan agreement a clause that required obtaining their permission before changing the nature of their business. Having failed to do so, the creditors bore the risk of the debtor's switch to sushi.

In essence, the *Moody* court decided that Jeannette's unsecured creditors bore a similar risk, which, though perhaps greater, was not so great as to be unreasonable. It was not the case, the court reasoned, that Jeannette's capitalization was so low that success was affirmatively *un*likely. That success was less likely after the LBO than before, the court concluded, was simply a cost to the creditors of doing business.

8C.6. The court might have, but did not, rely on the twice-reported fact that Jeannette's unsecured claims in bankruptcy arose *after* the LBO. These creditors came in with their eyes open and have the least reason of all to complain about the risks from the LBO transactions. The court chose not to rely on this fact because, as mentioned in footnote 27, some consensual creditors are unsophisticated and would not appreciate the high risks of a post-LBO debtor while others, such as tort victims, are nonconsensual and cannot adjust the terms of the obligation owed them to reflect risk.

Nonetheless, in light of decisions such as *Moody*, consensual creditors who are sophisticated have begun to protect themselves against the prospect of LBOs. An unsecured creditor might, for example, purchase a "poison put" at the time it lends at a low interest rate to a low-leverage firm. A "poison put" for a lender is a clause that allows it to terminate the loan and make the principal due and owing in the event the debtor engages in an LBO. Such a clause prevents a debtor's shareholders from increasing a firm's financial risk with a leveraged buyout on the backs of an earlier unsecured creditor.

8C.7. Finally, at the end of the opinion the *Moody* court makes a link between constructive and intentional fraud claims against the defendants. The court noted that the only ill the defendants intended was to increase the risk of Jeannette's returns. If, as the court held under its constructive fraud analysis, the imposition of such risk was legitimate, it could not be fraudulent to intend the same ends. Although this analysis seems sensible, consider the consequences if one finds that the LBO left the firm with unreasonably small capital. If a court concludes that the transfers in an LBO are constructively fraudulent, it would conclude as well that they are intentionally fraudulent. Thus, every knowing participant (i.e., everyone of interest) is deprived of the benefit of §548(c) and would have no lien for the amount paid in exchange for the property transferred. A court, then, could reject the questionable conduit-theory fiction and still eliminate the interest of an arm's-length secured lender such as Security Pacific. This was the approach taken by the court in Lippi v. Citibank, 955 F.2d 599 (9th Cir. 1992), for example. The question of good faith is explored further in Problem 8C-2 and in the next subsection of this book.

PROBLEM

8C-2. Manager is the president of Debtor Corporation, which runs a clothing-design business with a going-concern value of $2 million. Debtor owes $1 million in unsecured debt and has 1,000 shareholders. Manager has Debtor borrow $1 million from Bank and give Bank a security interest in all of Debtor's assets. Manager then has Debtor issue new stock, which Manager purchases from Debtor for $50,000 in cash. Next, Manager has Debtor redeem all outside shares, i.e., all shares other than Manager's, for a price of $1.05 million. A year later Debtor files for bankruptcy. Its assets are now worth only $1.5 million.

Was Manager foolish to pay $50,000 for shares in a company with a $2 million value subject to $2 million in debt? In answering this question assume that the $2 million value is, in reality, the center of a distribution of values that could be greater or less depending on Debtor's future revenues, which can only be estimated. Assuming these transactions did not alter this distribution, would Manager have been as anxious to proceed had the pretransaction creditors been secured rather than unsecured? How might the transactions have in fact altered the distribution?

Under the original assumptions, where the pretransaction creditors are unsecured, would Debtor's bankruptcy trustee be able to bring a fraudulent conveyance action against Bank? Against the pretransaction shareholders? Against Manager? Would any of these answers change if Manager did not purchase any new shares, but instead held shares prior to the transaction and simply retained them while the other shareholders sold after a secured loan from Bank of $1.05 million instead of $1 million? See Douglas G. Baird and Thomas H. Jackson, Fraudulent Conveyance Law and its Proper Domain, 38 Vand. L. Rev. 829 (1985).

3) GOOD-FAITH TRANSFEREE

The case below, *Manhattan Investment Fund*, as well as the notes and problem that follow ask you to consider when a transferee can claim to receive property in good faith for the purposes of §548(c), even where it might have discovered that the transfer was an element in the transferor's fraud. The case arises out of a set of transactions through which an investment fund engaged "short sales." That is, the fund committed to the future sale at the current price of stock. If the stock price falls between the time of the short-sale contract and the exercise date, a short seller makes a profit as it later can purchase the stock for less than it will receive under the contract. Of course, if the price rises, the short-seller loses. To assure its own performance on short-sale contracts, short sellers open margin accounts with stock brokers; the balance in a margin account is used to satisfy a short seller's net obligation should the price rise on the securities under contract. The transfers at issue in *Manhattan Investment Fund* are the transfers of money by a short seller to its margin account.

CASE

IN RE MANHATTAN INVESTMENT FUND LTD.

United States Bankruptcy Court, S.D.N.Y., 2007
359 Bankr. 510

LIFLAND, BANKRUPTCY JUDGE.

This adversary proceeding is an outgrowth of a massive Ponzi scheme executed by Michael Berger ('Berger') a convicted felon and fugitive, who created and used the Fund through his wholly owned company Manhattan Capital Management, Inc ("MCM"), as his vehicle to perpetrate fraud. On January 14, 2000, following an investigation into the Fund's trading activities, the Securities and Exchange Commission (the "SEC"), filed a complaint alleging securities fraud against the Fund, MCM and Berger. The SEC obtained an asset freeze and the appointment of Helen Gredd as Receiver for the Fund. On March 7, 2000 (the Petition Date"), the Receiver caused the Fund to file a voluntary petition for relief under [Chapter 11] of the Bankruptcy Code. * * *

In the year prior to the Petition Date, the Fund made eighteen separate transfers totaling $141.4 million (collectively, the "Transfers"), from its account at Bank of Bermuda to an account maintained by Bear Stearns at Citibank. Those monies were then transferred to the Fund's Bear Stearns account. The monies in the Fund's Bear Stearns account were used by the Fund to engage in securities trading. The Bear Stearns account was subject to a Professional Account Agreement (the "Agreement") between Berger and Bear Stearns which provided, in relevant part, that: (1) Bear Stearns had the right to set the level of maintenance margin; (2) Bear Stearns had a security interest in all monies held in the account; (3) Bear Stearns had sole discretion to prevent the Fund from withdrawing any money credited to its account as long as any short positions remained open; and (4) Bear Stearns had sole discretion to use any and all monies credited to the Fund's account to liquidate the Fund's open short positions with or without the Fund's consent. The Agreement and the account itself were governed by SEC Rule[s] which expressly preclude Bear Stearns from using the funds in the account for any purpose other than those outlined in the agreement.

After questions about the Fund and its activity arose and the SEC was investigating it, Bear Stearns put the Fund on "closing only" status in January 2000, meaning that no new positions could be opened by the Fund and no money withdrawn until all existing positions were closed out. Following Berger's confession of fraud Bear Stearns closed out all of the remaining short positions in the Fund's account using the monies in the account to do so. In March 2000, Trustee requested that Bear Stearns wire the remaining $16,288,746.46 in the Fund's account to the Fund's bank account at Chase Manhattan and in April 2000, Bear Stearns did so. As prime broker, Bear Stearns made approximately $2.4 million in revenue for its services over the course of its involvement with the Fund.

The Trustee now seeks summary judgment to avoid the Transfers under section 548(a)(1)(A) of the Bankruptcy Code. The Trustee contends that: (1) the Transfers were made with actual intent to hinder, delay or defraud the Fund's creditors and without which the Fund could not have continued to operate and further perpetrate its fraud; (2) Bear Stearns is not a mere conduit and is therefore a "transferee" under section 550(a) of the Bankruptcy Code; and (3) that Bear Stearns cannot prove that it accepted the Transfers in good faith. In opposition, Bear Stearns contends that: (1) the Trustee may not recover the Transfers because Bear Stearns lacked legal dominion and control over the Transfers and was therefore not a "transferee" under section 550(a) of the Bankruptcy Code; (2) the Trustee did not meet her burden in proving that the Transfers were made with an actual intent to hinder, delay or defraud the Fund's creditors; (3) the Transfers should not be recoverable from Bear Stearns based on public policy reasons; and (4) Bear Stearns acted in good faith in accepting the Transfers.

Avoiding Powers

The Bankruptcy Code bestows broad powers upon a trustee to avoid certain transfers of property made by the debtor before the filing of the bankruptcy petition. "In this way, the transferred property is returned to the estate for the benefit of all persons who have presented valid claims." See Christy v. Alexander & Alexander of NY, Inc. (In re Finley, Kumble, Wagner, Heine, Underberg, Manley, Myerson & Casey), 130 F.3d 52, 55 (2d Cir.1997). Specifically, section 548 of the Bankruptcy Code provides for the avoidance of any transfer of an interest in property made by the debtor in the [then applicable period of one] year prior to the filing of its bankruptcy petition as a fraudulent conveyance provided that the transfer was made with an actual fraudulent intent or with the badges of fraud constituting constructive fraud of the debtor's creditors. See 11 U.S.C. § 548(A) and (B). A fraudulent conveyance avoided under section 548 is recoverable by the Trustee under section 550(a) which provides, in relevant part, "the trustee may recover, … the property transferred, or, if the court so orders, the value of such property, from (1) the *initial transferee* of such transfer or the entity for whose benefit such transfer was made … . 11 U.S.C. § 550(a) (emphasis added).

However, section 546(e) of the Bankruptcy Code, commonly known as the "stockbroker defense," prevents the trustee from avoiding margin payments made to a stockbroker except where there is actual fraud. See §546(e). Legislative history reveals that Congress was concerned about the volatile nature of the commodities and securities markets, and decided that certain protections were necessary to prevent "the insolvency of one commodity or security firm from spreading to other firms and possibly threatening the collapse of the affected market."

Section 548(a)(1)(A), referred to as the "actual fraud" provision, requires that in order to avoid a transfer, it must be made with actual intent to hinder, delay, or defraud any entity to which the debtor was or became, on or after the date that such transfer was made or such obligation was incurred or indebted. 11 U.S.C. § 548(a)(1)(A).

Fraudulent Nature of the Transfers

The eighteen Transfers at issue in this matter were deposited by the Fund in its account at Bear Stearns to allow it to continue short selling activities within the year prior to the Petition Date. To engage in short sales, federal securities regulations required the Fund to maintain its margin account with Bear Stearns at a specified level. Bear Stearns, in turn, could, and did, make those requirements more stringent based on the level of risk at which it perceived the Fund's trading to be. The Transfers were made in order to open new short positions or to comply with the requirements of its margin account in order to continue trading. As such, the Transfers fit squarely within the definition of a margin payment as defined in sections 101, 741, and 761 of the Bankruptcy Code.

The Trustee argues that the Transfers are within the exception to section 546(e) of the Bankruptcy Code because the transfers were made in furtherance of a "Ponzi" scheme. "A 'Ponzi' or 'Pyramid' scheme is a fraudulent investment scheme in which money contributed by later investors is used to pay artificially high dividends to the original investors, creating an illusion of profitability, thus attracting new investors." See In re The Bennett Funding Group, Inc., 439 F.3d

155, 157 (2d Cir.2006) (citing *Black's Law Dictionary* 1198 (8th ed.2004)).

Actual intent to hinder, delay or defraud may be established as a matter of law in cases in which the debtor runs a Ponzi scheme or a similar illegitimate enterprise, because transfers made in the course of a Ponzi operation could have been made for no purpose other than to hinder, delay or defraud creditors. Thus, "courts nationwide have recognized that establishing the existence of a Ponzi scheme is sufficient to prove a Debtor's actual intent to defraud." Rieser v. Hayslip (In re Canyon Systems Corp., 343 Bankr. 615, 637 (Bankr. S.D. Ohio 2006). Moreover, acts taken in furtherance of the Ponzi scheme, such as paying brokers commissions, are also fraudulent. ...

Bear Stearns argues that there was no fraud. However, this Court, along with the District Court has already determined that issue. In ruling on Bear Stearns' motion to dismiss [related counts,] this Court explained that "[w]hen a debtor operating a Ponzi scheme makes a payment with the knowledge that future creditors will not be paid, that payment is presumed to have been made with actual intent to hinder, delay or defraud other creditors-regardless of whether payments were made to early investors, or whether the debtor was engaged in a strictly classic Ponzi scheme." In light of Berger's guilty plea and conviction coupled with the fact that the margin payments were made in connection with a massive Ponzi scheme, this Court finds sufficient evidence of actual fraudulent intent in connection with the Transfers. ... Accordingly, the issue is whether or not the payments may be recovered from Bear Stearns as an initial transferee under section 550(a)(1).

Initial Transferee

Bear Stearns argues that it is a "mere conduit" and not an initial transferee. The Bankruptcy Code does not define the term "transferee" and as such the "mere conduit" defense has arisen as a defense to liability in avoidance actions. In the course of examining the "mere conduit" defense, courts have used a "dominion and control" test to determine if an entity is an initial transferee from which an avoided transfer may be recovered under section 550(a)(1). In order to be an initial transferee courts require something more than being the "first hands" to touch the asset, but rather that the entity have the requisite dominion and control over the transferred asset. * * *

The Ninth Circuit recently explained the "mere conduit" or "dominion and control" test as actually being two distinct tests: the dominion test and the control test. Universal Service Administrative Co. v. Post Confirmation Committee of Unsecured Creditors of Incomnet Communications, 463 F.3d 1064, 1071 (9th Cir.2006). The court stated that the dominion test is one of legal dominion over the transfers and the control test instead focuses on the context of the situation and the actual control of the transfers taking the situation as a whole. The dominion test requires a higher standard of legal dominion; and the control test looks to who has actual control and focuses more on fairness under the circumstances. The Ninth Circuit, in its decision, acknowledged that while it draws a distinction between the dominion test and the control test that a number of circuits, including the Seventh Circuit and the Second Circuit, combine the two tests creating the "dominion and control test".

Bear Stearns contends that the Agreement relied upon by the Trustee to prove Bear Stearns' dominion and control over the transfers is standard in the industry and that such boilerplate provisions cannot give rise to initial transferee status. ... [But the] caselaw finding that an entity is a mere conduit differ from the facts here. In most cases, the recipient was held to be a mere conduit primarily because it did not receive consideration or compensation for its services nor did it have any liability in the transaction as a whole if the transfers had been made to the recipient. In this case, Bear Stearns made $2.4 million profit on the Fund's transactions during its tenure as the Fund's primary broker. Moreover, Bear Stearns used the funds in the account to cover all open positions the Fund had with Bear Stearns for which Bear Stearns would have been liable if the Transfers had not been made.

Under the terms of the Fund's Agreement with Bear Stearns, Bear Sterns had a security interest in any monies transferred; held the monies transferred as collateral for short sales; had the right to and did prohibit the Fund from withdrawing any of the monies transferred as long as any short position remained open; and had the right to and did use the monies transferred to purchase covering securities, with or without the Fund's consent. Thus, Bear Stearns had the ability to exercise control and use the Transfers to protect its own economic well-being and thus, is not a mere conduit with respect to those Transfers.

Bear Stearns Public Policy Argument

Bear Stearns further argues that allowing recovery of margin payments relating to short sale securities transactions is contrary to public policy, an argument previously addressed by this Court in the decision denying Bear Stearns' motion to dismiss. See In re Manhattan Investment Fund Ltd., 310 Bankr. at 513. This Court dismissed that argument finding that the Bankruptcy Code specifically provides for such a recovery under 546(e) and 548(a)(1)(A). Bear Stearns now argues that to find a securities brokerage such as itself an initial transferee based on its boilerplate provisions in its Agreement with Berger would expose all other broker-dealers to "massive" amounts of liability and would cripple the securities industry in the process. As stated in this Court's previous decision, "[a]ware of the necessity of the services provided by clearing brokers, Congress only *limited* trustees' ability to avoid margin payments in bankruptcy under section 546(e) of the Bankruptcy Code." Id. The provisions of the Bankruptcy Code work to permit margin payments to be avoided in only limited circumstances shielding brokers from the full reach of the creditor protections of the fraudulent conveyance laws. Id. Where the Bankruptcy Code specifically provides for the avoidance of margin payments it cannot be said that allowing just that would be contrary to public policy. *Id.* For all of the reasons articulated in this Court's prior ruling on the Motion to Dismiss as well as those above I find Bear Stearns' "public policy" argument meritless.

Good Faith Defense

Bear Stearns asserts that even should it be found to be an initial transferee within the meaning of section 550(a) of the Bankruptcy Code, that if Bear Stearns accepted the transfers from the Fund in good faith under 548(c), without knowledge of the fraud, then the Trustee will not be permitted to recover these monies. The Trustee contends that Bear Stearns' knowledge of the Fund's questionable activity put it on notice of the Ponzi scheme more than a year before the Fund was shut down and investigated by the SEC. She contends that Bear Stearns had the opportunity to discover the Ponzi scheme and therefore was on constructive notice of the Fund's continued fraud.

Section 548(c) provides, in relevant part, that to the "extent that a transfer is voidable, a transferee that takes for value and in good faith may retain any interest transferred to the extent that such transferee gave value to the debtor in exchange for such transfer or obligation." There is no dispute that Bear Stearns took the transfers in question for value, however the relevant issue herein is whether or not Bear Stearns took in good faith. Bear Stearns argues that the issue of good faith is one to be determined by a jury; the Trustee argues that the issue can be decided on summary judgment.

That an issue is factual does not necessarily preclude summary judgment. The party moving for summary judgment must only allege that there is an absence of evidence by which the nonmoving party can prove his case. The nonmoving party may not rest upon the mere allegations or denials in the pleadings. However, the burden on the nonmoving party is not a heavy one; the nonmoving party simply is required to show specific facts, as opposed to general allegations, that present a genuine issue worthy of trial. This rule does not direct courts to resolve questions of credibility or conflicting inferences. What it requires courts to do is assess whether the jury, drawing all inferences in favor of the nonmoving party, could reasonably render a verdict in favor of the nonmoving party in light of the substantive law. The determination requires application of the standard that courts apply in motions for a directed verdict or a judgment notwithstanding the verdict.

The Bankruptcy Code does not define good faith. However, courts have found that "good faith" includes not only "honest belief, the absence of malice and the absence of design to defraud or to seek an unconscionable advantage" but also "freedom from knowledge of circumstances which ought to put the holder on inquiry." In re M & L Business Mach. Co., Inc., 84 F.3d at 1335, citing Black's Law Dictionary (6th ed.1990). ... Further, a transferee may not remain willfully ignorant of facts that would cause it to be on notice of a debtor's fraudulent purpose, and then "put on 'blinders' prior to entering into transactions with the debtor and claim the benefit of 548(c)." In re World Vision Entertainment, Inc., 275 Bankr. 641, 659-60 (Bankr. M.D.Fla.2002) *quoting* In re Cannon, 230 Bankr. 546, 592 (Bankr. W.D.Tenn.1999) rev'd on other grounds, 277 F.3d 838 (6th Cir.2002).

The record reflects undisputed facts demonstrating that Bear Stearns was on inquiry notice as of December 1998 after Mr. Fredrik Schilling, Senior Managing Director and salesperson for Bear Stearns, had a conversation regarding the Fund at a party. In that conversation, Schilling was told by an individual who represented that he was affiliated with European Investment Management "EIM" who had clients that invested in the Fund, that the Fund was reporting a 20% profit for the year. At that time, Schilling was under the impression that the Fund was losing money based on his participation in risk-related conference calls in which the Fund had been mentioned, and consequently, what he was told by this investor did not "sound right."

Rather than respond to that individual, Schilling suggested that the individual have his boss call Schilling.

The day after this party conversation Schilling relayed the conversation with this investor to his boss, William Gangi, and the then-head of client services Michael Tumulty. The same day, Schilling spoke with the EIM representative's boss, Arpad Busson who inquired as to whether the Fund's performance matched Bear Stearns' books and records.

Schilling informed Busson that he would need to make a written inquiry in order to receive a response to that question. Thereafter, Schilling spoke with John Callanan in Bear Stearns' portfolio department about the Fund's performance and the books and records and Callanan confirmed that the Fund was losing money in its account at Bear Stearns. Schilling also passed on the written request from Busson to Bear Stearns' legal department as well as discussing the situation with senior management at Bear Stearns.

These discussions led to a conference call with two then managers in Bear Stearns' relationship management department, Peter Murphy and Christopher Welsh, Financial Asset Management ("FAM"), the Fund's introducing broker, and Michael Berger. Michael Berger explained that the discrepancy in the Fund's performance as described by EIM and Bear Stearns' records was due to the fact that Bear Stearns was only one of eight or nine prime brokers used by the Fund. While there is evidence that Berger's explanation could be plausible, Bear Stearns, apparently wearing "blinders," did nothing to verify this information despite the fact that a simple review of the Fund's financial statements—which was eventually done many months later—would have, and eventually did, reveal that Bear Sterns was the only prime broker for the Fund. Moreover, Bear Stearns' actions following the phone call with Berger demonstrate that it was not completely comfortable with Berger's explanation. For example, Schilling spoke with two partners at Deloitte & Touche, the Fund's auditor, to explain the nature of the inquiry with the Fund made by Busson and Bear Stearns. Schilling "asked that Deloitte & Touche be keen and careful during the Fund's upcoming audit because Deloitte & Touche, as the Fund's auditor, was in a position to oversee all of the Fund's assets."

In February 1999, Schilling coincidentally met Busson at a conference in Geneva where he learned that Busson further inquired into the Fund with Berger who would not release any information without a confidentiality agreement. Busson was advised by his counsel not to sign the agreement and told Schilling that EIM had either redeemed or was planning to redeem its clients' investments in the Fund. In the spring of 1999, Deloitte & Touche notified Schilling that the Fund's audit was completed without problem. Even after this call was made, however, Schilling continued to have discussions with investors about investigating Berger and the Fund, and asked the auditors to investigate the Fund again.

By August of 1999, the gap between the Fund's purported performance, as reported by Berger, and what the actual performance was had grown to $367 million. A month later, the gap was at nearly $399 million. By the time of the last transfers, in mid-December, the gap stood at more than $423 million. Bear Stearns' internal risk reports show an increase of concern about the Fund during November 1999 and the Fund received margin calls from Bear Stearns on almost a daily basis. "By late 1999" Bear Stearns raised the margin requirement on the Fund from 35% to 50%. When the Fund continued to lose money and with one stock comprising 70% of the portfolio, an email to members of Bear Stearns' risk department suggested that the Fund's position "necessitates higher requirements than 50%."

After another incident Bear Stearns finally took steps to determine what was really going on. In December of 1999, Schilling, while attending a meeting on unrelated business, spoke with Mark Nichols, a former third-party marketer for the Fund, and was told about the termination of Nichols' relationship with Berger and the Fund. Nichols informed Schilling that Nichols had had to sue Berger for a substantial amount money that Nichols was allegedly owed for past marketing efforts for the Fund. Learning that Berger breached contractual duties and broken Nichols' trust, Schilling became concerned that Berger may be "immoral" and that led him to initiating further inquiries into the Fund. * * *

Finally, after a phone call from Deloitte indicating that Deloitte could no longer discuss the Fund, Bear Stearns' senior management decided to notify the SEC that there was a potential problem with the Fund. By December 22, the Fund was put on "Closing only" status and asked to leave the firm. The following day, without Berger's permission, Bear Stearns covered all of the Fund's remaining open short positions at a realized loss to the Fund of more than $22 million.

It is clear from the record that Bear Stearns was on inquiry notice of Berger's fraud from December 1998 and throughout the following year. Based upon the information it had, Bear Stearns was required to do more than simply ask the wrongdoer if he was doing wrong. Diligence requires consulting easily obtainable sources of information that would bear on the truth of any explanation received from the potential wrongdoer. The simple steps Bear Stearns finally performed one year later, demonstrate that Bear Stearns failed to act diligently in a timely manner and accordingly, Bear Stearns cannot satisfy its burden of showing that it acted with the diligence required to establish good faith under section 548(c) of the Bankruptcy Code.

NOTES

8C.8. The essence of the Bear Stearns defense in *Manhattan Investment Fund* is that it was not its brother's keeper. Like other brokers, it holds numerous margin accounts and does not (or did not) typically pay close attention to any of them. The court makes much of the fact that Bear Stearns eventually uncovered the fraud, and thus held the broker responsible to have recovered it earlier, defining its failure to do so as lack of good faith. But whether a broker is required to discover a fraud that eventually becomes obvious is precisely the question before the court, and cannot be answered with the mere observation that eventually the fraud did become obvious. This said, the increased scrutiny encouraged by the opinion may well be beneficial to securities investors, though one might wonder whether the typical investor would want to pay the price brokers predictably will charge for such scrutiny. This theme is explored in Problem 8C-3. Also, compare Note 8C.7, above.

8C.9. The court in *Manhattan Investment Fund* expresses some doubt about (and little interest in) whether the transfers at issue were part of a classic "Ponzi scheme." For the court it was sufficient that as the investment fund lost money it kept itself afloat with false accounting and contributions from new investors. Those interested can find a classic Ponzi scheme described above in Note 6A-1 and discussed further in Cunningham v. Brown, 265 U.S. 1 (1924).

PROBLEM

8C-3. Debtor draws up plans to sell replicas of 19th century high wheel bicycles for $1,000 each, a price substantially less than that of its competitors, who typically charge more than $2,000 per bicycle. In its advertisements, Debtor claims a patented manufacturing process that permits it to achieve and pass along enormous cost-savings.

There is no patented process and the cost savings are accomplished simply by skimping on quality. A year after the first bikes are sold, they begin to collapse causing serious injury to some riders. Customers seek refunds for the defective bicycles and eventually file an involuntary Chapter 7 petition against Debtor, whose assets include $100,000 worth of manufacturing equipment and about $50,000 in cash. The trustee seeks to recover from Bank, Debtor's primary lender, the security interest it took in the equipment when Debtor began marketing the replica bikes. The trustee also seeks to recover from Debtor's landlord the rental payments on Debtor's factory used to manufacture the bikes and from Debtor's metal tubing supplier the purchase price for the tubing used in the bikes. Will the trustee prevail?

D. VOIDABLE PREFERENCES

The descent of a healthy firm into insolvency and then into bankruptcy is a long and slow one. Alert creditors are likely to anticipate the bankruptcy proceeding and the collective regime that puts all general creditors on an equal footing. These creditors would much rather be paid off in full than work things out with everyone else and ultimately take less than one hundred cents on the dollar. If we allowed creditors to keep payments they extracted when they knew bankruptcy was imminent, bankruptcy might do more harm than good. The prospect of a bankruptcy proceeding might have the effect of accelerating and exacerbating the creditors' race to the assets. In order to solve this gun-jumping problem, we need a bankruptcy rule that has the effect of turning back the clock and returning people to the positions they were in before bankruptcy was on the horizon. The rules in §547 on voidable preferences serve this function.

Although its rules are complicated, the basic purpose of preference law is quite straightforward and quite different from the role of fraudulent conveyance law. Except in unusual cases, a transfer to a creditor on account of an antecedent debt will not be a fraudulent conveyance. The antecedent debt counts as "fair consideration" or "reasonably equivalent value." Preferences to creditors are themselves unobjectionable so long as a collective proceeding is not in the works. Every creditor is "preferred" when it is paid, but for a creditor to be paid is an ordinary part of commercial life. Section 547 is designed to root out only preferences that are made on the eve of bankruptcy and interfere with the collective norms of bankruptcy law.

1) SCOPE OF PREFERENCE LAW

The Bankruptcy Code §547(b) tells us which transfers are pre-sumptively preferential: A transfer is presumptively a preference if it is made to or for the benefit of a creditor on account of an antecedent debt, during the ninety days before the bankruptcy petition, and while the debtor is insolvent (which §547(f) presumes for the ninety-day period), provided that the transfer leaves that creditor better off than it would have been had the transfer not been made and had the debtor's assets been liquidated. These transfers are presumptively preferential (and therefore voidable by the trustee) because they are likely to be last-minute attempts to opt out of an impending bankruptcy process. Because an insider (defined by §101(31)) is likely to know more about the debtor and be able to see the prospect of bankruptcy before others, transfers made to an insider on account of antecedent debts while the debtor was insolvent are suspect for the entire year before the filing of the petition, provided again that the transfer makes the insider better off.

Like any other bright-line rule, §547(b) is both under- and over-inclusive. Some creditors will see bankruptcy coming and act outside the ninety-day preference period. Other creditors will be paid within the ninety-day period, but will not have known anything about the bankruptcy petition. Section 547(c) cuts back on the breadth of the rule by excepting some transfers, but nothing is done to reach deliber-ate opt-out behavior by noninsiders that takes place before the ninety-day preference window. Hence, §547 is subject to manipulation. A big creditor can twist the debtor's arm, bleed the debtor dry, and then prop it up for ninety-one days. When you read bankruptcy cases, you will often note that the filing takes place just outside the preference window. It may not be a coincidence.

The most obvious voidable preference is that of an insolvent debtor who pays cash to an unsecured creditor a few days before fil-ing a bankruptcy petition. Preferences, however, can take many forms. A preference exists, for example, if the debtor gives a general creditor a security interest in its assets just before it files a petition or if the debtor acquires property just before bankruptcy and that prop-erty is subject to a preexisting security agreement. (See §547(e)(3).) In either case, even though the trustee cannot strike down the last-minute transfer of a properly perfected security interest using the strong-arm power of §544(a), the trustee can void the transfer under §547. The security interest gives the creditor priority over other general creditors and, assuming the debtor is insolvent, makes the creditor better off.

Section 547, moreover, covers more than transfers of cash or security interests. Imagine, for example, that a supplier agrees to ship a season's worth of fuel oil to a customer and the customer pays in advance. If the supplier delivers the fuel on schedule and then files a bankruptcy petition, the supplier's trustee may have a preference action against the customer. The customer became a creditor of the supplier when it paid for the oil in advance. The supplier had an obligation it owed the customer. Each shipment of fuel discharged some of that obligation and was therefore a transfer on account of an antecedent debt owed the customer. So long as the supplier was insolvent at the time it shipped the fuel, each shipment within the preference period is presumptively voidable.

A transfer is potentially voidable whether it is voluntary or involuntary. So a creditor cannot improve its position within the preference period before bankruptcy by cajoling or pressuring a debtor any more than it can by coercing payment through the judicial system. A creditor who is not behaving strategically, but instead innocently receives a transfer within the preference period, may have a chance to shield the transfer under safe harbor provisions located primarily in §547(c). These are explained in detail later in this section. Nevertheless, voluntary or involuntary, strategic or innocent, a transfer is presumptively voidable if the trustee can demonstrate that the transfer is caught in the screen of §547(b).

You cannot have a preference unless there is a transfer to or for the benefit of a creditor on account of an *antecedent* debt. In every case in which there is a potential preference problem, you have to determine the time of two events: You must know when the debt was incurred and you must know when the transfer occurred. A comparison of these times is the starting point for any preference inquiry.

We do not have a voidable preference unless the debt is incurred *before* the transfer. These questions keep us from being led astray. Consider the following example. Just before filing a bankruptcy petition, Debtor finds a new source for one of its raw materials. This new source, Supplier, sensing that bankruptcy is imminent, insists on being given $10,000 that it can use if Debtor ever fails to pay any of its bills. When Debtor files, the trustee cannot argue that the transfer of cash was a voidable preference. Supplier insisted on the cash advance because bankruptcy was on the horizon. It was in fact done specifically in contemplation of bankruptcy. But Debtor does not owe Supplier anything. Supplier is not a creditor and has never been a creditor. (Indeed, Supplier owes obligations. It is the debtor in the transaction.) The transfer was to secure future supplies. It was not on account of a debt. Hence, it cannot be a preference.

Many preference disputes involve secured creditors. Some cases are easy. Bank made an unsecured loan to Debtor several years ago. Now, after Debtor's fortunes have taken a turn for the worse, Bank insists that Debtor give it a security interest in all its assets. Bank properly perfects its interest. A month later Debtor files a bankruptcy petition. The trustee can strike down Bank's security interest. Bank is improving its position in anticipation of bankruptcy. One can argue that taking a security interest should not be treated the same way as a naked seizure of assets. Taking a security interest only affects how the pie is divided among creditors. It does not actually destroy value in the same way that seizure of assets does. Existing law, however, treats them the same. Whether it is paid off or takes collateral, Bank is receiving an interest in property within the ninety-day period, while Debtor is insolvent, on account of an antecedent debt. By receiving the transfer Bank ensures it will be paid in full, which is a lot better than it would have done if it had not tried to improve its place in line. Therefore this transaction is a voidable preference.

Not all cases in which a debtor grants a security interest on the eve of bankruptcy are preferences. Consider the following case. Debtor is in trouble. If it is to have any chance of surviving, Debtor needs to borrow additional money. Debtor comes to Bank. Bank agrees to lend, but only if Debtor grants it a security interest in all its assets. This transaction is not a voidable preference. There is no gun-jumping. Debtor transferred property to Bank, but Debtor did not make the transfer on account of an *antecedent* debt. Debtor gave up something (an interest in a machine) but got something in return at the same time (cash). Debtor's creditors cannot complain. If they think that Debtor is so far gone that they should take control, they should throw Debtor into bankruptcy. Until they do, Debtor is free to borrow money in arm's-length transactions and encumber assets that would otherwise go to the general creditors.

A secured creditor avoids a preference attack by ensuring that the security interest is "transferred" to it within the meaning of §547(e) at the same time it extends value to the debtor. As in §544, the relevant time is not the moment that the creditor enters into a security agreement with the debtor, but rather the moment that it perfects its interest. Section 547(e), however, provides a grace period to account for the case in which the filing takes place only a few days after the debt is incurred. If a creditor makes a secured loan, goes to sleep until the debtor is in trouble, and only then discovers that its security interest was not properly perfected, it should not be able to improve its position. But this case is distinguishable from the one in which a lender enters into a secured transaction inside the preference window and takes a few days to make the proper filing.

Section 547(e) provides for a grace period of thirty days. That is, a transfer takes place at the time it is effective between the parties, provided that it is perfected within thirty days. On January 1, Bank lends Debtor $100 and simultaneously takes a security interest in all assets. Five days later Bank files its financing statement. Two months later Debtor files a bankruptcy petition. There is no voidable preference. The debt was incurred on January 1 and the transfer of the security interest from Debtor to Bank took place at that time. Bank perfected within thirty days. If Bank had waited until February to file, there would be a voidable preference.

The hardest preference problems arise when there are three parties in the picture. Consider the following situation. Debtor has a long-standing relationship with Bank and it has a credit line that it can draw upon. Any obligations that Debtor owes Bank are secured by interest in all of Debtor's assets. Debtor's principal source of raw materials is Supplier. On January 1, Debtor owes Supplier $100,000. Supplier, sensing that Debtor will likely file for bankruptcy, wants to extricate itself. Rather than demanding payment, something that would subject it to a preference attack, Supplier persuades Debtor to have Bank issue a standby letter of credit, naming Supplier as the beneficiary. Supplier can draw on the letter of credit on March 1 to the extent of any obligations Debtor owes it. Bank knows nothing of Supplier's relationship with Debtor. It is willing to issue the standby letter of credit, however, because, under letter-of-credit doctrine, Debtor is obliged to reimburse it in the event the letter is drawn upon, and this obligation, like all of Debtor's other obligations to Bank, is fully secured. When March 1 arrives, Supplier does draw upon the letter of credit. On March 2, Debtor files a bankruptcy petition. The trustee discovers the transaction and seeks either to recover $100,000 from Supplier or reduce Bank's security interest by the same amount.

The trustee's task here is not easy. Supplier will argue that the letter-of-credit relationship between it and Bank is independent of its relationship with Debtor. The transfer of $100,000 of Bank's money *[margin top: i.e. security interest was made on account of antecedent debt for benefit of creditor (regardless of sexset mnsxn) — not 357 — 100,000 more secured by bank]*

under the draw on the letter of credit did not affect any of Debtor's general creditors. When the letter of credit was issued, there was the transfer of a security interest from Debtor to Bank supporting Bank's contingent obligation under the letter of credit, but this transfer took place because of the relationship between Debtor and Bank. It was independent of the relationship between Supplier and Bank.

[margin right: Makasek's argument]

Bank, for its part, will argue that the transfer of the security interest supporting its contingent obligation under the letter of credit was in return for issuing the letter of credit, not on account of the antecedent debt owed Supplier. In short, Supplier argues it never received anything from Debtor, while Bank argues that it never received a transfer on account of an antecedent debt.

[margin right: Bank: i.e. new debt new security interest.]

Our instincts, however, should tell us that something is amiss here. We should not allow Bank and Supplier to fragment this transaction into its separate pieces and find that no preference took place when, if we link the various transactions, there has been a transfer on account of the antecedent debt owed Supplier that left the general creditors worse off.

[interlinear: Trustee: same line of credit, letter just redirects it to new parts + security interest (antecedent debt)]

[margin right: Supplier: • no xfer → from D to S, the security interest taken by Bank. S is & does not, by itself, affect general creditors (the bank didn't have to ↑ security interest -- so unwind that)]

Courts have in fact allowed preference actions against creditors like Supplier in such cases. See In re Compton Corp., 831 F.2d 586 (5th Cir. 1987). These courts reason that the transfer of the security interest to Bank was a transfer on account of the antecedent debt owed Supplier. It was not a transfer directly to Supplier, but the language in §547(b) allows preference actions both when a transfer is made to a creditor on account of an antecedent debt and "for the benefit" of such a creditor. Section 550 allows the trustee to recover from Supplier the value of the transfer made for its benefit.

[margin left: But if it's same debt (type if not amount) → why ___]

These cases lead to an additional inquiry. We have to ask whether the trustee can recover from Bank instead of Supplier. Bank did not receive a transfer on account of an antecedent debt owed it, but it was the initial transferee and §550 allows the trustee to recover from transferees even if they were not themselves creditors who were preferred. See Levit v. Ingersoll Rand Financial Corp., 874 F.2d 1186 (7th Cir. 1989).

[margin left: Call it a new security interest (amount but not type)]

[margin right: → deal Supplier struck up bank could have been indep't of 2° security interest]

Section 550(c) limits the trustee's power to seek repayment from initial transferees, but only in one kind of three-party case. The following facts illustrate the kind of case at which §550(c) is aimed. A corporate debtor repays a general creditor that has a guarantee from an insider, such as the debtor's principal shareholder. The debtor files more than ninety days later, but within a year of the transfer. The

[bottom margin: i.e. Supplier held/inside antecedent debt for which it collected payment (through the bank) on the eve of BK. Direct impact was security interest which can be unwound under §550]

transfer is a voidable preference because it relieved the insider of her liability on the guarantee within a year of the bankruptcy petition. Section 550(c) provides that in this three-party case, the trustee's only recourse is against the insider. Given the unequivocal language of §550(a), however, the trustee apparently has unfettered rights to pursue initial transferees that were not themselves preferred in other kinds of transactions, one where the preference is not to an insider.

The above illustrations demonstrate the importance of substance over form in the application of preference law. One way to ensure that substance prevails over form is to combine (or 'step') discrete transactions together and thus allow a preference recovery. We also need to ask if the converse is also true: Do we step transactions together to prevent a preference attack when the transaction as a whole is not preferential? The case below, *P.A. Bergner*, as well as the related notes and problems address this and related questions. The material also asks you to consider whether preference law serves the asset-preservation objective described here and whether it might serve some other purpose as well or instead.

Before we turn to the case, however, the exercises below require you to work through some preference mechanics and ask you to consider further some of the themes developed here.

Key Provisions: Bankruptcy Code §547(b), (e), (f)

EXERCISES

8D(1) Debtor fully repays its $10,000 unsecured obligation to Bank. Immediately before the transfer, Debtor's total obligations are $100,000 and her total assets, none of which are exempt from collection, are worth $75,000. A month later nothing has changed except that Debtor files for bankruptcy. Assuming that there is no applicable exception, can Debtor's bankruptcy trustee avoid and collect the transfer to Bank? Would your answer change if Debtor's liabilities were still $100,000 at the time of the transfer, but her assets were just under $100,000 at the time of the transfer and $75,000 at the time of the bankruptcy petition? Would your answer change, assuming the original facts, if Debtor paid Bank only $7,000?

8D(2) Debtor, who is insolvent, owes Bank $10,000, an obligation secured by collateral worth $12,000. A month before Debtor files for bankruptcy, Debtor repays the loan in full. Assuming that there is no applicable exception, can Debtor's bankruptcy trustee avoid and collect the transfer to Bank? Would your answer change if the collateral were worth only $7,500? Would your answer change if the collateral were worth only $7,500 and Debtor repaid only $2,000?

8D(3) To secure an obligation, Debtor grants Bank an interest in equipment Debtor might acquire from time to time. Bank duly files an effective financing statement. A month later, Debtor buys a computer, then files for bankruptcy. Assuming that there is no applicable exception, can Debtor's bankruptcy trustee avoid the Bank's interest in the computer?

8D(4) Debtor operates a consignment store, where it sells goods provided by others and keeps ten percent of the proceeds. Just before Debtor files for bankruptcy it returns goods provided by Supplier. Assuming that there is no applicable exception, can Debtor's bankruptcy trustee avoid and collect the value of the transfer to Supplier? In answering this question consider, among other provisions, UCC §9-319.

8D(5) Debtor Corporation owes $100,000 to Baker, who is a Debtor shareholder. Four months prior to filing for bankruptcy, Debtor fully satisfies Baker's loan by granting her BlackAcre, a parcel of Debtor's unencumbered real estate. Two months later, Baker goes to the town real estate office and properly records her interest in BlackAcre. Assuming that there is no applicable exception, can Debtor's bankruptcy trustee avoid and collect the transfer to Baker? Would it make a difference if the grant had been made eleven months before the petition and the state filing two months thereafter?

8D(6) Bank holds insolvent Debtor Corporation's $100,000 obligation, which is unsecured but is guaranteed by Abel, Debtor's president. Nine months prior to Debtor's bankruptcy, Debtor repays Bank in full. Assuming that there is no applicable exception, can Debtor's bankruptcy trustee avoid the transfer to Bank? Can the trustee recover from Bank? From Abel? Would any of your answers change if Debtor secured Bank's loan nine months prior to bankruptcy rather than repaying the loan? Would any of your answers change if the repayment occurred within ninety days of Debtor's bankruptcy? In answering these questions, consider, among other provisions, Bankruptcy Code §547(i).

8D(7) Debtor pledges $100,000 to her church. One week later she pays $100,000 in satisfaction of that pledge. A month after that Debtor files for bankruptcy. Assuming that there is no applicable exception, can Debtor's trustee avoid the payment? Should the trustee be able to do so? In answering this question consider, among other provisions, Bankruptcy Code §548(a)(2).

CASE

P.A. BERGNER & CO. v. BANK ONE

United States Court of Appeals, Seventh Circuit, 1998
140 F.3d 1111

WOOD, CIRCUIT JUDGE.

* * * Bergner (now known as Carson Pirie Scott & Co.) is the holding company for a number of large retail department stores, principally located in the Midwest. At the time the events at issue here began to unfold Bank One was Bergner's primary cash management bank. It handled Bergner's primary operating account, and it also issued standby letters of credit in substantial amounts to entities with which Bergner did business, including suppliers and insurers. Bergner did not rely primarily on Bank One for credit; instead, it maintained a revolving line of credit with a group of mostly European banks led by the Swiss Bank Corporation (collectively, "the Swiss bank group").

On July 26, 1989, Bergner and Bank One entered into a Standby Letter of Credit Agreement ("SLCA") under which Bank One agreed to issue standby letters of credit as security for some of Bergner's credit obligations. This general agreement was to govern the terms of all irrevocable standby letters of credit Bank One might issue for Bergner. Under section 1, Bergner promised to pay Bank One the amount of any draft drawn under a letter of credit issued pursuant to the SLCA "at or before presentation of the draft" by the letter's beneficiary. If an "event of default" occurred, Bergner was obligated to pay Bank One the full amount of all drafts that could be presented under outstanding letters of credit, which sum Bank One would hold without interest for the purpose of honoring such drafts. Section 6 of the SLCA gave Bank One "a security interest in and lien on any deposit account or other money now or hereafter owed [Bergner] by [Bank One]." Bergner also agreed that Bank One could, "at any time after the occurrence of an Event of Default, without prior notice or demand set off against any such accounts or other money, all or part of the unpaid balance of the Obligations." * * *

At Bergner's request, Bank One issued standby letters of credit, under the SLCA, to several beneficiaries, two of which are relevant to this action: one of Bergner's suppliers, Associated Merchandising Corporation ("AMC"), and Bergner's insurance company, Liberty Mutual Insurance Company. These letters, like all letters of credit, had three relevant parties—the account party, or applicant (Bergner, the bank's customer), the issuer (Bank One), and the beneficiaries (AMC and Liberty Mutual). The relationship between each pair of parties involved in a letter of credit transaction is entirely independent, although each relationship is necessary to support a letter of credit, somewhat like the three legs of a tripod.

The first leg of our tripod—the agreement between Bank One and Bergner—was a contractual relationship, represented here by the SLCA we have already described. The letters of credit themselves, which embodied the direct arrangement between the issuer (Bank One) and the beneficiaries (AMC and Liberty Mutual) were the second leg. Third, of course, Bergner had distinct obligations to the beneficiaries that the standby letters of credit were designed to secure.

* * * The AMC letter of credit contained a so-called "evergreen" clause, under which, upon expiration, it would automatically be renewed for one year unless Bank One provided at least sixty days notice of nonrenewal. The bank also promised that if it sent such a notice, AMC would have the following right:

> [A]fter such notice is given … funds under this Letter of Credit will also be available against a sight draft drawn on us by AMC, accompanied by a signed written statement on its letterhead stating:
>
>> The proceeds of the accompanying draft will be held and applied against the obligations of CPS Department Stores, Carson Pirie Scott & Co. and/or P.A. Bergner & Co. of Illinois to The Associated Merchandising Corporation as they come due from time to time.

The AMC credit was first issued on July 31, 1990, for a face amount of $31,000,000. It was amended nine times to reflect increases or decreases in the amount of Bergner's outstanding orders with AMC. By July 2, 1991, the amount of the credit was $31,207,000, and the expiration date was July 31, 1991. * * *

Between March 1989, and September 1990, Bank One also issued four letters of credit at Bergner's request to Liberty Mutual. * * *

Bergner needed standby letters of credit to provide added security for its contract to purchase merchandise from AMC and for its insurance policy with Liberty Mutual. Bank One's irrevocable standby letters of credit served that purpose. The effect of standby letters of credit like these is to put the issuer (Bank One) itself behind the account party's (Bergner's) promises to pay. As long as Bergner paid those with which it contracted, the standby letters of credit did not come into play. If, however, one of the events entitling a beneficiary to draw on a letter of credit occurred, then the beneficiary was entitled to go straight to Bank One to collect its money, without worrying about Bergner's financial health. Bank One, in turn, promised to honor a demand from either beneficiary that conformed to the letters of credit, no matter what defenses Bergner may have had against either AMC's or Liberty Mutual's request for funds. A bank is willing to make such promises to a beneficiary both because its customer— the account party to the transaction—pays it a fee for the service (approximately $300,000 annually in this case) and because the bank is in the best position to ensure that the account party will be good for the money. Sometimes the bank may simply trust a long-time customer to reimburse the bank if a beneficiary draws on a letter of credit, but very often the bank will either demand collateral or, as Bank One did here, require its customer to prepay the bank in the amount of any demand that the beneficiary may present.

On May 23 and 24, 1991, Bank One sent certified letters both to its account party, Bergner, and to the two beneficiaries of the letters of credit, AMC and Liberty Mutual, announcing that it would not renew those letters of credit. This action prompted AMC to inform Bergner that it was planning to exercise its rights, under the special condition detailed above, to draw down the full amount of the credit in its favor. Bergner passed this word along to Bank One on July 16, 1991, which prompted Bank One to ask Bergner how it planned to prefund the AMC draw. Bank One suggested one possibility—that Bergner borrow the money from Bank One itself—but Bergner rejected this on the ground that the interest rate offered was unattractive. Bergner instead turned to the revolving line of credit it maintained with the Swiss bank group, which at that time was still approximately $74 million, believing that the interest rate would be more favorable. Bergner informed Bank One that it would make sure that it had enough money on deposit with Bank One before the AMC draw, as it was required to do under the SLCA.

On July 17, 1991, AMC presented documents to Bank One to try to draw down the full amount of the letter of credit. Those documents proved to be nonconforming, which bought the parties a brief amount of time. After correcting the technical problems with the documents, on July 19, 1991, AMC submitted conforming documents and drew $31,207,000 under the letter of credit. At 11:02 A.M. that day, the Swiss bank group wired $31,000,000 through the Federal Reserve Bank to Bergner's general operating account at Bank One (which already had enough to cover the remaining $207,000). At 1:24 P.M., Bank One began the process of transferring the funds from Bergner's operating account to AMC by "memo posting" Bergner's account in the amount of $31,207,000. "Memo posting" is a provisional internal bank process to record the transaction pending formal posting at the end of the day. At 2:10 P.M. Bank One transferred the full $31,207,000 through the Federal Reserve Bank to AMC.

Meanwhile, Liberty Mutual was also taking action in light of Bank One's earlier notification that its letters of credit would not be renewed. On July 22, 1991, it too notified Bank One that it intended to draw down its letters unless it received a replacement letter of credit. At Bergner's request, on July 29, 1991, Bank One replaced the expiring Liberty Mutual letters of credit with a new letter of credit in the amount of $6,358,000. (The new letter allowed draws on it only after July 31, the date the four old Liberty Mutual letters were scheduled to expire, and did expire, by their own terms.) Bergner's economic problems were becoming worse, however. On July 23, 1991, Bergner had presented its revised liquidity projections to the Swiss bank group, which was not impressed. On July 29, 1991, Bergner made another draw request on its revolving Swiss bank group credit facility. The next day, the Swiss bank group told Bergner that it would not honor the July 29 request, and it declared a "material adverse change" under its credit agreement with Bergner. This action had the effect of making unavailable the approximately $43 million that remained after the July 17 draw of $31,000,000 under the facility.

On July 31, Bergner notified Bank One that the Swiss bank group had declared a "material adverse change" under its credit agreement with Bergner. Bank One considered this an "event of default" under the SLCA, and told Bergner that it would start exercising its rights under the SLCA to offset letter of credit draws against Bergner's other accounts, unless Bergner maintained sufficient funds on deposit with Bank One to collateralize the full amount of the new Liberty Mutual letter of credit. (The offsetting procedure would have meant that large numbers of Bergner's ordinary checks would have been dishonored.) Although Bergner was not able to comply with this demand instantly, after August 2, 1991, it maintained at least enough in its account to cover the new Liberty Mutual letter of credit.

These measures were not enough to stabilize Bergner's financial position. On August 23, 1991, Bergner told Bank One that it intended to file a petition under Chapter 11 of the Bankruptcy Code. This too was an event of default under the SLCA. Bank One exercised its rights under section 6 of the SLCA by taking $6,358,000 from Bergner's account and placing it in a collateral account under Bank One's control, allocating these funds for any future claims by Liberty Mutual under the outstanding letter of credit in its favor. That same day, Bergner filed its Chapter 11 petition in the bankruptcy court for the Eastern District of Wisconsin.

By June 10, 1992, Liberty Mutual had drawn down the entire amount of its letter of credit from Bank One. On August 11, 1992, Bergner (now as the Chapter 11 debtor in possession) demanded from Bank One the return of $30,007,559, which represented an improvement in Bank One's position for the AMC letter of credit obligation, and $5,680,475, which represented an improvement in its position for the Liberty Mutual letter of credit obligation, citing §553(b) of the Bankruptcy Code. Bank One refused, and on August 26, 1992, Bergner commenced the present adversary proceeding to recover as preferential transfers both its July 19, 1991, payment of $31,207,000 to cover AMC's letter and the August 23, 1991, attachment of Bergner's cash deposits in the amount of $6,358,000. * * *

Bank One argues that the lower courts should not have followed the independence principle that normally governs letter of credit transactions under the circumstances presented here, because in reality in AMC's case there was only a single economic transaction orchestrated by Bergner, in which it moved $31,000,000 from its Swiss bankers, through Bank One, to AMC; in Liberty Mutual's case, Bank One argues, there was no diminution of Bergner's estate because the debit of $6,358,000 was inexorably tied to an equal credit in Bank One's "collateral account," and eventually to payments to Liberty Mutual. Bank One urges us to find that these transactions had no effect at all on the debtor's estate, and it argues that Bergner would receive a windfall if the debtor's estate were permitted to recoup the payments made to the bank. Bergner responds that Bank One's position ignores the independence of each part of the letter of credit transaction from each other part. If we were to follow Bank One's position, Bergner claims, we would be doing serious violence to the common business understanding of letters of credit and to the usefulness of the device in commercial transactions.

At first blush, one can understand Bank One's view of the transactions. Looking first at the AMC letter of credit, Bank One claims it was just a collection agent for Bergner. It points out that its SLCA with Bergner required Bergner to prefund all draws before Bank One would pay anything, from which it reasons that the money just flowed through the bank, much as this court described a transaction not involving a letter of credit in Bonded Financial Services, Inc. v. European American Bank, 838 F.2d 890, 896 (7th Cir. 1988). Bank One concedes that its position is not consistent with the independence principle that underlies letter of credit law, but it asks us not to "overemphasize" that principle so as to ignore the economic reality of a transaction for purposes of preference analysis.

The only problem with Bank One's argument is that letters of credit really are different from other financing mechanisms, and Bank One's position does not reflect the independent obligations that ran from the bank to the beneficiaries. From the point of view of the beneficiaries, AMC and Liberty Mutual, the way that Bank One settled its accounts with Bergner was of no importance, either legal or practical. As soon as Bank One issued the irrevocable letters in favor of each beneficiary (for a fee, as Bergner reminds us), it assumed the obligation of paying upon a draft supported by documents that conformed to the terms of the credit. Thus, when AMC presented its draft with conforming documents to Bank One on July 19, 1991, Bank One was required to pay AMC the full $31,207,000 that the letter of credit then provided, whether or not Bergner gave it a red cent. If Bergner did not comply with its own agreement with Bank One, under which it was required to give the bank the amount of the draw either before or at the time of the payment to the beneficiary, then Bank One would have had a perfectly good contract action against Bergner, but it would have had no defense against honoring the beneficiary's demand.

This means that at the moment AMC presented its draft, a debt arose between Bergner (as debtor) and Bank One (as creditor), in the amount of the requested draft. (This would not have been the case if, for example, AMC had demanded payment directly from Bergner, and Bergner had asked the bank to issue a cashier's check; in that situation the bank would have incurred no obligation to AMC if it had refused to write the check without sufficient funds from Bergner to cover it.) The debt was due, according to the SLCA, no later than the time when Bank One was required to honor the draft under its letter of credit to AMC. In order to pay its debt to Bank One, Bergner arranged for the transfer of $31,000,000 from the Swiss bank group to its account at Bank One. (Even though the time periods were quite short, as a result of the speed at which wire transfers can be accomplished through the Federal Reserve System, the underlying character of the transactions was no different than if these transfers had taken place over a period of weeks rather than hours or minutes.) Once Bergner placed the required amount of money in its account at Bank One, it authorized Bank One to take that money in satisfaction of its obligation under the SLCA, which Bank One did first by making its "memo posting," and later in the day by formally posting the transfer from Bergner to itself.

Still focusing on the AMC transaction ... this breakdown of the transaction shows that Bergner indeed had a debt to Bank One and that Bank One assured itself of payment in full within the preference period identified by §547(b). Looking at the elements of §547(b), we agree with Bergner that Bank One obtained a preferential transfer: there was a transfer in the amount of $31,207,000 of Bergner's funds to Bank One; the transfer was made on account of Bergner's antecedent obligation under the SLCA to pay Bank One the amount of a draw under the AMC letter of credit; the transfer was made while Bergner was insolvent; it occurred within ninety days of Bergner's filing its petition under Chapter 11; and the transfer allowed Bank One to be paid in full, even though other unsecured creditors would not have received full payment in a liquidation of Bergner. * * *

[T]he analysis of the Liberty Mutual letter of credit is identical in all relevant respects to that of AMC's, even though Liberty Mutual did not draw on the letter until long after the petition for bankruptcy protection had been filed. By August 23, Bergner had an existing obligation to Bank One under the SLCA for $6,358,000; Bank One took steps to gain full control of the funds on deposit to cover Bergner's obligations under the SLCA on the very day Bergner filed its Chapter 11 petition—obviously within the ninety day preference period. The substitution of the new letter of credit for the old series of letters makes no difference, at least in any way that would help Bank One's position. (The record reflects that Bank One issued the new letter because Liberty Mutual otherwise would have drawn down the full amount to which it was eligible under the four older letters; it was thus in Bank One's own interest to issue this new letter, regardless of any effect on Bergner.) ...

Bank One's actions seizing for itself both the $31,207,000 that Bergner paid it in satisfaction of Bergner's debt under the SLCA, and the $6,358,000 to assure its ability to collect from Bergner an amount equal to the new Liberty Mutual letter of credit were therefore avoidable preferential transfers under §547(b), which Bergner is entitled to recover under §550(a). * * *

NOTES

8D.1. AMC was not a general creditor of Bergner. The $31 million that it received when it drew on the letter of credit gave Bergner a credit that could be (and was in fact) used against goods that Bergner purchased from AMC. Before the transaction, Bergner had a $31 million credit line. After the transaction, Bergner had a right to receive $31 million in goods from AMC. If Bergner had taken money out of one bank account and put it in another, there would have been no preference. This transaction, from this point of view, is no different. Diminution of the estate is ordinarily thought to be necessary for any successful preference action. See Kapela v. Newman, 649 F.2d 887 (1st Cir. 1981).

Essential to the outcome in *Bergner* was the unwillingness of the court to connect the various transactions together. The court assumes that letter of credit doctrine compels this result, but one might take the opposite view. To be sure, bankruptcy should not affect the ability of a general creditor to draw on a standby letter of credit. As the court in *Bergner* notes, the relationship between the general creditor and the issuer of the letter of credit is independent of the relationships between the general creditor and the debtor and the debtor and the bank. But whether multiple transactions should be joined together to ask if a preference has taken place is arguably a question of bankruptcy law, not of the law governing letters of credit. We return to this question when we explore the earmarking doctrine in the next subsection.

8D.2. The issue in *Bergner*, as in any other preference case, is whether the trustee can avoid or collect the value of a transfer. There is no penalty for the receipt of a voidable preference. A transferee or beneficiary subject to a recovery order need not even pay interest. One might wonder, then, whether the preference rules actually deter the creditors' collection race. Problem 8D-2 explores this question. Problem 8D-3 asks you to consider an alternative role for preference law, deterrence of creditor loan *extension*.

Problems

8D-1. Debtor Corporation owes Finance Company $1 million secured by a perfected interest in Debtor's equipment worth $2 million. Among many other obligations, Debtor also owes Bank $800,000 on an unsecured loan. One month before Debtor files for bankruptcy, at a time when Debtor's assets other than the equipment are worth about $3 million and its other debts amount to about $12 million, Finance Company pays Bank $400,000 in exchange for Debtor's obligation to Bank. Debtor's security agreement with Finance Company includes a "dragnet clause," which automatically applies Finance Company's security interest to any obligation of Debtor later acquired by Finance Company. What, if anything, can Debtor's bankruptcy trustee recover from Bank or Finance Company?

8D-2. Debtor has two assets, worth $100 if kept together but worth only $40 each if separated even temporarily. Debtor is subject to three unsecured, past due loans of $40 each. Each of three creditors must decide simultaneously whether to attempt collection or refrain from collection. If at least one creditor refrains, Debtor will stay out of bankruptcy for at least ninety days. If each attempts collection, Debtor will enter bankruptcy immediately. You represent one of the creditors. Do you advise her to attempt collection or refrain? If any collection attempt is costless? If it costs $5?

8D-3. Can a debtor's grant of a security interest destroy going-concern value or synergy among assets? If not, is there any reason for preference rules to avoid the grant of an interest in assets as opposed to a transfer of the assets themselves? Consider the following. Debtor Corporation's business has declined for years to the point where Debtor is deeply insolvent and starved for cash. Debtor owes Bank $100,000 on an unsecured obligation due in a week. Debtor is unable to repay the loan in full and fears that default would lead immediately to bankruptcy and, perhaps, liquidation, which is a distinct possibility within the next few months in any case. Bank knows that it will receive less than $50,000 if Debtor enters bankruptcy now. But for the prospect of avoidance, Bank would accept cash or collateral of at least $70,000 in complete satisfaction of its obligation. Is Bank less likely to accept such a settlement given the preference rules? Much less likely? What is Bank's alternative? Are the creditors as a group or society likely served by Bank's reluctance to settle? See Prajit K. Dutta, *Strategies and Games: Theory and Practice* 128-32 (MIT Press, 1999); George G. Triantis and Ronald J. Daniels, The Role of

Debt in Interactive Corporate Governance, 83 Cal. L. Rev. 1073 (1995).

2) EARMARKING DOCTRINE

On occasion, the proceeds of a new loan are paid directly to an existing creditor. Sometimes the debtor has discretion over the use of the proceeds and asks the new lender to direct them to the existing creditor. Other times it is the new lender who insists that the new loan be used to repay an earlier obligation. The lender's reasons vary. The new lender may, for example, want to ensure the earlier creditor's release of collateral that the debtor has pledged to the new lender. In any case, when a new lender directly pays an antecedent debt, or the debtor is obligated to use the proceeds of a new loan to repay such debt, the new loan is called an earmarked loan. ⟹ ≈ balance x-fee

An insolvent debtor's use of a new loan's proceeds to repay an antecedent debt on the eve of bankruptcy may constitute a voidable preference. While there is no explicit statutory basis for an earmarked loan exception to the voidable preference rules, courts have established such an exception, known as the earmarking doctrine. The doctrine applies when the old loan is replaced with a new loan of equal priority. One can argue first that the proceeds of an earmarked loan are not an interest of the debtor in property, and thus not subject to §547(b) preference rules. Second, one can argue that unpaid creditors are not injured by an earmarked loan transaction. When one creditor replaces another, the whole of the transaction does not look like the grab race that preference law is designed to prevent. Thus, courts conclude, no purpose would be served by requiring reimbursement from the recipient of an earmarked loan's proceeds.

[margin handwriting: ← debtor doesn't transfer her interest in property (the old creditor does?)]

The exercises below ask you to apply the earmarking doctrine to a set of hypotheticals. The case, *In re Heitkamp*, provides a somewhat more detailed description of the doctrine and its history, as well as a twist on the doctrine's ordinary application. The notes and problem that follow ask you to question the premises of the earmarking doctrine and to consider whether the doctrine is sensible.

Key Provision: Bankruptcy Code §547(b)

EXERCISES

8D(8) Supplier sells $10,000 worth of raw materials to Debtor, and Debtor agrees to pay for them within ninety days. Debtor's fortunes take a turn for the worse, and eight months later Debtor is insolvent and Supplier is still unpaid. Debtor goes to Bank, and Bank agrees to pay Supplier $10,000 in return for Debtor's promise to repay it in six months. A month later, Debtor files a bankruptcy petition. Bank is still owed $10,000. Is Bank's payment to Supplier a voidable preference? Does it matter whether Supplier was a secured creditor? Would it matter if Debtor granted Bank a security interest in previously unencumbered property?

8D(9) A month before Debtor files a bankruptcy petition, and while Debtor is insolvent, Bank lends Debtor $1 million. Debtor agrees that it will use the money to satisfy an outstanding $1 million obligation owed Finance Company. Debtor uses the loan proceeds to pay Finance Company, which releases its collateral, worth $800,000. The released collateral as well as other of Debtor's property worth $200,000 is pledged to secure Bank's loan. To what extent, if any, is Debtor's payment to Finance Company a voidable preference?

CASE

IN RE HEITKAMP

United States Court of Appeals, Eighth Circuit, 1998
137 F.3d 1087

FAGG, CIRCUIT JUDGE.

Scott and Darcy Heitkamp build and sell homes in Wyndmere, North Dakota. In the course of their business, they borrowed money from Community First National Bank and maintained credit with several subcontractors. The bank initially loaned the Heitkamps $50,000 to build a certain house. A mortgage secured the loan. The Heitkamps ran out of cash before completing the project and obtained another loan for $40,000 from the bank in November 1995. Rather than giving the Heitkamps the money, the bank issued cashier's checks payable to specific subcontractors who supplied goods or services to construct the house. At the bank's direction, the Heitkamps obtained mechanic's lien waivers from the subcontractors in exchange for the checks. The Heitkamps also gave the bank a second mortgage on the house, but because of an oversight, the bank did not record the mortgage until March 1, 1996.

Three days later, the Heitkamps filed a Chapter 7 bankruptcy petition. The mortgaged house was sold, and the bank and several subcontractors asserted rights to the proceeds. The bankruptcy trustee brought an adversary proceeding to set aside the Heitkamps' transfer of the second mortgage interest to the bank under §547(b), which permits avoidance of certain transfers of the debtor's interest in property. The bankruptcy court set the transfer aside, rejecting the bank's argument that the earmarking doctrine prevented avoidance of the mortgage's transfer. The district court affirmed. The bank appeals, and we reverse.

According to the earmarking doctrine, there is no avoidable transfer of the debtor's property interest when a new lender and a debtor agree to use loaned funds to pay a specified antecedent debt, the agreement's terms are actually performed, and the transaction viewed as a whole does not diminish the debtor's estate. See In re Bohlen Enters., Ltd., 859 F.2d 561, 566 (8th Cir. 1988). No avoidable transfer is made because the loaned funds never become part of the debtor's property. See id. Instead, a new creditor merely steps into the shoes of an old creditor. Application of the earmarking doctrine is not limited to situations in which the new creditor is secondarily liable for the earlier debt, but extends to situations where "any third party ... pays down a debt of the debtor ... because [the] payments ... would have no effect on the estate of the debtor." In re Bruening, 113 F.3d 838, 841 (8th Cir. 1997); In re Safe-T-Brake of S. Fla., Inc., 162 Bankr. 359, 364 (S.D. Fla. 1993) ("caselaw has extended the earmarking doctrine beyond the guarantor scenario"). "Regardless of the lender's prior relationship with the debtor, or lack thereof, replacing one creditor with another of equal priority does not diminish the estate and thus no voidable [transfer] results." *In re Safe-T-Brake*, 162 Bankr. at 364. Thus, the doctrine applies when a security interest is given for funds used to pay secured debts, but not when a security interest is given for funds used to pay an unsecured debt.

The earmarking doctrine applies in this case. The bank and the Heitkamps agreed the secured funds would be used to pay specific preexisting debts, the agreement was performed, and the transfer of the mortgage interest did not diminish the amount available for distribution to the Heitkamps' creditors. Before the loan, the Heitkamps owed subcontractors $40,000 secured by the house for goods and services rendered. Afterwards, the Heitkamps owed the bank $40,000 secured by the house for a cash loan used to pay the subcontractors. The Heitkamps' assets and net obligations remained the same. Essentially, the bank took over the subcontractors' security interest in the house. The subcontractors had a statutory lien against the house and could have perfected a security interest in the house even after the Heitkamps filed for bankruptcy. §362(b)(3); §546(b)(1). The bank required the Heitkamps to obtain mechanic's lien waivers from the subcontractors, and the subcontractors specifically released their interest in the house. Because the transfer of the mortgage interest to the bank merely replaced the subcontractors' security interest, there was no transfer of the Heitkamps' property interest avoidable under §547(b). In these circumstances, recognition of the bank's security interest does not give the bank an unfair advantage over other creditors.

In sum, the trustee had the burden to prove the earmarking doctrine does not apply, and failed to do so. The trustee cannot avoid the second mortgage under §547(b) because the trustee cannot establish the mortgage was a "transfer of an interest of the debtor in property," an element of §547(b). We thus reverse and remand for further proceedings consistent with this opinion.

NOTES

8D.3. The *Heitkamp* court states that "[a]pplication of the earmarking doctrine is not limited to situations in which the new creditor is secondarily liable for the earlier debt." This comment implicitly refers to the fact that the earmarking doctrine has evolved from cases in which a guarantor advanced funds for repayment of an obligation on which the guarantor was liable. In such a case, the guarantor simply satisfies a preexisting obligation to the creditor and becomes subrogated to the creditor's rights against the debtor. The guarantor's payment does not constitute a new loan to the debtor even if the guarantor channels the funds through the debtor to the creditor. Thus, no property of the debtor is used to pay an antecedent debt and the preference rules are not implicated. See Newport v. National Herkimer County Bank, 225 U.S. 178 (1912).

As *Heitkamp* makes clear, the protection of transfers from a guarantor has been extended to encompass transfers from a new lender because, in the court's view, "replacing one creditor with another of equal priority does not diminish the estate." This conclusion seems unassailable when a preexisting obligation is simply transferred, through subrogation, from a creditor to a guarantor. When a lender negotiates at arm's length for a new loan to an insolvent debtor, however, the terms of that loan are unlikely to replicate those of the loan replaced. It is not clear, therefore, that the earmarked loan transaction is harmless to the estate. Problem 8D-4 asks you to explore possible injury to other creditors and ultimately to the bankruptcy estate.

8D.4. The substance of an earmarked loan transaction aside, one should not accept uncritically the courts' rhetoric in these cases. In applying the earmarking doctrine, courts invariably state that earmarked funds never become part of the debtor's property. Thus, a transfer of those funds to a creditor is not a "transfer of an interest of the debtor in property," the only sort of transfer to which §547(b) applies. This characterization is hard to sustain when earmarked funds are not paid by a guarantor but are instead proceeds of a new loan. Assume that at the time a debtor acquires a new loan, it had discretion to direct the proceeds. In this case, the loan proceeds would seem to be "an interest of the debtor in property," whether the debtor receives the funds itself or asks the lender to direct them to a creditor.

→ i.e. the debtor could keep funds (her proceeds)

8D.5. *Heitkamp* is a peculiar case because the earmarking doctrine is used to protect not the recipient of the earmarked funds, the subcontractors, but the provider of those funds, the bank. The subcontractors could have been shielded by the earmarking doctrine, but they likely did not need such protection. If fully secured, the subcontractors would have received full payment in a Chapter 7 liquidation. Consequently, the debtor's payment of the subcontractor's obligation would not run afoul of §547(b). The bank, in contrast, found itself in jeopardy because it did not perfect its security interest within the grace period provided by §547(e)(2). As a result, bank's mortgage was deemed to have been a transfer of a security interest on account of antecedent debt. This treatment of tardy perfection, left unexplained by the *Heitkamp* court, is discussed above in this section. To the extent §547(e) is designed to punish late perfection of a security interest—even if the actual transfer of the security interest is contemporaneous with a loan and thus not the result of a creditor's attempt to jockey for priority—it is not clear why the earmarking doctrine should come to a creditor's rescue.

late perfection should not fall under earmarking doctrine

8D.6. The *Heitkamp* opinion notes the subcontractors' right to perfect their mechanic's lien after the debtor filed for bankruptcy. The court cites §§362(b)(3) and 546(b)(1). These provisions are discussed above in chapter 4, section B.

PROBLEM

8D-4. Debtor is an insolvent retailer that has been losing money continually for more than a year. Debtor owes Supplier $100,000, due at once. Debtor also owes Finance Company $1 million, due in one year. Neither claim is secured. Debtor has little cash, and Supplier is threatening to file an involuntary bankruptcy petition against Debtor. To avoid immediate bankruptcy, Debtor borrows $100,000 from Bank, with the proceeds by agreement transferred to Supplier. A week later, one of Debtor's delivery trucks causes a serious accident, subjecting Debtor to $1 million in tort liability. The day after the accident, Debtor files a voluntary bankruptcy petition. Assume that previously unencumbered assets secure Bank's loan to Debtor. At the time of that loan, would Finance Company likely favor the loan? Now assume instead that Bank's loan to Debtor is unsecured. At the time of that loan, would Finance Company likely favor the loan? In answering this question, consider the loan terms—e.g., interest rate and maturity—that Bank would demand in an arm's-length transaction. If you conclude that Finance Company likely would be better off if Debtor did not borrow from Bank, would abolition of the earmarking doctrine help Finance Company? Would abolition of the doctrine maximize social welfare? Compare Problem 8D-3. See also Barry E. Adler, A Re-Examination of Near-Bankruptcy Investment Incentives, 62 U. Chi. L. Rev. 575 (1995).

3) SAFE HARBORS

Preferential transfers that are presumptively voidable under §547(b) and are not protected by the common law earmarking doctrine may nevertheless lie beyond the reach of a bankruptcy trustee. Section 547(c) lists a series of transfers that the trustee may not avoid. Most of these are parts of transactions that appear routine and not likely a last-minute attempt by a creditor to improve its position. There are, in addition, other miscellaneous exceptions to the trustee's avoiding powers.

Section 547(c)(1) excepts from avoidance a transfer to the extent that it was "intended by the debtor and the creditor" to be, and in fact was "substantially," "a contemporaneous exchange for new value given to the debtor." Suppose a customer purchases goods from a retailer with a check, and the customer's bank honors the check a few days later. The transfer of funds to the retailer is on account of antecedent debt established on the sale of the goods. Nevertheless,

§547(c)(1) sensibly excepts such regular transactions from attack as a voidable preference.

Section 547(c)(2) excepts from avoidance a transfer to the extent that it was "in payment of a debt incurred by the debtor in the ordinary course of business or financial affairs of the debtor in the ordinary course of business or financial affairs of the debtor and the transferee," and paid in "ordinary course of business or financial affairs of the debtor and the transferee" or otherwise "according to ordinary business terms." For many years, Retailer purchases inventory on credit from Supplier each month in the same way and on the same terms, just like others in its industry. Supplier ships at the start of each month, and Retailer pays at the end. Supplier may keep the three payments it receives in the ninety days before the filing of a bankruptcy petition. None of these transactions reflects opt-out behavior, as each was part of the way both parties and those similarly situated conduct their day-to-day affairs.

Section 547(c)(3) excepts from avoidance the transfer of certain purchase money security interests. (Recall that a purchase money security interest, or PMSI, is an interest granted by a debtor in exchange for new value given to enable, and in fact used by, the debtor to acquire the collateral.) Consider the case in which Debtor borrows $100 from Bank and grants it a security interest in the machine that it will buy with this loan. Bank immediately files. Buyer then goes out and buys the machine. This transaction runs afoul of §547(b). Section 547(e)(3) provides that Debtor cannot transfer a security interest in the new machine to Bank until it acquires rights in it. Debtor acquired rights in the machine *after* it received proceeds of the loan. Hence, Debtor transferred the security interest in the machine *after* the debt was incurred. There is a transfer on account of an antecedent debt. Section 547(c)(3) saves this transaction, which involves no opt-out behavior, from preference attack. The exception applies if and only if the debtor receives new value "at or after the signing" of the applicable security agreement and only if the PMSI "is perfected on or before 30 days after the debtor receives possession" of the collateral.

Section 547(c)(4) excepts from avoidance a transfer "to or for the benefit of a creditor, to the extent that, after such transfer, such creditor gave new value to or for the benefit of the debtor." This subsection provides, however, that the exception applies only to the extent that the new value is "not secured by an otherwise unavoidable security interest," and is not the proceeds of a loan that has itself been repaid with an "otherwise unavoidable transfer." This provision ensures that a trustee cannot launch a preference attack against a creditor who, after being repaid, turns around and makes a new loan of the same amount.

Consider a debtor who repays an old $100 unsecured loan two weeks before bankruptcy and then borrows $100 from the same creditor a week later. If the new loan is unsecured, and there is no other activity between the debtor and creditor prior to debtor's bankruptcy, the trustee cannot avoid the repayment. At the time of the bankruptcy, the lender is an unsecured creditor for $100, just as it was at the time of the repayment. If we allowed a preference attack, the lender would be forced to return $100 and become a general creditor for $200, an amount greater than it even lent debtor. Without this provision, debtors in financial trouble would not be able to maintain a revolving line of credit that varied in step with its repayments. This exception ensures that preference law leaves undisturbed a standard way of doing business.

Section 547(c)(5) deals with security interests in collateral that regularly turns over. It excepts from avoidance a transfer—

> that creates a perfected security interest in inventory or a receivable or the proceeds of either, except to the extent that the aggregate of all such transfers to the transferee caused a reduction, as of the date of the filing of the petition and to the prejudice of other creditors holding unsecured claims, of any amount by which the debt secured by such security interest exceeded the value of all security interests for such debt on the later of—

> (A)(i) with respect to a transfer to which subsection (b)(4)(A) of this section applies, 90 days before the date of the filing of the petition; or

> (ii) with respect to a transfer to which subsection (b)(4)(B) of this section applies, one year before the date of the filing of the petition; or

> (B) the date on which new value was first given under the security agreement creating such security interest.

This provision is designed to protect floating security interests in inventory or receivables. A receivable is any right to payment, see §547(a)(3). In practice, it is typically an obligation owed to the debtor by a customer who purchases goods or services on credit. Bank lends $100,000 and properly perfects a security interest in Debtor's inventory. Debtor runs a wholesale produce market and its inventory turns over every week, but its value remains the same. In the absence of

§547(c)(5), the trustee can argue that the inventory on hand at the time of the petition has been transferred to Bank on account of an antecedent debt. Under §547(e)(3), Bank does not acquire a security interest in Debtor's produce until Debtor acquires it, and all the produce on hand at the time of the bankruptcy petition had been acquired in the previous week. The transfer therefore took place long after Bank lent the money. Hence, it is a transfer on account of an antecedent debt, even though Bank did not engage in any opt-out behavior. Section 547(c)(5) and its two-point net improvement test protects Bank.

We do not, however, give a blanket exception to creditors who have security interests in inventory or accounts because there are ways in which opt-out behavior might take place. For example, ninety days before the filing of the petition, the inventory on hand might be worth much less than the amount of the loan. Because Bank is massively undersecured, repayment of its loan would be a voidable preference. By spending other assets and building up its inventory, Debtor could deliberately transform Bank into a fully secured creditor on the eve of bankruptcy at the expense of other creditors. Section 547(c)(5) is written to ensure that Debtor cannot prefer Bank by increasing the value of the inventory it has on hand.

We can imagine inventory or accounts as being like a river of collateral, which is fed by tributaries and empties into an estuary. At any time, the river has a height above its bed that reflects the total value of the inventory, the receivables, and proceeds. Over time, the river may rise or fall against its riverbank, which is marked periodically to reflect the amount of the loan then outstanding.

The key measurement is of the point at which the mark on the riverbank (amount of the loan outstanding) exceeds the waterline (total value of all collateral), if at all. This measurement is taken first at the beginning of the applicable preference period or, if the secured loan is made after this date, whenever the loan is made. The measurement is then taken again on the date of the debtor's bankruptcy petition. To the extent that the water has risen relative to the riverbank (the first measurement of loan excess over collateral value exceeds the second), the transfer of a security interest is subject to avoidance.

There is a common theme here, that transfers presumptively voidable under §547(b) are shielded if they likely reflect innocent events rather than an attempt by a creditor to opt out of, or gain advantage in, an imminent bankruptcy proceeding.

Not all exceptions follow this theme. Some exceptions are made for transfers on account of obligations the payment of which Congress particularly favors. For example, there is an exception for a transfer that is "the fixing of a statutory lien" and one for transfers that satisfy certain obligations owed for spousal or child support. See §547(c)(6) and (7), respectively. Other limited exceptions of this type protect a seller's right to reclaim goods sold (including fish or grain) and protect margin, settlement, or swap transactions in the securities industry. See §546(c)-(g). There are also de minimis exceptions: a transfer of less than $600 is not voidable in the bankruptcy case of an individual debtor who owes primarily consumer debts; in the case of a debtor whose debts are not primarily consumer debts, a transfer is not voidable if the aggregate value of all property "that constitutes or is affected by" the transfer is less than $5,475. See §547(c)(8) and (9), respectively. And for individual debtors, §547(h) prohibits avoidance of a payment made as part of a repayment plan adopted between the debtor and the creditor if the plan is one created by an approved credit counseling agency pursuant to the provisions of the 2005 Act. For the most part, however, these special cases contain few ambiguities and require little thought. The "innocent event" exceptions are far more interesting.

After the exercises below work through some of the basic exceptions to preference avoidance, the case that follows, *Union Bank v. Wolas*, provides the Supreme Court's view on the paradigmatic innocent-event exception, the exception for transfers in the ordinary course. The subsequent notes and problem ask you to consider what is meant by ordinary course and why an exception might depend on whether the loan was made as opposed to repaid in the ordinary course of business.

Key Provision: Bankruptcy Code §547(c)

EXERCISES

8D(10) Retailer sells Debtor a tractor on credit and retains a security interest in the tractor. Five weeks after the tractor is delivered, Retailer files to perfect its interest. A month later, Debtor files for bankruptcy. Can the trustee avoid Retailer's interest in the tractor? Would your answer change if applicable state law grants a purchase money secured lender priority over a lien creditor if the lender perfects its security interest in collateral within six weeks of Debtor's possession? See Fidelity Financial Services, Inc. v. Fink, 522 U.S. 211 (1998).

8D(11) Bank holds two of Debtor's obligations. The first is a $50,000 unsecured note. The second is a fully secured revolving line of credit with a $50,000 balance. Bank agrees to release its security interest on the line of credit, which Debtor desires to keep open, if Debtor immediately repays the note. Debtor repays the note and Bank releases the security interest. A few days later, Debtor files for bankruptcy. Can the trustee avoid the note repayment?

8D(12) Debtor Corporation sells long-term bonds that promise quarterly interest, principal upon maturity. Debtor never misses an interest payment but files for bankruptcy before the principal is due. Can the trustee avoid the last quarterly interest payment on the bonds?

8D(13) Finance Company lends Debtor $10,000 to purchase a mainframe computer. The loan is made pursuant to an agreement that grants Finance Company a security interest in the computer once it is purchased. Debtor deposits the loan proceeds in her checking account. Debtor then shops for the computer and purchases it a week later, at which time Finance Company files to perfect its interest. A month later Debtor files for bankruptcy. Can the trustee avoid Finance Company's interest in the computer?

8D(14) Debtor repays a $10,000 unsecured obligation to Bank. A week later, Bank lends Debtor $10,000. Five days after this second loan, Bank becomes concerned about Debtor's financial affairs and demands a security interest in Debtor's previously unencumbered equipment, which Debtor grants. The next day, Bank files to perfect its interest. A month later, Debtor files for bankruptcy. Can the trustee avoid Debtor's cash payment to Bank?

8D(15) Bank lends Debtor $100,000, the obligation secured by a perfected interest in Debtor's inventory, which completely turns over every thirty days, and in Debtor's equipment. Ninety days before Debtor files for bankruptcy, $90,000 of the loan is outstanding, the inventory on hand is worth $40,000, and the equipment is worth another $40,000. The day before bankruptcy, Debtor makes a $5,000 scheduled payment on the loan, leaving the balance at $85,000. On the date of Debtor's bankruptcy, the inventory on hand is worth $45,000 and the equipment remains worth $40,000. Can the trustee avoid Bank's security interest in the inventory?

8D(16) Bank lends Debtor $100,000, the obligation secured by a perfected interest in Debtor's inventory of fine art and receivables from the sale of that inventory. Ninety days before Debtor files for bankruptcy, her inventory consists of one painting, *Autumn*, worth $40,000. *Autumn* is a work by a recently discovered Renaissance artist. A few days later, Debtor trades *Autumn* for *Spring*, another work by the same artist. The day before Debtor files for bankruptcy, Debtor sells *Spring* on credit to Customer for $75,000. Can the trustee avoid any of Bank's security interest in Customer's obligation to Debtor?

8D(17) Nine months before Debtor Corporation files for bankruptcy, Lender, an insider of Debtor, lends Debtor $100,000, the obligation secured by a perfected interest in Debtor's inventory, worth $25,000 at the time. Despite his insider status, Lender pays little attention to Debtor for the next three months, over which period Debtor, while insolvent, acquires $50,000 in new inventory, raising the total value of inventory to $70,000 (as $5,000 of the new inventory replaces inventory sold). Lender then learns of Debtor's insolvency and persuades Debtor to raise the value of its inventory by another $20,000, so that at the time of bankruptcy Debtor has $90,000 worth of inventory, $80,000 of which Debtor has acquired since Debtor borrowed from Lender. At the time of bankruptcy, Debtor's obligation to Lender has increased to $110,000 with the accrual of interest. Can the trustee avoid any of Bank's security interest in the inventory? Would your answer change if during the three-month period of Lender's inattention the value of Debtor's inventory fell to nothing, and was later increased through Lender's intervention to $20,000?

CASE

UNION BANK v. WOLAS

Supreme Court of the United States, 1991
502 U.S. 151

JUSTICE STEVENS DELIVERED THE OPINION OF THE COURT.

Section 547(b) authorizes a trustee to avoid certain property transfers made by a debtor within 90 days before bankruptcy. The Code makes an exception, however, for transfers made in the ordinary course of business, §547(c)(2). The question presented is whether payments on long-term debt may qualify for that exception.

On December 17, 1986, ZZZZ Best Co., Inc. (Debtor) borrowed seven million dollars from petitioner, Union Bank (Bank). On July 8, 1987, the Debtor filed a voluntary petition under Chapter 7 of the Bankruptcy Code. During the preceding 90-day period, the Debtor had made two interest payments totaling approximately $100,000 and had paid a loan commitment fee of about $2,500 to the Bank. After his appointment as trustee of the Debtor's estate, respondent filed a complaint against the Bank to recover those payments pursuant to §547(b).

The Bankruptcy Court found that the loans had been made "in the ordinary course of business or financial affairs" of both the Debtor and the Bank, and that both interest payments as well as the payment of the loan commitment fee had been made according to ordinary business terms and in the ordinary course of business. As a matter of law, the Bankruptcy Court concluded that the payments satisfied the requirements of §547(c)(2) and therefore were not avoidable by the trustee. The District Court affirmed the Bankruptcy Court's summary judgment in favor of the Bank.

Shortly thereafter, in another case, the Court of Appeals held that the ordinary course of business exception to avoidance of preferential transfers was not available to long-term creditors. In reaching that conclusion, the Court of Appeals relied primarily on the policies underlying the voidable preference provisions and the state of the law prior to the enactment of the 1978 Bankruptcy Code and its amendment in 1984. Thus, the Ninth Circuit concluded, its holding in *CHG International, Inc.* dictated a reversal in this case. The importance of the question of law decided by the Ninth Circuit, coupled with the fact that the Sixth Circuit had interpreted §547(c)(2) in a contrary manner, persuaded us to grant the Bank's petition for certiorari.

I

We shall discuss the history and policy of §547 after examining its text. In subsection (b), Congress broadly authorized bankruptcy trustees to "avoid any transfer of an interest of the debtor in property" if five conditions are satisfied and unless one of seven exceptions defined in subsection (c) is applicable. In brief, the five characteristics of a voidable preference are that it (1) benefit a creditor; (2) be on account of antecedent debt; (3) be made while the debtor was insolvent; (4) be within 90 days before bankruptcy; and (5) enable the creditor to receive a larger share of the estate than if the transfer had not been made. Section 547 also provides that the debtor is presumed to have been insolvent during the 90-day period preceding bankruptcy. In this case, it is undisputed that all five of the foregoing conditions were satisfied and that the interest and loan commitment fee payments were voidable preferences unless excepted by subsection (c)(2).

Instead of focusing on the term of the debt for which the transfer was made, subsection (c)(2) focuses on whether the debt was incurred, and payment made, in the "ordinary course of business or financial affairs" of the debtor and transferee. Thus, the text provides no support for respondent's contention that §547(c)(2)'s coverage is limited to short-term debt, such as commercial paper or trade debt. Given the clarity of the statutory text, respondent's burden of persuading us that Congress intended to create or to preserve a special rule for long-term debt is exceptionally heavy. As did the Ninth Circuit, respondent relies on the history and the policies underlying the preference provision.

II

The relevant history of §547 contains two chapters, one of which clearly supports, and the second of which is not inconsistent with, the Bank's literal reading of the statute. Section 547 was enacted in 1978 when Congress overhauled the Nation's bankruptcy laws. The section was amended in 1984. For purposes of the question presented in this case, the original version of §547 differed in one significant respect from the current version: it contained a provision that the ordinary course of business exception did not apply unless the payment was made within 45 days of the date the debt was incurred. That provision presumably excluded most payments on long-term debt from the exception. In 1984 Congress repealed the 45-day limitation but did not substitute a comparable limitation.

Respondent contends that this amendment was intended to satisfy complaints by issuers of commercial paper and by trade creditors that regularly extended credit for periods of more than 45 days. Furthermore, respondent continues, there is no evidence in the legislative history that Congress intended to make the ordinary course of business exception available to conventional long-term lenders. Therefore, respondent argues, we should follow the analysis of the Ninth Circuit and read §547(c)(2) as protecting only short-term debt payments.

We need not dispute the accuracy of respondent's description of the legislative history of the 1984 amendment in order to reject his conclusion. For even if Congress adopted the 1984 amendment to redress particular problems of specific short-term creditors, it remains true that Congress redressed those problems by entirely deleting the time limitation in §547(c)(2). The fact that Congress may not have foreseen all of the consequences of a statutory enactment is not a sufficient reason for refusing to give effect to its plain meaning.

Respondent also relies on the history of voidable preferences prior to the enactment of the 1978 Bankruptcy Code. [T]he earlier Bankruptcy Act did not specifically include an exception for payments made in the ordinary course of business. The courts had, however, developed what is sometimes described as the "current-expense" rule to cover situations in which a debtor's payments on the eve of bankruptcy did not diminish the net estate because tangible assets were obtained in exchange for the payment. Without such an exception, trade creditors and other suppliers of necessary goods and services might have been reluctant to extend even short-term credit and might have required advance payment instead, thus making it difficult for many companies in temporary distress to have remained in business. Respondent argues that Congress enacted §547(c)(2) in 1978 to codify that exception, and therefore the Court should construe §547(c)(2) as limited to the confines of the current-expense rule.

This argument is not compelling for several reasons. First, it is by no means clear that §547(c)(2) should be construed as the statutory analogue of the judicially crafted current-expense rule because there are other exceptions in §547(c) that explicitly cover contemporaneous exchanges for new value. Those provisions occupy some (if not all) of the territory previously covered by the current-expense rule. Nor has respondent directed our attention to any extrinsic evidence suggesting that Congress intended to codify the current-expense rule in §547(c)(2).

The current-expense rule developed when the statutory preference provision was significantly narrower than it is today. To establish a preference under the Bankruptcy Act, the trustee had to prove that the challenged payment was made at a time when the creditor had "reasonable cause to believe that the debtor [was] insolvent." 1898 Act §96(b). When Congress rewrote the preference provision in the 1978 Bankruptcy Code, it substantially enlarged the trustee's power to avoid preferential transfers by eliminating the reasonable-cause-to-believe requirement for transfers made within 90 days of bankruptcy and creating a presumption of insolvency during that period. At the same time, Congress created a new exception for transfers made in the ordinary course of business, §547(c)(2). This exception was "intended to leave undisturbed normal financial relations, because it does not detract from the general policy of the preference section to dis-courage unusual action by either the debtor or his creditors during the debtor's slide into bankruptcy."

In light of these substantial changes in the preference provision, there is no reason to assume that the justification for narrowly confining the "current-expense" exception to trade creditors before 1978 should apply to the ordinary course of business exception under the 1978 Code. Instead, the fact that Congress carefully reexamined and entirely rewrote the preference provision in 1978 supports the conclusion that the text of §547(c)(2) as enacted reflects the deliberate choice of Congress.

III

The Bank and the trustee agree that §547 is intended to serve two basic policies that are fairly described in the House Committee Report. The Committee explained:

> A preference is a transfer that enables a creditor to receive payment of a greater percentage of his claim against the debtor than he would have received if the transfer had not been made and he had participated in the distribution of the assets of the bankrupt estate. The purpose of the preference section is two-fold. First, by permitting the trustee to avoid prebankruptcy transfers that occur within a short period before bankruptcy, creditors are discouraged from racing to the courthouse to dismember the debtor during his slide into bankruptcy. The protection thus afforded the debtor often enables him to work his way out of a difficult financial situation through cooperation with all of his creditors. Second, and more important, the preference provisions facilitate the prime bankruptcy policy of equality of distribution among creditors of the debtor. Any creditor that received a greater payment than others of his class is required to disgorge so that all may share equally. The operation of the preference section to deter "the race of diligence" of creditors to dismember the debtor before bankruptcy furthers the second goal of the preference section—that of equality of distribution.

[H.R. Rep. No. 95-595, pp. 177-178 (1977)]. As this comment demonstrates, the two policies are not entirely independent. On the one hand, any exception for a payment on account of an antecedent debt tends to favor the payee over other creditors and therefore may conflict with the policy of equal treatment. On the other hand, the ordinary course of business exception may benefit all creditors by deterring the "race to the courthouse" and enabling the struggling debtor to continue operating its business.

Respondent places primary emphasis, as did the Court of Appeals, on the interest in equal distribution. When a debtor is insolvent, a transfer to one creditor necessarily impairs the claims of the debtor's other unsecured and undersecured creditors. By authorizing the avoidance of such preferential transfers, §547(b) empowers the trustee to restore equal status to all creditors. Respondent thus contends that the ordinary course of business exception should be limited to short-term debt so the trustee may order that preferential long-term debt payments be returned to the estate to be distributed among all of the creditors.

But the statutory text—which makes no distinction between short-term debt and long-term debt—precludes an analysis that divorces the policy of favoring equal distribution from the policy of discouraging creditors from racing to the courthouse to dismember the debtor. Long-term creditors, as well as trade creditors, may seek a head start in that race. Thus, even if we accept the Court of Appeals' conclusion that the availability of the ordinary-business exception to long-term creditors does not directly further the policy of equal treatment, we must recognize that it does further the policy of deterring the race to the courthouse and, as the House Report recognized, may indirectly further the goal of equal distribution as well. Whether Congress has wisely balanced the sometimes conflicting policies underlying §547 is not a question that we are authorized to decide.

IV

In sum, we hold that payments on long-term debt, as well as payments on short-term debt, may qualify for the ordinary course of business exception to the trustee's power to avoid preferential transfers. We express no opinion, however, on the question whether the Bankruptcy Court correctly concluded that the Debtor's payments of interest and the loan commitment fee qualify for the ordinary course of business exception, §547(c)(2). In particular, we do not decide whether the loan involved in this case was incurred in the ordinary course of the Debtor's business and of the Bank's business, whether the payments were made in the ordinary course of business, or whether the payments were made according to ordinary business terms. These questions remain open for the Court of Appeals on remand.

The judgment of the Court of Appeals is reversed and the case is remanded for further proceedings consistent with this opinion.

JUSTICE SCALIA CONCURRING.

I join the opinion of the Court, including Parts II and III, which respond persuasively to legislative-history and policy arguments made by respondent. It is regrettable that we have a legal culture in which such arguments have to be addressed (and are indeed credited by a Court of Appeals), with respect to a statute utterly devoid of language that could remotely be thought to distinguish between long-term and short-term debt. Since there was here no contention of a "scrivener's error" producing an absurd result, the plain text of the statute should have made this litigation unnecessary and unmaintainable.

NOTES

8D.7. Wolas tells us that we cannot exclude a loan from the reach of §547(c)(2) simply because it is long term. Nevertheless, one can argue that when a firm such as the debtor typically incurs such a loan only once in its life, the loan is not incurred in ordinary course. As you will see in chapter 9, section D below, no one would doubt, for example, that a large operating loan would not be "in the ordinary course of business" within the meaning of §364(a) if the trustee were to obtain such a loan without court approval after the filing of a bankruptcy petition. Under one view, then, to discover whether a loan was incurred in "ordinary course" within the meaning of §547(c)(2) as well as of §364, one must ask not whether it is long or short term but whether obtaining such a loan is an everyday event for this debtor. One could also take exactly the opposite position, however, and argue that "ordinary course" in the context of §547 (as opposed to §364) requires us to focus merely on whether there was anything suspect about the loan or circumstances surrounding it, not on whether taking such a loan was something the debtor typically did. Problem 8D-5 asks you to consider how a loan might be suspect.

8D.8. Ambiguity also exists with respect to what payments are made in the ordinary course. The trustee can argue that even though payments made to the debtor's largest creditor were made like clockwork, they nevertheless cannot be considered ordinary course if the debtor had ceased to pay others. The decision to make timely payments to a firm's largest and most important creditor may cease to be ordinary if an implicit decision is made at the same time not to pay others. A payment made after a decision to prefer one creditor over another cannot be "ordinary." Such an argument would, of course, be more compelling if the debtor's president had guaranteed the loan.

8D.9. The 2005 Bankruptcy Act, which postdates *Wolas*, of course, changed the portion of §547(c)(2) that refers to the nature of the repayment (as opposed to the nature of the loan). Under the revised provision a repayment satisfies the requirement for exception if it is either made in the ordinary course of the debtor and creditor or made according to ordinary business terms; previously the repayment needed to be ordinary in both senses.

PROBLEM

8D-5. Debtor Corporation is insolvent and in danger that it will miss its next payroll, two weeks away. Debtor's president approaches a loan officer of Bank, which has lent to Debtor in the past. The president explains that Debtor is in desperate need of a loan so that it can meet payroll for the next year while Debtor pursues some aggressive strategies in an attempt to reverse its fortunes. Bank's loan officer rushes through the application and approves the loan. A year later, without prompting from Bank, Debtor repays the loan precisely according to the loan's terms, which are common. Two months later, Debtor files a bankruptcy petition, never having regained solvency. *Wolas* notwithstanding, the trustee likely can avoid the repayment to Bank. Can one argue that avoidance of this transfer reflects sound policy even though Bank did not attempt to improve its position during the preference period? Compare Problems 8D-3, 8D-4, and 13B. Compare Alan Schwartz, A Normative Theory of Business Bankruptcy, 91 Va. L. Rev. 1199 (2005).

E. SETOFFS

A debtor's assets may include an obligation owed to the debtor by one of the debtor's creditors. For example, a debtor might borrow money from a bank with which the debtor keeps a deposit account. The debtor's obligation on her loan is a debt she owes the bank. The funds in the debtor's deposit account represents an obligation owed by the bank to the debtor. By contract or operation of common or statutory law, the bank may have a right to cancel its obligation on the deposit account—i.e., remove the funds—to satisfy the debtor's loan obligation when that obligation comes due. This right is referred to as a right of setoff.

The Bankruptcy Code might simply have treated the right of setoff as a creditor's security interest in the creditor's own obligation to the debtor, the deposit account, for example. And the Code might simply have treated the exercise of a setoff right as a transfer in satisfaction of the debtor's obligation. No special rules for setoffs would have been required. This is not the course Congress chose, however. The setoff right is a security interest. See §506(a), discussed in chapter 5, section C above. And exercise of that right is a transfer. See §101(54). But there are special rules as well. Section 553 describes setoff rights that are to be honored (though not freely exercised) in bankruptcy, see chapter 4, section A above, and then lays out a scheme for disallowance and avoidance that tracks the preference rules discussed earlier in this section.

Section 553(a) provides, in general, that the Code "does not affect any right of a creditor to offset a mutual debt owing by such creditor to the debtor that arose before the commencement of [a bankruptcy case] against a claim of such creditor against the debtor that arose before the commencement of the case." There are then exceptions, including an exception to the extent that

(2) such claim was transferred, by an entity other than the debtor, to such creditor—

 (A) after the commencement of the case; or

 (B) (i) after 90 days before the date of the filing of the petition; and

  (ii) while the debtor was insolvent.

This provision is designed to prevent the prebankruptcy acquisition of an unsecured claim by a creditor at a discount and its transformation into an effectively secured claim. Imagine, for example, that a retailer owes a large sum to its insolvent supplier. If the retailer has a right of setoff against the supplier, the retailer might engage in arbitrage. To accomplish this, the retailer could contact other customers of the supplier and identify those to whom the supplier is obligated. Assume, for instance, that the retailer finds that the supplier owes one of its customers $10,000 as compensation for a defective shipment. The customer, however, expects to receive only ten cents on the dollar for its claim. The retailer could offer the customer, say, $5,000 for an assignment of this debt. Because the customer believes that it cannot get that much from the supplier directly, the customer might accept. If the retailer could then offset the entire $10,000 against the amount the retailer would otherwise have paid the supplier, the insolvent supplier would have indirectly paid its obligation to the customer in full, the proceeds divided between the customer and the retailer. If this transaction takes place within ninety days be-fore the supplier's bankruptcy, while the debtor is insolvent (which is presumed, see §553(c)), the retailer will lose its right in bankruptcy to set off against the $10,000 purchased claim. The retailer's attempt to augment its security interest just before bankruptcy would thus be thwarted. Compare Note 8D.3.

Section 553(a) also addresses a creditor's prebankruptcy attempt to improve its setoff position through transactions directly with the debtor. There is an exception to the setoff right to the extent that

(3) the debt owed to the debtor by such creditor was incurred by such creditor—

(A) after 90 days before the date of the filing of the petition;

(B) while the debtor was insolvent; and

(C) for the purpose of obtaining a right of setoff against the debtor.

Thus, a creditor may not pad its setoff right (in essence a security in-terest) against an insolvent debtor just before the debtor enters bank-ruptcy by nominally borrowing from a debtor rather than accepting a payment that would be voidable as a preference. A bank, for example, cannot protect its unsecured loan by persuading its debtor to make large deposits in its account instead of repaying the loan or giving it security.

While §553(a) addresses prebankruptcy accumulation of setoff rights, §553(b) deals with prebankruptcy exercise of those rights:

(b)(1) Except with respect to a setoff of a kind described in section 362(b)(6), 362(b)(7), 362(b)(14), 365(h), 546(h), or 365(i)(2) of this title, if a creditor offsets a mutual debt owing to the debtor against a claim against the debtor on or within 90 days before the date of the filing of the petition, then the trustee may recover from such creditor the amount so offset to the extent that any insuffi-ciency on the date of such setoff is less than the insufficiency on the later of—

(A) 90 days before the date of the filing of the petition; and

(B) the first date during the 90 days immediately preceding the date of the filing of the petition on which there is an insufficiency.

(2) In this subsection, "insufficiency" means amount, if any, by which a claim against the debtor exceeds a mutual debt owing to the debtor by the holder of such claim.

In general, this subsection resembles the two-point net improvement test of §547(c)(5), though the test is here applied to the satisfaction of an obligation rather than the acquisition of security for an obligation. On the first date within the ninety days prior to a debtor's bankruptcy that a creditor with a setoff right suffers an insufficiency, that insufficiency is measured and becomes a benchmark. Subject to limited exceptions stated in subsection (b)(1), the benchmark insufficiency cannot be reduced by exercise of a setoff right. That is, in most cases, the trustee can avoid and, under §550, recover any exercise to the extent a setoff accomplishes a reduction. (The exceptions are special interest exemptions, such as for the setoff of obligations in the securities trading industry.)

The exercises below ask you to work through some of the §553 mechanics. The case, *Braniff Airways*, illustrates an interaction between preference and setoff rules and addresses the §553(a) mutuality requirement for a setoff right under bankruptcy law. A note after the case asks you more broadly to consider the preference-setoff interaction and whether *Braniff*'s analysis has implications beyond its holding. Specifically, the note suggests that *Braniff* supports an expansion of §553(b) to disallow setoff rights that have *not* been exercised prior to bankruptcy. The remainder of the notes and a problem ask you to explore further the mutuality requirement for setoff and to compare this requirement with the requirement for recoupment, a conceptual sibling of setoff.

Key Provision: Bankruptcy Code §553

EXERCISES

8E(1) Factor is in the business of buying and selling debt obligations. Factor purchases from Supplier a $10,000 account receivable owed to Supplier by Retailer, who recently sold Factor $20,000 worth of office furniture on credit. Within a month, Retailer files for bankruptcy. Applicable state law would permit Factor to set off the account against its credit obligation. Is this right preserved in bankruptcy?

8E(2) Two months before Debtor files for bankruptcy, Debtor borrows $50,000 from Bank. A month later, Debtor opens an account with Bank and deposits $10,000. Does Bank's right to set off the account against its obligation survive bankruptcy?

8E(3) Ninety days before Debtor files for bankruptcy, Debtor owes Bank $100,000 on an unsecured business loan. At that time, Debtor's deposit account with Bank contains $120,000. The next day, Debtor withdraws $50,000 from the account. A week later, Debtor deposits another $10,000 in the account. Two weeks later, Bank exercises its setoff right against the entire contents of the account. A month after this, Bank lends Debtor another $100,000. Can the trustee recover from Bank any amount of the setoff? Would your answer change if Bank had set off all but $10,000 of the account? (For simplicity, ignore the accrual of interest.)

CASE

BRANIFF AIRWAYS INC. v. EXXON CO.

United States Court of Appeals, Fifth Circuit, 1987
814 F.2d 1030

HILL, CIRCUIT JUDGE.

In this bankruptcy appeal, Exxon Company, U.S.A., argues that the district court erred in concluding that Exxon could not setoff prepetition claims owed to it by debtor Braniff Airways, Inc., against prepetition debts that it owed to Braniff. We find that Exxon does have a right of setoff pursuant to §553(a), but that any setoff is potentially subject to being recovered by Braniff pursuant to §553(b). Since the record is not sufficient to allow us to decide whether a §553(b) recovery by Braniff is appropriate, we reverse and remand this case for further proceedings as outlined herein.

I

The facts in this case are undisputed and have been stipulated to by both parties. Prior to Braniff's filing its petition on May 13, 1983, for relief under Chapter 11 of the Bankruptcy Code, Exxon and Braniff were parties to a contract for the sale of jet turbo fuel. Pursuant to the contract, Braniff made a prepayment by wire transfer each week based on its estimated fuel needs for the following week. On May 11 Braniff made one of these weekly prepayments in the amount of $530,000 for estimated fuel purchases for the week beginning May 12. By May 13 when Braniff filed its bankruptcy petition, it had used $96,252 in fuel. The unused prepayment of $434,972 was owed to Braniff.

As of the date of the bankruptcy petition, Exxon also had prepetition claims against Braniff in the amount of $1,824. An agreed turnover order pursuant to §542(b) was subsequently entered in the bankruptcy court authorizing Exxon to setoff mutual prepetition claims and debts in the amount of $1,824 under §553. The remaining $433,148 of the prepayment was ordered remitted to Braniff.

Prior to the filing of Braniff's bankruptcy petition, Braniff and Exxon also had a contract for the sale of turbo oil, lubricating oil, gasoline, and other miscellaneous products that were sold on open account. During the ninety-day period prior to bankruptcy, Braniff had made payments totaling $145,745 to cover purchases it made pursuant to this account.

Braniff commenced this action by filing suit in the district court seeking to recover as voidable preferences the payments it made to Exxon on the open account during the ninety days prior to its filing for bankruptcy protection. Braniff stipulated that $80,753 of the $145,745 in open account payments fall within the exception in §547(c)(2) and are not recoverable as voidable preferences. The dispute regarding these payments revolves around the remaining $64,992.

As a result of a stipulation by the parties as to the facts, the only issue to be decided by the district court was whether Braniff's open account payments to Exxon allowed Exxon to receive more than it would have if the payments had not been made and Braniff were liquidated under Chapter 7. The resolution of that question depended on whether Exxon was secured by a right of setoff of its claim against Braniff in the amount of $64,992 against the debt that it owed to Braniff in the amount of $433,148.

The district court ruled in Braniff's favor. The court found that Exxon did not have a right of setoff under §553 because the debt owed by Exxon to Braniff was created by a judgment of the bankruptcy court, which occurred after the bankruptcy petition was filed. Thus, because the debt arose postpetition, the court held that the debts were not mutual, prepetition debts, and the requirements of §553 prior to a setoff being allowed were not met.

Exxon now appeals, contending that the debts were mutual and prepetition and therefore it was entitled to setoff the amount owed by Braniff against the amount owed to Braniff. This right of setoff, Exxon claims, has the status of a secured claim and thus the payments made by Braniff to it on the open account were not preferential because, ~~being secured~~, it did not receive more than it would have in a Chapter 7 liquidation.

II

Section 547(b) allows a trustee to recover as a preferential payment certain transfers made by a debtor to a creditor within the ninety-day period prior to bankruptcy. This section provides the elements of a preference. ... The first four elements are not in dispute; Exxon has stipulated to the applicability of each one. The controversy revolves around the fifth element. This is the requirement that before a trustee in bankruptcy can avoid a preferential payment, the trustee must establish that the payment enabled the creditor to receive more than the creditor would have received upon liquidation under Chapter 7 of the Bankruptcy Code. It must be determined, then, whether Exxon, in receiving the prepetition open account payments from Braniff, received more than it would have if the payments had not been made and Braniff were liquidated.

[handwritten margin notes: §547(b) Voidable preference; "what level of generality?"; "but Braniff was not liquidated so court has to run Ch. 7 counterfactual"]

To compare what the creditor would have received in a Chapter 7 liquidation with what it received prepetition, it is necessary to consider how the debt would have been treated in a Chapter 7 liquidation. ... That is, if the debtor had not made the payment to the creditor, and the debtor were liquidated, it must be determined what amount the creditor would receive.

Exxon argues that it was secured by a right of setoff, so that if there were a Chapter 7 liquidation it would have been able to setoff its claim to the open account payments made by Braniff against its debt to Braniff growing out of Braniff's jet fuel prepayments. Exxon contends that this amount that it would be entitled to in a liquidation would be the same amount that it received as prepetition payments from Braniff because of this setoff right, and therefore the payments did not enable it to receive more than it would have in a liquidation.

The issue therefore becomes whether Exxon had a right of setoff, because if such a right exists Exxon would be secured and would therefore have a permissible preference to the degree of the allowable setoff. ... This conclusion is based on §506(a), which provides that a claim subject to setoff under §553 is secured to the extent of the amount subject to setoff. ...Thus, since §553 bestows secured status upon a creditor for the amount of the setoff, and payments to a secured creditor are not preferential, §547 cannot be used to avoid the amount of the setoff. * * *

[handwritten margin notes: "set off right = security interest (permissible preference)"]

Exxon argues that it is entitled to setoff because it had a prepetition debt to Braniff in the amount of $434,972 and a prepetition claim of $1,824, which were setoff, and that if Braniff had not paid the $64,992, Exxon would merely have had a larger claim to setoff. Thus, if the open account payments had not been made, Exxon asserts that it would have merely remitted a lesser amount back to the bankrupt estate. For the reasons set forth below, we agree with Exxon that it had a right of setoff. * * *

A

The first question is whether Exxon's debt to Braniff is prepetition. Braniff argues that Exxon's debt was postpetition because it was a debt created by the judgment of the bankruptcy court. Exxon responds that the debt was created at the time of the prepayment from Braniff to it for the purchase of jet fuel, which occurred prior to bankruptcy. Thus, it must be determined when the debt arose.

A "debt" is defined as "a liability on a claim." [§101(12)]. A "claim" is defined as a "right to payment, whether or not such right is reduced to judgment, liquidated, unliquidated, fixed, contingent, natural, unnatural, disputed, undisputed, legal, equitable, secured, or unsecured. ... " [§101(5)] Exxon asserts that its debt fits within these definitions because when the prepayment was made Braniff became entitled to either jet fuel or to a refund, and Exxon thus incurred the liability when it received the money. While the actual amount was not fixed, it argues the debt was absolutely owed. * * *

[The] debt owed the debtor does not have to be calculated prior to the filing of the bankruptcy petition in order for setoff to be available to a creditor. In this case, prepetition, Exxon clearly owed Braniff either fuel or a refund of the fuel prepayments. The debt was absolutely owed; it just was not due until a calculation of the amount of fuel that was used was made. To say that Exxon did not have a prepetition debt to Braniff would be to say that Exxon could have retained the fuel prepayment funds and not have delivered any fuel to Braniff. Braniff could have certainly brought an action against Exxon in such a case, alleging that Exxon owed it either money or fuel. Thus, as in [In re Delta Energy Resources, Inc., 67 Bankr. 8 (Bankr. W.D. La. 1986)], "all the transactions which gave rise to this debt occurred prior to the petition date. The genesis of the debt is clearly prepetition and although the refund order was entered later," Exxon owed Braniff before the petition was filed. We hold, therefore, that Exxon's debt to Braniff was prepetition.

B

Braniff also argues that the mutuality requirement is not present and thus setoff should not be permitted. We disagree. "[I]t is essential to the establishment of a setoff that the claims or debts be mutual. ... " In re Braniff Airways, Inc., 42 Bankr. 443, 449 (Bankr. N.D. Tex. 1984). For mutuality to exist, "each party must own his claim in his own right severally, with the right to collect in his own name against the debtor in his own right and severally." In re DePrizio Construction Co., 52 Bankr. 283, 287 (Bankr. N.D. Ill. 1985). The mutuality element is lacking if a party attempts to setoff a prepetition debt against a postpetition claim. See *Braniff*, 42 Bankr. at 449 ("As a general rule, neither a creditor nor a debtor may offset prepetition debts and claims against postpetition debts and claims because of the absence of mutuality of the parties.").

Based upon our conclusion that Exxon's debt owed to Braniff was prepetition, and the uncontested fact that Braniff's debt to Exxon was also prepetition, this mutuality requirement has been met. * * *

Braniff also argues that mutuality is lacking because Exxon held the money as either a trustee or bailee for the benefit of Braniff. Because of this status of Exxon, Braniff asserts that it and Exxon are not standing in the same capacity, and there is no mutuality. * * *

* * * Braniff, however, never states how a bailment arose; instead Braniff merely states that Exxon never treated the funds as its own, and that Braniff owned them. There is no contention that an express bailment agreement existed. Nor do we believe that there exists a bailment relationship by implication. The elements of a bailment are delivery of personal property by one person to another in trust for a specific purpose and acceptance of such delivery, and an express or implied contract that the trust will be carried out and the property returned to the bailor or dealt with as he directs. ... These elements are not met in this case. First, assuming the funds qualify as property that can be subject to a bailment, the money in this case was not given in trust. It was given as payment for fuel. Moreover, once the "specific purpose" was carried out, the funds became Exxon's property. The property was not returned to Braniff nor did Braniff have any right to direct how Exxon should deal with the money. There is no bailment relationship.

For the foregoing reasons we hold that the debt owed by Exxon to Braniff and the claim possessed by Exxon against Braniff are mutual obligations.

C

Braniff next attempts to add an additional requirement to the elements of §553. Braniff's argument in support of the district court's decision denying Exxon the right to setoff is that "Exxon received more money than it would have had the preferential payments not been made because Exxon did not possess 'secured status' by virtue of the right of a setoff at the time the preferential transfers were made." Thus, Braniff is arguing that to determine whether a creditor has the right to setoff claims, the court must examine the status of the parties at the time the preferential payment was made. And, since at the time the open account payments were made Braniff had not yet transferred the payment for fuel, Exxon did not owe Braniff anything and did not have a right to offset. Since that right did not exist, argues Braniff, Exxon was not secured by §553 and the preferential payment can be avoided under §547(b).

We disagree with this analysis. Nowhere in §553 do we find such a requirement. Rather, §553 requires only that the debts arise "before the commencement of the case." * * *

* * * We therefore decline to adopt Braniff's view that the order [in which] the debts arise does matter, and following the plain language of §553, and the numerous cases applying it, hold that the only timing requirement relevant to deciding if setoff is allowed is that the debts arise prepetition.

In conclusion, we find that the debts were mutual prepetition debts and Exxon was secured by this right to setoff. * * *

III

Braniff argues, however, that if Exxon is allowed to setoff its claim against its debt, Exxon will have improved its position in violation of §553(b)(1) and thus the setoff should not be allowed. Based on the record before us, there is some indication that this argument may have merit, but because there is an insufficient factual development, we must remand the case for further fact finding. * * *

* * * If §553(b) is applicable, prepetition setoffs within the 90-day period before filing that improve the creditor's position can be recovered by the trustee. * * *

The application of this statute is strictly mathematical, and the test is whether the insufficiency on the date of the setoff is less than the insufficiency 90 days before the date of the filing of the petition. * * *

The key factor, then, is the term "insufficiency." This term is defined as the "amount, if any, by which a claim against the debtor exceeds a mutual debt owing to the debtor by the holder of such a claim." §553(b)(2). Thus, we must determine (a) the amount of any insufficiency on the date of the setoff and (b) the insufficiency 90 days prior to the date of the filing of the petition, or the first date during the 90 days when an insufficiency existed.

At the time the setoff would have occurred,[11] Exxon's claim against Braniff was $64,992, and the debt owing to Braniff was $433,148. Exxon's claim against Braniff did not exceed the debt Exxon owed to Braniff. Thus, the insufficiency at the time of setoff was zero.

The second inquiry involved in determining the extent of the recovery permitted by the trustee under §553(b) cannot be made based on the factual development in the record before us. At the time of Braniff's payment to Exxon, it is not clear whether Exxon was indebted to Braniff. Other than the stipulated facts, there has been no development of the financial relationship existing between the parties. Therefore, we cannot resolve this issue, and must remand the case to the district court for such proceedings.[13] Upon doing so, the court can then rule on whether Exxon has improved its position in violation of §553(b) in light of its right to setoff the prepetition claim in the amount of $64,992 owed to it by Braniff against prepetition debt in the amount of $434,972 it owed to Braniff.

---

[11] The fact that a setoff never actually took place does not affect the analysis. The issue is whether Exxon hypothetically had the right to a setoff, and because of this right it was secured and therefore the payment received from Braniff was not a voidable preference.

[13] Exxon argues that §553(b) is inapplicable because the setoff occurred postpetition. If Exxon had a postpetition setoff, it appears that §553(b) would be inapplicable. . . . Exxon is arguing is that by reason of §553(a) it was fully secured at all times during the 90-day period prior to bankruptcy. But Exxon is also arguing that for purposes of §553(b) the setoff should be calculated postpetition. Such an analysis would allow Exxon to avoid the improvement in position test. Exxon wants it both ways; we decline to let Exxon have it both ways. If Exxon wants to rely on a prepetition right to setoff pursuant to §553, it must comply with both §§553(a) and 553(b). * * *

IV

For the foregoing reasons, we reverse the district court's decision that Exxon was not entitled to a setoff, and remand for further proceedings consistent with this opinion.

NOTES

8E.1. Exxon argues in *Braniff* that at the time of the challenged transfer it possessed a setoff right that secured its claim. One might imagine that the trustee could challenge this position under §553(a), which disallows the acquisition of setoff rights in some circumstances. But part 3 of the court's opinion addresses a challenge based on §553(b), which disallows in some circumstances the *exercise* of a setoff right. Exxon did not execute a setoff before Braniff's bankruptcy. There was no need, as Braniff paid its debt. Exxon argues the irrelevance of any obligation it *might* otherwise have had to pay *had it* offset funds before Braniff's bankruptcy. Exxon's position seems compelling. In response to a turnover order, Exxon paid Braniff all it owed. (Turnover orders are described below in chapter 9, section A.) It seems that the trustee came back for the money a second time.

The trustee's position, adopted by the court, must rest on an expansion of §553(b) to disallow setoff rights regardless of whether those rights are exercised before the debtor's bankruptcy. Assume, for example, that between ninety days before Braniff's bankruptcy and the date of the challenged transfer, Exxon's insufficiency declined by at least the amount of that transfer. Now assume that such decline, *without more*, invalidates Exxon's setoff right. The trustee would then win a complete victory, as Exxon could neither use setoff to resist the turnover order of all funds owed nor claim that the transfer was on account of secured debt and thus outside the scope of §547(b). This result may be defensible as a matter of policy, but it is an aggressive reading of the Bankruptcy Code.

8E.2. The *Braniff* court was on more solid statutory ground when it noted that a setoff right is limited to "mutual" obligations. This limitation comes from §553(a), which protects a right to "offset a mutual debt" that is, like the claim to be offset, incurred prepetition. Mutuality generally requires that each party stand in the same capacity with respect to each obligation as the other party stands with respect to the other. So, for example, under bankruptcy law, a jeweler bailee of a customer's watch cannot offset her obligation to return the watch against a simple contract debt owed by the customer to the jeweler. Mutuality is lacking because the jeweler is a bailee of the customer's watch and a simple creditor, while the customer is a bailor of the watch and a simple debtor. It is unclear why bankruptcy law should not honor a setoff right here if one existed under applicable nonbankruptcy law. But little turns on this quandary, as in most circumstances such as this, state law would not provide a setoff right, either. The parties might contract explicitly for a right to set off obligations that lacked mutuality. Whatever the label, however, such a contractual right would be treated under state and bankruptcy law as an ordinary security interest. For instance, the jeweler would have a security interest in the customer's watch.

8E.3. Sometimes apparently offsetting obligations arise out of the same transaction. One might ask whether, or assume that, these obligations are mutual debts. But an altogether different approach may be appropriate. For example, a good sold on credit might be defective in breach of the seller's warranty. Uniform Commercial Code §2-717 permits the purchaser to notify the seller and then deduct her damages from the purchase price. This deduction might be characterized as a setoff, but might alternatively be thought of as an adjustment to a single obligation—the buyer's obligation to pay for the goods. Courts that adopt the latter characterization refer to the adjustment as a "recoupment," which is not subject to the limitations in preference or setoff law. Consider the problem that follows.

PROBLEM

8E. State prepays $1 million for Hospital's medical services. Hospital is deeply insolvent and files for bankruptcy before it earns any of this fee. Hospital continues to operate during bankruptcy and provides State with $1 million worth of services. The trustee sends State a bill for $1 million. Must State pay? Should it be forced to pay? See United States v. Consumer Health Services of America, Inc., 108 F.3d 390 (D.C. Cir. 1997); In re University Medical Center, 973 F.2d 1065 (3d Cir. 1992).

IX. MANAGING THE ESTATE

Bankruptcy proceedings take time. It may not be clear at the start who all the debtor's creditors are or what claims they have. Rarely will much of a debtor's assets be in the form of cash. Months may pass before a buyer for the assets is found. Even more time consuming may be efforts to reorganize the debtor corporation's capital structure and then compensate the creditors (and perhaps shareholders) with interests in the new firm according to their nonbankruptcy entitlements. As designed, bankruptcy law should ensure that the passage of time itself does not change the value of various creditors' rights relative to one another. At the same time, bankruptcy law should have as small an effect as possible on the debtor's relationships with the rest of the world. In this chapter, we explore the problems that arise as the law attempts to achieve these dual objectives in a world where things take time.

As we have seen, many of the most important issues in bankruptcy are connected with sorting out the rights of secured creditors. A secured creditor is entitled to have its priority respected, but unlike a third party that can deal with the debtor or not as it chooses, the secured creditor must participate in the bankruptcy process. As we shall see in the first part of this chapter, the obligation to participate is imposed even on the secured creditor who has repossessed, but not disposed of, its collateral before the petition is filed. The security interest is respected, but the asset itself must be returned to the trustee. The Bankruptcy Code protects secured creditors by requiring that their rights be "adequately protected." The next part of the chapter asks what amount of protection is "adequate."

A trustee (or debtor in possession) who retains or recaptures collateral typically does so because the assets are needed to continue the debtor's business. In the last two parts of this chapter, we address more broadly the challenges that arise when the trustee or debtor in possession must operate the business. Outside of bankruptcy, loan covenants limit the ability of managers to make major decisions that adversely affect the rights of creditors. These covenants often require that the debtor obtain creditor approval before selling capital assets or taking on another large loan. Inside of bankruptcy, the court monitors the debtor by requiring the trustee or debtor to obtain the bankruptcy judge's blessing for transactions that are outside the ordinary course of business, whether it is to buy or sell assets or to incur new debt.

A. TURNOVER OF PROPERTY

Bankruptcy Code §541 establishes an "estate," and §362 is designed to keep that estate together for purposes of the bankruptcy proceeding. As we discussed above in chapter 6, the bankruptcy estate consists of interests in property. To move from the notional to the practical, the trustee must be able to obtain possession of or control over the property itself. Section 542 generally requires the turnover of property that "the trustee may use, sell, or lease under §363 of [the Code], or that the debtor may exempt under §522." We shall discuss §363 at length later in this chapter, and we shall address exempt property in the context of the fresh start for individuals in part 3 below. For now suffice it to say that the trustee can gather property in which the debtor has an interest even if another, such as a secured creditor, also has an interest, and no matter to whom the bankruptcy process will ultimately award the property or its value.

Sometimes, prior to bankruptcy, a custodian takes possession or control of assets and collects the rents or proceeds of those assets for the benefit of others, including perhaps the debtor's creditors. Section 543, in essence, requires that the custodian relinquish its role to the bankruptcy trustee, who will take the property and protect the interests of others, including creditors, according to the rules of the bankruptcy process.

Ordinarily, the Bankruptcy Code's turnover provisions can be applied in a straightforward manner. The exercises below give examples of some relatively simple applications. But hard questions may arise about whether the debtor's interest in property exists at the time of bankruptcy or has been extinguished so that there is no property to which a turnover obligation can attach. The case below, *Whiting Pools*, as well as the related notes and problem address these questions.

Key Provisions: Bankruptcy Code §§542; 543

EXERCISES

9A(1) Debtor, an individual real estate dealer of questionable ethics, files for bankruptcy a few days before Customer's obligation to Debtor comes due. On the day Customer's obligation matures, Debtor demands payment. Should Customer pay Debtor? Does it matter whether Customer knows of Debtor's bankruptcy? In answering these questions consider, among other provisions, Bankruptcy Code §542(b), (c).

9A(2) After Debtor Corporation fails both economically and financially, its managers give up and transfer all of Debtor's assets to Custodian with instructions that Custodian pay creditors, to the extent possible, according to state law priority. About a month after the transfer, Custodian completes the sale of all assets and announces its repayment plan. Immediately thereafter, three of Debtor's general creditors, dissatisfied with the plan, file an involuntary petition against Debtor. Custodian receives notice of the bankruptcy, but wants to execute its repayment plan anyway. May Custodian do so?

CASE

UNITED STATES v. WHITING POOLS, INC.

United States Supreme Court, 1983
462 U.S. 198

JUSTICE BLACKMUN DELIVERED THE OPINION OF THE COURT.

Promptly after the Internal Revenue Service (IRS or Service) seized respondent's property to satisfy a tax lien, respondent filed a petition for reorganization under the Bankruptcy Reform Act of 1978, hereinafter referred to as the "Bankruptcy Code." The issue before us is whether §542(a) of that Code authorized the Bankruptcy Court to subject the IRS to a turnover order with respect to the seized property.

Respondent Whiting Pools, Inc., a corporation, sells, installs, and services swimming pools and related equipment and supplies. As of January 1981, Whiting owed approximately $92,000 in Federal Insurance Contribution Act taxes and federal taxes withheld from its employees, but had failed to respond to assessments and demands for payment by the IRS. As a consequence, a tax lien in that amount attached to all of Whiting's property.[1]

---

[1] Section 6321 of the Internal Revenue Code of 1954, 26 U.S.C. 6321, provides:

> If any person liable to pay any tax neglects or refuses to pay the same after demand, the amount . . . shall be a lien in favor of the United States upon all property and rights to property, whether real or personal, belonging to such person.

On January 14, 1981, the Service seized Whiting's tangible personal property—equipment, vehicles, inventory, and office supplies—pursuant to the levy and distraint provision of the Internal Revenue Code of 1954.[2] According to uncontroverted findings, the estimated liquidation value of the property seized was, at most, $35,000, but its estimated going-concern value in Whiting's hands was $162,876. The very next day, January 15, Whiting filed a petition for reorganization, under the Bankruptcy Code's Chapter 11 in the United States Bankruptcy Court for the Western District of New York. Whiting was continued as debtor-in-possession.

The United States, intending to proceed with a tax sale of the property,[4] moved in the Bankruptcy Court for a declaration that the automatic stay provision of the Bankruptcy Code, §362(a), is inapplicable to the IRS or, in the alternative, for relief from the stay. Whiting counterclaimed for an order requiring the Service to turn the seized property over to the bankruptcy estate pursuant to §542(a) of the Bankruptcy Code. Whiting intended to use the property in its reorganized business.

The Bankruptcy Court determined that the IRS was bound by the automatic stay provision. Because it found that the seized property was essential to Whiting's reorganization effort, it refused to lift the stay. Acting under §543(b)(1), rather than under §542(a), the

---

[2] Section 6331 of that Code, 26 U.S.C. §6331, provides:

(a) Authority of Secretary

If any person liable to pay any tax neglects or refuses to pay the same within 10 days after notice and demand, it shall be lawful for the Secretary to collect such tax (and such further sum as shall be sufficient to cover the expenses of the levy) by levy upon all property and rights to property . . . belonging to such person or on which there is a lien provided in this chapter for the payment of such tax. . . .

(b) Seizure and sale of property

The term "levy" as used in this title includes the power of distraint and seizure by any means. . . . In any case in which the Secretary may levy upon property or rights to property, he may seize and sell such property or rights to property (whether real or personal, tangible or intangible).

[4] Section 6335 provides for the sale of seized property after notice. The taxpayer is entitled to any surplus of the proceeds of the sale. §6342(b).

court directed the IRS to turn the property over to Whiting on the condition that Whiting provide the Service with specified protection for its interests.[7]

The United States District Court reversed, holding that a turnover order against the Service was not authorized by either §542(a) or §543(b)(1). ... The United States Court of Appeals for the Second Circuit, in turn, reversed the District Court. It held that a turnover order could issue against the Service under §542(a), and it remanded the case for reconsideration of the adequacy of the Bankruptcy Court's protection conditions. The Court of Appeals acknowledged that its ruling was contrary to that reached by the United States Court of Appeals for the Fourth Circuit in Cross Electric Co. v. United States, 664 F.2d 1218 (4th Cir. 1981), and noted confusion on the issue among bankruptcy and district courts. We granted certiorari to resolve this conflict in an important area of the law under the new Bankruptcy Code. * * *

By virtue of its tax lien, the Service holds a secured interest in Whiting's property. We first examine whether §542(a) generally authorizes the turnover of a debtor's property seized by a secured creditor prior to the commencement of reorganization proceedings. Section 542(a) requires an entity in possession of "property that the trustee may use, sell, or lease under §363" to deliver that property to the trustee. Subsections (b) and (c) of §363 authorize the trustee to use, sell, or lease any "property of the estate," subject to certain conditions for the protection of creditors with an interest in the property. Section 541(a)(1) defines the "estate" as "comprised of all the following property, wherever located: (1) ... all legal or equitable interests of

---

[7] Section 363(e) of the Bankruptcy Code provides:

> Notwithstanding any other provision of this section, at any time, on request of an entity that has an interest in property used, sold, or leased, or proposed to be used, sold, or leased by the trustee, the court shall prohibit or condition such use, sale, or lease as is necessary to provide adequate protection of such interest. In any hearing under this section, the trustee has the burden of proof on the issue of adequate protection.

Pursuant to this section, the Bankruptcy Court set the following conditions to protect the tax lien: Whiting was to pay the Service $20,000 before the turnover occurred; Whiting also was to pay $1,000 a month until the taxes were satisfied; the IRS was to retain its lien during this period; and if Whiting failed to make the payments, the stay was to be lifted. [§363(e) was reworded slightly in 1984 and a portion of it was moved to §363(o).—Eds.]

the debtor in property as of the commencement of the case." Although these statutes could be read to limit the estate to those "interests of the debtor in property" at the time of the filing of the petition, we view them as a definition of what is included in the estate, rather than as a limitation.

In proceedings under the reorganization provisions of the Bankruptcy Code, a troubled enterprise may be restructured to enable it to operate successfully in the future. Until the business can be reorganized pursuant to a plan under §§1121-1129, the trustee or debtor-in-possession is authorized to manage the property of the estate and to continue the operation of the business. See §1108. By permitting reorganization, Congress anticipated that the business would continue to provide jobs, to satisfy creditors' claims, and to produce a return for its owners. Congress presumed that the assets of the debtor would be more valuable if used in a rehabilitated business than if "sold for scrap." The reorganization effort would have small chance of success, however, if property essential to running the business were excluded from the estate. ... Thus, to facilitate the rehabilitation of the debtor's business, all the debtor's property must be included in the reorganization estate.

This authorization extends even to property of the estate in which a creditor has a secured interest. §363(b) and (c); see H.R. Rep. No. 95-595, p. 182 (1977). Although Congress might have safeguarded the interests of secured creditors outright by excluding from the estate any property subject to a secured interest, it chose instead to include such property in the estate and to provide secured creditors with "adequate protection" for their interests. At the secured creditor's insistence, the bankruptcy court must place such limits or conditions on the trustee's power to sell, use, or lease property as are necessary to protect the creditor. The creditor with a secured interest in property included in the estate must look to this provision for protection, rather than to the nonbankruptcy remedy of possession.

Both the congressional goal of encouraging reorganizations and Congress' choice of methods to protect secured creditors suggest that Congress intended a broad range of property to be included in the estate.

The statutory language reflects this view of the scope of the estate. As noted above, §541(a) provides that the "estate is comprised of all the following property, wherever located ... all legal or equitable interests of the debtor in property as of the commencement of the case."[8] The House and Senate Reports on the Bankruptcy Code indicate that §541(a)(1)'s scope is broad. Most important, in the context of this case, §541(a)(1) is intended to include in the estate any property made available to the estate by other provisions of the Bankruptcy Code. ... Several of these provisions bring into the estate property in which the debtor did not have a possessory interest at the time the bankruptcy proceedings commenced.

§541(a)(1) includes property w/o possessory interest

Section 542(a) is such a provision. It requires an entity (other than a custodian) holding any property of the debtor that the trustee can use under §363 to turn that property over to the trustee. Given the broad scope of the reorganization estate, property of the debtor repossessed by a secured creditor falls within this rule, and therefore may be drawn into the estate. While there are explicit limitations on the reach of §542(a), none requires that the debtor hold a possessory interest in the property at the commencement of the reorganization proceedings.

As does all bankruptcy law, §542(a) modifies the procedural rights available to creditors to protect and satisfy their liens. ... In effect, §542(a) grants to the estate a possessory interest in certain property of the debtor that was not held by the debtor at the commencement of reorganization proceedings.[15] The Bankruptcy

---

[8] Section 541(a)(1) speaks in terms of the debtor's interests . . . in property," rather than property in which the debtor has an interest, but this choice of language was not meant to limit the expansive scope of the section. The legislative history indicates that Congress intended to exclude from the estate property of others in which the debtor had some minor interest such as a lien or bare legal title. See 124 Cong. Rec. 32399, 32417 (1978) (remarks of Rep. Edwards); id., at 33999, 34016-34017 (remarks of Sen. DeConcini); cf. §541(d) (property in which debtor holds legal but not equitable title, such as a mortgage in which debtor retained legal title to service or to supervise servicing of mortgage, becomes part of estate only to extent of legal title); 124 Cong. Rec. 33999 (1978) (remarks of Sen. DeConcini) (§541(d) "reiterates the general principle that where the debtor holds bare legal title without any equitable interest, . . . the estate acquires bare legal title without any equitable interest in the property"). Similar statements to the effect that §541(a)(1) does not expand the rights of the debtor in the hands of the estate were made in the context of describing the principle that the estate succeeds to no more or greater causes of action against third parties than those held by the debtor. See H.R. Rep. No. 95-595, pp. 367-368 (1977). These statements do not limit the ability of a trustee to regain possession of property in which the debtor had equitable as well as legal title.

[15] Indeed, if this were not the effect, §542(a) would be largely superfluous in light of §541(a)(1). Interests in the seized property that could have been exercised

Code provides secured creditors various rights, including the right to adequate protection, and these rights replace the protection afforded by possession.

This interpretation of §542(a) is supported by the section's legislative history. Although the legislative reports are silent on the precise issue before us, the House and Senate hearings from which §542(a) emerged provide guidance. Several witnesses at those hearings noted, without contradiction, the need for a provision authorizing the turnover of property of the debtor in the possession of secured creditors. Section 542(a) first appeared in the proposed legislation shortly after these hearings. ... The section remained unchanged through subsequent versions of the legislation.

Moreover, this interpretation of §542 in the reorganization context is consistent with judicial precedent predating the Bankruptcy Code. Under Chapter X, the bankruptcy court could order the turnover of collateral in the hands of a secured creditor. Reconstruction Finance Corp. v. Kaplan, 185 F.2d 791, 796 (1st Cir. 1950). ... Nothing in the legislative history evinces a congressional intent to depart from that practice. Any other interpretation of §542(a) would deprive the bankruptcy estate of the assets and property essential to its rehabilitation effort and thereby would frustrate the congressional purpose behind the reorganization provisions.

We conclude that the reorganization estate includes property of the debtor that has been seized by a creditor prior to the filing of a petition for reorganization.

We see no reason why a different result should obtain when the IRS is the creditor. The Service is bound by §542(a) to the same extent as any other secured creditor. The Bankruptcy Code expressly states that the term "entity," used in §542(a), includes a governmental unit. [§101(15)]. ... Moreover, Congress carefully considered the effect of the new Bankruptcy Code on tax collection, and decided to provide protection to tax collectors, such as the IRS, through grants of enhanced priorities for unsecured tax claims, [§507(a)(8)], and by the

---

by the debtor—in this case, the rights to notice and the surplus from a tax sale—are already part of the estate by virtue of §541(a)(1). No coercive power is needed for this inclusion. The fact that §542(a) grants the trustee greater rights than those held by the debtor prior to the filing of the petition is consistent with other provisions of the Bankruptcy Code that address the scope of the estate. See, e.g., §544 (trustee has rights of lien creditor); §545 (trustee has power to avoid statutory liens); §549 (trustee has power to avoid certain postpetition transactions).

nondischarge of tax liabilities, §523(a)(1). Tax collectors also enjoy the generally applicable right under §363(e) to adequate protection for property subject to their liens. Nothing in the Bankruptcy Code or its legislative history indicates that Congress intended a special exception for the tax collector in the form of an exclusion from the estate of property seized to satisfy a tax lien.

Of course, if a tax levy or seizure transfers to the IRS ownership of the property seized, §542(a) may not apply. The enforcement provisions of the Internal Revenue Code do grant to the Service powers to enforce its tax liens that are greater than those possessed by private secured creditors under state law. ... But those provisions do not transfer ownership of the property to the IRS.

The Service's interest in seized property is its lien on that property. The Internal Revenue Code's levy and seizure provisions, 26 U.S.C. §§6331 and 6332, are special procedural devices available to the IRS to protect and satisfy its liens ... and are analogous to the remedies available to private secured creditors. ... They are provisional remedies that do not determine the Service's rights to the seized property, but merely bring the property into the Service's legal custody. ... At no point does the Service's interest in the property exceed the value of the lien. ... The IRS is obligated to return to the debtor any surplus from a sale. 26 U.S.C. §6342(b). Ownership of the property is transferred only when the property is sold to a bona fide purchaser at a tax sale. ... In fact, the tax sale provision itself refers to the debtor as the owner of the property after the seizure but prior to the sale. Until such a sale takes place, the property remains the debtor's and thus is subject to the turnover requirement of §542(a).

When property seized prior to the filing of a petition is drawn into the Chapter 11 reorganization estate, the Service's tax lien is not dissolved; nor is its status as a secured creditor destroyed. The IRS, under §363(e), remains entitled to adequate protection for its interests, to other rights enjoyed by secured creditors, and to the specific privileges accorded tax collectors. Section 542(a) simply requires the Service to seek protection of its interest according to the congressionally established bankruptcy procedures, rather than by withholding the seized property from the debtor's efforts to reorganize.

The judgment of the Court of Appeals is affirmed.

It is so ordered.

NOTES

9A.1. The lessons of *Whiting Pools* apply generally to all secured creditors who have repossessed collateral before the filing of the petition but have not yet disposed of it. Special considerations arise, however, when the secured creditor is a governmental entity. Unless the governmental entity files a claim in the bankruptcy proceeding, the trustee will be unable to force it to turn over collateral because of sovereign immunity. Hoffman v. Connecticut Department of Income Maintenance, 492 U.S. 96 (1989). It remains possible, moreover, that a state entity will be able to resist turnover even if the entity files a claim. Recall our discussion of sovereign immunity and bankruptcy in chapter 2, section C.

9A.2. Section 542 requires the turnover of property "that the trustee may use, sell, or lease under §363." But as noted above, the definition of "property of the estate" in §541, which §363 uses, refers to "interests" in property, not the property itself. The debtor's only "interests" remaining in repossessed property are those of redemption and surplus. Justice Blackmun avoids this issue by stating that "[a]lthough these statutes could be read to limit the estate to those 'interests of the debtor in property' at the time of the filing of the petition, we view them as a definition of what is included in the estate, rather than as a limitation." But definitions function as limitations. Perhaps Justice Blackmun would have been on more solid ground had he noted that, in order for the trustee to protect even a partial interest in property, the trustee needs to obtain possession of or control over that property. Nothing in a turnover order eliminates the interests of others in property subject to that order. Problem 9A further explores the distinction, if any, between property of the estate and the property in which the debtor maintains an interest.

9A.3. The 2005 Bankruptcy Act adds §541(b)(8), which excludes from the estate tangible personal property in the possession of a licensed lender and pledged (or formally sold) to such lender on a nonrecourse basis, so long as the debtor has not exercised a right to redeem the property. The result in *Whiting Pools* would not change, however, as the creditor was the IRS, not a licensed lender.

PROBLEM

9A. Debtor pledges a bearer note as security for any obligation Debtor may owe Lender from time to time. (A bearer note is an obligation to pay the holder a fixed sum on a date certain.) Lender takes possession of the note, which matures in one year and entitles the holder to $100,000 at that time. Six months later, Debtor defaults on its obligation to Lender. At the time of the default, Debtor owes Lender $150,000. According to the terms of the agreement between Debtor and Lender, after a default, Lender may sell the note and apply the proceeds to Debtor's obligation. Lender notifies Debtor of its intent to sell the note. Before Lender can execute the sale, Debtor files for bankruptcy under Chapter 11. Is the note subject to a turnover order by the trustee? In answering this question consider, among other factors, the phrase "inconsequential value or benefit to the estate" as used in Bankruptcy Code §542(a). Consider this problem again after you have read the next section.

B.   ADEQUATE PROTECTION

Once in possession or control of property that makes up property of the estate, the trustee (or debtor in possession) is charged with maintaining that property for the benefit of the creditors. There are limitations on the trustee's or debtor's exercise of this charge. The first of the limitations that we shall address is the requirement that the trustee or debtor protect the interest of others in property. A secured creditor, for example, has an interest in collateral that the trustee may wish to retain for the benefit of the estate. In principle, the trustee retains collateral only when the collateral is worth more to the debtor as a continuing enterprise than to another who would purchase the collateral in a liquidation sale. Thus, the trustee should be able to compensate the secured creditor fully for the creditor's forgone opportunity to foreclose, and the debtor should still benefit from retention of the property.

Section 552(b) generally permits the postpetition attachment of a security interest in the proceeds, product, offspring, profits, and rents of or from collateral subject to an unavoided security interest. Yet maintenance of a security interest, whether in original collateral or its proceeds, is not by itself a guarantee that the secured creditor will realize the full value of its property interest. The creditor may fear that the trustee will dissipate the value of the creditor's security, even if the interest formally survives. The creditor can seek protection of its security interest by requesting that a court lift the automatic stay under §362(d), which provides:

On request of a party in interest and after notice and a hearing, the court shall grant relief from the stay provided under subsection (a) of this section, such as by terminating, annulling, modifying, or conditioning such stay—

(1) for cause, including the lack of adequate protection of an interest in property of such party in interest;

(2) with respect to a stay of an act against property under subsection (a) of this section, if—

   (A) the debtor does not have an equity in such property; and

   (B) such property is not necessary to an effective reorganization; or

(3) with respect to a stay of an act against single asset real estate under subsection (a), by a creditor whose claim is secured by an interest in such real estate, unless, not later than the date that is 90 days after the entry of the order for relief (or such later date as the court may determine for cause by order entered within that 90-day period) or 30 days after the court determines that the debtor is subject to this paragraph, whichever is later—

   (A) the debtor has filed a plan of reorganization that has a reasonable possibility of being confirmed within a reasonable time; or

   (B) the debtor has commenced monthly payments that—

      (i) may, in the debtor's sole discretion, notwithstanding section 363(c)(2), be made from rents or other income generated before, on, or after the date of the commencement of the case by or from the property to each creditor whose claim is secured by such real estate (other than a claim secured by a judgment lien or by an unmatured statutory lien); and

      (ii) are in an amount equal to interest at the then applicable nondefault contract rate of interest on the value of the creditor's interest in the real estate.

Look first at §362(d)(2). Suppose a debtor owes a bank $500,000 secured by a parcel of land worth no more than $300,000. Assume that the debtor files a petition for Chapter 7 bankruptcy or attempts to reorganize under Chapter 11 but does not intend to retain the parcel of land. In either case, there is no reason for the trustee to retain the parcel. When it is sold, the entire proceeds will go to the bank. The debtor has no equity in the property. Moreover, none of the debtor's other assets will become less valuable by virtue of the parcel's removal from bankruptcy jurisdiction. Hence, the property is not "necessary to an effective reorganization." Under these circumstances, therefore, the bank can demand that the stay be lifted so that it can foreclose on its collateral. Section 362(d)(2) leaves the trustee no ground on which to object.

If a parcel of land generates substantially all of the debtor's gross income and is otherwise single-asset real estate as defined by §101(51B), then §362(d)(3) (revised by the 2005 Bankruptcy Act) makes it easier for a creditor with a security interest in it to obtain relief from the automatic stay. To avoid foreclosure, the debtor must either (A) file a plan of reorganization that has a reasonable possibility of being confirmed within a reasonable time, or (B) begin monthly interest payments to the creditor on the secured portion of its claim at contract rate of the related loan. When a debtor has but one piece of real estate subject to a mortgage, there is little chance of collective action problems among the creditors as the holder of the mortgage, typically to secure what is by far the debtor's largest loan, can count on receipt of the property. Nor is there a threat to a going concern nearly comparable to what one would encounter if, for example, the debtor were a manufacturer with multiple assets synergistically connected. After foreclosure, the new owner can either keep the existing real estate managers in place or hire new ones. These characteristics of the single-asset real estate case may explain these more stringent requirements. *for the debtor*

A more difficult situation arises when the debtor does have equity in collateral that is part of a more complex enterprise or when the collateral is necessary to keep a business running. In either case, but particularly in the latter, there is a reason for the trustee to maintain the collateral and not surrender it to foreclosure by the secured creditor. Imagine that a debtor retailer owes a bank $500,000 secured by the debtor's computer and proprietary customer-tracking software, worth at least $600,000 if sold to another business. After the debtor files for bankruptcy, the trustee might wish to retain this collateral for two reasons. First, the trustee would want to be sure that the computer and software fetch the highest possible price if they are sold, because sale proceeds in excess of $500,000 would go to the debtor's general creditors. (Even if the debtor had no equity in the collateral, the trustee would have some interest, though a lesser one, in obtaining the highest possible sale price if that price were used to establish the secured creditor's deficiency claim. The smaller that claim, the greater the return to the general creditors.) Second, the computer and software might be essential to the debtor's continued operation. Removal could destroy the debtor's going-concern value to the detriment of the debtor's general creditors.

Section 362(d)(1) gives creditors the ability to lift the automatic stay for cause. Secured creditors most commonly argue that they are entitled to have the stay lifted because their interests are not being adequately protected. "Adequate protection" requires the debtor to protect the secured creditor from any loss of the collateral's value. Moreover, if the adequate protection provided ultimately proves inadequate, the secured creditor is entitled to a first priority claim against any of the debtor's unencumbered assets. See §507(b), discussed more fully later in this section.

The concept of adequate protection appears elsewhere in the Bankruptcy Code. As described more fully in section C below, §363 provides for the debtor's use, sale, or lease of collateral, including, under some circumstances, sale free from liens. See §363(b), (c), (f). To protect the secured creditor in such cases, §363(e) gives an entity with an interest in property the ability to condition any use, sale, or lease on the provision of adequate protection. Similarly, adequate protection is required in the rare case in which the debtor alters the priority of a valid security interest to obtain a new loan under §364(d). Section 363(c)(2), moreover, provides that the debtor cannot use, sell, or lease "cash collateral"—defined by §363(a) to include cash, negotiable instruments, deposit accounts, and the like—without explicit permission of the secured party or, after notice and hearing, the court. Thus, for cash or the equivalent, the value of which is easily spent, the burden is on the trustee or the debtor in possession, rather than on the creditor, to raise the issue of adequate protection.

Although the general principle of "adequate protection" is straightforward, the precise meaning of the term was one of the most hotly debated bankruptcy questions in the early 1980s. Because inflation during this time sometimes ran in double digits, the issue was of considerable moment. To understand the debate, consider the following example. Bank is owed $100 and has a security interest in a machine that is worth $100 at the time the petition is filed. Under §506, Bank has a secured claim for $100. The interest of Bank that had to be "adequately protected" under §362, however, was not clear. Everyone agreed that if the machine depreciated in value and was worth $10 less every month—$90 instead of $100—Bank would be entitled to something worth at least $10 each month, such as an additional lien on other property. (Bank, however, could not be forced to accept a $10 share in the reorganized debtor as compensation for the decline in

§361(3)
adequate protection
excludes shares
in reorged
entity

value. See §361(3). In the words of the legislative history, such protection is "too uncertain to be meaningful.") What divided courts was whether the time value of the undersecured claim needed to be adequately protected—the change in value caused over time when the machine that could be sold for $100 today could be sold for only $100 still in a year's time. While in nominal terms nothing has changed ($100 is still $100), in *real* terms, $100 a year from now is not as valuable as $100 today.

voidable preference

Recall our discussion of §547(b)(5) in chapter 8, section D above. If Bank were paid in full in cash the day before the filing of the petition, the trustee could not argue that Bank had received a voidable preference because the transfer of cash did not make it any better off. A fully secured creditor is supposed to be as well as off if it is paid in full or if it has a secured claim for the amount it is owed. But in practice this would be true only if the bankruptcy proceeding lasted an instant. Bank would not be indifferent between payment on the day before the filing of the petition and payment of that same nominal amount at the end of the reorganization, which might last years.

Bank argued that, at the end of the day, it should receive an amount equal in value to what it would have recovered had the bankruptcy petition not been filed. Bank has no right to interest for the period between the default (or the filing of the petition as a proxy therefor) and the time it would have been able to foreclose, but it ordinarily takes much longer to reorganize a company than to foreclose on property. To have its nonbankruptcy position respected in full, Bank needs to be compensated for the amount its claim declines in value between the time it would have foreclosed and the time the bankruptcy is over.

← starting point is really foreclosure NOT petition

The trustee argued that Bank was entitled only to have the nominal value of its interest protected. If the machine is worth $100 at the time Bank asks for adequate protection, Bank should be entitled to liens (or other interests in other property) that will ensure that Bank will receive $100 whenever the bankruptcy process ends. If the property is of a kind that does not depreciate (such as a perpetual annuity or a piece of undeveloped real estate in a stable market), the secured creditor needs nothing more to be adequately protected.

Nominal vs. Real value

In *Timbers*, the case that follows below, the Supreme Court decided that nominal values rather than real values should be used. The related notes and problem ask you to consider whether the Court confronted the secured creditor's argument as seriously as it should have.

You should also consider which result makes sense in light of the policies that the Bankruptcy Code should serve.

Before turning to *Timbers*, however, consider the following exercises, which cover some basic ground discussed above and also ask you to address two new sets of provisions added by the 2005 Bankruptcy Act, one designed to defeat a fraudulent scheme of lien evasion and the other designed to hasten an individual debtor's decision about personal property subject to a security interest.

Key Provisions: Bankruptcy Code §§362(d); 363(a), (e); 506(a); 552(b)

EXERCISES

9B(1) Bank takes a mortgage in WhiteAcre, rental property owned by Debtor. According to the terms of the mortgage agreement, in the event of Debtor's default on the mortgage note, Bank is entitled to all rental income from WhiteAcre. Bank never records its mortgage. Debtor defaults on the loan and files for bankruptcy. Does Bank have a security interest in the postpetition rental income? Does it matter whether applicable state law would enforce Bank's unrecorded mortgage? In answering these questions consider and compare the language of §552(b)(1) and (b)(2) and reconsider Exercise 8A(1).

9B(2) Debtor Corporation files for bankruptcy under Chapter 7 after years of losing money. Debtor's most valuable asset is its manufacturing machinery, which is worth between $500,000 and $1 million and is mortgaged to Bank as collateral for a still outstanding $2 million loan. While the trustee is still sorting out the difficult case, she values the collateral at $650,000 and establishes Bank's deficiency claim at $1.35 million. Bank moves to lift the stay. The trustee resists and offers protection for Bank's interest in the collateral. Should Bank's motion be granted? Would your answer change if you knew that the trustee sought to keep the machinery so that Debtor could fill its current orders prior to liquidation?

9B(3) Debtor owns a single asset, a commercial warehouse in which Debtor leases space to customers. Bank holds a mortgage on the warehouse as collateral on a $1 million loan. When Debtor defaults on this loan and files for bankruptcy under Chapter 11, Debtor still owes Bank $1 million, having paid only interest, but has few other debts. At this time, the warehouse is worth slightly less than $1 million. Debtor seeks to reorganize rather than liquidate because tax law would treat liquidation as a realization event requiring Debtor to pay taxes on the difference between the sale price of the property and Debtor's "basis" in the property. (Basis here is, in essence, the amount Debtor paid for the property less depreciation previously deducted from Debtor's taxes.) Because Debtor has (lawfully) deducted more depreciation than actually occurred to the warehouse, liquidation would leave Debtor with a large tax bill. Bank moves to have the stay lifted so that it can foreclose on the warehouse. Will this motion be granted?

9B(4) Finance Company maintains a security interest in Debtor's deposit account with Bank. After Debtor files for bankruptcy under Chapter 11, Debtor seeks to use the account to meet payroll, a step essential to the survival of Debtor's business. Finance Company has not moved to have the stay lifted. Can Debtor use the account to pay its employees?

9B(5) Owner is the sole shareholder of Investment Corp., a small business with a single asset, a parcel of undeveloped commercial real estate called BlackAcre. The land, which has a current market value of $800,000, is subject to Bank's $1 million mortgage. When Investment Corp. defaults on the bank loan, Bank threatens to foreclose. Owner asks Bank for more time to turn things around. When Bank refuses, Investment Corp. files a Chapter 11 bankruptcy petition. The bankruptcy court soon dismisses the Investment Corp. case on the ground that no viable reorganization plan has been proposed or is possible. Within a month of the dismissal, as Bank is, again, set to foreclose, Owner forms a new corporation, Investment Corp. II, the shares of which are owned by Owner and her brother-in-law. Owner then has Investment Corp. transfer its interest in BlackAcre to Investment Corp. II, which promptly files its own Chapter 11 bankruptcy petition. Bank ignores the petition and proceeds to foreclose on BlackAcre, over the debtor's objection. What result? See Bankruptcy Code §§362(d)(4),(n); 101(51D). Consider this exercise again after reading chapter 13 of this book.

9B(6) Debtor, a corporate executive by trade, is a passionate photographer who desires the best equipment for his hobby. Debtor purchases on credit a new $25,000 medium format digital camera from Vendor, who duly takes a security interest in the camera, which depreciates modestly once it cannot be sold as new. Shortly thereafter, Debtor loses his job and files a Chapter 7 bankruptcy petition. Vendor promptly seeks to have the stay lifted. Two months later, while the bankruptcy case is still open, Debtor has taken no action with respect to his ownership of the camera and Vendor seeks to foreclose, over Debtor's objection. What result? See Bankruptcy Code §521(a)(6). Would it have mattered if two weeks after the petition Debtor filed with the court a statement of intention to redeem the camera by paying for it with postpetition earnings? See §362(e)(2), (h). What result if Debtor leased the camera but did not promptly assume the lease? See §365(p). Compare In re Park, 275 Bankr. 253 (Bankr. E.D. Va. 2002). Would any of your answers change if the camera had appreciated rather than depreciated? Consider this exercise again after reading chapter 11 of this book.

CASE

UNITED SAVINGS ASSOCIATION v. TIMBERS OF INWOOD FOREST ASSOCIATES, LTD.

United States Supreme Court, 1988
484 U.S. 365

JUSTICE SCALIA DELIVERED THE OPINION OF THE COURT.

Petitioner United Savings Association of Texas seeks review of an en banc decision of the United States Court of Appeals for the Fifth Circuit, holding that petitioner was not entitled to receive from respondent debtor, which is undergoing reorganization in bankruptcy, monthly payments for the use value of the loan collateral which the bankruptcy stay prevented it from possessing. ... We granted certiorari, ... to resolve a conflict in the Courts of Appeals regarding application of §§361 and 362(d)(1). * * *

I

On June 29, 1982, respondent Timbers of Inwood Forest Associates, Inc. executed a note in the principal amount of $4,100,000. Petitioner is the holder of the note as well as of a security interest created the same day in an apartment project owned by respondent in Houston, Texas. The security interest included an assignment of rents from the project. On March 4, 1985, respondent filed a voluntary petition under Chapter 11 in the United States Bankruptcy Court for the Southern District of Texas.

On March 18, 1985, petitioner moved for relief from the automatic stay of enforcement of liens triggered by the petition on the ground that there was lack of "adequate protection" of its interest within the meaning of §362(d)(1). At a hearing before the Bankruptcy Court, it was established that respondent owed petitioner $4,366,389, and evidence was presented that the value of the collateral was somewhere between $2,650,000 and $4,250,000. The collateral was appreciating in value, but only very slightly. It was therefore undisputed that petitioner was an undersecured creditor. Respondent had agreed to pay petitioner the postpetition rents from the apartment project (covered by the after-acquired property clause in the security agreement), minus operating expenses. Petitioner contended, however, that it was entitled to additional compensation. The Bankruptcy Court agreed and on April 19, 1985, it conditioned continuance of the stay on monthly payments by respondent, at the market rate of 12% per annum, on the estimated amount realizable on foreclosure, $4,250,000—commencing six months after the filing of the bankruptcy petition, to reflect the normal foreclosure delays. ... The court held that the postpetition rents could be applied to these payments. ... Respondent appealed to the District Court and petitioner cross-appealed on the amount of the adequate protection payments. The District Court affirmed but the Fifth Circuit en banc reversed.

We granted certiorari to determine whether undersecured creditors are entitled to compensation under §362(d)(1) for the delay caused by the automatic stay in foreclosing on their collateral.

II

When a bankruptcy petition is filed, §362(a) of the Bankruptcy Code provides an automatic stay of, among other things, actions taken to realize the value of collateral given by the debtor. The provision of the Code central to the decision of this case is §362(d). ... The phrase "adequate protection" in [§362(d)(1)] is given further content by §361, which reads in relevant part as follows:

> When adequate protection is required under §362 ... of this title of an interest of an entity in property, such adequate protection may be provided by—
>
> (1) requiring the trustee to make a cash payment or periodic cash payments to such entity, to the extent that the stay under §362 of this title ... results in a decrease in the value of such entity's interest in such property;
>
> (2) providing to such entity an additional or replacement lien to the extent that such stay ... results in a decrease in the value of such entity's interest in such property; or

(3) granting such other relief ... as will result in the realization by such entity of the indubitable equivalent of such entity's interest in such property.

It is common ground that the "interest in property" referred to by §362(d)(1) includes the right of a secured creditor to have the security applied in payment of the debt upon completion of the reorganization; and that that interest is not adequately protected if the security is depreciating during the term of the stay. Thus, it is agreed that if the apartment project in this case has been declining in value petitioner would have been entitled, under §362(d)(1), to cash payments or additional security in the amount of the decline, as §361 describes. The crux of the present dispute is that petitioner asserts, and respondent denies, that the phrase "interest in property" also includes the secured party's right (suspended by the stay) to take immediate possession of the defaulted security, and apply it in payment of the debt. If that right is embraced by the term, it is obviously not adequately protected unless the secured party is reimbursed for the use of the proceeds he is deprived of during the term of the stay.

The term "interest in property" certainly summons up such concepts as "fee ownership," "life estate," "co-ownership," and "security interest" more readily than it does the notion of "right to immediate foreclosure." Nonetheless, viewed in the isolated context of §362(d)(1), the phrase could reasonably be given the meaning petitioner asserts. Statutory construction, however, is a holistic endeavor. A provision that may seem ambiguous in isolation is often clarified by the remainder of the statutory scheme—because the same terminology is used elsewhere in a context that makes its meaning clear ... or because only one of the permissible meanings produces a substantive effect that is compatible with the rest of the law. ... That is the case here. Section 362(d)(1) is only one of a series of provisions in the Bankruptcy Code dealing with the rights of secured creditors. The language in those other provisions, and the substantive dispositions that they effect, persuade us that the "interest in property" protected by §362(d)(1) does not include a secured party's right to immediate foreclosure.

Section 506 of the Code defines the amount of the secured creditor's allowed secured claim and the conditions of his receiving post-petition interest. In relevant part it reads as follows:

(a) An allowed claim of a creditor secured by a lien on property in which the estate has an interest ... is a secured claim to the extent of the value of such creditor's interest in the estate's interest in such property, ... and is an unsecured claim to the extent that the value of such creditor's interest ... is less than the amount of such allowed claim. * * *

(b) to the extent that an allowed secured claim is secured by property the value of which ... is greater than the amount of such claim, there shall be allowed to the holder of such claim, interest on such claim, and any reasonable fees, costs, or charges provided for under the agreement under which such claim arose.

In subsection (a) of this provision the creditor's "interest in property" obviously means his security interest without taking account of his right to immediate possession of the collateral on default. If the latter were included, the "value of such creditor's interest" would increase, and the proportions of the claim that are secured and unsecured would alter, as the stay continues—since the value of the entitlement to use the collateral from the date of bankruptcy would rise with the passage of time. No one suggests this was intended. The phrase "value of such creditor's interest" in §506(a) means "the value of the collateral." H.R. Rep. No. 95-595, pp. 181, 356 (1977); see also S. Rep. No. 95-989, p. 68 (1978). We think the phrase "value of such entity's interest" in §361(1) and (2), when applied to secured creditors, means the same.

Even more important for our purposes than §506's use of terminology is its substantive effect of denying undersecured creditors postpetition interest on their claims—just as it denies oversecured creditors postpetition interest to the extent that such interest, when added to the principal amount of the claim, will exceed the value of the collateral. Section 506(b) provides that " *[t]o the extent that* an allowed secured claim is secured by property the value of which ... is greater than the amount of such claim, there shall be allowed to the holder of such claim, interest on such claim." (Emphasis added.) Since this provision permits postpetition interest to be paid only out of the "security cushion," the undersecured creditor, who has no such cushion, falls within the general rule disallowing postpetition interest. See §502(b)(2). If the Code had meant to give the undersecured creditor, who is thus denied interest on his *claim,* interest on the value of his *collateral,* surely this is where that disposition would have been set forth, and not obscured within the "adequate protection" provision of §362(d)(1). Instead of the intricate phraseology set forth above, §506(b) would simply have said that the secured creditor is entitled to interest "on his allowed claim, or on the value of the property securing his allowed claim, whichever is lesser." Petitioner's interpretation of §362(d)(1) must be regarded as contradicting the carefully drawn disposition of §506(b).

Petitioner seeks to avoid this conclusion by characterizing §506(b) as merely an alternative method for compensating oversecured creditors, which does not imply that no compensation is available to undersecured creditors. This theory of duplicate protection for oversecured creditors is implausible even in the abstract, but even more so in light of the historical principles of bankruptcy law. Section 506(b)'s denial of postpetition interest to undersecured creditors merely codified pre-Code bankruptcy law, in which that denial was part of the conscious allocation of reorganization benefits and losses between undersecured and unsecured creditors. "To allow a secured creditor interest where his security was worth less than the value of his debt was thought to be inequitable to unsecured creditors." Vanston Bondholders Protective Committee v. Green, 329 U.S. 156, 164 (1946). It was considered unfair to allow an undersecured creditor to recover interest from the estate's unencumbered assets before unsecured creditors had recovered any principal. ... We think it unlikely that §506(b) codified the pre-Code rule with the intent, not of achieving the principal purpose and function of that rule, but of providing oversecured creditors an alternative method of compensation. Moreover, it is incomprehensible why Congress would want to favor undersecured creditors with interest if they move for it under §362(d)(1) at the inception of the reorganization process—thereby probably pushing the estate into liquidation—but not if they forbear and seek it only at the completion of the reorganization.

Second, petitioner's interpretation of §362(d)(1) is structurally inconsistent with §552. Section 552(a) states the general rule that a prepetition security interest does not reach property acquired by the estate or debtor postpetition. Section 552(b) [now divided into §552(b)(1) and (b)(2)] sets forth an exception, allowing postpetition "proceeds, product, offspring, rents, or profits" of the collateral to be covered only if the security agreement expressly provides for an interest in such property, and the interest has been perfected under "applicable nonbankruptcy law." ... Section 552(b) therefore makes possession of a perfected security interest in postpetition rents or profits from collateral a condition of having them applied to satisfying the claim of the secured creditor ahead of the claims of unsecured creditors. Under petitioner's interpretation, however, the undersecured creditor who lacks such a perfected security interest in effect achieves the same result by demanding the "use value" of his collateral under

§362. It is true that §506(b) gives the *over*secured creditor, despite lack of compliance with the conditions of §552, a similar priority over unsecured creditors; but that does not compromise the principle of §552, since the interest payments come only out of the "cushion" in which the oversecured creditor does have a perfected security interest.

Third, petitioner's interpretation of §362(d)(1) makes nonsense of §362(d)(2). On petitioner's theory, the undersecured creditor's inability to take immediate possession of his collateral is always "cause" for conditioning the stay (upon the payment of market rate interest) under §362(d)(1), since there is, within the meaning of that paragraph, "lack of adequate protection of an interest in property." But §362(d)(2) expressly provides a different standard for relief from a stay "of an act against property," which of course includes taking possession of collateral. It provides that the court shall grant relief "if ... (A) the debtor does not have an equity in such property (i.e., the creditor is undersecured); *and* (B) such property is not necessary to an effective reorganization." (Emphasis added.) By applying the "adequate protection of an interest in property" provision of §362(d)(1) to the alleged "interest" in the earning power of collateral, petitioner creates the strange consequence that §362 entitles the secured creditor to relief from the stay (1) if he is undersecured (and thus not eligible for interest under §506(b)), *or* (2) if he is undersecured *and* his collateral "is not necessary to an effective reorganization." This renders §362(d)(2) a practical nullity and a theoretical absurdity. If §362(d)(1) is interpreted in this fashion, an undersecured creditor would seek relief under §362(d)(2) only if its collateral was not depreciating (or it was being compensated for depreciation) and it was receiving market rate interest on its collateral, but nonetheless wanted to foreclose. Petitioner offers no reason why Congress would want to provide relief for such an obstreperous and thoroughly unharmed creditor.

Section 362(d)(2) also belies petitioner's contention that undersecured creditors will face inordinate and extortionate delay if they are denied compensation for interest lost during the stay as part of "adequate protection" under §362(d)(1). Once the movant under §362(d)(2) establishes that he is an undersecured creditor, it is the burden of the *debtor* to establish that the collateral at issue is "necessary to an effective reorganization." See §362(g). What this requires is not merely a showing that if there is conceivably to be an effective reorganization, this property will be needed for it; but that the property is essential for an effective reorganization *that is in prospect.* This means, as many lower courts, including the en banc court in this case, have properly said, that there must be "a reasonable possibility of a successful reorganization within a reasonable time." ... The cases are numerous in which §362(d)(2) relief has been provided within less than a year from the filing of the bankruptcy petition. And while the bankruptcy courts demand less detailed showings during the four months in which the debtor is given the exclusive right to put together a plan, even within that period lack of any realistic prospect of effective reorganization will require §362(d)(2) relief.

III

A

Petitioner contends that denying it compensation under §362(d)(1) is inconsistent with sections of the Code other than those just discussed. Petitioner principally relies on the phrase "indubitable equivalent" in §361(3), which also appears in §1129(b)(2)(A)(iii). Petitioner contends that in the latter context, which sets forth the standards for confirming a reorganization plan, the phrase has developed a well-settled meaning connoting the right of a secured creditor to receive present value of his security—thus requiring interest if the claim is to be paid over time. It is true that under §1129(b) a secured claimant has a right to receive under a plan the present value of his collateral. This entitlement arises, however, not from the phrase "indubitable equivalent" in §1129(b)(2)(A)(iii), but from the provision of §1129(b)(2)(A)(i)(II) that guarantees the secured creditor "deferred cash payments ... of a value, *as of the effective date of the plan,* of at least the value of such [secured claimant's] interest in the estate's interest in such property." (Emphasis added.) Under this formulation, even though the undersecured creditor's "interest" is regarded (properly) as solely the value of the collateral, he must be rendered payments that assure him that value *as of the effective date of the plan.* In §361(3), by contrast, the relief pending the stay need only be such *"as will result in the realization ... of the indubitable equivalent"* of the collateral. (Emphasis added.) It is obvious (since §§361 and 362(d)(1) do not entitle the secured creditor to immediate payment of the principal of his collateral) that this "realization" is to "result" not at once, but only upon completion of the reorganization. It is *then* that he must be assured "realization ... of the indubitable equivalent" of his collateral. To put the point differently: similarity of outcome between §361(3) and §1129 would be demanded only if the former read "such other relief ... as will give such entity, as of the date of the relief, the indubitable equivalent of such entity's interest in such property."

Nor is there merit in petitioner's suggestion that "indubitable equivalent" in §361(3) connotes reimbursement for the use value of collateral because the phrase is derived from In re Murel Holding Corp., 75 F.2d 941 (2d Cir. 1935), where it bore that meaning. *Murel* involved a proposed reorganization plan that gave the secured creditor interest on his collateral for 10 years, with full payment of the secured principal due at the end of that term; the plan made no provision, however, for amortization of principal or maintenance of the collateral's value during the term. In rejecting the plan, *Murel* used the words "indubitable equivalence" with specific reference not to interest (which was assured), but to the jeopardized principal of the loan:

> Interest is indeed the common measure of the difference [between payment now and payment ten years hence], but a creditor who fears the safety of his principal will scarcely be content with that; he wishes to get his money or at least the property. We see no reason to suppose that the statute was intended to deprive him of that in the interest of junior holders, unless by a substitute of the most indubitable equivalence.

Id. at 942. Of course *Murel,* like §1129, proceeds from the premise that in the confirmation context the secured creditor is entitled to present value. But no more from *Murel* than from §1129 can it be inferred that a similar requirement exists as of the time of the bankruptcy stay. The reorganized debtor is supposed to stand on his own two feet. The debtor in process of reorganization, by contrast, is given many temporary protections against the normal operation of the law.

Petitioner also contends that the Code embodies a principle that secured creditors do not bear the costs of reorganization. It derives this from the rule that general administrative expenses do not have priority over secured claims. See §§506(c); 507(a). But the general principle does not follow from the particular rule. That secured creditors do not bear one kind of reorganization cost hardly means that they bear none of them. The Code rule on administrative expenses merely continues pre-Code law. But it was also pre-Code law that undersecured creditors were not entitled to postpetition interest as compensation for the delay of reorganization. ... Congress could hardly have understood that the readoption of the rule on administrative expenses would work a change in the rule on postpetition interest, which it also readopted.

Finally, petitioner contends that failure to interpret §362(d)(1) to require compensation of undersecured creditors for delay will create an inconsistency in the Code in the (admittedly rare) case when the debtor proves solvent. When that occurs, §726(a)(5) provides that postpetition interest is allowed on unsecured claims. Petitioner contends it would be absurd to allow postpetition interest on unsecured claims but not on the secured portion of undersecured creditors' claims. It would be disingenuous to deny that this is an apparent anomaly, but it will occur so rarely that it is more likely the product of inadvertence than are the blatant inconsistencies petitioner's interpretation would produce. Its inequitable effects, moreover, are entirely avoidable, since an undersecured creditor is entitled to "surrender or waive his security and prove his entire claim as an unsecured one." United States Nat. Bank v. Chase Nat. Bank, 331 U.S. 28, 34 (1947). Section 726(a)(5) therefore requires no more than that undersecured creditors receive postpetition interest from a solvent debtor on equal terms with unsecured creditors rather than ahead of them—which, where the debtor is solvent, involves no hardship.

B

Petitioner contends that its interpretation is supported by the legislative history of §§361 and 362(d)(1), relying almost entirely on statements that "[s]ecured creditors should not be deprived of the benefit of their bargain." H.R. Rep. No. 95-595, at 339; S. Rep. No. 95-989, at 53. Such generalizations are inadequate to overcome the plain textual indication in §506 and §362(d)(2) of the Code that Congress did not wish the undersecured creditor to receive interest on his collateral during the term of the stay. If it is at all relevant, the legislative history tends to subvert rather than support petitioner's thesis, since it contains not a hint that §362(d)(1) entitles the undersecured creditor to postpetition interest. Such a major change in the existing rules would not likely have been made without specific provision in the text of the statute ... ; it is most improbable that it would have been made without even any mention in the legislative history.

Petitioner makes another argument based upon what the legislative history does *not* contain. It contends that the pre-Code law gave the undersecured creditor relief from the automatic stay by permitting him to foreclose; and that Congress would not have withdrawn this entitlement to relief without any indication of intent to do so in the legislative history, unless it was providing an adequate substitute, to wit, interest on the collateral during the stay.

The premise of this argument is flawed. As petitioner itself concedes, ... the undersecured creditor had no absolute entitlement to foreclosure in a Chapter X or XII case; he could not foreclose if there was a reasonable prospect for a successful rehabilitation within a reasonable time. ... Thus, even assuming petitioner is correct that the undersecured creditor had an absolute entitlement to relief under Chapter XI, Congress would have been faced with the choice between adopting the rule from Chapters X and XII or the asserted alternative rule from Chapter XI, because Chapter 11 of the current Code "replaces Chapters X, XI and XII of the Bankruptcy Act" with a "single chapter for all business reorganizations." S. Rep. No. 95-989, at 9; see also H.R. Rep. No. 95-595, at 223-224. We think §362(d)(2) indicates that Congress adopted the approach of Chapters X and XII. In any event, as far as the silence of the legislative history on the point is concerned, that would be no more strange with respect to alteration of the asserted Chapter XI rule than it would be with respect to alteration of the Chapters X and XII rule.

Petitioner's argument is further weakened by the fact that it is far from clear that there was a distinctive Chapter XI rule of absolute entitlement to foreclosure. At least one leading commentator concluded that "a Chapter XI court's power to stay lien enforcement is as broad as that of a Chapter X or XII court and that the automatic stay rules properly make no distinctions between the Chapters." Countryman, Real Estate Liens in Business Rehabilitation Cases, 50 Am. Bankr. L.J. 303, 315 (1976). Petitioner cites dicta in some Chapter XI cases suggesting that the undersecured creditor was automatically entitled to relief from the stay, but the courts in those cases uniformly found in addition that reorganization was not sufficiently likely or was being unduly delayed. ... Moreover, other Chapter XI cases held undersecured creditors not entitled to foreclosure under reasoning very similar to that used in Chapters X and XII cases. ... The at-best divided authority under Chapter XI removes all cause for wonder that the alleged departure from it should not have been commented upon in the legislative history. * * *

The Fifth Circuit correctly held that the undersecured petitioner is not entitled to interest on its collateral during the stay to assure adequate protection under §362(d)(1). Petitioner has never sought relief from the stay under §362(d)(2) or on any ground other than lack of adequate protection. Accordingly, the judgment of the Fifth Circuit is affirmed.

NOTES

9B.1. The Court in *Timbers* relies heavily on inferences from §506, suggesting that "[i]f the Code had meant to give the under-secured creditor, who is thus denied interest on his *claim,* interest on the value of his *collateral,* surely this [§506(b)] is where that disposition would have been set forth, and not obscured within the 'adequate protection' provision of §362(d)(1)" (emphasis in original). It may not follow, however, that the secured claim to be adequately protected has the same characteristics as the secured claim under §506 before the creditor asks for adequate protection.

If the secured creditor outside of bankruptcy wants to assert its rights of repossession and resale against a recalcitrant debtor, it has to institute a foreclosure action. The analog inside of bankruptcy is a motion to lift the stay, which the court must grant unless the secured claim is adequately protected. The foreclosure action would provide the creditor with cash, which the creditor could then reinvest at market rates. It is this reinvestment income for which the undersecured creditor in *Timbers* seeks protection. By contrast, if a secured creditor outside of bankruptcy does not foreclose, it continues with a loan in default and the debtor keeps possession of the collateral. When that happens, instead of getting market returns on the sale of the collateral, the creditor's claim continues to accrue contract-rate interest. It is the right of such accrual that §506(b) protects, at least arguably. See In re Dixon, 228 Bankr. 166, 172 (W.D. Va. 1998). From this perspective, one would expect that adequate protection—where the value of foreclosure rights are protected—and the baseline rule of §506(b) would be *different,* and that §362(d) is *exactly* where one would expect to find protection of an interest in the value of collateral.

9B.2. One needs to identify the right of the secured creditor that is to be valued. One might look to the amount that the secured creditor could realize if it repossessed and sold the collateral. After all, its property right was the right to repossess and sell upon default. Those who argue that time value should be taken into account also argue that a secured creditor should be entitled only to what it would have realized in a nonbankruptcy foreclosure and should not benefit from any going-concern value that the bankruptcy process preserved. Because the secured creditor is opting out by asking for adequate protection, it should not get any benefit of the value of the machine in the debtor's operations. What was to be adequately protected was liquidation value, not going-concern value. But when one makes the secured creditor bear some of the costs of the reorganization, the answer might not be the same.

9B.3. There is another silver lining to *Timbers* for undersecured creditors. Lower courts often point to the Court's discussion of §362(d)(2):

> [I]t is the burden of the *debtor* to establish that the collateral at issue is "necessary to an effective reorganization." ... What this requires is ... that the property is essential for an effective reorganization *(that is in prospect.)* This means ... that there must be "a reasonable possibility of a successful reorganization within a reasonable time." (Emphasis in original.)

[handwritten margin note: reorganization really must be in PROSPECT]

This dictum in *Timbers* may be as important as the holding. Many bankruptcy judges, at a time when secured creditors used to ask for adequate protection, consider lifting the stay altogether because a reorganization may not be "in prospect." A §362(d) motion to lift the stay sometimes becomes a mini-confirmation hearing. *Timbers* gave debtors an incentive to procrastinate but also made bankruptcy judges less inclined to tolerate delay. *[handwritten note: b/c they don't have to pay interest]*

9B.4. Congress, as well, responded to *Timbers*, though in small measure. Section 362(d)(3), noted in the essay above, provides special treatment for single-asset real estate cases. This provision was added after, and likely in reaction to, the *Timbers* decision. Note, though, that §362(d)(3) offers no relief to creditors with an interest in property other than single-asset real estate. Thus, an undersecured creditor remains without general recourse for protection of its interest in property held by a debtor throughout a prolonged bankruptcy reorganization.

[handwritten margin note: what if the asset isn't depreciating, still no interest right, c'mon?]

9B.5. The Court in *Timbers* notes that §552(b) permits a secured creditor to acquire a security interest in proceeds, rent, and the like generated by collateral postpetition. Thus, if an undersecured creditor's collateral is something like an apartment building, the rental stream (such as was given to the secured creditor in *Timbers*) may in fact be the same as adequate protection of reinvestment income. This is so because if the property is properly managed, the rental income should compensate the owner, or the secured creditor, for the forgone opportunity to sell the property now. Indeed, in a well-functioning market, the former determines the value of the latter. Even if the property is not put to its highest use, and thus does not earn to its full potential, the rental income to some extent protects the secured creditor from the costs of delay. Problem 9B explores how a combination of §552(b) and *Timbers* creates arbitrary distinctions based on type of collateral.

9B.6. The negative implication of §506(b) continues to play out in the courts. In Travelers Casualty & Surety Co. v. Pacific Gas & Electric Co., 127 S. Ct. 1199 (2007), Travelers Casualty sought post-petition attorneys' fees from debtor PG &E, which had contractually committed to paying attorneys' fees. Travelers' position was that its (unsecured) claim for post-petition fees, while unaccrued at the time of the bankruptcy petition, was contingent at that time and should thus have been allowed under §502. PG & E responded that the reasoning of *Timbers* forbids such allowance, as §506(b) awards "reasonable fees" to the holder of an oversecured claim and thus, implicitly, *only* to the holder of such a claim. The Supreme Court decided the case on other grounds and remanded for consideration of the *Timbers* issue.

PROBLEM

9B. Debtor is in the business of leasing road-building equipment. Bank holds separate perfected security interests in Debtor's main-frame computer, which tracks customer and employee accounts, and in one of Debtor's road graders held for lease to customers. Debtor defaults on its loans to Bank, which believes that Debtor may soon file for Chapter 11 bankruptcy. Bank intends to take possession of and sell at least one item of collateral. Debtor explains that it could more easily afford to part with the grader than with the computer. The computer and grader have about the same value. Which item of collateral should Bank take now?

C. ADMINISTERING PROPERTY

In bankruptcy cases where some or all assets will be kept to-gether—either for purposes of a going-concern sale under Chapter 7 or a reorganization under Chapter 11—it will be necessary to keep the debtor's business running at least for a time. This requires not just that the assets are kept together in the face of individual creditor incen-tives to pull them apart (the subject of §362), but that the business continues to function more or less as usual. The trustee (or more likely in a reorganization, the debtor in possession) must deal with suppliers and with buyers to whom the debtor's end product or service is sold. Such activity does not inherently protect any given asset. By its nature, business operation entails a *risk* to all assets. When the debtor uses cash to purchase inventory, for example, that expenditure is worthwhile only if the debtor can sell the inventory profitably.

Whether operation is truly worth the risk is not always clear. And a debtor's constituents—secured creditors, general creditors, equity holders, and interested third parties—may differ on what they would like done with a debtor's assets. The bankruptcy process tries to ensure that decisions about the use of the assets are in the joint interests of all those with rights in them.

The primary provision governing the use, sale, or lease of property of the estate is §363. "Property of the estate" here refers to property in which the estate has an interest—i.e., any property in the possession or control of the trustee or debtor—even though in other contexts (see, e.g., §541(a), described above in chapter 6, section A) the term refers only to the debtor's interest in property. Were this not the case, despite authorization to use "property of the estate" under §363, the debtor could not use property subject to a perfected lien, say the debtor's bulldozer, as the bulldozer embodies both the debtor's interest and that of the secured creditor. Such absurdity is avoided by a less than precise parsing of the provision. This does not, however, imply that the debtor may disregard the perfected interests of others.

In its general application, §363 draws a distinction between cases in which "the business of the debtor is authorized to be operated" and cases without such authorization. See §363(c)(1). Operation in bankruptcy of a debtor's business is authorized automatically in a case of reorganization or debt adjustment under Chapter 11, 12, or 13 unless the court orders otherwise. See §§1108, 1203, and 1304. In a Chapter 7 liquidation, continuation of business is not ordinarily contemplated, so bankruptcy operation requires court authorization. See §721. When operation is authorized, the debtor may use, sell, or lease property "in the ordinary course of business" without court permission. See §363(c)(1). Use, sale, or lease outside the ordinary course of business must be specifically approved by a court after notice and hearing. See §363(b)(1). When operation is not authorized, no use, sale, or lease is presumed to be in the ordinary course, and again court permission is required.

When others have an interest in property that the debtor seeks to use, some special provisions of §363 come into play. For example, under conditions specified by §363(f)—such as when collateral is worth more than all obligations it secures—the trustee or debtor can sell property free from encumbrance. This is not a disaster for the interested party, however. As noted in the previous section, an entity with an interest in property can by request condition use, sale, or lease on the debtor's provision of adequate protection for its interest. See §363(e). Also as noted above, the debtor may not use cash collateral, the value of which is easily spent and thus lost as collateral, unless the secured creditor consents to such use or is notified of a hearing at which it can request adequate protection. See §363(a), (c)(2). With respect to adequate protection, §363 merely reinforces the provisions of §362(d). In addition, there is a variety of restrictions on the sale of property in which a party other than the debtor has an ownership interest rather than an ordinary lien or security interest. See §363(f)-(j). These subsections primarily protect the interest of a debtor's spouse in co-owned property.

While §363 dictates how the debtor may use property for the benefit of the estate, sometimes the debtor has no use for a particular item of property. The property may be worthless or, more commonly, it may be so encumbered by liens or security interests that it has no value to the general creditors. For example, a trustee in a Chapter 7 liquidation may want to abandon the debtor's equipment to the secured lender. The trustee is likely to favor this course if all agree that the secured lender is owed more than the equipment is worth and there is no synergy between the equipment and the debtor's other assets. To deal with these cases, §554 permits the trustee or debtor, after notice and hearing, to "abandon any property of the estate that is burdensome to the estate or that is of inconsequential value and benefit to the estate."

These provisions implement the notion that in a proceeding designed to sort out the debtor's past, its future should not be made unnecessarily difficult relative to businesses not in bankruptcy. But the provision of a notice and hearing for unusual transactions also recognizes that some mechanism is needed to replace the control that creditors have over a firm's decisions outside of bankruptcy. Once the automatic stay is in place, creditors can no longer enforce their loan covenants, let alone exercise their default rights. The fiduciary duties of the managers run to the creditors once the firm is insolvent, but the lax business judgment rule under which they operate outside of bankruptcy may not be sufficient to ensure that they act in the creditors' interests inside of bankruptcy. In addition to the constraints the automatic stay imposes, decision making in this environment is difficult because prepetition creditors and equity holders alike have strong incentives to engage in strategic behavior.

The exercises below require you to work through some mechanics of asset administration in bankruptcy. The material that follows then asks you to take a closer look at the issues of use, sale, and abandonment.

Key Provisions: Bankruptcy Code §§363; 554

EXERCISES

9C(1) Debtor Corporation is in the process of converting its business from a bakery to a pizza restaurant when it runs low on cash and files for bankruptcy. While still operating as a bakery, Debtor intends to use the little money it has left for bakery supplies. To raise more money, Debtor intends to sell two of its ovens and to modify a third so that it can properly bake pizza. Does Debtor need court permission to take these steps? In answering this question consider who might favor and who might oppose this conversion.

9C(2) Debtor pledges BlackAcre to Bank as security for Bank's $1 million loan, which remains unpaid at the time of Debtor's bankruptcy. Bank moves to have Debtor's bankruptcy "abandon" BlackAcre, which all agree is worth less than $1 million. Anxious to determine Bank's deficiency claim, the trustee instead proposes a sale of BlackAcre to Purchaser, free of Bank's interest, for $600,000. Can the trustee make this sale over the objection of Bank? In answering this question consider, among other provisions, §§363(d), (f)(3), (5) and 554(b).

1) USE OF ASSETS

The cases that follow, *Official Committee of Equity Security Holders v. Mabey* and *Kmart* along with the related notes and problem involve payment of prepetition claims to general creditors before the conclusion of the bankruptcy case. A payment to creditors before the end of a case is ordinarily not permitted. Consider, however, whether in these cases such payment would leave the estate better off.

CASES

OFFICIAL COMMITTEE OF EQUITY SECURITY HOLDERS v. MABEY

United States Court of Appeals, Fourth Circuit, 1987
832 F.2d 299

CHAPMAN, CIRCUIT JUDGE.

This is an appeal arising from the Dalkon Shield litigation in the A.H. Robins Co. Chapter 11 bankruptcy proceedings. The Official Committee of Equity Security Holders (Equity Committee) appeals the May 21, 1987 order of the district court which directed

> that the Debtor shall, within sixty (60) days of this date, establish an emergency treatment fund in the sum of $15 million for the purpose of assisting in providing tubal reconstructive surgery or in-vitro fertilization to eligible Dalkon Shield claimants on the terms and conditions set forth in paragraphs 12 through 23 of said motion as if fully set out in this Order.

The clerk was directed to forward notice of the program to approximately one hundred eight thousand people who have filed timely notice of a claim and responded to the Court Questionnaire. Paragraphs 12 through 23 of the motion set forth in detail the Emergency Treatment Program which will provide funds for tubal reconstructive surgery or in-vitro fertilization for Dalkon Shield claimants who have asserted that they have been rendered infertile as a consequence of their use of the product. The Program names an administrator, who "may employ others to assist in the administration of the program." It also creates a court appointed medical expert agreeable to the Dalkon Shield Claimants' Committee and a court appointed medical expert agreeable to Robins. These two medical experts shall agree upon a third expert to be appointed by the court to make any medical decisions required under the Program and further provides that the court may appoint "a nationally recognized fertility institute to make all eligibility and other medical determinations." The Program is to be financed by a $15 million fund to be set aside by Robins in an interest bearing account. The Program is to be audited by an accounting firm approved by the court; the administrator, experts and others employed in connection with the Program will be compensated as allowed by the court, and the program will "be terminated prior to or superseded by a confirmed plan of reorganization and all unexpended funds will be reallocated as provided by a confirmed plan of reorganization."

The Program also sets out the eligibility requirements for claimants seeking treatment or surgery. Payment will be made directly to the doctor and hospital and no money will be paid directly to the claimant or her attorney. Any amounts paid under the Program on behalf of a participating claimant will be deducted from the amount of disbursement the claimant would otherwise receive under a confirmed Chapter 11 plan of reorganization of Robins.

We find that the establishment and funding of the Program would benefit only certain unsecured holders of Dalkon Shield claims and that the program would afford preferential treatment to such claimants over other similarly situated unsecured Dalkon Shield claimants and over general unsecured creditors. The disbursement of such funds prior to the confirmation of a plan of reorganization for Robins would violate the Bankruptcy Code. We, therefore, reverse the district court.

I

The history of this litigation is well known and will not be repeated in detail. A.H. Robins Co. is operating its business as a Debtor in possession pursuant to the Bankruptcy Code, having filed a voluntary petition for relief under Chapter 11. The United States District Court for the Eastern District of Virginia, retained jurisdiction of certain aspects of this bankruptcy, including the Dalkon Shield litigation and claims. In September 1985 the district court ordered the appointment of The Official Committee of Equity Security Holders to represent the interest of Robins public shareholders. The common stock of Robins is traded on the New York Stock Exchange. There are more than twenty million shares of common stock outstanding.

Robins sought refuge in Chapter 11 because of a multitude of civil actions filed against it by women who alleged they were injured by use of the Dalkon Shield intrauterine device. As a result of the District Court's Bar Date Order of November 21, 1985, and worldwide notice of the effect of this order, approximately 325,000 notices of claim have been filed against Robins in the Bankruptcy Court alleging Dalkon Shield injuries. Robins and the Equity Committee have challenged the validity and amount of many of these claims, and none of these alleged Dalkon Shield claims have yet been "estimated" pursuant to 502(c) or "allowed" pursuant to 502(a).

In April 1987 Robins filed a proposed plan of reorganization and shortly thereafter filed a proposed disclosure statement. No action has been taken on the proposed plan of reorganization because of a merger proposal submitted by Rorer Group, Inc. under which Dalkon

Shield claimants would be compensated out of a $1.75 billion fund and all other creditors would be paid in full. Robins' stockholders would receive stock of the merged corporation. As a result of the merger proposal a revised plan of reorganization and disclosure statement must be filed, but, as of the date of the district court's order creating the $15 million "Emergency Treatment Fund," a revised plan of reorganization had not been submitted nor confirmed.

On August 13, 1986, the court appointed Ralph R. Mabey as an examiner "to evaluate and suggest proposed elements of a plan of reorganization." Examiner Mabey together with Robins, the Dalkon Shield Claimants' Committee and the Future Claimants' Representative filed the motion seeking the establishment of the Emergency Treatment Fund. In this motion they assert that one kind of injury allegedly caused by the Dalkon Shield is infertility, and that a number of claimants alleging such infertility are candidates for tubal reconstructive surgery or in-vitro fertilization. The program provides:

> A claimant is considered a candidate for reconstructive surgery if:
> (a) she is less than 40 years old; (b) she claims infertility; and (c) she is not surgically infertile.

It is alleged that the rate of success in restoring fertility by reconstructive surgery is 30% to 60% in cases where proper screening techniques have been utilized. The cost of such surgery runs $10,000 to $15,000. It is further stated "upon information and belief, in-vitro fertilization may be effective in certain cases in which tubal reconstructive surgery is unlikely to be successful."

The motion further states:

> If we assume that a Dalkon Shield claimant who has a compensable infertility claim would receive at least Fifteen Thousand Dollars under any plan of reorganization, the net financial cost of the program should not exceed the sum of the program administrative expenses and the time value of the monies disbursed. In effect, a participating claimant is simply electing to take a portion of her ultimate distribution in the form of medical assistance now rather than cash later. (However, if the claim of a participant is ultimately disallowed under a plan of reorganization, or valued at $15,000 or less, the claimant, while not being required to repay any amounts paid on her behalf for reconstructive surgery, will receive no additional distribution.)

II

The May 21, 1987 order of the district court approving the Emergency Treatment Fund makes no mention of its authority to establish such a fund prior to the allowance of the claim of the women who would benefit from the fund, and prior to the confirmation of a plan of reorganization of Robins. However, in its order denying The Equity Committee's Motion for a Stay Pending Appeal of the May 21, 1987 order, the district court relied upon the "expansive equity power" of the court.

> The court recognizes that the establishment of an emergency treatment fund is unusual and, indeed, may be unprecedented. Nevertheless, the Code provides the Court, pursuant to §105(a) with an expansive equity power to "issue any order, process or judgment that is necessary or appropriate to carry out the provisions of this title." The dire circumstances of this case required the Court to invoke its power under §105(a) and take those steps needed to treat these claimants equitably. See also Midlantic Natl. Bank. v. New Jersey Dept. of Envtl. Protection, 474 U.S. 494 (1986).

We have searched *Midlantic* without finding any reference to the equitable powers under §105(a), and we find such decision has no relevance to the issues presently before us. While the equitable powers emanating from §105(a) are quite important in the general bankruptcy scheme, and while such powers may encourage courts to be innovative, and even original, these equitable powers are not a license for a court to disregard the clear language and meaning of the bankruptcy statutes and rules. In In re Chicago, Milwaukee, St. Paul & Pacific Railroad Co., 791 F.2d 524, 528 (7th Cir. 1986), the court stated

> the fact that a proceeding is equitable does not give the judge a free-floating discretion to redistribute rights in accordance with his personal views of justice and fairness, however enlightened those views may be.

The same rule was stated earlier by Judge Augustus Hand in Guerin v. Weil, Gotshal & Manges, 205 F.2d 302, 304 (2d Cir. 1953).

> Although it has been broadly stated that a Bankruptcy Court is a court of equity, the exercise of its equitable powers must be strictly confined within the prescribed limits of the Bankruptcy Act.

While one may understand and sympathize with the district court's concern for the Dalkon Shield claimants, who may desire reconstructive surgery or in-vitro fertilization, the creation of the Emergency Treatment Fund at this stage of the Chapter 11 bankruptcy proceedings violates the clear language and intent of the Bankruptcy Code, and such action may not be justified as an exercise of the court's equitable powers under §105(a).

The Bankruptcy Code does not permit a distribution to unsecured creditors in a Chapter 11 proceeding except under and pursuant to a plan of reorganization that has been properly presented and approved. Section §1121 provides for the filing of a plan of reorganization. Sections 1122-1129 set forth the required contents of a plan, the classification of claims, the requirements of disclosure of the contents of the plan, the method for accepting the plan, any modification thereof, the hearing required on confirmation of the plan and the requirements for confirmation. The clear language of these statutes, as well as the Bankruptcy Rules applicable thereto, does not authorize the payment in part or in full, or the advance of monies to or for the benefit of unsecured claimants prior to the approval of the plan of reorganization. The creation of the Emergency Treatment Program has no authority to support it in the Bankruptcy Code and violates the clear policy of Chapter 11 reorganizations by allowing piecemeal, preconfirmation payments to certain unsecured creditors. Such action also violates Bankruptcy Rule 3021 which allows distribution to creditors only after the allowance of claims and the confirmation of a plan. * * *

Equally without merit is the appellee's claim that the order of the district court establishing the Emergency Treatment Fund was justified under what it refers to as a "business judgment" standard. We can find no support for such a standard, and if such a standard does exist, it would not allow the court to violate the clear dictates of the Bankruptcy Code, by paying certain unsecured claimants before their claims have been allowed and before a confirmed plan of reorganization is in place.

Reversed.

IN RE KMART CORP.

United States Court of Appeals, Seventh Circuit, 2004
359 F.3d 866

EASTERBROOK, CIRCUIT JUDGE

On the first day of its bankruptcy, Kmart sought permission to pay immediately, and in full, the prepetition claims of all "critical vendors." (Technically there are 38 debtors: Kmart Corporation plus 37 of its affiliates and subsidiaries. We call them all Kmart.) The theory behind the request is that some suppliers may be unwilling to do business with a customer that is behind in payment, and, if it cannot obtain the merchandise that its own customers have come to expect, a firm such as Kmart may be unable to carry on, injuring all of its creditors. Full payment to critical vendors thus could in principle make even the disfavored creditors better off: they may not be paid in full, but they will receive a greater portion of their claims than they would if the critical vendors cut off supplies and the business shut down. Putting the proposition in this way implies, however, that the debtor must *prove,* and not just allege, two things: that, but for immediate full payment, vendors *would* cease dealing; and that the business will gain enough from continued transactions with the favored vendors to provide some residual benefit to the remaining, disfavored creditors, or at least leave them no worse off.

Bankruptcy Judge Sonderby entered a critical-vendors order just as Kmart proposed it, without notifying any disfavored creditors, without receiving any pertinent evidence (the record contains only some sketchy representations by counsel plus unhelpful testimony by Kmart's CEO, who could not speak for the vendors), and without making any finding of fact that the disfavored creditors would gain or come out even. The bankruptcy court's order declared that the relief Kmart requested—open-ended permission to pay any debt to any vendor it deemed "critical" in the exercise of unilateral discretion, provided that the vendor agreed to furnish goods on "customary trade terms" for the next two years—was "in the best interests of the Debtors, their estates and their creditors". The order did not explain why, nor did it contain any legal analysis, though it did cite 11 U.S.C. § 105(a). (The bankruptcy court issued two companion orders covering international vendors and liquor vendors. Analysis of all three orders is the same, so we do not mention these two further.)

Kmart used its authority to pay in full the prepetition debts to 2,330 suppliers, which collectively received about $300 million. This came from the $2 billion in new credit (debtor-in-possession or DIP financing) that the bankruptcy judge authorized, granting the lenders super-priority in postpetition assets and revenues. See In re Qualitech Steel Corp., 276 F.3d 245 (7th Cir.2001). Another 2,000 or so vendors were not deemed "critical" and were not paid. They and 43,000 additional unsecured creditors eventually received about 10¢ on the dollar, mostly in stock of the reorganized Kmart. Capital Factors, Inc., appealed the critical-vendors order immediately after its entry on January 25, 2002. A little more than 14 months later, after all of the critical vendors had been paid and as Kmart's plan of reorganization was on the verge of approval, District Judge Grady reversed the order authorizing payment. 291 Bankr. 818 (N.D. Ill. 2003). He concluded that neither §105(a) nor a "doctrine of necessity" supports the orders. * * *

Section 105(a) allows a bankruptcy court to "issue any order, process, or judgment that is necessary or appropriate to carry out the provisions of" the Code. This does not create discretion to set aside the Code's rules about priority and distribution; the power conferred by §105(a) is one to implement rather than override. Every circuit that has considered the question has held that this statute does not allow a bankruptcy judge to authorize full payment of any unsecured debt, unless all unsecured creditors in the class are paid in full. We agree with this view of §105. "The fact that a [bankruptcy] proceeding is equitable does not give the judge a free-floating discretion to redistribute rights in accordance with his personal views of justice and fairness, however enlightened those views may be." In re Chicago, Milwaukee, St. Paul & Pacific R.R., 791 F.2d 524, 528 (7th Cir. 1986).

A "doctrine of necessity" is just a fancy name for a power to depart from the Code. Although courts in the days before bankruptcy law was codified wielded power to reorder priorities and pay particular creditors in the name of "necessity"—see Miltenberger v. Logansport Ry., 106 U.S. 286 (1882); Fosdick v. Schall, 99 U.S. 235 (1878)—today it is the Code rather than the norms of nineteenth century railroad reorganizations that must prevail. *Miltenberger* and *Fosdick* predate the first general effort at codification, the Bankruptcy Act of 1898. Today the Bankruptcy Code of 1978 supplies the rules. Congress did not in terms scuttle old common-law doctrines, because it did not need to; the Act curtailed, and then the Code replaced, the entire apparatus. Answers to contemporary issues must be found within the Code (or legislative halls). Older doctrines may survive as glosses on ambiguous language enacted in 1978 or later, but not as freestanding entitlements to trump the text.

So does the Code contain any grant of authority for debtors to prefer some vendors over others? Many sections require equal treatment or specify the details of priority when assets are insufficient to satisfy all claims. Appellants rely on §363(b), §364(b), and §503 as sources of authority for unequal treatment. Section 364(b) . . . authorizes the debtor to obtain credit (as Kmart did) but has nothing to say about how the money will be disbursed or about priorities among creditors. To the extent that In re Payless Cashways, Inc., 268 Bankr. 543 (Bankr. W.D. Mo. 2001), and similar decisions, hold otherwise, they are unpersuasive. Section 503, which deals with administrative expenses, likewise is irrelevant. Pre-filing debts are not administrative expenses; they are the antithesis of administrative expenses. Filing a petition for bankruptcy effectively creates two firms: the debts of the pre-filing entity may be written down so that the post-filing entity may reorganize and continue in business if it has a positive cash flow. See Boston & Maine Corp. v. Chicago Pacific Corp., 785 F.2d 562 (7th Cir. 1986). Treating pre-filing debts as "administrative" claims against the post-filing entity would impair the ability of bankruptcy law to prevent old debts from sinking a viable firm.

[handwritten margin note: severs the tie between pre- and post-petition liens]

That leaves §363(b)(1). This is more promising, for satisfaction of a prepetition debt in order to keep "critical" supplies flowing is a use of property other than in the ordinary course of administering an estate in bankruptcy. Capital Factors insists that §363(b)(1) should be limited to the commencement of capital projects, such as building a new plant, rather than payment of old debts—as paying vendors would be "in the ordinary course" but for the intervening bankruptcy petition. To read §363(b)(1) broadly, Capital Factors observes, would be to allow a judge to rearrange priorities among creditors (which is what a critical-vendors order effectively does), even though the Supreme Court has cautioned against such a step. See United States v. Reorganized CF & I Fabricators of Utah, Inc., 518 U.S. 213 (1996). Yet what these decisions principally say is that priorities do not change unless a statute supports that step; and if §363(b)(1) is such a statute, then there is no insuperable problem. If the language is too open-ended, that is a problem for the legislature. Nonetheless, it is prudent to read, and use, §363(b)(1) to do the least damage possible to priorities established by contract and by other parts of the Bankruptcy Code. We need not decide whether §363(b)(1) could support payment of some prepetition debts, because *this* order was unsound no matter how one reads §363(b)(1).

[handwritten margin note: §363(b)(1)?]

[handwritten note: — avoids question of whether it should be interpreted broadly]

The foundation of a critical-vendors order is the belief that vendors not paid for prior deliveries will refuse to make new ones. Without merchandise to sell, a retailer such as Kmart will fold. If paying the critical vendors would enable a successful reorganization and make even the disfavored creditors better off, then all creditors favor payment whether or not they are designated as "critical." This sug-

[handwritten note at bottom: ↳ existing vendors · brand equity, reputation, loyalty]

gests a use of §363(b)(1) similar to the theory underlying a plan crammed down the throats of an impaired class of creditors: if the impaired class does at least as well as it would have under a Chapter 7 liquidation, then it has no legitimate objection and cannot block the reorganization. For the premise to hold true, however, it is necessary to show not only that the disfavored creditors will be as well off with reorganization as with liquidation—a demonstration never attempted in this proceeding—but also that the supposedly critical vendors would have ceased deliveries if old debts were left unpaid while the litigation continued. If vendors will deliver against a promise of current payment, then a reorganization can be achieved, and all unsecured creditors will obtain its benefit, without preferring any of the unsecured creditors.

Some supposedly critical vendors will continue to do business with the debtor because they must. They may, for example, have long-term contracts, and the automatic stay prevents these vendors from walking away as long as the debtor pays for new deliveries. Fleming Companies, which received the largest critical-vendors payment because it sold Kmart between $70 million and $100 million of groceries and related goods weekly, was one of these. No matter how much Fleming would have liked to dump Kmart, it had no right to do so. It was unnecessary to compensate Fleming for continuing to make deliveries that it was legally required to make. Nor was Fleming likely to walk away even if it had a legal right to do so. Each new delivery produced a profit; as long as Kmart continued to pay for new product, why would any vendor drop the account? That would be a self-inflicted wound. To abjure new profits because of old debts would be to commit the sunk-cost fallacy; well-managed businesses are unlikely to do this. Firms that disdain current profits because of old losses are unlikely to stay in business. They might as well burn money or drop it into the ocean. Again Fleming illustrates the point. When Kmart stopped buying its products after the contract expired, Fleming collapsed (Kmart had accounted for more than 50% of its business) and filed its own bankruptcy petition. Fleming was hardly likely to have quit selling of its own volition, only to expire the sooner.

Doubtless many suppliers fear the prospect of throwing good money after bad. It therefore may be vital to assure them that a debtor will pay for new deliveries on a current basis. Providing that assurance need not, however, entail payment for prepetition transactions. Kmart could have paid cash or its equivalent. (Kmart's CEO told the bankruptcy judge that COD arrangements were not part of Kmart's business plan, as if a litigant's druthers could override the rights of third parties.) Cash on the barrelhead was not the most convenient way, however. Kmart secured a $2 billion line of credit when it entered bankruptcy. Some of that credit could have been used to assure vendors that payment would be forthcoming for all postpetition transactions. The easiest way to do that would have been to put some of the $2 billion behind a standby letter of credit on which the bankruptcy judge could authorize unpaid vendors to draw. That would not have changed the terms on which Kmart and any of its vendors did business; it just would have demonstrated the certainty of payment. If lenders are unwilling to issue such a letter of credit (or if they insist on a letter's short duration), that would be a compelling market signal that reorganization is a poor prospect and that the debtor should be liquidated post haste.

Yet the bankruptcy court did not explore the possibility of using a letter of credit to assure vendors of payment. The court did not find that any firm would have ceased doing business with Kmart if not paid for prepetition deliveries, and the scant record would not have supported such a finding had one been made. The court did not find that discrimination among unsecured creditors was the only way to facilitate a reorganization. It did not find that the disfavored creditors were at least as well off as they would have been had the critical-vendors order not been entered. For all the millions at stake, this proceeding looks much like the Chapter 13 reorganization that produced In re Crawford, 324 F.3d 539 (7th Cir. 2003). Crawford had wanted to classify his creditors in a way that would enable him to pay off those debts that would not be discharged, while stiffing the creditors whose debts were dischargeable. We replied that even though classification (and thus unequal treatment) is possible for Chapter 13 proceedings, see §1322(b), the step would be proper only when the record shows that the classification would produce some benefit for the disfavored creditors. Just so here. Even if §363(b)(1) allows critical-vendors orders in principle, preferential payments to a class of creditors are proper only if the record shows the prospect of benefit to the other creditors. This record does not, so the critical-vendors order cannot stand.

NOTES

9C.1. Although the *Mabey* opinion is not clear on this point, the examiner was able to show that such a fund would ultimately *lower* the aggregate cost of claims submitted by the tort victims. The fund was set up to treat infertility, the primary injury caused by Robins' conduct. For the many women who would have benefited from the treatment, Robins' liability would have been reduced significantly. Creditors as a whole would very likely be made better off even if they were not paid in full. It is better to pay someone a small amount for surgery (and thus compensate them completely for their injury) than to prevent them from having the surgery and thereby generate a much larger claim against the estate. A general creditor who stands to receive about fifty cents on the dollar would much rather have a tort creditor paid in full for a $15,000 claim at the start of the bankruptcy than share the Debtor's assets at the end of the case based on a tort claim that has increased to $150,000. Hence, it should come as little surprise that the creditors did not object.

Instead, the objection came from the equity holders. Under state law, equity holders are entitled to a corporation's assets only after all creditors—including tort claimants—are paid in full. As we will see in part 3 below, bankruptcy law generally follows this priority scheme. So the only *legitimate* ground for equity's objection would be that the debtor was solvent and could pay its creditors in full but that the treatment would not bring benefits to the tort victims worth the cost. The evidence the examiner presented made this possibility quite implausible. The equity holders may instead have thought that by objecting to this plan (as well as others) that were otherwise in the interests of the firm, they would extract greater concessions under the plan of reorganization. A common feature of Chapter 11 bargaining (though not often as shocking as the one seen in this case) is the willingness of some players to lodge strategic objections.

9C.2. The *Mabey* court did not reject the examiner's estimates in favor of the equity committee's. Instead, the court held that the bankruptcy law "does not authorize the payment in part or in full, or the advance of monies to or for the benefit of unsecured claimants prior to the approval of the plan of reorganization." The court was not persuaded that a bankruptcy judge's general equitable powers under §105 could provide such authorization in the face of clear direction on how assets of a bankruptcy estate or their value are to be distributed. But the court might have looked elsewhere in the Bankruptcy Code. Section 549(a)(2), for example, though addressed to the avoidance of unauthorized transfers, arguably implies that a transfer of assets prior to the conclusion of the bankruptcy case can be authorized by *either* the Code or the court.

As discussed in the *Kmart* opinion, however, alternative means of justifying the Emergency Treatment Fund rests on §363. There is no doubt, for example, that the trustee may spend resources to maintain the value of a firm's assets. The trustee can spend money to repair machines or buy insurance. As we shall see, such expenses are entitled to priority because they ultimately are designed to increase the value of the assets and hence the distribution to the general creditors. When a payment to a prepetition creditor will increase the return to general creditors, it is arguably a use of assets within the ambit of §363. Such a payment is not an ordinary course expenditure, but §363 requires in such cases only that there be notice and a hearing so that the examiner can show that the payments will have the promised effect. One might fear that such payments, especially when made at the outset of the case by the debtor in possession, might not benefit the general creditors. But one might account for this by placing a heavy burden on the party proposing the payment or requiring that it be supported by a third party such as an examiner. In *Mabey,* the case for making the payment was so compelling that the examiner might well have been able to meet even an arbitrarily high burden of proof.

9C.3. Notwithstanding *Mabey* or any doubts about statutory authorization, a firm that wants to stay in business in Chapter 11 typically will pay its workers their prepetition wages on schedule. If the workers are not paid, they may not continue to work. Even if a refusal to work violates §362(a)(6) because it is an act to obtain payment on a prepetition claim, the Norris-LaGuardia Act prevents the bankruptcy court from issuing an injunction against the workers. See *Northwest Airlines* in chapter 7, section C above. Given that the workers are diverse and in many cases judgment-proof, the threat of monetary sanctions for violating the automatic stay may not loom large, either. Moreover, because wages are entitled to a priority under §507(a), as we shall discuss in part 3 below, there may be little danger that workers will receive more at the outset than they would have received at the end of the process.

Nonetheless, in the unusual case that someone objects to payments of prepetition wages, and those wages are in excess of the workers' §507(a) priority, courts are split on whether to authorize the payments. Some refuse. See, e.g., In re FCX, Inc., 60 Bankr. 405 (E.D.N.C. 1986). Others accept the argument that such payments are in the interests of everyone as the workers are necessary. See, e.g., In re Ionosphere Clubs, Inc., 98 Bankr. 174 (Bankr. S.D.N.Y. 1989). Courts that take the latter view sometimes cite the doctrine of necessity or the necessity-of-payment rule developed in the era of equity receiverships and first set forth in Miltenberger v. Logansport, C. & S.W. Railway Co., 106 U.S. 286 (1882). According to this doctrine, the payment is made because of the benefit that will accrue to the estate as a whole, not because of any entitlement of the individual creditor. The doctrine thus tracks the argument, stated above, that §363 authorized the Emergency Treatment Fund in *Mabey* and follows the dicta of *Kmart*.

9C.4. As illustrated by *Kmart*, the doctrine of necessity, along with its (better grounded) §363 analog, applies not only to employees, of course. Suppliers of goods, like workers, may have the power to shut down a debtor that seeks to reorganize and stay in business. Even an insolvent debtor in bankruptcy, therefore, may consider full payment of prepetition general claims to a supplier. With this in mind, the 2005 Bankruptcy Act added §503(b)(9), which provides the vendor an administrative expense for goods delivered to the debtor in the ordinary course of business within 20 days of the commencement of the case. (The Act also broadened a supplier's reclamation rights under §546(c).) But an administrative expense priority, addressed later in this section of the book, does not provide the holder an immediate right to payment or cover long overdue obligations (and reclamations rights are not always effective). So *Kmart* remains a significant case.

9C.5. As may be apparent, *Kmart* does not reject §363 as a basis to pay prepetition debts to critical vendors. Rather the case stands for the proposition that a debtor's payment of prepetition claims is extraordinary and requires a demonstration of necessity, which is not assumed. For a case that reaches a similar conclusion, though under the doctrine of necessity and §105, see In re Coserv, LLC, 273 Bankr. 487 (Bankr. N.D. Tex. 2002). Problem 9C-1 further explores the issues that may arise when a supplier, of labor or goods, is also a prepetition creditor.

9C.6. One should not uncritically accept either the doctrine of necessity or the use of §363 to support this doctrine even if it is clear that a debtor could not remain in operation without payment of prepetition claims. Application of the doctrine assumes that a debtor in reorganization should continue and that the use of the debtor's assets toward that end is beneficial to the estate. This assumption is not always prudent. Sometimes, debtors fail financially and enter bankruptcy because they have failed economically as well. In these cases, the debtor's assets are more valuable sold off to other enterprises, and the creditors will benefit from such liquidation (though the debtor's employees or communities likely will not). When liquidation rather than reorganization is efficient, it may well be that §363 should authorize no ordinary transfer of assets to employees, much less extraordinary transfers such as the payment of prepetition wages as a bribe to assure continuation. If a firm is losing money, there is a danger that the assets spent to preserve the estate may leave everyone worse off. *In re Ionosphere Clubs*, cited above in Note 9C.3 as doctrine of necessity case, involved the reorganization of Eastern Airlines. The company lost hundreds of millions of dollars before it ceased operations and left nothing for the general creditors.

PROBLEM

9C-1. Debtor is a retailer that sells Manufacturer Brand shoes. As cash becomes short, Debtor permits holes to develop in its lines. For example, Debtor might stock sizes 6 through 8 and 11 through 12 of a certain shoe but not sizes 9 and 10. Customers become frustrated with the lack of choice. Debtor files for bankruptcy under Chapter 11. While in bankruptcy, Debtor obtains a loan from a bank and attempts to fill the holes in its inventory with purchases from Manufacturer. To Debtor's surprise, Manufacturer responds that it will not sell Debtor any new shoes, even for cash, unless Debtor pays in full for shoes Manufacturer sold Debtor, prepetition, on general credit. Does the Bankruptcy Code authorize payment for the prepetition shoes? Should it? Do Manufacturer's terms violate the automatic stay? (See chapter 4, section A above.) Would any of your answers change if Manufacturer simply raised the shoe price for Debtor by exactly enough to satisfy Debtor's prepetition obligation? How, if at all, do the facts of this problem differ from those of *Mabey*? See In re Ike Kempner & Bros. 4 Bankr. 31 (Bankr. E.D. Ark. 1980).

2) *SALE OF ASSETS*

In the next cases, *Lionel* and *TWA* the courts examine the extent to which the procedures in Chapter 11 set implicit limits on whether a debtor may sell assets under §363. In *Lionel* the question was whether the sale could occur at all, while in *TWA* the question was whether the assets sold would be free and clear from claims. As a practical matter, though, anticipated disallowance of a free-and-clear sale will prevent the sale itself. While reading the cases, as well as the related notes and problem, consider how a sale under §363 may create opportunities for advantage-taking and abuse.

CASES

IN RE LIONEL CORP.

United States Court of Appeals, Second Circuit, 1983
722 F.2d 1063

CARDAMONE, CIRCUIT JUDGE.

This expedited appeal is from an order of United States District Judge Dudley B. Bonsal dated September 7, 1983, approving an order entered earlier that day by the United States Bankruptcy Court for the Southern District of New York (Ryan, J.). The order authorized the sale by Lionel Corporation, a Chapter 11 debtor in possession, of its 82% common stock holding in Dale Electronics, Inc. to Peabody International Corporation for $50 million.

I. Facts

On February 19, 1982 the Lionel Corporation—toy train manufacturer of childhood memory—and two of its subsidiaries, Lionel Leisure, Inc. and Consolidated Toy Company, filed joint petitions for reorganization under Chapter 11. Resort to Chapter 11 was precipitated by losses totaling $22.5 million that Lionel incurred in its toy retailing operation during the two-year period ending December 1982.

There are 7.1 million shares of common stock of Lionel held by 10,000 investors. Its consolidated assets and liabilities as of March 31, 1983 were $168.7 million and $191.5 million, respectively, reflecting a negative net worth of nearly $23 million. Total sales for 1981 and 1982 were $295.1 million and $338.6 million. Lionel's creditors hold approximately $135.6 million in prepetition claims, and they are represented in the ongoing bankruptcy proceedings by an Official Creditors' Committee whose 13 members hold $80 million of those claims. The remaining $55 million is scattered among thousands of small creditors.

Lionel continues to operate its businesses and manage its properties pursuant to §§1107-1108, primarily through its wholly-owned subsidiary, Leisure. Leisure operates Lionel's presently owned 56 specialty retail stores, which include a number of stores formerly managed by Lionel's other subsidiary, Consolidated Toy. In addition to the stock of Leisure and Consolidated Toy, Lionel has other assets such as the right to receive royalty payments relating to the manufacture of toy trains.

Lionel's most important asset and the subject of this proceeding is its ownership of 82% of the common stock of Dale, a corporation engaged in the manufacture of electronic components. Dale is not a party to the Lionel bankruptcy proceeding. Public investors own the remaining 18% of Dale's common stock, which is listed on the American Stock Exchange. Its balance sheet reflects assets and liabilities as of March 31, 1983 of $57.8 million and $29.8 million, respectively, resulting in shareholders equity of approximately $28.0 million. Lionel's stock investment in Dale represents approximately 34% of Lionel's consolidated assets, and its interest in Dale is Lionel's most valuable single asset. Unlike Lionel's toy retailing operation, Dale is profitable. For the same two-year period ending in December 1982 during which Lionel had incurred its substantial losses, Dale had an aggregate operating profit of $18.8 million.

On June 14, 1983 Lionel filed an application under §363(b) seeking bankruptcy court authorization to sell its 82% interest in Dale to Acme-Cleveland Corporation for $43 million in cash. Four days later the debtor filed a plan of reorganization conditioned upon a sale of Dale with the proceeds to be distributed to creditors. Certain issues of the reorganization remain unresolved, and negotiations are continuing; however, a solicitation of votes on the plan has not yet begun. On September 7, 1983, following the Securities and Exchange Commission's July 15 filing of objections to the sale, Bankruptcy Judge Ryan held a hearing on Lionel's application. At the hearing, Peabody emerged as the successful of three bidders with an offer of $50 million for Lionel's interest in Dale.

The Chief Executive Officer of Lionel and a Vice-President of Salomon Brothers were the only witnesses produced and both testified in support of the application. Their testimony established that while the price paid for the stock was "fair," Dale is not an asset "that is wasting away in any sense." Lionel's Chief Executive Officer stated that there was no reason why the sale of Dale stock could not be accomplished as part of the reorganization plan, and that the sole reason for Lionel's application to sell was the Creditors' Committee's insistence upon it. The creditors wanted to turn this asset of Lionel into a "pot of cash," to provide the bulk of the $70 million required to repay creditors under the proposed plan of reorganization.

In confirming the sale, Judge Ryan made no formal findings of fact. He simply noted that cause to sell was sufficiently shown by the Creditors' Committee's insistence upon it. Judge Ryan further found cause—presumably from long experience—based upon his own opinion that a present failure to confirm would set the entire reorganization process back a year or longer while the parties attempted to restructure it.

The Committee of Equity Security Holders, statutory representatives of the 10,000 public shareholders of Lionel, appealed this order claiming that the sale, prior to approval of a reorganization plan, deprives the equity holders of the Bankruptcy Code's safeguards of disclosure, solicitation and acceptance and divests the debtor of a dominant and profitable asset which could serve as a cornerstone for a sound plan. The SEC also appeared and objected to the sale in the bankruptcy court and supports the Equity Committee's appeal, claiming that approval of the sale side-steps the Code's requirement for informed suffrage which is at the heart of Chapter 11.

The Creditors' Committee favors the sale because it believes it is in the best interests of Lionel and because the sale is expressly authorized by §363(b). Lionel tells us that its ownership of Dale, a nonoperating asset, is held for investment purposes only and that its sale will provide the estate with the large block of the cash needed to fund its plan of reorganization.

From the oral arguments and briefs we gather that the Equity Committee believes that Chapter 11 has cleared the reorganization field of major preplan sales—somewhat like the way Minerva routed Mars—relegating §363(b) to be used only in emergencies. The Creditors' Committee counters that a bankruptcy judge should have absolute freedom under §363(b) to do as he thinks best. Neither of these arguments is wholly persuasive. Here, as in so many similar cases, we must avoid the extremes, for the policies underlying the Bankruptcy Reform Act of 1978 support a middle ground—one which gives the bankruptcy judge considerable discretion yet requires him to articulate sound business justifications for his decisions.

II. Discussion

The issue now before this Court is to what extent Chapter 11 permits a bankruptcy judge to authorize the sale of an important asset of the bankrupt's estate, out of the ordinary course of business and prior to acceptance and outside of any plan of reorganization. Section 363(b), the focal point of our analysis, provides that "[t]he trustee, after notice and a hearing, may use, sell, or lease, other than in the ordinary course of business, property of the estate."

On its face, §363(b) appears to permit disposition of any property of the estate of a corporate debtor without resort to the statutory safeguards embodied in Chapter 11. Yet, analysis of the statute's history and over seven decades of case law convinces us that such a literal reading of §363(b) would unnecessarily violate the congressional scheme for corporate reorganizations. * * *

Section 116(3) of the 1938 Act, which was the immediate predecessor of §363(b), was originally enacted as §77B(c) in 1937. Section 116(3) provided:

> Upon the approval of a petition, the judge may, in addition to the jurisdiction, powers and duties hereinabove and elsewhere in this chapter conferred and imposed upon him and the court ... (3) authorize a receiver or a trustee or a debtor in possession, upon such notice as the judge may prescribe and upon cause shown, to lease or sell any property of the debtor, whether real or personal, upon such terms and conditions as the judge may approve.

This section applied in Chapter X proceedings, and a similar provision, §313(2), pertained to Chapter XI cases. Thus, when reorganization became part of the bankruptcy law, the long established administrative powers of the court to sell a debtor's property prior to adjudication were extended to cover reorganizations with a debtor in possession under Chapter XI pursuant to §313(2), as well as a trustee in control under Chapter X pursuant to §116(3). These sections, as their predecessors, were designed to handle leases or sales required during the time lag between the filing of a petition for reorganization and the date when the plan was approved.

The Rules of Bankruptcy Procedure applicable in Chapters X and XI, the Act's reorganization procedures, provided for a sale of all or part of a bankrupt's property after application to the court and "upon cause shown." Rules 10-607(b), 11-54. Despite the provisions of this Rule, the "perishable" concept, expressed in the view that a preconfirmation or pre-adjudication sale was the exception and not the rule, persisted. As one commentator stated, "[o]rdinarily, in the absence of perishable goods, or depreciation of assets, or actual jeopardy of the estate, a sale will not be ordered, particularly prior to adjudication." 1 Collier on Bankruptcy ¶2.28(3) (14th ed. 1978). * * *

[Courts have recently] upheld sales prior to plan approval under the [1898 Act] where the bankruptcy court outlined the circumstances in its findings of fact indicating why the sale was in the best interest of the estate. E.g., In re Equity Funding Corp., 492 F.2d 793, 794 (9th Cir. 1974) (finding of fact that because market value of asset was likely to deteriorate substantially in the near future, sale was in the estate's best interests); In re Dania Corp., 400 F.2d 833, 835-837 (5th Cir. 1968) (upholding sale of stock representing debtor's major asset where its value was rapidly deteriorating causing the reorganizing estate to diminish); In re Marathon Foundry & Machine Co., 228 F.2d 594 (7th Cir. 1955) (heavy interest charges justified sale of stock which had been pledged to secure loan). In essence, these cases evidence the continuing vitality under the old law of an "emergency" or "perishability" standard. As we shall see, the new Bankruptcy Code no longer requires such strict limitations on a bankruptcy judge's authority to order disposition of the estate's property; nevertheless, it does not go so far as to eliminate all constraints on that judge's discretion. * * *

363(b) seems on its face to confer upon the bankruptcy judge virtually unfettered discretion to authorize the use, sale or lease, other than in the ordinary course of business, of property of the estate. Of course, the statute requires that notice be given and a hearing conducted, but [no] reference is made to an "emergency" or "perishability" requirement nor is there an indication that a debtor in possession or trustee contemplating sale must show "cause." Thus, the language of §363(b) clearly is different from the terms of its statutory predecessors. And, while Congress never expressly stated why it abandoned the "upon cause shown" terminology of §116(3), arguably that omission permits easier access to §363(b). Various policy considerations lend some support to this view.

First and foremost is the notion that a bankruptcy judge must not be shackled with unnecessarily rigid rules when exercising the undoubtedly broad administrative power granted him under the Code. As Justice Holmes once said in a different context, "[s]ome play must be allowed for the joints of the machine. ... " Missouri, Kansas & Texas Ry. Co. v. May, 194 U.S. 267, 270 (1904). To further the purposes of Chapter 11 reorganization, a bankruptcy judge must have substantial freedom to tailor his orders to meet differing circumstances. This is exactly the result a liberal reading of §363(b) will achieve.

Support for this policy is found in the rationale underlying a number of earlier cases that had applied §116(3) of the Act. In particular, this Court's decision in [In re Sire Plan, Inc., 332 F.2d 497 (2d Cir. 1964)] was not hinged on an "emergency" or "perishability" concept. Lip service was paid to the argument that a partially constructed building is a "wasting asset"; but the real justification for authorizing the sale was the belief that the property's value depended on whether a hotel could be built in time for the World's Fair and that an advantageous sale after the opening of the World's Fair seemed unlikely. Thus, the reason was not solely that a steel skeleton was deteriorating, but rather that a good business opportunity was presently available, so long as the parties could act quickly. In such cases therefore the bankruptcy machinery should not straightjacket the bankruptcy judge so as to prevent him from doing what is best for the estate.

Just as we reject the requirement that only an emergency permits the use of §363(b), we also reject the view that §363(b) grants the bankruptcy judge carte blanche. Several reasons lead us to this conclusion: the statute requires notice and a hearing, and these procedural safeguards would be meaningless absent a further requirement that reasons be given for whatever determination is made; similarly, appellate review would effectively be precluded by an irreversible order; and, finally, such construction of §363(b) swallows up Chapter 11's safeguards. In fact, the legislative history surrounding the enactment of Chapter 11 makes evident Congress' concern with rights of equity interests as well as those of creditors.

Chapter 5 of the House bill dealing with reorganizations states that the purpose of a business reorganization is to restructure a business' finances to enable it to operate productively, provide jobs for its employees, pay its creditors and produce a return for its stockholders. The automatic stay upon filing a petition prevents creditors from acting unilaterally or pressuring the debtor. The plan of reorganization determines how much and in what form creditors will be paid, whether stockholders will continue to retain any interests, and in what form the business will continue. Requiring acceptance by a percentage of creditors and stockholders for confirmation forces negotiation among the debtor, its creditors and its stockholders. A fair analysis of the House bill reveals that reorganization under the 1938 Chandler Act, though designed to protect creditors had, over the years, often worked to their detriment and to the detriment of shareholders as well.

The primary reason reorganization under the [1898 Act] had not served well was that disclosure was minimal and reorganization under the Act was designed to deal with trade debt, not secured or public debt or equity. ... The key to the reorganization Chapter, therefore, is disclosure. To make disclosure effective, a provision was included that there be a disclosure statement and a hearing on the adequacy of the information it contains. The essential purpose served by disclosure is to ensure that public investors are not left entirely at the mercy of the debtor and its creditors. For that reason the Securities and Exchange Commission, for example, has an absolute right to appear and be heard on behalf of the public interest in an orderly securities market.

The Senate hearings similarly reflect a concern as to how losses are to be apportioned between creditors and stockholders in the reorganization of a public company. S. Rep. No. 95-989, 95th Cong. 2d Sess. 9 (1978). Noting that "the most vulnerable today are public investors," the Senate Judiciary Committee Report states that the bill is designed to counteract "the natural tendency of a debtor in distress to pacify large creditors with whom the debtor would expect to do business, at the expense of small and scattered public investors." S. Rep. No. 95-989 at 10. The Committee believed that investor protection is most critical when the public company is in such financial distress as to cause it to seek aid under the bankruptcy laws. The need for this protection was plain. Reorganization under the 1938 Act was often unfair to public investors who lacked bargaining power, and these conditions continued. Echoing the conclusion of the House Committee, the Senate Committee believed that the bill would promote fairer and more equitable reorganizations granting to public investors the last chance to conserve values that corporate insolvency has jeopardized.

III. Conclusion

History surrounding the enactment in 1978 of current Chapter 11 and the logic underlying it buttress our conclusion that there must be some articulated business justification, other than appeasement of major creditors, for using, selling or leasing property out of the ordinary course of business before the bankruptcy judge may order such disposition under §363(b).

The case law under §363's statutory predecessors used terms like "perishable," "deteriorating," and "emergency" as guides in deciding whether a debtor's property could be sold outside the ordinary course of business. The use of such words persisted long after their omission from newer statutes and rules. The administrative power to sell or lease property in a reorganization continued to be the exception, not the rule. Collier on Bankruptcy ¶2.28(b). In enacting the 1978 Code Congress was aware of existing case law and clearly indicated as one of its purposes that equity interests have a greater voice in reorganization plans—hence, the safeguards of disclosure, voting, acceptance and confirmation in present Chapter 11.

Resolving the apparent conflict between Chapter 11 and §363(b) does not require an all or nothing approach. Every sale under §363(b) does not automatically short-circuit or side-step Chapter 11; nor are these two statutory provisions to be read as mutually exclusive. Instead, if a bankruptcy judge is to administer a business reorganization successfully under the Code, then—like the related yet independent tasks performed in modern production techniques to ensure good results—some play for the operation of both §363(b) and Chapter 11 must be allowed for.

The rule we adopt requires that a judge determining a §363(b) application expressly find from the evidence presented before him at the hearing a good business reason to grant such an application. In this case the only reason advanced for granting the request to sell Lionel's 82% stock interest in Dale was the Creditors' Committee's insistence on it. Such is insufficient as a matter of fact because it is not a sound business reason and insufficient as a matter of law because it ignores the equity interests required to be weighed and considered under Chapter 11. The court also expressed its concern that a present failure to approve the sale would result in a long delay. As the Supreme Court has noted, it is easy to sympathize with the desire of a bankruptcy court to expedite bankruptcy reorganization proceedings for they are frequently protracted. "The need for expedition, however, is not a justification for abandoning proper standards." Protective Committee for Independent Stockholders of TMT Trailer Ferry, Inc. v. Anderson, 390 U.S. 414, 450 (1968). Thus, the approval of the sale of Lionel's 82% interest in Dale was an abuse of the trial court's discretion.

In fashioning its findings, a bankruptcy judge must not blindly follow the hue and cry of the most vocal special interest groups; rather, he should consider all salient factors pertaining to the proceeding and, accordingly, act to further the diverse interests of the debtor, creditors and equity holders, alike. He might, for example, look to such relevant factors as the proportionate value of the asset to the estate as a whole, the amount of elapsed time since the filing, the likelihood that a plan of reorganization will be proposed and confirmed in the near future, the effect of the proposed disposition on future plans of reorganization, the proceeds to be obtained from the disposition vis-à-vis any appraisals of the property, which of the alternatives of use, sale or lease the proposal envisions and, most importantly perhaps, whether the asset is increasing or decreasing in value. This list is not intended to be exclusive, but merely to provide guidance to the bankruptcy judge.

Finally, we must consider whether appellants opposing the sale produced evidence before the bankruptcy court that such sale was not justified. While a debtor applying under §363(b) carries the burden of demonstrating that a use, sale or lease out of the ordinary course of business will aid the debtor's reorganization, an objectant, such as the Equity Committee here, is required to produce some evidence respecting its objections. Appellants made three objections below: First, the sale was premature because Dale is not a wasting asset and there is no emergency; second, there was no justifiable cause present since Dale, if anything, is improving; and third, the price was inadequate. No proof was required as to the first objection because it was stipulated as conceded. The second and third objections are interrelated. Following Judge Ryan's suggestion that objections could as a practical matter be developed on cross-examination, Equity's counsel elicited testimony from the financial expert produced by Lionel that Dale is less subject than other companies to wide market fluctuations. The same witness also conceded that he knew of no reason why those interested in Dale's stock at the September 7, 1983 hearing would not be just as interested six months from then. The only other witness who testified was the Chief Executive Officer of Lionel, who stated that it was only at the insistence of the Creditors' Committee that Dale stock was being sold and that Lionel "would very much like to retain its interest in Dale." These uncontroverted statements of the two witnesses elicited by the Equity Committee on cross-examination were sufficient proof to support its objections to the present sale of Dale because this evidence demonstrated that there was no good business reason for the present sale. Hence, appellants satisfied their burden.

Accordingly, the order appealed from is reversed and the matter remanded to the district court with directions to remand to the bankruptcy court for further proceedings consistent with this opinion.

WINTER, Circuit Judge, dissenting.

In order to expedite the decision in this matter, I set forth my dissenting views in summary fashion.

The following facts are undisputed as the record presently stands: (i) Lionel sought a buyer for the Dale stock willing to condition its purchase upon confirmation of a reorganization plan. It was unsuccessful since, in the words of the bankruptcy judge "the confirmation of any plan is usually somewhat iffy," and few purchasers are willing to commit upwards of $50 million for an extended period without a contract binding on the other party; (ii) every feasible reorganization plan contemplates the sale of the Dale stock for cash; (iii) a reorganization plan may be approved fairly soon if the Dale stock is sold now. If the sale is prohibited, renewed negotiations between the creditors and the equity holders will be necessary, and the submission of a plan, if any, will be put off well into the future; and (iv) the Dale stock can be sold now at or near the same price as it can be sold later.

The effect of the present decision is thus to leave the debtor in possession powerless as a legal matter to sell the Dale stock outside a reorganization plan and unable as an economic matter to sell it within one. This, of course, pleases the equity holders who, having introduced no evidence demonstrating a disadvantage to the bankrupt estate from the sale of the Dale stock, are now given a veto over it to be used as leverage in negotiating a better deal for themselves in a reorganization.

The likely results of today's decision are twofold: (i) The creditors will at some point during the renewed protracted negotiations refuse to extend more credit to Lionel, thus thwarting a reorganization entirely; and (ii) notwithstanding the majority decision, the Dale stock will be sold under §363(b) for exactly the same reasons offered in support of the present proposed sale. However, the ultimate reorganization plan will be more favorable to the equity holders, and they will not veto the sale.

It seems reasonably obvious that result (i) is something that the statutory provisions governing reorganizations, including §363(b), are designed to avoid. Result (ii) not only is contrary to the purpose of the reorganization provisions in causing delay and further economic risk but also suffers from the legal infirmity which led the majority to reject the proposed sale, the only difference between the two sales being the agreement of the equity holders.

The equity holders offered no evidence whatsoever that the sale of Dale now will harm Lionel or that Dale can in fact be sold at a reasonable price as part of a reorganization plan. The courts below were quite right in not treating their arguments seriously for they are the legal equivalent of the "Hail Mary pass" in football.

IN RE TRANS WORLD AIRLINES

United States Court of Appeals, Third Circuit, 2003
322 F.3d 283

FUENTES, CIRCUIT JUDGE

The issues in this bankruptcy appeal involve the doctrine of successor liability and arise out of the Bankruptcy Court's order approving the sale of the assets of Trans World Airlines ("TWA") to American Airlines ("American"). The primary question is whether the District Court erred in affirming the Bankruptcy Court's order, which had the effect of extinguishing the liability of American, as successor to TWA, for (1) employment discrimination claims against TWA and (2) for the Travel Voucher Program awarded to TWA's flight attendants in settlement of a sex discrimination class action. Because §363(f) permits a sale of property "free and clear" of an "interest in such property[,]" and because the claims against TWA here were connected to or arise from the assets sold, we affirm the Bankruptcy Court's order approving the sale "free and clear" of successor liability. * * *

[In 2001], TWA filed a Chapter 11 bankruptcy petition. Although it was the nation's eighth largest airline at the time, it had not earned a profit in over a decade. Months earlier, in the Spring of 2000, TWA determined that it could not continue to operate as an independent airline and that it needed to enter into a strategic transaction, such as a merger with, or sale of, TWA as a going concern to another airline. Throughout 2000, TWA held intermittent discussions with American concerning the possibility of a strategic partnership. On January 3, 2001, American contacted TWA with a proposal to purchase substantially all of TWA's assets. On January 9, 2001, American agreed to a purchase plan subject to an auction and Bankruptcy Court approval.

Though TWA's assets were being sold under a court-approved bidding process, as of February 28, 2001, the deadline for the submission of bids, TWA had not received any alternate proposals other than American's that conformed with the bidding procedures. Accordingly,

TWA's Board of Directors voted to accept American's proposal to purchase TWA's assets for $742 million.

The EEOC and the Knox-Schillinger class objected to the sale to American. After conducting an evidentiary hearing, the Bankruptcy Court approved the sale to American over the objections of the EEOC and the Knox-Schillinger plaintiffs. In approving the Sale Order, the Bankruptcy Court determined that there was no basis for successor liability on the part of American and that the flight attendants' claims could be treated as unsecured claims. In keeping with the Bankruptcy Court's conclusions, the Sale Order extinguished successor liability on the part of American for the Travel Voucher Program and any discrimination charges pending before the EEOC. Specifically, the Order provided that, in accordance with §363(f) of the Bankruptcy Code:

> the free and clear delivery of the Assets shall include, but not be limited to, all asserted or unasserted, known or unknown, employment related claims, payroll taxes, employee contracts, employee seniority accrued while employed with any of the Sellers and successorship liability accrued up to the date of closing of such sale.

The Sale Order also enjoined all persons from seeking to enforce successor liability claims against American. The Court's order provided that:

> Pursuant to §105(a) and §363, all Persons are enjoined from taking any action against Purchaser or Purchaser's Affiliates including, without limitation, TWA Airlines LLC, to recover any claim which such Person had solely against Sellers or Sellers' Affiliates. * * *

The parties' dispute in this case concerns the meaning of the phrase "interest in such property" (hereafter "interest in property") as that phrase is used in § 363(f). This section "permits sale of property free and clear of any interest in the property of an entity other than the estate." S. Rep. No. 95-989, at 56 (1978). Appellants assert that the Travel Voucher Program and the pending EEOC charges are not interests in property within the meaning of this section and that, therefore, these claims were improperly extinguished by the Sale Order. They assert that interests in property are limited to "liens, mortgages, money judgments, writs of garnishment and attachment, and the like, and cannot encompass successor liability claims arising under federal antidiscrimination statutes and judicial decrees implementing those statutes." Appellants also assert that their claims are outside the scope of §363(f), and therefore cannot be extinguished, because they could not "be compelled, in a legal or equitable proceeding, to accept a money satisfaction of [their] interest[s]." The Airlines, on the other hand, argue that, while Congress did not expressly define "interest in property," the phrase should be broadly read to authorize a bankruptcy court to bar any interest that could potentially travel with the property being sold, even if the asserted interest is unsecured. They also assert that appellants' claims lie within the scope of §363(f)(5), and therefore, can be extinguished because appellants can be compelled to accept a money satisfaction of their claims. We agree with the Airlines.

The contentions of the parties require us to consider whether the claims in this case constitute an interest in property as understood within the meaning of §363(f). Some courts have narrowly interpreted interests in property to mean *in rem* interests in property, such as liens. See, e.g., In re White Motor Credit Corp., 75 Bankr. 944, 948 (Bankr. N.D. Ohio 1987); In re New England Fish Co., 19 Bankr. 323, 326 (Bankr. W.D. Wash. 1982). However, the trend seems to be toward a more expansive reading of "interests in property" which "encompasses other obligations that may flow from ownership of the property."

In Folger Adam Sec., Inc. v. DeMatteis/MacGregor, 209 F.3d 252 (3d Cir. 2000), we addressed the issue of whether certain affirmative defenses to a claim for breach of contract constituted an interest in property within the meaning of section 363(f). Specifically, we were asked to decide "whether the affirmative defenses of setoff, recoupment, and other contract defenses ... constitute an 'interest' under §363(f) such that a sale of the debtors' assets in a consolidated Bankruptcy Court auction free and clear, extinguished such affirmative defenses ... ." Id. at 253-54. We observed that there was no support in the case law for the proposition that *a defense* may be extinguished as a result of a free and clear sale. Accordingly, we held that "a right of recoupment is a defense and not an interest and therefore is not extinguished by a §363(f) sale."

In arriving at this conclusion, we explored the significance of the Fourth Circuit's decision in In re Leckie Smokeless Coal Co., 99 F.3d 573 (4th Cir. 1996). In *Leckie,* the Fourth Circuit held that, irrespective of whether the purchasers of the debtors' assets were successors in interest, under §363(f), the Bankruptcy Court could properly extinguish all successor liability claims against the purchasers arising under the Coal Act by entering an order transferring the debtors' assets free and clear of those claims. The Fourth Circuit held that the two employer-sponsored benefit plans that sought to collect Coal Act premium payments from the debtors' successors in interest were asserting interests in property that had already been sold through the §363 sale. The Fourth Circuit explained that:

> while the plain meaning of the phrase "interest in such property" suggests that not all general rights to payment are encompassed by the statute, Congress did not expressly indicate that, by employing such language, it intended to limit the scope of §363(f) to *in rem* interests, strictly defined, and we decline to adopt such a restricted reading of the statute here.

Id. at 582. The Court explained that the employer-sponsored benefit plans had interests in the property of the debtors which had been transferred under §363(f) in the sense that there was a relationship between their right to demand premium payments from the debtors and the use to which the debtors had put their assets. Importantly, in the course of our review of *Leckie,* we noted that "the term 'any interest' is intended to refer to obligations that are connected to, or arise from, the property being sold." *Folger Adam,* 209 F.3d at 259.

Here the Airlines correctly assert that the Travel Voucher and EEOC claims at issue had the same relationship to TWA's assets in the §363(f) sale, as the employee benefits did to the debtors' assets in *Leckie.* In each case it was the assets of the debtor which gave rise to the claims. Had TWA not invested in airline assets, which required the employment of the EEOC claimants, those successor liability claims would not have arisen. Furthermore, TWA's investment in commercial aviation is inextricably linked to its employment of the Knox-Schillinger claimants as flight attendants, and its ability to distribute travel vouchers as part of the settlement agreement. While the interests of the EEOC and the Knox-Schillinger class in the assets of TWA's bankruptcy estate are not interests in property in the sense that they are not *in rem* interests, the reasoning of *Leckie* and *Folger Adam* suggests that they are interests in property within the meaning of §363(f) in the sense that they arise from the property being sold.

Indeed, to equate interests in property with only *in rem* interests such as liens would be inconsistent with §363(f), which contemplates that a lien is but one type of interest. In this regard, we find ourselves in agreement with Collier's observation that:

Section 363(f) permits the bankruptcy court to authorize a sale free of "any interest" that an entity has in property of the estate. Yet the Code does not define the concept of "interest," of which the property may be sold free. Certainly a lien is a type of "interest" of which the property may be sold free and clear. This becomes apparent in reviewing section 363(f)(3), which provides for particular treatment when "such interest is a lien." Obviously there must be situations in which the interest is something other than a lien; otherwise section 363(f)(3) would not need to deal explicitly with the case in which the interest is a lien.

3 Collier on Bankruptcy ¶363.06[1].

In addition to asserting that their claims are not interests in property within the meaning of §363(f), appellants also assert that their claims are outside the scope of §363(f)(5) because neither the vouchers nor the EEOC claims are interests on account of which they could be compelled to accept money satisfaction. As noted above, under §363(f), assuming the "interest in property" at issue falls within the meaning of the statute, a sale free and clear of such interest can occur if any one of five conditions has been satisfied. The Bankruptcy Court determined that, because the travel voucher and EEOC claims were both subject to monetary valuation, the fifth condition had been satisfied. We agree. Had TWA liquidated its assets under Chapter 7, the claims at issue would have been converted to dollar amounts and the claimants would have received the distribution provided to other general unsecured creditors on account of their claims. A travel voucher represents a seat on an airplane, a travel benefit that can be reduced to a specific monetary value. Indeed, TWA arrived at a valuation for tax purposes, as noted in the Annex to the settlement agreement. Likewise, the EEOC discrimination claims are reducible to, and can be satisfied by, monetary awards even if the relief sought is injunctive in nature.

Even were we to conclude that the claims at issue are not interests in property, the priority scheme of the Bankruptcy Code supports the transfer of TWA's assets free and clear of the claims. The statutory scheme defines various classes of creditors entitled to satisfaction before general unsecured creditors may access the pool of available assets. In *New England Fish,* the Bankruptcy Court held that the civil rights claims before it were *not* interests in property but decided that the claimants were general unsecured creditors and that the debtor's assets could be transferred free and clear of such claims. See 19 Bankr. at 326-29.

In *New England Fish Co.,* the issue was whether the Bankruptcy Court could extinguish the right to payment of claimants asserting civil rights claims in the Bankruptcy Court. The civil rights claims at issue in *New England Fish* were based on allegations of racial discrimination in employment. In that case, two class actions had been brought against the debtor by its employees. One of the suits went to trial and the plaintiffs obtained a damages award for job discrimination, housing discrimination and attorneys fees. In the other suit, there had been no determination of liability at the time of the bankruptcy filing. The Bankruptcy Court recognized the claimants holding a judgment as being general unsecured creditors with liquidated claims and recognized the other class of claimants as being general unsecured creditors to the extent they could prove liability. The prospective purchaser of the assets of the debtor and its trustee sought an adjudication that the assets of the debtor were transferred free and clear of the interests of the civil rights claimants. The prospective purchaser also sought a declaration that it did not qualify as a successor employer of the debtor, and, therefore, could not be held liable to the civil rights claimants. * * *

Other courts have followed the rationale set forth in *New England Fish.* For instance, in Forde v. Kee-Lox Mfg. Co., Inc., 437 F. Supp. 631 (W.D.N.Y. 1977), the District Court dismissed a suit brought under Title VII by an employee of a bankrupt debtor against the purchaser of its assets on a successor liability theory. The Court rejected the civil rights claimant's assertion that the Court could not reduce his demand for reinstatement to a fixed amount of money that could be satisfied out of the proceeds of the sale of the assets of the debtor's bankruptcy estate. See id. at 633. The Court explained:

> There are two major difficulties with the plaintiff's position. First, the plaintiff would allow claimants such as himself to assert their claims against purchasers of the bankrupt's assets, while relegating lienholders to the proceeds of the sale. This elevates claims that have not been secured or reduced to judgment to a position superior to those that have. Yet the Bankruptcy Act is clearly designed to give liens on the bankrupt's property preference over unliquidated claims.

> An additional difficulty with the plaintiff's position is that it would seriously impair the trustee's ability to liquidate the bankrupt's estate. If the trustee in a liquidation sale is not able to transfer title to the bankrupt's assets free of all claims, including civil rights claims, prospective purchasers

may be unwilling to pay a fair price for the property, leaving less to distribute to the creditors.

Id. at 633-34.

Appellants here assert that *Forde* is no longer good law because it was decided under the Bankruptcy Act, which lacked a provision expressly authorizing asset sales free and clear of interests in property. We reject this argument based on the Supreme Court's teaching in Van Huffel v. Harkelrode, 284 U.S. 225 (1931), that although the Bankruptcy Act did not expressly authorize bankruptcy courts to do so, the power to sell property of the bankruptcy estate free of encumbrances was "granted by implication." Id. at 227.

We are sensitive to the concerns raised in *Forde*. We recognize that the claims of the EEOC and the Knox-Schillinger class of plaintiffs are based on congressional enactments addressing employment discrimination and are, therefore, not to be extinguished absent a compelling justification. At the same time, in the context of a bankruptcy, these claims are, by their nature, general unsecured claims and, as such, are accorded low priority. To allow the claimants to assert successor liability claims against American while limiting other creditors' recourse to the proceeds of the asset sale would be inconsistent with the Bankruptcy Code's priority scheme.

Moreover, the sale of TWA's assets to American at a time when TWA was in financial distress was likely facilitated by American obtaining title to the assets free and clear of these civil rights claims. Absent entry of the Bankruptcy Court's order providing for a sale of TWA's assets free and clear of the successor liability claims at issue, American may have offered a discounted bid. This is particularly likely given that the EEOC has been unable to estimate the number of claims it would pursue or the magnitude of the damages it would seek. The arguments advanced by appellants do not seem to account adequately for the fact that American was the only entity that came forward with an offer that complied with the court-approved bidding procedures for TWA's assets and provided jobs for TWA's employees.

The Bankruptcy Court found that, in the absence of a sale of TWA's assets to American, "the EEOC will be relegated to holding an unsecured claim in what will very likely be a piece-meal liquidation of TWA. In that context, such claims are likely to have little if any value." The same is true for claims asserted pursuant to the Travel Voucher Program, as they would be reduced to a dollar amount and would receive the same treatment as the unsecured claims of the EEOC. Given the strong likelihood of a liquidation absent the asset sale to American, a fact which appellants do not dispute, we agree with the Bankruptcy Court that a sale of the assets of TWA at the expense of preserving successor liability claims was necessary in order to preserve some 20,000 jobs, including those of Knox-Schillinger and the EEOC claimants still employed by TWA, and to provide funding for employee-related liabilities, including retirement benefits.

After carefully considering the arguments discussed above and all other arguments advanced by appellants, we join the District Court in affirming the Bankruptcy Court's authorization of the sale of TWA's assets to American free and clear of the claims of the EEOC and the Knox-Schillinger class.

NOTES

9C.7. Lionel is a case in which everything turns on starting presumptions. A judge is not in the business of trying to outguess the market. The price of a publicly traded stock today is as likely to rise as it is to fall tomorrow. There may be some who can consistently outguess the market, but they surely have missed their calling in life if they become bankruptcy judges. The court could not decide the case by asking whether selling the stock of Dale Electronics was a good idea. Holding onto the stock or selling it was equally likely to benefit everyone as a group. For this reason, everything turned on which party had the burden of persuasion. The stock would be sold sooner or later. If the party who wanted it sold now had to explain why, it would lose. There was no reason to sell the stock early. If the party who wanted to delay the sale had to justify the delay, it would lose. There was no reason to sell the stock later, either.

To say that the creditors or equity holders could not *justify* their desires is not to say that they lacked reasons. The creditors in *Lionel* stand to lose, and the shareholders stand to gain, when the debtor holds on to assets that may change in value prior to allocation of the debtor's assets. Assume the creditors were owed $100 and the Dale stock could be sold for $100 today. If the sale took place today, the creditors would be paid in full. If the sale were delayed six months, the stock might go up, in which case the creditors would still receive only $100 (ignoring, for simplicity, the accrual of interest), or the stock might go down, in which case they would receive less. The creditors can do no better from delay but they can do worse. The shareholders have exactly the opposite incentives. When the creditors want assets whose value fluctuates to be converted into assets whose value does not, the shareholders want the reverse. This is the essence of Judge Winter's dissent. Compare Note 9C.1.

9C.8. Most cases will not be like *Lionel,* in which the only question is whether to sell an asset with a readily attainable market value sooner rather than later. Usually, those who advocate the use, sale, or lease of property will be able to articulate some business reason for the move. And it is noteworthy that not all transactions under §363 convert assets of uncertain value to cash, as was the case in *Lionel.* A proposal under §363 can make the firm a riskier proposition. See, e.g., In re Continental Air Lines, Inc., 780 F.2d 1223 (5th Cir. 1986) (debtor wants to lease airplanes to service new routes).

One of the greatest risks we see in Chapter 11 arises when assets are sold to finance the debtor's continued operation. When parties come to the court proposing to sell off assets to keep the firm running, the bankruptcy judge realizes that denying such a request could be tantamount to shutting the firm down. The bankruptcy judge is in the position of a venture capitalist who must decide whether to pull the plug on a project. Among other things, the bankruptcy judge must be alert to the problem of escalating commitment, the cognitive bias that arises when a new decision requires an assessment of a course of action already chosen. Once one makes a decision to follow a certain course (such as a decision to keep the firm intact as a going concern), one may be prone to remain on that course. Most people find it costly to admit error. Cases such as Eastern Airlines, in which a firm is kept in business until all its assets are gone, provide vivid examples of how the decision to liquidate the firm can come much too late.

9C.9. In *TWA,* the holders of employment discrimination and travel voucher claims apparently wanted to have their cake and to eat it too. They did not dispute that the sale of TWA assets to American maximized the debtor's value. Thus, if the choice were between a free-and-clear sale and no sale, presumably the claimants would have preferred the former. After the fact, though, the claimants coveted American's deep pockets. The court reasonably takes an ex ante perspective. Problem 9C-2 further explores this dynamic.

9C.10. Lionel was decided in 1983, while *TWA* was decided in 2003. The cases well reflect their times. In the interim between the decisions, a sea change occurred through which an auction of the debtor's assets has become a commonplace alternative to a traditional corporate reorganization. This change is explored in the last section of this chapter as well as later in the book. Another recent change, to §363(b), is a restriction on the sale of private information. Such restriction is not relevant to the cases presented here.

PROBLEM

9C-2. Debtor Aircraft Corporation manufactures small planes. After years of production, Debtor discovers a design defect in the engine of its most popular product. This defect can be corrected easily in future production but cannot be repaired in planes already sold. Debtor calculates that the present value of future liability for this defect is $100 million. At the time of the discovery, Debtor's assets are worth $75 million if held together as part of a going concern. The same assets are worth $50 million if liquidated piecemeal in sales to other aircraft manufacturers. Debtor's aggregate outstanding debt obligation, exclusive of any product liability claims, is unsecured in the amount of $50 million.

After Debtor files for bankruptcy, its managers seek to have Debtor's future liability declared a "claim" under §101(5), but the bankruptcy court rules against them. The managers then propose to sell Debtor's assets from the bankruptcy estate, not piecemeal, but as a unit to Competitor. The sale proceeds would then be distributed to Debtor's creditors. Competitor will pay $75 million for Debtor's assets but only if the sale can be free from any future product liability claims, which would follow the assets as a unit under the state's successor liability doctrine. Can such a sale be free from future claims? Should it be? In answering this question consider, among other provisions, Bankruptcy Code §363(f) and compare Problem 5A-2. See also In re Savage Industries, Inc., 43 F.3d 714 (1st Cir. 1994).

3) ABANDONMENT

Sometimes a trustee will not want to use, sell, lease, or even hold property of the estate. Note that under §541, discussed above in chapter 6, section A, much property comes into the estate automatically because it was property of the debtor. Some of that property is burdensome or worthless to the estate, and a rational trustee wants to rid the estate of detritus. Thus, Bankruptcy Code §554 permits abandonment. For example, if the estate includes property subject to a lien that exceeds the property's value, a trustee might abandon it if it is not needed for reorganization rather than administer it for the benefit of the lienholder. Once the property is abandoned, the secured creditor can quickly foreclose under state law and take the proceeds.

To illustrate a more difficult case, assume that a corporate debtor owns several dozen drums of waste oil containing PCBs. The corporation also has other assets, but owes creditors who have security interests in those assets far more than the assets are worth. The corporation files for bankruptcy. Under applicable state law, the owner of such waste oil is required to dispose of it safely (an expensive proposition) regardless of how that person came to own the waste oil. But the state statute does not give the state any special priority with respect to the debtor's other assets if the state seeks to enforce this obligation.

Outside of bankruptcy, the corporation could not continue to operate unless it disposed of the oil. The state would simply enjoin the corporation from spending the assets on other activity, and would order those assets directed to disposing of the waste oil. As we saw in chapter 4, section C above, the state can do the same inside of bankruptcy, the automatic stay notwithstanding. If the corporation ceases operation, however, it is another question whether the state can force the corporation to dispose of the oil by using the assets that serve as collateral for others. Outside of bankruptcy, state law might force a race between the state, which would seek to impose a cleanup order, and the secured creditors, who would seek to foreclose on the assets that might become subject to such an order. (If the state lost the race, or if the clean assets could not be converted to cash free from a valid security interest, the state would have a remediless right to order a cleanup from an empty shell.) Inside bankruptcy, this race would be replicated with an additional obstacle placed before the secured creditors, who could not foreclose until the automatic stay was lifted under §362(d), discussed in the previous section.

The creditors, of course, might like the corporation to continue operating free from the state's rights or to liquidate without fear of state interference. Once the corporation files for bankruptcy, §554 might seem to provide the creditors, or the trustee or debtor in possession on their behalf, with a means to these ends, abandonment of the oil drums that give rise to the state cleanup obligation. As the *Midlantic* case and notes that follow suggest, however, abandoning an asset is different from ridding oneself of a liability.

CASE

MIDLANTIC NATIONAL BANK v. NEW JERSEY DEPARTMENT OF ENVIRONMENTAL PROTECTION

United States Supreme Court, 1986
474 U.S. 494

JUSTICE POWELL DELIVERED THE OPINION OF THE COURT.

* * * Quanta Resources Corporation (Quanta) processed waste oil at two facilities, one in Long Island City, New York, and the other in Edgewater, New Jersey. At the Edgewater facility, Quanta handled the oil pursuant to a temporary operating permit issued by the New Jersey Department of Environmental Protection (NJDEP). In June 1981, Midlantic National Bank provided Quanta with a $600,000 loan secured by Quanta's inventory, accounts receivable, and certain equipment. The same month, NJDEP discovered that Quanta had violated a specific prohibition in its operating permit by accepting more than 400,000 gallons of oil contaminated with PCB, a highly toxic carcinogen. NJDEP ordered Quanta to cease operations at Edgewater, and the two began negotiations concerning the cleanup of the Edgewater site. But on October 6, 1981, before the conclusion of negotiations, Quanta filed a petition for reorganization under Chapter 11. The next day, NJDEP issued an administrative order requiring Quanta to clean up the site. Quanta's financial condition remained perilous, however, and the following month, it converted the action to a liquidation proceeding under Chapter 7. Thomas J. O'Neill was appointed trustee in bankruptcy, and subsequently oversaw abandonment of both facilities.

After Quanta filed for bankruptcy, an investigation of the Long Island City facility revealed that Quanta had accepted and stored there over 70,000 gallons of toxic, PCB-contaminated oil in deteriorating and leaking containers. Since the mortgages on that facility's real property exceeded the property's value, the estimated cost of disposing of the waste oil plainly rendered the property a net burden to the estate. After trying without success to sell the Long Island City property for the benefit of Quanta's creditors, the trustee notified the creditors and the Bankruptcy Court for the District of New Jersey that he intended to abandon the property pursuant to §554(a). No party to the bankruptcy proceeding disputed the trustee's allegation that the site was "burdensome" and of "inconsequential value to the estate" within the meaning of §554.

The City and the State of New York (collectively New York) nevertheless objected, contending that abandonment would threaten the public's health and safety, and would violate state and federal environmental law. New York rested its objection on "public policy" considerations reflected in applicable local laws, and on the requirement of 28 U.S.C. §959(b), that a trustee "manage and operate" the property of the estate "according to the requirements of the valid laws of the State in which such property is situated." New York asked the Bankruptcy Court to order that the assets of the estate be used to bring the facility into compliance with applicable law. After briefing and argument, the court approved the abandonment, noting that "[t]he City and State are in a better position in every respect than either the Trustee or debtor's creditors to do what needs to be done to protect the public against the dangers posed by the PCB-contaminated facility." * * *

Upon abandonment, the trustee removed the 24-hour guard service and shut down the fire-suppression system. It became necessary for New York to decontaminate the facility, with the exception of the polluted subsoil, at a cost of about $2.5 million.

On April 23, 1983, shortly after the District Court had approved abandonment of the New York site, the trustee gave notice of his intention to abandon the personal property at the Edgewater site, consisting principally of the contaminated oil. The Bankruptcy Court approved the abandonment on May 20, over NJDEP's objection that the estate had sufficient funds to protect the public from the dangers posed by the hazardous waste. * * *

Before the 1978 revisions of the Bankruptcy Code, the trustee's abandonment power had been limited by a judicially developed doctrine intended to protect legitimate state or federal interests. This was made clear by the few relevant cases. In Ottenheimer v. Whitaker, 198 F.2d 289 (4th Cir. 1952), the Court of Appeals concluded that a bankruptcy trustee, in liquidating the estate of a barge company, could not abandon several barges when the abandonment would have obstructed a navigable passage in violation of federal law. The court stated:

> The judge-made [abandonment] rule must give way when it comes into conflict with a statute enacted in order to ensure the safety of navigation; for we are not dealing with a burden imposed upon the bankrupt or his property by contract, but a duty and a burden imposed upon an owner of vessels by an Act of Congress in the public interest.

Id. at 290.

In In re Chicago Rapid Transit Co., 129 F.2d 1 (7th Cir. 1942), the Court of Appeals held that the trustee of a debtor transit company could not cease its operation of a branch railway line when local law required continued operation. While the court did not forbid the trustee to abandon property (i.e., to reject an unexpired lease), it conditioned his actions to ensure compliance with state law. Similarly, in In re Lewis Jones, Inc., 1 B.C.D. 277 (Bankr. E.D. Pa. 1974), the bankruptcy court invoked its equitable power to "safeguard the public interest" by requiring the debtor public utilities to seal underground steam lines before abandoning them.

Thus, when Congress enacted §554, there were well-recognized restrictions on a trustee's abandonment power. In codifying the judicially developed rule of abandonment, Congress also presumably included the established corollary that a trustee could not exercise his abandonment power in violation of certain state and federal laws. The normal rule of statutory construction is that if Congress intends for legislation to change the interpretation of a judicially created concept, it makes that intent specific. ... The Court has followed this rule with particular care in construing the scope of bankruptcy codifications. ... Although these cases do not define for us the exact contours of the trustee's abandonment power, they do make clear that this power was subject to certain restrictions when Congress enacted §554(a).

Neither the Court nor Congress has granted a trustee in bankruptcy powers that would lend support to a right to abandon property in contravention of state or local laws designed to protect public health or safety. As we held last Term when the State of Ohio sought compensation for cleaning the toxic waste site of a bankrupt corporation:

> Finally, we do not question that anyone in possession of the site—whether it is [the debtor] or another in the event the receivership is liquidated and the trustee abandons the property, or a vendee from the receiver *or the bankruptcy trustee*—must comply with the environmental laws of the State of Ohio. Plainly, that person or firm may not maintain a nuisance, pollute the waters of the State, or refuse to remove the source of such conditions.

Ohio v. Kovacs, 469 U.S. 274, 285 (1985) (emphasis added).

Congress has repeatedly expressed its legislative determination that the trustee is not to have carte blanche to ignore nonbankruptcy law. Where the Bankruptcy Code has conferred special powers upon the trustee and where there was no common-law limitation on that power, Congress has expressly provided that the efforts of the trustee to marshal and distribute the assets of the estate must yield to governmental interest in public health and safety. ... One cannot assume that Congress, having placed these limitations upon other aspects of trustees' operations, intended to discard a well-established judicial restriction on the abandonment power. As we held nearly two years ago in the context of the National Labor Relations Act, "[T]he debtor-in-possession is not relieved of all obligations under the [Act] simply by filing a petition for bankruptcy." NLRB v. Bildisco & Bildisco, 465 U.S. 513, 534 (1984).

> The automatic stay provision of the Bankruptcy Code, §362(a), has been described as "one of the fundamental debtor protections provided by the bankruptcy laws." S. Rep. No. 95-989, p. 54 (1978); H.R. Rep. No. 95-595, p. 340 (1977). Despite the importance of §362(a) in preserving the debtor's estate, Congress has enacted several categories of exceptions to the stay that allow the Government to commence or continue legal proceedings. For example, [§362(b)(4)] permits the Government to enforce "nonmonetary" judgments against a debtor's estate. * * *

Petitioners have suggested that the existence of an express exception to the automatic stay undermines the inference of a similar exception to the abandonment power: had Congress sought to restrict similarly the scope of §554, it would have enacted similar limiting provisions. This argument, however, fails to acknowledge the differences between the predecessors of §554 and §362. As we have noted, the exceptions to the judicially created abandonment power were firmly established. But in enacting §362 in 1978, Congress significantly broadened the scope of the automatic stay, ... an expansion that had begun only five years earlier with the adoption of the Bankruptcy Rules in 1973. ... Between 1973 and 1978, some courts had stretched the expanded automatic stay to foreclose States' efforts to enforce their antipollution laws, and Congress wanted to overrule these interpretations in its 1978 revision. In the face of the greatly increased scope of §362, it was necessary for Congress to limit this new power expressly.

Title 28 U.S.C. §959(b) provides additional evidence that Congress did not intend for the Bankruptcy Code to pre-empt all state laws. Section 959(b) commands the trustee to "manage and operate the property in his possession ... according to the requirements of the valid laws of the State." The petitioners have contended that §959(b) is relevant only when the trustee is actually operating the business of the debtor, and not when he is liquidating it. Even though §959(b) does not directly apply to an abandonment under §554(a)—and therefore does not delimit the precise conditions on an abandonment—the section nevertheless supports our conclusion that Congress did not intend for the Bankruptcy Code to pre-empt all state laws that otherwise constrain the exercise of a trustee's powers.

Although the reasons elaborated above suffice for us to conclude that Congress did not intend for the abandonment power to abrogate certain state and local laws, we find additional support for restricting that power in repeated congressional emphasis on its "goal of protecting the environment against toxic pollution." Chemical Manufacturers Assn., Inc. v. Natural Resources Defense Council, Inc., 470 U.S. 116, 143 (1985). Congress has enacted a Resource Conservation and Recovery Act, 42 U.S.C. §§6901-6987, to regulate the treatment, storage, and disposal of hazardous wastes by monitoring wastes from their creation until after their permanent disposal. That Act authorizes the United States to seek judicial or administrative restraint of activities involving hazardous wastes that "may present an imminent and substantial endangerment to health or the environment." 42 U.S.C. §6973; see also S. Rep. No. 98-284, p. 58 (1983). Congress broadened the scope of the statute and tightened the regulatory restraints in 1984. In the Comprehensive Environmental Response, Compensation, and Liability Act, Congress established a fund to finance cleanup of some sites and required certain responsible parties to reimburse either the fund or the parties who paid for the cleanup. The Act also empowers the Federal Government to secure such relief as may be necessary to avert "imminent and substantial endangerment to the public health or welfare or the environment because of an actual or threatened release of a hazardous substance." 42 U.S.C. §9606. In the face of Congress' undisputed concern over the risks of the improper storage and disposal of hazardous and toxic substances, we are unwilling to presume that by enactment of §554(a), Congress implicitly overturned longstanding restrictions on the common-law abandonment power.

In the light of the Bankruptcy trustee's restricted pre-1978 abandonment power and the limited scope of other Bankruptcy Code provisions, we conclude that Congress did not intend for §554(a) to pre-empt all state and local laws. The Bankruptcy Court does not have the power to authorize an abandonment without formulating conditions that will adequately protect the public's health and safety. Accordingly, without reaching the question whether certain state laws imposing conditions on abandonment may be so onerous as to interfere with the bankruptcy adjudication itself, we hold that a trustee may not abandon property in contravention of a state statute or regulation that is reasonably designed to protect the public health or safety from identified hazards.[9] Accordingly, we affirm the judgments of the Court of Appeals for the Third Circuit.

It is so ordered.

NOTES

9C.11. With abandonment, the trustee in *Midlantic* sought to rid Quanta of its maintenance obligations under applicable environmental law. But §554 speaks only of abandonment of the asset. It does not suggest that Quanta could absolve itself of the *liability* by abandoning the asset. (If you commit a tort with your car, you do not absolve yourself of tort liability by selling the car.) CERCLA may impose cleanup liability on any buyer of the property, but it does not relieve past owners of environmental tort liability when they sell the property. Such liability could, of course, be "abandoned" if only existing owners were liable, but liability under statutes like CERCLA is not extinguished on sale. In any event, Quanta's liability stemmed not from its ownership of previously polluted land, but from its causing the pollution in the first instance. Consider this issue again after you read section D2 below.

9C.12. Arguably, the Court did not go far enough in its conclusions. The Court stated that "Congress did not intend for the abandonment power to abrogate *certain* state and local laws" (emphasis added). But the structure of the Bankruptcy Code as well as the rationale of the *Midlantic* opinion itself suggests that abandonment can abrogate *no* state or local law. Just as the trustee's power to use or sell property (cocaine, for example) under §363 is surely limited by nonbankruptcy law regulating use and sale, so too should the power to abandon property under §554 be implicitly limited. This reading is in accord with the general thrust of 28 U.S.C. §959(b), which the Court discusses but relies on only as "evidence."

---

[9] This exception to the abandonment power vested in the trustee by §554 is a narrow one. It does not encompass a speculative or indeterminate future violation of such laws that may stem from abandonment. The abandonment power is not to be fettered by laws or regulations not reasonably calculated to protect the public health or safety from imminent and identifiable harm.

D. Financing the Estate

A debtor who runs a business in bankruptcy may require more than the freedom to use, sell, or lease property of the estate, as permitted (within limits) by §363. Businesses often must be able to borrow on an ongoing basis. In many industries, it is common to ship goods in return for the buyer's promise to pay in thirty days. One cannot be competitive in such industries if one does business any other way. To extend such short-term credit to their customers, firms must often borrow money themselves either from their suppliers or from a financial institution to pay their suppliers and employees. Firms in bankruptcy have no less a need for such financing. In addition, a bankruptcy reorganization is itself costly, and those who provide the requisite services typically insist on being paid on an ongoing basis.

Sections 364 and 503 govern finance of a debtor in bankruptcy. Section 364 parallels §363. In cases for which §363 authorizes the trustee to use property in the ordinary course of business, §364(a) authorizes the trustee (and thus a debtor in possession) to obtain ordinary credit extensions or loans without special permission from the court. Such an extension or loan is unsecured, but is entitled to priority over prepetition unsecured claims. This priority is provided, albeit indirectly, by allowance of the new debt as an "administrative expense," defined by §503(b) generally to include "the actual, necessary costs and expenses of preserving the estate." See §503(b)(1)(A). (Similarly, in an involuntary bankruptcy case, ordinary course obligations incurred by a debtor between commencement and an order for relief are granted special status under §502(f).)

There is a perfectly plausible reason for postpetition debt to have priority over unsecured prepetition claims. If the debtor's business continues in bankruptcy, it is presumed that the debtor's assets are worth more as part of a going concern than in liquidation. Otherwise liquidation should be immediate. This implies that the value of the debtor as a going concern exceeds the aggregate piecemeal value of any loan collateral, at least as the latter value could be realized in a liquidation. Thus, the holders of unsecured claims should profit from continuation, even if those claims (or any junior interests) bear the entire cost of new credit. That is, if continuation is worthwhile, but not otherwise, the owners of a debtor's residual will gladly pay the cost of continuation. Sections 364(a) and 503 reflect this presumption.

Not all postpetition debts are in the ordinary course of business. The trustee or debtor can borrow under unusual circumstances—a large loan to finance a new project, for example—but only with court approval after notice and hearing. Just as unusual uses of property require court approval under §363, unusual loans require court approval for similar reasons. Once a court is satisfied that an unusual loan is in the debtor's interest, it can approve an unsecured obligation that will be entitled to administrative expense priority, just like an ordinary course unsecured obligation and on the same theory. See §364(b).

For the trustee to give a security interest of any sort when borrowing money, §364(c) applies. All subparts of this provision require the trustee or debtor to obtain court permission. Section 364(c) deals with three types of extra "security" that do not interfere with holders of other property rights: (1) priority over other administrative expenses; (2) liens on property not previously encumbered; (3) junior liens on property previously encumbered. All three of these are similar to §364(a) in two respects: They all give priority over unsecured claims, and none give priority over other secured creditors. Such financing is merely a continuation of the debtor's financial affairs past the filing of a bankruptcy petition. Any priority granted under §364(c) could have been granted by the debtor prior to bankruptcy under applicable nonbankruptcy law.

In contrast, §364(d), explicitly designed as a refuge of last resort, permits a deviation from nonbankruptcy priority. The provision permits the court to authorize new obligations that have a security interest in property equal or senior to that of a prepetition claim. But the court may authorize such an obligation only if the trustee or debtor shows both that such credit is not otherwise obtainable and that the existing secured creditor is adequately protected. Consider how these twin tests are in tension. If a debtor cannot get money from anyone without interfering with the priority rights of a secured creditor, there may be good reason to believe that the debtor cannot adequately protect the creditor. The debtor's inability to borrow money from anyone else, using the same package it offers the secured creditor as adequate protection, provides at least some evidence that the debtor's prospects are not as bright as the debtor might suggest to the court.

There may be some consolation to a secured creditor deprived of priority under §364(d). As noted above, administrative expense priorities are set out in §503(b), which works in conjunction with §507. If the trustee offers adequate protection under §364 (or under §§362 or 363, for that matter), and if, despite that assurance of adequate protection, the creditor in fact turns out not to have been adequately protected, §507(b) provides that the creditor gets a kind of "super-priority" over all other administrative expense claims. This provision creates a ranking *within* the category of administrative expense claimants by creating a category of claims that is first among firsts. Still, there is no certainty that even first priority among administrative expense priority will be fully satisfied.

Turning to other provisions, §503(b) also grants administrative expense status to costs of ownership or operation not linked to §364. For example, obligations under a new executory contract or lease, or under an assumed prepetition executory contract or lease (presumably a net asset when assumed), give rise to administrative expenses if breached during the bankruptcy (though priority for obligations on an assumed then abandoned nonresidential lease is limited by §503(b)(7)). For another example, §503(b)(1)(B) classifies certain of a debtor's postpetition tax obligations as an administrative expense. And, not surprisingly, §503(b)(2)-(6) specifically grant administrative expense status for actual administrative expenses such as compensation owed for services rendered by a trustee or creditor on behalf of the estate. When a bankruptcy case concludes, §507(a) grants an unpaid administrative expense (as well as §502(f) claims) priority over all prepetition unsecured claims.

After some basic exercises, the material below is divided into two parts. The first explores in more detail the nature of postpetition borrowing, sometimes called debtor-in-possession or DIP financing. Special attention is drawn to cases in which the debtor wishes to borrow anew from prepetition creditors. The second part is devoted to postpetition obligations incurred by the debtor incidentally through operation rather than by any affirmative action. The question sometimes arises whether such obligations are entitled to administrative expense priority.

Key Provisions: Bankruptcy Code §§364; 503(b)

EXERCISES

9D(1) After Debtor Corporation files for bankruptcy, it needs $50,000 to operate its business. May it borrow this amount from Lender, giving Lender administrative expense priority without court permission?

9D(2) After Debtor Corporation files for bankruptcy, it needs $50,000 to operate its business. Lender wants more than an administrative expense priority. Debtor offers Lender a security interest on some previously unencumbered assets. May Debtor grant this interest without court permission? Compare this exercise with the prior one. Is there any reason to have a different standard? Whose rights are affected as a result of the different treatment? What, if anything, should Debtor have to show before it can grant the interest Lender requests?

9D(3) Debtor owes Manufacturer $300,000. This debt is secured by an interest in Debtor's equipment. Debtor files a Chapter 11 bankruptcy petition. Shortly thereafter, Debtor seeks authorization to borrow $100,000 from Bank and to give Bank a security interest on the equipment with priority over Manufacturer's interest. Debtor argues that Manufacturer is adequately protected because, Debtor says, the value of the equipment is $500,000. Should the bankruptcy court approve Debtor's request if it agrees with Debtor's valuation of the equipment? If the court does approve Bank's security interest over Manufacturer's objection, does Manufacturer have an effective avenue for appeal? In answering these questions consider §364(e).

9D(4) After Debtor files for bankruptcy under Chapter 11, it enters into a long-term contract with Supplier. Shortly thereafter, before the bankruptcy case concludes, Debtor realizes that the contract was a mistake and repudiates the contract. Are Supplier's damages entitled to administrative expense priority? Would your answer change if the contract predated the bankruptcy, but was assumed under §365 prior to repudiation? Would your answer change if Debtor breached the contract inadvertently rather than by repudiation? What if the contract were a real estate lease rather than for supply acquisition?

9D(5) At the time Debtor files a Chapter 11 petition, Debtor's only valuable assets are a $5,000 bank account and an industrial truck worth $100,000, collateral for Bank's $150,000 loan. After the bankruptcy filing, the truck begins to have engine trouble. Debtor spends its $5,000 in cash for an emergency repair on the truck and avoids a $25,000 repair later. Soon thereafter the court converts Debtor's case to Chapter 7. Assuming that the truck's value does not change and that the trustee is diligent, how much will Bank receive on account of its secured claims and how much will be available to holders of administrative expenses or unsecured claims? In answering this question consider, among other provisions, §506(c). Now assume that Mechanic does the repairs on credit and the trustee fails to pay the bill.

Does Mechanic have a right to insist on payment? See Hartford Underwriters Insurance Co. v. Union Planters Bank, 530 U.S. 1 (2000).

9D(6) Debtor files a bankruptcy petition on January 1. On February 1, Debtor negligently drives his car into Bystander's house. Is Bystander's claim entitled to administrative expense priority under §503(b)? Would your answer change if Debtor were a corporation and its employee caused the accident? Would your answer change if Debtor is an individual in Chapter 7 and the accident is caused by the trustee driving to a meeting with Debtor's creditors?

1) *DEBTOR-IN-POSSESSION FINANCING*

A new loan—credit from a supplier or cash from a bank—is a common early objective of a debtor once it files a bankruptcy reorganization petition. Such a loan is called debtor-in-possession or DIP financing. Often, the source of this financing is the lender who was the debtor's principal source of credit before bankruptcy. The debtor will often turn to this lender because the exigencies of business leave little time to find another credit source. Even if a new lender were available in time, it might charge more than the old lender, who already has a relationship with and thus reliable information about the debtor. A new lender would incur some cost to obtain and verify such information.

Take the case of a trucking firm that has just filed a Chapter 11 petition. The payroll checks issued yesterday will bounce unless postpetition financing is found. From a theoretical perspective, one might think that all the payroll checks *should* bounce. The workers, after all, have only prepetition claims. They should not be paid until the end of the case. But the debtor will likely take a more practical view. If the checks bounced, the workers likely would not work anymore and the firm would have to close down. If the debtor's trucking business is viable despite the bankruptcy, this would be a loss to all.

When the best source of DIP financing is the same creditor who provided the debtor with a credit line before the petition, that creditor may ask for a "cross-collateralization" clause in its loan agreement. Such a clause would grant the bank an interest in debtor's property, say its trucks, as security not only for the bank's new loan but for its unsecured prepetition claim as well. Such a clause would effectively elevate the priority of the bank's unsecured claim over that of the debtor's other unsecured claims even though the latter are otherwise entitled to the same priority as the former. When a debtor asks for approval of a cross-collateralization clause, a court may be torn between the debtor's need for new financing on one hand and its desire to honor nonbankruptcy priority on the other.

In the case that follows, *Saybrook Manufacturing*, after the bankruptcy court approved a DIP loan with a cross-collateralization clause, the Eleventh Circuit reversed. As you read the case, along with the related notes and problems, you should ask yourself not only whether §364 permits cross-collateralization clauses but also how, assuming it does permit them, a court should assess such requests in individual cases. In this regard, consider also the Southern District of New York guidelines for DIP lending, which appear after the case. As you can see, although the guidelines treat cross collateralization and similar provisions as extraordinary, they reflect a belief that such provisions are permissible. Think about the effects of a cross-collateralization clause or similar clause when such a clause *is* necessary to obtain a new loan on terms favorable to the debtor. Contemplate these questions not only from the perspective of the firm as a whole but also from that of the each of the affected players.

CASE

IN RE SAYBROOK MANUFACTURING CO.

United States Court of Appeals, Eleventh Circuit, 1992
963 F.2d 1490

COX, CIRCUIT JUDGE.

Seymour and Jeffrey Shapiro, unsecured creditors, objected to the bankruptcy court's authorization for the Chapter 11 debtors to "cross-collateralize" their prepetition debt with unencumbered property from the bankruptcy estate. The bankruptcy court overruled the objection and also refused to grant a stay of its order pending appeal. The Shapiros appealed to the district court, which dismissed the case as moot under §364(e) of the Bankruptcy Code because the Shapiros had failed to obtain a stay. We conclude that this appeal is not moot and that cross-collateralization is not authorized under the Bankruptcy Code. Accordingly, we reverse and remand.

Saybrook Manufacturing Co., Inc., and related companies (the "debtors"), initiated proceedings seeking relief under Chapter 11 of the Bankruptcy Code on December 22, 1988. On December 23, 1988, the debtors filed a motion for the use of cash collateral and for authorization to incur secured debt. The bankruptcy court entered an emergency financing order that same day. At the time the bankruptcy petition was filed, the debtors owed Manufacturers Hanover approximately $34 million. The value of the collateral for this debt, however, was less than $10 million. Pursuant to the order, Manufacturers Hanover agreed to lend the debtors an additional $3 million to facilitate their reorganization. In exchange, Manufacturers Hanover received a security interest in all of the debtors' property—both property owned prior to filing the bankruptcy petition and that which was acquired subsequently. This security interest not only protected the $3 million of postpetition credit but also secured Manufacturers Hanover's $34 million prepetition debt.

This arrangement enhanced Manufacturers Hanover's position vis-à-vis other unsecured creditors, such as the Shapiros, in the event of liquidation. Because Manufacturers Hanover's prepetition debt was undersecured by approximately $24 million, it originally would have shared in a pro rata distribution of the debtors' unencumbered assets along with the other unsecured creditors. Under the financing order, however, Manufacturers Hanover's prepetition debt became fully secured by all of the debtors' assets. If the bankruptcy estate were liquidated, Manufacturers Hanover's entire debt—$34 million prepetition and $3 million postpetition—would have to be paid in full before any funds could be distributed to the remaining unsecured creditors. * * *

The Shapiros filed a number of objections to the bankruptcy court's order on January 13, 1989. After a hearing, the bankruptcy court overruled the objections. The Shapiros then filed a notice of appeal and a request for the bankruptcy court to stay its financing order pending appeal. The bankruptcy court denied the request for a stay on February 23, 1989.

The Shapiros subsequently moved the district court to stay the bankruptcy court's financing order pending appeal; the court denied the motion on March 7, 1989. On May 20, 1989, the district court dismissed the Shapiros' appeal as moot under §364(e) because the Shapiros had failed to obtain a stay of the financing order pending appeal, rejecting the argument that cross-collateralization is contrary to the Code. ... The Shapiros then appealed to this court. * * *

We begin by addressing the lenders' claim that this appeal is moot under §364(e) of the Bankruptcy Code. ... The purpose of this provision is to encourage the extension of credit to debtors in bankruptcy by eliminating the risk that any lien securing the loan will be modified on appeal.

The lenders suggest that we assume cross-collateralization is authorized under §364 and then conclude the Shapiros' appeal is moot under §364(e). This is similar to the approach adopted by the Ninth Circuit in Burchinal v. Central Washington Bank (In re Adams Apple, Inc.), 829 F.2d 1484 (9th Cir. 1987). That court held that cross-collateralization was "authorized" under §364 for the purposes of §364(e) mootness but declined to decide whether cross-collateralization was illegal per se under the Bankruptcy Code. * * *

We reject the reasoning of *In re Adams Apple* ... because [it] "put[s] the cart before the horse." By its own terms, §364(e) is only applicable if the challenged lien or priority was authorized under §364. ... We cannot determine if this appeal is moot under §364(e) until we decide the central issue in this appeal—whether cross-collateralization is authorized under §364. Accordingly, we now turn to that question.

Cross-collateralization is an extremely controversial form of Chapter 11 financing. Nevertheless, the practice has been approved by several bankruptcy courts. ... Even the courts that have allowed cross-collateralization, however, were generally reluctant to do so. * * *

In [In re Vanguard Diversified Industries, Inc., 31 Bankr. 364, 366 (Bankr. E.D.N.Y. 1983)], for example, the bankruptcy court noted that cross-collateralization is "a disfavored means of financing" that should only be used as a last resort. In order to obtain a financing order including cross-collateralization, the court required the debtor to demonstrate:

    (1) that its business operations would fail absent the proposed financing;

    (2) that it is unable to obtain alternative financing on acceptable terms;

    (3) that the proposed lender will not accept less preferential terms; and

    (4) that the proposed financing is in the general creditor body's best interest.

This four-part test has since been adopted by other bankruptcy courts which permit cross-collateralization. * * *

The issue of whether the Bankruptcy Code authorizes cross-collateralization is a question of first impression in this court. Indeed, it is essentially a question of first impression before any court of appeals. * * *

The Second Circuit expressed criticism of cross-collateralization in In re Texlon, [596 F.2d 1092 (2d Cir. 1979)]. The court, however, stopped short of prohibiting the practice altogether. At issue was the bankruptcy court's ex parte financing order granting the lender a security interest in the debtor's property to secure both prepetition and postpetition debt. The court, in an exercise of judicial restraint, concluded that:

> In order to decide this case we are not obliged, however, to say that under no conceivable circumstances could "cross-collateralization" be authorized. Here it suffices to hold that ... a financing scheme so contrary to the spirit of the [1898 Act] should not have been granted by an ex parte order, where the bankruptcy court relies solely on representations by a debtor in possession that credit essential to the maintenance of operations is not otherwise obtainable.

In re Texlon, 596 F.2d at 1098. ... Although *In re Texlon* was decided under the earlier Bankruptcy Act, the court also considered whether cross-collateralization was authorized under the Bankruptcy Code. "To such limited extent as it is proper to consider the new Bankruptcy Act, which takes effect on October 1, 1979, in considering the validity of an order made in 1974, we see nothing in §364(c) or in other provisions of that section that advances the case in favor of 'cross-collateralization.'" * * *

Cross-collateralization is not specifically mentioned in the Bankruptcy Code. ... We conclude that cross-collateralization is inconsistent with bankruptcy law for two reasons. First, cross-collateralization is not authorized as a method of postpetition financing under §364. Second, cross-collateralization is beyond the scope of the bankruptcy court's inherent equitable power because it is directly contrary to the fundamental priority scheme of the Bankruptcy Code. * * *

Section 364 authorizes Chapter 11 debtors to obtain secured credit and incur secured debt as part of their reorganization. ... By their express terms, §364(c) and (d) apply only to future—i.e., postpetition—extensions of credit. They do not authorize the granting of liens to secure prepetition loans. * * *

Given that cross-collateralization is not authorized by §364, we now turn to the lenders' argument that bankruptcy courts may permit the practice under their general equitable power. Bankruptcy courts are indeed courts of equity, see, e.g., §105(a), and they have the power to adjust claims to avoid injustice or unfairness. Pepper v. Litton, 308 U.S. 295 (1939). This equitable power, however, is not unlimited.

> [T]he bankruptcy court has the ability to deviate from the rules of priority and distribution set forth in the Code in the interest of justice and equity. The Court cannot use this flexibility, however, merely to establish a ranking of priorities within priorities. Furthermore, absent the existence of some type of inequitable conduct on the part of the claimant, which results in injury to the creditors of the bankrupt or an unfair advantage to the claimant, the court cannot subordinate a claim to claims within the same class.

In re FCX, Inc., 60 Bankr. 405, 409 (E.D.N.C. 1986).

Section 507 of the Bankruptcy Code fixes the priority order of claims and expenses against the bankruptcy estate. Creditors within a given class are to be treated equally, and bankruptcy courts may not create their own rules of superpriority within a single class. ... Cross-collateralization, however, does exactly that. ... As a result of this practice, postpetition lenders' unsecured prepetition claims are given priority over all other unsecured prepetition claims. * * *

The Second Circuit has noted that, if cross-collateralization were initiated by the bankrupt while insolvent and shortly before filing a petition, the arrangement "would have constituted a voidable preference." In re Texlon, 596 F.2d at 1097. The fundamental nature of this practice is not changed by the fact that it is sanctioned by the bankruptcy court. We disagree with the district court's conclusion that, while cross-collateralization may violate some policies of bankruptcy law, it is consistent with the general purpose of Chapter 11 to help businesses reorganize and become profitable. ... Rehabilitation is certainly the primary purpose of Chapter 11. This end, however, does not justify the use of any means. Cross-collateralization is directly inconsistent with the priority scheme of the Bankruptcy Code. Accordingly, the practice may not be approved by the bankruptcy court under its equitable authority.

Cross-collateralization is not authorized by §364. Section 364(e), therefore, is not applicable and this appeal is not moot. Because *Texlon*-type cross-collateralization is not explicitly authorized by the Bankruptcy Code and is contrary to the basic priority structure of the Code, we hold that it is an impermissible means of obtaining postpetition financing. The judgment of the district court is reversed and the case is remanded for proceedings not inconsistent with this opinion.

JUDICIAL GUIDELINES

United States Bankruptcy Court
Southern District of New York
General Order No. M-274
Guidelines for Financing Requests

The purpose of this document is to establish guidelines for cash collateral and financing requests under sections 363 and 364 of the Bankruptcy Code in the United States Bankruptcy Court for the Southern District of New York (the "Court"). Although it is recognized that each case is different, the Guidelines are designed to help practitioners identify common material issues that typically are of concern to the Court (at least on the first day of a case and/or where there is limited notice), and to highlight such matters so that, among other things, determinations can be made, if necessary, on an expedited basis.

Substantively, these Guidelines do not purport to establish rules that cannot be varied, but they do require disclosure of the "Extraordinary Provisions," discussed below, that ordinarily will not be approved in interim orders without substantial cause shown, compelling circumstances and reasonable notice.

It will be evident that many of the following guidelines are designed to deal with debtor in possession financing requests documented with a loan agreement and (for want of a better term) a long-form financing order. However, the Court would welcome the use of simplified orders, whenever possible, particularly in smaller cases and in connection with the debtor's use of cash collateral not involving the extension of new funds.

These guidelines are intended to supplement the requirements of sections 363 and 364 of the Bankruptcy Code and Bankruptcy Rules 4001(b) and (c).

I. MOTIONS

* * * 2. *Description of use of cash collateral or the material provisions of DIP financing.* The motion should ordinarily contain the following disclosure relative to the use of cash collateral or the financing, either in the text of the motion or in an attached term sheet:

(a) amount of cash to be used or borrowed, including (if applicable) committed amount, maximum borrowings (if less), any borrowing base formula, availability under the formula, and the purpose of the borrowing;

(b) material conditions to closing and borrowing, including any budget provisions;

(c) pricing and economic terms, including interest rates, letter of credit fees, commitment fees, any other fees, and the treatment of costs and expenses of the lender (and its professionals);

(d) collateral or adequate protection provided to the lender and any priority or superpriority provisions, including the effect thereof on existing liens, and any carve-outs from liens or superpriorities;

(e) maturity, termination and default provisions, including events of default, effect on the automatic stay and any cross-default provisions; and

(f) any other material provisions, including any Extraordinary Provisions, as defined in Section II, any provisions relating to change of control, and key covenants.

3. *Adequacy of Budget.* Any motion for new financing or use of cash collateral must also include disclosure by the debtor as to whether it has reason to believe that any budget to which the debtor will be subject under the order will be adequate (in the context of all assets available to the debtor) to pay all administrative expenses due and payable during the period covered by the financing or the budget.

4. *Extraordinary Provisions.* The motion must disclose prominently whether the financing includes any of the Extraordinary Provisions set forth in section II of these Guidelines, and any accompanying order must also set forth these provisions prominently and conspicuously.

5. *Efforts to Obtain Financing.* The motion should describe in general terms the debtor's efforts to obtain financing, the basis on which the debtor determined that the proposed financing was on the best terms available, and material facts bearing on the issue of whether the extension of credit is being extended in good faith.

6. *Emergency Applications.* A motion that seeks entry of an Emergency Order or Interim Order should also describe the amount and purpose of funds sought to be borrowed on an emergency or interim basis and set forth facts to support a finding that immediate or irreparable harm will be caused to the estate if immediate financing is not obtained at a preliminary hearing or on an emergency basis. * * *

II. ORDERS

The following provisions in a cash collateral or DIP financing order, or in a financing agreement to be approved under such an order, called "Extraordinary Provisions," must be disclosed conspicuously in the motion and order and justification therefor separately set forth:

1. *Cross-Collateralization.* Extraordinary Provisions include all provisions that elevate prepetition debt to administrative expense (or higher) status or secure prepetition debt with liens on postpetition assets that such debt would not have by virtue of the prepetition security agreement or applicable law (for the purposes of these Guidelines, "Cross-Collateralization"), unless such status and liens are limited in extent to that necessary to accord the prepetition lender in a reorganization case adequate protection against a decline in the value of its collateral during the postpetition period. In connection with a request for Cross-Collateralization, the Court will consider, among other factors:

(i) the extent of the notice provided;

(ii) the terms of the DIP financing and a comparison to the terms that would be available absent the Cross-Collateralization;

(iii) the degree of consensus among parties in interest supportive of Cross-Collateralization;

(iv) the extent and value of the prepetition liens held by the prepetition lender (and in particular the amount of any "equity cushion" that the prepetition lender may have), and

(v) whether Cross-Collateralization will give an undue advantage to prepetition lenders without a countervailing benefit to the estate. An order approving Cross-Collateralization must ordinarily reserve the right of the Court to unwind the postpetition protection provided to the prepetition lender in the event that there is a timely and successful challenge to the validity, enforceability, extent, perfection, and (where appropriate) priority of the prepetition lender's claims or liens, or a determination that the prepetition debt was undersecured as of the petition date, and the Cross-Collateralization unduly advantaged the lender.

2. *"Rollups."* Rollups include the application of proceeds of postpetition financing to pay, in whole or in part, prepetition debt. Determination of the propriety of a rollup will normally take into account, to the extent applicable, the factors mentioned above in connection with Cross-Collateralization, and, in addition, the following:

(a) the nature and amount of new credit to be extended, beyond the application of proceeds of postpetition financing used to pay in whole or in part the prepetition debt;

(b) whether the advantages of the postpetition financing justify the loss to the estate of the opportunity to satisfy the prepetition secured debt otherwise in accordance with applicable provisions of the Bankruptcy Code, and the burdens on the estate of incurring an administrative claim;

(c) whether the rollup can be unwound (see below);

(d) availability under the terms of the DIP financing and a comparison to the terms that would be available in the absence of the rollup;

(e) the extent to which prepetition and postpetition collateral can, as a practical matter, be identified and/or segregated;

(f) the extent to which difficult "priming" issues would have to be addressed in the absence of a rollup; and

(g) whether the postpetition advances are used to repay a pre-bankruptcy, "emergency" liquidity facility secured by first priority liens on the same collateral as the postpetition financing, where the prepetition facility was provided in anticipation of, or in an effort to avoid, a bankruptcy filing.

An order approving a rollup must ordinarily reserve the right of the Court to unwind the paydown of the prepetition debt in the event that there is a timely and successful challenge to the validity, enforceability, extent, perfection, and (where appropriate) priority of the prepetition lender's claims or liens, or a determination that the prepetition debt was undersecured as of the petition date.

3. *Waivers and concessions as to validity of prepetition debt.* The Court will not consider as extraordinary the debtor's stipulation as to validity, perfection, enforceability, priority and non-avoidability of a prepetition lender's claim and liens, and the lack of any defense thereto, provided that:

(a) the Official Committee of Unsecured Creditors (the "Committee"), appointed under section 1102 of the Bankruptcy Code, has a minimum of 60 days (or such longer period as the Committee may obtain for cause shown before the expiration of such period) from the date of the order approving the appointment of counsel for the Committee to investigate the facts and bring any appropriate proceedings as representative of the estate; or

(b) if no Committee is appointed, any party in interest has a minimum of 75 days (or a longer period for cause shown before the expiration of such period) from the entry of the final financing order to investigate the facts and file a motion seeking authority to bring any appropriate proceedings as representative of the estate; provided that

(c) the foregoing periods may be shortened in prepackaged or prearranged cases for cause shown.

4. *Waivers.* Extraordinary Provisions include those that divest the Court of its power or discretion in a material way, or interfere with the exercise of the fiduciary duties of the debtor or Creditors Committee in connection with the operation of the business, administration of the estate, or the formulation of a reorganization plan, such as provisions that deprive the debtor or the Creditors Committee of the ability to file a request for relief with the Court, to grant a junior postpetition lien, or to obtain future use of cash collateral. Notwithstanding the foregoing, and where duly disclosed, it will not be considered "extraordinary" for the debtor to agree to repay the postpetition financing in connection with any plan; for the debtor to waive any right to incur liens that prime or are pari passu with liens granted under section 364; for a financing order to contain reasonable limitations and conditions regarding future borrowings under section 364 or cash collateral usage under section 363 (including consent of the lender, subordination of future borrowings to the priorities and liens given to the initial lender, and repayment of the initial loan with the proceeds of a subsequent borrowing); and for an order to provide that the lender has no obligation to fund certain activities of the debtor or the Committee, so long as the debtor or Committee is free to engage therein.

5. *Section 506(c) waivers.* Extraordinary Provisions include any waiver of the debtor's right to a surcharge against collateral under section 506(c); factors to be considered in connection with any order seeking such a waiver include whether the debtor's rights are (to the extent permitted by law) delegated to the Committee (or, if a Committee is not appointed, to any party in interest) and whether the carveout includes expenses under section 726(b) (see below).

6. *Liens on avoidance actions.* Extraordinary Provisions include the granting of liens on the debtor's claims and causes of action arising under sections 544, 545, 547, 548 and 549 (but not liens on recoveries under section 549 on account of collateral as to which the lender has a postpetition lien), and the proceeds thereof, or a superpriority

administrative claim payable from the proceeds of such claims and causes of action.

7. *Carve-outs.* Provisions relating to a carve-out that will be considered "extraordinary" include those that provide disparate treatment for the professionals retained by the Committee compared to professionals retained by the debtor or that do not include the fees of the U.S. Trustee, the reasonable expenses of Committee members, and reasonable fees and expenses of a trustee under section 726(b); however, reasonable allocations among such expenses can be proposed, and the lender may refuse to include in a carve-out the costs of litigation against it (but not the costs of investigating whether any claims or causes of action exist). Provisions relating to carve-outs should make clear when the carve-out takes effect (and, in this connection, whether it remains unaltered after payment of interim fees made before an event of default under the facility), and any effect of the carve-out on availability under the postpetition loan.

8. *Termination; Default; Remedies.* Extraordinary Provisions include terms that provide that the use of cash collateral will cease, or the financing agreement will default, on (i) the filing of a challenge to the lender's prepetition lien or to the lender's prepetition conduct; (ii) entry of an order granting relief from the automatic stay (except as to material assets); (iii) the grant of a change of venue with respect to the case or any adversary proceeding; (iv) the making of a motion by a party in interest seeking any relief (as distinct from an order granting such relief); and (v) management changes or the departure, from the debtor, of any identified employees. Clauses providing a reasonable maturity date for the postpetition debt and for termination of the loan or default of the postpetition debt (if not repaid) on dismissal of the case or on confirmation of a plan of reorganization, or on conversion to Chapter 7, or on the appointment of a trustee or an examiner with expanded powers, will not be considered to be extraordinary. Termination of the postpetition lender's commitment to continue to advance funds after an event of default will not be considered extraordinary, but the following provisions will:

> (a) failure to provide at least five business days' notice to the debtor and the Committee before the automatic stay terminates and the lender's remedies can be enforced; and

> (b) failure to provide at least three business days' notice before use of cash collateral ceases, provided that the use of cash collateral conforms to any budget in effect. * * *

NOTES

9D.1. The facts of Saybrook may not have been as egregious as the opinion suggests. The value of the debtor's unencumbered collateral may have been worth only as much as the new loan. The cross-collateralization clause may have improved the creditor's recovery on its prepetition loan only by a small amount and may have been included primarily for administrative convenience. See Karen M. Gebbia & Lawrence E. Oscar, *Saybrook Manufacturing*: Is Cross-Collateralization Moot?, 2 J. Bankr. Law & Practice 163, 194 n.136 (1993).

The Eleventh Circuit's hostility to cross-collateralization in *Saybrook* is, nevertheless, understandable. Courts are badly positioned to understand the effects of a cross-collateralization clause when they must approve a DIP loan on an emergency basis a few days before Christmas. A flat prohibition on such clauses does not mean that funding from prepetition creditors will be unavailable. Manufacturers Hanover might still have provided the funds even if cross-collateralization clauses were forbidden. So long as the terms of the new loan independently offered fair compensation, Manufacturers Hanover, as the holder of a prepetition *un*secured claim, might well have benefited from Saybrook's continued activity financed by the infusion of funds. Moreover, another lender might have been induced to lend. (Note that the Southern District Guidelines require a debtor to exhaust a search for external finance before an extraordinary provision such as cross-collateralization is approved; this suggests that external sources of finance are sometimes available.) Despite the risk of forgone opportunity, a rule that bans cross collateralization may, on balance, be the right one, as much mischief may result under the guise of administrative convenience or the like.

That said, there are times that the only plausible lender, particularly on short notice, will be a prepetition lender, one familiar with the debtor, and such a lender may in fact offer better terms if it can rely on cross collateralization or a similar provision. See, e.g., In re Calpine Corp., 2007 WL 685595 (Bankr. S.D.N.Y.), where a prepetition lender was the only initial source for a DIP loan even though substitute finance was later obtained. In this regard, it may not be meaningful to talk about the terms of the new loan independent from collateralization of the old. Saybrook may have had to choose between a new loan with a high interest rate and no cross-collateralization and a new loan with a low interest rate and cross-collateralization. Either might constitute fair terms for the funds that Saybrook needed to survive. As such, it would seem that the pledge of assets for a cross-collateralization clause in the low-interest loan would be a reasonable use of property authorized not by §364, but by *§363*, a provision that the court did not consider. Compare the notes in section 9C above and Problem 9C-1.

Given these multiple factors, the propriety of a cross-collateralization clause is not easy to determine in the abstract, particularly if there is dissent among prepetition creditors. Problem 9D-1 asks you to consider how a court should deal with a cross-collateralization clause when not all general creditors approve.

9D.2. Section 364(e) is designed to assure postpetition lenders that the terms on which they lend will not be rewritten after the fact. Otherwise, lenders would hesitate to provide new funds and DIP financing would face a considerable obstacle. The court in *Saybrook* reasons that this is all well and good for new loans that are authorized by §364, but that because a cross-collateralized loan is not so authorized, such a loan is not protected by §364(e). This proves too much, however, as *no* loan term reversed on appeal is authorized in the view of the appellate court. Thus, the Eleventh Circuit's reasoning in *Saybrook*, if extended to other cases, may limit the protection §364(e) offers. That said, other appellate courts have declined to follow *Saybrook* on the §364(e), question. See, e.g., In re Cooper Commons, LLC, 430 F.3d. 1215 (9th Cir. 2005). And, as the Southern District of New York Guidelines indicate, bankruptcy courts have continued to approve cross-collateralization clauses.

9D.3. It is noteworthy that the Southern District Guidelines address not only cross-collateralization clauses, but a number of related provisions as well. These include, e.g., "rollups" and waivers of lien challenge. Such provisions, while formally distinct, have a common effect, an improvement of a lender's position with respect to prepetition debt in exchange for postpetition finance. Thus, they can be analyzed similarly.

9D.4. Cash collateral orders, also addressed by the Guidelines, are somewhat different. When a debtor requests the use of cash collateral, it takes the position that the benefits of such use will be sufficient to compensate the affected secured creditor and will, in addition, enhance the value of the estate. Consider the merits of such a position in connection with §364(d), discussed in section B of this chapter.

9D.5. The Southern District Guidelines contain other important provisions as well. The Guidelines anticipate loan provisions "that divest the Court of its power or discretion in a material way, or interfere with the exercise of the fiduciary duties of the debtor or Creditors

Committee in connection with the operation of the business, administration of the estate, or the formulation of a reorganization plan." These are extraordinary indeed and, along with cross-collateralization, rollups, and the like form the basis of a change in the conduct of Chapter 11 bankruptcy cases. It has now become common for a corporate debtor to enter bankruptcy in desperate need of an immediate cash infusion. Prepetition lenders, particularly secured creditors, are often there waiting with the necessary funds but only with significant strings attached, including a requirement that the debtor hand over control. Not infrequently, the DIP loan, and its terms, are arranged and agreed to in advance of the petition. The logic of these provisions is that discussed above: Even a burdensome loan may on balance be better than the alternative.

Problem 9D-2 ask you to explore this scenario. The recent trend in Chapter 11 bankruptcy practice, including the increase in Chapter 11 sales, is mentioned above in section C of this chapter of the book and is described more fully below in chapter .13, section A.

PROBLEMS

9D-1. Debtor Corporation enters bankruptcy after years of declining sales. Despite recent losses and insolvency, Debtor wants to reorganize and immediately after the bankruptcy petition seeks a loan from Bank. In the deal reached, Bank would provide Debtor with $1 million in exchange for Debtor's obligation to repay principal plus interest at 4 percent per annum. The note is secured by Debtor's previously unencumbered real estate, worth $2 million. By the terms of the agreement, Bank's prepetition unsecured obligation of $1 million is also to be secured by this real estate. At the hearing to consider this loan, Union as representative of Debtor's employee-creditors approves. Supplier, however, objects to offering security for Bank's prepetition loan. Debtor responds through its prebankruptcy shareholder-managers, who serve as debtor in possession. The managers explain that the interest rate Bank would charge for even a secured loan would be too high, more than 10 percent, unless Bank received cross-collateralization. Should the court approve the new loan terms? Compare Problem 8D-4.

9D-2. Debtor Corporation, which manufactures aircraft engines, founders after its largest customer ceases operation. By the time Debtor files for bankruptcy under Chapter 11, Debtor has no cash on hand and is subject to Investment Bank's secured loan on all of

Debtor's assets, including inventory, receivables, and intangibles. Despite its financial crisis, Debtor is economically viable and requires a cash infusion to operate efficiently. On the first day after Debtor's bankruptcy petition, it files a motion for court approval of a DIP loan by Investment Bank on terms that give Investment Bank complete control over Debtor and the reorganization process. In its motion, Debtor recites that it has tried to obtain finance from an alternative source but could not acquire such finance within the necessarily narrow time frame. Debtor's value as a going concern is approximately equal to the amount of Investment Bank's secured claim and proposed DIP loan combined (conditional on receipt of that loan), and Investment Bank proposes a reorganization plan that would sell all of Debtor's assets in a prenegotiated deal with one of Debtor's competitors. Debtor's general creditors object to the terms of the DIP loan, citing what they call Investment Bank's complicity in the Debtor's dire straights at the time of the petition. Specifically, the general creditors allege that Investment Bank used its overarching prepetition security interest to block a prior workout that might have yielded a higher return to creditors as a group. The general creditors concede that a delay now in obtaining DIP finance would reduce the value of Debtor's assets somewhat, but argue that an open auction for those assets might yield a price that more than makes up the difference. Should the bankruptcy court grant Debtor's motion?

2) ADMINISTRATIVE EXPENSES

The administrative expense priority, defined by Bankruptcy Code §503, is an integral part of bankruptcy's solution to the debtor's problem of maintaining relationships with suppliers, customers, and others. If keeping the business operating is in the collective interest of the general creditors, they should be willing to allow priority for "newcomers" who supply materials, labor, office space, and so on, or the cash to purchase or lease the same.

Administrative expenses are not restricted to explicit extensions of credit (the topic discussed immediately above). When a debtor in bankruptcy enters or assumes a contract, the debtor incurs obligations under that contract necessary to obtain the promised performance of the other party. Thus, the debtor's obligations under such a contract are administrative expenses entitled to priority, in the event of debtor's breach, just as a postpetition loan obligation is entitled to priority. Similarly, taxes incurred postpetition are a cost of operation or ownership that the prepetition creditors, as beneficiaries of such operation or ownership, are required to pay through administrative expense priority.

Difficult cases sometimes arise when a postpetition debtor incurs an expense that is not the product of a postpetition decision to become indebted and is not explicitly covered by the Bankruptcy Code (as are postpetition taxes). Each of the three cases below, *Reading Co. v. Brown* (a pre-Code case), *Wall Tube*, and *Microsoft v. DAK*, along with the related notes and problem address an aspect of this issue. As you read this material, consider the purpose of the administrative expense priority.

CASES

READING CO. v. BROWN

United States Supreme Court, 1968
391 U.S. 471

JUSTICE HARLAN DELIVERED THE OPINION OF THE COURT.

On November 16, 1962, I. J. Knight Realty Corporation filed a petition for an arrangement under Chapter XI of the Bankruptcy Act. The same day, the District Court appointed a receiver, Francis Shunk Brown, a respondent here. The receiver was authorized to conduct the debtor's business, which consisted principally of leasing the debtor's only significant asset, an eight-story industrial structure located in Philadelphia.

On January 1, 1963, the building was totally destroyed by a fire which spread to adjoining premises and destroyed real and personal property of petitioner Reading Company and others. On April 3, 1963, petitioner filed a claim for $559,731 in the arrangement, based on the asserted negligence of the receiver. It was styled a claim for "administrative expenses" of the arrangement. Other fire loss claimants filed 146 additional claims of a similar nature. The total of all such claims was in excess of $3,500,000, substantially more than the total assets of the debtor.

On May 14, 1963, Knight Realty was voluntarily adjudicated a bankrupt and respondent receiver was subsequently elected trustee in bankruptcy. The claims of petitioner and others thus became claims for administration expenses in bankruptcy which are given first priority under §64a(1) of the Bankruptcy Act. The trustee moved to expunge the claims on the ground that they were not for expenses of administration. It was agreed that the decision whether petitioner's claim is provable as an expense of administration would establish the status of the other §146 claims. It was further agreed that, for purposes of deciding whether the claim is provable, it would be assumed that the damage to petitioner's property resulted from the negligence of the receiver and a workman he employed. The United States, holding a claim for unpaid prearrangement taxes admittedly superior to the claims of general creditors and inferior to claims for administration expenses, entered the case on the side of the trustee.

The referee disallowed the claim for administration expenses. He also ruled that petitioner's claim was not provable as a general claim against the estate, a ruling challenged by neither side. On petition for review, the referee was upheld by the District Court. On appeal, the Court of Appeals for the Third Circuit, sitting en banc, affirmed the decision of the District Court by a 4-3 vote. We granted certiorari because the issue is important in the administration of the bankruptcy laws and is one of first impression in this Court. For reasons to follow, we reverse.

Section 64a of the [1898 Act] provides in part as follows:

> The debts to have priority, in advance of the payment of dividends to creditors, and to be paid in full out of bankrupt estates, and the order of payment, shall be (1) the costs and expenses of administration, including the actual and necessary costs and expenses of preserving the estate subsequent to filing the petition. * * *

It is agreed that this section, applicable by its terms to straight bankruptcies, governs payment of administration expenses of Chapter XI arrangements. Furthermore, it is agreed that for the purpose of applying this section to arrangements, … the words "preserving the estate" include the larger objective, common to arrangements, of operating the debtor's business with a view to rehabilitating it.

The question in this case is whether the negligence of a receiver administering an estate under a Chapter XI arrangement gives rise to an "actual and necessary" cost of operating the debtor's business. The [1898 Act] does not define "actual and necessary," nor has any case directly in point been brought to our attention. We must, therefore, look to the general purposes of §64a, Chapter XI, and the [1898 Act] as a whole.

The trustee contends that the relevant statutory objectives are (1) to facilitate rehabilitation of insolvent businesses and (2) to preserve a maximum of assets for distribution among the general creditors should the arrangement fail. He therefore argues that first priority as "necessary" expenses should be given only to those expenditures without which the insolvent business could not be carried on. For example, the trustee would allow first priority to contracts entered into by the receiver because suppliers, employees, landlords, and the like would not enter into dealings with a debtor in possession or a receiver of an insolvent business unless priority is allowed. The trustee would exclude all negligence claims, on the theory that first priority for them is not necessary to encourage third parties to deal with an insolvent business, that first priority would reduce the amount available for the general creditors, and that first priority would discourage general creditors from accepting arrangements.

In our view the trustee has overlooked one important, and here decisive, statutory objective: fairness to all persons having claims against an insolvent. Petitioner suffered grave financial injury from what is here agreed to have been the negligence of the receiver and a workman. It is conceded that, in principle, petitioner has a right to recover for that injury from their "employer," the business under arrangement, upon the rule of respondeat superior. Respondents contend, however, that petitioner is in no different position from anyone else injured by a person with scant assets: its right to recover exists in theory but is not enforceable in practice.

That, however, is not an adequate description of petitioner's position. At the moment when an arrangement is sought, the debtor is insolvent. Its existing creditors hope that by partial or complete postponement of their claims they will, through successful rehabilitation, eventually recover from the debtor either in full or in larger proportion than they would in immediate bankruptcy. Hence the present petitioner did not merely suffer injury at the hands of an insolvent business: it had an insolvent business thrust upon it by operation of law. That business will, in any event, be unable to pay its fire debts in full. But the question is whether the fire claimants should be subordinated to, should share equally with, or should collect ahead of those creditors for whose benefit the continued operation of the business (which unfortunately led to a fire instead of the hoped-for rehabilitation) was allowed.

Recognizing that petitioner ought to have some means of asserting its claim against the business whose operation resulted in the fire, respondents have suggested various theories as alternatives to "administration expense" treatment. None of these has case support, and all seem to us unsatisfactory.

Several need not be pursued in detail. The trustee contends that if the present claims are not provable in bankruptcy they would survive as claims against the shell. He also suggests that petitioner may be able to recover from the receiver personally, or out of such bond as he posted. Without deciding whether these possible avenues are indeed open, we merely note that they do not serve the present purpose. * * *

The United States, as a respondent, suggests instead that tort claims arising during an arrangement are, if properly preserved, provable general claims in any subsequent bankruptcy under §63a of the Act. * * *

In any event, we see no reason to indulge in a strained construction of the relevant provisions, for we are persuaded that it is theoretically sounder, as well as linguistically more comfortable, to treat tort claims arising during an arrangement as actual and necessary expenses of the arrangement rather than debts of the bankrupt. In the first place, in considering whether those injured by the operation of the business during an arrangement should share equally with, or recover ahead of, those for whose benefit the business is carried on, the latter seems more natural and just. Existing creditors are, to be sure, in a dilemma not of their own making, but there is no obvious reason why they should be allowed to attempt to escape that dilemma at the risk of imposing it on others equally innocent.

More directly in point is the possibility of insurance. An arrangement may provide for suitable coverage, and the court below recognized that the cost of insurance against tort claims arising during an arrangement is an administrative expense payable in full under §64a(1) before dividends to general creditors. It is of course obvious that proper insurance premiums must be given priority, else insurance could not be obtained; and if a receiver or debtor in possession is to be encouraged to obtain insurance in adequate amounts, the claims against which insurance is obtained should be potentially payable in full. In the present case, it is argued, the fire was of such incredible magnitude that adequate insurance probably could not have been obtained and in any event would have been foolish; this may be true, as it is also true that allowance of a first priority to the fire claimants here will still only mean recovery by them for a fraction of their damages. In the usual case where damages are within insurable limits, however, the rule of full recovery for torts is demonstrably sounder.

Although there appear to be no cases dealing with tort claims arising during Chapter XI proceedings, decisions in analogous cases suggest that "actual and necessary costs" should include costs ordinarily incident to operation of a business, and not be limited to costs without which rehabilitation would be impossible. It has long been the rule of equity receiverships that torts of the receivership create claims against the receivership itself; in those cases the statutory limitation to "actual and necessary costs" is not involved, but the explicit recognition extended to tort claims in those cases weighs heavily in favor of considering them within the general category of costs and expenses.

In some cases arising under Chapter XI it has been recognized that "actual and necessary costs" are not limited to those claims which the business must be able to pay in full if it is to be able to deal at all. For example, state and federal taxes accruing during a receivership have been held to be actual and necessary costs of an arrangement. The United States, recognizing and supporting these holdings, agrees with petitioner that costs that form "an integral and essential element of the continuation of the business" are necessary expenses even though priority is not necessary *to* the continuation of the business. Thus the Government suggests that "an injury to a member of the public—a business invitee—who was injured while on the business premises during an arrangement would present a completely different problem [i.e., could qualify for first priority]" although it is not suggested that priority is needed to encourage invitees to enter the premises.

The United States argues, however, that each tort claim "must be analyzed in its own context." Apart from the fact that it has been assumed throughout this case that all 147 claimants were on an equal footing and it is not very helpful to suggest here for the first time a rule by which lessees, invitees, and neighbors have different rights, we perceive no distinction: No principle of tort law of which we are aware offers guidance for distinguishing, within the class of torts committed by receivers while acting in furtherance of the business, between those "integral" to the business and those that are not.

We hold that damages resulting from the negligence of a receiver acting within the scope of his authority as receiver give rise to "actual and necessary costs" of a Chapter XI arrangement.

The judgment of the Court of Appeals is reversed, and the case remanded for further proceedings consistent with this opinion.

It is so ordered.

CHIEF JUSTICE WARREN, with whom JUSTICE DOUGLAS joins, dissenting.

In my opinion, the Court has misinterpreted the term "costs and expenses of administration" as intended by §64a(1) of the [1898 Act] and, by deviating from the natural meaning of those words, has given the administrative cost priority an unwarranted application. The effect of the holding in this case is that the negligence of a workman may completely wipe out the claims of all other classes of public and private creditors. I do not believe Congress intended to accord tort claimants such a preference. Accordingly, I would affirm the judgment below.

On other occasions, this Court has observed that "[t]he theme of the [1898 Act] is 'equality of distribution' ... ; and if one claimant is to be preferred over others, the purpose should be clear from the statute." Nathanson v. NLRB, 344 U.S. 25, 29 (1952). ... More particularly, the [1898 Act] expressly directs that eligible negligence claims are to share *equally* with the unsecured claims in a pro rata distribution of the debtor's nonexempt assets. Departing from this statutory scheme, the Court today singles out one class of tort claims for special treatment. After today's decision, the status of a tort claimant depends entirely upon whether he is fortunate enough to have been injured after rather than before a receiver has been appointed. And if the claimant is in the select class, he may be permitted to exhaust the estate to the exclusion of the general creditors as well as of the wage claims and government tax claims for which Congress has shown an unmistakable preference. In my view, this result frustrates rather than serves the underlying purposes of a Chapter XI proceeding, and I would not reach it without a clear indication that Congress so intended.

Congress enacted Chapter XI as an alternative to straight bankruptcy for individuals and small businesses which might be successfully rehabilitated instead of being subjected to economically wasteful liquidation. The success of a Chapter XI proceeding depends largely on two factors: first, whether creditors will take the chance of permitting an arrangement; second, whether other businesses will continue to deal with the distressed business. With respect to the first of these considerations, today's decision will undoubtedly discourage creditors from permitting arrangements, because it subjects them to unpredictable and probably uninsurable tort liability. I do not believe the statutory language requires such an interpretation. I would construe §64a(1) with reference to the second consideration mentioned above. In my opinion, the Court would reach a result more in line with congressional intent and the [1898 Act] generally by regarding as administrative costs only those costs required for a smooth and successful arrangement. Accordingly, the administrative cost priority should be viewed as a guaranty to the receiver and those who deal with or are employed by him that they will be paid for their goods and services. Any broader interpretation will discourage creditors from permitting use of the rehabilitative machinery of Chapter XI and tend to force distressed businesses into straight bankruptcy.

It is equitable, the Court believes, that the general creditors (and wage and tax claimants) bear the loss in this case because they have "thrust" an insolvent business upon petitioner for their own benefit. I respectfully submit that this is a most unfair characterization of arrangements. An economically distressed businessman seeks an arrangement for his own and not for his creditors' benefit. Of course the creditors will benefit if the arrangement is successful, just as they would have benefited if the businessman had been successful without resorting to an arrangement. But a business in arrangement is no more thrust on the public than is any other business enterprise which is conducted for the mutual prosperity of the owners, the wage earners and the creditors. Realistically, the only difference is that a business administered under Chapter XI has not been prosperous. If the arrangement is successful, the owners, wage earners and creditors will all benefit; if it is not, they will all be injured. Thus, I would not distinguish in this case between petitioner and the other general creditors, none of whom was responsible for the catastrophe for which all of them must sustain some loss. Instead, in deciding this case, I would adhere to the Act's basic theme of equality of distribution.

The Court states that its decision will encourage Chapter XI receivers to obtain "adequate" insurance. The Court fairly well concedes, however, that in this case "adequate" insurance "probably could not have been obtained and in any event would have been foolish." In other words, so far as this Court knows, the insurance taken out by the receiver in this case was in fact "adequate," in the sense that no reasonable receiver could or should obtain fire insurance in the amount of $3,500,000 on the assumption that his workman might accidentally cause a fire of the proportions which occurred here. Moreover, quite apart from the case at bar, there is absolutely no indication that today's decision is needed to encourage receivers to obtain insurance. I see no basis in the [1898 Act] or in sound policy for a ruling that the creditors of an estate under a Chapter XI arrangement become involuntary insurers against a liability which probably would not and should not be insurable by more traditional means.

The Court also relies, in my opinion mistakenly, upon analogies to equity receiverships. In reorganizations under Chapter X and §77, Congress has directed the courts to apply the rules of priority developed in equity. However, arrangements under Chapter XI are governed strictly by the statutory priorities fixed by §64a. These statutory priorities differ in many respects from those applicable to equity receiverships, and they have been amended repeatedly to narrow the class of claimants which may participate ahead of the general creditors. * * *

I see no basis in equity or in the statutory language or purpose for subjecting every class of creditors except petitioner's to a loss caused by the negligence of a workman. Consequently, I would construe "actual and necessary costs" as limited to those costs actually and necessarily incurred in preserving the debtor's estate and administering it for the benefit of the creditors. I would not include ordinary negligence claims within this class.

IN RE WALL TUBE & METAL PRODUCTS CO.

United States Court of Appeals, Sixth Circuit, 1987
831 F.2d 118

KEITH, Circuit Judge.

This case concerns two federal statutes: the Bankruptcy Code ... and the Comprehensive Environmental Response Compensation and Liability Act. CERCLA allows a state to recover all costs incurred by it in responding to the improper disposal of hazardous substances. The statute makes the owner and operator of the disposal site, among others, liable for those response costs. The issue before us is whether the response costs, recoverable by the State of Tennessee ("State") under federal law, are allowable as administrative expenses in a Chapter 7 bankruptcy proceeding. In proceedings before the bankruptcy court, the State filed a request and application for administrative expenses pursuant to §503(b)(1)(A) and §507(a)[(2)]. The bankruptcy court denied the State's request. The district court affirmed the bankruptcy court. We reverse. * * *

Debtor Wall Tube & Metal Co. ("Wall Tube") occupied property in Newport, Tennessee under a twenty-year lease. The company manufactured automobile bumpers, outdoor furniture, steel tubing and other metal fabrications on the leased premises. The company's manufacturing processes generated hazardous waste substances which were drummed and stored on the site. Sometime in October, 1983, Wall Tube halted operations and shut down the Newport facility. On December 8, 1983, an inspector for the Tennessee Department of Health and Environment ("TDHE") inspected the site and found that an open storage tank containing 1, 1, 1 trichloroethane was almost overflowing due to rainwater accumulation. The inspector also found several drums filled with lime sludge and "pickle liquor" (a substance containing hydrofluoric acid for the treatment of steel). These substances are defined as hazardous substances under CERCLA. The inspector issued a notice of violation of the Tennessee Hazardous Waste Management Act of 1977 ("Tennessee Act"), Tenn. Code Ann. 68-46-101 et seq., and recommended that Wall Tube immediately dispose of the wastes on the site in a proper manner. A subsequent inspection by the TDHE on February 1, 1984 found the situation basically unchanged.

Wall Tube filed a voluntary petition in bankruptcy under Chapter 7 on February 22, 1984. The trustee of the debtor's estate, William Lancaster, was notified of the hazardous substances and the violation of the State's environmental law by receipt of the TDHE February inspection report. On June 11, 1984, the State requested its standard hazardous waste removal contractor to inspect the facility and present a proposal for the facility's emergency cleanup. The inspection, undertaken on June 15, 1984, revealed evidence of dumping or spilling of various wastes onto the ground and inside the buildings, the presence of nonhazardous and hazardous substances in drums inside and outside the buildings, tanks or vats containing sludges, a tank leaking a corrosive liquid, and bottles of nitric and hydrochloric acid. On July 23, 1984, the Chapter 7 trustee gave notice, pursuant to Bankruptcy Rule 6007, of his intent to convey most of the property to its original lessors, two corporations owned by a M.E. Bullard.

On November 9, 1984, the State authorized its contractor to sample and analyze the substances on the Wall Tube site. The contractor undertook the analysis in late November and late December of 1984. On December 3, 1984, the bankruptcy court approved the conveyance announced by the trustee in July. While the property transfer conveyed some of the hazardous substances, other drums and tanks containing hazardous wastes remained part of the debtor's estate. The State's contractor submitted its reports from the 1984 analysis in January, February and April of 1985. According to an affidavit submitted by Margaret E. Dew, a chemist and staff member of TDHE, the contractor's reports and the TDHE's own inspection revealed that the drums still within the estate constituted up to four separate "threatened release locations" of hazardous substances. These substances, if contacted or inhaled, could have caused as many as fifteen different health hazards, including loss of consciousness, vomiting, internal organ damage, skin burns, birth defects and death.

On May 2, 1985, the State filed a formal request for administrative expense treatment of its expenses. After a hearing, the bankruptcy court denied the request, finding that the expenses were not "actual, necessary costs and expenses of preserving the estate" within the meaning of §503(b). The bankruptcy court also concluded that 28 U.S.C. §959(b), which requires a trustee to "manage and operate the property in his possession ... according to the requirements of the valid laws of the State ... " does not apply to a Chapter 7 trustee liquidating the estate. The court held that since the State's activity neither benefited the estate nor fulfilled a legal obligation under State law, the State's recovery costs could not be accorded administrative expense status.

The district court affirmed, relying on Midlantic National Bank v. New Jersey Dept. of Environmental Protection, 474 U.S. 494 (1986), to hold that 28 U.S.C. §959(b) does not apply to liquidation trustees. The State appeals. * * *

Wall Tube violated the Tennessee Act's requirement of proper disposal and storage of hazardous wastes. The violation was discovered before the bankruptcy petition was filed and continued after the Wall Tube trustee was notified. The Tennessee Act is, of course, one "designed to protect the public health or safety" from readily identified hazards. In this case, the hazards were identified by the TDHE's series of inspections. Wall Tube's trustee, under those circumstances, could not have abandoned the property. If he had done so, the public would have been faced with the same threat the court in *Midlantic* sought to avoid—a continuing, potentially disastrous environmental health hazard with no one clearly responsible for remedial action.

It follows that if the Wall Tube trustee could not have abandoned the estate in contravention of the State's environmental law, neither then should he have *maintained or possessed* the estate in continuous violation of that same law. Otherwise, the result avoided in *Midlantic* would (and in this case did) remain—an ongoing, potentially disastrous health hazard without remedy from those at fault. The only difference here is that the danger arose because of the trustee's and the debtor's failure to correct the violation, not because of the trustee's exercise of the abandonment power as in *Midlantic*. We find that difference, however, as unpersuasive as the difference between omission and action, especially when the deleterious effect on the public health and safety is the same.

Nor are we convinced that §959(b) is inapplicable to liquidating trustees, as respondents argue. The *Midlantic* Court found that §959(b) *supported* its conclusion that the Bankruptcy Code does "not pre-empt all state laws that otherwise constrain the exercise of a trustee's powers." ... Furthermore, the Court noted Congress' intentions that the trustee's efforts "to marshal and distribute the assets of the estate" give way to the governmental interest in public health and safety. [474 U.S.] at 502. We believe that whether a trustee is liquidating, managing or reorganizing the debtor's estate, his efforts under the Code remain the same—the consolidation and distribution of the estate's assets to the benefit of the creditors. As such, that the trustee in this case is liquidating the estate rather than reorganizing it is inconsequential, especially in the critical context of the public's welfare. In either case, an environmental hazard on the estate's property is within the control of the trustee.

* * * Wall Tube and later its trustee should have complied with the State's hazardous substance laws. Since they did not comply, despite ample opportunity to do so both before and after the December 1984 conveyance, the State was compelled to remedy the environmental health hazard at public expense. We now turn to whether the expense incurred by the State was an actual, necessary cost and expense of preserving the estate.

* * * In Reading v. Brown, 391 U.S. 471 (1968), the Supreme Court expanded the concept of administrative expenses to include damages resulting from the estate's postpetition negligence. The creditors argued then that making the response costs an administrative expense is unfair to the generally innocent creditors who suffer at the expense of the petitioner's higher priority claim. The *Reading* Court's response is applicable to this case: "Existing creditors are, to be sure, in a dilemma not of their own making; but there is no obvious reason why they should be allowed to escape that dilemma at the risk of imposing it on others equally innocent." 391 U.S. at 482, 483. Indeed,

the protection of innocent creditors would not be furthered by a contrary holding that permits creditors to benefit from their silence while the debtor violates the law. See U.S. v. Elliott, 761 F.2d 168 (4th Cir. 1985).

Moreover, the *Midlantic* and *Kovacs* cases have created a special emphasis on the importance of complying with laws that protect the public health and safety. * * *

It is undisputed that the hazardous wastes still within the debtor's estate after the 1984 conveyance presented a danger to the public's health and safety. The State of Tennessee, in the absence of compliance by the debtor's estate, was entitled by its own law to expend funds to assess the gravity of the environmental hazard. We thus find those expenses to be actual and necessary, both to preserve the estate in required compliance with state law and to protect the health and safety of a potentially endangered public.

We therefore reverse the decision of the Bankruptcy and District Court below, remand the case to the Bankruptcy Court and direct the Bankruptcy Court to enter an order granting the State of Tennessee's request seeking the response cost of $23,670 as an administrative expense.

MICROSOFT CORP. v. DAK INDUSTRIES, INC.

United States Court of Appeals, Ninth Circuit, 1995
66 F.3d 1091

BRUNETTI, CIRCUIT JUDGE.

* * * In April 1991, Microsoft, a distributor of computer software, and DAK Industries, Inc., a distributor of computer hardware, entered into a "License Agreement" granting DAK certain nonexclusive, worldwide "license rights" to Microsoft's Word for Windows software (Word). The agreement gave DAK the right to adapt Word to enable it to run on computer systems sold by DAK, to copy Word, and to distribute and license Word to consumers during a specified term. DAK also received the right to accept updates and new versions of Word, as well as the right to distribute copyrighted documentation that explained how to use Word. As a practical matter, the agreement provided that Microsoft would furnish DAK with a master disk containing Word, and that DAK would copy the program and load it onto computer hardware units, which it then sold to end consumers.

The agreement provided that DAK would pay a "royalty rate" of $55 per copy of Word that it distributed. Upon signing the agreement, DAK became obligated to pay Microsoft a "minimum commitment" of $2,750,000 in five installments, regardless of how many copies of Word it sold. The payment schedule was:

1. Signing of agreement:	$250,000
2. First payment date:	$406,250
3. 3 months after first payment date:	$697,917
4. 6 months after first payment date:	$697,917
5. 9 months after first payment date:	$697,917

The first payment date depended upon when DAK first sold a copy of Word to a consumer. The term of the agreement expired one year after the first payment date.

DAK's $2,750,000 minimum commitment paid Microsoft royalties at the $55 per unit price for the distribution of 50,000 copies of Word. DAK could sell any and all of those copies to consumers at any time during the term. The agreement provided that if DAK sold more copies than those paid for by the minimum commitment, DAK would pay Microsoft $55 for each additional copy sold. However, if DAK sold fewer copies than those paid for by the minimum commitment, Microsoft would not refund any of the commitment. Microsoft did not perfect a security interest in any of DAK's property, which might have protected it against DAK's failure to pay the entire minimum commitment in the event of bankruptcy.

Sometime between July and December of 1991, the parties amended the agreement by reducing the royalty rate to $45. As a result of the amendment, the minimum commitment paid royalties for the sale of more than 50,000 copies of Word.

The first payment date was December 30, 1991. In accordance with the payment schedule, DAK paid the first three installments, totaling $1,354,167. On June 11, 1992, DAK filed a petition for bankruptcy. The debtor has not paid the final two installments, totaling $1,395,833.

On December 1, 1992, Microsoft moved in the bankruptcy court for an order compelling the debtor to assume or reject the executory contract with Microsoft. On January 12, 1993, Microsoft filed a motion for the payment of an administrative expense, claiming it should be compensated for the debtor's postbankruptcy petition "use" of the license agreement, because the debtor continued to distribute Word.

On February 3, 1993, the bankruptcy court denied Microsoft's administrative expense claim. The court concluded that the payment structure of the agreement was more analogous to payments on a sale of goods than to royalty payments for the continuing use of an intellectual property. As such, the debt was a prepetition unsecured claim, not a postpetition administrative expense claim. The court also concluded that the agreement was an executory contract, and that the debtor had until May 4, 1993, to assume or reject the agreement.

In April 1993, Microsoft moved for reconsideration of the denial of its administrative expense claim. The bankruptcy court denied that motion on June 16, 1993.

The debtor rejected the agreement on May 4, 1993. The parties agree that DAK had sold approximately 13,244 copies of Word prior to filing for bankruptcy on June 11, 1992. They also agree that the debtor sold approximately another 7,600 copies between June 11, 1992, and January 21, 1993, a date one week before the bankruptcy court hearing on Microsoft's administrative expense claim. The record does not reflect how many copies of Word the debtor sold between January 21, 1993, and May 4, 1993, the date when it formally rejected the agreement and stopped selling Word.[1]

Microsoft appealed the bankruptcy court's denial of its administrative expense claim to the district court. The district court concluded that the debtor had received benefits from its postpetition distribution of Word. However, the court concluded that the payment schedule resembled installment payments for the sale of goods, not periodic royalties for the use of intellectual property. Therefore, the obligations for the amounts due under the agreement were incurred prepetition. The court also concluded that Microsoft was neither in-

---

[1] In its brief to this court, DAK calculates that at the amended royalty rate of $45 per copy, it could have sold a total of 30,092 copies before exceeding the number for which it had paid prior to bankruptcy. According to this calculation, DAK could have sold 9,248 additional copies between January 21, 1993, and May 4, 1993 (9,248 + 7,600 + 13,244 = 30,092). In its reply brief, Microsoft states that DAK's brief admits that DAK sold 9,248 copies during that time. This mischaracterizes the statement in DAK's brief. DAK did not state how many units it actually sold during that time, but only that it never exceeded the amount for which it had paid. The record before this court does not establish how many copies of Word DAK sold between January 21, 1993, and May 4, 1993, when it stopped selling Word.

duced to nor continued to provide software units at its expense after the filing of the petition. Accordingly, Microsoft had provided no postpetition consideration to debtor. The court rejected Microsoft's administrative expense claim, thereby leaving the remaining amount due under the agreement as a prepetition, unsecured claim. * * *

The burden of proving an administrative expense claim is on the claimant. The claimant must show that the debt asserted to be an administrative expense (1) arose from a transaction with the debtor in possession as opposed to the preceding entity (or, alternatively, that the claimant gave consideration to the debtor in possession); and (2) directly and substantially benefited the estate. The bankruptcy court has broad discretion to determine whether to grant such a claim. In order to keep administrative costs to the estate at a minimum, "the actual, necessary costs and expenses of preserving the estate," §503(1)(A), are construed narrowly.

In this case, the debtor rejected an executory contract without ever assuming it. Under §365(g)(1), for purposes of bankruptcy proceedings, that rejection constitutes breach of the contract immediately prior to the date on which the bankruptcy petition was filed. Nonetheless, after the petition, the debtor continued to distribute copies of the software provided under that contract. The estate directly and substantially benefited from these postpetition sales of Word. Therefore, Microsoft is entitled to an administrative expense claim if the debt outstanding on the contract arose after the petition or if Microsoft provided consideration to the debtor after the petition. Otherwise, Microsoft is entitled only to a prepetition, unsecured claim.

Microsoft argues that this transaction should be viewed as an agreement granting DAK the use of intellectual property. Accordingly, Microsoft claims that the debt arose after the petition as periodic payments for use of the property became due. Microsoft also argues that even though the transaction was initiated prior to the petition, Microsoft provided consideration after the petition by continuing to make the intellectual property available for the debtor's use. Characterized this way, the transaction is analogous to a debtor's postpetition use of leased property under an agreement signed prepetition. Such use gives rise to an administrative expense claim for the payment of rent.

DAK, the Tokai Bank, (DAK's largest creditor), and the committee of unsecured creditors all respond that this transaction should be viewed as a prepetition sale by Microsoft of software units to

DAK. Accordingly, DAK claims that the entire debt arose prior to the petition, when the sale took place. DAK also argues that Microsoft did not provide consideration to DAK after the petition; rather, DAK only sold software units which it had already purchased from Microsoft prepetition. Characterized this way, the transaction is analogous to a debtor selling goods out of its inventory postpetition that it bought prepetition on unsecured credit. While the estate benefits, the creditor is not entitled to an administrative expense claim. Rather, it simply has an unsecured claim.

When applying the Bankruptcy Code to this transaction, we must look through its form to the "economic realities of th[e] particular arrangement." In re Moreggia & Sons, Inc., 852 F.2d 1179, 1182 (9th Cir. 1988).[2] We conclude that this agreement is best characterized as a lump sum sale of software units to DAK, rather than a grant of permission to use an intellectual property. Accordingly, debt arose prepetition and Microsoft gave no consideration postpetition. We reach this conclusion for several reasons.

First, DAK's entire debt to Microsoft arose prepetition. ... The agreement here provided that upon signing, DAK was absolutely obligated to pay $2,750,000, even if it sold only one copy of Word. The fact that some of the payments became due postpetition does not alter the fact that the entire debt was absolutely owed prepetition, and was therefore prepetition debt.

Second, the pricing structure of the agreement indicates that it was more akin to a sale of an intellectual property than to a lease for use of that property. The amount of the minimum commitment, as well as any additional payments, was calculated based upon quantity of units DAK obtained, as in most sales arrangements, not upon the duration of the "use" of the property, as in most rental arrangements.

Third, as in a sale, DAK received all of its rights under the agreement when the term of the agreement commenced. Initially, DAK made a down payment on its $2,750,000 minimum commitment. At that point, the agreement permitted DAK to distribute immediately the full quantity of units covered by its $2,750,000 commitment. The remaining amount due on that commitment was to

---

[2] Because we look to the economic realities of the agreement, the fact that the agreement labels itself a "license" and calls the payments "royalties," both terms that arguably imply periodic payment for the use rather than sale of technology, does not control our analysis.

be paid in future installments. This arrangement is similar to a purchase of goods on unsecured credit: The purchaser makes a down payment, obtains and can dispose of the goods immediately, and then pays the remainder of the purchase price in subsequent installments. The timing of DAK's installment payments confirms this analysis. The installment dates did not correlate with when DAK could sell the 50,000 programs in the way that rent payment dates generally correlate with time during which rental property is used. Instead, DAK could sell all of the programs at the outset of the term, even though the installments were due three, six and nine months into the term.

Fourth, it is more accurate to describe this agreement as granting DAK a "right to sell" than "permission to use" an intellectual property. Microsoft relies upon various cases in which the claimant granted debtor temporary permission to employ the claimant's property to run its operation. ... Unlike those cases, DAK did not employ Word over a period of time in order to run its operation. Rather, it sold the program to consumers. Accordingly, DAK's postpetition distribution of Word is more like the sale of inventory than the utilization of the claimant's trademark or device. * * *

Finally, Microsoft did not provide anything at its expense to the debtor after the petition. As discussed above, at the time of the petition, Microsoft had already granted DAK the right to sell at least 50,000 copies of Word. Microsoft does not contend that DAK sold more than this amount. Furthermore, the district court found that the debtor did not accept any Word updates offered by Microsoft after the petition. The district court also found that Microsoft did not incur any additional expense postpetition by making its generally available software hotline service also available to DAK's customers. * * *

For these reasons, the economic realities of this agreement indicate that it was basically a sale, not a license to use. The debt arose prepetition, and Microsoft did not provide the debtor any consideration postpetition. Microsoft was not entitled to an administrative expense claim.[3]

---

[3] We also note that Microsoft's reliance upon In re Prize Frize, 150 Bankr. 456 (9th Cir. BAP 1993), aff'd, 32 F.3d 426 (9th Cir. 1994), is misplaced. In that case, Prize Frize had granted a licensee an exclusive license to manufacture, use and sell its patented french fry vending machine. In exchange, the licensee agreed to pay certain license fees to Prize Frize. After Prize Frize filed for bankruptcy, it rejected the agreement. The court held that the license fees still owed by the licensee were "royalty payments" within the meaning of §365(n), and that therefore §365(n) re-

Several policy considerations also counsel against granting Microsoft an administrative expense claim, which has priority over other unsecured claims. First, denying Microsoft's claim will not unjustly enrich the estate for the benefit of all other creditors. DAK paid Microsoft $1,354,167 prior to filing for bankruptcy. At the $45 per copy royalty rate provided by the amended agreement, DAK paid for up to 30,092 copies of Word. While the record is not clear as to the total number of copies sold, Microsoft does not contend that DAK sold more than 30,092. Therefore, DAK has not sold any copies for which it did not pay Microsoft at least the $45 royalty rate. Under these circumstances, granting Microsoft a priority over other unsecured creditors would be unjust. In addition, Microsoft might still recover some of the outstanding amount due under the agreement. That amount remains an unsecured claim. If any proceeds from the bankruptcy are distributed to unsecured creditors, Microsoft will receive a share.

Secondly, granting Microsoft priority over other unsecured creditors would not serve the purpose of §503. Section 503's principal purpose is to induce entities to do business with a debtor after bankruptcy by insuring that those entities receive payment for services rendered. Payment of administrative expenses allows the debtor to secure goods and services necessary to administer the estate, which ultimately accrues to the benefit of all creditors. In this case, Microsoft was not induced to and did not do business with the debtor postpetition. As we have described above, the transaction in this case took place before bankruptcy ... .

The bankruptcy court and the district court properly denied Microsoft's administrative expense claim.

---

quired the licensee to pay those fees to the debtor in order to retain its rights under the agreement. Microsoft claims that *Prize Frize* supports its argument that the "royalty payments" owed by DAK in this case were payments for continuous "use" of Word. However, the question in this case is not whether the payments owed are "royalty payments" under §365(n), but rather whether either the debt arose postpetition or Microsoft provided postpetition consideration to the debtor, such that Microsoft is entitled to a §503 administrative expense claim. Furthermore, the balance struck by §365(n) and the policies underlying that section are entirely different from those underlying §503. "Royalty payments" owed to the debtor under §365(n) are interpreted broadly in order to insure that the estate receives full payment when a licensee takes advantage of the debtor's intellectual property. On the other hand, administrative expenses under §503 are construed narrowly because they give one unsecured creditor absolute priority in payment over other unsecured creditors and over the estate. The narrow construction of administrative expenses insures that payments out of the estate are kept to a minimum.

NOTES

9D.6. In *Reading Co. v. Brown*, Chief Justice Warren, writing for the minority, sees the principal purpose of the bankruptcy process—initiated, as he sees it, by the debtor for its benefit and not for the benefit of its creditors—as one of achieving equality of treatment among those similarly situated. Accordingly, Warren thinks that there should be no better treatment for postpetition tort claimants based on the "fortuity" of their being postpetition. Justice Harlan, in contrast, writing for the majority, sees such postpetition torts as a cost of running the bankrupt's business. As such, the costs of those torts, he believes, should be borne by the prepetition creditors (including prepetition tort creditors), on whose behalf, in his view, the debtor's business is being run.

9D.7. Chief Justice Warren's dissent may be seen in light of the principle of *Butner*. If the creditors try to negotiate a nonbankruptcy workout and the firm commits any torts during these negotiations, the tort victims will have only general claims against the firm. They would enjoy no special priority. Similarly, if the firm were to dissolve under nonbankruptcy law, any tort claims that arose during the dissolution proceeding are ordinarily treated the same way as other general claims. In the absence of a nonbankruptcy rule that gives tort victims priority whenever the firm is insolvent, a bankruptcy rule that has that effect discourages the use of bankruptcy. The dissenters in *Reading Co.*, one can suggest, take the view that the rule should be the same in bankruptcy as out.

One may question, however, whether Chief Justice Warren is correct in asserting that a rule that forced general creditors to bear the cost of tort liability will create an *improper* bias toward liquidation. Justice Harlan does ensure that the trustee in bankruptcy has the right set of incentives. The risk of tort liability might lead creditors to close down a firm, but tort law is intended to have this effect when a firm is worth keeping intact as a going concern only if the firm can impose costs on others. The vice of Justice Harlan's approach, if any, is not that it creates a bias toward liquidation, but rather that it creates a bankruptcy solution to something that is not a bankruptcy problem.

9D.8. In *Wall Tube & Metal Products,* there is no pretense that the cleanup obligation is a way of minimizing the potential tort liability of the general creditors. The court is relying on the trustee's status as a new owner as an independent source of liability. Environmental laws typically impose liability in multiple ways. Hence, there is no inconsistency is asserting that pollution gives rise both to a claim against the debtor as a prepetition polluter and to an action against the debtor by virtue of its postpetition ownership of the property. As the court notes, this is essentially the same issue that arose in *Midlantic*. The cleanup obligation is a liability that attaches to ownership of the polluted property and thus permits a claim against untainted property. To be sure, outside of bankruptcy, Wall Tube's creditors might have taken the clean assets before the state could have ordered those assets converted to pay for the cleanup (whatever the social merit of such action). But it is uncertain who would have won this race, and because bankruptcy replaces the nonbankruptcy process it can emulate nonbankruptcy outcomes only roughly. Compare section C3 above. Moreover, as noted above with regard to *Reading Co.*, there is good reason to afford high priority for nonconsensual claims such as that of the state in *Wall Tube*. Otherwise, a debtor's consensual creditors and equity holders could join together to impose on others the costs of operation.

9D.9. In *Microsoft v. DAK*, Microsoft argued that DAK's debt arose after the petition as periodic payments for continued use of Microsoft's intellectual property. "Characterized this way," the court remarked, "the transaction is analogous to a debtor's postpetition use of leased property under an agreement signed prepetition. Such use gives rise to an administrative expense claim for the payment of rent." The court rejected this characterization, however. Relying largely on the fact that "Microsoft did not provide anything at its expense to the debtor after the petition," the court concluded that DAK's obligation was more akin to one incurred from inventory purchased on credit prepetition and sold postpetition. Microsoft, therefore, held an ordinary prepetition claim. An ordinary lessor, however, need not "provide anything at its expense to the debtor after the petition." The case should not turn on Microsoft's obligations postpetition, but rather on the nature of its relationship to DAK. On one hand, one might find that it is merely an unperfected secured creditor, someone that has sold a piece of intellectual property and agreed to be paid over time. On the other, it might be seen as more like a lessor that has conveyed an interest in its intellectual property for a limited period of time for a fixed amount.

If Microsoft's position more closely resembles that of a lessor, the *Butner* principle suggests that we should look toward substantive nonbankruptcy law. If, under nonbankruptcy law, Microsoft could enjoin DAK's distribution of Word until DAK made its installment payments, then that right to enjoin arguably should be entitled to protection in bankruptcy. Priority for Microsoft's claim would protect this right, just as administrative priority for lease obligations protects the right of a lessor. Administrative expense priority and adequate protection serve the same purpose: Each allows the debtor to benefit from property in which others have an interest, but only if others are fully compensated for that interest. Given the holding of *Microsoft v. DAK*, those in Microsoft's position in the future should perhaps seek adequate protection for their right of injunction, if one exists. Adequate protection is discussed earlier in this section. Problem 9D-3 asks a question left unanswered by the case.

PROBLEM

9D-3. Software Designers Inc. and Debtor Corp. enter into what is described as a "licensing agreement." Under this agreement, for a period of five years, Debtor is permitted to sell any quantity of Software's "Word Right," Software's newly designed word processing program. Software is also to provide continuing technical support. At the end of each month, Debtor is to pay Software $50 for each unit of Word Right sold to customers. Debtor makes all monthly payments prior to its filing a Chapter 11 bankruptcy petition. After entering bankruptcy, Debtor sells 10,000 units of Word Right. Debtor then rejects the agreement with Software without making any payment with respect to these units. Is Debtor's $500,000 obligation to Software an administrative expense?

Part Three

DISPOSITION OF THE CASE

Once claims against the estate are allowed, property of the estate is gathered, and the estate is administered, all that is left is disposition of the case. The disposition of the case has consequences for the debtor that vary by type of debtor and by bankruptcy chapter. Chapter 7 contains provisions that direct how the estate will be liquidated and distributed. Although Chapter 7 can be used by almost any debtor—corporation, partnership, or individual—this chapter is most useful for an individual. Chapter 13 applies only to individuals, and permits an eligible debtor to retain all her assets as she adjusts her debt obligations. The most important bankruptcy chapter for a corporation, or similar entity such as a business partnership, is Chapter 11, which permits the reorganization of a debtor's capital structure. Chapter 11 is also available for individual debtors, but the disposition of a Chapter 11 case affects the individual debtor in largely the same way as does the disposition of a Chapter 7 case. Chapter 11 procedures are sometimes better suited to individual debtors who have substantial business debts, but the substantive consequences are frequently similar.

Each of these chapters is described below. The mechanisms of each chapter are best seen as variations on a common theme. The differences stem from the policies that are implicated. While it is important to keep these different policies in mind, it is also useful to note the basic structural similarities. As we shall see, for example, one must know the distribution scheme of Chapter 7 in order to evaluate a plan of adjustment under Chapter 13 or a plan of reorganization under Chapter 11. Similarly, Chapter 13 and Chapter 11 share a number of features that protect the interest of secured creditors. Mastery of any chapter helps with mastery of the others. We do not review Chapter 9 for municipal debtors or Chapter 12 for family farmers, but these too have structures that can be largely understood by reference to the more commonly used chapters. Chapter 12, for example, employs many of the features of Chapter 13 but takes into account that family farms often do business in corporate form.

A survey of the bankruptcy chapters begins with the simplest type of bankruptcy, a Chapter 7 liquidation. In Chapter 7, the trustee releases to secured creditors or sells the assets that she has gathered and distributes any proceeds, for the most part, according to the priority scheme applicable under substantive nonbankruptcy law. There are exceptions to this principle. One such exception already discussed occurs when priorities are established or altered as part of the administrative process. These alterations of nonbankruptcy priority can be seen as a cost of doing business for the subordinated creditors. Without the administrative expense priority there might be no one willing to finance maintenance of the estate and thus a smaller estate to divide among the prebankruptcy creditors. The priority scheme in Chapter 7 alters nonbankruptcy entitlements in an additional way. The priority scheme—detailed through an interaction primarily among §§725, 726, 507, and 503—includes a series of special priorities that reflect congressional preferences, such as those for employees and taxing authorities. (Similarly, as we have seen in chapter 5 above, some state law claims are disallowed altogether under §502.) Moreover, bankruptcy courts sometimes engage in "equitable subordination" of claims held by those the courts believe to have misbehaved.

So one must look not only to state law but also to bankruptcy law for substantive priorities in distribution. Priorities are formally established in Chapter 7, but provide the baseline of entitlement for distribution in other bankruptcy chapters as well. Keep this in mind as you work through these priority provisions in the next chapter of this book.

As important as the priority in distribution of assets is to bankruptcy, one must not focus on it myopically. Distribution tells only half the story. Central to the disposition of the case is what happens to the debtor. The simplest and least important case is that of the corporation that files a Chapter 7 petition. When the case is over, the corporation leaves bankruptcy without any change in its obligations. Because the corporation loses all its assets in Chapter 7, however, it is irrelevant whether the corporation receives a discharge of unpaid obligations. After bankruptcy, the next step for the corporation is dissolution under the state law that created it. (A partnership would end similarly.) Thus, even without a discharge, there would be no assets and no entity for unpaid creditors to pursue. Of much greater importance is the treatment accorded individuals seeking relief from debt.

In chapters 11 and 12 below we explore the fresh start for individual debtors, focusing first on Chapter 7 and then on Chapter 13 of the Bankruptcy Code. The concept of a fresh start for individuals is simple enough: Individual debtors receive a discharge and leave bankruptcy with their exempt assets—such as the clothes on their backs and their tools of trade. In Chapter 7, this is accomplished through §§727 and 522. To support the discharge, and thus the debtor's right to enjoy the fruits of subsequent labor, future earnings are specifically excluded from the bankruptcy estate under §541(a)(6).

Not all debtors have a right to a discharge, however. Since the 2005 Bankruptcy Act, some relatively high-income debtors are ineligible for Chapter 7. Also, even a debtor of modest means who abuses the bankruptcy process—such as one who runs up debts on the eve of filing with no intent to repay them or one who hides assets—may see the Chapter 7 case dismissed under §707(b) or might be denied a discharge under §727. Moreover, some debts are not dischargeable. For example, alimony and child support payments as well as certain student loans and many tax obligations are excluded, some under any circumstances, others unless repayment would impose undue hardship. Upon leaving Chapter 7, the debtor is still obliged to pay these in full. The repayment of certain obligations that arise from some kinds of misconduct, such as drunken driving, also survive bankruptcy. These exceptions are contained in §523. The effect is to privilege these obligations. Not only is the debtor obliged to pay them out of future earnings, but, after the discharge of the other obligations, other creditors are no longer in the picture. Claimants who hold nondischargeable obligations thus face less competition for the debtor's assets.

Some individuals, then, cannot obtain relief under Chapter 7. Others would rather keep more of their nonexempt assets and give up in return some of their future income. For some of these individuals, those with regular income and with debts below a certain level, Chapter 13 provides an avenue of relief. The individual debtor creates a repayment plan that satisfies the restrictions Chapter 13 imposes. The essence of these restrictions, contained in §1325, is that the debtor must promise to pay all of her disposable income for a specified time toward her debts. Creditors can also insist on receiving at least as much as they would have received from a Chapter 7 liquidation. After making the payments under the plan for up to five years, the debtor receives a discharge.

Unlike Chapter 7, a Chapter 13 case arises only when a debtor affirmatively wants it. There are no involuntary Chapter 13 petitions. The reasons why a debtor files for Chapter 13 vary. A debtor might choose Chapter 13 over Chapter 7 because she places a value on her nonexempt property greater than the market value the creditors would receive under Chapter 7. Chapter 13 may allow a debtor breathing space in which to renegotiate a home mortgage that is in default (though Chapter 13 does not generally permit a debtor to restructure a home mortgage as a matter of right). Chapter 13 also excepts fewer debts from discharge than does Chapter 7. And, as noted above, for some high-income debtors, the 2005 Bankruptcy Act removes Chapter 7 as an option, leaving Chapter 13 as the best alternative.

Before we begin a more thorough examination of the individual debtor, it is useful to bear in mind the substantively different treatment that awaits corporations in Chapter 11. As we have noted, the animating principle of bankruptcy law in the case of the individual debtor is the fresh start—the right to discharge past debts, free future income, and exempt property. A different principle—the need for a new capital structure—animates the law of corporate reorganizations.

A corporation (or other business entity) in Chapter 11, like an individual in Chapter 7, receives a discharge at the end of the bankruptcy proceeding, but this discharge has radically different consequences. In the case of the individual debtor, the discharge works in conjunction with other parts of the Bankruptcy Code to ensure that an individual can enjoy a fresh start. What matters in the case of an individual is not simply that debts are formally discharged, but also that future earnings do not become property of the estate under §541. Hence, these earnings are beyond the reach of creditors in the bankruptcy proceeding itself. We need both the discharge and the carving out of future income from property of the estate to ensure an individual debtor a fresh start.

In contrast to the case of an individual in Chapter 7, a corporation's future earnings do become property of the estate. For this reason, the discharge itself does not put future income beyond the reach of those who held rights against the debtor before the petition was filed. The discharge of corporate debt, provided for in §1141, serves a purpose altogether different from the discharge of individual debt in §727. Rather than freeing the debtor from its obligation, the discharge is part of the mechanism that divides future income among creditors.

The Bankruptcy Code generally requires that the new capital structure recognize the priority claims and interests enjoyed under nonbankruptcy law. The "absolute priority rule," contained in §1129, is the bedrock of Chapter 11. Unless holders of claims or interests in a class make a concession, each class must be paid in full, typically with a claim against or interest in the reorganized firm, before any junior class or any equity holders are paid anything. Moreover, even if a class decides as a group to make a concession, no single dissenter can be silenced unless awarded at least as much as the dissenter would have received in a Chapter 7 liquidation. The discharge of prepetition claims, then, is not intended to give anyone a break. Instead discharge is the means employed to implement a new capital structure. Without discharge, unpaid junior claims could be asserted against the reorganized debtor, the ownership of which had been transferred to holders of senior claims. Collection on the junior claims could upset absolute priority and might threaten a firm's viability.

The principles of Chapter 11 and its absolute priority rule are more easily stated than executed. A debtor firm should be reorganized rather than sold piecemeal if it is worth more alive than dead. When a firm is kept in operation as a going concern, however, it is harder to value both the firm as a whole and the discrete assets in which creditors hold security interests. Furthermore, creditors who enjoy different priorities will favor different approaches to the reorganization. Senior creditors, who are entitled to the entire value of the firm's assets up to a limit, argue for low valuation of the firm and, until there is a definitive determination of that value, favor the safest course even when such course is not in the interests of the group. Junior creditors and equity owners have opposite incentives. They tend to argue for a high enough valuation to justify their continuing interest in the firm and favor even foolish gambles with a high upside potential that might be realized prior to the determination of their stake.

In an attempt to facilitate the resolution of conflicts among holders of claims and interests, the Bankruptcy Code groups similar claims or interests in a class and allows holders in each class a voice in the reorganization. Even here, however, problems arise. Those who hold identical legal rights might nevertheless see reorganization plans differently. A creditor is more likely to look favorably on a plan that keeps the firm in place if that creditor would benefit from doing business with the firm in the future. By contrast, a creditor with the same priority but with no such plans might prefer liquidation if that course would maximize the creditor's immediate payoff. Hence, a debtor's suppliers might view the case differently from a debtor's bank lenders. We explore corporate reorganizations in the last chapter of this book.

X. PRIORITIES IN DISTRIBUTION

The trustee's primary job in a Chapter 7 case is to release or sell the assets she has gathered and to distribute any proceeds. Throughout this book, we have seen, at least in rough contours, the basic order in which claimants are paid. As a general matter, if particular rights are recognized outside of bankruptcy, the claimant holding these rights will be able to assert them fully in bankruptcy. Thus, when assets are distributed at the end of a bankruptcy case, a holder of an unavoided security interest or other property interest is entitled to have that claim satisfied first, up to the extent of the value of that property right. Section 725 directs the trustee "to dispose of any property in which an entity other than the estate has an interest." The force of §725 is explained in the accompanying legislative report:

> The purpose of this section is to give the court appropriate authority to ensure that collateral or its proceeds is returned to the proper secured creditor, that consigned or bailed goods are returned to the consignor or bailor, and so on. ... The section is in lieu of a section that would direct a certain distribution to secured creditors. It gives the court greater flexibility to meet the circumstances, and it is broader, permitting disposition of property subject to a co-ownership interest.

After claimants holding nonavoided property interests have had those interests satisfied under §725, the question becomes how to divide up the remaining assets among the debtor's remaining obligations. In a Chapter 7 liquidation, we start with §726. It refers to §507, which provides a basic list of bankruptcy priorities. This list, in turn, refers to §§502 and 503 for further distinctions in the hierarchy. It is important to note at the outset that the subject of "priorities," as the Bankruptcy Code uses that term, is the ranking among creditors who do not hold property interests. The omission of secured claims from the priority list in §507 is not a subordination of those claims, but merely a recognition that secured claims are satisfied first under §725.

The first set of priorities under §726(a)(1) is that established by §507. The list in §507 begins with domestic support obligations, a special priority, applicable by nature only to individual debtors and established by the 2005 Bankruptcy Act to protect these obligations from competition with other obligations a debtor might not discharge in bankruptcy. Next come administrative expenses. As we saw at the end of the last chapter, fees owed to the trustee and money owed on an unsecured postpetition loan authorized by §364 are not prepetition claims but rather administrative expenses entitled to priority over the general creditors. The trustee, like anyone else who conducts a sale, incurs costs that must be deducted from the sale's gross proceeds. These expenses, and any incurred through the trustee's management of the debtor's business, come ahead of all prepetition claims. The remaining priorities in §507 reflect a set of claims that, at one time or another, Congress thought especially worthy of protection. These priorities do not necessarily track nonbankruptcy rights, but many of the claims that enjoy priority under §507 are also singled out for special treatment under nonbankruptcy law. For example, unpaid workers, whose claims within specified limits have priority under §§503(b) and 507(a)(4), are protected under the Fair Labor Standards Act, which limits a firm's ability to sell goods when the firm's workers go unpaid. For another example, the tax collector, whose claims may have priority under §507(a)(8), often enjoys a lien under substantive nonbankruptcy law.

Once a debtor's assets or the proceeds therefrom are applied to claims given priority under §507, any property that remains is applied under §726's own priority provisions. Section 726(a)(2) grants priority next to unsecured claims allowed under §502 (which include any portion of a claim that remains after a limited §507 priority has been exhausted). There are exceptions, however, for certain allowed claims that are singled out, not for priority as under §507, but for subordination to other general claims. The disfavored claims include, under §726(a)(3), certain tardy claims and, under §726(a)(4), punitive damages. Beyond such subordination, the remainder of §726 more or less complies with nonbankruptcy priority. If all allowed claims are satisfied, §726(a)(5) provides for the payment of postpetition interest on those claims. (Recall from chapter 5, section B above that such interest is not itself a "claim.") If property still remains—that is, if the debtor proves to be solvent—§726(a)(6) directs that the debtor receive the residual.

Byzantine though it is, the priority schedule established by these provisions is not the extent of the Bankruptcy Code's priority provisions. Section 510 addresses subordination. Section 510(a) honors a contractual subordination agreement to the extent enforceable under applicable law. Section 510(b) specifically subordinates claims that arise from the purchase or sale of a security of the debtor. Such a claim is subordinated to the security sold or, if common stock is the security sold, is subordinated to the priority of common stock. This provision is significant, for example, if an insolvent corporation violates securities law when it issues its stock. Under securities law, this liability is an ordinary debt obligation. In bankruptcy, however, all other creditors will be paid ahead of the claim based on the securities violation. The notion is that one victimized by the sale of an equity security should not be made better off by that violation than if the sale had been lawful. And if the debtor proves insolvent without regard to the securities law liability, not even an honest transaction would have benefited the victim of the violation. Whether this justification of subordination succeeds depends on why one believes an issuer, and thus its investors, should ever be liable for fraud committed by corporate managers in the issuer's name. Finally, §510(c) provides for "equitable subordination," applied when courts find that justice requires an alteration of the statutory priorities.

The first section below addresses statutory priorities. The second section describes how bankruptcy courts may exercise their discretion to depart from such priorities.

A. CODIFIED PRIORITIES

As we shall see in the following exercises, most of the priority provisions discussed above are straightforward. An important exception is the provision in §507(a)(8) for priority of certain tax obligations. As you work through the exercises on §507(a)(8), it will be useful to consider the structure of a withholding tax. An employer is often obligated to withhold from its employees, and pay to the government, a portion of salary that the employee will likely owe the government as an income tax. Whether ultimately the government keeps or the employee receives the portion of salary withheld is a matter between the government and the employee. The employer is merely a stakeholder, with an obligation to hold and pay funds over to the government. The obligation is *derivative* of the employee's obligation to pay income taxes. Because the employee owes no taxes on salary owed but never received, an employer has no obligation to withhold taxes on salary owed but never paid.

The case that follows the exercises, *Dana*, along with the related notes and problem, ask you to consider Congress' manipulation of bankruptcy priority in the wake of the Enron and WorldCom scandals, which included at least the perception of insiders enriching themselves at the companies' expense. The 2005 Bankruptcy Act adds §503(c), which contains a number of provisions that restrict executive compensation. *Dana* provides an early glimpse of §503(c) in action, and reveals the great flexibility a judge has in its application.

Key Provisions: Bankruptcy Code §§502; 503; 506; 507; 725; 726

EXERCISES

10A(1) Debtor decides to open a foreign language school as a sole proprietorship. After setting up business, Debtor receives $1,200 from each of twenty students as tuition for a course. Before classes start, however, Debtor files for bankruptcy. Debtor's assets are gathered and liquidated. Debtor has a computer, worth $10,000, subject to an unavoidable security interest in favor of Bank for a $5,000 loan. Debtor also has other nonexempt assets (office furniture, video equipment, bank account, and so forth) worth $62,500. In addition to the loan from Bank, Debtor is subject to the following obligations:

1. a claim by the landlord for $1,000 rent for use of the leased property while Debtor was in bankruptcy;

2. a claim by Debtor's fifteen employees for aggregate wages of $10,000 accrued by them while Debtor was in bankruptcy;

3. the government's claim for $3,000 of those wages in item (2) as a withholding obligation;

4. a wage claim by an individual employee of $12,500 for wages earned during the last month before Debtor filed for bankruptcy;

5. the government's claim of $3,750 for those wages in item (4) as a withholding obligation;

6. a claim of $500 for each of Debtor's fifteen employees that aggregate $7,500. These claims are based on Debtor's failure to make a contribution to the employee benefit plan for their last month's services;

7. claims by the twenty students for a refund of their money, aggregating $24,000;

8. a claim of $8,000 for child support obligations owed Debtor's spouse;

9. a claim of $4,000 by the government for Debtor's withholding obligation with respect to wages paid to employees before bankruptcy; and

10. other general unsecured claims in the amount of $20,000.

How will Debtor's property be distributed? In answering this question consider, among other provisions, Bankruptcy Code §104.

10A(2) Debtor ran a failed foreign language school just as in the prior exercise. There is one more creditor on the scene. Finance Company lent Debtor $5,000 and took a security interest in the video equipment. Because the video equipment was depreciating, Finance asked for and the bankruptcy court granted Finance a security interest in Debtor's office furniture to protect Finance in the event that the value of the video equipment dropped below $5,000. During the course of the bankruptcy, both the video equipment and the office furniture lose virtually all their value. The accounts prove uncollectible as well. Debtor's only nonexempt asset of any worth is the computer, which is now worth $14,000 but still secures Bank's $5,000 loan. How will Debtor's property be distributed?

10A(3) Debtor ran a failed foreign language school just as in Exercise 10A(1), with the exception that Debtor now has $85,000 in nonexempt assets other than the computer. How will Debtor's property be distributed?

10A(4) Debtor ran a failed foreign language school just as in Exercise 10A(1), with the exception that Debtor now has $85,000 in nonexempt assets other than the computer. There is also an additional claim for punitive damages. Just before the bankruptcy petition was filed, a disgruntled student was awarded punitive as well as compensatory damages on account of Debtor's fraudulent advertisements. How will Debtor's property be distributed?

CASE

IN RE DANA CORPORATION

United States Bankruptcy Court, S.D.N.Y., 2006
358 Bankr. 567

LIFLAND, BANKRUPTCY JUDGE

The Debtors [the "Dana Companies"] are leading suppliers of modules, systems and components for original equipment manufacturers and service customers in the light, commercial and off-highway vehicle markets. The products manufactured and supplied are used in cars, vans, sport-utility vehicles, light, medium and heavy trucks, and a wide range of off-highway vehicles. … [T]he Dana Companies recorded revenue of more than $8.6 billion and had assets of approximately $7.4 billion and liabilities totaling $6.8 billion. As of the Petition Date, the Dana Companies had approximately 44,000 employees. * * *

EXECUTIVE COMPENSATION

In addition to base salary and an annual incentive plan (the "AIP"), the Employment Agreements of the CEO and Senior Executives, as modified, include the following terms:

Pension Benefits

Dana proposes to assume one hundred percent of the Senior Executives' pension plans (ranging between $999,000 and $2.7 million) and sixty percent of the CEO's pension plan (60% of $5.9 million), with the remaining forty percent being allowed as a general unsecured claim. Assumption would take place upon emergence from bankruptcy or the Senior Executives' involuntary termination without cause, and with respect to the CEO, voluntary termination for good reason. The pension benefits would only be assumed on the condition that the salaried and bargaining unit defined benefit pension plans of Dana employees have not been terminated.

To the extent not assumed, one hundred percent of the pension benefits of CEO and Senior Executives would be treated as allowed general unsecured claims in their vested amount as of the Petition Date, with all postpetition accruals and credits allowed as administrative claims.

Severance

Should the need arise, the Debtors propose to pay the CEO and Senior Executives severance in an amount that complies with section 503(c)(2) of the Bankruptcy Code. To quell the fears of objecting parties, the Debtors agreed to submit a statement, upon the termination of the CEO or Senior Executive, detailing a calculation of the severance payment for which they are eligible, and allow sufficient notice of such payment.

Non-Disclosure Agreement and Pre-Emergence or Post-Emergence Claim

In consideration for the assumption of their Employment Agreements and receipt of payments under the [long-term performance based incentive plan (the "LTIP")], the Senior Executives would execute a new non-compete, non-solicitation, non-disclosure and non-disparagement agreement (collectively, the "NDA Agreements") that would prohibit the Senior Executives from accepting a position with a competitor of Dana, disclosing Dana's confidential information to third parties, soliciting any employees of Dana or disparaging Dana for twelve months.

The CEO's Employment Agreement would be modified to include a provision that in the event the CEO is involuntarily terminated without cause or resigned for good reason prior to the Debtors' emergence from Chapter 11, the CEO would be prohibited from accepting a position with a competitor of Dana, disclosing Dana's confidential information to third parties, soliciting any employees of Dana or disparaging Dana for six months. The pre-emergence claim (the Pre-Emergence Claim) of the CEO would be an allowed *general unsecured claim* in the amount of $4 million (with recovery limited to $3 million, less any severance actually paid under section 503(c)(2) of the Bankruptcy Code) on account of the CEO's claim relating to damages from termination of the Employment Agreement. The Pre-Emergence Claim would be freely assignable after termination.

In the event that the CEO is involuntarily terminated without cause or resigns for good reason *after* Dana's emergence from Chapter 11, the CEO would be prohibited from accepting a position with a competitor of Dana, disclosing Dana's confidential information to third parties, soliciting any employees of Dana or disparaging Dana for twelve months (the "Post-Emergence NDA Agreement"). The post-emergence claim (the "Post-Emergence Claim") of $3 million would be paid ratably over the term of the Post-Emergence NDA Agreement on account of the CEO's claim for damages under the Employment Agreement.

In addition to the request to approve the assumption of the Employment Agreements, the Executive Compensation Motion requests approval of the LTIP. Under the LTIP, the CEO and Senior Executives would be eligible for a long-term incentive bonus if the company reaches a certain [earnings benchmarks] and the amount of the incentive payment would increase if additional, higher … benchmarks were reached. In order for the CEO to qualify for the minimum amount of the LTIP ($3 million), the company must achieve [2007 earnings] of $250 million. The CEO would earn an additional $750,000 for each $100 million increase in [earnings], with a maximum payout of $4.5 million for 2007. In 2007, the first $3 million, if earned, would be paid in cash, with payment deferred to the post-emergence period, and any additional amounts would be paid in stock of the reorganized company. In 2008, a similar structure of minimum [earnings] with incremental increases applies, but all payments would be made in the form of stock. ... In sum, as Debtors' counsel noted at the hearing, if all [earnings] goals were reached, over a three year period, the LTIP provides for $11 million payments in total to the six executives, $5 million of which is in cash, with the remainder in stock. The LTIP is a substantial reduction from the long-term incentives that were available prepetition to the CEO and Senior Executives prior to the bankruptcy filing.

In sum, Dana contends that the compensation provided in the Executive Compensation Motion is necessary and appropriate, and represents a reasonable exercise of the Debtors' business judgment, pursuant to sections 363, 365 and 502 of the Bankruptcy Code, and are permissible under section 503(c) of the Bankruptcy Code. In denying the [an earlier] Compensation Motion because it violated section 503(c), I specifically expressed concern about certain aspects of the plan [then before the Court], including: the guaranteed completion bonus, the targets set for additional bonuses, and payments classified as non-compete payments. The Executive Compensation Motion currently before the Court arguably contains some similar provisions to the previous motion, but ... [the] plan before the Court today, unlike the previous iteration, has *no guaranteed payments* to the CEO or Senior Executives other than base salary and is a substantial retreat from the original proposals.

DISCUSSION

Senator Edward Kennedy proposed the amendment to section 503 of the Bankruptcy Code as a last-minute addition to the [2005 Bankruptcy Act], expressing his concern over the "glaring abuses of the bankruptcy system by the executives of giant companies like Enron Corp. and WorldCom Inc. and Polaroid Corporation, who lined their own pockets, but left thousands of employees and retirees out in the cold." Other members of Congress were concerned that Senator Kennedy's amendment would prevent responsible companies that needed to retain key employees to reorganize successfully and suggested that section 503(c) of the Bankruptcy Code should only prevent payments to insiders in the event of fraud, mismanagement, and conduct contributing to the debtor's insolvency. The modified language proposed by Senator Hatch that would have addressed the above concern was never included in the final bill.

Section 503(c) of the [Bankruptcy Code as provided by the Bankruptcy Act] restricts transfers or payments by debtors to the extent that such payments are outside the ordinary course. The predominate focus of the amendments to section 503(c) is on payments made to "insiders" of the debtor(s). However, section 503(c) was not intended to foreclose a Chapter 11 debtor from *reasonably* compensating employees, including "insiders," for their contribution to the debtors' reorganization.

Section 503(c)(1) prohibits the allowance and payment of sums to "insiders" "for the purpose of inducing such person to remain" with the business "absent a finding by the court based on the evidence in the record" that (1) the payment is "essential" to the retention of the individual "because the individual has a bona fide job offer from another business at the same or greater rate of compensation;" and (2) the services of that individual are "essential to the survival of the debtor's business." The ... statute also fixes the measure of acceptable retention bonuses for insiders by linking them to a multiple of bonuses available to non-management employees. The Debtors are not moving under section 503(c)(1).

Section 503(c)(2) of the Bankruptcy Code allows severance payments to be made to insiders only if they are part of a generally applicable program and are less than ten times the amount of the mean severance pay given to non-management employees. * * *

If sections 503(c)(1) and (c)(2) are not operative, a court may consider whether the payments are permissible under section 503(c)(3), which limits payments made to management and employees, among others, outside of the ordinary course, unless such payments are shown to be justified under the facts and circumstances of the Chapter 11 case. [T]he test in section 503(c)(3) appears to be no more stringent a test than the one courts must apply in approving any administrative expense under section 503(b)(1)(A). Any expense must be an actual, necessary cost or expense of preserving the estate. Accordingly, section 503(c)(3) gives the court discretion as to bonus and incentive plans, which are not primarily motivated by retention or in the nature of severance.

Courts consider the following in determining if the structure of a compensation proposal and the process for developing the proposal meet the "sound business judgment" test:

- Is there a reasonable relationship between the plan proposed and the results to be obtained, i.e., will the key employee stay for as long as it takes for the debtor to reorganize or market its assets, or, in the case of a performance incentive, is the plan calculated to achieve the desired performance?

- Is the cost of the plan reasonable in the context of the debtor's assets, liabilities and earning potential?

- Is the scope of the plan fair and reasonable; does it apply to all employees; does it discriminate unfairly?

- Is the plan or proposal consistent with industry standards?

- What were the due diligence efforts of the debtor in investigating the need for a plan; analyzing which key employees need to be incentivized; what is available; what is generally applicable in a particular industry?

- Did the debtor receive independent counsel in performing due diligence and in creating and authorizing the incentive compensation? * * *

The Employment Agreements

The Unions, Non-Union Retiree Committee and the U.S. Trustee (the "Objecting Parties") object to the assumption of the Employment Agreements on several grounds. First, they argue that the pension benefit is severance pay and is retentive in nature. These pension benefits are essentially the entire retirement package from Dana for the CEO and Senior Executives. The pension benefits do not vest until the executive has been at Dana for five years, and various interim accruing factors determine the actual amount of the benefits, making this a true pension plan. The Senior Executives have already earned certain of the assumption of such benefits does not increase the amount of pension benefits to which they are currently entitled. Moreover, such assumption is not contingent upon any Senior Executive continuing to be employed by Dana for any particular period of time after assumption. To the extent these conditions have any retentive impact, it is merely incidental to the terms of the pension plans and are ordinary and customary in such plans.

Richard Priory, the Chairman of the Compensation Committee at Dana, testified that the CEO and Senior Executives gave up retirement plans at their former employers with the expectation that similar benefits would be provided by Dana. The pension benefits would be assumed as part of the Employee Agreement, which originally provided for more lucrative pension benefits for the CEO. Additionally, the assumption of the CEO and Senior Executives' pension plans is expressly tied to the non-termination of Dana's salaried and bargained unit defined benefit pension plans, which ensures parity of treatment of the pensions of the CEO and Senior Executives and Dana's other employees. The pension benefits, therefore, are not retentive in nature and are not severance, rather they are customary pension plans and their assumption is subject to the Debtors' business judgment.

Second, the Objecting Parties contend that the Pre-Emergence Claim and Post-Emergence Claim violate section 503(c). The Pre-Emergence Claim is a general unsecured claim. Section 503(c) of the Bankruptcy Code, which on its face only limits the allowance and payment of *administrative* claims, is not violated. The U.S. Trustee suggests that Congress meant to prevent debtors from providing *any* sort of compensation to executives of debtors in possession that might in any way be construed as retentive, however the language of section 503(c) is clear and unambiguous that *only administrative claims* are subject to section 503(c) restrictions.

The Post-Emergence Claim would be earned only if the CEO continues to comply with the terms of the agreement after dismissal (and not merely upon dismissal). Debtors point out that the payment is not for the loss of employment, but rather it is to compensate the employee for losses attributable to foregoing post-termination opportunities that if accepted, could result in direct detriment of Dana.

Dana contends that the $3 million post-emergence payment to the CEO is permissible because it would be paid only after the Debtors emerge from Chapter 11 and therefore the Debtors will no longer be constrained by section 503(c). However, to the extent that the $3 million payment is subject to further review and must be passed upon as a provision in a disclosure statement and plan of reorganization, the Court cannot, at this early point in the cases, guarantee that the payment will be ultimately approved.

The Board believes that given the CEO and Senior Executives' extensive knowledge of Dana's operations, customers and strategies, the continuing presence of the CEO and Senior Executives is crucial for the Debtors' operations and challenges of restructuring. The Board came to the conclusion that this CEO and the Senior Executive team that he had assembled was the "right team" to run the company.

At the Hearing, Mr. Priory, testified that the Compensation Committee, with advice from Dana's outside expert on executive compensation, Mercer Human Resources Consulting, and the Compensation Committee's own independent compensation consultant, Frederic W. Cook & Co., Inc., worked to determine the appropriate level of compensation for the CEO and Senior Executives after the Petition Date. Mr. Priory noted, "[b]y the time Mr. Burns went through the process of having his compensation stripped away Mr. Burns was not only below mean, but way below the median." After the Initial Compensation Motion was denied by this Court, the team went back to the drawing board, and included the Creditors' Committee and Equity Committee in its deliberations. Together, they devised the Executive Compensation Motion before the Court today.

This uncontroverted evidence supports the Debtors' contention that they exercised fair and reasonable business judgment in determining to assume the Employment Agreements of the CEO and Senior Executives.

The AIP (Annual Incentive Plan)

The 2006 Annual Incentive Plan (the "AIP"), is a refinement of the 2005 short-term incentive program, reflecting current business conditions and a reduction in the number of participants, and is similar to Dana's previous short-term incentive programs. Dana contends that the continuance of the AIP is a transaction in the ordinary course of business for which no court approval is needed, and contends that no approval was sought. The parties opposing the Debtors' motion contend that the AIP is not in the ordinary course and that it was restructured just before the Petition Date. Dana's Board of Directors authorized the bonuses payable under the AIP on February 28, 2006; in the same timeframe the AIP is typically authorized. The AIP, like its predecessor programs, provides short-term performance-based incentives to hundreds of key employees of Dana and its subsidiaries for 2006, including the Senior Executives and CEO.

The Bankruptcy Code is designed to allow a debtor-in-possession the flexibility to engage in ordinary transactions without unneeded oversight by creditors or the court, while at the same time giving creditors an opportunity to contest those transactions that are not ordinary. This balance between allowing businesses to continue their *daily* operations on the one hand, and protecting creditors from squandering the estate's assets on the other, is reflected in section 363(c)(1) of the Bankruptcy Code:

If the business of the debtor is authorized to be operated under ... this title and unless the court orders otherwise, the trustee may enter into transactions ... in the ordinary course of business, without notice or a hearing, and may use property of the estate in the ordinary course of business without notice or a hearing. * * *

[A] short-term incentive plan has been a common component of compensation plans at Dana for the past fifty years and does not differ significantly from Dana's prepetition practice. Accordingly, it is within the ordinary course of Debtors' business. However, the payments to be made under the AIP to the Executives must be considered in the context of determining whether the overall compensation proposal is a proper exercise of Debtors' business judgment.

The LTIP

The LTIP requires that the company reach certain [earnings] benchmarks before the CEO and Senior Executives will be eligible for any payment under the long-term incentive plan. This aspect of the bonus is a significant change from the terms of the doomed Initial Compensation Motion, where Debtors' sought approval of a completion bonus, awarded upon emergence from Chapter 11 and a separate bonus based on total enterprise value of the company upon emergence, with a bonus being awarded even if the total enterprise value of the company declined by the time the company emerged. The Debtors assert that the proposed [earnings] minimum benchmarks will require management to "stretch" in order to achieve superior operating results for the Debtors, particularly in the difficult and rapidly deteriorating auto industry. The Objecting Parties argue that [earnings] required over the first six months of 2006 indicates that the 2007 [earnings] for the CEO and Senior Executives to be paid their minimum LTIP is "virtually guaranteed." Based upon the uncontroverted evidence at the hearing, however, achievement of the [earnings] benchmarks is uncertain, at best.

Ted Stenger, a managing director at Alix Partners and the Debtors' Chief Restructuring Officer, testified that although, as of September 30, 2006, the Debtors had reached [earnings] of $235 million, the remainder of the year would finish at about that level. Mr. Stenger explained that the first half of the year resulted in $175 million [earnings] with the second half only expected to add only $750,000 due to a significant decline in sales. Much of the Debtors' negative performance is due to the state of the automotive industry in general, the increasing cost of materials, and Dana's dependency on Ford, General Motors and Daimler-Chrysler (the "Detroit 3") which have recently instituted unprecedented cutbacks. Specifically with respect to Dana's automotive systems group, which manufactures parts for pick-up trucks and SUVs, Dana has suffered severe losses and anticipates a $750 million decline in sales of light trucks in 2007. In addition, Mr. Stenger noted that due to pre-buying of medium and heavy-duty trucks in 2006 in advance of changes in regulatory emissions standards that will take effect in the United States in the beginning of 2007, the Debtors anticipate decreases of approximately 47% in North American heavy-duty truck build and 19% in medium-duty truck build, compared to 2006. This reduction will have a significant adverse impact on the Debtors, reducing their sales in these markets by an estimated $500 million in 2007. Mr. Stenger stated that although the Debtors are planning major cost cutting initiatives, the benefits depend upon the speed at which the Debtors can institute those measures, and some involve negotiations with third parties and are therefore unpredictable.

Due to these factors, among others, Mr. Stenger expects 2007-2008 [earnings] levels will not reach the 2006 number. ... As such, the benchmarks for the LTIP are difficult targets to reach and are clearly not "lay-ups." In sum, the LTIP is not a [key employee retention program], but is a program designed to incentivize the CEO and Senior Executives, and may be assumed by the Debtors if it is a fair and reasonable exercise of business judgment. *.*.*

Returning to the holistic approach discussed earlier, in order to determine the reasonableness and cost effectiveness of the compensation levels, one must consider the total compensation that could potentially be earned by the CEO and Senior Executives during the Chapter 11 proceedings. The information before this Court indicates that the only compensation to be earned by the CEO and Senior Executives in 2006 is their salary and the potential for AIP payments of up to $2 million for the CEO and between $336,000 to $528,000 for the Senior Executives. The 2007 compensation packages, however, include salary, an AIP and a LTIP. In 2007, when the CEO and Senior Executives are eligible for significant long-term incentive bonuses, they may also be eligible for AIPs of up to 200% of the their salary.

Looking at the packages through the previously identified prism of whether the cost or expense is reasonable and in the best interests of the estate, the present record is not sufficiently transparent to support an affirmative finding. The Debtors have made a record supporting the reasonableness and cost effectiveness of providing a base salary and LTIP for 2007. However, if *augmented* by an AIP bonus, the potential compensation earned for services during the course of the pre-confirmation period (2007, *et. seq.*) is not transparent from this record and may well be outside the realm of reasonableness, disproportionate and overly generous. Although this Court has considered the "no guarantee" aspect of the package and the different timing of the long-term versus the short-term payments, the inclusion of both incentive programs in 2007 and 2008, in their current form, may not accomplish the "sharing the pain" objective.

This Court is inclined to approve the LTIP provided that an appropriate yearly ceiling is placed on each of the CEO and Senior Executives' total compensation earned during the reorganization period. * * *

CONCLUSION

By presenting an executive compensation package that properly incentivizes the CEO and Senior Executives to produce and increase the value of the estate, the Debtors have established that section 503(c)(1) does not apply to the Executive Compensation Motion. Additionally, the Debtors have satisfactorily established that none of the payments proposed violate section 503(c)(2), as the Executive Compensation Motion specifically limits "severance" payments to those permissible under section 503(c)(2) and any other payments are non-severance in nature.

With the exceptions noted herein, pursuant to sections 503(c)(3), 363(b) and 365, the Debtors have presented this Court with unconverted evidence that the assumption of the Employment Agreements and the adoption of the LTIP is fair and reasonable and well within the Debtors' business judgment. Accordingly, the Executive Compensation Motion is granted, conditioned on the submission of an order including an appropriate ceiling or cap on the total level of yearly compensation to be earned by the CEO and Senior Executives during the course of the bankruptcy proceedings.

NOTES

10A.1. As noted in the introductory material to this section, Congress enacted §503(c) as a reaction to the public outcry over corporate scandal. It is not clear, however, that the new provision accomplishes much beyond the symbolic, or is well advised. As *Dana* itself illustrates, the provision is almost infinitely flexible in the hands of a judge who wants to approve a debtor's compensation package. Moreover, inasmuch as insider self-enrichment tends to occur prior to bankruptcy, and because creditors are now frequently in control of the bankruptcy process (a development discussed below in chapter 13, section A of this book), these provisions may have limited effect. One might wonder, in any case, about the wisdom of specifying the terms under which a particular expense is necessary, given the myriad sorts of expenses that a corporate debtor can incur if it continues in business during the bankruptcy process.

10A.2. Pay particular attention to §503(c)(2), which addresses severance packages and is summarized in *Dana*. One might wonder whether this provision in fact restricts the ability of a debtor to pay executives whom the debtor wishes to favor. Problem 10A explores this question.

PROBLEM

10-A. As Debtor Corporation begins to suffer setbacks in the market place its employees begin to fear that Debtor will not survive and leave for other jobs. At the suggestion of Debtor's chief executive officer, Debtor puts in place a "retention program" through which all full-time employees are promised substantial severance payments should they be terminated for any reason. The CEO's own severance package is ten times that of the average (non-management) full-time worker in Debtor's employ. After the retention program is instituted, Debtor begins to lay off nonmanagement employees, paying them their severance, while the managers remain on the job. Soon, though, despite the cuts, it becomes clear that Debtor will not be able to pay its obligations and it files for bankruptcy under Chapter 11. Debtor's general creditors succeed in having a trustee appointed to wind up Debtor's affairs and to sell its assets in an open auction. The first thing the trustee does is terminate all of Debtor's officers and announce a rejection of their employment contracts, including Debtor's obligations to the officers under the retention program. The officers challenge such . What result?

B.   JUDICIAL SUBORDINATION

The priorities established by the tangle of provisions described above do not end the distribution inquiry. Bankruptcy Code §510(c) permits a bankruptcy court to employ principles of equitable subordination to alter the distribution priorities that would otherwise apply. Using these principles, a court may subordinate, in whole or part, any claim or interest and may eliminate a lien that secures a claim thus subordinated.

Equitable subordination can best be understood with a canonical illustration. Suppose a single shareholder owns all the stock in a debtor corporation, which is subject to a substantial loan from a bank creditor. The debtor becomes insolvent, or arrives at the brink of insolvency, at which point the bank's loan has become highly risky. The shareholder, who controls the firm, either converts some of her stock to debt or, somewhat less nefariously, lends the debtor new funds in a last ditch effort to revive the failing firm. When the firm fails, the shareholder dons her creditor's hat and attempts to collect with or ahead of the creditors that dealt with the debtor at arm's length.

As we know from chapter 8, section C above, a shareholder's conversion of worthless stock to valuable debt would be a fraudulent conveyance because in such an exchange the insolvent corporation would necessarily receive less than fair value. Even a last-minute loan on seemingly fair terms might be considered a fraudulent conveyance. Such a loan can substantially increase the risk that the arm's-length creditors will not recover. Given the potential loss to creditors, moreover, a court might move beyond fraudulent conveyance doctrine and equitably subordinate a controlling shareholder's last-minute exchange with the debtor. Hence, equitable subordination may be seen as an alternative or supplement to fraudulent conveyance law.

Equitable subordination is not always limited to the case of an overreaching insider. Some courts will, at times, subordinate the loan of a third-party creditor who, in the court's view, acts selfishly at the expense of the debtor or other creditors. The exercises below, the *Clark Pipe* case that follows, and the related notes address aspects of this scenario. The second case in this section, *Owens Corning*, as well as the related note and problem ask you to think about the principles of equitable subordination in the context of a "substantive consolidation," in which a court combines two or more bankruptcy cases of related debtors.

Key Provision: Bankruptcy Code §510(c)

EXERCISES

10B(1) Bank has a security interest in Debtor's entire inventory, whenever acquired. In February, Bank learns that Debtor's sales are falling. Debtor plans to reduce inventory, but Bank threatens to call its loan unless Debtor uses revenues to increase inventory instead. By the beginning of March, despite decreased sales, Debtor holds more inventory than ever before. As a result, Debtor lacks funds to improve its business and, by early July, files for bankruptcy. At the time of liquidation, Debtor's only valuable asset is the inventory, worth $100,000, roughly the amount of Bank's claim. Debtor also owes other creditors amounts in excess of $100,000. How will Debtor's property be distributed?

10B(2) Debtor runs a clothing store that is in desperate financial distress. Suppliers, still unpaid from past deliveries, will no longer sell on credit. Unless Debtor can obtain an immediate cash infusion, the business will shut down within a matter of days. Bank offers to lend Debtor the needed cash at a not extraordinarily high interest rate but only on the condition that Bank have a right to call the loan on short notice "for any reason or no reason at all." Without this right, Bank explains, it would be foolhardy to invest in an already failing business. Debtor quickly agrees and borrows the money. The new money does not help, however, and Debtor continues to founder. Bank calls the loan and threatens to sue for collection unless Debtor turns over Debtor's entire cash reserves, which at that time constitute about three-fourths of Bank's principal. Debtor acquiesces, and after a brief and futile attempt to attract replacement funds, Debtor files for bankruptcy. Bank concedes that its collection was a voidable preference and turns over the collected funds. Suppliers claim that Bank's return of this money is insufficient. According to Suppliers, had Bank not called its loan, Debtor's business would have survived and Suppliers would have been paid more than the few cents on the dollar that they will now receive. Suppliers want Debtor's obligation to Bank subordinated.

Will Suppliers prevail? Should they? How do you assess Suppliers' further contention that beyond subordination, under the doctrine of lender liability, Bank should be liable for any deficiency of Debtor's assets to satisfy Suppliers' claims? Would your answer to the last question change if Debtor voluntarily repaid Bank before Bank threatened to sue? See Barry E. Adler, Accelerated Solution of Financial Distress, 76 Wash. U. L.Q. 1169 (1998); George G. Triantis, A Theory of the Regulation of Debtor-in-Possession Financing, 46 Vand. L. Rev. 901 (1993).

IN RE CLARK PIPE & SUPPLY CO., INC.

United States Court of Appeals. Fifth Circuit, 1990
893 F.2d 693

JOLLY, CIRCUIT JUDGE.

* * * Clark Pipe and Supply Company, Inc., ("Clark") was in the business of buying and selling steel pipe used in the fabrication of offshore drilling platforms. In September 1980, Associates and Clark executed various agreements under which Associates would make revolving loans secured by an assignment of accounts receivable and an inventory mortgage. Under the agreements, Clark was required to deposit all collections from the accounts receivable in a bank account belonging to Associates. The amount that Associates would lend was determined by a formula, i.e., a certain percentage of the amount of eligible accounts receivable plus a certain percentage of the cost of inventory. The agreements provided that Associates could reduce the percentage advance rates at any time at its discretion.

When bad times hit the oil fields in late 1981, Clark's business slumped. In February 1982 Associates began reducing the percentage advance rates so that Clark would have just enough cash to pay its direct operating expenses. Clark used the advances to keep its doors open and to sell inventory, the proceeds of which were used to pay off the past advances from Associates. Associates did not expressly dictate to Clark which bills to pay. Neither did it direct Clark not to pay vendors or threaten Clark with a cut-off of advances if it did pay vendors. But Clark had no funds left over from the advances to pay vendors or other creditors whose services were not essential to keeping its doors open.

One of Clark's vendors, going unpaid, initiated foreclosure proceedings in February and seized the pipe it had sold Clark. Another attempted to do so in March. The resulting priority dispute was resolved only in litigation. . . . When a third unpaid creditor initiated foreclosure proceedings in May, Clark sought protection from creditors by filing for reorganization under Chapter 11 of the Bankruptcy Code.

The case was converted to a Chapter 7 liquidation on August 31, 1982, and a trustee was appointed. In 1983, the trustee brought this adversary proceeding against Clark's lender, Associates. The trustee sought the recovery of alleged preferences and equitable subordination of Associates' claims. Following a one-day trial on August 28, 1986, the bankruptcy court entered judgment on April 10, 1987, and an amended judgment on June 9, 1987. The court required Associates to turn over $370,505 of payments found to be preferential and subordinated Associates' claims. The district court affirmed on May 24, 1988. * * *

[The] issue before us is whether the bankruptcy court was justified in equitably subordinating Associates' claims. This court has enunciated a three-pronged test to determine whether and to what extent a claim should be equitably subordinated: (1) the claimant must have engaged in some type of inequitable conduct, (2) the misconduct must have resulted in injury to the creditors of the bankrupt or conferred an unfair advantage on the claimant, and (3) equitable subordination of the claim must not be inconsistent with the provisions of the Bankruptcy Code. In re Missionary Baptist Foundation, 712 F.2d 206, 212 (5th Cir. 1983) (*Missionary Baptist I*). Three general categories of conduct have been recognized as sufficient to satisfy the first prong of the three-part test: (1) fraud, illegality or breach of fiduciary duties; (2) undercapitalization; and (3) a claimant's use of the debtor as a mere instrumentality or alter ego.

In essence, the bankruptcy court found that once Associates realized Clark's desperate financial condition, Associates asserted total control and used Clark as a mere instrumentality to liquidate Associates' unpaid loans. Moreover, it did so, the trustee argues, to the detriment of the rights of Clark's other creditors.

Associates contends that its control over Clark was far from total. Associates says that it did no more than determine the percentage of advances as expressly permitted in the loan agreement; it never made or dictated decisions as to which creditors were paid. Thus, argues Associates, it never had the "actual, participatory, total control of the debtor" required to make Clark its instrumentality under Krivo Industrial Supply Co. v. National Distillers & Chemical Corp., 483 F.2d 1098, 1105 (5th Cir. 1973), modified factually, 490 F.2d 916 (5th Cir. 1974). If it did not use Clark as an instrumentality or engage in any other type of inequitable conduct under *Missionary Baptist I,* argues Associates, then it cannot be equitably subordinated. * * *

We first consider whether Associates asserted such control over the activities of Clark that we should consider that it was using Clark as its mere instrumentality. In our prior opinion, we agreed with the district court and the bankruptcy court that, as a practical matter, Associates asserted total control over Clark's liquidation, and that it used its control in a manner detrimental to the unsecured creditors. Upon reconsideration, we have concluded that we cannot say that the sort of control Associates asserted over Clark's financial affairs rises to the level of unconscionable conduct necessary to justify the application of the doctrine of equitable subordination. We have reached our revised conclusion primarily because we cannot escape the salient fact that, pursuant to its loan agreement with Clark, Associates had the right to reduce funding, just as it did, as Clark's sales slowed. We now conclude that there is no evidence that Associates exceeded its authority under the loan agreement, or that Associates acted inequitably in exercising its rights under that agreement.

We think it is important to note at the outset that the loan and security agreements between Associates and Clark, which are at issue here, were executed in 1980, at the inception of their relationship. There is no evidence that Clark was insolvent at the time the agreements were entered into. Clark was represented by counsel during the negotiations, and there is no evidence that the loan documents were negotiated at anything other than arm's length or that they are atypical of loan documents used in similar asset-based financings.

The loan agreement between Associates and Clark established a line of credit varying from $2.2 million to approximately $2.7 million over the life of the loan. The amount that Associates would lend was determined by a formula: 85% of the amount of eligible accounts receivables plus 60% of the cost of inventory. Under the agreement, Clark was required to deposit all collections from the accounts receivable in a bank account belonging to Associates. Associates would, in turn, re-advance the agreed-upon portion of those funds to Clark on a revolving basis. The agreement provided that Associates could reduce the percentage advance rates at any time in its discretion.

When Clark's business began to decline, along with that of the oil patch generally, Associates advised Clark that it would reduce the advance ratio for the inventory loan by 5% per month beginning in January 1982. After that time, the company stopped buying new inventory and, according to the Trustee's expert witness, Clark's monthly sales revenues amounted to less than one-fifth of the company's outstanding accounts payable. Clark prepared a budget at Associates' request that indicated the disbursements necessary to keep the company operating. The budget did not include payment to vendors for previously shipped goods. Associates' former loan officer, Fred Slice, testified as to what he had in mind:

> If he [the comptroller of Clark] had had the availability [of funds to pay a vendor or other trade creditor] that particular day, I would have said, "Are you sure you've got that much availability, Jim," because he shouldn't have that much. The way I had structured it, he wouldn't have any money to pay his suppliers. . . .

> But you know, the possibility that—this is all hypothetical. I had it structured so that there was no—there was barely enough money—there was enough money, if I did it right, enough money to keep the doors open. Clark could continue to operate, sell the inventory, turn it into receivables, collect the cash, transfer that cash to me, and reduce my loans.

> And, if he had ever had availability for other things, that meant I had done something wrong, and I would have been surprised. To ask me what I would have done is purely hypothetical[;] I don't think it would happen. I think it's so unrealistic, I don't know.

Despite Associates' motive, which was, according to Slice, "to get in the best position I can prior to the bankruptcy, i.e., I want to get the absolute amount of dollars as low as I can by hook or crook," the evidence shows that the amount of its advances continued to be based on the applicable funding formulas. Slice testified that the lender did not appreciably alter its original credit procedures when Clark fell into financial difficulty.

In our original opinion, we failed to focus sufficiently on the loan agreement, which gave Associates the right to conduct its affairs with Clark in the manner in which it did. In addition, we think that in our previous opinion we were overly influenced by the negative and inculpatory tone of Slice's testimony. Given the agreement he was working under, his testimony was hardly more than fanfaronading about the power that the agreement afforded him over the financial affairs of Clark. Although his talk was crass (e.g., "I want to get the absolute dollars as low as I can, by hook or crook"), our careful examination of the record does not reveal any conduct on his part that was inconsistent with the loan agreement, irrespective of what his personal motive may have been.

Through its loan agreement, every lender effectively exercises "control" over its borrower to some degree. A lender in Associates' position will usually possess "control" in the sense that it can foreclose or drastically reduce the debtor's financing. The purpose of equitable subordination is to distinguish between the unilateral remedies that a creditor may properly enforce pursuant to its agreements with the debtor and other inequitable conduct such as fraud, misrepresentation, or the exercise of such total control over the debtor as to have essentially replaced its decision-making capacity with that of the lender. The crucial distinction between what is inequitable and what a lender can reasonably and legitimately do to protect its interests is the distinction between the existence of "control" and the exercise of that "control" to direct the activities of the debtor. As the Supreme Court stated in Comstock v. Group of Institutional Investors, 335 U.S. 211, 229 (1947): "It is not mere existence of an opportunity to do wrong that brings the rule into play; it is the unconscionable use of the opportunity afforded by the domination to advantage itself at the injury of the subsidiary that deprives the wrongdoer of the fruits of his wrong."

In our prior opinion, we drew support from In re American Lumber Co., 5 Bankr. 470 (D. Minn. 1980), to reach our conclusion that Associates' claims should be equitably subordinated. Upon reconsideration, however, we find that the facts of that case are significantly more egregious than we have here. In that case, the court equitably subordinated the claims of a bank because the bank "controlled" the debtor through its right to a controlling interest in the debtor's stock. The bank forced the debtor to convey security interests in its remaining unencumbered assets to the bank after the borrower defaulted on an existing debt. Immediately thereafter, the bank foreclosed on the borrower's accounts receivable, terminated the borrower's employees, hired its own skeleton crew to conduct a liquidation, and selectively honored the debtor's payables to improve its own position. The bank began receiving and opening all incoming mail at the borrower's office, and it established a bank account into which all amounts received by the borrower were deposited and over which the bank had sole control. The bankruptcy court found that the bank exercised control over all aspects of the debtor's finances and operation including: payments of payables and wages, collection and use of accounts receivable and contract rights, purchase and use of supplies and materials, inventory sales, a lumber yard, the salaries of the principals, the employment of employees, and the receipt of payments for sales and accounts receivable.

Despite its decision to prohibit further advances to the debtor, its declaration that the debtor was in default of its loans, and its decisions to use all available funds of the company to offset the company's obligations to it, the bank in *American Lumber* made two specific representations to the American Lumbermen's Credit Association that the debtor was not in a bankruptcy situation and that current contracts would be fulfilled. Two days after this second reassurance, the bank gave notice of foreclosure of its security interests in the company's inventory and equipment. Approximately two weeks later the bank sold equipment and inventory of the debtor amounting to roughly $450,000, applying all of the proceeds to the debtor's indebtedness to the bank.

Associates exercised significantly less "control" over the activities of Clark than did the lender in *American Lumber*. Associates did not own any stock of Clark, much less a controlling block. Nor did Associates interfere with the operations of the borrower to an extent even roughly commensurate with the degree of interference exercised by the bank in *American Lumber*. Associates made no management decisions for Clark, such as deciding which creditors to prefer with the diminishing amount of funds available. At no time did Associates place any of its employees as either a director or officer of Clark. Associates never influenced the removal from office of any Clark personnel, nor did Associates ever request Clark to take any particular action at a shareholders meeting. Associates did not expressly dictate to Clark which bills to pay, nor did it direct Clark not to pay vendors or threaten a cut-off of advances if it did pay vendors. Clark handled its own daily operations. The same basic procedures with respect to the reporting of collateral, the calculation of availability of funds, and the procedures for the advancement of funds were followed throughout the relationship between Clark and Associates. Unlike the lender in *American Lumber,* Associates did not mislead creditors to continue supplying Clark. Perhaps the most important fact that distinguishes this case from *American Lumber* is that Associates did not coerce Clark into executing the security agreements after Clark became insolvent. Instead, the loan and security agreements between Clark and Associates were entered into at arm's length prior to Clark's insolvency, and all of Associates' activities were conducted pursuant to those agreements.

Associates' control over Clark's finances, admittedly powerful and ultimately severe, was based solely on the exercise of powers found in the loan agreement. Associates' close watch over Clark's affairs does not, by itself, however, amount to such control as would justify equitable subordination. "There is nothing inherently wrong with a creditor carefully monitoring his debtor's financial situation or with suggesting what course of action the debtor ought to follow." In re Teltronics Services, Inc., 29 Bankr. 139, 172 (Bankr. E.D.N.Y. 1983). Although the terms of the agreement did give Associates potent leverage over Clark, that agreement did not give Associates total control over Clark's activities. At all material times Clark had the power to act autonomously and, if it chose, to disregard the advice of Associates; for example, Clark was free to shut its doors at any time it chose to do so and to file for bankruptcy.

Finally, on reconsideration, we are persuaded that the rationale of In re W. T. Grant Co., 699 F.2d 599 (2d Cir. 1983), should control the case before us. In that case, the Second Circuit recognized that

> a creditor is under no fiduciary obligation to its debtor or to other creditors of the debtor in the collection of its claim. The permissible parameters of a creditor's efforts to seek collection from a debtor are generally those with respect to voidable preferences and fraudulent conveyances proscribed by the Bankruptcy Act; apart from these there is generally no objection to a creditor's using his bargaining position, including his ability to refuse to make further loans needed by the debtor, to improve the status of his existing claims.

699 F.2d at 609-10. Associates was not a fiduciary of Clark, it did not exert improper control over Clark's financial affairs, and it did not act inequitably in exercising its rights under its loan agreement with Clark. * * *

Finally, we should note that in our earlier opinion, we found that, in exercising such control over Clark, Associates engaged in other inequitable conduct that justified equitable subordination. Our re-examination of the record indicates, however, that there is not really any evidence that Associates engaged in such conduct. Our earlier opinion assumed that Associates knew that Clark was selling pipe to which the suppliers had a first lien, but the issue of whether the vendors had a first lien on the pipe was not decided by our court until a significantly later time. In addition, although the trustee made much of the point on appeal, after our re-study of the record, we conclude that it does not support the finding that Associates encouraged Clark to remove decals from pipe in its inventory.

We also note that the record is devoid of any evidence that Associates misled other Clark creditors to their detriment.

When the foregoing factors are considered, there is no basis for finding inequitable conduct upon which equitable subordination can be based. We therefore conclude that the district court erred in affirming the bankruptcy court's decision to subordinate Associates' claims. * * *

IN RE OWENS CORNING CORP.

United States Court of Appeals, Third Circuit, 2005
419 F.3d 195

AMBRO, CIRCUIT JUDGE

We consider under what circumstances a court exercising bankruptcy powers may substantively consolidate affiliated entities. Appellant Credit Suisse First Boston ("CSFB") is the agent for a syndicate of banks (collectively, the "Banks") that extended in 1997 a $2 billion unsecured loan to Owens Corning, a Delaware corporation ("OCD"), and certain of its subsidiaries. This credit was enhanced in part by guarantees made by other OCD subsidiaries. The District Court granted a motion to consolidate the assets and liabilities of the OCD borrowers and guarantors in anticipation of a plan of reorganization.

The Banks appeal and argue that the Court erred by granting the motion, as it misunderstood the reasons for, and standards for considering, the extraordinary remedy of substantive consolidation, and in any event did not make factual determinations necessary even to consider its use. ... [W]e reverse the ruling of the District Court .... * * *

While this area of law is difficult and this case important, its outcome is easy with the facts before us. Among other problems, the consolidation sought is "deemed." Should we approve this nonconsensual arrangement, the plan process would proceed as though assets and liabilities of separate entities were merged, but in fact they remain separate with the twist that the guarantees to the Banks are eliminated. From this we conclude that the proponents of substantive consolidation request it not to rectify the seldom-seen situations that call for this last-resort remedy but rather as a ploy to deprive one group of creditors of their rights while providing a windfall to other creditors.

OCD and its subsidiaries (which include corporations and limited liability companies) comprise a multinational corporate group. Different entities within the group have different purposes. Some, for example, exist to limit liability concerns (such as those related to asbestos), others to gain tax benefits, and others have regulatory reasons for their formation.

Each subsidiary was a separate legal entity that observed governance formalities. Each had a specific reason to exist separately, each maintained its own business records, and intercompany transactions were regularly documented. Although there may have been some "sloppy" bookkeeping, two of OCD's own officers testified that the financial statements of all the subsidiaries were accurate in all material respects. Further, through an examination of the subsidiaries' books, OCD's postpetition auditors (Ernst & Young) have eliminated most financial discrepancies, particularly with respect to the larger guarantor subsidiaries.

In 1997 OCD sought a loan to acquire Fibreboard Corporation. At this time OCD faced growing asbestos liability and a poor credit rating that hindered its ability to obtain financing. When CSFB was invited to submit a bid, it included subsidiary guarantees in the terms of its proposal. The guarantees gave the Banks direct claims against the guarantors for payment defaults. They were a "credit enhancement" without which the Banks would not have made the loan to OCD. All draft loan term sheets included subsidiary guarantees.

A $2 billion loan from the Banks to OCD closed in June 1997. The loan terms were set out primarily in a Credit Agreement. Among those terms were the guarantee provisions and requirements for guarantors, who were defined as "present or future Domestic Subsidiar[ies] … having assets with an aggregate book value in excess of $30,000,000." [T]he Agreement provided that the guarantees were "absolute and unconditional" and each "constitute[d] a guarant[ee] of payment and not a guarant[ee] of collection." A "No Release of Guarantor" provision … stated that "the obligations of each guarantor … shall not be reduced, limited or terminated, nor shall such guarantor be discharged from any such obligations, for any reason whatsoever," except payment and performance in full or through waiver or amendment of the Credit Agreement. Under … the Credit Agreement, a guarantor could be released only through (i) the unanimous consent of the Banks for the guarantees of Fibreboard subsidiaries or through the consent of Banks holding 51% of the debt for other subsidiaries, or (ii) a fair value sale of the guarantor if its cumulative assets totaled less than 10% of the book value of the aggregate OCD group of entities.

CSFB negotiated the Credit Agreement expressly to limit the ways in which OCD could deal with its subsidiaries. For example, it could not enter into transactions with a subsidiary that would result in losses to that subsidiary. Importantly, the Credit Agreement contained provisions designed to protect the separateness of OCD and its subsidiaries. The subsidiaries agreed explicitly to maintain themselves as separate entities. To further this agreement, they agreed to keep separate books and financial records in order to prepare separate financial statements. The Banks were given the right to visit each subsidiary and discuss business matters directly with that subsidiary's management. The subsidiaries also were prohibited from merging into OCD because both entities were required to survive a transaction under … the Credit Agreement. This provision also prohibited guarantor subsidiaries from merging with other subsidiaries unless there would be no effect on the guarantees' value.

On October 5, 2000, facing mounting asbestos litigation, OCD and seventeen of its subsidiaries (collectively, the "Debtors") filed for reorganization under Chapter 11 of the Bankruptcy Code. Twenty-seven months later, the Debtors and certain unsecured creditor groups (collectively, the "Plan Proponents") proposed a reorganization plan (as amended, the "Plan") predicated on obtaining "substantive consolidation" of the Debtors along with three non-Debtor OCD subsidiaries. Typically this arrangement pools all assets and liabilities of the subsidiaries into their parent and treats all claims against the subsidiaries as transferred to the parent. In fact, however, the Plan Proponents sought a form of what is known as a "deemed consolidation," under which a consolidation is deemed to exist for purposes of valuing and satisfying creditor claims, voting for or against the Plan, and making distributions for allowed claims under it. Yet "the Plan would not result in the merger of or the transfer or commingling of any assets of any of the Debtors or Non-Debtor Subsidiaries, … [which] will continue to be owned by the respective Debtors or Non-Debtors." Despite this, on the Plan's effective date "all guarantees of the Debtors of the obligations of any other Debtor will be deemed eliminated, so that any claim against any such Debtor and any guarantee thereof … will be deemed to be one obligation of the Debtors with respect to the consolidated estate." Put another way, "the Plan eliminates the separate obligations of the Subsidiary Debtors arising from the guarantees of the 1997 Credit Agreement."

The Banks objected to the proposed consolidation. … [In the lower court,] Judge Fullam concluded that there existed "substantial identity between … OCD and its wholly-owned subsidiaries." He further determined that "there [was] simply no basis for a finding that, in extending credit, the Banks relied upon the separate credit of any of the subsidiary guarantors." In Judge Fullam's view, it was "also clear that substantive consolidation would greatly simplify and expedite the successful completion of this entire bankruptcy proceeding. More importantly, it would be exceedingly difficult to untangle the financial affairs of the various entities." As such, he held substantive consolidation should be permitted, as not only did it allow "obvious advantages ... [, but was] a virtual necessity." In any event, Judge Fullam wrote, "[t]he real issue is whether the Banks are entitled to participate, *pari passu,* with other unsecured creditors, or whether the Banks' claim is entitled to priority, in whole or in part, over the claims of other unsecured creditors.". But this issue, he stated, "cannot now be determined."

CSFB appeals on the Banks' behalf. ... We consider four factors in determining whether we should exercise jurisdiction over a bankruptcy appeal: "(1) [t]he impact on the assets of the bankrupt estate; (2)[the][n]ecessity for further fact-finding on remand; (3) [t]he preclusive effect of [the Court's] decision on the merits of further litigation; and (4)[t]he interest of judicial economy." Buncher Co. v. Official Comm. of Unsecured Creditors of GenFarm Ltd. P'ship IV, 229 F.3d 245, 250 (3d Cir.2000). All four factors weigh heavily in favor of our jurisdiction to consider the appeal of an order granting substantive consolidation. * * *

Substantive consolidation, a construct of federal common law, emanates from equity. It "treats separate legal entities as if they were merged into a single survivor left with all the cumulative assets and liabilities (save for inter-entity liabilities, which are erased). The result is that claims of creditors against separate debtors morph to claims against the consolidated survivor." Genesis Health Ventures, Inc. v. Stapleton (In re Genesis Health Ventures, Inc.), 402 F.3d 416, 423 (3d Cir.2005). Consolidation restructures (and thus revalues) rights of creditors and for certain creditors this may result in significantly less recovery. * * *

Prior to substantive consolidation, other remedies for corporate disregard were (and remain) in place. For example, where a subsidiary is so dominated by its corporate parent as to be the parent's "alter ego," the "corporate veil" of the subsidiary can be ignored (or "pierced") under state law. Or a court might mandate that the assets transferred to a corporate subsidiary be turned over to its parent's trustee in bankruptcy for wrongs such as fraudulent transfers, in effect bringing back to the bankruptcy estate assets wrongfully conveyed to an affiliate. If a corporate parent is both a creditor of a subsidiary and so dominates the affairs of that entity as to prejudice unfairly its other creditors, a court may place payment priority to the parent below that of the other creditors, a remedy known as equitable subordination, which is now codified in § 510(c) of the Bankruptcy Code.

Adding to these remedies, the Supreme Court, little more than six decades ago, approved (at least indirectly and perhaps inadvertently) what became known as substantive consolidation. Sampsell v. Imperial Paper & Color Corp., 313 U.S. 215 (1941). In *Sampsell* an individual in bankruptcy had transferred assets prepetition to a corporation he controlled. (Apparently these became the corporation's sole assets.) When the bankruptcy referee ordered that the transferred assets be turned over by the corporation to the individual debtor's trustee, a creditor of the non-debtor corporation sought distribution priority with respect to that entity's assets. In deciding that the creditor should not be accorded priority (thus affirming the bankruptcy referee), the Supreme Court turned a typical turnover/fraudulent transfer case into the forebear of today's substantive consolidation by terming the bankruptcy referee's order (marshaling the corporation's assets for the benefit of the debtor's estate) as "consolidating the estates."

Each of these remedies has subtle differences. "Piercing the corporate veil" makes shareholders liable for corporate wrongs. Equitable subordination places bad-acting creditors behind other creditors when distributions are made. Turnover and fraudulent transfer bring back to the transferor debtor assets improperly transferred to another (often an affiliate). Substantive consolidation goes in a direction different (and in most cases further) than any of these remedies; it is not limited to shareholders, it affects distribution to innocent creditors, and it mandates more than the return of specific assets to the predecessor owner. It brings all the assets of a group of entities into a single survivor. Indeed, it merges liabilities as well. "The result," to repeat, "is that claims of creditors against separate debtors morph to claims against the consolidated survivor." *Genesis Health Ventures*, 402 F.3d at 423. The bad news for certain creditors is that, instead of looking to assets of the subsidiary with whom they dealt, they now must share those assets with all creditors of all consolidated entities, raising the specter for some of a significant distribution diminution.

Though the concept of consolidating estates had Supreme Court approval, Courts of Appeal (with one exception) were slow to follow suit. Stone v. Eacho (In re Tip Top Tailors, Inc.), 127 F.2d 284 (4th Cir.1942), cert. denied, 317 U.S. 635 (1942), was the first to pick up on *Sampsell's* new remedy. Little occurred thereafter for more than

two decades, until the Second Circuit issued several decisions—
Soviero v. National Bank of Long Island, 328 F.2d 446 (2d Cir.1964);
Chemical Bank New York Trust Co. v. Kheel (In re Seatrade Corp.),
369 F.2d 845 (2d Cir.1966); Flora Mir Candy Corp. v. R.S. Dickson
& Co. (In re Flora Mir Candy Corp.), 432 F.2d 1060 (2d Cir.1970);
and Talcott v. Wharton (In re Continental Vending Machine Corp.),
517 F.2d 997 (2d Cir.1975)—that brought substantive consolidation
as a remedy back into play and premise its modern-day understanding.

The reasons of these courts for allowing substantive consolidation as a possible remedy span the spectrum and often overlap. For
example, *Stone* and *Soviero* followed the well-trod path of alter ego
analysis in state "pierce-the-corporate-veil" cases. *Stone,* 127 F.2d at
287-89; *Soviero,* 328 F.2d at 447-48. *Kheel* dealt with, *inter alia,* the
net-negative practical effects of attempting to thread back the tangled
affairs of entities, separate in name only, with "interrelationships ...
hopelessly obscured." 369 F.2d at 847. See also, e.g., In re
Augie/Restivo, 860 F.2d 515, 518-19 (2nd Cir. 1988). *Continental
Vending Machine* balanced the "inequities" involved when substantive rights are affected against the "practical considerations" spawned
by "accounting difficulties (and expense) which may occur where the
interrelationships of the corporate group are highly complex, or perhaps untraceable." 517 F.2d at 1001.

Ultimately most courts slipstreamed behind two rationales—
those of the Second Circuit in *Augie/Restivo* and the D.C. Circuit in
Drabkin v. Midland-Ross Corp. (In re Auto-Train Corp.), 810 F.2d
270, 276 (D.C.Cir.1987). The former found that the competing "considerations are merely variants on two critical factors: (i) whether
creditors dealt with the entities as a single economic unit and did not
rely on their separate identity in extending credit, ... or (ii) whether
the affairs of the debtors are so entangled that consolidation will benefit all creditors ... ." *Augie/Restivo,* 860 F.2d at 518 (internal quota-
tion marks and citations omitted). *Auto-Train* touched many of the
same analytical bases as the prior Second Circuit cases, but in the end
chose as its overarching test the "substantial identity" of the entities
and made allowance for consolidation in spite of creditor reliance on
separateness when "the demonstrated benefits of consolidation 'heavily' outweigh the harm." *Auto-Train,* 810 F.2d at 276 (citation omitted). Whatever the rationale, courts have permitted substantive
consolidation as an equitable remedy in certain circumstances. No
court has held that substantive consolidation is not authorized, though

there appears nearly unanimous consensus that it is a remedy to be used "sparingly." *Augie/Restivo,* 860 F.2d at 518.

Substantive consolidation exists as an equitable remedy. But when should it be available and by what test should its use be measured? ... The *Auto-Train* approach (requiring "substantial identity" of entities to be consolidated, plus that consolidation is "necessary to avoid some harm or realize some benefit," 810 F.2d at 276) adopts, we presume, one of the *Augie/Restivo* touchstones for substantive consolidation while adding the low bar of avoiding some harm or discerning some benefit by consolidation. To us this fails to capture completely the few times substantive consolidation may be considered and then, when it does hit one chord, it allows a threshold not sufficiently egregious and too imprecise for easy measure. For example, we disagree that "[i]f a creditor makes [a showing of reliance on separateness], the court may order consolidation ... if it determines that the demonstrated benefits of consolidation 'heavily' outweigh the harm." Id. at 276 (citation omitted). If an objecting creditor relied on the separateness of the entities, consolidation cannot be justified *vis-a-vis* the claims of that creditor.

In assessing whether to order substantive consolidation, courts consider many factors ... . Too often the factors in a check list fail to separate the unimportant from the important, or even to set out a standard to make the attempt. This often results in rote following of a form containing factors where courts tally up and spit out a score without an eye on the principles that give the rationale for substantive consolidation (and why, as a result, it should so seldom be in play). What, then, are those principles? We perceive them to be as follows.

(1) Limiting the cross-creep of liability by respecting entity separateness is [fundamental]. As a result, the general expectation of state law and of the Bankruptcy Code, and thus of commercial markets, is that courts respect entity separateness absent compelling circumstances calling equity (and even then only possibly substantive consolidation) into play.

(2) The harms substantive consolidation addresses are nearly always those caused by *debtors* (and entities they control) who disregard separateness. Harms caused by creditors typically are remedied by provisions found in the Bankruptcy Code (*e.g.,* fraudulent transfers, §§ 548 and 544(b)(1), and equitable subordination, § 510(c)).

(3) Mere benefit to the administration of the case (for example, allowing a court to simplify a case by avoiding other issues or to

make postpetition accounting more convenient) is hardly a harm calling substantive consolidation into play.

(4) Indeed, because substantive consolidation is extreme (it may affect profoundly creditors' rights and recoveries) and imprecise, this "rough justice" remedy should be rare and, in any event, one of last resort after considering and rejecting other remedies (for example, the possibility of more precise remedies conferred by the Bankruptcy Code).

(5) While substantive consolidation may be used defensively to remedy the identifiable harms caused by entangled affairs, it may not be used offensively (for example, having a primary purpose to disadvantage tactically a group of creditors in the plan process or to alter creditor rights).

The upshot is this. In our Court what must be proven (absent consent) concerning the entities for whom substantive consolidation is sought is that (i) prepetition they disregarded separateness so significantly their creditors relied on the breakdown of entity borders and treated them as one legal entity, or (ii) postpetition their assets and liabilities are so scrambled that separating them is prohibitive and hurts all creditors. Proponents of substantive consolidation have the burden of showing one or the other rationale for consolidation. * * *

With the principles we perceive underlie use of substantive consolidation, the outcome of this appeal is apparent at the outset. Substantive consolidation fails to fit the facts of our case and, in any event, a "deemed" consolidation cuts against the grain of all the principles. * * *

Despite the Plan Proponents' pleas to the contrary, there is no evidence of the prepetition disregard of the OCD entities' separateness. To the contrary, OCD (no less than CSFB) negotiated the 1997 lending transaction premised on the separateness of all OCD affiliates. Even today no allegation exists of bad faith by anyone concerning the loan. * * *

There also is no meaningful evidence postpetition of hopeless commingling of Debtors' assets and liabilities. Indeed, there is no question which entity owns which principal assets and has which material liabilities. ... As we have explained, commingling justifies consolidation only when separately accounting for the assets and liabilities of the distinct entities will reduce the recovery of *every* creditor—that is, when every creditor will benefit from the consolidation. Moreover, the benefit to creditors should be from cost savings that make assets available rather than from the shifting of assets to benefit one group of creditors at the expense of another. Mere benefit to some creditors, or administrative benefit to the Court, falls far short.

NOTES

10B.1. The court in *Clark* thought it "important to note at the outset that the loan and security agreements between Associates and Clark, which are at issue here, were executed . . . at the inception of their relationship. There is no evidence that Clark was insolvent at the time the agreements were entered into," perhaps even if the negotiations were fully at arm's length. This suggests a possibly different result if the agreements were executed after Clark had suffered financial distress. It is not at all clear why that should be so. Imagine that a debtor, while insolvent, were able to borrow money only on terms that permitted the new creditor priority as well as far-reaching collection powers. A rule that subordinated the new loan if the creditor exercises its collection option—or worse, a rule that established the new lender's liability to the debtor's other creditors—undoubtedly would discourage such a loan. And without the loan the debtor's business might not have even the chance to survive.

To be sure, one might argue that the quick demise of an insolvent business will, on average, maximize societal resources. Managers of a business that has failed both financially and economically may borrow and keep the business alive too long, hoping in vain for a reversal of fortune. In this event, a rule that reduced the opportunity to borrow would be productive. Even so, there is nothing in the *Clark* opinion that even suggests this rationale for equitable subordination.

10B.2. The *Clark* court seemed to lack the courage of its convictions. At one point, the court notes that the Associates loan should not be subordinated because Associates did no more than that to which it was contractually entitled. The court qualifies this statement, however, with the observation that Associates did not exercise "total control" over Clark. In the court's view, this lack of total control distinguished *Clark* from *American Lumber*. This statement and its qualification logically do not sit well together. Presumably, the creditor in *American Lumber* did not exceed its contractual rights whether it acted with the rights of a creditor or a shareholder. So the *Clark* court offers no easy way to distinguish the permissible control exercised by Associates, which the court describes as "admittedly powerful and ultimately severe," from the impermissible control exercised by the creditor in *American Lumber*.

More illuminating than the *Clark* court's abstract rhetoric is its description of "[p]erhaps the most important fact that distinguishes this case from *American Lumber*." In *American Lumber*, the creditor controlled the debtor's management and directed the debtor to issue new security interests while the debtor was insolvent, apparently with lack of fair consideration. Thus, the court seems to suggest that self-dealing is grounds for equitable subordination, while even the most aggressive collection on a debt contract negotiated at arm's length is permissible (at least if that contract is negotiated before the debtor becomes insolvent). This distinction comports with traditional equitable subordination doctrine but arguably yields a remedy that overreaches if a lender's entire obligation is subordinated rather than just that portion acquired through self-dealing.

10B.3. Consider the significance of the following statement in *Owens Corning*: "The harms substantive consolidation addresses are nearly always those caused by *debtors* (and entities they control) who disregard separateness." This distinguishes substantive consolidation cases from those where creditor misbehavior is alleged, as in *Clark Pipe*. Yet, for the reasons discussed in *Owens Corning*, and explored further by Problem 10B, the effect of substantive consolidation can be the functional equivalent of subordination even absent the sort of creditor misbehavior discussed in *Clark Pipe*.

PROBLEM

10B. Owner is the sole shareholder of two new companies, Manufacturer Corp. and Service Corp. Manufacturer is established as a sizeable enterprise with $1 million in equipment. Bank carefully examines Manufacturer's affairs, discovers the equipment as well as about $1 million in unsecured debt, and agrees to lend Manufacturer $2 million, which Owner says she will use for expansion. Service is established with minimal capital, but, through the efforts of Owner, enters into a number of lucrative contracts for the repair of industrial vehicles. In each of these contracts, Service receives a substantial engagement fee up front.

Over time, Owner siphons cash from both Manufacturer and Service and illegitimately shuttles funds between the two companies.

Moreover, after Owner repays some small loans, she borrows additional funds from new creditors under circumstances that make it unclear which of the two companies is the debtor. Owner eventually disappears. Manufacturer is left with $1.5 million in assets and with $2 million of debt. Service is left with no assets and debts of $1 million. Both companies are forced into bankruptcy.

It would be difficult or impossible fully to separate the assets and liabilities of Manufacturer and Service. Consequently, those creditors subject to Service's unfulfilled service contracts request that the court substantively consolidate the two cases. Bank opposes such consolidation. Should the cases be consolidated?

XI. THE FRESH START FOR INDIVIDUAL DEBTORS

The typical individual debtor in bankruptcy is honest but unlucky or improvident. Perhaps the debtor's spouse has suffered from a catastrophic illness, or the debtor loses a high-paying job and is unable to cut back on expenses before drowning in debt. In other cases, debtors mismanage their affairs. They accept too many credit-card offers and succumb to the temptation of paying only the minimum payment each month. When some event finally forces them to take stock of their finances, they discover that they owe twice their annual income and that interest is running at a double-digit rate. Although the 2005 Bankruptcy Act imposes a means test that limits the availability of the fresh start to some high-income debtors, as discussed in chapter 3, section C above, the fresh start remains available for the vast majority of those who have traditionally sought bankruptcy protection: lower middle class working people who have fallen on hard times.

For many of these traditional debtors, there are no assets upon which the general creditors can levy. The house and car are subject to security interests. The secured creditors will be able to reach such assets outside of bankruptcy as well as in, so the general creditors cannot look to these assets for payment. The debtor's other property consists of such things as clothes and household goods that are exempt from creditor levy outside of bankruptcy as well as in. Thus, general creditors largely rely on a debtor's future earnings. Even under nonbankruptcy law, however, garnishment laws limit the amount of each month's check that can be reached to pay the debt.

In assessing the benefits of bankruptcy's fresh start or the cost of denying it, one must take into account the powers that creditors enjoy outside of bankruptcy. The effect of allowing debtors to use Chapter 7, then, is to insulate all of the debtor's future income from creditors as opposed to just that portion protected by limitations on garnishment. One should keep in mind, however, that there are limits to this protection and its benefits.

The requirement that those seeking a fresh start give up any non-exempt assets limits the number of opportunists who might take advantage of the system. The unscrupulous could, of course, attempt to hide assets, but those who seek the protection of bankruptcy law must disclose the whereabouts of all their assets and submit to questioning from creditors. Under §727, a debtor who is not forthcoming or who is found to have perpetrated a recent fraud on creditors loses, among other things, the right to a fresh start. The ability to scrutinize the debtor's affairs is a substantial benefit to many creditors. Indeed, some creditors might willingly give up their pursuit of the debtor once they satisfy themselves that the debtor cannot repay them. The procedure that bankruptcy law puts in place reassures creditors that the debtor does not have other assets and that nothing is hidden from them.

A bankruptcy petition imposes costs even on the honest individual who has no nonexempt assets. Most obviously, a debtor who has filed a bankruptcy petition will find it harder to borrow in the future. (Immediately after the petition, however, the debtor may find it easier to borrow because at that moment, the debtor will have no creditors and will not be able to take advantage of bankruptcy's fresh start again for eight years. See §727(a)(8).) The other costs of bankruptcy are harder to measure, but are probably more important. For example, in our society, a social stigma still attaches to those who do not pay their creditors. Many individuals see their own filing of a bankruptcy petition as a confession of failure.

One can argue that neither stigma nor guilt should follow in the wake of a bankruptcy petition, but the fact that they do deters most from filing bankruptcy petitions until their financial situation is desperate. Lenders recognize the force of stigma and guilt and are willing to lend even to those who have no assets other than their ability to earn money in the future. Indeed, some who favor narrowing the availability of the fresh start focus on the role that stigma plays. They assert that the stigma associated with bankruptcy has declined over time and that bankruptcy filings increased as a result. Under this view, reducing the availability of the fresh start is a way of returning to the old equilibrium.

A right to a fresh start in bankruptcy is a kind of insurance. All debtors pay a higher rate of interest at the outset and, in return, the creditor bears part of the loss that arises when a particular debtor falls on hard times. One must ask if it makes sense to make this "insurance policy" part of every debt contract. A number of different factors determine whether a given risk is insurable. No insurance company will sell a policy that will pay someone's gambling losses in Las Vegas. Once you have such a policy, you will gamble more recklessly than you would otherwise. (This is called the moral hazard problem.) Moreover, those who seek such a policy and are willing to pay its premium are the ones most likely to have large losses. (This is called the adverse selection problem.) When insurance companies cannot control these problems or see a limit to them, they cannot sell insurance. The premiums they would charge to cover claims would be much larger than people would be willing to pay.

The "insurance" that bankruptcy's fresh start gives the individual debtor creates both moral hazard and adverse selection problems. If you can get a fresh start when you encounter financial disaster, you might be tempted to borrow too much. Similarly, if lenders raise their interest rates to compensate themselves for the risk of a bankruptcy's fresh start, the borrowers most willing to pay the high interest rate may be the ones most likely to take advantage of the fresh start. Because the moral hazard and adverse selection problems exist in some measure, the argument in favor of bankruptcy's fresh start must begin with the claim that these problems do not loom large enough to destroy the market for consumer loans or cause dramatic distortions of it.

One might argue that a right to a fresh start in bankruptcy is more like fire insurance than gambling insurance. Although individuals are more apt to be careless when their house is insured and arsonists are especially eager to buy fire insurance, a thriving market exists for such insurance nevertheless. Individuals may become more careless when they have fire insurance, but not significantly so. Moreover, rules can and have been written to punish arsonists, who are not entitled to the benefits of fire insurance. Similarly, individuals have so much to lose when they go broke that the existence of a fresh start may not significantly encourage carelessness. Adverse selection problems can be controlled as well. The rules governing the fresh start are written in such a way that they screen out many of those who borrow and spend with the intent of using bankruptcy to avoid paying their creditors.

The preceding paragraphs, however, make the fresh start in bankruptcy seem somewhat easier to justify than it is. Insurance policies are a good thing, but the law usually does not force people to buy them. To complete the insurance analysis, we need to explain why individuals are prevented from waiving their right to a fresh start. Section 727(a)(10) permits a court-approved waiver of discharge *after* an order for relief in bankruptcy, but it does not allow waiver of discharge at the time the debtor borrows. Thus, individuals are free to decide whether they want to pay for fire insurance, but they are not similarly free to waive the right to a fresh start and save the premium associated with it. Debtors must "buy" the right to a fresh start regardless of whether the benefits of this insurance policy are worth the costs in the form of higher rates of interest and less available credit.

One might object to free waiver of discharge on the ground that no waiver could ever be fully informed and truly voluntary. But we allow individuals to waive many rights, such as the right to counsel or the right to be protected from unreasonable search and seizure, that have far greater consequences than looking only to nonbankruptcy law for protection from creditors. Moreover, the law might condition waiver on stringent creditor disclosure requirements. Yet few lawmakers or commentators would permit a debtor to waive her right of discharge in advance of financial crisis.

Our society's reluctance to allow the waiver goes beyond doubts about whether there could ever be adequate disclosure. Identifying the source of our reluctance, however, is not easy. It seems insufficient to say that lenders would insist on waivers because of their superior bargaining position. The presence or absence of a right to a fresh start will not keep a creditor with bargaining power from using that power. To be sure, at a given interest rate, a lender would rather make a nondischargeable loan than one the debtor can discharge. Nevertheless, lenders should still be willing to give borrowers a right to a fresh start in return for a higher interest rate. The "fresh start" is a form of insurance. Like other kinds of insurance, lenders should be willing to offer a fresh start, assuming individuals valued it at an amount greater than its cost. Even if lenders did not offer the equivalent of bankruptcy's fresh start, others might enter the market and offer insurance to debtors that protects them in the event of financial misfortune at the appropriate risk-adjusted price.

This outcome is not assured. A market failure is possible. A market for insurance does not always exist even when people as a group value it more than it costs to supply. There might be an adverse selection problem known as a "lemons" problem. Borrowers who were the best credit risks might not buy the fresh-start insurance. The price of the policy is set by the average risk of default. Given the low probability of encountering financial difficulty, the best risks would find the price of insurance too high. As soon as the safest borrowers opt out, however, the price of the fresh-start insurance rises for everyone else. The remaining borrowers are, on average, more likely to default than when the safest borrowers were in the pool. But when the price rises, the safest risks among those still remaining, might opt out for the same reason. The price rises again and more borrowers opt out. The market may unravel entirely or to a large extent. Just as it is hard to sell a used car because buyers are afraid that only lemons are sold, it may be hard to buy fresh-start insurance because lenders may rationally believe that only those who are bad credit risks ask for it. A mandatory legal rule is a possible solution to this problem. By mandating that everyone buy this insurance, this unraveling cannot take place.

Mandatory rules, however, come with their own costs. Instead of consumers who want such insurance not being able to acquire it, some who do not want it are forced to pay for it. Indeed, some may not be able to borrow. In any event, showing that unraveling can happen in theory is not the same as showing that it is empirically important. The lemons problem exists only when borrowers know their own likelihood of default but their lenders do not, that is, only when from the lenders' perspective potential borrowers look the same. The ability of modern lenders to gather individualized information on prospective borrowers suggests that this is not strictly the case. In short, we cannot simply assume that the fresh start would be unavailable in the marketplace even when it made consumers in the aggregate better off. Thus, other explanations for the nonwaivability of bankruptcy's fresh-start policy may be more important.

The avoidance of "externalities" may justify the mandatory right to discharge in bankruptcy. That is, a belief that the right to a fresh start should not be waivable may result from a recognition of the effects that a debtor's financial misfortunes might have on others. A debtor's own financial failure can leave him unable to support his children. Even if a coolly rational borrower reasonably thought the right to a fresh start was not worth its price, he might come to a different decision were he forced to internalize the costs imposed on family members. The argument against waiver on this ground is particularly strong if a debtor borrows to make frivolous purchases now and leaves his family in dire straits later. In contrast, a loan now to attend college may be worthy of a waiver discharge. This argument meshes with the way in which the Bankruptcy Code makes alimony and support obligations as well as student loans nondischargeable. See §523. Alimony and child support obligations are nondischargeable to minimize the costs a potentially frivolous borrower can impose on others. Student loans, in contrast, are nondischargeable to permit the finance of an important expenditure despite the risk that a penurious borrower will become unable to support his family.

Another problem with free waiver of discharge stems from the fact that individuals are not coolly rational, at least not all the time. Individuals may not behave rationally when they borrow in their personal capacities. The temptation to borrow at a lower rate in return for waiver of discharge might be one to which a debtor would succumb at the moment of the loan; but the debtor might prefer not to be put in a position in which she were exposed to the temptation. One who favors a bankruptcy law bar on time-of-loan waiver is like Ulysses, who ordered himself chained to the mast of his ship, not to be released when the ship sailed passed the Sirens, however much he might *then* protest. Such a person might also place her alarm clock across the room from her bed rather than on a nearby night table, not trusting that her half-asleep self will appreciate the importance of an early meeting. The prudence that would lead a debtor to insist on the right to a fresh start might desert her at the crucial time.

In addition, unlike corporate decision makers disciplined by the pressures of the marketplace, individuals in their personal capacity may not be well equipped to judge the probability that they will encounter hard financial times in the future. One may not fully realize that, while the chance of any particular financial downturn can be small, the chance of one of these events coming to pass may be substantial. Although the evidence is not free from doubt, a substantial body of empirical literature suggests that people systematically underestimate aggregate probabilities such as this. This misunderstanding could lead to improvident waivers of the insurance inherent in discharge and the fresh start.

One should not, however, assume that these cognitive justifications for forbidding the waiver of the right to a fresh start are unassailable. Their most significant failing is that they prove too much. Many other activities, such as skydiving and cigarette smoking, might be banned for similar reasons. Moreover, arguments in favor of making the discharge mandatory rest on the assumption that borrowers are less able than others to assess their risk of defaulting. Recall that a competing justification, that a right to waive the fresh start gave rise to a lemons problem, assumed that individual borrowers were *better* able to make this assessment.

Whatever the merits, the fresh start is part of bankruptcy law and may not be waived in advance of bankruptcy. This chapter of the book explores some of the more difficult issues in the application of the fresh-start policy. The first two sections below analyze property that the debtor can take into her postbankruptcy life. The last two sections conclude with an analysis of the discharge that shields the postbankruptcy debtor from her prebankruptcy obligations. An alternative version of bankruptcy's fresh start, under Chapter 13, is left for the book's next chapter.

A. UNBUNDLING INTERESTS IN PROPERTY

The Bankruptcy Code distinguishes between assets that become property of the estate under §541 and assets that are kept outside of §541. As we have discussed, the individual debtor's fresh start derives from two sources. First, the Bankruptcy Code's discharge provisions, §727 for Chapter 7, ensures that a debtor who gives up existing assets can prevent creditors from reaching any of the debtor's future income or assets acquired with such income. Second, §522, which works in conjunction with nonbankruptcy state and federal law, allows a debtor to keep exempt property (unless subject to certain unavoidable liens). Because the definitions of "property of the estate" and "exemptions" of property are not coordinated, each must be interpreted independently. The fresh start is the sum of future income, which is *not* property of the estate, and exempt property, which is. These sources must be considered specifically. It is not possible to rest on the general concept of the fresh start.

Determining property of the estate for an individual with an independent life after bankruptcy requires determining what constitutes "earnings from services" within the meaning of §541(a)(6). As discussed above in chapter 6, section A, §541(a) provides generally that the estate comprises "interests of the debtor in property *as of the commencement of the case*," while §541(a)(6) provides that property of the estate also includes items such as proceeds, rents, and profits from such property "except such as are earnings from services performed by an individual debtor after the commencement of the case." In principle, then, postpetition earnings from the individual debtor's assets belong to the estate while postpetition earnings from the debtor's labor belong to the debtor.

This is simple in theory, but the required distinctions are sometimes difficult in application. Many of the hard cases arise when the individual who seeks a fresh start runs a business. For this reason, many of the cases that examine the reach of §541(a)(6) are cases in which individuals use Chapter 11. That bankruptcy chapter offers both a fresh start for the individual and a mechanism for ensuring that the debtor's business continues. The earnings of the business in the future will derive both from the value of its existing assets and from the future work of the debtor. A lawyer or a physician builds up a practice over the course of many years and hires a number of associates who work with her. She invests on the side in real estate deals that turn sour and discovers that she owes much more than her practice will generate. She wants to continue her practice after leaving bankruptcy and she is entitled to her future earnings. But not all of the earnings of the practice will be due to her future work. The Ninth Circuit expressed the point in In re Fitzsimmons, 725 F.2d 1208 (9th Cir. 1984):

> [S]ection 541(a)(6) excepts from the proceeds of the estate only those earnings generated by services personally performed by the individual debtor. [The debtor] is thus entitled to monies generated by his law practice only to the extent that they are attributable to personal services that he himself performs. To the extent that the law practice's earnings are attributable not to [the debtor's] personal services but to the business' invested capital, accounts receivable, good will, employment contracts with the firm's staff, client relationships, fee agreements, or the like, the earnings of the law practice accrue to the estate.
>
> Our interpretation accords with the plain meaning of the language of §541(a)(6). The section speaks only of "services performed by an *individual* debtor," reinforcing our conclusion that it excepts only earnings from services personally performed by an *individual* debtor, since the services of a debtor's employee or return on capital are not services of the individual debtor himself.

The challenge posed is that of disaggregating the earnings of the debtor from the earnings of the business itself. The practice may have substantial goodwill. Clients come because they know that this firm is one that will provide them with good service, but the reputation is built, at least in part, upon the debtor's past labors. As the Seventh Circuit observed in In re Prince, 85 F.3d 314, 323 n.5 (7th Cir. 1996):

> [T]he mere fact that [the debtor's] goodwill was created through years of his practicing in the community does not alter the conclusion that it is an asset separate from his human capital. If [the debtor] were to have fashioned one of the practice's physical assets with his own hands, this would not change the fact that the asset could be sold and, therefore, that the asset had value independent of [the debtor]. The earnings exception does not exclude earnings from an asset created by a debtor's past labors, only the earnings from actual services performed by the debtor in the *future*.

In *Prince*, as in other cases, however, it may be worth reflecting on the nonbankruptcy background. Earnings one derives in the future depend in some measure on past efforts. A medical or legal practice that a person builds up over time is, in this respect, the same as the knowledge of law or medicine that a person also devoted past labor to acquire. Section 541(a)(6), however, allows individuals to keep their earnings independent of how much past labor was an investment in "human capital." Human capital is not an asset of the bankruptcy estate. To be sure, a practice can be sold in a way that one's legal or medical knowledge cannot. But transfers of professional practices require active cooperation. The lawyer or doctor who sells a practice usually, as part of the sale, agrees to vouch for the buyer, introduce her to clients or patients, and perhaps work with her through a transitional period. In addition, the new buyer will ordinarily insist on a covenant not to compete. Hence, the amount for which a cooperative debtor could sell the practice outside of bankruptcy may not be the relevant benchmark. A better approximation of asset value distinct from the individual debtor might be the value of the practice that would remain if the debtor were to die or otherwise cease all connections with the business.

There is another important wrinkle in distinguishing property of the estate from property of the postpetition individual debtor. Property that exists at the time of a debtor's bankruptcy may be beyond the reach of either the creditor or the debtor. The paradigm is the spendthrift trust. A parent might establish a trust for a child prone to impulsive spending and provide that the child could not convey future income from the trust in exchange for a fixed sum today. Nonbankruptcy law respects such provisions and would shield the trust funds from buyers or creditors. Section 541(c)(2) tells us that bankruptcy law respects the provisions as well. This provision's reach extends beyond those trusts that are denominated "spendthrift trusts." The provision applies equally to any beneficial interest in a trust that has the crucial attribute of being beyond the reach of the debtor and the debtor's creditors under applicable nonbankrupty law.

The Bankruptcy Code contains still another aspect to the separation of property between debtor and creditors. The bankruptcy discharge extinguishes claims against the individual debtor, but it does not extinguish the liens that secured such claims. Let us assume, for example, that the debtor has a car subject to a security interest that supports a claim equal to the value of the car. The trustee might sell the car and remit the proceeds to the secured creditor. Because the car has no value to the general creditors, the trustee might well decide to abandon it to the debtor. After the Chapter 7 case is over, the secured creditor can no longer assert a claim against the debtor. The claim has been discharged. Nevertheless, the lien the creditor has on the debtor's car survives bankruptcy. The general, oft-stated, rule is that liens "pass through" bankruptcy unaffected. This principle was established in the venerable pre-Code case of Long v. Bullard, 117 U.S. 617 (1886). As we shall see later in this section, the rule in general survives to this day. There are, however, exceptions to lien pass-through that are needed to protect the fresh start.

An assignment of wages or any device that gives a creditor a security interest in the debtor's future wages does not pass through bankruptcy. This doctrine, set out in another long-lived case, Local Loan Company v. Hunt, 292 U.S. 234 (1934), supplements the carve-out of future earnings in §541(a)(6). How far we extend the doctrine is not clear.

The bankruptcy of Tia Carrere, for example, raised the question of the scope of *Local Loan Company*. See In re Carrere, 64 Bankr. 156 (Bankr. C.D. Cal. 1986). Tia Carrere is an actress who wanted to escape from a long-term contract with ABC that required her to appear on *General Hospital,* a daytime television soap opera. A clause in that contract prevented her from becoming a regular on *The A-Team*, a prime-time show. The court had to decide whether bankruptcy's fresh start freed her from the unfavorable employment contract. If Carrere had foolishly borrowed money from ABC and lost it all, she would have been able to file a bankruptcy petition and keep her earnings from whatever job she happened to take. Similarly, if a creditor of Carrere's had garnished her wages, the garnishment would not survive bankruptcy. Conceptually, Carrere's promise not to appear elsewhere, or indeed any covenant not to compete, can be characterized as a pledge of future wages to support an obligation. *Local Loan Company* requires that such a pledge not survive bankruptcy. To be sure, if one could discharge a covenant not to compete in bankruptcy, it would be harder for actresses like Carrere to find jobs in the first instance. ABC would be less willing to take on new actors if it were not able to keep them. But this does not distinguish *Carrere* from *Local Loan Company*. Any limit on the doctrine of lien pass-through reduces the ability of debtors to commit themselves and hence makes it less attractive for others to enter into agreements with them.

Nonetheless, in *Carrere*, the court enforced the covenant in part on the ground that Carrere's primary purpose in filing for bankruptcy was to escape the ABC contract, an act of bad faith in the court's view (a view now codified by §707(b) as amended by the 2005 Bankruptcy Act). But *every* bankruptcy of an individual involves a debtor's attempt to escape burdensome obligations. Perhaps aware of this observation (and in an opinion that predates the 2005 Act), the *Carrere* court did not rely on its bad-faith determination alone. It decided as well that the covenant not to compete was a right of ABC unaffected by Carrere's breach or, thus, rejection of the executory contract the covenant in part formed. Compare the *Register* case discussed above in chapter 7, section C.

No matter how one addresses this issue, the substantive problem is the same and presents a special case for an individual as opposed to a corporation, for which a pledge of all future value is unobjectionable. The exercises below work through some of the issues involved in unbundling an individual debtor's interest in property from the estate's interest.

The prohibition of liens on human capital aside, there are, in addition, narrower statutory protections of an individual debtor's interest in property. Section 522(f) permits the debtor to remove some liens on exempt property without any postpetition payment to the lienholder. (The fact that §522(f) does not cover all liens on all exempt property should make one cautious in thinking of "exempt property" as truly exempt.) Section 722, moreover, allows a debtor to redeem and remove any lien on abandoned or exempt "tangible personal property intended primarily for personal, family, or household use" if that property secures dischargeable consumer debt. But to extinguish a lien under §722, the debtor must pay the holder "the amount of the secured claim of such holder that is secured by such lien."

We discuss exempt property and liens thereon more fully in the next section. It will be useful now, though, to focus on §722 and its effect on liens that cannot be removed under §522(f). Imagine that Bank lends Debtor $10,000 and takes a security interest in Debtor's diamond necklace. When Debtor enters bankruptcy several years later, the price of diamonds has dropped and the necklace is worth less than what Bank is owed. The trustee abandons the necklace under §554, discussed above in chapter 9, section C, because Bank's lien will absorb the entire value and leave nothing for the general creditors as the estate's residual beneficiaries. In a hearing under §506(a), discussed above in chapter 5, section C, the bankruptcy court determines that the necklace is worth only $6,000 and that Bank can assert in Debtor's bankruptcy proceeding an unsecured claim for $4,000—the difference between the value of the necklace and the amount Bank is owed. This claim, like those of the general creditors, is likely to be paid only a few cents on the dollar.

After bankruptcy, Debtor's discharge prevents Bank from pursuing its claim against Debtor, but the discharge does not cut off Bank's lien on the necklace. Section 722, however, provides that Debtor can redeem the jewelry for $6,000 because that is the amount of the "allowed secured claim" under §506(a). Assume that Debtor raises $6,000 from family and friends and exercises her redemption right solely because the necklace once belonged to her grandmother. In this case, Debtor will have preserved her heirloom and Bank will have lost nothing but the opportunity to hold up Debtor for the sentimental value she attaches to the property. That is, in this case, §722 will have worked exactly as intended.

There is another possibility, however. Debtor may have redeemed the necklace not because of any sentimental value, but because the bankruptcy judge undervalued the jewelry or because the piece had appreciated since the judge's valuation. In either case, the "strip down" of Bank's lien to the judicial valuation of its collateral deprives Bank of its interest in nonexempt property. Outside of bankruptcy, that interest would include the full actual value of the necklace up to the amount of Bank's unpaid loan and lien—$10,000 less whatever Bank recovered prior to foreclosure—regardless of whether Debtor exercised her state law right of redemption. This result may not have been intended by Congress in the Bankruptcy Code's balance of the debtor's fresh start with creditor recovery, but the outcome will seldom be important because a consumer debtor's personal household or family property rarely has substantial value, this illustration notwithstanding.

The prospect of lien strip-down looms much larger in a different setting. Imagine that Bank's collateral is not household property but the house itself. Just as with the necklace, §506(a) would bifurcate an undersecured loan and reduce the secured claim on such a loan to the value of the collateral, here real estate. Now, however, given the typically high value of real estate compared to personal property, there may be more at stake in a lien strip-down if the court's valuation proved to be low, initially or after appreciation. In this case, if the trustee abandoned the property, strip-down would permit Debtor to profit, perhaps significantly, by redemption for the amount of the reduced lien or by return of any foreclosure sale proceeds above that amount. Although state law would govern both redemption and foreclosure postabandonment, for neither process could state law define the amount of the lien contrary to federal bankruptcy law. If bankruptcy law permits lien strip-down, then, a debtor may retain a substantial interest in property even if that property is nonexempt and not subject to bankruptcy redemption under §722.

At first glance, it does appear that the Bankruptcy Code permits lien strip-down of a claim bifurcated by §506(a). Section 506(d) provides:

> To the extent that a lien secures a claim against the debtor that is not an allowed secured claim, such lien is void.

Thus, it seems that §506(d) voids a creditor's lien to the extent of the unsecured portion of the creditor's claim. The lien would survive, but only to the extent of the amount of the secured claim under §506(a).

In the next case that we examine, *Dewsnup v. Timm*, the Supreme Court considers whether there is a reason to give §506(d) an interpretation different from the one that appears on its face. The related notes and problem further delve into the issue of lien strip-down under §506(d).

Key Provisions: Bankruptcy Code §§506(d); 541(a)(6), (c)(2)

EXERCISES

11A(1) Debtor, an insolvent individual, has a lucrative contract to be the sole provider of maintenance services for a local manufacturer. Debtor files for bankruptcy and continues to provide maintenance for which the manufacturer pays. Debtor's bankruptcy trustee argues that the contract is property of the estate and that Debtor's income therefrom is proceeds of that property, which the trustee, therefore, wants for the estate. Will the trustee prevail? Is it relevant whether Debtor used valuable tools to fulfill her obligations under the contract? Should it matter whether those tools are exempt from creditor collection? See In re FitzSimmons, 725 F.2d 1208 (9th Cir. 1984).

11A(2) Debtor is a physician with a successful practice. Bad investments, however, have left her hopelessly in debt, and she files a Chapter 7 bankruptcy petition. Despite the bankruptcy, Debtor continues to earn $200,000 from her medical practice. The trustee reasons that if the Debtor were to move to a new city and start afresh, she would be able to earn only $125,000 in her first year. She would return to her current income only after three years of work building up a new practice. The additional income she enjoys now depends upon the goodwill that she has built up in the past. Can the trustee insist that as a condition of receiving a discharge, Debtor turn over $75,000 a year for the next three years?

CASE

DEWSNUP v. TIMM

United States Supreme Court, 1992
502 U.S. 410

JUSTICE BLACKMUN DELIVERED THE OPINION OF THE COURT.

We are confronted in this case with an issue concerning §506(d). May a debtor "strip down" a creditor's lien on real property to the value of the collateral, as judicially determined, when that value is less than the amount of the claim secured by the lien?

I

On June 1, 1978, respondents loaned $119,000 to petitioner Aletha Dewsnup and her husband, T. LaMar Dewsnup, since deceased. The loan was accompanied by a Deed of Trust granting a lien on two parcels of Utah farmland owned by the Dewsnups.

Petitioner defaulted the following year. Under the terms of the Deed of Trust, respondents at that point could have proceeded against the real property collateral by accelerating the maturity of the loan, issuing a notice of default, and selling the land at a public foreclosure sale to satisfy the debt. * * *

Respondents did issue a notice of default in 1981. Before the foreclosure sale took place, however, petitioner ... filed a petition seeking liquidation under Chapter 7. Because of the pendency of these bankruptcy proceedings, respondents were not able to proceed to the foreclosure sale.

In 1987, petitioner filed the present adversary proceeding in the Bankruptcy Court for the District of Utah seeking, pursuant to §506, to "avoid" a portion of respondents' lien. ... Petitioner represented that the debt of approximately $120,000 then owed to respondents exceeded the fair market value of the land and that, therefore, the Bankruptcy Court should reduce the lien to that value. According to petitioner, this was compelled by the interrelationship of the security-reducing provision of §506(a) and the lien-voiding provision of §506(d). Under §506(a) ("An allowed claim of a creditor secured by a lien on property in which the estate has an interest ... is a secured claim to the extent of the value of such creditor's interest in the estate's interest in such property"), respondents would have an "allowed secured claim" only to the extent of the judicially determined value of their collateral. And under §506(d) ("To the extent that a lien secures a claim against the debtor that is not an allowed secured claim, such lien is void"), the court would be required to void the lien as to the remaining portion of respondents' claim, because the remaining portion was not an "allowed secured claim" within the meaning of §506(a). * * *

II

As we read their several submissions, the parties and their amici are not in agreement in their respective approaches to the problem of statutory interpretation that confronts us. Petitioner-debtor takes the position that §506(a) and §506(d) are complementary and to be read together. Because, under §506(a), a claim is secured only to the extent of the judicially determined value of the real property on which the lien is fixed, a debtor can void a lien on the property pursuant to §506(d) to the extent the claim is no longer secured and thus is not "an allowed secured claim." In other words, §506(a) bifurcates classes of claims allowed under §502 into secured claims and unsecured claims; any portion of an allowed claim deemed to be unsecured under §506(a) is not an "allowed secured claim" within the lien-voiding scope of §506(d). Petitioner argues that there is no exception for unsecured property abandoned by the trustee. * * *

Respondents primarily assert that §506(d) is not, as petitioner would have it, "rigidly tied" to §506(a). ... They argue that §506(a) performs the function of classifying claims by true secured status at the time of distribution of the estate to ensure fairness to unsecured claimants. In contrast, the lien-voiding §506(d) is directed to the time at which foreclosure is to take place, and, where the trustee has abandoned the property, no bankruptcy distributional purpose is served by voiding the lien.

In the alternative, respondents, joined by the United States as amicus curiae, argue more broadly that the words "allowed secured claim" in §506(d) need not be read as an indivisible term of art defined by reference to §506(a), which by its terms is not a definitional provision. Rather, the words should be read term-by-term to refer to any claim that is, first, allowed, and, second, secured. Because there is no question that the claim at issue here has been "allowed" pursuant to §502 and is secured by a lien with recourse to the underlying collateral, it does not come within the scope of §506(d), which voids only liens corresponding to claims that have not been allowed and secured. This reading of §506(d), according to respondents and the United States, gives the provision the simple and sensible function of voiding a lien whenever a claim secured by the lien itself has not been allowed. It ensures that the Code's determination not to allow the underlying claim against the debtor personally is given full effect by preventing its assertion against the debtor's property.

Respondents point out that pre-Code bankruptcy law preserved liens like respondents' and that there is nothing in the Code's legislative history that reflects any intent to alter that law. Moreover, according to respondents, the "fresh start" policy cannot justify an impairment of respondents' property rights, for the fresh start does not extend to an in rem claim against property but is limited to a discharge of personal liability.

III

The foregoing recital of the contrasting positions of the respective parties and their amici demonstrates that §506 and its relationship to other provisions of that Code do embrace some ambiguities. ... Hypothetical applications that come to mind and those advanced at oral argument illustrate the difficulty of interpreting the statute in a single opinion that would apply to all possible fact situations. We therefore focus upon the case before us and allow other facts to await their legal resolution on another day.

We conclude that respondents' alternative position, espoused also by the United States, although not without its difficulty, generally is the better of the several approaches. Therefore, we hold that §506(d) does not allow petitioner to "strip down" respondents' lien, because respondents' claim is secured by a lien and has been fully allowed pursuant to §502. Were we writing on a clean slate, we might be inclined to agree with petitioner that the words "allowed secured claim" must take the same meaning in §506(d) as in §506(a). But, given the ambiguity in the text, we are not convinced that Congress intended to depart from the pre-Code rule that liens pass through bankruptcy unaffected.

The practical effect of petitioner's argument is to freeze the creditor's secured interest at the judicially determined valuation. By this approach, the creditor would lose the benefit of any increase in the value of the property by the time of the foreclosure sale. The increase would accrue to the benefit of the debtor, a result some of the parties describe as a "windfall."

We think, however, that the creditor's lien stays with the real property until the foreclosure. That is what was bargained for by the mortgagor and the mortgagee. The voidness language sensibly applies only to the security aspect of the lien and then only to the real deficiency in the security. Any increase over the judicially determined valuation during bankruptcy rightly accrues to the benefit of the creditor, not to the benefit of the debtor and not to the benefit of other unsecured creditors whose claims have been allowed and who had nothing to do with the mortgagor-mortgagee bargain.

Such surely would be the result had the lienholder stayed aloof from the bankruptcy proceeding (subject, of course, to the power of other persons or entities to pull him into the proceeding pursuant to §501), and we see no reason why his acquiescence in that proceeding should cause him to experience a forfeiture of the kind the debtor proposes. It is true that his participation in the bankruptcy results in his having the benefit of an allowed unsecured claim as well as his allowed secured claim, but that does not strike us as proper recompense for what petitioner proposes by way of the elimination of the remainder of the lien. * * *

Apart from reorganization proceedings, ... no provision of the pre-Code statute permitted involuntary reduction of the amount of a creditor's lien for any reason other than payment on the debt. Our cases reveal the Court's concern about this. In Long v. Bullard, 117 U.S. 617, 620-21 (1886), the Court held that a discharge in bankruptcy does not release real estate of the debtor from the lien of a mortgage created by him before the bankruptcy. And in Louisville Joint Stock Land Bank v. Radford, 295 U.S. 555 (1935), the Court considered additions to the Bankruptcy Act effected by the Frazier-Lemke Act, 48 Stat. 1289 (1934). There the Court noted that the latter Act's "avowed object is to take from the mortgagee rights in the specific property held as security; and to that end 'to scale down the indebtedness' to the present value of the property." ... The Court invalidated that statute under the Takings Clause. It further observed: "No instance has been found, except under the Frazier-Lemke Act, of either a statute or decision compelling the mortgagee to relinquish the property to the mortgagor free of the lien unless the debt was paid in full." * * *

Congress must have enacted the Code with a full understanding of this practice.

When Congress amends the bankruptcy laws, it does not write "on a clean slate." See Emil v. Hanley, 318 U.S. 515, 521 (1943).

Furthermore, this Court has been reluctant to accept arguments that would interpret the Code, however vague the particular language under consideration might be, to effect a major change in pre-Code practice that is not the subject of at least some discussion in the legislative history. ... Of course, where the language is unambiguous, silence in the legislative history cannot be controlling. But, given the ambiguity here, to attribute to Congress the intention to grant a debtor the broad new remedy against allowed claims to the extent that they become "unsecured" for purposes of §506(a) without the new remedy's being mentioned somewhere in the Code itself or in the annals of Congress is not plausible, in our view, and is contrary to basic bankruptcy principles.

The judgment of the Court of Appeals is affirmed.

It is so ordered.

JUSTICE SCALIA, with whom JUSTICE SOUTER joins, dissenting.

With exceptions not pertinent here, §506(d) provides: "To the extent that a lien secures a claim against the debtor that is not an allowed secured claim, such lien is void. ... " Read naturally and in accordance with other provisions of the statute, this automatically voids a lien to the extent the claim it secures is not both an "allowed claim" and a "secured claim" under the Code. In holding otherwise, the Court replaces what Congress said with what it thinks Congress ought to have said—and in the process disregards, and hence impairs for future use, well-established principles of statutory construction. I respectfully dissent.

I

This case turns solely on the meaning of a single phrase found throughout the Bankruptcy Code: "allowed secured claim." Section 506(d) unambiguously provides that to the extent a lien does not secure such a claim it is (with certain exceptions) rendered void. ... Congress did not leave the meaning of "allowed secured claim" to speculation. Section 506(a) says that an "allowed claim" (the meaning of which is obvious) is also a "secured claim" "to the extent of the value of [the] creditor's interest in the estate's interest in [the securing] property." (This means, generally speaking, that an allowed claim "is secured only to the extent of the value of the property on which the lien is fixed; the remainder of that claim is considered unsecured." United States v. Ron Pair Enterprises, Inc., 489 U.S. 235, 239 (1989).) When §506(d) refers to an "allowed secured claim," it can only be referring to that allowed "secured claim" so carefully described two brief subsections earlier.

The phrase obviously bears the meaning set forth in §506(a) when it is used in the subsections of §506 other than §506(d)—for example, in §506(b), which addresses "allowed secured claim[s]" that are oversecured. Indeed, as respondents apparently concede, ... even when the phrase appears outside of §506, it invariably means what §506(a) describes: the portion of a creditor's allowed claim that is secured after the calculations required by that provision have been performed. See, e.g., §722 (permitting a Chapter 7 debtor to redeem certain tangible personal property from certain liens "by paying the holder of such lien the amount of the allowed secured claim of such holder that is secured by such lien"). ... The statute is similarly consistent in its use of the companion phrase "allowed unsecured claim" to describe (with respect to a claim supported by a lien) that portion of the claim that is treated as "unsecured" under §506(a). See, e.g., §507(a)(7) (fixing priority of "allowed unsecured claims of governmental units"); §726(a)(2) (providing for payment of "allowed unsecured claim[s]" in Chapter 7 liquidation). ... When, on the other hand, the Bankruptcy Code means to refer to a secured party's entire allowed claim, i.e., to both the "secured" and "unsecured" portions under §506(a), it uses the term "allowed claim"—as in §363(k), which refers to "a lien that secures an allowed claim." Given this clear and unmistakable pattern of usage, it seems to me impossible to hold, as the Court does, that "the words 'allowed secured claim' in §506(d) need not be read as an indivisible term of art defined by reference to §506(a)." * * *

The Court makes no attempt to establish a textual or structural basis for overriding the plain meaning of §506(d), but rests its decision upon policy intuitions of a legislative character, and upon the principle that a text which is "ambiguous" (a status apparently achieved by being the subject of disagreement between self-interested litigants) cannot change pre-Code law without the imprimatur of "legislative history." Thus abandoning the normal and sensible principle that a term (and especially an artfully defined term such as "allowed secured claim") bears the same meaning throughout the statute, the Court adopts instead what might be called the one-subsection-at-a-time approach to statutory exegesis. "[W]e express no opinion," the Court amazingly says, "as to whether the words 'allowed secured claim' have different meaning in other provisions of the Bankruptcy Code." ... "We ... focus upon the case before us and allow other facts to await their legal resolution on another day." * * *

III

Although the Court makes no effort to explain why petitioner's straightforward reading of §506(d) is textually or structurally incompatible with other portions of the statute, respondents and the United States do so. They point out, to begin with, that the two exceptions to §506(d)'s nullifying effect both pertain to the disallowance of claims, and not to the inadequacy of security, see §506(d)(1) and (2)—from which they conclude that the applicability of §506(d) turns only on the allowability of the underlying claim, and not on the extent to which the claim is a "secured claim" within the meaning of §506(a). But the fact that the statute makes no exceptions to invalidation by reason of inadequate security in no way establishes that such (plainly expressed) invalidation does not exist. The premise of the argument—that if a statute qualifies a noun with two adjectives ("allowed" and "secured"), and provides exceptions with respect to only one of the adjectives, then the other can be disregarded—is simply false. The most that can be said is that the two exceptions in §506(d) do not contradict the United States' and respondents' interpretation; but they in no way suggest or support it.

Respondents and the United States also identify supposed inconsistencies between petitioner's construction of §506(d) and other sections of the Bankruptcy Code; they are largely illusory. The principal source of concern is §722, which enables a Chapter 7 debtor to "redeem" narrow classes of exempt or abandoned personal property from "a lien securing a dischargeable consumer debt." The price of redemption is fixed as "the amount of the allowed secured claim of [the lienholder] that is secured by such lien." ... This provision, we are told, would be largely superfluous if §506(d) automatically stripped liens securing undersecured claims to the value of the collateral, i.e., to the value of the allowed secured claims.

This argument is greatly overstated. Section 722 is necessary, and not superfluous, because §506(d) is not a redemption provision. It reduces the value of a lienholder's equitable interest in a debtor's property to the property's liquidation value, but it does not insure the debtor an opportunity to "redeem" the property at that price, i.e., to "free [the] property ... from [the] mortgage or pledge by paying the debt for which it stood as security." Black's Law Dictionary 1278 (6th ed. 1990). Congress had good reason to be solicitous of the debtor's right to redeem personal property (the exclusive subject of §722), since state redemption laws are typically less generous for personalty than for real property. ... The most that can be said regarding §722 is that petitioner's construction of §506(d) would permit a more concise formulation: Instead of describing the redemption price as "the amount of the allowed secured claim ... that is secured by such lien" it would have been possible to say simply "the amount of the claim ... that is secured by such lien"—since §506(d) would automatically have cut back the lien to the amount of the allowed secured claim. I would hardly call the more expansive formulation a redundancy—not when it is so far removed from the section that did the "cutting back" that the reader has likely forgotten it.

Respondents and their amicus also make much of the need to avoid giving Chapter 7 debtors a better deal than they can receive under the other Chapters of the Bankruptcy Code. They assert that, by enabling a Chapter 7 debtor to strip down a secured creditor's liens and pocket any postpetition appreciation in the property, petitioner's construction of §506(d) will discourage debtors from using the preferred mechanisms of reorganization under Chapters 11, 12, and 13. This evaluation of the "finely reticulated" incentives affecting a debtor's behavior rests upon critical—and perhaps erroneous—assumptions about the meaning of provisions in the reorganization chapters. In any event, reorganization contains other enticements to lure a debtor away from Chapter 7. It not only permits him to maintain control over his personal and business assets, but affords a broader discharge from prepetition in personam liabilities. * * *

Finally, respondents and the United States find it incongruous that Congress would so carefully protect secured creditors in the context of reorganization while allowing them to be fleeced in a Chapter 7 liquidation by operation of §506(d). This view mistakes the generosity of treatment that creditors can count upon in reorganization. There, no more than under Chapter 7, can they demand the benefit of postevaluation increases in the value of property given as security. See §1129(b)(2)(A) and §1325(a)(5) (permitting "cram-down" of reorganization plan over objections of secured creditors if creditors are to receive payments equal in present value to the cash value of the collateral, and if creditors retain liens securing such payments).

IV

I must also address the Tenth Circuit's basis for the decision affirmed today ... that §506 does not apply to property abandoned by the bankruptcy trustee under §554. Respondents' principal argument before us was a modified (and less logical) version of the same basic point—viz., that although §506(a) applies to abandoned property,

§506(d) does not. I can address the point briefly, since the plain-language obstacles to its validity are even more pronounced than those raised by the Court's approach.

The Court of Appeals' reasoning was as follows: §506(d) effects lien-stripping only with respect to property subject to §506(a); but by its terms §506(a) applies only to property "in which the estate has an interest"; since "[t]he estate has no interest in, and does not administer, abandoned property," §506(a), and hence §506(d), does not apply to it. ... The fallacy in this is the assumption that the application of §506(a) (and hence §506(d)) can be undone if and when the estate ceases to "have an interest" in property in which it "had an interest" at the outset of the bankruptcy proceeding. The text does not read that way. Section 506 automatically operates upon all property in which the estate has an interest at the time the bankruptcy petition is filed. Once §506(a)'s grant of secured-creditor rights, and §506(d)'s elimination of the right to "underwater" liens and liens securing unallowed claims have occurred, they cannot be undone by later abandonment of the property. Nothing in the statute expressly permits such an unraveling, and it would be absurd to imagine it. If, upon the collateral's abandonment, the claim bifurcation accomplished by §506(a) were nullified, the status of the creditor's allowed claim—i.e., whether (and to what extent) it is "secured" or "unsecured" for purposes of the bankruptcy distribution—would be impossible to determine. Instead, the claim would have to be treated as either completely "secured" or completely "unsecured," neither of which disposition would accord with the Code's distribution principles. The former would deprive the secured claimant of a share in the distribution to general creditors altogether. See §726 (providing for distribution of property of the estate to unsecured claimants). The latter (treating the claim as completely unsecured) would permit the lienholder to share in the pro rata distribution to general creditors to the full amount of his allowed claim (rather than simply to the amount of §506(a)-defined "unsecured claim") while reserving his in rem claim against the security. Respondents' variation on the Tenth Circuit's holding avoids these alternative absurdities only by embracing yet another textual irrationality—asserting that, even though the language that is the basis for the "abandonment" theory (the phrase "in which the estate has an interest") is contained in §506(a), and only applies to §506(a) through §506(d), nonetheless only the effects of §506(d) and not the effects of §506(a) are undone by abandonment. This hardly deserves the name of a theory.

V

As I have said, the Court does not trouble to make or evaluate the foregoing arguments. Rather, in Part II of its opinion it merely describes (uncritically) "the contrasting positions of the respective parties and their amici" concerning the meaning of §506(d), ... and concludes, because the positions are contrasting, that there is "ambiguity in the text." ... (This mode of analysis makes every litigated statute ambiguous.) Having thus established "ambiguity," the Court is able to summon down its deus ex machina: "the pre-Code rule that liens pass through bankruptcy unaffected"—which cannot be eliminated by an ambiguous provision, at least where the "legislative history" does not mention its demise. * * *

We have, of course, often consulted pre-Code behavior in the course of interpreting gaps in the express coverage of the Code, or genuinely ambiguous provisions. And we have often said in such cases that, absent a textual footing, we will not presume a departure from long-standing pre-Code practice. ... But we have never held pre-Code practice to be determinative in the face of what we have here: contradictory statutory text. * * *

The principal harm caused by today's decision is not the misinterpretation of §506(d). The disposition that misinterpretation produces brings the Code closer to prior practice and is, as the Court irrelevantly observes, probably fairer from the standpoint of natural justice. (I say irrelevantly, because a bankruptcy law has little to do with natural justice.) The greater and more enduring damage of today's opinion consists in its destruction of predictability, in the Bankruptcy Code and elsewhere. By disregarding well-established and oft-repeated principles of statutory construction, it renders those principles less secure and the certainty they are designed to achieve less attainable. When a seemingly clear provision can be pronounced "ambiguous" sans textual and structural analysis, and when the assumption of uniform meaning is replaced by "one-subsection-at-a-time" interpretation, innumerable statutory texts become worth litigating. In the bankruptcy field alone, for example, unfortunate future litigants will have to pay the price for our expressed neutrality "as to whether the words 'allowed secured claim' have different meaning in other provisions of the Bankruptcy Code." ... Having taken this case to resolve uncertainty regarding one provision, we end by spawning confusion regarding scores of others. I respectfully dissent.

NOTES

11A.1. The Court in *Dewsnup* argues that lien strip-down serves no particular bankruptcy policy and that §506(d) is better understood as preventing liens from surviving bankruptcy when the underlying claim is disallowed. Consider the following. In anticipation of Debtor's bankruptcy, Lawyer provides legal services at an exorbitant fee and secures that fee with a lien on Debtor's property. In bankruptcy, the court disallows the fee under §329, which limits such fees. But this provision does not explicitly void Lawyer's lien. And one might imagine that a court would enforce the full lien despite the reduced claim (though this is by no means certain). With such an example in mind, one might conclude, as did the Court, that the purpose of §506(d) is not to strip down liens but rather to make sure that a creditor's lien fares no better than her claim. Section 506(d) ensures that Lawyer cannot go after the property, in anyone's hands, after the bankruptcy is over.

11A.2. In his dissent, Justice Scalia rejects the interpretation the *Dewsnup* majority offers for §506(d). In Scalia's view, to have the effect the Court claims, the subsection should have been written differently. It should have provided:

> To the extent that a lien secures a claim against the debtor that is not an allowed claim, such lien is void.

Yet the provision in fact refers to an "allowed *secured* claim." Justice Scalia does not disagree with the Court that the plain meaning of §506(d), as actually written, is undesirable from the perspective of creditors, unsound as a matter of bankruptcy policy, and contrary to preexisting practice. But for him this is all quite beside the point. The straightforward reading of §506(d) might be a bad idea with dubious pedigree, but this should not deny the statutory language a meaning that both makes sense on its own and is consistent with the way the language is used elsewhere in the Code. The majority and dissenting opinions in *Dewsnup* are two of the major landmarks in the Supreme Court's ongoing debate over statutory interpretation, in bankruptcy and elsewhere.

11A.3. Although §506(d) applies to corporate debtors as well as to individuals who file for bankruptcy under Chapters 13 or 11, interpretation of this provision is significant primarily for individual debtors in Chapter 7. Corporate debtors in Chapter 7 receive no discharge. Unlike an individual, therefore, a corporation that has been through Chapter 7 cannot raise new funds to purchase property free from old creditor claims and thus usually dissolves shortly after bankruptcy. Consequently, even before *Dewsnup*, abandonment of a corporate asset typically resulted in its turnover to the secured creditor, not its retention or redemption by the debtor postbankruptcy. Moreover, as we shall see in the last two chapters of this book, any debtor in Chapter 13 or 11 can, in essence, strip a lien down to a court's valuation with provisions other than §506(d), *Dewsnup* notwithstanding. Indeed, the prospect of an individual debtor's Chapter 13 case following closely after a Chapter 7 case remains a problem for secured creditors of abandoned property despite *Dewsnup*. With this in mind, Problem 11A asks you to explore possible strategies for a secured creditor in the face of a proposed abandonment.

PROBLEM

11A. Debtor is an individual in the real estate business whose only substantial asset is BlackAcre, a commercial parcel subject to Bank's mortgage. The mortgage supports a note well in excess of BlackAcre's current value. After Debtor files for bankruptcy under Chapter 7, the trustee announces her intention to abandon BlackAcre and requests a §506(a) hearing with regard to the property. Bank is concerned that the court will undervalue BlackAcre. Does Bank have anything to fear from any such undervaluation? Assume that Bank does have something to fear, if not from the undervaluation itself, then from the abandonment. What position would you advise Bank to take with regard to the trustee's proposed course? Consider this problem again after you read about Chapter 13 bankruptcy cases in the next chapter of this book. See Barry E. Adler, Creditor Rights After *Johnson* and *Dewsnup*, 10 Bankr. Dev. J. 1 (1993).

B. EXEMPT PROPERTY

In addition to allowing the debtor to keep everything that is not property of the estate and allowing the debtor to nullify liens on future income under the principle of *Local Loan Company,* the debtor is also able to keep "exempt" assets. These assets are exempt under §522 even though they are property of the estate within the meaning of §541. Under the old Bankruptcy Act of 1898, the definition of exempt property was entirely dependent on state and federal nonbankruptcy law. Hence, the scope of the fresh start to which a debtor was entitled varied from one state to another. The Constitution gives Congress the power to pass only "uniform" laws on the subject of bankruptcy. The Supreme Court has held, however, that deferring to state exemption statutes does not prevent a bankruptcy statute from being "uniform." Hanover National Bank v. Moyses, 186 U.S. 181 (1902).

Section 522 is a compromise between those who wanted federal exemptions and those who favored the old regime. Section 522 divides conceptually into two halves. First, there is the debtor's power to remove property from the trustee's hands (and therefore from the prepetition unsecured creditors). Second, there is the debtor's power to avoid liens—property rights—that otherwise would impair exemptions.

Section 522(b) defines exempt property, which the debtor may remove from the estate. Given that bankruptcy law is layered upon the state laws that already protect debtors, it is not surprising that there is great deference to state law. Under §522(b), the debtor makes a choice between the (b)(2) bankruptcy exemptions and the (b)(3) state (as well as substantive nonbankruptcy federal) exemptions, unless the domiciliary state makes its exemptions (plus nonbankruptcy federal exemptions) mandatory.

Under §522(b)(2), when a state allows it (and most opt out instead), a debtor may forgo otherwise applicable nonbankruptcy exemptions and choose the special bankruptcy exemptions. The federal bankruptcy exemption list is set forth in §522(d). The largest exemption in §522(d) is the $20,200 federal homestead exemption. But §522(d)(1), the source of this exemption, must be read in conjunction with §522(d)(5), for §522(d)(5) gives the debtor $1,075 plus up to $10,125 of the unused portion of §522(d)(1) to apply wherever the debtor wants—the "wild card" exemption. Conversely, the $1,075 from §522(d)(5) can be combined with §522(d)(1) to give the debtor a $21,275 federal homestead exemption. Section 522(d)(3) provides for an exemption of $525 per item on household goods, subject to a cap of $10,755 (not counting the wild card). (These amounts are adjusted periodically, per Bankruptcy Code §104.) Other §522(d) provisions exempt the debtor's interest in household goods, health aids, tools of the trade, and a motor vehicle, as well as the debtor's right to receive alimony, support payments, life insurance payments, veteran's benefits, and victim's compensation payments, among other items, some limited in scope or amount, others not.

The state nonbankruptcy exemptions vary in detail from jurisdiction to jurisdiction. Some are firmly rooted in the nineteenth century and include such things as homesteads, church pews, and the family bible. Modern exemption statutes also include pensions and insurance policies. The most controversial issue with respect to exemptions is not the type of property exempted, but the value of the property that can be exempted.

As noted above in chapter 1, some states, notably Florida and Texas, exempt a debtor's homestead without a cap. Other states provide similar treatment for some insurance and pension plans. Suppose a wealthy investor lives in a large house in Florida that he owns outright. He might file for bankruptcy, discharge all debts, and still be a millionaire. So long as the debtor was a resident of Florida and owned the house when he borrowed, creditors have nothing to complain about. They can take this risk into account. A more complicated issue arises, however, if the debtor bought the expensive house on the eve of bankruptcy or moved to Florida only after borrowing the money and after encountering financial trouble.

With the 2005 Bankruptcy Act Congress drew a line between permissible and impersmisible prebankruptcy planning. Section 522(b)(3)(A) provides that a debtor who, at the time of bankruptcy, has not resided in the same state for the past 730 days is bound by the exemptions of the state in which he resided for the greatest portion of the 180-day period immediately prior to the 730-day period. Similarly, §522(o) denies a state homestead exemption to the extent a debtor, within ten years of his bankruptcy filing, fraudulently converts nonexempt assets into a homestead. In the same vein, for a debtor "electing" state exemptions, §522(p) caps at $136,875 the exemption for a homestead not purchased, and not the result of an interest transferred from a home in the same state purchased, more than 1,215 days prior to the bankruptcy petition. See also, e.g., In re Kane, 336 Bankr. 477 (Bankr. D. Nev. 2006) (applying the cap in opt-out state, where debtor has no election). (There are other exemption limitations as well, unrelated to planning, such as a $136,875 homestead exemption cap for a debtor who violates federal securities law. See §522(q).)

Homestead exemptions aside, property that is exempt for purposes of §522(b)(3) may extend beyond what a state explicitly calls exempt. All agree that exempt property in §522(b)(3) includes what state and federal nonbankruptcy law labels exempt. Some have argued that the (b)(3) exemption should also include any property that has the attributes of exempt property, whatever label the state (or substantive federal law) applies.

Litigation over Keogh plans (tax-favored retirement savings fund) provides a good illustration of the label problem. A debtor might save for retirement by putting money in a Keogh plan. The assets in the plan contain property of the estate because the debtor can reach them outside of bankruptcy. That is, the debtor has an "interest" in the property for the purposes of §541(a). See chapter 6, section A above. Prior to the 2005 Bankruptcy Act, one still needed to ask if these assets were exempt. Substantive federal law provides that outside of bankruptcy, creditors cannot levy on assets in a Keogh plan. Federal law and the laws of many states, however, do not label Keogh plans as exempt property. The question therefore arose whether a debtor could keep the assets in a Keogh plan under §522. By and large, courts did not allow (b)(3) debtors to keep any property except that which state law labels exempt. Under this view, creditors in many states were able to reach the assets in a Keogh plan, even though they could not reach any of them outside of bankruptcy. A Keogh plan has the distinctive attribute of exempt property under substantive nonbankruptcy law, but for some courts the substance made no difference.

In response, the 2005 Bankruptcy Act amended §522, albeit with a blunt and potentially overbroad instrument. Under the new law, assets of an individual debtor's retirement fund are now exempt from the bankruptcy estate, whether the debtor elects state or federal exemptions, if the fund receives a favorable tax exemption determination under the Internal Revenue Code, or at least has not been denied such tax exemption. The exempt amounts in individual retirement accounts are generally limited to $1 million, but in exceptional cases, a bankruptcy judge may even exempt more than $1 million. (In a related provision, the 2005 Act amended §541 to exclude from the estate, subject to specified conditions and limitations, funds placed in an education individual retirement account, or used to purchase tuition credit, at least a year before the bankruptcy petition.)

Beyond the definition of exempt property (or property of the estate), §522 also allows the debtor to "avoid the fixing of" certain liens on such property. This power exists regardless of whether the debtor uses the special bankruptcy exemptions or the state and federal nonbankruptcy exemptions. More precisely, for example, §522(f)(1)(A) generally allows the individual debtor to free exempt property from judicial liens—e.g., a lien created by levy on behalf of a general creditor—subject only to limited exceptions such as liens that secure a domestic support obligation, defined by §101(14A).

Moreover, §522(f)(1)(B) allows the debtor to avoid a nonpossessory, nonpurchase money security interest in specified property. That property, listed in §522(f)(1)(B)(i), (ii), and (iii), turns out to be some of the same type of property set forth in §522(d). For example, §522(f)(1)(B)(i) and §522(d)(3) each refer to "household goods," defined for purposes of the former by §522(f)(4) (added by the 2005 Bankruptcy Act). The words in §522(f), however, do not necessarily mean the same thing as the ones in §522(d) because the former implicitly refers to property exempt under nonbankruptcy law and arguably incorporates a nonbankruptcy definition, while the latter is a special term of bankruptcy law.

The exercises below ask you to work through some of the mechanics of §522. The cases, *Geise* and *Owen*, as well as the related notes and problems, further explore the question of exemption definition.

Key Provisions: Bankruptcy Code §522(b), (d), (f)

EXERCISES

11B(1) Debtor, one of the last remaining traveling salesmen, files a Chapter 7 bankruptcy petition at a time that he possesses only a single valuable asset, an automobile worth $10,000. Total claims against Debtor well exceed this amount. Will Debtor emerge from bankruptcy with his car?

11B(2) Debtor, an individual, files a Chapter 7 bankruptcy petition and duly opts for the special bankruptcy exemptions under §522(b)(2). Just before filing, Debtor's spouse, an unsecured creditor, garnishes Debtor's right to receive a veteran's benefit. Will that garnishment survive bankruptcy?

11B(3) Debtor, a carpenter, files a Chapter 7 bankruptcy petition and seeks to exempt from property of the estate his valuable trained bird of a species known in Shakespeare's time as a handsaw. As luck would have it, in Debtor's home state a statute specifically exempts from creditor collection "a carpenter's hammers, drills, . . . and handsaws." Can Debtor make use of the state exemption? If the state would allow an exemption here, may Debtor also remove a judicial lien on the bird?

11B(4) A divorce court awards Debtor the couple's home and awards Debtor's spouse a lien on the house as security for the court's order that Debtor pay his spouse an amount required to equalize the net marital assets. Debtor files for bankruptcy under Chapter 7. The house qualifies for an exemption. Can Debtor avoid his spouse's lien? See Farrey v. Sanderfoot, 500 U.S. 291 (1991).

11B(5) Debtor's home state exempts from creditor collection "household goods" including an "engagement ring or wedding ring" without limitation as to value. At the time that Debtor loses her job and files for bankruptcy under Chapter 7, she owns an engagement ring worth $150,000. Debtor's husband gave her the ring when they were married ten years before the bankruptcy petition. Two years before the petition, when Debtor's husband died, Debtor pledged the ring as collateral for a Bank loan, $100,000 of which is still outstanding. Can Bank reach the ring? Would your answer change if the collateral were a wedding ring instead of an engagement ring?

CASES

IN RE GEISE

United States Court of Appeals. Seventh Circuit, 1993
992 F.2d 651

RIPPLE, CIRCUIT JUDGE.

* * * On February 29, 1988, the debtor, Gerald E. Geise, Jr., filed a voluntary petition for relief under Chapter 13. This case was later converted to a Chapter 7 liquidation proceeding. In his personal property schedule (Schedule B-2), Mr. Geise listed a personal injury cause of action then pending in Nevada. Pursuant to §522, Mr. Geise elected to file exemptions under Wisconsin law and listed the personal injury claim as exempt from property of the estate. . . . The bankruptcy trustee objected on the ground that, at the time of Mr. Geise's filing, Wisconsin law provided no statutory exemption for personal injury actions or their proceeds. * * *

As the bankruptcy and district courts have recognized in confronting this question, the starting point of the analysis must be an understanding of the Bankruptcy Code's approach to exemptions, an approach that differs radically from the methodology employed in the [1898 Act]. Except where otherwise provided in the section, §541(a)(1) defines property of the bankruptcy estate to include "all legal or equitable interests of the debtor in property as of the commencement of the case." The scope of §541 is broad and includes causes of action. * * *

In contrast, §70(a)(5) of the [1898 Act], the predecessor statute to §541, included in the estate

> rights of property, which prior to the filing of the petition [the bankrupt] could by any means have transferred or which might have been levied upon and sold under judicial process against him, or otherwise seized, impounded, or sequestered: Provided, That rights of action [for] injuries to the person of the bankrupt ... shall not vest in the trustee unless by the law of the State such rights of action are subject to attachment, execution, garnishment, sequestration, or other judicial process. * * *

Thus, the new Bankruptcy Code changed the legal landscape by dramatically expanding the definition of property included in the estate. In re Hunter, 970 F.2d 299, 302 (7th Cir. 1992). Section 541 eliminated the requirement that property must be transferable or subject to process in order to become initially part of the estate.

Moreover, with the enactment of the Code, a revised exemption scheme was also implemented under §522. As we explained in *Hunter*:

> Under this section, two alternative sets of exemptions are created. Subsection [522(b)(2)] affords the debtor the federal exemptions set forth in subsection 522(d); alternatively, under subsection [522(b)(3)], the debtor may choose the exemptions provided by his domicile state along with exemptions provided by federal, non-Code bankruptcy law ... . The Code also allows individual states to take this choice away from the debtor by "opting out" of the federal exemptions altogether. See [§522(b)(2)].

Id. at 303. Thus, while state law is no longer relevant to define property of the estate, state law is extremely pertinent if a debtor is attempting to exempt property under the laws of the state of his domicile.

This court has long recognized the difficulties that attend the task of interpreting the state law exemptions allowed by the new Bankruptcy Code. [S]ection 522(b) was a last-minute legislative compromise that left virtually no legislative history. Consequently, the courts of appeals that have addressed the issue have concluded that the states have great latitude in formulating their own exemptions and in establishing eligibility requirements for these exemptions. ... Indeed, courts have noted candidly that state exemption schemes can be quite inconsistent with the general goals of the federal Bankruptcy Code. * * *

In taking advantage of the ability to provide state exemptions, therefore, Wisconsin has a great deal of freedom, under the consistent precedent of this and other circuits, in how it proceeds. With this background, we turn to the available, but sparse, evidence of what Wisconsin has done. Our goal is to discern, from this paucity of material, whether Wisconsin has exempted from the bankrupt estate a cause of action for personal injuries.

We begin with the Wisconsin Constitution. Article I, section 17 provides that

> [t]he privilege of the debtor to enjoy the necessary comforts of life shall be recognized by wholesome laws, exempting a reasonable amount of property from seizure or sale for the payment of any debt or liability hereafter contracted.

In interpreting this section, the Wisconsin courts have discerned two underlying policy concerns that bear on our analysis. Legislation creating exemptions in favor of a debtor must be liberally construed. ... Nevertheless, this general principle of liberal construction cannot be employed to write exemptions into statutes. ... The right of a debtor to keep property free from the claims of creditors is not a common-law right. ... In the absence of a statutory provision, therefore, all the debtor's property may be subjected to the payment of debts. * * *

As we have noted earlier, the Wisconsin legislature has enacted an exemption section that implements explicitly the constitutional provision. See Wis. Stat. Ann. §815.18 (listing property exempt from execution). At the present time, although not at the time of the filing of the bankruptcy petition in this case, the statute specifically lists payments, not in excess of $25,000, resulting from bodily injury claims as exempt from property of the estate. From the available legislative history, we cannot tell whether this amendment was considered a matter of addition or clarification. It was added at the time of a general revision of the statutory section. Just as importantly, there is no indication that this section is the sole source of legislative exemptions. Indeed, there appears to be at least one other section that sets up other exemptions under the Wisconsin Consumer Act. As we have already noted, there is no federal requirement that a state exemption provision be so self-contained. Indeed, as a brief glance at a collection of the state exemption statutes confirms, even in those states that have enacted specific statutory listings of exempt property, other statutory sections also have been considered exemptions.

Mr. Geise contends that §128.19 of the Wisconsin Code, while not providing an explicit exemption, may be construed as establishing an exemption for personal injury actions and their proceeds. That section provides:

> 128.19. Title to property (1) The receiver or assignee upon his qualification shall be vested by operation of law with the title of the debtor as of the date of the filing of the petition or assignment hereunder ... including ... (a) Property transferred by him in fraud of his creditors. (b) Property which prior to the filing of the petition or assignment he could by any means have transferred or which might have been levied upon and sold under judicial process against him. (c) Rights of action arising upon contracts or from the unlawful taking or detention of or injury to his property. (2) The receiver or assignee may avoid any transfer by the debtor of his property which any creditor might have avoided and may recover the property so transferred or its value from the person to whom it was transferred unless he was a bona fide holder for value prior to the filing of the petition or assignment hereunder.

On its face, the statute says nothing about personal injury actions. Nevertheless, Mr. Geise submits that such a construction is warranted. In this regard, he relies on this court's decision in In re Buda, 323 F.2d 748 (7th Cir. 1963). In that case, this court was required to determine whether under Wisconsin law a cause of action for personal injuries ought to be included in the bankruptcy estate under §70(a)(5) of the old Bankruptcy Act. As we have noted previously, §70(a)(5) exempted personal injury causes of action "unless by the law of the State such rights are subject to attachment, execution, garnishment, sequestration or other judicial process." The trustee had conceded (although the basis for this concession is not clear) that such a right of action was not subject to attachment, execution, or garnishment under Wisconsin law. Therefore, this court had to determine whether the cause of action was "subject to sequestration or other judicial process." The court held that

> [i]t is our opinion that if the Wisconsin legislature intended that "property" subject to "sequestration" should include a right of action for injuries to one's person it would not obscure that intention by the general language of paragraph (1)(b) of §128.19 but would have placed the words "his person or" following the word "to" in paragraph (1)(c). We conclude on this point that because the right

of action was transferable by assignment it was not ipso facto property which vested under §128.19.

Id. at 750.

In the present case, the district court was of the view that this court's holding in *Buda* cannot constitute an exemption because, in Wisconsin, all exemptions must be based on specific constitutional or statutory provisions. We do not believe, however, that invocation of this principle of Wisconsin law, standing alone, is sufficient to preclude a determination that §128.19 constitutes an exemption. The decision in *Buda* is, at bottom, a judicial interpretation of a statute. This court held, in essence, that §128.19 ought to be construed as forbidding, by implication, the sequestration of a cause of action for personal injury. Therefore, consistent with Wisconsin law, the exemption would be grounded in a statute.

While we do not believe that the Wisconsin rule that an exemption be constitutionally or statutorily based is an impediment to determining that §128.19 is an exemption, a more fundamental issue must be addressed before we can hold that §128.19 can be treated as providing an exemption. We must determine whether the immunity of tort causes of action from sequestration, the interpretation of §128.19 suggested by this court in *Buda*, amounts to an exemption for purposes of §522(b)(3)(A).

The term "exemption" is not defined in either the Bankruptcy Code or Wisconsin law as it existed at the time of Mr. Geise's filing. As we have noted earlier, our prior case law makes clear that the Code places few restrictions on the manner in which a state structures its exemption scheme. Nevertheless, as the following paragraphs will demonstrate, we are not entirely without guideposts.

As a starting point, we recall that the purpose of §522(b)(3)(A) is to afford a state an opportunity to substitute its judgment for that of the Congress with respect to what property ought to be excluded from the bankruptcy estate. Our basic task, therefore, is to discern the will of the state legislature: what was the exemption scheme that the legislature wished to make available to the state's residents as an alternative to the federal exemptions set forth in the Bankruptcy Code? It is not unreasonable to expect that the state's policy judgment will be set forth with sufficient clarity to permit the bankruptcy court administering the estate to identify the state exemptions with reasonable certainty. While state courts frequently refer to statutes which prohibit only certain forms of judicial process as "exemption" statutes, the term "exemption" "conventionally connotes protection against all forms of process. ... William T. Vukowich, Debtors' Exemption Rights, 62 Geo. L.J. 779, 816 (1974). Therefore, it is appropriate, in our view, to give the word its common meaning in the absence of any legislative indication to the contrary. ... This approach not only provides us with the best opportunity to discern the otherwise unknown intent of the state legislature but also promotes an important congressional policy underlying the enactment of the new Bankruptcy Code: avoidance of "cumbersome ... state law analysis." Sierra Switchboard Co. v. Westinghouse Electric Corp., 789 F.2d 705, 709 (9th Cir. 1985). A fundamental purpose behind enactment of the new Code was to avoid such a quagmire:

> The bill makes significant changes in what constitutes property of the estate. Current law is a complicated melange of references to State law, and does little to further the bankruptcy policy of distribution of the debtor's property to his creditor in satisfaction of his debts. ... The bill determines what is property of the estate by a simple reference to what interests in property the debtor has at the commencement of the case. This includes all interests, such as interests in ... tangible and intangible property . . . [and] causes of action ... whether or not transferable by the debtor.

H.R. Rep. No. 595, 95th Cong., 2d Sess. 175 (1977). It would indeed frustrate this congressional policy if, while avoiding such "cumbersome ... state law analysis" in defining initially the bankruptcy estate, a court was required to engage in the same analysis in determining whether property is exempt from the estate.

In applying these considerations to the case before us, it is quite clear, we believe, that the district court was correct in refusing to consider Mr. Geise's personal injury claim to be an "exemption" under Wisconsin law. If the Wisconsin legislature had wished to exempt personal injury causes of action at the time Mr. Geise filed for bankruptcy, it certainly was under no obligation to include this property right within its general list of "exemptions" in order to preserve it for its residents. However, it was obliged to identify it with reasonable certainty as an exemption. [A]t no place in its statutes, or in the case law interpreting its statutes is there more than a whisper of an echo of the Wisconsin legislature's intent, during the relevant time period, to afford such protection to a personal injury action. ... While our decision in *Buda* held that such claims were not subject to sequestration, our opinion did not, literally or functionally, characterize the immunity from process found in §128.19 as an "exemption." As the district court discerned, *Buda* is simply too thin a reed to support a determination that at the time Mr. Geise filed for bankruptcy, the Wisconsin legislature had determined that personal injury causes of action were to be considered exemptions, as that term is normally used.

Because we believe the district court was correct in its decision that Mr. Geise's personal injury cause of action cannot be considered exempt from the bankruptcy estate, we affirm the judgment. * * *

OWEN v. OWEN

United States Supreme Court, 1991
500 U.S. 305

JUSTICE SCALIA DELIVERED THE OPINION OF THE COURT.

The Bankruptcy Code allows the States to define what property a debtor may exempt from the bankruptcy estate that will be distributed among his creditors. §522(b). The Code also provides that judicial liens encumbering exempt property can be eliminated. §522(f). The question in this case is whether that elimination can operate when the State has defined the exempt property in such a way as specifically to exclude property encumbered by judicial liens.

In 1975, Helen Owen, the respondent, obtained a judgment against petitioner Dwight Owen, her former husband, for approximately $160,000. The judgment was recorded in Sarasota County, Florida, in July 1976. Petitioner did not at that time own any property in Sarasota County, but under Florida law, the judgment would attach to any after-acquired property recorded in the county. ... In 1984, petitioner purchased a condominium in Sarasota County; upon acquisition of title, the property became subject to respondent's judgment lien. * * *

One year later, Florida amended its homestead law so that petitioner's condominium, which previously had not qualified as a homestead, thereafter did. Under the Florida Constitution, homestead property is "exempt from forced sale ... and no judgment, decree or execution [can] be a lien thereon ... ," Fla. Const., Art. 10, §4(a). The Florida courts have interpreted this provision, however, as being inapplicable to pre-existing liens, i.e., liens that attached before the property acquired its homestead status. ... Pre-existing liens, then, are in effect an exception to the Florida homestead exemption.

In January 1986, petitioner filed for bankruptcy under Chapter 7, and claimed a homestead exemption in his Sarasota condominium. The condominium, valued at approximately $135,000, was his primary asset; his liabilities included· approximately $350,000 owed to the respondent. The bankruptcy court discharged petitioner's personal liability for these debts, and sustained, over respondent's objections, his claimed exemption.

The condominium, however, remained subject to respondent's pre-existing lien, and after discharge, petitioner moved to reopen his case to avoid the lien pursuant to §522(f)(1). The Bankruptcy Court refused to decree the avoidance; the District Court affirmed, finding that the lien had attached before the property qualified for the exemption, and that Florida law therefore did not exempt the lien-encumbered property. ... The Court of Appeals for the Eleventh Circuit affirmed on the same ground. ... We granted certiorari. * * *

An estate in bankruptcy consists of all the interests in property, legal and equitable, possessed by the debtor at the time of filing, as well as those interests recovered or recoverable through transfer and lien avoidance provisions. An exemption is an interest withdrawn from the estate (and hence from the creditors) for the benefit of the debtor. Section 522 determines what property a debtor may exempt. Under §522(b), he must select between a list of federal exemptions (set forth in §522(d)) and the exemptions provided by his State, "unless the State law that is applicable to the debtor ... specifically does not so authorize"—that is, unless the State "opts out" of the federal list. If a State opts out, then its debtors are limited to the exemptions provided by state law. Nothing in subsection (b) (or elsewhere in the Code) limits a State's power to restrict the scope of its exemptions; indeed, it could theoretically accord no exemptions at all.

Property that is properly exempted under §522 is (with some exceptions) immunized against liability for prebankruptcy debts. §522(c). No property can be exempted (and thereby immunized), however, unless it first falls within the bankruptcy estate. Section 522(b) provides that the debtor may exempt certain property "from property of the estate"; obviously, then, an interest that is not possessed by the estate cannot be exempted. Thus, if a debtor holds only bare legal title to his house—if, for example, the house is subject to a purchase-money mortgage for its full value—then only that legal interest passes to the estate; the equitable interest remains with the mortgage holder, §541(d). And since the equitable interest does not pass to the estate, neither can it pass to the debtor as an exempt interest in property. Legal title will pass, and can be the subject of an exemption; but the property will remain subject to the lien interest of the mortgage holder. This was the rule of Long v. Bullard, 117 U.S. 617 (1886), codified in §522. Only where the Code empowers the court to avoid liens or transfers can an interest originally not within the estate be passed to the estate, and subsequently (through the claim of an exemption) to the debtor.

It is such an avoidance provision that is at issue here, to which we now turn. Section 522(f) reads as follows:

(f)[(1)] Notwithstanding any waiver of exemptions[...], the debtor may avoid the fixing of a lien on an interest of the debtor in property to the extent that such lien impairs an exemption to which the debtor would have been entitled under subsection (b) of this section, if such lien is—

[(A)] a judicial lien [...]; or

[(B)] a nonpossessory, nonpurchase-money security interest. * * *

The lien in the present case is a judicial lien, and we assume without deciding that it fixed "on an interest of the debtor in property." See Farrey v. Sanderfoot, 500 U.S. 291 (1991). The question presented by this case is whether it "impairs an exemption to which [petitioner] would have been entitled under subsection (b)." Since Florida has chosen to opt out of the listed federal exemptions, the only subsection (b) exemption at issue is the Florida homestead exemption described above. Respondent suggests that, to resolve this case, we need only ask whether the judicial lien impairs that exemption. It obviously does not, since the Florida homestead exemption is not assertable against pre-existing judicial liens. To permit avoidance of the lien, respondent urges, would not preserve the exemption but would expand it.

At first blush, this seems entirely reasonable. Several Courts of Appeals in addition to the Eleventh Circuit here have reached this result with respect to built-in limitations on state exemptions, though others have rejected it. What must give us pause, however, is that this result has been widely and uniformly rejected with respect to built-in limitations on the federal exemptions. Most of the federally listed exemptions (set forth in §522(d)) are explicitly restricted to the "debtor's aggregate interest" or the "debtor's interest" up to a maximum amount. See §522(d)(1)-(6), (8). If respondent's approach to §522(f) were applied, all of these exemptions (and perhaps others as well) would be limited by unavoided encumbering liens, see §522(c). The federal homestead exemption [applicable at the time of this case], for example, allows the debtor to exempt from the property of the estate "the debtor's aggregate interest, not to exceed $7,500 in value, in ... a residence." §522(d)(1). If respondent's interpretation of §522(f) were applied to this exemption, a debtor who owned a house worth $10,000 that was subject to a judicial lien for $9,000 would not be entitled to the full homestead exemption of $7,500 [applicable at the time of this case]. The judicial lien would not be avoidable under §522(f), since it does not "impair" the exemption, which is limited to the debtor's "aggregate interest" of $1,000. The uniform practice of bankruptcy courts, however, is to the contrary. To determine the application of §522(f) they ask not whether the lien impairs an exemption to which the debtor is in fact entitled, but whether it impairs an exemption to which he *would have been* entitled but for the lien itself.

As the preceding italicized words suggest, this reading is more consonant with the text of §522(f)—which establishes as the baseline, against which impairment is to be measured, not an exemption to which the debtor "is entitled," but one to which he "would have been entitled." The latter phrase denotes a state of affairs that is conceived or hypothetical, rather than actual, and requires the reader to disregard some element of reality. "Would have been" but for what? The answer given, with respect to the federal exemptions, has been but for the lien at issue, and that seems to us correct.

The only other conceivable possibility is but for a waiver—harking back to the beginning phrase of §522(f), "Notwithstanding any waiver of exemptions. ... " The use of contrary-to-fact construction after a "notwithstanding" phrase is not, however, common usage, if even permissible. Moreover, though one might employ it when the "notwithstanding" phrase is the main point of the provision in question ("Notwithstanding any waiver, a debtor shall retain those exemptions to which he would have been entitled under subsection (b)"), it would be most strange to employ it where the "notwithstanding" phrase, as here, is an aside. The point of §522(f) is not to exclude waivers (though that is done in passing, waivers are addressed directly in §522(e)) but to provide that the debtor may avoid the fixing of a lien. In that context, for every instance in which "would have been entitled" may be accurate (because the incidentally mentioned waiver occurred) there will be thousands of instances in which "is entitled" should have been used. It seems to us that "would have been entitled" must refer to the generality, if not indeed the universality, of cases covered by the provision; and on that premise the only conceivable fact we are invited to disregard is the existence of the lien.

This reading must also be accepted, at least with respect to the federal exemptions, if §522(f) is not to become an irrelevancy with respect to the most venerable, most common and most important exemptions. The federal exemptions for homestead (§522(d)(1)), for motor vehicles (§522(d)(2)), for household goods and wearing apparel (§522(d)(3)), and for tools of the trade (§522(d)(6)), are all defined by reference to the debtor's "interest" or "aggregate interest," so that if respondent's interpretation is accepted, no encumbrances of these could be avoided. Surely §522(f) promises more than that—and surely it would be bizarre for the federal scheme to prevent the avoidance of liens on those items, but to permit it for the less crucial items (for example, an "unmatured life insurance contract owned by the debtor," §522(d)(7)) that are not described in such fashion as unquestionably to exclude liens.

We have no doubt, then, that the lower courts' unanimously agreed-upon manner of applying §522(f) to federal exemptions—ask first whether avoiding the lien would entitle the debtor to an exemption, and if it would, then avoid and recover the lien—is correct. The question then becomes whether a different interpretation should be adopted for state exemptions. We do not see how that could be possible. Nothing in the text of §522(f) remotely justifies treating the two categories of exemptions differently. The provision refers to the impairment of "exemption[s] to which the debtor would have been entitled under subsection (b)," and that includes federal exemptions and state exemptions alike. Nor is there any overwhelmingly clear policy impelling us, if we possessed the power, to create a distinction that the words of the statute do not contain. Respondent asserts that it is inconsistent with the Bankruptcy Code's "opt-out" policy, whereby the States may define their own exemptions, to refuse to take those exemptions with all their built-in limitations. That is plainly not true, however, since there is no doubt that a state exemption which purports to be available "unless waived" will be given full effect, even if it has been waived, for purposes of §522(f)—the first phrase of which, as we have noted, recites that it applies "[n]otwithstanding any waiver of exemptions." ... Just as it is not inconsistent with the policy of permitting state-defined exemptions to have another policy disfavoring waiver of exemptions, whether federal or state-created; so also it is not inconsistent to have a policy disfavoring the impingement of certain types of liens upon exemptions, whether federal or state-created. We have no basis for pronouncing the opt-out policy absolute, but must apply it along with whatever other competing or limiting policies the statute contains.

On the basis of the analysis we have set forth above with respect to federal exemptions, and in light of the equivalency of treatment accorded to federal and state exemptions by §522(f), we conclude that Florida's exclusion of certain liens from the scope of its homestead protection does not achieve a similar exclusion from the Bankruptcy Code's lien avoidance provision. * * *

The judgment of the Court of Appeals is reversed, and the case remanded for proceedings consistent with this opinion.

It is so ordered.

Notes

11B.1. At its narrowest, *Geise* might seem to suggest that property is exempt only if a state labels it as exempt. But the court explicitly denies that its decision goes this far, noting that Wisconsin "certainly was under no obligation to include this property right within its general list of 'exemptions' in order to preserve it for its residents." Instead, the court said that it ruled against the exemption because the state was not clear enough. The court wanted to avoid a "cumbersome state law analysis." Consider Problem 11B-1 and ask yourself whether the holding in *Geise* will always save a court such cumbersome analysis.

11B.2. The question of labels versus attributes, presented by *Geise*, is important for a debtor faced with an election between bankruptcy exemptions and state (as well as substantive federal) exemptions. The bankruptcy exemptions need to be compared to the nonbankruptcy items that would be found on a list of exempt property, together with whatever other items (if any) a court might consider exempt because of similar attributes. Problem 11B-2 asks you to consider the possibility that the disregard for labels in a slightly different context could lead a debtor to choose the bankruptcy exemptions even when the state list of explicit exemptions is more generous.

11B.3. One should not jump to the conclusion that the *Owen* Court relied on labels in its disregard for the substance of Florida exemption law. An unencumbered homestead in Florida would be free from creditor reach even though, as the Court notes, "[p]re-existing liens . . . are in effect an exception to the Florida homestead exemption." That is, Florida law contemplated property that would be exempt but for an unavoidable lien. As the Supreme Court points out in *Owen*, albeit in belabored fashion, §522(f)(1) is about this very circumstance as it avoids otherwise enforceable liens on such property. It is quite another question why Congress would so limit a state's choice of exemption rules.

The *Owen* Court's common sense description of what "impairment" by a lien must mean is now codified in §522(f)(2). Problem 11B-3 revisits the larger issue the Court confronts in *Owen*.

PROBLEMS

11B-1. The state of Debtor's domicile lists as exempt property "a debtor's interest in household furnishings up to an aggregate value of $50,000." Debtor's only property is an eighteenth century collectible chair worth almost $100,000. Debtor attempts to exempt $50,000 of that value. Will Debtor succeed?

11B-2. Debtor is the beneficiary of a pension plan. Under applicable nonbankruptcy law, Debtor's interest in the plan is inalienable and beyond the reach of Debtor's creditors. Debtor's interest in the plan qualifies as an exempt asset on his home state's list of such assets, but it is not a qualified plan or exempt from taxation under the Internal Revenue Code. Should Debtor elect the §522(b)(2) or (b)(3) exemptions, assuming that Debtor's interest in the plan is his most important asset? In answering this question consider, among other provisions, §§522(d)(10)(E) and 541(c)(2). Consider also Note 6A.2. See also Patterson v. Shumate, 504 U.S. 753 (1992).

11B-3. Debtor's home state requires that Debtor use its exempt property list, which includes "a debtor's interest in a homestead unless the homestead is subject to a lien." At the time of Debtor's bankruptcy petition, her home is subject to a judicial lien. Can Debtor avoid this lien?

C. SCOPE OF THE DISCHARGE

Whatever the disposition of an individual debtor's property, an important reason for an individual to file for bankruptcy is the discharge that protects her future income from prebankruptcy claims. The basic discharge provision for an individual is Bankruptcy Code §727(b), which generally discharges a Chapter 7 debtor from all debts that arose before the bankruptcy case. In Chapter 13, after the debtor completes his plan payments §1328(a) similarly provides a discharge, in this case of all debts provided for under the debtor's plan, that is, up to all prepetition obligations. Also in Chapter 13, under §1328(b), (c), even a debtor who fails to complete his plan payments can, under specified circumstances and with court permission, receive a discharge of unsecured claims provided for under the plan if the debtor has paid on these claims an amount of a value at least equal to what the holders of the claims would have received in a Chapter 7 liquidation. This is discussed in the book's next chapter. Turning to Chapter 11, in the unusual case of an individual debtor, §1141 discharges all debts incurred prior to the confirmation of the plan. Chapter 11 is addressed in the book's final chapter.

Against the background is a litany of specific exceptions. (Grounds for overall denial of, rather than exceptions to, discharge are discussed in the next section.) Section 523(a) applies to any discharge other than that of a debtor who completes all payments under a Chapter 13 plan. It excepts from discharge, among other claims, many income tax liabilities (including those granted priority under §507(a)(8), discussed in the previous chapter), debts for loans fraudulently obtained, debts for fraud while acting as a fiduciary, claims that the debtor failed to disclose to the bankruptcy court, domestic support obligations (as defined by §101(14A)), obligations to repay student loans, liability for willful or malicious injury, liability for death or personal injury caused by driving while intoxicated, and payments required as restitution for a criminal violation of federal law. In addition, a Chapter 13 debtor granted a discharge despite her failure to make all plan payments cannot discharge a long-term obligation the payments on which she chose to maintain under the plan. See §1328(c)(1). The maintenance of such obligation, typically in connection with a mortgage, is discussed below in chapter 12, section B of this book.

For a debtor who completes all payments under a Chapter 13 plan, there is a separate list of exceptions to discharge under §1328, which is narrower than §523(a), presumably to reflect the debtor's voluntary payment of prebankruptcy debts from postbankruptcy income. The list of debts excepted from discharge in Chapter 13 despite completion of plan payments includes those for the debtor's bad acts as well as domestic support obligations; moreover, no Chapter 13 discharge is allowed at all unless the debtor is current on domestic support obligations.

The treatment of domestic support obligations in Chapter 13 reflects the controversy generated in the debate over the 2005 Bankruptcy Act. As described above in chapter 3, section C of this book, the 2005 Act limits access to a Chapter 7 discharge by high-income debtors. It was expected that these debtors would either not file for bankruptcy or be channeled into Chapter 13. There was a concern that, in either case, nondischargeable domestic support obligations would compete with debts that would have been discharged in Chapter 7. This raises the more general point that a creditor owed a nondischargeable obligation is not merely indifferent to a debtor's bankruptcy. Such a creditor welcomes the debtor's bankruptcy and the debtor's relief from *other* obligations.

As you consider the individual exceptions to dischargeable debt, don't lose sight of the broader fact that the discharge is limited to debt itself. As you will recall from chapter 5, section A above, "debt" is defined in §101 by reference to a "claim," which is in turn defined as a right to payment. Consequently, whatever one thinks an individual debtor's fresh start should include, the bankruptcy discharge is in fact limited to financial obligations. So a debtor cannot use a bankruptcy filing to evade a prison sentence or a child-custody order, for example, even though neither obligation is listed as an exception to discharge.

Where discharge is applicable, at a minimum it operates as an injunction against the commencement or continuation of any lawsuit to collect, recover, or offset a discharged claim. This is provided by §524, which describes the effects of discharge. Section 524 further protects the individual's fresh start by providing that a discharge generally operates as an injunction against *any act* to collect, recover, or offset such a claim. The coverage of the injunction is not limited to a legal action. So, for example, after bankruptcy a creditor cannot telephone its debtor and exhort it to pay. But application of the prohibition will not always be easy or clear. Issues will arise similar to those presented by questions of what creditor actions fall outside the automatic stay because they are not efforts to collect a debt. For example, a college might regularly provide transcripts to its graduates, but it may refuse to do so for those who fell behind on their student loan payments.

There is, in addition, another protection related to discharge that is afforded an individual debtor in bankruptcy. Bankruptcy Code §525 limits the ability of two parties, the government and the debtor's employer, to discriminate against someone who has filed a bankruptcy petition, even if neither party had been a creditor of the debtor at all. In general, a government may not refuse to grant a license to, and an employer may not discriminate with respect to employment of, an individual (or an associate of a person) who has been a debtor in bankruptcy, who has been insolvent prior to or during bankruptcy, or who has not paid a dischargeable debt. This nondiscrimination provision constrains only a government in its capacity as grantor and an employer qua employer. Moreover, it does not apply against anyone to protect a debtor who has financially foundered again after the debtor's (most recent) bankruptcy relief. Thus, it is incorrect to state broadly that the law bars discrimination based on bankruptcy or financial distress.

The exercises below ask you to work through the mechanics in some of these discharge and antidiscrimination provisions. (In this regard, you may also want to consider the exercises in this book's next section.) The case that follows, *Edgeworth*, as well as the related notes and problem explore the question of how one should distinguish between an obligation owed by a debtor, which is discharged in bankruptcy, and an obligation owed by any other entity, even an entity associated with the debtor, explicitly excluded from discharge by Bankruptcy Code §524(e).

Key Provisions: Bankruptcy Code §§523; 524; 525

EXERCISES

11C(1) A month before Debtor files for bankruptcy under Chapter 7, Debtor borrows $15,000 on her credit cards and goes on a cruise. Are these credit card obligations dischargeable? Would it matter whether Debtor's employer went out of business shortly after Debtor returned from vacation? In answering these questions consider §523(a)(2)(C).

11C(2) Debtor has a loan from Bank. Debtor encounters financial difficulties and returns to Bank for an additional loan, which Debtor obtains through false statements. Debtor then files for bankruptcy under Chapter 7. To what extent, if any, is Debtor's obligation to Bank dischargeable?

11C(3) Abel lends money to Baker and holds Baker's coin collection as collateral. In violation of their agreement, Abel sells Baker's coins and spends the proceeds, which exceed the amount Baker owes Abel. When Baker learns of this act he sues Abel for the excess value of the coin collection. Abel files for bankruptcy under Chapter 7. Is Abel's obligation to Baker dischargeable?

11C(4) Debtor, a destitute student with a family to support, files for bankruptcy and receives a general discharge while he owes his last semester's tuition to University, a private institution. Shortly after the discharge, Debtor applies for a variety of jobs. Debtor wishes to provide his potential employers with his academic record and requests a transcript from University, which cites a policy not to provide transcripts to deadbeats. May Debtor demand the transcript? In answering this question consider, among other factors, §523(a)(8). Recall Problem 4A-2.

11C(5) Debtor is liable for damages she negligently inflicted in a traffic accident. More than a year after the tort judgment against her, Debtor files for bankruptcy while the judgment remains unpaid. Shortly after Debtor's bankruptcy, Debtor applies to renew her driver's license. State refuses to renew the license unless she posts a $25,000 bond against any future liability from traffic accidents. State does not require this bond from all drivers, just those who have allowed a liability from an accident to go unpaid for more than one year. May State withhold the license?

CASE

HOUSTON v. EDGEWORTH

United States Court of Appeals, Fifth Circuit, 1993
993 F.2d 51

JONES, CIRCUIT JUDGE.

Christine Genson, [appellant Houston's] mother, died on June 7, 1989, while under the care of appellee Dr. Lewis Edgeworth. A month later, Edgeworth filed for protection under Chapter 7. Appellants did not participate in the bankruptcy case but, after Edgeworth received a discharge, they sought and obtained bankruptcy court approval to file a medical malpractice claim in state court. Shortly afterward, Edgeworth persuaded the bankruptcy court to reverse itself—to enforce his discharge by enjoining the lawsuit pursuant to §524(a). The district court affirmed. The question before us is whether the appellants may pursue their lawsuit against Dr. Edgeworth in order to collect any judgment solely from the proceeds of his malpractice liability policy. We hold that they may do so, because §524(e) excludes the liability insurance carrier from the protection of bankruptcy discharge and the proceeds of the policy were not property of Edgeworth's estate. * * *

The bankruptcy court and district court enjoined appellants from proceeding with their state court lawsuit against Dr. Edgeworth because they apparently believed that the malpractice claim was discharged under §727 and §524. In general, §524 protects a debtor from any subsequent action by a creditor whose claim has been discharged in a bankruptcy case. To ensure that a discharge will be completely effective, it operates as an injunction against enforcement of a judgment or the commencement or continuation of an action in other courts to collect or recover a debt as a personal liability of the debtor. A discharge in bankruptcy does not extinguish the debt itself, but merely releases the debtor from personal liability for the debt. Section 524(e) specifies that the debt still exists and can be collected from any other entity that might be liable.

In the liability insurance context, of course, a tort plaintiff must first establish the liability of the debtor before the insurer becomes contractually obligated to make any payment. The question, then, is whether §524(a) acts to bar such liability-fixing suits even if a plaintiff has agreed to forswear recovery from the debtor personally and to look only to the policy proceeds.

Most courts have held that the scope of a §524(a) injunction does not affect the liability of liability insurers and does not prevent establishing their liability by proceeding against a discharged debtor. This interpretation is grounded in both textual and equitable foundations. Section 524(a)(2) enjoins only suits "to collect, recover or offset" a debt as the "personal liability of the debtor," a phrase that has been interpreted to exclude merely nominal liability. In re Fernstrom Storage and Van Co., [938 F.2d 731, 733-34 (7th Cir. 1991)].

The foundation of this reading of §524(a)(2) is that it makes no sense to allow an insurer to escape coverage for injuries caused by its insured merely because the insured receives a bankruptcy discharge. "The 'fresh-start' policy is not intended to provide a method by which an insurer can escape its obligations based simply on the financial misfortunes of the insured." [In re Jet Florida Systems, Inc., 883 F.2d 970, 975 (11th Cir. 1989).] * * *

Finally, allowing commencement or continuation of such actions does not inequitably burden the debtor. Burden there is, in the sense that attending depositions and trial may take up Edgeworth's time. But this is not a burden alleviated by §524 when the purpose of the suit is to establish Edgeworth's nominal liability in order to collect from his insurance policy. Edgeworth has not asserted that he will be required to pay the costs of his defense against appellants' suit or that the insurance company denied coverage or is defending under a reservation of rights. Such threats to Edgeworth's pocketbook might require a different result under §524. Thus, as long as the costs of defense are borne by the insurer and there is no execution on judgment against the debtor personally, §524(a) will not bar a suit against the discharged debtor as the nominal defendant.

Edgeworth makes much of the fact that the appellants never filed a claim in the bankruptcy proceeding, and it is true that their failure to do so waived their ability to recover from Edgeworth personally. But, at least in a case like this where no question has been raised about the sufficiency of the liability insurance coverage, a plaintiff's failure to file in the bankruptcy proceeding should not impair the right to file suit against another party who may be liable on the debt. * * *

As part of his argument that Houston's claim is barred, Edgeworth also asserts that the insurance proceeds sought by Houston were part of the bankruptcy estate and may not now be recovered. Edgeworth does not argue that these "insurance proceeds" literally came into the estate and were distributed as part of his Chapter 7 liquidation. In fact, Edgeworth never explicitly tendered the insurance policy or any insurance proceeds into the bankruptcy estate. Instead, Edgeworth argues that the insurance proceeds were part of the estate as a matter of law and that his discharge acted to bar forever any prepetition claims against the insurance policy.

"Property of the estate," defined in §541(a), includes all legal or equitable interests of the debtor in property as of the commencement of the case. This definition is intended to be broadly construed, and courts are generally in agreement that an insurance policy will be considered property of the estate. Insurance policies are property of the estate because, regardless of who the insured is, the debtor retains certain contract rights under the policy itself. Any rights the debtor has against the insurer, whether contractual or otherwise, become property of the estate.

Acknowledging that the debtor owns the policy, however, does not end the inquiry. "The question is not who owns the policies, but who owns the liability proceeds." [In re Louisiana World Exposition, Inc., 832 F.2d 1391, 1399 (5th Cir. 1987).] In In re Louisiana World Exposition, Inc., for example, even though the policy was property of the estate, the proceeds of the liability policy were payable to the directors and officers of the corporation and were not part of the debtor's estate. Likening the circumstances before it to cases in which a purchaser of an insurance policy assigned its proceeds to other entities, the court noted that ownership of a policy "does not inexorably lead to ownership of the proceeds." [Id. at 1401.]

The overriding question when determining whether insurance proceeds are property of the estate is whether the debtor would have a right to receive and keep those proceeds when the insurer paid on a claim. When a payment by the insurer cannot inure to the debtor's pecuniary benefit, then that payment should neither enhance nor decrease the bankruptcy estate. In other words, when the debtor has no legally cognizable claim to the insurance proceeds, those proceeds are not property of the estate.

Examples of insurance policies whose proceeds are property of the estate include casualty, collision, life, and fire insurance policies in which the debtor is a beneficiary. Proceeds of such insurance policies, if made payable to the debtor rather than a third party such as a creditor, are property of the estate and may inure to all bankruptcy creditors. But under the typical liability policy, the debtor will not have a cognizable interest in the proceeds of the policy. Those proceeds will normally be payable only for the benefit of those harmed by the debtor under the terms of the insurance contract.

Although Dr. Edgeworth's liability policy was part of the Chapter 7 estate, the proceeds of that policy were not. Dr. Edgeworth has asserted no claim at all to the proceeds of his medical malpractice liability policy, and they could not be made available for distribution to the creditors other than victims of medical malpractice and their relatives. Moreover, no secondary impact has been alleged upon Edgeworth's estate, which might have occurred if, for instance, the policy limit was insufficient to cover appellants' claims or competing claims to proceeds. Consequently, in this case the insurance proceeds were not part of the estate as a matter of law, and §524 does not bar appellants from pursuing their state court suit against Dr. Edgeworth so they can recover against policy proceeds.

NOTES

11C.1. The court's opinion in *Edgeworth* might be understood as a triumph of substance over form. The plaintiff's suit in the case does seem to be "an action" to collect a discharged debt "as a personal liability of the debtor" as proscribed by §524(a)(2). But the plaintiff did not seek collection of this personal liability *from* the debtor. And, as the court notes, §524(e) provides that discharge of a debtor's liability does not affect anyone else's liability on the same obligation. It seems, therefore, that the spirit of subsection (e) would be violated if subsection (a) prohibited establishment of the insurance company's liability. Keep in mind, however, that Dr. Edgeworth contested this suit against him and thus must have had something at stake despite the discharge. One might argue, therefore, that any such suit over the debtor's objection deprives the debtor of the benefits discharge is designed to provide. Problem 11C asks you to consider this argument in a context in which the grounds for a debtor's objection are more apparent and substantial.

11C.2. Courts have wrestled with the question of the extent to which proceeds of an insurance policy are "property of the estate." See Homsy v. Floyd, 51 F.3d 530 (5th Cir. 1995). To get a sense of the difficulties, consider the case that arises when two physicians are in practice together and share a malpractice policy. Each has malpractice claims that exceed the policy limits. One files for bankruptcy. The extent to which the proceeds are property of the estate may affect the extent to which victims of the bankrupt physician's malpractice recover on their claims.

PROBLEM

11C. Debtor, a livery cab driver, rents his vehicle from Lessor, who arranges for its lessee's auto insurance. To give its drivers the proper incentives, Lessor maintains a policy of rebating annually 50 percent of all "excess" insurance premiums to the drivers. Excess premiums are total annual premiums less claims paid on accidents that occur during the year. If an accident case is pending at the close of any year, Lessor holds any excess premium until the case is resolved. Debtor negligently causes an auto accident that injures Victim. Debtor promptly files for bankruptcy to discharge liability from the accident. Later, Victim sues Debtor for damages from Victim's injuries. Should the trial court permit this suit? If so, and Victim wins, can Lessor deduct the award from any prior excess owed Debtor?

D. DENIAL OF DISCHARGE

Aside from the §523 exceptions described above, the Bankruptcy Code offers an individual debtor relief that is usually an all-or-nothing affair. Our focus here is on the conditions that can yield an entire denial of discharge. Most, but not all, of these are related to bad conduct.

Section 727 lists acts that lead to an outright denial of discharge under Chapter 7, which, through §1141(d)(3)(C), also constitute grounds for denial of discharge under Chapter 11. Many of these activities have one attribute in common: They can be considered forms of fraud or related egregious misbehavior directed against creditors or their collection efforts. An intentional fraudulent conveyance of assets, or other act to deprive creditors of assets, within a year prior to the bankruptcy case is ground for denial of discharge under §727(a)(2). Other acts of fraud or obstruction in connection with the bankruptcy process are grounds for denial of discharge under §727(a)(3)-(7).

Many forms of behavior that we might consider more egregious do not deny the debtor a discharge. There is, for example, no exception in §727 for individuals who have committed arson or murder. The fact that society wants to deter the types of activities listed in §727 does not itself suggest that the proper or only way to achieve such deterrence is through denial of discharge. Fines, prison terms, and other such criminal or quasi-criminal sanctions are alternatives (sometimes used in conjunction with denial of discharge). That is, it is not clear why a con artist who hides assets is denied a discharge while an armed robber who is caught with the loot is not. Either activity may be discouraged or punished with denial of discharge or prison or both, yet only the con artist faces both.

There are other grounds to deny discharge. For example, §727(a)(1) denies a Chapter 7 discharge to any debtor that is not an individual. This leaves a legally constructed debtor, such as a corporation, an empty shell harmlessly subject to unpaid debt, and leaves investors in such a debtor to rely on limited liability, if available, under applicable nonbankruptcy law. Chapter 7 also limits successive filings. Section 727(a)(8) prohibits discharge under Chapter 7 if a discharge has been granted in a Chapter 7 or 11 case commenced within eight years of the petition in the case at issue. Section 727(a)(9) similarly denies a discharge within six years of a case under Chapter 13 (or 12) where a discharge was granted unless the earlier discharge followed at least 70% of plan payments on unsecured claims and debtor made an honest effort at full compliance. Also, in a provision added by the 2005 Bankruptcy Act, §727(a) conditions discharge of an individual in bankruptcy on completion of an instructional course in personal financial management if such debtor is capable of taking such course and such course is available.

A discharge in Chapter 13 will not be granted until four years since the debtor's most recent discharge in Chapter 7, 11, or 12 and two years since the debtor's most recent discharge in Chapter 13. Also, as in Chapter 7, a discharge is conditioned on completion of a course in financial management if the debtor is capable of taking such a course and the course is available. Note that discharge under Chapter 13 (or 12) is not as restrictive as under Chapters 7 and 11, presumably because, as will be discussed in this book's next chapter, under Chapter 13 (or 12) creditors can require a debtor to pay disposable income toward satisfaction of prebankruptcy obligations as a condition of discharge. Thus, there is presumably less reason to deny a discharge outright.

The exercises below ask you to consider some specific cases of discharge. The case that follows, *Norwest Bank Nebraska*, as well as the related notes and problem ask you to explore the extent to which conscious planning in anticipation of bankruptcy can lead to a denial of discharge. The case grows out of a debtor with substantial business debts who chose to use Chapter 11. The scope of the discharge and the relevant legal principles, however, would be the same under Chapter 7.

Key Provisions: Bankruptcy Code §§707(b); 727

EXERCISES

11D(1) While drunk, Debtor commits vehicular homicide. The civil liability from the accident combined with Debtor's loan obligations overwhelms Debtor, who files for bankruptcy under Chapter 7. Will Debtor obtain a discharge?

11D(2) Debtor is a refrigerator mechanic who sold Christmas trees in an otherwise empty lot as a part-time, unincorporated business during the Christmas season. Debtor's business was cash-and-carry. Debtor never maintained any books or records. When Debtor filed for bankruptcy under Chapter 7, Debtor could not comply with the trustee's request to produce all business records. Will Debtor obtain a discharge?

11D(3) While a senior in college, Debtor joins her friends in an annual ritual of harvesting a Christmas tree from campus grounds and placing it in the lobby of a student dorm. This year, the students pick the wrong tree, which was part of a science experiment at the college's agriculture department. The college, within its rights, agrees to grant Debtor the computer science degree she had earned only on the condition that she and her friends agree to pay the school $200,000 over ten years as compensation for the lost experiment. Shortly after graduation, Debtor's friends disappear, leaving Debtor to pay the entire $20,000 per year. Three years into the payments, Debtor, a well-compensated engineer at a software company, finishes repayment of her student loans and files for bankruptcy under Chapter 7. Debtor has no assets, and her only debt is the Christmas tree obligation. Will Debtor obtain a discharge? Would your answer change if, just before filing for bankruptcy, Debtor unexpectedly incurred modest but significant uninsured medical expenses?

11D(4) Slightly more than two months before Debtor files for bankruptcy under Chapter 7, Debtor maxes out his credit cards, borrowing $15,000 for a luxury cruise. Will Debtor obtain a discharge? Would your answer change if the stock market crashed while Debtor was away? If there were no crash of the market as a whole, but Debtor's single investment, bought on a hunch, plummeted in value? If Debtor had no stock investment but lost all his money betting "red" on the cruise-ship roulette wheel? If Debtor neither had a stock market investment nor gambled, but arrived home from the cruise three days late and was fired for his failure to show up to work on schedule?

11D(5) Debtor runs a small, unincorporated business that hits on hard times. Debtor, already deeply indebted, obtains a new loan from Bank. In Debtor's written application for the loan Debtor exaggerates his business revenues from the prior year. The new loan does not help, and Debtor files for bankruptcy under Chapter 7. In response to a request for information from the bankruptcy trustee, Debtor turns over records that include the false information used to obtain the loan from Bank. Will Debtor obtain a discharge? Would your answer change if Debtor's prepetition fraud were to hide assets from Bank when Bank attempted to collect on its loan? Would your answer change if Debtor filed under Chapter 11?

CASE

NORWEST BANK NEBRASKA v. TVETEN

United States Court of Appeals, Eighth Circuit, 1988
848 F.2d 871

TIMBERS, CIRCUIT JUDGE.

Appellant Omar A. Tveten, a physician who owed creditors almost $19,000,000, mostly in the form of personal guaranties on a number of investments whose value had deteriorated greatly, petitioned for Chapter 11 bankruptcy. He had converted almost all of his nonexempt property, with a value of about $700,000, into exempt property that could not be reached by his creditors. The bankruptcy court, on the basis of its findings of fact and conclusions of law, entered an order on February 27, 1987, denying a discharge in view of its finding that Tveten intended to defraud, delay, and hinder his creditors. The district court . . . affirmed the bankruptcy court's order. On appeal, Tveten asserts that his transfers merely constituted astute prebankruptcy planning. We hold that the bankruptcy court was not clearly erroneous in inferring fraudulent intent on the part of Tveten. We affirm. * * *

Tveten is a 59-year-old physician in general practice. He is the sole shareholder of Omar A. Tveten, P.A., a professional corporation. He has no dependents. He began investing in various real estate developments. These investments initially were quite successful. Various physician friends of Tveten joined him in organizing a corporation to invest in these ventures. These investments were highly leveraged. The physicians, including Tveten, personally had guaranteed the debt arising out of these investments. In mid-1985, Tveten's investments began to sour. He became personally liable for an amount close to $19,000,000—well beyond his ability to pay. * * *

Before filing for bankruptcy, Tveten consulted counsel. As part of his prebankruptcy planning, he liquidated almost all of his nonexempt property, converting it into exempt property worth approximately $700,000. This was accomplished through some seventeen separate transfers. The nonexempt property he liquidated included land sold to his parents and his brother, respectively, for $70,000 and $75,732 in cash; life insurance policies and annuities with a for-profit company with cash values totaling $96,307; his net salary and bonuses of $27,820; his KEOGH plan and individual retirement fund of $20,487; his corporation's profit-sharing plan worth $325,774; and a home sold for $50,000. All of the liquidated property was converted into life insurance or annuity contracts with the Lutheran Brotherhood, a fraternal benefit association, which, under Minnesota law, cannot be attached by creditors. Tveten concedes that the purpose of these transfers was to shield his assets from creditors. Minnesota law provides that creditors cannot attach *any* money or other benefits payable by a fraternal benefit association. Unlike most exemption provisions in other states, the Minnesota exemption has no monetary limit. Indeed, under this exemption, Tveten attempted to place $700,000 worth of his property out of his creditors' reach.

Tveten sought a discharge with respect to $18,920,000 of his debts. Appellees objected to Tveten's discharge. In its order of February 27, 1987, the bankruptcy court concluded that, although Tveten's conversion of nonexempt property to exempt property just before petitioning for bankruptcy, standing alone, would not justify denial of a discharge, his inferred intent to defraud would. The bankruptcy court held that, even if the exemptions were permissible, Tveten had abused the protections permitted a debtor under the Bankruptcy Code (the "Code"). His awareness of Panuska's judgment against him and of several pending lawsuits, his rapidly deteriorating business investments, and his exposure to extensive liability well beyond his ability to pay, all were cited by the court in its description of the circumstances under which Tveten converted his property. Moreover, the court concluded that Tveten intended to hinder and delay his creditors. Accordingly, the bankruptcy court denied Tveten a discharge. * * *

The sole issue on appeal is whether Tveten properly was denied a discharge in view of the transfers alleged to have been in fraud of creditors.

At the outset, it is necessary to distinguish between (1) a debtor's right to exempt certain property from the claims of his creditors and (2) his right to a discharge of his debts. The Code permits a debtor to exempt property either pursuant to the provisions of the Code if not forbidden by state law, or pursuant to the provisions of state law and federal law other than the minimum allowances in the Code. When the debtor claims a state-created exemption, the scope of the claim is determined by state law. It is well established that under the Code the conversion of nonexempt to exempt property for the purpose of placing the property out of the reach of creditors, without more, will not deprive the debtor of the exemption to which he otherwise would be entitled. . . . Both the House and Senate Reports regarding the debtor's right to claim exemptions state:

> As under current law, the debtor will be permitted to convert non-exempt property into exempt property before filing a bankruptcy petition. The practice is not fraudulent as to creditors, and permits the debtor to make full use of the exemptions to which he is entitled under the law.

H.R. Rep. No. 595, 95th Cong., 1st Sess. 361 (1977); S. Rep. No. 989, 95th Cong., 2d Sess. 76 (1978). The rationale behind this policy is that "[t]he result which would obtain if debtors were not allowed to convert property into allowable exempt property would be extremely harsh, especially in those jurisdictions where the exemption allowance is minimal." 3 Collier on Bankruptcy ¶522.08[4], at 40 [(15th ed. 1984)]. This blanket approval of conversion is qualified, however, by denial of discharge if there was extrinsic evidence of the debtor's intent to defraud creditors. . . .

A debtor's right to a discharge, however, unlike his right to an exemption, is determined by *federal,* not state, law. . . . The Code provides that a debtor may be denied a discharge under Chapter 7 if, among other things, he has transferred property "with intent to hinder, delay, or defraud a creditor" within one year before the date of the filing of the petition. §727(a)(2). Although Tveten filed for bankruptcy under Chapter 11, the proscription against discharging a debtor with fraudulent intent in a Chapter 7 proceeding is equally applicable against a debtor applying for a Chapter 11 discharge. The reason for this is that the Code provides that confirmation of a plan does not discharge a Chapter 11 debtor if "the debtor would be denied a discharge under §727(a) of this title if the case were a case under Chapter 7 of this title." §1141(d)(3)(C) (1982).

Although the determination as to whether a discharge should be granted or denied is governed by federal law, the standard applied consistently by the courts is the same as that used to determine whether an exemption is permissible, i.e. absent extrinsic evidence of fraud, mere conversion of nonexempt property to exempt property is not fraudulent as to creditors even if the motivation behind the conversion is to place those assets beyond the reach of creditors. . . .

As the bankruptcy court correctly found here, therefore, the issue in the instant case revolves around whether there was extrinsic evidence to demonstrate that Tveten transferred his property on the eve of bankruptcy with intent to defraud his creditors. The bankruptcy court's finding that there was such intent to defraud may be reversed by us only if clearly erroneous. . . .

There are a number of cases in which the debtor converted non-exempt property to exempt property on the eve of bankruptcy and was granted a discharge because there was no extrinsic evidence of the debtor's intent to defraud. In [In re] Forsberg, [15 F.2d 499 (8th Cir. 1926)], an old decision of our Court, a debtor was granted a discharge despite his trade of nonexempt cattle for exempt hogs while insolvent and in contemplation of bankruptcy. Although we found that the trade was effected so that the debtor could increase his exemptions, the debtor "should [not] be penalized for merely doing what the law allows him to do." 15 F.2d at 501. We concluded that "before the existence of such fraudulent purpose can be properly found, there must appear in evidence some facts or circumstances which are extrinsic to the mere facts of conversion of nonexempt assets into exempt and which are indicative of such fraudulent purpose." Id. at 502. * * *

There also are a number of cases, however, in which the courts have denied discharges after concluding that there was extrinsic evidence of the debtor's fraudulent intent. In [In re] Ford, [773 F.2d 52 (4th Cir. 1985)], the debtor had executed a deed of correction transferring a tract of land to himself and his wife as tenants by the entirety. The debtor had testified that his parents originally had conveyed the land to the debtor alone, and that this was a mistake that he corrected by executing a deed of correction. Under relevant state law, the debtor's action removed the property from the reach of his creditors who were not also creditors of his wife. The Fourth Circuit, in upholding the denial of a discharge, found significant the fact that this "mistake" in the original transfer of the property was "corrected" the day after an unsecured creditor obtained judgment against the debtor. The Fourth Circuit held that the bankruptcy court, in denying a discharge, was not clearly erroneous in finding the requisite intent to defraud, after "[h]aving heard . . . [the debtor's] testimony at trial and having considered the circumstances surrounding the transfer." [773 F.2d at 55.] In In re Reed, [700 F.2d 986 (5th Cir. 1983)], shortly after the debtor had arranged with his creditors to be free from the payment obligations until the following year, he rapidly had converted nonexempt assets to extinguish one home mortgage and to reduce another four months before bankruptcy, and had diverted receipts from his business into an account not divulged to his creditors. The Fifth Circuit concluded that the debtor's "whole pattern of conduct evinces that intent." 700 F.2d at 991. The court went further and stated:

> It would constitute a perversion of the purposes of the Bankruptcy Code to permit a debtor earning $180,000 a year to convert every one of his major nonexempt assets into sheltered property on the eve of bankruptcy with actual intent to defraud his creditors and then emerge washed clean of future obligation by carefully concocted immersion in bankruptcy waters.

Id. at 992.

In most, if not all, cases determining whether discharge was properly granted or denied to a debtor who practiced "prebankruptcy planning," the point of reference has been the state exemptions if the debtor was claiming under them. Although discharge was not denied if the debtor merely converted his nonexempt property into exempt property as permitted under state law, the exemptions involved in these cases comported with federal policy to give the debtor a "fresh start"—by limiting the monetary value of the exemptions. This policy has been explicit, or at least implicit, in these cases. In *Fosberg,* for example, we stated that it is not fraudulent for an individual who knows he is insolvent to convert nonexempt property into exempt property, thereby placing the property out of the reach of creditors

> because the statutes granting exemptions have made no such exceptions, and because the policy of such statutes is to favor the debtors, at the expense of the creditors, *in the limited amounts allowed to them, by preventing the forced loss of the home and of the necessities of subsistence,* and because such statutes are construed liberally in favor of the exemption.

15 F.2d at 501 (emphasis added). Similarly, in In re Ellingson, 63 Bankr. 271 [(N.D. Iowa 1986)], in holding that the debtors' conversion of nonexempt cash and farm machinery did not provide grounds for denial of a discharge, the court relied on the social policies behind the exemptions. The court found that the debtors' improvement of their homestead was consistent with several of these policies, such as protecting the family unit from impoverishment, relieving society from the burden of supplying subsidized housing, and providing the debtors with a means to survive during the period following their bankruptcy filing when they might have little or no income. The court held that exemptions should further one or more of the following social policies:

> (1) To provide the debtor with property necessary for his physical survival; (2) To protect the dignity and the cultural and religious identity of the debtor; (3) To enable the debtor to rehabilitate himself financially and earn income in the future; (4) To protect the

debtor's family from the adverse consequences of impoverishment; (5) To shift the burden of providing the debtor and his family with minimal financial support from society to the debtor's creditors.

Id. at 277-78. * * *

In the instant case, however, the state exemption relied on by Tveten was unlimited, with the potential for unlimited abuse. Indeed, this case presents a situation in which the debtor liquidated almost his entire net worth of $700,000 and converted it to nonexempt property in seventeen transfers on the eve of bankruptcy while his creditors, to whom he owed close to $19,000,000, would be left to divide the little that remained in his estate. Borrowing the phrase used by another court, Tveten "did not want a mere *fresh* start, he wanted a *head* start." In re Zouhar, 10 Bankr. [154] at 156 [(Bankr. D. N. Mex. 1981)]. His attempt to shield property worth approximately $700,000 goes well beyond the purpose for which exemptions are permitted. Tveten's reliance on his attorney's advice does not protect him here, since that protection applies only to the extent that the reliance was reasonable. * * *

The bankruptcy court, as affirmed by the district court, examined Tveten's entire pattern of conduct and found that he had demonstrated fraudulent intent. We agree. While state law governs the legitimacy of Tveten's exemptions, it is federal law that governs his discharge. Permitting Tveten, who earns over $60,000 annually, to convert all of his major nonexempt assets into sheltered property on the eve of bankruptcy with actual intent to defraud his creditors "would constitute a perversion of the purposes of the Bankruptcy Code." In re Reed, 700 F.2d at 992. Tveten still is entitled to retain, free from creditors' claims, property rightfully exempt under relevant state law.

We distinguish our decision in Hanson v. First National Bank, 848 F.2d 866 (8th Cir. 1988), decided today. *Hanson* involves a creditor's objection to two of the debtors' claimed exemptions under South Dakota law, a matter governed by state law. The complaint centered on the Hansons' sale, while insolvent, of nonexempt property to family members for fair market value and their use of the proceeds to prepay their preexisting mortgage and to purchase life insurance policies in the limited amounts permissible under relevant state law. The bankruptcy court found no extrinsic evidence of fraud. The district court . . . affirmed. We also affirmed, concluding that the case fell within the myriad of cases which have permitted such a conversion on the eve of bankruptcy. * * *

We hold that the bankruptcy court was not clearly erroneous in inferring fraudulent intent on the part of the debtor, rather than astute prebankruptcy planning, with respect to his transfers on the eve of bankruptcy which were intended to defraud, delay and hinder his creditors.

Affirmed.

ARNOLD, Circuit Judge, dissenting.

The Court reaches a result that appeals to one's general sense of righteousness. I believe, however, that it is contrary to clearly established law, and I therefore respectfully dissent.

Dr. Tveten has never made any bones about what he is doing, or trying to do, in this case. He deliberately set out to convert as much property as possible into a form exempt from attachment by creditors under Minnesota law. Such a design necessarily involves an attempt to delay or hinder creditors, in the ordinary, non-legal sense of those words, but, under long-standing principles embodied both in judicial decisions and in statute, such a purpose is not unlawful. The governing authority in this Court is Forsberg v. Security State Bank, 15 F.2d 499 (8th Cir. 1926). There we said:

> It is well settled that it is not a fraudulent act by an individual who knows he is insolvent to convert a part of his property which is not exempt into property which is exempt, for the purpose of claiming his exemptions therein, and of thereby placing it out of the reach of his creditors.

Id. at 501. Thus, under the controlling law of this Circuit, someone who is insolvent may convert property into exempt form for the very purpose of placing that property beyond the reach of his creditors. * * *

If there ought to be a dollar limit, and I am inclined to think that there should be, and if practices such as those engaged in by the debtor here can become abusive, and I admit that they can, the problem is simply not one susceptible of a judicial solution according to manageable objective standards. A good statement of the kind of judicial reasoning that must underlie the result the Court reaches today appears in In re Zouhar, 10 Bankr. 154 (Bankr. D. N.M. 1981), where the amount of assets converted was $130,000. The Bankruptcy Court denied discharge, stating, among other things, that "there is a principle of too much; phrased colloquially, when a pig becomes a hog it is slaughtered." Id. at 157. If I were a member of the Minnesota Legislature, I might well vote in favor of a bill to place an over-all dollar maximum on any exemption. But as a sitting judge, by what criteria do I determine when this pig becomes a hog? If $700,000 is too much, what about $70,000? * * *

Debtors deserve more definite answers to these questions than the Court's opinion provides. In effect, the Court today leaves the distinction between permissible and impermissible claims of exemption to each bankruptcy judge's own sense of proportion. As a result, debtors will be unable to know in advance how far the federal courts will allow them to exercise their rights under state law.

Where state law creates an unlimited exemption, the result may be that wealthy debtors like Tveten enjoy a windfall that appears unconscionable, and contrary to the policy of the bankruptcy law. I fully agree with Judge Kishel, however, that

> [this] result . . . cannot be laid at [the] Debtor's feet; it must be laid at the feet of the state legislature. Debtor did nothing more than exercise a prerogative that was fully his under law. It cannot be said that his actions have so tainted him or his bankruptcy petition as to merit denial of discharge.

[In re Johnson, 80 Bankr. 953, 963 (Bankr. D. Minn. 1987).] I submit that Tveten did nothing more fraudulent than seek to take advantage of a state law of which the federal courts disapprove.

I would reverse this judgment and hold that the debtor's actions in converting property into exempt form do not bar a discharge in bankruptcy.

NOTES

11D.1. The court in *Tveten* emphasized that a debtor's right to a discharge, "unlike his right to an exemption, is determined by *federal, not state, law.*" One might argue that this is a highly formal distinction. If §727(a)(2) makes it impossible for a debtor to take advantage of a state's exemption provisions, then federal law in effect trumps state law on exemptions as well. To honor state law exemptions, it would follow, the federal courts would have to define the actions proscribed by §727(a)(2) so that they exclude investment in or the purchase of exempt property.

In response to such an argument, the court might have stressed less the size of the exemption Tveten sought and relied almost exclusively on the fact that the conversion of nonexempt to exempt property occurred on the "eve of bankruptcy." Nothing in §522, which grants states the right to determine exemptions, allows the states to permit eve-of-bankruptcy conversions. But "eve of bankruptcy" is not defined in the Code, so even this response fails to address the point made in dissent that denial of discharge in a case such as this would leave future debtors in doubt as to what conversions are or are not permissible under federal law.

11D.2. The propriety of asset conversion has become a politically contentious issue in the context of what is sometimes called "deadbeat jumping," in which a debtor borrows in a state with few exemptions and moves to a state with many. Problem 11D asks you to consider this issue further.

PROBLEM

11D. Debtor, a highly compensated architect, borrows $500,000 from Bank in a jurisdiction that has only a modest homestead exemption. Debtor then gets a new job and moves to another jurisdiction with an unlimited homestead exemption. Upon arrival, Debtor borrows an additional $100,000 from Finance Company and purchases a new home for $600,000. Just short of a year later, with no principal paid on either loan, Debtor files for bankruptcy under Chapter 7. Will Debtor obtain a discharge? Should she?

XII. ADJUSTMENT OF INDIVIDUAL DEBT IN CHAPTER 13

In Chapter 7, an individual debtor turns over her nonexempt property and in return is allowed to enjoy all of her future income. In Chapter 13, an individual debtor keeps all her nonexempt property, but she must give up some of her future income. A debtor might make a similar arrangement with creditors outside of bankruptcy through debt renegotiation. Even so, Chapter 13 can be valuable to a debtor because it allows the debtor to reach the same outcome even if some creditors prove recalcitrant. Moreover, Chapter 13 allows a debtor to discharge some claims that are not dischargeable under Chapter 7.

In contrast to Chapter 7, not every individual debtor is eligible for Chapter 13. Under §109, Chapter 13 is unavailable to those whose debts exceed set amounts—$336,900 and $1,010,650 for unsecured and secured debt respectively. (The dollar caps in §109 are adjusted every three years by regulation to reflect inflation as required by §104.) Chapter 13 is designed for working individual debtors or couples with limited financial affairs, typically consumers or proprietors of small businesses. Individuals with more at stake cannot use Chapter 13, perhaps because Chapter 11 is available to individuals, even those with sizeable personal or business obligations. Chapter 12 serves those who are farmers. But for others the only alternative to Chapter 7 is Chapter 11. As we shall see in the next chapter of this book, Chapter 11 is designed primarily for corporations. Its procedures are more elaborate and can be much more expensive than those of Chapter 13, but may be appropriate nonetheless for individuals with large obligations, particularly obligations generated by an individual's operation of a business.

As in Chapter 7, there is a trustee in every Chapter 13 case. See §1302. The debtor herself, however, is charged with moving the process forward. She must file a plan with the court that sets out the way in which her future income will be used to pay creditors. See §1321. The plan, which may modify or reduce the debtor's obligations, must oblige the debtor to pay her creditors from some or all of the debtor's future income. See §1322(b). Plan payments are generally limited to three years for low-income debtors, but the court may extend the period up to five years for cause (including the need to satisfy domestic support obligations, defined by §101(14A)), while higher-income debtors may propose a plan of up to five years without showing cause.

See §1322(a)(1), (d). The distinction between low- and high-income debtors, defined by reference to the median household income of the debtor's home state adjusted for family size, was added by the 2005 Bankruptcy Act.

The plan must also satisfy a series of important payment conditions. First, the plan must provide for the full satisfaction, in deferred cash payments, of all allowed claims and administrative expenses entitled to priority under §507 unless the holder of such a priority claim (or expense) agrees to some other treatment. See §1322 and chapter 10, section A above. Second, the plan must provide for the satisfaction of all allowed unsecured claims with property (including the debtor's new or continuing obligations) whose value, as of the effective date of the plan, is at least equal to the amount that the creditors would receive under Chapter 7 on that date. See §1325(a)(4). In theory, these provisions together ensure that creditors are no worse off than they would be if the debtor filed under Chapter 7.

The conditions imposed on Chapter 13 plans protect unsecured creditors in one more way. The holder of an allowed unsecured claim, or the trustee on a creditor's behalf, can demand that either the plan provide for full payment of a claim with interest or that the plan commit the debtor's "projected disposable income" to the repayment of creditors over the commitment period of the plan, a period that cannot be less than three years for a low-income debtor if general claims are not to be paid in full and cannot be less than five years for a high-income debtor if general claims are not to be paid in full or for any debtor if domestic support obligations are not to be paid in full. §§1325(b)(1), (4); 1322(a)(4). Disposable income is defined generally as "current monthly income," that term, as defined by §101(10A), "not reasonably necessary to be expended" for the maintenance or support of the debtor or a dependent of the debtor, for domestic support obligations, for limited charitable contributions, or for the continuation, preservation, and operation of the debtor's business. §1325(b)(2). For high-income debtors, amounts "reasonably necessary to be expended" are determined by reference to the means test applied to individuals in Chapter 7—see chapter 3, section C above— and include a combination of deemed and actual expenditures. §1325(b)(3).

Another important condition imposed on Chapter 13 plans protects holders of secured claims. If the plan provides that the debtor retain property securing a claim, the plan must provide for full payment of the secured claim unless the creditor consents to less. Recall, however, that under §506(a) claims are bifurcated. A creditor's claim is *secured* to the extent of the value of the collateral. The balance is the creditor's unsecured claim. Payment on the secured claim may occur over time, if paid with interest, but the debtor's obligation under the plan must be secured by a lien on the original collateral, which continues until the debtor either pays the loan in full under applicable nonbankruptcy law or earns a discharge in the Chapter 13 case. See §1325(a)(5). Note also that several provisions of Chapter 13, when taken together, cut back sharply on a debtor's ability to restructure a mortgage on her principal residence. See §1322(b)(2), (5), and (c). We focus on these provisions in section B below.

If a plan meets the requirements described above and otherwise complies with the provisions of Chapter 13—the requirements that the plan be made in good faith (see §1325(a)(3)) and that it be feasible (see §1325(a)(6)), e.g.—the court must confirm the plan. Keep in mind that confirmation does not conclude the bankruptcy case. In important respects, confirmation is a beginning. Even after the plan is confirmed, the bankruptcy case remains open. The debtor's creditors remain stayed from collection by §362 (and an individual co-liable with the debtor generally is protected by §1301). The debtor's postpetition acquisitions and earnings become property of the estate under §1306.

A debtor who successfully completes performance under a Chapter 13 plan holds property "free and clear of any claim or interest of any creditor provided for under the plan." See §1327(c). She also earns a discharge under §1328(a), provided that she satisfies a number of additional conditions. For example, she must complete a course in personal financial management if she is able to do so and must be current on any domestic support obligations. See §1328(a), (g). The discharge is subject to exceptions, set out primarily in §523. Note that there are fewer exceptions to discharge under Chapter 13 than under Chapter 7. For example, some tax obligations cannot be discharged in Chapter 7, but can be discharged in Chapter 13 even when the plan does not provide for paying them in full. Congress continues to expand the number of nondischargeable debts in Chapter 13, however, so this difference between the two chapters is likely to lessen over time.

If the debtor cannot meet payments under the plan, she may seek to modify it. See §1329. She may also request a discharge if creditors have already received as much as they would have received under Chapter 7. Such a discharge will be granted only if modification of the plan is not practicable and if the reason for the debtor's failure was an event beyond the debtor's control. See §1328(b). Moreover, as in the case of a discharge after completion of the plan, a debtor who makes partial payments is not eligible for a discharge unless she completes a course in personal financial management if able to do so. (And although the Code, as amended by the 2005 Act, is less than clear on this point, a debtor who seeks a discharge after only partial plan payments likely must comply with all other conditions applicable to one who completes payments, such as the condition that she remain current on domestic support obligation.) Even where a debtor qualifies for a discharge after partial plan payments, in such a case, the discharge does not extend beyond those debts that could have been discharged in Chapter 7. Thus, the debtor could not discharge any debt listed in §523(a). Moreover, a Chapter 13 debtor who makes only partial plan payments cannot discharge any secured claim or any long-term claim the debtor chose to maintain under the plan. See §1328(c) and the next section of this chapter.

The provisions of Chapter 13, in the main, are consistent with the notion that Chapter 13 is a procedure intended for the debtor's benefit. Involuntary petitions are not permitted under Chapter 13. See §303(a), discussed above in chapter 3, section B. And the debtor can always dismiss the case. See §1307(b). Until recently, moreover, a debtor under Chapter 13 could freely convert the case to one under Chapter 7. See §1307(a).However, matters have changed somewhat. In the 2005 Bankruptcy Act, Congress responded to those who argued that Chapter 13 should be the primary avenue of relief for those with substantial incomes and with the ability to repay a significant amount of their debt, Now individual debtors with relatively high incomes and the means to repay much of their debt are ineligible for a Chapter 7 discharge and thus are channeled into Chapter 13 cases. (Such debtors remain eligible for Chapter 11, but individuals cannot use that chapter to escape the payment obligations of Chapter 13. See §1129(a)(15).) This "means test" (as it is called), is described more fully above in chapter 3, section C of this book.

The logic of the 2005 reforms is straightforward. That is, those who can afford to repay their debts should be forced to do so, at least to some extent. The wisdom of making a means test part of the Bankruptcy Code, however, cannot rest on the notion that Chapter 13 has been an historical success. It hasn't been. Prior to means testing, only about one-third of those who filed under Chapter 13 completed their plans.

The means test notwithstanding, most debtors choose between using Chapter 7 and Chapter 13. Prior to the 2005 Bankruptcy Act, some tried to use the two in sequence. The typical case arose when a debtor owned commercial real estate that had fallen in value since the debtor subjected the property to a mortgage. By filing in Chapter 7, this debtor discharged his personal obligations, including his personal obligation to the real estate lender for the difference between the amount of the loan and the value of the collateral. After receiving a Chapter 7 discharge, however, the debtor still faced a lender with a lien on the real property for the entire amount of the debt. (Recall that, under *Dewsnup*, which appears above in chapter 11, part A of this book, debtors cannot strip down liens in Chapter 7.) The lender could foreclose unless the debtor paid the entire amount owed on the mortgage loan. The discharge of the lender's unsecured claim prevented the creditor only from seeking a deficiency judgment from the debtor on what it is still owed. The debtor, however, could prevent foreclosure if it then filed under Chapter 13 and proposed a plan that provided the lender with a payment stream equal to the present value of its secured claim, a claim worth considerably less than the outstanding amount of the mortgage loan. A debtor who has invested in commercial real estate may initially owe more than the Chapter 13 limit for debt obligations, but Chapter 7 discharges those debts and hence puts the debtor under the limit. The 2005 Act closed this "Chapter 20" loophole, which some courts allowed despite allegations of debtor bad faith, by imposing time limits on successive discharges. Now a debtor is ineligible for a Chapter.13 discharge if she has received a discharge under Chapter 7, 11, or 12 in the past 4 years or a discharge under Chapter 13 in the past 2 years.

The material below explores these issues further. Section A addresses the debtor's repayment obligation on unsecured claims. This obligation includes paying all disposable income to creditors if there is an objection from the trustee or the holder of an unsecured claim who is not paid in full. Section B addresses the treatment of secured claims, including the special treatment of claims secured only by the debtor's principal residence.

A.   REPAYMENT OBLIGATION ON UNSECURED CLAIMS

A debtor's Chapter 13 plan must propose to pay allowed unsecured claims at least the amount those claims would have received in Chapter 7. See §1325(a)(4). The trustee (or a creditor who is not being paid in full) may insist that, in addition, all of the debtor's projected disposable income for three or five year (depending on the debtor's income), be paid out under the plan. See §1325(b). In response to such insistence, the debtor can threaten to convert her case to Chapter 7. See §1307(a), (f). But this threat may not be credible. The debtor may have nonexempt assets that have a high subjective value. She would rather pay a creditor out of future income an amount even greater than what these assets are worth. Alternatively, the debtor may have a debt that is dischargeable in Chapter 13 but not in Chapter 7. Or the debtor may have already tried to use Chapter 7 but had her case dismissed under §707(b), perhaps because she failed the means test there. Under any of these circumstances, the disposable-income test can become the central focus of a Chapter 13 case.

After the exercises below explore some basics of the debtor's repayment obligation in Chapter 13, the next case, *Lanning*, addresses a series of issues related to the definition of projected disposable income under the 2005 Bankruptcy Act revisions; of particular interest there is the distinction, if any, between disposable income and *projected* disposable income. In *Jones*, the case that follows, the court examines a fundamental question of how to characterize expenses for the purpose of determining projected disposable income. When reading *Jones*, keep in mind that it was decided prior to the 2005 Bankruptcy Act. The related notes describe how the Act would have affected the holding in the case and, like the related problem, further explore the requirements for plan confirmation when disposable income is at issue.

Key Provisions: Bankruptcy Code §1325(a), (b)

EXERCISES

12A(1) Debtor, who is single and works as a finance professor at a local college, files for bankruptcy under Chapter 13. Debtor's only substantial obligation is to Bank for $200,000 on an unsecured loan. Debtor's only substantial asset is a diamond necklace. At a reasonably conducted auction, the necklace would be expected to bring $75,000 more than the applicable exemption for jewelry. Debtor earns $100,000 per year and lives modestly. She proposes a plan under which she would retain the necklace and would pay Bank $20,000 per year for five years. The plan would pay all miscellaneous claims and expenses in full. Bank alone objects to the plan. What are Bank's likely grounds for objection? Will Bank prevail? Might your answer depend on whether Debtor lives in Alaska or New York? Are Debtor's plan and Bank's objection easier to understand if the necklace is a family heirloom?

12A(2) Debtor runs a small grocery that she inherited from her parents. Debtor defaults on her only substantial obligation, a still unpaid $200,000 unsecured loan to Bank. After reviewing the business, Bank tells Debtor that it is time to call it quits. Bank finds a buyer for the grocery willing to pay $100,000 and run it as part of a chain, with Debtor hired on as a manager if she wishes. Debtor wants to continue her independent family business and declines the offer. Debtor then files for bankruptcy under Chapter 13. Debtor's plan calls for her to retain the grocery, her only asset, and to pay Bank $100,000 in cash immediately. The cash for Bank would be a gift to Debtor from Debtor's cousin, who loved Debtor's parents and would hate to see the family lose the grocery. The plan provides for no other payments to Bank. Debtor argues that no other payments are necessary, as "every free penny is needed to keep the business afloat." Bank does not contest that statement, but argues that this is precisely why Debtor should not keep the business. Bank believes that Debtor is just wasting her money on this business, which in Bank's view can survive in the long run only as part of a chain. Can Bank block Debtor's plan?

12A(3) Debtor, a deeply religious church deacon, has tithed for his entire adult life, paying his church 10 percent of his wages, earned as a social worker. After Debtor's son suffers a serious accident that wipes out Debtor's life savings, Debtor files for bankruptcy under Chapter 13. Debtor chooses Chapter 13 rather than Chapter 7 because he wants to keep his family home, the value of which is mainly nonexempt, and which his injured son has come to love. Debtor's plan proposes to pay unsecured creditors substantially more than they would receive under Chapter 7, but withholds from creditors the amount of the tithe, which Debtor intends to continue. Assuming that the plan has no defects other than perhaps the tithe, can the court confirm over the objection of the bankruptcy trustee? Would your answer change if Debtor were not a church deacon but a self-employed ne'er-do-well who lost his money at the track and intends to make the first charitable contributions of his life because he despises his creditors, to whom he refers as "bloodsucking leaches"?

12A(4) Debtor files for bankruptcy under Chapter 13. Debtor's plan, which is confirmed by the bankruptcy court, proposes to pay the holders of unsecured claims 75 percent of their claims, plus interest, over three years, an amount calculated to pay something more than on the unsecured claims than they would have received in a Chapter 7 liquidation. Six months after confirmation of the plan, Debtor's mother becomes seriously ill. Debtor's mother cannot pay her medical bills, and has no one local to care of her. Debtor quits his job and moves to his mother's town, accepting a lower paying job. Perhaps as a karmic reward, he then promptly wins the lottery. Debtor's prepetition unsecured creditors move to have both the length of the plan and the payments under the plan increased. Debtor moves to have the payments under the plan reduced. Will either prevail? In answering this question consider, among other provisions, §1329 and compare §1323.

12A(5) Debtor files for bankruptcy under Chapter 13. At the time of the filing, Debtor owes $100,000 on unsecured claims and owns $25,000 of nonexempt, unencumbered assets. Debtor's plan, which is confirmed by the bankruptcy court, proposes to pay the holders of unsecured claims 50 percent over five years. Four months after filing for Chapter 13, Debtor receives an inheritance of $200,000. Can the creditors require the Debtor to increase the payments under the Chapter 13 plan? In answering this question consider, among other provisions, §1329 and compare §§541(a)(5), 1306. Would your answer change if Debtor received the inheritance eight months after filing for Chapter 13? See In re Koonce, 54 Bankr. 643 (Bankr. D. S.C. 1985); In re Euerle, 70 Bankr. 72 (Bankr. D. N.H. 1987); In re Arnold, 869 F.2d 240 (4th Cir. 1989).

CASES

IN RE LANNING

United States Bankruptcy Court, D. Kansas, 2007
2007 WL 1451999

KARLIN, BANKRUPTCY JUDGE.

The Chapter 13 Trustee has objected to confirmation of the plans in these two cases. In each case, the Debtor's actual income is considerably less than his or her historical income as a result of changes in employment that occurred in the six-month period prior to filing. The Court must interpret certain provisions of the Bankruptcy Code, as recently amended by the Bankruptcy Abuse Prevention and Consumer Protection Act of 2005 to decide whether the income shown on [Official Bankruptcy] Form B22C is determinative, or whether circumstances exist under which the Court may use [an alternative measure] to determine such debtors' projected disposable income. The Court must also determine over how many months an above-median income debtor must pay his or her creditors under the facts of these cases. * * *

Facts

Debtor [Lanning] filed her bankruptcy petition on October 26, 2006. Her Statement of Financial Affairs reflected income of $43,147 in 2004, and $56,516 in 2005, both of which put her above the median family income for a family of one in Kansas. Within the six months prior to filing, however, she took a buyout from her then employer, which caused her April 2006 gross income to total $11,990.03, and her May 2006 gross income to total $15,356.42—over three times her previous regular monthly income. Because of this buyout, her "current monthly income," (hereafter "CMI") as defined by [Bankruptcy Code] §101(10A), was skewed upwards to $64,124 per annum, or $5,343 a month.

In reality, at the time of filing, Debtor was no longer employed by the employer from whom she had earned the above-median income wages. Debtor's [Official Bankruptcy] Schedule I reflects net monthly income of $1,922, which, annualized, equals $23,064— considerably below the median income in Kansas. Debtor's [Official Bankruptcy] Schedule J reflects expenses of $1,772.97. A comparison of those two Schedules thus showed $149 excess income. Debtor's plan proposes to pay $144 per month for 36 months.

In contrast, through use of the expense deductions now required of above-median income debtors, Debtor's Form B22C reflects monthly expenses of $4,228. After subtracting Debtor's monthly expenses from her CMI, Line 58 of Form B22C indicates Debtor has "Monthly Disposable Income Under §1325(b)(2)" of $1,114 to pay to unsecured creditors. Obviously, because Debtor's income precipitously dropped since the six month look-back period, Debtor is unable to pay $1,114 per month to the Trustee, which amount represents almost 60% of Debtor's actual gross monthly income.

Although the Trustee acknowledges that Debtor would be unable to cash flow a plan at the $1,114 rate, that Debtor can only afford to pay the amount her plan proposes to pay, and makes no argument that her reduction in income occurred in bad faith, the Trustee nevertheless filed an objection to confirmation solely on the basis that "[t]he

Plan fails to provide that all of the Debtor's projected disposable income to be received in the applicable commitment period will be applied to make payments to unsecured creditors under the plan as required by 11 U.S.C. § 1325." In his brief, he argues that " ... 1325(b)(2) ... provide[s] a rigid, mechanical test by which a debtor's projected disposable income is to be determined, despite the potential for a different result under [a more flexible] analysis."

Debtor [Avila] filed his bankruptcy petition on December 8, 2006. Debtor's Form B22C shows that he is also an above-median income debtor based on the §101(10A) definition of current monthly income. During the six-month look back period, Debtor held one full time and two part time jobs, resulting in CMI of $5,686. At the time of filing, however, he had quit his two part time jobs because of the stress created by working over 14 hours a day. His "actual" income, as shown on Schedule I, was $5,200, which is still above-median income.

Debtor's Form B22C reflected expenses of $5,531.57, resulting in $155.09 monthly disposable income on Line 58. The expenses Debtor listed on Schedule J, however, totaled $3,489, leaving net excess disposable income of $411, after deducting those expenses from the actual income shown on Schedule I. Debtor's plan proposes payment of $195 two times a month, the exact amount of "excess income" noted on Schedule J, which is $256 per month more than the "rigid, mechanical test" advocated by the Trustee. Since creditors will receive more under Debtor's plan than that mechanical test would require, the Trustee obviously does not object to the higher amount.

Although Debtor's plan provides that the "commitment period is 60 months," it also provides that "[t]he commitment period does not deal with the length of the plan. In so providing, Debtor does not commit to making payments for a full 60 months, or to payment of unsecured creditors." The Trustee's objection states that "Debtor does not propose to pay the net result of Form B22C to unsecured creditors. Trustee contends that changes in circumstances cannot modify this result as Congress' intent was to remove from the Court, Trustee and Counsel the discretion to effect a number at odds with these computations."

The Trustee's position is that §1325(b)(3) requires, for above-median income debtors, that the court look only at the dollar amount contained on Line 58 of Form B22C, and if it is a positive number, that the debtor must then pay that amount to unsecured creditors over not less than 60 months. As in Lanning, the Trustee does not dispute that Debtor can only afford to pay the amount his plan proposes to pay, or allege that the reduction in income occurred in bad faith.

Discussion

In its passage of BAPCPA, Congress clearly intended that debtors with the financial ability to pay something to unsecured creditors should be required to do so. To implement this goal, debtors wishing to liquidate their assets under Chapter 7 are now subject to a "means test." National and regional expense standards used by the Internal Revenue Service in determining a taxpayer's ability to repay delinquent taxes are used to determine whether debtors have the ability to repay a portion of their debts. If it is determined, pursuant to §707(b)(2)(A)(I), that a debtor can pay the stated percentage or amount of his or her debt, the debtor must choose to either convert his or her case, or suffer its dismissal. The means test is incorporated into Chapter 13 proceedings to determine what amount a debtor must pay to unsecured creditors, and over what period of time.

A. The Statutory Predicate (and Predicament)

To answer the questions raised by these two cases, the Court is required to follow the plain meaning of the relevant statutes, unless to do so would lead to an absurd or futile result. The Court must consider the statute as a whole, interpreting it in a fashion that the entire Code can function in a workable manner. Pivotal to this Court's decision is how to interpret the undefined phrase "projected disposal income" found in §1325(b)(1)(B), which implicates several sections of the recently amended Bankruptcy Code.

The sections that must be considered are §101(10A) and §1325(b)(1), (4). Section 1325(b)(1)(B) is the starting point for this analysis; it provides:

> If the trustee or the holder of an allowed unsecured claim objects to the confirmation of the plan, then the court may not approve the plan unless, as of the effective date of the plan—

> (B) the plan provides that all of the debtor's projected disposable income to be received in the applicable commitment period beginning on the date that the first payment is due under the plan will be applied to make payments to unsecured creditors under the plan.

Although the term "projected disposable income" is not defined, "disposable income" is defined[, by §1325(b)(2)], as follows:

For purposes of this subsection, "disposable income" means current monthly income received by the debtor (other than child support payments, foster care payments, or disability payments for a dependent child made in accordance with applicable nonbankruptcy law to the extent reasonably necessary to be expended for such child) less amounts reasonably necessary to be expended

(A)(I) for the maintenance or support of the debtor or a dependent of the debtor, or for a domestic support obligation, that first becomes payable after the date the petition is filed; and

(ii) for charitable contributions (that meet the definition of 'charitable contribution' under section 548(d)(3) to a qualified religious or charitable entity or organization (as defined in section 548(d)(4)) in an amount not to exceed 15 percent of gross income of the debtor for the year in which the contributions are made; and

(B) if the debtor is engaged in business, for the payment of expenditures necessary for the continuation, preservation, and operation of such business.

This statute then requires us to look at the definition of "current monthly income," which is defined, in §101(10A), as essentially " ... the average monthly income from all sources that the debtor receives ... during the 6-month period ... " before filing. In other words, "current monthly income" is a snapshot of a debtor's income for the six-month period prior to the filing of his or her bankruptcy petition; it is not the actual, monthly income the debtor has available to fund a Chapter 13 plan when the bankruptcy is filed.

Subsection 1325(b)(3) is also relevant to this analysis, because it defines what amounts are "reasonably necessary to be expended"— i.e., what expenses are appropriate for an above-median debtor, under §1325(b)(2). It provides that appropriate expenses shall be determined in accordance with §707(b)(2)(A) and (B), which limits expenses to the categories and amounts specified therein. The expenses allowed are those contained in the National and Local Standards established by the Internal Revenue Service, as well as some actual expenses in the categories specified by the Internal Revenue Service as "Other Necessary Expenses."

Finally, §1325(b)(4) defines "applicable commitment period" as three years, or not less than five years for an above-median debtor, unless all allowed unsecured creditors are paid in full earlier.

1. Income

In construing these code sections together to determine how to calculate "projected disposable income" for above-median debtors, most courts have focused on whether the undefined term, "projected disposable income," has the same meaning as the defined term, "disposable income." In other words, did Congress mean the word "projected" to add anything to its definition of "disposable income?" Two competing interpretations have emerged, and interestingly, both claim their opposite conclusions are supported by the plain meaning of the relevant statutes.

The first camp reasons that the addition of the word "projected" to the defined phrase "disposable income" "suggests that Congress intended to refer to the income actually to be received by the debtor during the commitment period, rather than the income received during the six-month look back period prior to filing. Courts adopting this view opine that it is appropriate for courts to consider each debtor's actual income, as shown on Schedule I, to determine what they can realistically pay over the life of a plan when there has been a substantial change in circumstances that Form B22C could not, or did not, contemplate. These courts also rely on the maxim of statutory construction that when Congress includes particular language in one section of a statute, but omits it in another, Congress must have intended different meanings. Thus, they argue that "projected disposable income" was intended to mean something different than "disposable income."

The other camp holds that Congress intended to, and did, adopt a specific test to be rigidly applied for above-median income debtors, that the test is codified by completion of Form B22C, and that debtors, trustees, and the Court are bound by the mathematical calculations resulting from completion of Form B22C in formulating any plan, regardless of any change in circumstances. The courts adopting this reasoning suggest that one must not isolate the word "projected" and inflate its importance, but instead, that the courts' new role is to simply confirm the math on Form B22C and require debtors pay the net number over the proper period of time, without more.

This Court respectfully agrees with the majority of courts, which have found that the term "projected" is a forward-looking concept that not only allows, but requires, this Court to consider at confirmation the debtor's actual income as it is reported on Schedule I, as well as any reasonably anticipated changes in that income during the life of the proposed Chapter 13 plan. First, Congress' reference in §1325(b)(1)(B) to *projected* disposable income *to be received* in the applicable commitment period would be superfluous if the historical average was the start and end of the equation. * * *

Accordingly, in those cases where the debtor's income at confirmation has not appreciably changed from the historical number contained in Form B22C, Schedule I will contain essentially the same "income" number. In cases like Avila's and Lanning's, however, where a debtor's financial situation has significantly deteriorated over the six months prior to filing, strict adherence to the net results of Form B22C would result in the anomalous situation where those who most need bankruptcy protection would be precluded from seeking it. Experience shows that individuals who lose jobs, or who have a sudden (albeit temporary) reduction in income as a result of a strike, layoff, medical condition for them or a dependent requiring time off work, and the like, are among those who most frequently seek Chapter 13 protection, in an attempt to save homes and cars for which they have failed to make timely payments due to the reduction in income. If these debtors are forced to file quickly after the income reduction (when their "current monthly income" is still above-median as averaged over the prior six months), in an attempt to forestall the repossession of a car, or the foreclosure of a home, they will, as a class, be denied the opportunity to reorganize under Chapter 13.[25]

This Court will not adopt a reading of the statute that results in this absurd result—a result that would effectively preclude Chapter 13 relief for those most in need. Furthermore, the reading of the statute preferred by the minority, which minimizes the importance of the word "projected," similarly results in an absurd result when a debtor's financial picture has appreciably improved since the six-month look back period. The following example demonstrates that situation:

> A debtor takes unpaid family leave for the first two months of the historical six-month look back period required by § 101(10A), but then returns to her $6,000 a month job for the remaining four

---

[25] They might also be denied relief under Chapter 7, as a presumption of abuse could well arise under § 707(b)(2). They would then have to either convert to Chapter 13 (which would be futile because they could not propose a feasible plan) or dismiss their Chapter 7. Again, the scant legislative history would indicate this was likely not the intent of Congress. See 151 Cong. Rec. 2462-02 at S2470, 2005 WL 562943 (March 10, 2005) (statement of Senator Nelson: "It is important to note that no American will be denied access to the bankruptcy system under these reforms.").

months. She would still be an above-median income debtor, but her Form B22C would only show monthly income of $4,000. The net dividend payable to unsecured creditors, shown on Line 58 of Form B22C, would almost inevitably be considerably less than her actual ability to pay.

Nevertheless, the Court would be required to confirm the plan, even though the debtor was not paying what she was able to pay her unsecured creditors. * * *

2. Expenses

The next issue the Court must decide is whether it should subtract the expenses shown on Form B22C, some of which are formulaic and some of which are "actual," or those shown on Schedule J, which are allegedly "actual" expenses, from the appropriate income number, to determine the dividend that should be paid to unsecured creditors by above-median income debtors under §1325(b)(1)(B). The plain language of §1325(b)(3) summarily decides the issue.

That statute requires that "[a]mounts reasonably necessary to be expended under paragraph (2) *shall* be determined in accordance with subparagraphs (A) and (B) of section 707(b)(2)." Section 707(b)(2)(A)(ii)(I)-(V) establishes very definitive deductions from income, based on Internal Revenue Service National and Local Standards as well as on some of a debtor's actual monthly expenses for "the categories specified as Other Necessary Expenses issued by the Internal Revenue Service for the area in which the debtor resides ... ." (Emphasis added). In this statute, Congress expressly contrasted when the standardized (or "applicable") allowance must be used, and when actual expenses were to be used, in determining "disposable income."

This demonstrates that Congress clearly understood the difference between actual expenses and "standardized" expenses, and elected to establish a means test formula that used a mix of those two. Accordingly, if the Court were to use Schedule J (which reflects actual expenses in every expense category), in determining which expenses to deduct from income, it would be reading all references to National and Local IRS Standards out of the relevant statutes, which of course it cannot do. This Court finds that above-median income debtors must deduct from income the expenses they itemize on Form B22C to arrive at the minimum amount that they must pay to unsecured creditors, except for limited exceptions not expressly argued here.

B. Duration of plan payments

The final issue this Court must decide is whether the plans of Debtors Avila and Lanning can be confirmed in light of the inference or provision in each plan that their plans will not necessarily run a full 60 months. Again, this question is easily answered by the plain meaning of §1325(b)(1)(B). The Code does not require a set dividend to unsecured creditors , only a minimum number of months for debtors to commit their projected disposable income to payment into their Chapter 13 plan. Neither plan satisfies this requirement.

[T]he applicable commitment period for above-median income debtors is 60 months (unless their plan earlier pays unsecured creditors in full), even when the amount on B22C or Schedule I, minus the expenses shown on Form B22C, is a negative number .... * * * [A]doption of [a] "monetary" or "multiplier" theory[, where an above-median debtor could satisfy the period requirement by paying 60 times the monthly requirement over a shorter period,] would allow debtors to cash out unsecured creditors at a discount at any time, without requiring a debtor make his or her best efforts over some required period of time to repay creditors. * * *

[Moreover], what little legislative history we have supports that Congress believed that requiring debtors to make plan payments for 36-60 months would assist debtors in acquiring the financial discipline they would need to really get a fresh start, post-discharge. Senator Sessions, one of the proponents of the legislation, stated that

> [i]f a debtor files under Chapter 13 and learns how to manage money under a structured repayment plan that requires some discipline, the debtor learns financial responsibility and should be able to avoid future financial turmoil. Chapter 13 bankruptcies allow debtors to keep their assets and pay back a portion of their debts over a 5 year period. In exchange, the remaining portions of their debt are discharged and the debtor gets a fresh start.

FN38. 151 Cong. Rec. S2462-02 at S2472 -S2473, 2005 WL 562943 (March 10, 2005).

To obtain a confirmable plan, both Lanning and Avila will be required to make payments over 60 months.

Because Debtor Lanning's Schedule I showed actual income of $1,922, and her B22C showed expenses of $4,228, the means test would result in Debtor not having to pay anything to unsecured creditors, because the remainder is a negative number. If she pays zero, however, she cannot formulate a feasible plan that meets all the other requirements of §1325(a) [such as the requirement under §1325(a)(4) that unsecured creditors are to receive property under the plan of a value at least equal to what they would receive in a Chapter 7 liquidation]. Nothing prevents debtors from electing to pay more than the statutory means test requires, in order to meet the requirement that a plan must be feasible, so long as the payment continues for 60 months. Accordingly, since Debtor Lanning has proposed to pay $144 per month, her plan is confirmable so long as it continues 60 months.

Similarly, Debtor Avila's Schedule I showed actual income of $5,200 and his B22C showed expenses of $5,531.57, resulting in the finding that nothing need be paid to unsecured creditors. The Trustee has not objected that Debtor's plan to pay $195 biweekly is not feasible, only that his plan must run 60 months. Accordingly, the Court may well confirm the plan if his heirs wish to proceed, and if the standard confirmation order is modified to require payment for a full 60 months.

IN RE JONES

United States Bankruptcy Court, D. Minnesota, 1985
55 Bankr. 462

MAHONEY, BANKRUPTCY JUDGE.

* * * Lynnel L. Jones (Debtor) filed a Chapter 13 petition on May 14, 1985. At that time Debtor was an unemployed lawyer, formerly of the firm of Lynnel L. Jones & Associates, P.A.

Debtor has three children aged 12, 14 and 18 years. Two of them live with the Debtor and her husband on a full-time basis. The eldest child attends Carleton College in Northfield, Minnesota. Debtor's husband suffers from Parkinson's Disease, and receives $2,000 per month in disability income. Since the date of the petition, the Debtor and her family have moved from Minnesota to the State of Kentucky, where Debtor is currently employed.

Debtor's Chapter 13 statement indicates that current income, including her husband's disability income, is $4,324 per month. Debtor's monthly expenditures, as estimated by her, are:

House Payment	$989
Utilities	230
Food	515

Clothing	250
Laundry and Cleaning	40
Periodicals and Books	30
Husband's Medical Expenses	200
Insurance: Auto	50
Health	250
Transportation	110
Recreation	0
Real Estate Taxes	165
Son's College Tuition	500
Secondary School Tuition	500
Household Insurance	30
Car Payment	175
Student Loan	144
TOTAL MONTHLY EXPENSE	$4,178

The Debtor's Chapter 13 plan indicates total unsecured debts of approximately $66,000. However, as listed in Debtor's statement, total undisputed, unsecured claims amount to $56,744. The payment provisions in this plan refer to this amount, not the $66,000 estimate. Debtor's undisputed, unsecured creditors are:

Fifth Norwest Bank-Calhoun Isles	$12,776
Dennis J. Johnson	29,328
Loring Hill Partnership	14,640
TOTAL	$56,744

In addition, Debtor lists a disputed, unsecured claim by James Beal in an amount stated to be in excess of $50,000. [The Beal claim is a tort claim against the Debtor for alleged legal malpractice.]

The plan proposes that the unsecured creditors shall receive 13.95% of their claims, amounting to $7,916. The amount is to be paid over a five-year period in monthly installments of $132 plus 10% for the Trustee. The total proposed monthly payment under the plan is $146, that being the amount of disposable monthly income projected by the Debtor.

Dennis J. Johnson (Creditor) is an unsecured judgment creditor of Debtor. He raises several objections to the Debtor's Chapter 13 plan, and moves that the plan not be confirmed. He further moves that the Chapter 13 proceedings be dismissed due to bad faith and fraud on the Debtor's part. * * *

Creditor objects to Debtor's listed monthly expenditures of $500 for her eldest son's college tuition, and $500 for one of her younger children's secondary school tuition. He contends that these expenditures are not "reasonably necessary" for the support or maintenance of the Debtor or a dependent of Debtor within the meaning of §1325(b)(1) and (2).

. . . These provisions are part of ... §1325(b) which was added to the Bankruptcy Code by Congress in 1984. Th[is] subsection incorporates into Chapter 13 the "ability to pay" test, which requires debtors to pay as much as they are able, but only as much as they are able, into the plan. As a result, a debtor's Chapter 13 plan cannot be confirmed over the objections of an allowed unsecured creditor unless the debtor proposes to pay all of his or her projected disposable income for the Chapter 13 period into the plan. . . .

The basic question is, therefore, whether Debtor has proposed to pay all of her projected disposable income into the plan. The definition of "disposable income" in §1325(b)(2) leads me to the dispositive issue in this matter, which is whether the Debtor's listed monthly expenditures are reasonably necessary for the maintenance or support of the Debtor or the Debtor's dependents.

By raising this issue, Creditor's objection leads me onto new ground. There appear to be no cases dealing with §1325(b)(2)(A) or the standard to be applied thereunder. Furthermore, the legislative history to §1325(b) is singularly vague and unenlightening. As a result, the immediate question is what standard is to be applied in determining the portion of a debtor's income that is not reasonably necessary for the maintenance or support of the debtor or the debtor's dependents.

The legislative history, such as there is, expressly leaves the development of an appropriate standard to the courts. Chapter 13, it states, "contemplates a substantial effort by the debtor to pay his debts," and furthermore, "[s]uch an effort may require some sacrifices by the debtor." S. Rep. No. 65, 98th Cong. 1st Sess. 22 (1983). Where, as here, Congress has provided little guidance as to the meaning of a statutory provision, the courts must employ other methods of construction to determine that meaning. * * *

Fortunately, the provision contained in §1325(b)(2)(A) is not unique in the Bankruptcy Code. Similar provisions are found in §522(d)(10)(E) and §523(a)(2)(C).

Section 523 deals with exceptions to the discharge provisions under Chapters 7, 11 and 13. Subsection (a)(2)(C) provides that certain consumer debts for "luxury goods or services" are nondischargeable. "Luxury goods or services" is defined as "goods or services [not] reasonably acquired for the support or maintenance of the debtor or a dependent of the debtor." Extending this definition to §1325(b)(2)(A) would provide a standard which excludes expenditures for luxury goods or services. I think this is clearly appropriate, but it falls short of providing a workable standard to be applied under §1325.

Section 522(d)(10)(E) exempts from the property of the estate in bankruptcy certain benefit payments made to a debtor "to the extent reasonably necessary for the support of the debtor and any dependent of the debtor." The "reasonably necessary" standard in §522(d)(10)(E) was first interpreted in In re Taff, 10 Bankr. 101 (Bankr. D. Conn. 1981). *Taff* involved a Chapter 7 debtor who was seeking to exempt payments received by him under a pension plan. The pension payments could only be exempt if they were reasonably necessary for the support of the debtor or a dependent of the debtor. In holding that the payments were not exempt, the court was called upon to interpret the "reasonably necessary" provision under §522(d)(10)(E). After a thorough examination of the legislative background to the exemption and of exemption laws in general, the court decided that:

> . . . the reasonably necessary standard requires that the Court take into account other income and exempt property of the debtor, present and anticipated . . . and that the appropriate amount to be set aside for the debtor ought to be sufficient to sustain basic needs not related to [the debtor's] former status in society or the life style to which he is accustomed. . . .

10 Bankr. at 107. Since 1981, the *Taff* standard has been embraced by the courts in several cases involving §522(d)(10)(E). . . .

I find the *Taff* construction of §522(d)(10)(E) to be compelling in the present case. Section 522(d)(10)(E) and §1325(b)(2)(A) are similar in so far as they both provide the opportunity for a debtor to retain certain income for his or her own needs. In doing so, they both limit the extent of this retention to that which is reasonably necessary for the maintenance or support of the debtor or a dependent of the debtor. In view of this essential similarity between the two sections, I think the standard to be applied under them should be the same. Furthermore, as I see it, the purpose of Chapter 13 is to provide the maximum recovery to creditors while at the same time leaving the debtor sufficient money to pay for his or her basic living expenses. The "reasonably necessary" standard set out by the court in *Taff* is in accord with my views. Accordingly, I am adopting that standard and applying it to the present matter arising under §1325(b).

Before I consider the Debtor's listed monthly expenditures under this standard, I need to note that Creditor has objected only to the $500 college tuition expense and the $500 secondary school expense. Under §1325(b), however, it is the court's duty to consider the listed expenditures individually and as a whole to determine whether the debtor has proposed to pay all of his or her disposable income into the plan. Accordingly, I am not limited in my inquiry by the scope of Creditor's objection. Rather, it is my duty to examine Debtor's entire budget.

Applying the "reasonably necessary" standard to the Debtor's listed monthly expenditures, I find that the list includes several items that are not within the standard. The $500 per month for college tuition, and the $500 per month for secondary school tuition are both excessive. An expensive private school education is not a basic need of the Debtor's dependents, particularly in view of the high quality public education available in this country at both the collegiate and secondary school levels. The $515 per month that Debtor claims for food for a family of four is high in my judgment. Lastly, the monthly house payment of $989 is well above the amount necessary to provide adequate housing for a family of four.

Debtor has listed monthly income in the amount of $4,324. Her claimed monthly expenditures amount to $4,178. After considering the Debtor's listed monthly expenditures and the circumstances of this case, I find that the Debtor reasonably needs $3,800 for the maintenance or support of herself or her dependents.

In order for me to confirm Debtor's Chapter 13 plan over the objections of Creditor, the plan must have proposed to apply all of Debtor's disposable income … under the plan. Debtor's plan proposes to apply $131.93 per month to payments under the plan. I find that the proper amount should be $510 per month. Accordingly, I am denying confirmation of the Debtor's Chapter 13 plan as presently constituted. * * *

NOTES

12A.1. The *Lanning* court certainly seems on solid ground when it suggests that Congress must have had a reason to include the word "projected" in §1325(b)(1)(B). But another plausible explanation is sloppy draftsmanship. Consider that "projected" was not added by the 2005 Bankruptcy Act, but part of the preexisting language that may simply have been overlooked. Moreover, as part of the new Chapter 7 means test (described above in chapter 3, section C of this book), §707(b)(2)(B) expressly permits an adjustment of income based on changed circumstances, but limits those circumstances to those such as "a serious medical condition" or "a call or order to active duty in the Armed Forces." It might seem odd that Congress would prescribe limitations on adjustment in the means test of Chapter 7 but permit open-ended adjustments in Chapter 13. This said, it would seem equally odd if Chapter 13 permitted *no* adjustment for changed circumstances, and so whatever Congress intended, if it intended anything at all, the holding of *Lanning* seems reasonable. As the opinion itself states, however, not all courts agree. For a contrary result, see, e.g., In re Alexander, 344 Bankr. 742 (Bankr. E.D.N.C. 2006).

12A.2. Harder to defend than its holding on projected disposable income, is *Lanning*'s opinion on the length of the plan. The requirement that a debtor who will not repay her creditors in full pay disposable income over a minimum specified period is sometimes called a "pay-til-it-hurts" provision. The notion is that in exchange for retaining even nonexempt property, the debtor must award some of her human capital, in the form of disposable income, to prepetition creditors. Prior to the 2005 Bankruptcy Act, this tradeoff was an option of the debtor, and while it still is to some extent, as no one can be forced into Chapter 13, the new Chapter 7 means test was designed to steer above-median-income debtors into Chapter 13 and thus encourage them to pay disposable income under their plans. Consistent with this design is the new §1325(b)(4), which applies a five-year rather than three-year commitment period to above-median debtors. With this as background, once a court determines that a debtor has *no* disposable income, there does not seem to be a reason for even an above-median debtor to make payments over five years. Some courts so hold. See, e.g., In re Frederickson, 2007 WL 1453061 (Bankr. E.D. Ark.) This issue is explored further in Problem 12A-1.

12A.3. The court in *Jones* concludes that an "expensive private school education is not a basic need of the Debtor's dependents, particularly in view of the high quality public education available in this country at both the collegiate and secondary school levels." This sort of subjective judgment makes it hard for the "reasonably necessary" standard of §1325(b)(2) to be applied consistently across cases. A number of courts, for example, have come to different conclusions about whether private schooling is "reasonably necessary." See, e.g., In re Nicola, 244 Bankr. 795 (N.D. Ill. 2000). Problem 12A-2 further illustrates the difficulties of a subjective standard.

12A.4. As noted in the introductory material to this section, the 2005 Bankruptcy Act added some guidance in the quest to determine what constitutes "amounts reasonably necessary to be expended." Section 1325(b)(3) defines that term by reference to the Chapter 7 means test in §707(b), which in turn refers to the "applicable monthly expense amounts specified under the National Standards and Local Standards" issued by the Internal Revenue Service. §707(b)(2)(A)(ii). But 2005 Act falls far short of providing a beacon here. There are multiple reasons. First, §1325(b)(3) applies only to high-income debtors as defined by the means test, thus offering courts no guidance for many debtors. Second, the reference to standards provides only some of the permitted expenditures, while others include actual expenses if justified by the debtor. For example, the debtor's necessary expenses "may include the actual expenses for each dependent child less than 18 years of age, not to exceed $1,650 per year per child, to attend a private or public elementary or secondary school if the debtor provides ... a detailed explanation of why such expenses are reasonable and necessary [and not accounted for otherwise]." §707(b)(2)(A)(ii)(IV). This provision, if applicable, would have resolved the dispute in *Jones*, by implication, both because one tuition there was for college, not elementary or secondary school, and because the amounts (even without adjustment to current dollars) exceeded the limit. But it is easy to imagine a similar case in which the dilemma of the *Jones* court remains unresolved.

PROBLEM

12A-1. Debtor earns just above the applicable median income for her home state at the time she files for bankruptcy under Chapter 13. She completes all the required forms and it is determined that she has no disposable income under the applicable formulas. Debtor has a single, unencumbered asset, a thoroughbred horse given to her by her terminally ill (and unemployed) husband. The horse, which Debtor loves, is worth $20,000 more than any applicable exemption. Debtor proposes a plan that would repay her unsecured creditors $670 per month for 36 months. Assuming that this amount reflects the appropriate interest rate on a $20,000 obligation, is the plan confirmable? Would a plan for $440 per month for 60 months be confirmable, again assuming the correct interest rate? Would your answer change if Debtor's disposable income were not zero but trivially positive? Is there any legitimate reason for a debtor's unsecured creditors to prefer the first plan over the second?

12A-2. Debtor is a rookie police officer who is required by her employer to live in the city for which she works. The public elementary schools in the city are notoriously poor, both in resources available to them and in the results they yield. The private school is excellent but expensive. Debtor sends her daughter to the private school. Debtor becomes unable to repay obligations, including a substantial tax penalty that she incurred when the small business she ran failed just before Debtor joined the police force. Debtor files for bankruptcy under Chapter 13. Debtor's now estranged cousin, and her largest unsecured creditor, objects to the plan on the ground that the school tuition is too high and that Debtor's plan thus does not devote enough to repayment of unsecured claims, which will not be paid in full. The cousin knows, and tells the court, that Debtor has been offered a well-paying job in the suburbs, where public schools are good, though not as good as the private school Debtor's daughter now attends. Will cousin's argument prevail? In answering this question consider, among other provisions, §1328(a). Would your analysis change if the schools in question were not elementary schools but universities, and Debtor's daughter sought a graduate degree? Compare Exercise 3C(2).

B.   TREATMENT OF SECURED CLAIMS

A Chapter 13 plan may propose the debtor's retention of collateral for a secured claim and generally "may modify the rights of holders of secured claims." §1322(b). But Chapter 13 protects holders of secured claims from modifications that leave them worse off. The most basic protection is found in §1325(a)(5), which provides that the plan must distribute to the secured creditor on account of its secured claim property that has a value, as of the effective date of the plan, at least equal to the amount of the claim. Moreover, according to the same provision, if the debtor is to retain the collateral, the plan must grant the holder of the secured claim a continuing lien on the collateral until the new obligation is fully paid or the debtor receives a discharge in the case. Put plainly, a debtor cannot retain collateral unless the plan proposes to pay the secured claim in full, though not necessarily at once. The requirement of a continuing lien supports this full-payment obligation in the event the debtor fails to complete payments under the plan.

Home mortgages often figure centrally in Chapter 13 cases. A debtor who has fallen behind on her mortgage payments is one of those most likely to file under Chapter 13. When a debtor encounters hard times, it may be that outside of bankruptcy she can prevent foreclosure and loss of her home only by paying off a bank's entire loan in full or by reaching a negotiated settlement with the bank. Particularly where the home has fallen in value, the debtor may find the bank uncooperative. The debtor, if eligible, might file for bankruptcy under Chapter 7, but she will find little relief there, as liquidation of the estate will throw the house back to the bank and state law. Chapter 13 offers the debtor breathing space and a last chance to sort things out. This breathing space does not come without its cost to lenders, who in turn can be expected to pass on the cost to new borrowers. The treatment of home mortgages in Chapter 13 has the potential to affect the important home purchase market. Not surprisingly, then, Chapter 13 contains a number of special provisions that primarily affect home mortgages.

The greatest limitation on a debtor's right to affect a home mortgage is the general prohibition on modification of the rights of holders provided by §1322(b)(2). For other kinds of mortgages, a plan will bifurcate an ordinary undersecured claim under §506(a) into a secured and unsecured claim, then treat each part separately. The plan will provide the holder with two new loan obligations, one on account of the secured claim and one on account of the deficiency, which as an unsecured claim may well receive only cents on the dollar. The terms of these loans can be different from each other and from the term of the original loan. These new obligations replace the old claim, which may be discharged even if the terms of the original loan are never fully satisfied. Under §1322(b)(2), however, the debtor's ability to modify the "rights of holders of secured claims" does not extend to "a claim secured only by a security interest in real property that is the debtor's principal residence."

The scope of this provision is not clear from the text alone. Consider the following example. Debtor buys a home and borrows $100,000 from Bank. A recession hits, unemployment rises, and housing prices fall. Debtor loses his high-paying job, accepts a new job with a lower salary, and files under Chapter 13. The home is now worth only $60,000. Under §506(a), Bank has a secured claim for $60,000 and an unsecured claim for $40,000. Nevertheless, the plan may not give effect to such bifurcation with new loans on terms different from Bank's original loan. Such modification would illegitimately modify the *rights* of a holder of the claim secured by the debtor's home even though the secured claim itself, as defined by §506(a), is not the same as Bank's original loan supported by the house as collateral. So said the Supreme Court in Nobelman v. American Savings Bank, 508 U.S. 324, 329 (1993). As a result, §1322(b)(2) prevents a plan from altering the terms of the original loan, including the right, if there is such a right, to bring an action against the debtor for any deficiency.

Even after *Nobelman*, however, Chapter 13 provides some relief to debtors for their home mortgages. Under §1322(b)(5), notwithstanding §1322(b)(2) and applicable nonbankruptcy law, a Chapter 13 debtor may cure a default on secured or unsecured obligations for which the last payment is due after the date on which the last payment is due under the debtor's plan. Such a cure must occur within a reasonable time and must reinstate a mortgage on its original terms. In short, Chapter 13 gives debtors a way to keep their homes after a default, even after a default that would give the lender a right to foreclose under state law. But during the Chapter 13 plan period and afterward debtors must continue to pay off the mortgage in full, even if the value of the home has fallen far below the outstanding amount of the debt. The ability to cure only returns debtors to the situation they were in before they defaulted. Unless there has been a change in their circumstances, debtors can quickly find themselves unable to meet these same obligations once again.

When creditors pursue their nonbankruptcy remedies, sooner or later they must have gone so far in the foreclosure process that a debtor can no longer file for bankruptcy and cure outstanding defaults. As originally enacted, Chapter 13 did not identify this point. In 1994, §1322(c)(1) was added. It tells us that a debtor loses the right to cure defaults once the residence is sold at a foreclosure sale that is conducted in accordance with applicable nonbankruptcy law.

Home mortgages can run for twenty years or longer. Typically, the term of the mortgage is longer than the term of the plan and the rule of modification or cure just described will apply. Also in 1994, however, Congress amended Chapter 13 to provide for the case in which the remaining term of the home mortgage is less than the length of the Chapter 13 plan. In such a case, "the plan may provide for the payment of the claim as modified pursuant to §1325(a)(5)," notwithstanding the §1322(b)(2) anti-modification clause. §1322(c)(2). Chapter 13 thus gives the debtor some maneuvering room with respect to home mortgages that are close to the end of their term. Unfortunately, neither the intent nor the full implication of this amendment is uniformly understood.

The exercises below rehearse some basics of these and related provisions. The first two cases that follow, *Witt* and *Mattson*, delve more deeply into the rules for the modification or cure of home mortgages. The third case, *Wright* explores what has come to be known as the "hanging paragraph" of §1325(a), a paragraph that governs security interests in a type of collateral second in importance only to that of a home: the automobile. The related notes and problems further explore these issues.

Key Provisions: Bankruptcy Code §§1322; 1325(a)

EXERCISES

12B(1) Debtor opens a nursery and borrows $125,000 from Bank. To secure the loan, Bank takes a mortgage on Debtor's home and his hunting cabin. After the nursery fails, Debtor obtains a high-paying job as a tree surgeon and files for bankruptcy under Chapter 13. At the time of the filing, Debtor owes Bank $100,000 on the loan. Debtor's home is then worth between $50,000 and $75,000, and his cabin is worth about $5,000. These are debtor's only assets. Debtor proposes a plan that would have Debtor retain the home, release the cabin to Bank, and pay Bank $60,000 plus interest for three years. The plan provides for no other distribution of property and leaves Debtor with no projected disposable income. Bank objects to the plan. Why? Assuming that the plan has no defects in the terms not presented, and assuming that the court accepts Debtor's valuation of the home, can the court confirm the plan despite Bank's objection? Would it matter if the original mortgage loan had ten years to maturity at the time of the proposed confirmation?

12B(2) Debtor is a truck driver who files for bankruptcy under Chapter 13. At that time Debtor owes bank $50,000 on a loan secured by Debtor's truck. Debtor also owes his brother-in-law $25,000 for an injury the brother-in-law suffered at Debtor's apartment. In addition to his truck, Debtor owns Treasury bonds with a value that exceeds by $25,000 the total exemptions available to Debtor. Debtor proposes a plan that would have Debtor retain the truck, which Debtor values at $25,000, as well as the bonds. The plan would have Debtor pay Bank $25,000 on account of Bank's secured loan. This amount would be paid with interest over two years. The plan would also have Debtor pay $12,500 each to Bank on account of its deficiency claim and to the brother-in-law on account of his claim. These amounts would be paid with interest over three years. The court confirms the plan. Debtor makes all payments for two years, and then discontinues all payments. The court converts the case to Chapter 7. At this time, Debtor's truck is worth $40,000. Bank attempts to foreclose on the truck. What will be the result? In answering this question consider, among other factors, the Supreme Court's opinion in *Dewsnup*, discussed in the previous chapter. Would your answer change if Debtor were discharged after payments for two years following a personal tragedy that disabled him from making further payments?

12B(3) Debtor earns a good living and has never missed a bill payment. After an uninsured illness depletes her savings, however, she files for bankruptcy under Chapter 13. Debtor's only asset is her home, on which Bank holds a mortgage to support a loan with fifteen years until maturity and $150,000 still outstanding. The home is worth somewhat more than that amount. Debtor's plan does not explicitly provide for a payment to Bank except to say that the loan and mortgage are continued according to their original terms. Bank has no right to accelerate the loan under state law, but would like to do so anyway because market interest rates have risen substantially since the loan. Can Bank block Debtor's plan? Consider this exercise again after you read the material on §§1124 and 1126(f) in the next chapter.

12B(4) In January, Debtor ceases monthly payments and thus defaults on a home mortgage loan from Bank. In April, after negotiation with Debtor fails, Bank begins the foreclosure process, but Debtor files for bankruptcy under Chapter 13 before the foreclosure sale. Debtor proposes a cure for the default as part of a plan to become effective in December. Bank objects to the terms of the cure and insists that the plan be revised so that Bank would receive not only interest on the outstanding principal between January and December but also interest on the interest payments that should have been made between January and December. The plan proposes to pay the aggregate sum of the monthly interest payments but not interest on those payments. Applicable state law prohibits the collection of interest on interest in the enforcement of a home mortgage. The mortgage loan does not mature for more than five years. At all relevant times, the value of the mortgaged real estate exceeds the value of the loan. Will Bank prevail? In answering this question consider, among other provisions, §1322(e).

12B(5) Debtor files a bankruptcy petition under Chapter 13 and in connection with her three-year payment plan proposes to maintain a mortgage on her residence, the last payment under which is due in fifteen years. Debtor makes every payment under the plan on time and receives a discharge. At the time of her discharge, her home has depreciated greatly in value and she releases it to her mortgagee, whom she declines to pay further, citing the discharge. What result? In answering this question consider, among other provisions, §1328(a)(1).

CASES

WITT v. UNITED COMPANIES LENDING CORP.

United States Court of Appeals, Fourth Circuit, 1997
113 F.3d 508

MICHAEL, CIRCUIT JUDGE.

* * * On April 13, 1995, the Witts filed their petition for relief under Chapter 13. Their principal debt was $22,561 due to United on a note executed September 15, 1989, which matures in 1999. The note was secured by a first deed of trust on the Witts' only residence, a mobile home and lot located in Appomattox County, Virginia. According to the Witts, the current fair market value of their home is $13,100. In their proposed Chapter 13 plan the Witts bifurcated the obligation to United into two claims, one secured and one unsecured. The $13,100 secured claim (representing the value of United's interest in the home) would be paid out in full over five years, beginning July 1, 1995. Interest at 10% per annum would be paid on the secured claim. The rest ($9,461) of the obligation to United would be unsecured. In their plan the Witts propose to pay only 30% of each allowed unsecured claim. * * *

The Witts' Chapter 13 plan bifurcates United's claim into secured and unsecured components even though the underlying note was entirely secured by a first deed of trust on the Witts' home. Bifurcation is generally permitted under §506(a), which states:

An allowed claim of a creditor secured by a lien on property in which the estate has an interest ... is a secured claim to the extent of the value of such creditor's interest ... and is an unsecured claim to the extent that the value of such creditor's interest ... is less than the amount of such allowed claim.

However, in Nobelman v. American Savings Bank, 508 U.S. 324 (1993), the Supreme Court held that §506(a) did not apply to claims that were secured only by an interest in the debtor's principal residence. To reach this result, the Court looked to §1322(b)(2), which provides that a Chapter 13 plan may "modify the rights of holders of secured claims, other than a claim secured only by a security interest in real property that is the debtor's principal residence." The Court held that "to give effect to §506(a)'s valuation and bifurcation of secured claims through a Chapter 13 plan ... would require a modification of the rights of the holder of the security interest." Id. at 332. According to the Court, "§1322(b)(2) prohibits such a modification where, as here, the lender's claim is secured only by a lien on the debtor's principal residence." Id.

The Witts readily admit that their plan's proposed bifurcation is similar in all relevant respects to the one proposed in *Nobelman* and would therefore be barred under *Nobelman* if that decision still controls. However, subsequent to *Nobelman* Congress passed the Bankruptcy Reform Act of 1994. Section 301 of the Act amended §1322 to add subsection (c), which states in relevant part:

Notwithstanding subsection (b)(2) and applicable nonbankruptcy law— * * *

(2) in a case in which the last payment on the original payment schedule for a claim secured only by a security interest in real property that is the debtor's principal residence is due before the date on which the final payment under the plan is due, the plan may provide for the payment of the claim as modified pursuant to §1325(a)(5) of this title.

§1322(c)(2). Both sides agree that the Witts' plan meets the condition that "the last payment on the original payment schedule" be due "before the date on which the final payment under the plan is due." Since the Witts' plan meets this condition, their plan "may provide for the payment of the claim as modified pursuant to §1325(a)(5) of this title."

The parties differ, however, over whether the phrase "as modified pursuant to §1325(a)(5)" should be read as applying to "claim" or "payment." The Witts argue that the phrase should be interpreted to apply to "claim." This interpretation would allow the Witts to "modif[y]" United's "claim" pursuant to §1325(a)(5), which (the Witts say) permits bifurcation. United contends, however, that the phrase "as modified pursuant to §1325(a)(5)" should be read as applying to "payment" rather than "claim." This interpretation would only permit the Witts to "modif[y]" the amount or scheduling of the individual payments on the claim; the amount of the underlying claim itself could not be modified. . . .

In interpreting §1322(c)(2), we begin by examining the text of the statute. . . . Unfortunately, we find the language of §1322(c)(2)—"payment of the claim as modified"—to be ambiguous. It cannot be determined, merely from the statute's text, whether the words "as modified" should apply to "payment" or to "claim."

We recognize that under the "rule of the last antecedent," a phrase should be read to modify its immediate antecedent. According to this rule, the phrase "as modified" would apply to its immediate antecedent, "claim." However, although this reading may be "quite sensible as a matter of grammar," we find, as did the *Nobelman* Court (in interpreting another section, §1322(b)(2)), that such a reading "is not compelled." In the section we must interpret, §1322(c)(2), the term "claim" is part of the phrase "of the claim," which modifies "payment." It is quite plausible as a matter of common sense, we believe, that the phrase "as modified" also modifies "payment" and not "claim." After all, the subject of payment is the focus of §1322(c)(2); it only deals with plan payment provisions when "the last payment on the original payment schedule" on a home mortgage loan "is due before the date on which the final payment under the plan is due."

Moreover, in the final clause of §1322(c)(2) ("the plan may provide for the payment of the claim as modified") the word "payment" becomes superfluous if the Witts' interpretation is adopted. According to their interpretation, "as modified" can only be read as applying to "claim," and "payment" is left unmodified. If Congress had intended this reading, however, there was no need for it to talk about the "payment" of the claim. Instead, it could have simply ended §1322(c)(2) by saying "the plan may provide for the claim to be modified." But Congress said something else in the last clause of §1322(c)(2), that is, "the plan may provide for the payment of the claim as modified." Under the Witts' interpretation, this reference to "payment" becomes wholly unnecessary and superfluous. As the Supreme Court counseled in Connecticut Nat'l Bank v. Germain, 503 U.S. 249, 253 (1992), "courts should disfavor interpretations of statutes that render language superfluous."

The legislative history provides further support for the interpretation that only payment may be modified. See Green v. Bock Laundry Machine Co., 490 U.S. 504, 511 (1989) ("Because the plain text does not resolve these issues, we must examine the history leading to enactment. ... "). Although both the Senate and the House were working on similar bills to reform the Bankruptcy Code in the 103d Congress, it was the House bill that eventually became the Bankruptcy Reform Act of 1994. In House Report 835, the House Committee on the Judiciary set forth the purpose of the Act and also set forth individual analyses of each section. The Report notes in the "Summary and Purpose" section that among the problems addressed by the Act were "a number of problematic court opinions construing the Bankruptcy Code." H.R. Rep. No. 103-835 at 32 (1994). The Report states that the Act "addresses the most pressing of these problems in a moderate and carefully balanced fashion." Id. In summarizing some of the proposed solutions, the Report notes that the Act "makes several changes pertaining to consumer bankruptcies, including strengthening a debtor's right to cure a home mortgage default in a Chapter 13 plan." Id. at 34.

The Report also includes a separate section explaining §301 of the Act, codified at §1322(c). This section, entitled "Period for curing default relating to principal residence," first discusses the changes made by the addition of §1322(c)(1). The Report says that §301 "allow[s] the debtor to cure home mortgage defaults at least through the completion of a foreclosure sale under applicable nonbankruptcy law." Id. at 52. According to the Report, §1322(c)(1) was meant to overrule In re Roach, 824 F.2d 1370 (3d Cir. 1987), which held that the right to cure was extinguished after the issuance of a foreclosure judgment. The Report then discusses the impact of the section we must interpret in this case, §1322(c)(2):

> The changes made to this section, in conjunction with those made in §305 of this bill, would also overrule the result in First National Fidelity Corp. v. Perry, 945 F.2d 61 (3d Cir. 1991) with respect to mortgages on which the last payment on the original payment schedule is due before the date on which the final payment under the plan is due. In that case, the Third Circuit held that subsequent to foreclosure judgment, a Chapter 13 debtor cannot provide for a mortgage debt by paying the full amount of the allowed secured claim in accordance with §1325(a)(5), because doing so would

constitute an impermissible modification of the mortgage holder's right to immediate payment under §1322(b)(2).

Report at 52. This passage makes clear Congress's intent in enacting §1322(c)(2). Under *Perry* a Chapter 13 debtor could not "provide for a mortgage debt by paying the full amount of the allowed secured claim" through a bankruptcy plan if the creditor had previously obtained a foreclosure judgment. Instead, the creditor was entitled to "immediate payment" because §1322(b)(2) did not permit any modification of the mortgage holder's rights. Section 1322(c)(2), however, "overrule[s]" *Perry* and allows for payment of the full amount over time. Thus, §1322(c)(2) was only intended to allow payments to be stretched out over time; the debtor is still required to pay the "full amount of the allowed secured claim." Report at 52.

The Report is also instructive for what it does not say. It makes no mention of the *Nobelman* decision or of any intention to overrule that decision. The Witts' interpretation of the statute, however, would directly overrule *Nobelman*. Had Congress intended to overrule *Nobelman*, we expect Congress would have discussed that in the legislative history. Although the Report directly refers to forty cases, including three Supreme Court cases, that the Act was intended to overrule, *Nobelman* is not one of them. The Witts offer no reason why Congress would have failed to include *Nobelman* in this list if it was actually overruled by §1322(c)(2).

"It is firmly entrenched that Congress is presumed to enact legislation with knowledge of the law." United States v. Langley, 62 F.3d 602, 605 (4th Cir. 1995) (en banc). The upshot of this canon of statutory interpretation is that "absent a clear manifestation of contrary intent, a newly-enacted or revised statute is presumed to be harmonious with existing law and its judicial construction." Id. Congress certainly intended the Bankruptcy Reform Act of 1994 to overrule judicial precedent in a number of different areas. There is no "clear manifestation," however, that Congress intended to overrule *Nobelman*. We believe it ill-advised to give such a drastic interpretation to §1322(c)(2) without congressional support. . . .

Based on all of this, we hold that §1322(c)(2) does not permit the bifurcation of an undersecured loan into secured and unsecured claims if the only security for the loan is a lien on the debtor's principal residence. Because the Witts' bankruptcy plan proposed such a bifurcation, United's objection to the plan was well taken. * * *

IN RE MATTSON

United States Bankruptcy Court, D. Minnesota, 1997
210 Bankr. 157

KRESSEL, BANKRUPTCY JUDGE.

* * * The debtor purchased a home for herself and her son in June of 1994 for $49,900. She obtained a $47,405 loan from Norwest Mortgage, Inc., secured by a first priority mortgage on her home and borrowed an additional $1,500 from a special loan program. She paid the balance in cash. The $1,500 loan has been repaid. Norwest has not filed a claim, but the debtor's Schedule D indicates a debt to Norwest of $46,500.

In the fall of 1995, the debtor received an unsolicited letter in the mail from Commercial Credit. In response to the solicitation the debtor contacted Commercial Credit and went to its office in Burnsville on approximately November 2, 1995. While the debtor filled out an application to borrow $5,000 to refinance some credit card debt, Commercial Credit offered to loan her $10,000 secured by a second mortgage on her home. There apparently was no discussion about the value of the home or current encumbrances.

On November 2, 1995, the debtor signed a promissory note in the amount of $10,202 and granted Commercial Credit a second mortgage on her home to secure repayment. The repayment was amortized over five years with the last payment on the mortgage due November 7, 2000. The debtor was current on her payments until about a month before she filed her Chapter 13 case on February 27, 1997. She has filed a plan in which she proposes to treat Commercial Credit as an unsecured creditor.

The debtor claims that she can treat the Commercial Credit claim as an unsecured claim. It is her belief that the value of the home is less than the amount of Norwest's first mortgage, leaving Commercial Credit totally unsecured. As a result, she feels that she can utilize the cramdown provisions of Chapter 13 and pay Commercial Credit as an unsecured creditor.

Commercial Credit, on the other hand, believes that the value of the debtor's homestead is in excess of the first mortgage and therefore its claim is secured in whole or in part. In addition, Commercial Credit argues that, regardless of the value of the home, its claim must be paid in full as a result of the special protection granted to holders of security interests in real property that is the debtor's principal residence. * * *

Commercial Credit's position is supported by a recent opinion of the Fourth Circuit. Witt v. United Companies Lending Corp. (In re Witt), 113 F.3d 508 (4th Cir. 1997). Its opinion is flawed, however, in that it attempts to divine the will of Congress and then combine the results of its understanding with a misapplication of the Supreme Court's holding in *Nobelman* to reach an erroneous result. The correct result is easily reached by a straightforward reading of the statute, which is consistent with both the scant legislative history of §1322(c)(2) and the opinion in *Nobelman*. * * *

Cramdown is the centerpiece of the reorganization chapters. Cramdown starts with §506(a) which basically provides that a creditor holding a security interest in property has a secured claim only to the extent that there is value in that property to provide actual security for its claim. In a situation like ours, this means that Commercial Credit has a secured claim only to the extent of the difference between the value of the debtor's homestead and Norwest Mortgage, Inc.'s, debt, less any other prior encumbrances on the property, such as real estate taxes. The basic rule of cramdown is that, under a plan, a debtor must make payments to a secured creditor which have a value equal to the debtor's allowed secured claim, which is not necessarily its entire claim.

Cramdown as a general principle is recognized in Chapter 13. With one major exception which I will get to later, §1322(b)(2) provides that a plan may "modify the rights of holders of secured claims ... or of holders of unsecured claims." Section 1325(a)(5)(B) then goes on to specify that, as to secured creditors, unless the debtor surrenders the creditor's collateral or the creditor accepts some other treatment, that the creditor must retain its lien and receive value, as of the effective date of the plan, not less than the allowed amount of such claim. This is the essence of cramdown and, in the absence of other applicable provisions, the debtor would be correct and the only issue would be one of valuation.

There is more, of course. The provision in §1322(b)(2), quoted in the previous paragraph above, providing for the modification of the rights of holders of secured claims, specifically provides that the debtor may not modify such rights if the claim is "secured only by a security interest in real property that is the debtor's principal residence." The parties agree that Commercial Credit has such a claim and that if there were no more applicable provisions, then Commercial Credit would be right. The debtor would have to pay Commercial Credit in full according to the terms of its mortgage and note. This is what the Supreme Court's opinion in *Nobelman* settled.

There is yet more. Section 1322(b)(5) provides:

> notwithstanding paragraph (2) of this subsection, [a plan may] provide for the curing of any default within a reasonable time and maintenance of payments while the case is pending on any unsecured claim or secured claim on which the last payment is due after the date on which the final payment under the plan is due.

This provision has been in the Bankruptcy Code since it was enacted in 1978. This language acts as an exception to the exception that we just talked about. It provides that, even though §1322(b)(2) says that the rights of a home mortgagee may not be modified, that a plan may modify them to a limited extent. The only modification allowed under §1322(b)(5) is a modification dealing with the payment of defaults. Those defaults can be paid over a reasonable time. Since §1322(b)(5) applies only to those creditors whose last payment is due after the final payment under the plan, it does not apply in this case. However, it is important to understand the full framework of these provisions.

The last piece of this puzzle is a new one. Congress added a new §1322(c) in 1994, and renumbered the old §1322(c) as §1322(d). In particular, §1322(c)(2) applies to this case. * * *

Since the last payment to Commercial Credit comes due before the last payment under the plan, the parties agree that this subsection applies to the Commercial Credit debt. What the parties cannot agree on and what the cases are split on is what this provision says. In *Witt*, the Fourth Circuit parses the sentence in a very odd way, by holding that the last clause "as modified pursuant to §1325(a)(5) of this title" modifies the word "payment" rather than its direct antecedent "claim." Such a reading is unnatural and violates rules of both common sense and grammar, not to mention the last antecedent rule of statutory construction. The Fourth Circuit seems to have a preconceived notion about what this section is trying to do, based primarily on its scant bit of legislative history. They use this understanding of congressional intent to thereby create this strained meaning, or at least create an ambiguity, which they then proceed to resolve by resorting to the same legislative history they used to create the ambiguity in the first place.

The [court in In re Young, 199 Bankr. 643 (Bankr. E.D. Tenn. 1996),] uses a more straightforward and, if I can use the phrase, "plain meaning" analysis of the section. It begins with the words "notwithstanding subsection (b)(2)." We are therefore to ignore subsection (b)(2), at least to the extent that it is inconsistent with the language that follows. While part of §1322(b)(2) says that the rights of home mortgagees may not be modified, §1322(c)(2) says ignore that language. In certain limited circumstances which obtain here, the debtor may in fact utilize the provisions of §1325(a)(5) to cram down on the secured creditor, i.e., a return to the general rule of treatment of secured claims.

If Congress had wanted to adopt the rule proposed by Commercial Credit it could have done so much more easily by mimicking the language of §1322(b)(5). It did not do so; instead it chose to adopt a whole new subsection and use different language.

* * * Those of us who deal with bankruptcy laws are forever vexed by the paucity of appropriate legislative history. Instead of committee reports, which constitute the customary legislative history of federal statutes, we are left with conference committee statements, floor statements, and even ex post facto statements by key legislators. The statute at hand is a good example. The briefly stated purpose of the provision suggests that it was to overrule First Nat'l Fidelity Corp. v. Perry, 945 F.2d 61 (3d Cir. 1991). However, the new §1322(c)(2) has little, if anything, to do with *Perry*. *Perry* had to do with whether or not there were defaults still existing in a mortgage to be cured. In fact, if anything, it is §1322(c)(1) which deals with the situation in *Perry* and a lot of other cases which struggled with determining at what point, in a mortgage foreclosure process, there are no longer "defaults." Section 1322(c)(1) settled that issue by stating a rule that the courts could rely on in making that determination. * * *

The Fourth Circuit makes much about the fact that the commentary to §1322(c)(2) does not mention an intent to overrule *Nobelman*. First, while §1322(c)(2) provides an additional exception to §1322(b)(2) as interpreted in *Nobelman*, the new section does not purport to overrule *Nobelman*, so it is no surprise that the legislative history does not say it does. In addition, when notes are cobbled together at the last minute as it was for the Bankruptcy Reform Act of 1994, we should not put too much stock in what it says, much less what it does not say. * * *

The reason for the rule against modification of home mortgages seems to be an intent to encourage the flow of capital into the home lending market. Section 1322(c) addresses mortgages that have nothing to do with the home mortgage market. The section will typically apply to second mortgages such as this one, which are based very little on the value of the home and more on the leverage provided by having a mortgage on a debtor's homestead. A true first mortgage, payable over a longer term (typically 30 years), will rarely, if ever, be undersecured, especially when the last payment is coming due during the terms of a plan. While I will concede that occasionally this provision could catch such a home mortgage, it will be so rare as to have no effect on the home mortgage market. Thus, it is not at all unlikely that Congress saw a distinction between the type of mortgage that exists here and the type of mortgage that it sought to protect in §1322(b)(2). * * *

It is worth repeating that the effect of the provision is really not extraordinary. It provides only that such mortgages are treated like bankruptcy treats virtually all other secured creditors, save only the special provisions provided for the more traditional home purchase lender.

I will overrule Commercial Credit's objection to the extent that it relies on §1322(c)(2). However, an evidentiary hearing is still necessary. Depending on the value of the debtor's homestead, Commercial Credit may or may not have an allowed secured claim. If it does, the debtor's plan would be unconfirmable since it proposes to treat Commercial Credit as a totally unsecured creditor. * * *

IN RE WRIGHT

United States Court of Appeals, Seventh Circuit, 2007
2007 WL 1892502

EASTERBROOK, CIRCUIT JUDGE.

Bankruptcy judges across the nation have divided over the effect of the unnumbered hanging paragraph that the Bankruptcy Abuse Prevention and Consumer Protection Act of 2005 added to §1325(a) of the Bankruptcy Code. Section 1325, part of Chapter 13, specifies the circumstances under which a consumer's plan of repayment can be confirmed. The hanging paragraph says that, for the purpose of a Chapter 13 plan, §506 of the Code does not apply to certain secured loans.

Section 506(a) divides loans into secured and unsecured portions; the unsecured portion is the amount by which the debt exceeds the current value of the collateral. In a Chapter 13 bankruptcy, consumers may retain the collateral (despite contractual provisions entitling creditors to repossess) by making monthly payments that the judge deems equal to the market value of the asset, with a rate of interest that the judge will set (rather than the contractual rate). This procedure is known as a "cramdown"—the court crams down the creditor's throat the substitution of money for the collateral, a situation that creditors usually oppose because the court may underestimate the collateral's market value and the appropriate interest rate, and the debtor may fail to make all promised payments, so that the payment stream falls short of the collateral's full value. (The effect is asymmetric: if a judge overestimates the collateral's value or the interest rate, the debtor will surrender the asset and the creditor will realize no more than the market price. When the judge errs in the debtor's favor, however, the debtor keeps the asset and pays at the reduced rate. Creditors systematically lose from this asymmetry-and in the long run solvent borrowers must pay extra to make up for creditors' anticipated loss in bankruptcy.)

The question we must decide is what happens when, as a result of the hanging paragraph, §506 vanishes from the picture. The majority view among bankruptcy judges is that, with §506(a) gone, creditors cannot divide their loans into secured and unsecured components. Because §1325(a)(5)(C) allows a debtor to surrender the collateral to the lender, it follows (on this view) that surrender fully satisfies the borrower's obligations. If this is so, then many secured loans have been rendered nonrecourse, no matter what the contract provides. See, e.g., In re Payne, 347 Bankr. 278 (Bankr. S.D. Ohio 2006); In re Ezell, 338 Bankr. 330 (Bankr. E.D. Tenn.2006). The minority view[, which we adopt here], is that Article 9 of the Uniform Commercial Code plus the law of contracts entitle the creditor to an unsecured deficiency judgment after surrender of the collateral, unless the contract itself provides that the loan is without recourse against the borrower. That unsecured balance must be treated the same as other unsecured debts under the Chapter 13 plan.

Craig Wright and LaChone P. Giles-Wright, debtors in this proceeding, owe more on their purchase-money automobile loan than the car is worth. Because the purchase occurred within 910 days of the bankruptcy's commencement, the hanging paragraph in § 1325(a)(5) applies. This paragraph reads:

For purposes of paragraph (5), section 506 shall not apply to a claim described in that paragraph if the creditor has a purchase money security interest securing the debt that is the subject of the claim, the debt was incurred within the 910-day [sic] preceding the date of the filing of the petition, and the collateral for that debt consists of a motor vehicle (as defined in section 30102 of title 49) acquired for the personal use of the debtor, or if collateral for that debt consists of any other thing of value, if the debt was incurred during the 1-year period preceding that filing.

Debtors proposed a plan that would surrender the car to the creditor and pay nothing on account of the difference between the loan's balance and the collateral's market value. After taking the minority position on the effect of bypassing §506, the bankruptcy judge declined to approve the Chapter 13 plan, because debtors did not propose to pay any portion of the shortfall. * * *

Like the bankruptcy court, we think that, by knocking out § 506, the hanging paragraph leaves the parties to their contractual entitlements. True enough, §506(a) divides claims into secured and unsecured components. ... Yet it is a mistake to assume, as the majority of bankruptcy courts have done, that §506 is the *only* source of authority for a deficiency judgment when the collateral is insufficient. The Supreme Court held in Butner v. United States, 440 U.S. 48 (1979), that state law determines rights and obligations when the Code does not supply a federal rule.

The contract between the Wrights and their lender is explicit: If the debt is not paid, the collateral may be seized and sold. Creditor "must account to Buyer for any surplus. Buyer shall be liable for any deficiency." In other words, the contract creates an ordinary secured loan with recourse against the borrower. Just in case there were doubt, the contract provides that the parties enjoy all of their rights under the Uniform Commercial Code. Section 9-615(d)(2) of the UCC, enacted in Illinois as 810 ILCS 5/9-615(d)(2), provides that the obligor must satisfy any deficiency if the collateral's value is insufficient to cover the amount due.

If the Wrights had surrendered their car the day before filing for bankruptcy, the creditor would have been entitled to treat any shortfall in the collateral's value as an unsecured debt. It is hard to see why the result should be different if the debtors surrender the collateral the day after filing for bankruptcy when, given the hanging paragraph, no operative section of the Bankruptcy Code contains any contrary rule. Section 306(b) of the 2005 Act, Pub. L. 109-8, 119 Stat. 23, 80 (Apr.

20, 2005), which enacted the hanging paragraph, is captioned "Restoring the Foundation for Secured Credit". This implies replacing a contract-defeating provision such as §506 (which allows judges rather than the market to value the collateral and set an interest rate, and may prevent creditors from repossessing) with the agreement freely negotiated between debtor and creditor. Debtors do not offer any argument that "the Foundation for Secured Credit" could be "restored" by making all purchase-money secured loans non-recourse; they do not argue that non-recourse lending is common in consumer transactions, and it is hard to imagine that Congress took such an indirect means of making non-recourse lending *compulsory*.

Appearing as *amicus curiae,* the National Association of Consumer Bankruptcy Attorneys makes the bold argument that loans covered by the hanging paragraph cannot be treated as secured in any respect. Only §506 provides for an "allowed secured claim," *amicus* insists, so the entire debt must be unsecured. This also would imply that a lender is not entitled to any post-petition interest. *Amicus* recognizes that §502 rather than §506 determines whether a claim should be "allowed" but insists that only § 506 permits an "allowed" claim to be a "secured" one.

This line of argument makes the same basic mistake as the debtors' position: it supposes that contracts and state law are irrelevant unless specifically implemented by the Bankruptcy Code. *Butner* holds that the presumption runs the other way: rights under state law count in bankruptcy unless the Code says otherwise. Creditors don't need §506 to create, allow, or recognize security interests, which rest on contracts (and the UCC) rather than federal law. Section 502 tells bankruptcy courts to allow claims that stem from contractual debts; nothing in §502 disfavors or curtails secured claims. Limitations, if any, depend on §506, which the hanging paragraph makes inapplicable to purchase-money interests in personal motor vehicles granted during the 910 days preceding bankruptcy (and in other assets during the year before bankruptcy).

Both the debtors and the *amicus curiae* observe that many decisions … state that §506 governs the treatment of secured claims in bankruptcy. No one doubts this, but the question at hand is what happens when §506 does not apply. The fallback under *Butner* is the parties' contract (to the extent the deal is enforceable under state law), rather than non-recourse secured debt (the Wrights' position) or no security interest (the *amicus curiae's* position). And there is no debate about how the parties' contract works: the secured lender is entitled to an (unsecured) deficiency judgment for the difference between the value of the collateral and the balance on the loan.

By surrendering the car, debtors gave their creditor the full market value of the collateral. Any shortfall must be treated as an unsecured debt. It need not be paid in full, any more than the Wrights' other unsecured debts, but it can't be written off *in toto* while other unsecured creditors are paid some fraction of their entitlements.

NOTES

12B.1. A debtor already in Chapter 13, no doubt, would prefer *Mattson* to *Witt* for an interpretation of §1322(c)(2). *Mattson*, however, represents only a partial victory for a debtor. According to *Mattson*, a Chapter 13 debtor can use §506(a) to reduce even an obligation secured only by debtor's home when the obligation has only a short time to run. Recall, however, the Supreme Court's opinion in *Dewsnup*, excerpted and discussed in chapter 11, section A above. In *Dewsnup*, the Court held that §506(d) does not strip down a lien even when §506(a) reduces the amount of a secured claim. If *Dewsnup* applies in Chapter 13, a matter the Court explicitly declined to decide, a debtor could find its property encumbered by the amount of a lender's original mortgage loan even though the bankruptcy process has reduced the debtor's personal obligation on that loan. To take an extreme example, imagine that a debtor's house is worth half the amount of an outstanding mortgage loan and that a confirmed Chapter 13 plan consequently reduces the lender's secured claim by half, after which the debtor completes plan payments and receives a discharge. One could argue that, whatever the "secured claim," the lien on the house, for twice the amount of the payments, itself rides through Chapter 13 unaffected. This result seems unlikely, however, and inconsistent with new §1325(A)(5)(B)(II), which permits lien pass through in a case that is dismissed or converted (rather than completed). Compare Exercise 12B(2).

12B.2. Whether you are more persuaded by the arguments in *Witt* or in *Mattson*, do not overlook the significance of *Mattson*'s distinction between first and second mortgages. A residential first mortgage—i.e., one with first priority—ordinarily secures a long-term loan for the purchase price of a home. As the court notes, thirty years is a common maturity. A Chapter 13 plan cannot last for more than five years. Thus, for a debtor to avail herself of §1322(c) with respect to a typical first mortgage she would have had to file for bankruptcy after paying down the loan for a long time, perhaps twenty-five years or more. As the court suggests, it would be extraordinary for such a loan to be undersecured in such a situation, the facts of *Witt* notwithstanding. By contrast, a residential second mortgage—i.e., one with second priority—may support a loan with a shorter maturity and, because it is second in priority, may frequently be undersecured even if the home has substantial value. *Mattson* concludes, therefore, that Congress intended to permit only cures and reinstatements for first mortgages but any modification consistent with §1325(a)(5) for second mortgages. Such an intent could well explain the otherwise mysterious combination of §1322(b)(5) and (c)(2). Nevertheless, as the opinion in *Witt* makes clear, the matter is not free from doubt. Problem 12B-1 asks you to explore a related wrinkle on the question of home mortgage strip down under Chapter 13 where the mortgage has little time to run before maturity.

12B.3. Neither *Witt* nor *Mattson* needed to confront the issue whether a wholly unsecured second mortgage is subject to the anti-modification clause of §1322(b)(2) in the first instance, before consideration of any exception. Imagine that a debtor's home is worth less than the amount of a loan subject to a first mortgage. Assume that the home is also subject to a second mortgage. When one applies §506(a) to the second mortgage, the holder of that mortgage has *no* "secured claim" because "the value of such creditor's interest in the estate's interest" in the home is zero. Thus, the question becomes whether the holder of the second mortgage can benefit from §1322(b)(2), which implicitly prevents modification of "a claim secured only by a security interest" in a debtor's principal residence. *Witt* didn't need to confront this question because that case involved a first mortgage. *Mattson* didn't need to confront the question because its interpretation of §1322(c)(2) permitted modification whether or not the loan in that case was partially secured.

Other courts have squarely addressed the issue. The minority of courts read "a claim secured by a security interest" to mean "a claim supported by collateral," and apply the anti-modification clause even to a second mortgage that is not a "secured claim" as that term is defined by §506(a). The majority, however, conclude that a claim must be a "secured claim" or it cannot be a "claim secured by a security interest." These courts refuse to apply the clause. See, e.g., In re Bartee, 212 F.3d 277 (5th Cir. 2000) (adopting the majority view and describing both views).

12B.4. The opinion in *Wright* addresses only one of the conundrums presented by the hanging paragraph, an astonishingly sloppy piece of legislation by any standard. In *Wright*, the debtors surrendered the collateral. The question arises what Congress intended with respect to collateral retained by the debtor. Problem 12B-2 asks you to consider this question along with the "personal use" condition for application of the hanging paragraph to an interest in a motor vehicle, relevant when the purchase money loan is made between one year and 910 days prior to the bankruptcy petition.

PROBLEM

12B-1. After Debtor lost his high-paying job, he took one with a significantly lower salary and then struggled for some time to pay debts incurred before the change. Eventually, he gave up and filed a Chapter 13 bankruptcy petition. At the time Debtor seeks confirmation of her Chapter 13 plan her only asset is her home, a house worth between $150,000 and $250,000. The house is subject to Bank's first mortgage loan, of which $150,000 is outstanding, and Finance Company's second mortgage loan, of which $100,000 is outstanding. The first mortgage loan matures in fifteen years. The second mortgage loan matures in just under four years. Prior to her bankruptcy petition, Debtor defaulted on both loans, but at the time she seeks confirmation, she is current on each. Debtor values the house at $200,000 and proposes a plan for payments over four years. The plan would reinstate Bank's first mortgage loan. The plan also bifurcates Finance Company's loan into equal secured and unsecured portions. Debtor's income is regular, but not high enough to provide for significant payments on her unsecured obligations. Finance Company argues that the house is worth $250,000 and on that basis opposes the plan. Assuming no defects in terms not presented here, will the court confirm the plan?

Would your answer change if Debtor's plan valued the house at $150,000 and characterized Finance Company's loan as wholly unsecured? In answering these questions consider, among other factors, §1322(d).

12B-2. Eighteen months before Debtor files for bankruptcy under Chapter 13, she buys a car on credit from Auto Dealer, which takes and properly perfects a security interest in the vehicle. Debtor uses the car as a commuter vehicle for her salaried job, to transport her children, and for grocery shopping, but she also uses it occasionally to transport goods she sells on weekends at local flea markets. At the time of the bankruptcy petition, the car has a value between $8,000 and $12,000, the latter also the outstanding balance of Dealer's loan. Debtor proposes to retain the car and to pay Dealer $2,400 per year for each of the five years of her plan. Dealer, which argues that the car is worth $12,000, objects to the plan. What result? In answering this question consider, among other factors, Bankruptcy Code §1111(b), discussed in the book's next chapter. See also, e.g., In re Philips, 2007 WL 706834 (Bankr. E.D. Va. 2007), In re Carver, 338 Bankr. 521 (Bankr. S.D. Ga. 2006).

XIII. CORPORATE REORGANIZATIONS IN CHAPTER 11

The dynamics of the typical large Chapter 11 are different from what they were even less than a decade ago. To understand the modern Chapter 11 process, one must understand these differences, which are summarized here and described in more depth by Douglas G. Baird and Robert K. Rasmussen, Chapter 11 at Twilight, 56 Stan. L. Rev. 673 (2003) and by Douglas G. Baird and Robert K. Rasmussen, The End of Bankruptcy, 55 Stan. L. Rev. 751 (2002).

The traditional account of corporate reorganizations assumes a financially distressed business faces three conditions simultaneously: (1) It has substantial value as a going concern; (2) its investors cannot sort out the financial distress through ordinary bargaining and instead require Chapter 11's collective forum; and (3) the business cannot be readily sold in the market as a going concern. A review of large Chapter 11s shows that these conditions are not routinely found in a financially distressed business today. It is even less likely that all three of them will exist at the same time.

In December 2002, for example, the bankruptcy court in Delaware confirmed Global Crossing's plan of reorganization. One of the largest corporations ever to go through Chapter 11, Global Crossing is emblematic of Chapter 11's past and its future. Global Crossing was formed in 1997 to close one of the last gaps in the Internet. The telecommunications cables connecting the continents were too small to accommodate the expected growth in Internet use outside of North America. In 1997, those outside North America accounted for only 20% Internet use. By 2000, they would account for almost half.

To take advantage of this change, Global Crossing laid a trans-Atlantic cable within 10 months and embarked on ambitious plans to create a global fiber network. It reached $1 billion in revenues within its first 20 months. Global Crossing continued to invest billions in creating the first network of fiber optic cable across the world's oceans. Global Crossing was to be a major player in the Digital Age, and its market capitalization soon exceeded that of General Motors.

Global Crossing's fall, however, was as swift as its rise. Competitors appeared. Internet traffic grew, but it doubled only every year, not every hundred days as some had predicted. Moreover, technological innovation allowed much more information to be carried over the same cable. As a result, there was massive overcapacity. Global

Crossing's revenue barely paid its ongoing expenses. Its stock price collapsed as people quickly came to see that Global Crossing would never make back the billions it spent building its fiber optic network.

Fiber optic cable was to the 1990s what iron rails and wooden ties were to the 1880s. A promising technology in a heavily regulated environment will bring people together as never before. An entrepreneur makes the enormous capital investment the technology requires, but demand falls far short of expectations. A visionary business that attracted capital from all over the world and that employs thousands cannot generate the funds needed to pay its creditors. Games are played with the business's finances to hide this reality for a time, but the truth is discovered soon enough.

At this point we have to make the best of a bad situation. While we investigate the financial frauds and those who perpetrated them, we have to accept that the railroad has been built and the fiber optic cable has been laid. We need to sort through the financial mess and still ensure these assets are put to their best use. The equity receivership allowed nineteenth century investors to take control of the business, throw out bad managers, and agree upon a new capital structure consistent with the less-than-expected revenue of the railroad going forward. Chapter 11 provides a similar forum today. From this perspective, Global Crossing is merely old wine in a new bottle. The technology is different, but the legal challenge is the same.

Closer examination, however, reveals fundamental differences between nineteenth century railroads on the one hand and Global Crossing and the many casualties of the dot-com era on the other. The railroads had to raise capital in bits and pieces. No one source of capital was large enough to build the entire project. Dozens of different types of bonds were secured by different parts of the road. Bondholders were scattered in New York, London, and Amsterdam. Creditors could not work together to hold a single foreclosure sale. Even if they could, no one buyer would be able to muster the resources to bid.

Today creditors of insolvent businesses—even those as large as Global Crossing—no longer need a substitute for a market sale. Instead of providing a substitute for a market sale, Chapter 11 now frequently serves as the forum where such sales are conducted. In the equity receivership, judges protected minority investors when valuations could not be set in the market. To carry out this task, they developed the absolute priority rule. In modern Chapter 11, the judge ensures that sale is conducted in a way that brings the highest price. Lock-up agreements and bust-up fees are now bankruptcy issues.

In the equity receivership, no actual sale could take place, but as Global Crossing illustrates, sales are now part of the warp and woof of Chapter 11 practice. Of the 10 largest Chapter 11s of 2002, for instance, eight used the bankruptcy court as a way of selling their assets to the highest bidder, whether piecemeal or as a going concern. Of the large publicly traded firms in Chapter 11, the assets of more than half were sold in Chapter 11 or were transferred to a new owner under the plan of reorganization. In some cases, the sales are more or less completed before the fact and the Chapter 11 merely insures that no one else will bid more. In other cases, the bankruptcy judge conducts an auction in open court.

If we take a snapshot of the business before and after the Chapter 11, we would not be able to tell whether there has been a Chapter 11 or a traditional corporate control transaction. The business may now be folded into another. Even if it is not, the old shareholders are gone as are the old managers and the old board. New managers run a business whose operations have been streamlined and whose workforce has been reduced. The process itself resembles the takeover battles we see elsewhere. Corporate raiders square off against each other in a bidding war, while the board's independent directors pay careful heed to their fiduciary duty to maximize the sale price. The lawyers shuttle between their offices in New York and a courtroom in Wilmington. Chapter 11 has morphed largely into a branch of the law governing mergers and acquisitions.

There continue to be some Chapter 11 cases in which the sale of the business is never in prospect. In these cases, the embers of the equity receivership still burn. Here again, however, the differences between the equity receivership and modern Chapter 11 are enormous. The railroads possessed primitive, and needlessly complex, capital structures. When the Atchison, Topeka, and Santa Fe entered receivership, there were 43 different types of bonds. By contrast, corporations today have far simpler capital structures. Their form is the product of deliberate design. Global Crossing's capital structure was structured so that it had to return repeatedly to capital markets. A bank group held much of the senior debt and was well-positioned to monitor the business and negotiate with it as its condition deteriorated.

The elaborate committee structure of the equity receivership provided investors with a way to communicate with each other that did not exist elsewhere. The ability of creditors to control their debtor and negotiate with each other outside of Chapter 11 is now vastly greater than it was during the equity receivership—or even in Chapter 11 just 20 years ago. Often Chapter 11 is needed only to put in place a plan that the key players negotiated before the petition was filed.

Of the large businesses whose assets are not sold in Chapter 11, perhaps half enter Chapter 11 with a prenegotiated plan. The judge usually confirms it within several months after only minor modifications. In looking at recent large Chapter 11s, there is one other striking contrast between these businesses and the railroads reorganized in the Nineteenth Century. The railroads generated substantial operating profits. Value would be lost if the railroad did not stay intact. The value of keeping the business intact is far less obvious with businesses in Chapter 11 today.

Even in Global Crossing, the value of keeping the assets together was not self-evident. Global Crossing has to compete in a market in which one can create networks through contract. As long as these contracting costs are low, Global's ability to offer direct connections between Tokyo and London may not be worth much. A pulse of light can be transferred between multiple carriers much more easily than rail freight. A detour of thousands of miles is irrelevant. A route that is twice as long matters if one is moving coal or wheat, but not if one is moving electrons. The value of what is being preserved by keeping the business intact is much smaller than in the case of railroads.

The difference between the receivership and the large businesses in reorganization today is even more manifest in other large businesses in Chapter 11. Outside the telecommunications sector, they often lack large infrastructure investments. Some are holding companies. Their operating subsidiaries were not in Chapter 11. Chapter 11 provides a relatively cheap way to put a new capital structure in place, but the value being preserved is only that of the holding company. The worst thing that would happen in the absence of a reorganization would be for the equity of the operating companies to be spread among diverse creditors.

In many other large Chapter 11s, particularly those in which there was neither a prenegotiated plan nor an asset sale, the corporation is a collection of discrete businesses, such as movie theaters, nursing homes, or hotels. What is at risk is the synergy gained from putting these different discrete businesses under one umbrella. This synergy itself, however, is often of recent vintage. The business itself was formed through the same highly leveraged acquisitions that precipitated the financial distress and the need to reorganize. Unlike a railroad, the synergy that these businesses possess is intangible and often quite small.

During the 1980s, nine of ten large businesses entered Chapter 11, crafted a plan of reorganization there, and then emerged intact. Today, this was true in fewer than one in four. The disappearance of the traditional reorganization stems not from changes in the law, but from changes in the economy that have been underway for a long period of time. The equity receivership of the nineteenth century railroad was desirable because of a conjunction of a number of different conditions. There was a huge capital investment in a particular business and the assets were worth far more if kept together than if sold off piecemeal. The creditors were scattered across the globe and could not effectively control the railroad or shape its future outside the kind of collective forum that the receivership provided. Finally, the capital markets were not liquid enough to have a sale of the railroad as a going concern.

Any one of these conditions can still exist today, but each is less likely. In particular, while large operating companies continue in business and new ones form, presumably because it is efficient for them to do so, going-concern surplus is less evident now than in the time of the great railroads. Fewer businesses today center around specialized long-lived assets. In a service-oriented economy, the assets walk out the door at 5:00. Today the costs of starting a business are those involved in creating and implementing a business plan. Millions are spent training staff, building a client base, and cementing relationships with suppliers. But these investments are fundamentally different from those involved with building a railroad. The ability to outsource has left even large-scale manufacturers less dependent on their factories and workers. Third-party vendors in Japan are making more than a third of Boeing's latest airplane. If one can design and build a large commercial jet through a network of contracts, the value of ensuring that production remains inside a given firm is necessarily smaller than it once was.

The disappearance of going-concern value reduces the benefits that can be had through a traditional reorganization. Among the large cases that have been concluded recently, one resembling the traditional Chapter 11 was that of Pillowtex, the manufacturer of Cannon and Royal Velvet towels and Fieldcrest sheets and pillows. It cost millions to build the factories, hire thousands of employees, and create all the relationships that made Pillowtex's business work, but these have no value as a going concern in a world in which the towels, pillows, and sheets can be made under the same labels for less off shore. The Chapter 11 from which Pillowtex emerged in 2002 only postponed the inevitable. It filed for Chapter 11 again in July 2003, and its factories were closed, its remaining assets sold off piecemeal. The second bankruptcy was not so much the result of some failure of the first, but the natural consequence of a world in which there is increasingly less value associated with discrete business entities. The absence of going-concern value makes the traditional role that Chapter 11 is supposed to serve increasingly irrelevant. There are no railroads here.

And there has been another change. By comparison to creditors of distressed businesses in an earlier era, creditors today (ranging from banks and other financial institutions to universities, mutual funds and hedge funds) increasingly tend to be professional investors who are often willing to forego a market sale in order to recapitalize the debtor through a stand-alone reorganization. The more sophisticated the investors and the more promptly they can reach agreement on a plan of reorganization, the less tolerant they will be of imperfections in the market for sale of the business as a going concern. The players in a large corporate reorganization, even those that most resemble the nineteenth century railroad no longer see a Hobson's choice between a sale in an illiquid market or a costly reorganization. Instead, they see the choice as one between selling the business to other investors in a developed, but not perfect, market or keeping it themselves in a proceeding that has become cheaper and easier to control over time.

All this said, the law of bankruptcy reorganization itself is not irrelevant, even if it is increasingly outdated. When businesses, particularly large businesses, fail today they still resolve insolvency within Chapter 11, and even where such resolution is prenegotiated, that negotiation takes place in the shadow of the Bankruptcy Code. Despite the modern use of Chapter 11 as a tool for asset sales, not every business is sold whole for cash with no strings attached. Partial liquidations leave assets behind and these must be redeployed. And Chapter 11 remains the vehicle for distribution of a debtor's value, whether that distribution is of a continuing interest in the debtor or cash. The mechanics of Chapter 11 thus remain important.

Take, for example, the role of the secured creditor in a modern Chapter 11 case. The Bankruptcy Code continues to provide that the debtor's prebankruptcy management, as the debtor-in-possession ("DIP"), controls the debtor throughout the bankruptcy process and has an exclusive period in which to propose a reorganization plan unless the unusual step is taken to appoint a trustee. As described more fully below, the 2005 Bankruptcy Act limits the debtor's exclusive period, but it still exists and has existed throughout the period of change described here. Despite this, secured creditors have increasingly taken control of both the debtor and the reorganization process. The secured creditor's tool of choice has been DIP finance. Frequently, now, a dominant secured lender gains a pledge of debtor's liquid capital prior to bankruptcy. Liquidity is lifeblood for a business and thus, once the debtor files for bankruptcy, the secured creditor with such collateral has at its mercy a debtor who hopes to continue in business, even just long enough to be sold. The secured creditor can and does use this leverage to condition DIP finance on terms favorable to the lender. Outside lenders, who might, in principle, offer finance on more favorable terms, are often unable to act quickly enough.

The terms of conditional DIP loans may be generally beneficial, as when they assure a quick sale of a debtor that is floundering under current management. (DIP loans are discussed more fully in chapter 9, section D of this book.) But the secured lenders that provide such loans are not charitable institutions and there is a risk that they will use control of the process to their own ends perhaps at the expense of other creditors and of efficient resolution of the debtor's financial distress. It is possible, therefore, that the secured creditor can use the confirmation process, including the threat of cramdown, to achieve private and not socially optimal ends. So the formal rules of Chapter 11 as well as the incentives for strategic behavior created by these rules, remain a live topic even if there is a new hand on the tiller of the reorganization process.

With this as background, it is useful to have a sense of the terrain. Bankruptcy Code §103 states that generally the rules in Chapters 1, 3, and 5 of the Bankruptcy Code apply in Chapter 11 as well as in Chapters 7 and 13 (and 12). For example, the automatic stay of §362, the voidable preference rules of §547, and the definition of a claim under §101(5) apply in Chapter 11 as in the other chapters. Moreover, the priority rules applicable in Chapter 7 are also relevant in Chapter 11. Indeed, because the stakes are typically larger in Chapter 11 cases, many of the general rules we have looked at so far have involved debtors in Chapter 11. What concerns us now are those features of Chapter 11 that are distinctive.

Although an individual or partnership is eligible for Chapter 11 bankruptcy reorganization, we shall focus on the corporation—or an essentially similar entity such as a limited partnership—and the way in which it fares differently from how it would in Chapter 7. A fundamental difference is in who controls the debtor. In every Chapter 7 case, a trustee is appointed to assemble the assets and make the most of them. By contrast, in Chapter 11, the old directors and officers remain in place in the absence of fraud or some other special circumstance such as a demonstrable diminution of the estate without reasonable prospect of rehabilitation . See §1104. These managers are known collectively as the "debtor in possession." They continue to run the business and enjoy all the powers of the trustee, see §1106, including the right to sell, use, and lease property under §363, as well as the right to borrow money under §364.

The debtor in possession has responsibilities beyond management of the debtor. It enjoys the same strong-arm powers as the trustee and, like the trustee, can resist efforts to lift the automatic stay. Throughout part 2 of this book, cases exploring the powers of the trustee often involved debtors in possession asserting the powers of the trustee. Bankruptcy Code §§1104 and 1106 permit the appointment of a trustee or an "examiner." In some cases, an examiner is appointed to oversee the reorganization process, while the debtor in possession remains in control of the debtor's business affairs. An examiner played exactly this role in *Official Committee of Equity Security Holders v. Mabey*, the Dalkon Shield case in chapter 9, section C. Section 1106 gives the bankruptcy judge the ability to shape the role of the examiner to accommodate the specific needs of the case.

Both Chapter 7 and Chapter 11 permit continuation of the business while the firm is in bankruptcy. If the business is to continue after the close of the case, however, Chapter 7 is far less flexible than Chapter 11. At the end of a Chapter 7 case, the trustee must abandon or distribute the bankruptcy estate, or the proceeds thereof, to the holders of claims or interests. Thus, while a trustee can run a firm as a going concern while the debtor is in Chapter 7, the trustee must sell the business as a unit if it is to remain a going concern after the bankruptcy case is over. In contrast, Chapter 11 does not require such a sale. Chapter 11 replaces old claims and interests against the firm with new ones. The new claims and interests, like the old ones, reflect the rights that the creditors and shareholders enjoy outside of bankruptcy, but they also reflect the economic condition in which the firm finds itself. A general creditor of an insolvent firm, for example, cannot expect to be paid in full and will not be paid in full whether the debtor is restructured or sold. When the firm is restructured, new claims and interests from what may be described as a hypothetical sale are distributed instead of proceeds from an actual one.

The division of such new claims and interests is contained in a "plan of reorganization." In broad strokes, the reorganization process is relatively simple. Typically, the debtor proposes a plan of reorganization. The claims of the creditors and the interests of the shareholders are then placed in classes, and each class votes on the plan. If all classes accept the plan and the plan otherwise satisfies Chapter 11's requirements, the court confirms the plan. If a class dissents, then the court can confirm a plan only if the plan is fair and equitable and does not discriminate unfairly. The contours of the fair and equitable standard and the unfair-discrimination standard are set out in §1129(b). These in turn must be read in light of a series of Supreme Court opinions spanning almost a century. The core idea, however, is quite straightforward. A class of claims is entitled to insist that the plan comply with the principle of "absolute priority." Holders of unsecured claims, for example, can insist on being paid in full if equity holders receive any property on account of their old interests. Moreover, a class of claims or interests can insist on being treated at least as well as those in another class that enjoys the same priority outside of bankruptcy.

Even if a class as a group votes to accept a plan, an individual within that class can block confirmation unless the plan gives the individual dissenter at least the amount she would have received under a hypothetical Chapter 7 liquidation. (This protection is sometimes called the "best interests" test.) In principle, a Chapter 11 reorganization will not make anyone worse off than would a Chapter 7 liquidation, and the reorganization can make some better off. A successful Chapter 11 preserves the extra value a firm has as a going concern. Hence, there is more value to be distributed. Critics of Chapter 11, however, have argued that the absolute priority rule and the best-interests test often fall short in practice. These devices do not always ensure that creditors are in fact at least well as off as they would have been in a speedy liquidation. The protections they offer depend on whether the valuations are being done accurately. Moreover, the Chapter 11 process takes both time and money. Creditors may be better off settling for much less than their theoretical entitlements if settlement brings the reorganization to a speedy conclusion.

Replacing the old capital structure with a new one requires the termination of the rights inherent in the old structure. Section 1141 accomplishes this by providing for a discharge of old claims and interests. One should not, however, assume that, because the same word is used, the discharge under §1141 serves the same purpose here for a corporate debtor as it does in the case of the individual debtor. As we have seen in the last two chapters, the discharge of an insolvent individual shelters that individual's future earnings from prebankruptcy creditors. In contrast, the discharge of the debt of an insolvent corporate debtor is merely a necessary step in capital reorganization. Accompanying it is the parceling out of new rights against the firm back to the creditors. The new rights creditors receive back reflect the priority of claims over interests. When the corporation is insolvent, creditors as a group can insist on being paid in full before the shareholders receive anything. There is no provision comparable to §541(a)(6), which puts the future income of a corporate debtor beyond the reach of creditors. Indeed, when §1141 is read in conjunction with §1129(b), "discharge" serves exactly the opposite function. By creating a new and presumably more stable capital structure, the discharge ensures that the debtor's future income will go to creditors.

These are just the broad strokes, and much is glossed over. For example, as intimated above, a plan puts all claims against and interests in the corporate debtor into various classes. A claim secured by the debtor's real property might be in one class, a claim secured by debtor's equipment in another, the claims of the trade creditors and other general creditors in a third, and the interests of shareholders in the last. The debtor or other plan proponent will form classes in a way that is most likely to lead to confirmation of the plan. Chapter 11 classification rules limit, but do not completely prevent, strategic manipulation of classes. Then there is the question whether a class has voted to accept a plan. Section 1126 provides rules, but these are not always easy to apply. Finally, while it is easy in the abstract to describe the absolute priority or best-interests rule, applying these rules to the facts of a given case is often hard. We discuss these topics in a more detailed description of the reorganization process below in section A.

In the last two sections we connect the lessons learned about the reorganization process to two areas that have become increasingly important. As the economy has become more global, many firms operate in more than one jurisdiction. Hence transnational bankruptcy law, the focus of section B, matters more than it did only a few years ago. Also in flux is the role that lawyers themselves play in the Chapter 11 process. As discussed in section C, the duties of lawyers who represent different players in the Chapter 11 process now form a growing body of law distinct from general bankruptcy law. The ordinary rules of professional responsibility draw a sharp line between a lawyer's duties when representing a client in litigation and when representing one in a transaction. In bankruptcy, however, these lines are often impossible to define. Moreover, so many parties are involved or potentially involved in a large bankruptcy case that conflicts invariably surface in a Chapter 11 case of any size.

Before launching into a detailed study of Chapter 11, consider whether the structure of Chapter 11 as it exists today is well suited to achieving its basic goals. Chapter 11 is designed to ensure the survival of those firms in financial distress that are worth keeping intact as going concerns. A railroad that has proved unexpectedly costly to build, but that is otherwise a success, is a prototypical example. Although the railroad's revenues exceed its operating costs, the railroad cannot generate enough income to meet its debt obligations. Its assets, however, are worth more if kept together as a railroad than if used for anything else. By restructuring its obligations, the railroad can continue to operate and the creditors are repaid to the extent possible. But the process that Chapter 11 uses to create the new capital structure is not the only one that might be used, or even the most straightforward.

The simplest way to accomplish the same goal is to sell the railroad as a unit stripped of its old obligations. The proceeds of the sale can be divided among the creditors and, if anything remains, distributed to shareholders. There might still be disputes that need to be resolved. A secured creditor, for example, might argue about the value of its collateral, but this issue would be cleanly separated from the operations of the railroad after it is sold and put into a third party's hands. Such a sale might simplify significantly the reorganization of firms in financial distress. Chapter 11 permits such sales and, in recent years, some bankruptcy judges push the parties to take this course. The difficulties inherent in selling small firms, however, may render such sales infeasible in many cases.

The law does not have to mandate a particular reorganization regime. It might simply require that entrepreneurs and investors specify a reorganization mechanism in their corporate charters. The corporate charter, for example, might specify that in the event of specific conditions of default, some or all of the debtor's obligations would automatically become equity, thus extinguishing the former equity shares. In effect, instead of holding ordinary debt instruments, investors would hold an instrument that is debt under some circumstance and equity under others. A charter that provided for such "chameleon" equity would also have to cover a variety of other issues, such as the rights of tort claimants and those of secured creditors. But if these challenges were met, such an automatic transfer scheme would avoid the costs of Chapter 11 and not impose the costs of a sale.

None of these options—current Chapter 11, sale, or chameleon equity—dominates the others. That is, depending on the circumstances of an insolvent debtor, and considering what might go wrong, investors and entrepreneurs might choose any (or none) of them for a particular firm. Current law, however, does not begin with the idea of a reorganization mechanism as one that parties can shape to their mutual advantage at the time the corporation is formed. Unlike corporate law generally, Chapter 11 is not a set of default rules but rather a mandatory regime that parties can contract around only with great difficulty. For better or worse, Chapter 11's procedures in practice tend to extend the life of a business enterprise and, critically, the employment of its workers, *regardless* of whether the business is more valuable continued than liquidated. Keep this in mind as you work through the material below.

A. PLAN OF REORGANIZATION

We now turn in some more detail to the plan of reorganization and the reorganization process. The sequence in the best of worlds is as follows. A corporation that is unable to make its loan payments but is worth keeping intact files a Chapter 11 petition. The old managers continue to run the business. Some business decisions they may wish to make require notice and a hearing under §§363 and 364, but mostly they stick to business as usual. The rest of the world continues to do business with the corporation as before. Shortly after the petition is filed, the United States Trustee, a government administrator who serves a general oversight function, appoints a committee of creditors. This committee usually consists of the creditors with the seven largest unsecured claims who are willing to serve on the committee. If a group of creditors had attempted to restructure the debt outside of bankruptcy (a process that is typically called a "workout"), that group may be appointed to serve as the creditors committee. Additional creditors committees or equity holders committees may be appointed as well. An authorized committee may hire professionals to look into the debtor's affairs. The creditors committee, as well as any other committee, provides a vehicle for negotiations between the debtor and the creditors generally. See §§1102 and 1103.

While the debtor's business continues, the debtor, typically through its management, tries to come up with a plan of reorganization. Under §1121, the debtor has the exclusive right to propose a plan of reorganization during the first 120 days after the order for relief at the start of the case. If the debtor files a plan within the first 120 days, the exclusivity period is extended for an additional 60 days to give the debtor a chance to solicit acceptance of its plan without competition from any competing plan. Moreover, the exclusivity period can be extended further with court approval, up to 18 months from commencement of the case for the filing of a plan and up to 20 months from commencement if a plan has been filed. The court may also shorten the exclusivity period, and the period is terminated if the court appoints a trustee. But curtailment of exclusivity is not the general practice. Instead, courts commonly grant extensions, especially in relatively large cases, so long as the debtor is able to generate enough revenue to meet ongoing operating expenses.

If the exclusivity period expires because a plan is not filed or not accepted within the specified time limits, any party in interest may propose a plan. Nondebtor plans that continue the debtor as a going concern are relatively rare, however. If a creditor cannot persuade the court to lift the automatic stay or convert the case to Chapter 7, the creditor is likely to find it in its interest to negotiate with the debtor rather than have protracted litigation over competing plans of reorganization.

Under §1123, a reorganization plan must divide the claims of the creditors, as well as any interests of shareholders, into various classes. The plan must propose a treatment for each class. Section 1122 explicitly prohibits the common classification of dissimilar claims or interests. Thus, courts generally agree that each secured claim belongs in a class by itself. As cases such as *Woodbrook Associates* below suggest, however, courts are divided on what makes one claim "substantially similar" to another. This determination is particularly difficult where holders of claims with the same priority have dramatically different relationships with the debtor. There is, in addition, an issue over whether similar claims generally must be classified together. Section 1122(b) explicitly permits the separate classification of all similar small claims or interests—sometimes called the "administrative class." But courts disagree on whether or under what circumstances claims that have the same legal entitlements must be put together. Again, much turns on the different relationships the claimholders have with the debtor. The bank that made a one-time unsecured loan and the long-term supplier that has shipped the debtor goods on an unsecured open account for years have identical legal rights, but each may have different views about whether the debtor should remain as a going concern.

A class is deemed to accept a plan if the class is unimpaired within the meaning of §1124. Generally speaking, a class is unimpaired under a plan if the plan would cure any default, other than ipso facto clauses triggered by bankruptcy or financial crisis, and reinstate the claim or interest according to its original terms. (Such terms include interest rate and maturity date.) The holders of unimpaired claims or interests may well want to be cashed out. Interest rates, for example, might have moved in the wrong direction. But the Bankruptcy Code does not permit this. Rather, it adopts the idea that if a reorganization leaves holders of claims or interests after the reorganization with exactly what they had before, they have nothing to complain about.

Impaired classes have a choice. They must study the plan and vote. For this reason, after the debtor proposes a plan, it must write and get court approval for a disclosure statement. The disclosure statement functions in bankruptcy the same way a prospectus functions outside of bankruptcy. It explains the plan to those who must vote for or against the plan. Disclosure and solicitation are governed by §1125. After the disclosure statement is approved, the debtor is able to solicit acceptance of the plan from any and all impaired classes.

Actual approval of a class of claims or interests is governed by §1126. Approval requires positive votes by those who hold two-thirds in amount and a majority by number of the allowed claims duly voted in a class. In the case of equity interests, actual approval requires positive votes only by those who hold two-thirds in amount of the shares duly voted.

So long as at least one class of claims is impaired under a plan, at least one class must vote to approve the plan. As a result, unless all classes of claims are unimpaired, creditors cannot be forced to accept a plan unless at least those who hold one class of claims think the plan is a good idea. This provision, codified in §1129(a)(10), is one of the many Chapter 11 rules designed to protect creditors. Holders of equity interests are not similarly protected. The typical debtor in bankruptcy is insolvent. Hence, classes of interests are more easily eliminated after a determination that absolute priority entitles equity to nothing. Moreover, inasmuch as the debtor in possession is usually the management originally appointed by equity, it may be that creditors need protection from equity holders, but not the other way around, at least when the debtor is the plan's proponent. The level of protection that §1129(a)(10) affords creditors, however, turns crucially on how much freedom the debtor has to create different classes of claims.

If at least one impaired class of claims accepts the plan, the proponent of the plan (in most cases the debtor) can seek to have it confirmed over the objection of other classes. To do this (that is, to "cram down" the plan), the debtor must show that the plan complies with §1129(b). Under §1129(b), the plan must not discriminate unfairly against the dissenting class and it must treat the dissenting class in a way that is fair and equitable. These two terms of art embody the idea of absolute priority. Each class can insist on being treated at least as well as classes that enjoy the same priority under nonbankruptcy law, and each class can insist on being paid in full before any junior class is paid anything.

Cramdown is a time consuming and expensive affair. Among other things, it requires a valuation of the debtor as a going concern. Creditors may be better off accepting a plan even if §1129(b) gives them the right to insist on better treatment. For example, creditors may be better off getting paid eighty cents on the dollar today than invoking the absolute priority rule and succeeding to all of a firm's assets a year later. In addition, creditors may be willing to allow old equity holders to retain an interest in the firm because of the role these shareholders play. Many small firms depend on the skill and commitment of their owner-managers. For example, a firm's principal asset might be an unfinished software program and the firm's founder may be the only person who can complete the job. If she can condition her future work on retaining an equity interest in the firm, the creditors are well advised not to insist on strict adherence to absolute priority. So class dissents are less common than one might expect if one looked merely at naked legal entitlements.

Dissent by an individual creditor (or rarely, an interest holder), as opposed to a class of creditors, happens more often. But a reorganization plan is more easily confirmed over the objection of an individual creditor than over the objection of a class. A dissenter may block a plan only if the dissenter is not to receive a distribution at least equal in value to the distribution she would have received had the debtor been liquidated under Chapter 7. See §1129(a)(7). This is sometimes called the "best interests" test. Where a debtor has substantial going-concern surplus in excess of its liquidation value, a court may easily reach this determination even without a precise estimate of the debtor's going-concern value. The lower level of protection can be justified because similarly situated creditors (or interest holders) have approved the plan. (If the claims or interests were not substantially similar, they could not be classified together under §1122.) Here as elsewhere, Chapter 11 strikes a balance between protecting the rights of creditors and preventing holdout behavior.

Even if a plan meets these conditions of class and individual protection, the court must still ensure that the plan meets other requirements of Chapter 11, many of which are spelled out in §1129(a). One noteworthy rule of reorganization is that to be confirmed, a plan must pay off administrative expense obligations in full in cash on the effective date of the plan. §1129(a)(9)(A). This requirement is not likely to be burdensome for a large firm that has ready access to capital markets. Moreover, practices have emerged that make this requirement less rigid than it might first appear. Administrative creditors are free to scale back or modify their claims in a side deal. Their willingness to do so depends on their past and future relationship with the debtor. For example, among the largest administrative claims may be payments owed to debtor's counsel, and these are often structured initially with a schedule over time.

Nevertheless, §1129(a)(9)(A) sets a baseline that matters for smaller firms. The success of some Chapter 11s depends on the debtor's ability to bring a preference or fraudulent conveyance action. Failing that, the sole source of new cash may be the old equity holder. For such a firm, a reorganization may be possible only if the old equity holder has enough cash to pay administrative expenses. The longer the reorganization lasts, the greater this amount will be and the harder it will be for the debtor to confirm a plan of reorganization, at least without extraordinarily understanding accountants and lawyers. Professional fees for even a closely held firm in Chapter 11 routinely run into hundreds of thousands of dollars.

Similarly, §1129(a)(9)(B) requires that a plan provide cash for specified prebankruptcy claims, such as obligations to employees and employee benefit plans, afforded high priority by §507(a)(3)-(7). Immediate full payment is required for such claims if the class of claims has not accepted the plan. If the class has accepted the plan, an individual creditor cannot demand immediate payment, but may insist on full payment over time, including appropriate interest. This is true even of a claim that is not of a high enough priority to have warranted payment in full under Chapter 7. Other obligations to employees, retiree benefits as opposed to contributions, are also given special treatment. Section 1129(a)(13) requires that the plan provide for the continued full payment of such obligations.

Perhaps the most important rule in this family of requirements is the condition stated in §1129(a)(9)(C) that a plan provide for the regular installment payments of taxes afforded priority by §507(a)(8), including income, excise, and withholding taxes. These cash payments must be made within a six-year period and must have a value, as of the date of the plan, equal to the amount of taxes owing, whether or not the claim would have been paid in full under Chapter 7. These provisions are clear and give rise to few reported decisions. Nevertheless, tax claims may loom large in the landscape of many debtor firms. A debtor in bankruptcy may not have been earning enough before bankruptcy to become liable for significant corporate income tax, but even an unprofitable firm owes or must withhold taxes related to the firm's role as an employer. An example of this is social security taxes. A firm often fails to meet these obligations when it encounters trouble, despite the risk of criminal liability to the firm's managers. (Tax laws treat the failure to turn over taxes withheld from employees' paychecks much more seriously than a failure to pay the firm's own taxes.) Negotiations over how these tax obligations will be paid are often the primary focus of Chapter 11 when the debtor is a small, family-run business.

Another generally important condition for confirmation of a plan is set out in §1129(a)(11). According to this provision, a bankruptcy court cannot confirm a plan unless the court is satisfied that confirmation is not likely to be followed by the liquidation or further reorganization of the debtor (unless such is contemplated by the plan itself). This requirement is often called the feasibility test. The standard for feasibility is subjective, but the court can seek guidance from the capital structure of other firms in the debtor's industry. A reorganization plan that leaves a firm too highly leveraged compared with its peers may be so likely to need to be reorganized again that it fails to satisfy §1129(a)(11).

A court must confirm a plan that satisfies all conditions set out in §1129. If exclusivity has been lifted and more than one plan satisfies

§1129, the court must pick one, taking into account the preferences of both creditors and equity holders. See §1129(c). If no plan satisfies the requirements for confirmation, the court can permit the debtor or another proponent to try again. At the request of the debtor or other party, the court can also convert the case to Chapter 7 or dismiss it. See §1112.

Confirmation of a plan discharges all debts that arose prior to *confirmation*—not merely as of the order for relief—except for (and insofar as) those debts are reestablished by the plan. See §1141. On its face, Chapter 11 permits the discharge of *all* debts of a corporation. A corporate debtor's §1141 discharge is not subject to the exceptions in §523(a). There is not even a provision parallel to §523(a)(3), which excepts from an individual debtor's discharge certain claims not disclosed by the debtor. By its terms, then, §1141 seems to release the new entity from liability on a claim even if the creditor was never notified and never learned about the proceeding. The due process clause of the Constitution, however, mandates a minimum level of notice and this ultimately places a check on the scope of the discharge in Chapter 11.

An additional limitation on the seemingly sweeping §1141 discharge is one inherent in the nature of some obligations. Consider, for example, a debtor that remains the owner of a piece of property on which it (or someone else) dumped toxic waste before the bankruptcy petition was filed. The environmental claims that arose before confirmation are discharged, but the discharge of these claims is not sufficient to insulate the debtor from cleanup obligations that attach to whoever happens to own the property. In such a case the reorganized debtor may be liable not because of past actions but because of present ownership, in the same way that someone to whom the debtor sold the property would be liable. Thus, when a debtor lacks the ability to sell or abandon the property, it may have no way of escaping from responsibility for environmental damage. This is just what the environmental protection laws intend.

In sum, for the prototypical Chapter 11 case, the old claims against the firm disappear with the discharge and the new obligations of the firm take their place. The firm sails off happily into the future. A financial reorganization of the firm takes place in such a way that the firm survives as a going concern. This scenario is common with respect to large firms that file for Chapter 11. Most of these emerge from bankruptcy and continue as going concerns. These cases, however, while they involve a substantial portion of the assets that are reorganized in Chapter 11 and most of the jobs, are but a small minority of the Chapter 11 cases filed each year. More than half of the firms that file for Chapter 11 reorganization have assets of less than $500,000, and two thirds of them have assets of less than $1 million. Of these, most never leave Chapter 11 as going concerns. Hence, it is important not to equate the course of an abstract case through Chapter 11 as we have sketched out above with the day-to-day realities of Chapter 11 practice.

In too many cases, a Chapter 11 filing is simply a way to play for time. The managers or the debtor's shareholders seek delay in the hope of a miraculous reversal of fortune. By their nature, however, miracles are rare. Section 1112(b) authorizes the bankruptcy judge to dismiss a bankruptcy proceeding for want of good faith. "The clearest case of bad faith is where the debtor enters Chapter 11 knowing that there is no chance to reorganize his business and hoping merely to stave off the evil day when the creditors take control of his property." In re James Wilson Associates, 965 F.2d 160, 170 (7th Cir. 1992). Still, hope springs eternal, and debtors frequently file doomed petitions after which resources are wasted (mostly to the detriment of creditors) until the evil day finally arrives.

To address the problem of Chapter 11 cases filed by a debtor set on delay, Congress has taken a number of steps to reshape Chapter 11 in recent years. One place in which Congress has acted concerns the "single asset real estate," which is, in general, real property of a debtor that generates substantially all of the debtor's revenues; small residential properties are excluded but, since the 2005 Bankruptcy Act, there is no ceiling on value. See §101(51)(B). If a court denies relief from the stay to a creditor with a security interest in single-asset real estate, the debtor must expedite the reorganization or make monthly payments. See §362(d)(3). Being impatient in these cases may make sense. In a single-asset real estate case, a management company usually runs the day-to-day operations. The general partner might run the management company, but the debtor itself has no employees to speak of. No jobs are at issue. There is no going concern. The only creditor of any consequence is a bank that holds a nonrecourse mortgage on the land. The collective action problem that drives bankruptcy policy does not exist. The only problem is the inability of the lender and the partners to reach a deal.

Congress has also taken some steps to formalize the fast-track procedures that some bankruptcy judges had instituted on their own for small cases. A "small business debtor" is, in general, a commercial or business entity that has entered bankruptcy with no more than $2 million in fixed obligations, excluding those to insiders and affiliates, and for which there is not an active committee of unsecured creditors. See §101(51)(D). A bankruptcy case for such a debtor is defined as a "small business case." §101(51)(C). In a small business case there is no requirement of a creditors' committee (active or otherwise) and relaxed disclosure and solicitation obligations. See §§1102(a)(3), 1125(f). Also, although the debtor's exclusive period for filing a plan is longer in a small business case than in a standard case—180 days instead of 120—the plan must filed along with any disclosure statement not later than 300 days after commencement, with confirmation to occur, if at all, within 45 days of the filing of the plan. The debtor bears an express burden of proof that an extension of these periods is warranted. See §§1121(e); 1129(e).

Prior to the 2005 Bankruptcy Act, these or similar provisions operated only when the debtor elected to be put on a fast track, but now they apply to any small business debtor. The goal is to advance the case quickly when the debtor wants Chapter 11 merely to play for time. In the same spirit, the 2005 Act also added §§308 and 1116, which require that a small business debtor file with the court periodic statements of its financial situation and of compliance with bankruptcy rules and tax laws. Moreover, new §362(n) provides that the automatic stay does not apply to the voluntary petition of a small-business debtor that has another case pending or has had a case confirmed or dismissed in the prior two years unless the court is convinced that, among other factors, the new case will lead to confirmation in a reasonable time. This provision is designed to address the perceived problem of an entrepreneur who employs serial bankruptcy filings for their corporate entities to forestall creditor collection.

Taken together, these provisions address what is widely regarded as the shortcomings of the bankruptcy process, particularly as it relates to small firms. Proponents of these provisions argued, successfully, that the costs of a longer Chapter 11 process outweigh the benefits of giving debtors additional time. The affairs of a firm that has only a few hundred thousand dollars in debt are sufficiently straightforward, this reasoning goes, that if it cannot reorganize within a short time, it is unlikely ever to do so. Thus, where creditors do not take an active role in the bankruptcy process of a small business debtor—perhaps because none have enough at stake—the rules themselves expedite the case on the creditors' behalf. There is growing evidence that bankruptcy judges have become adept at identifying quickly those debtors that try to abuse the system, see Edward R. Morrison, Bankruptcy Decisionmaking: An Empirical Study of Continuation Bias in Small Business Bankruptcies, 50 J.L. & Econ. (forthcoming 2007). But the 2005 Act may help combat what abuse remains, perhaps at the expense of firms that would otherwise reorganize successfully.

The material below highlights the most important elements of the Chapter 11 reorganization process. The first three subsections—on classification, voting, and the absolute priority rule—explore aspects of Chapter 11 dynamics where there is conflict between or among the debtor and classes of creditors. The fourth subdivision focuses on the best-interests test. It examines a different sort of conflict, the conflict between an individual creditor and others who hold claims in that creditor's class.

Although this chapter of the book is devoted primarily to the treatment of corporations in Chapter 11, remember that it is available to individual debtors as well. Consider, for example, an individual debtor who runs a business in her personal capacity and files for Chapter 11. The individual might be a lawyer or a doctor. She does not do business in corporate form, and her personal finances have become intertwined with those of her practice. If no trustee is appointed, it is the individual debtor, rather than the debtor in possession, who runs the business and proposes a plan for a new set of obligations to replace the old. The rules for confirmation are the same. Unlike the corporate debtor, however, the individual maintains an identity separate from the productive assets she owns. Thus, an individual debtor under Chapter 11 commits only that future income promised by the plan. Through discharge, she retains the rest of her human capital and achieves a fresh start as she would in Chapter 7. Correspondingly, as in Chapter 7, there are exceptions to discharge for certain obligations, including child support and some taxes.

1) CLASSIFICATION

A plan of reorganization must sort a debtor's claims and interests into different classes. All claims or interests in a class must be treated the same unless the holder of any less favorably treated claim or interest consents. See §1123(a)(4). A plan cannot give one type of claim in a class ten cents on the dollar and another five cents on the dollar.

Nor can it provide that some claims in a class be paid in cash and others in long-term promissory notes. This much is clear.

The Bankruptcy Code does not set out in detail how much freedom the debtor or any other plan proponent enjoys in the way in which claims are sorted into different classes. Section 1122(a) provides that only substantially similar claims or interests can occupy a single class. This provision requires at least that claims with different legal rights be classified separately. For this reason, each secured claim is typically in a class by itself. Two claims are not substantially similar if they are secured by different collateral, for example. Indeed, they are not substantially similar even when secured by the same collateral if one claim enjoys priority over the other.

Other determinations are harder to make. Consider a deficiency claim held by a secured creditor for the difference between the amount it is owed and the value of its collateral, on the one hand, and on the other the claim of a trade creditor who looks forward to continuing business with the reorganized debtor. If these claims are placed in different classes, the trade creditor and the secured creditor each control a class and hence each can invoke the absolute priority rule. When claims are put in one class, the ability of one of them to invoke the absolute priority rule may turn on whether the other member wants to as well. A court must decide whether a plan proponent must put different claims in the same class, must put them in separate classes, or enjoys the freedom to do either.

From one point of view, one can argue that deficiency and trade claims belong in the same class. Section 1122(a) talks about putting together substantially similar claims "except as provided by subsection (b)." The latter subsection allows a plan to designate a separate class of unsecured claims below a plan-specified threshold if necessary for administrative convenience. The "except as provided by subsection (b)" language in §1122(a), therefore, suggests that, except for administrative convenience claims, substantially similar claims *must* be put into the same class. The trade and deficiency claims therefore must be put together if they are substantially similar—and they are, because both are unsecured claims and neither enjoys a priority higher than the other.

An alternative approach starts with the observation that while §1122(a) provides that substantially similar claims may be put in the same class, it does not explicitly require it. In any event, the Bankruptcy Code does not tell us what makes a claim substantially similar.

One can argue that the deficiency claim and the trade claim are not substantially similar merely because they are both unsecured claims that enjoy no special priority. It may be that their relationships with the debtor (and other rights each may have against) are sufficiently different that we should not assume they will look on the plan from the same vantage point.

In choosing among different interpretations, one should bear in mind the potential consequences of each. Neither interpretation is free from potential abuse. Consider, for example, a rule that required common classification of all claims with the same legal attributes. Assume that as a result of this rule a small deficiency claim is placed in the same class as trade claims more than twice as large. Assume also that the holders of the trade claims are willing to accept a small distribution under a reorganization plan because the trade creditors hope to profit from continued business with the debtor, which will emerge from bankruptcy under the control of the plan proponents. In this case, the trade creditors, who control the vote of the class under §1126, might approve even a plan that would distribute some property to the debtor's equity holders, even if the debtor is insolvent and equity is thus entitled to no distribution. Under these circumstances the holder of the deficiency claim could suffer a violation of absolute priority, from which it would not benefit, and yet would have no opportunity to invoke the absolute priority rule. Without a right to oppose classification here, the holder of the deficiency claim would have no recourse and could be forced to accept the plan if it provided the holder merely what it would have received in a liquidation.

A rule that permitted separate classification of claims or interests with the same legal attributes would allow a holder to oppose an improper combination of classes, but such a rule would create the opportunity for a different sort of abuse that can arise when the debtor can create multiple classes. Section 1129(a)(10) bars the confirmation of a plan that includes an impaired class unless at least one impaired class has voted to accept the plan (not counting the votes of any insider). In single-asset real estate cases, the deficiency claim of the creditor that holds the mortgage on the property dwarfs all other claims. If this deficiency claim is placed in the same class as all the unsecured claims, this creditor will have a veto power in any reorganization. In these and many other cases, a debtor struggles to create a separate class of claims that approves the plan to ensure it can at least have a chance to cram down the plan. Courts routinely strike down crude gerrymandering, but, especially outside the single-asset real estate setting, it is sometimes hard to distinguish a gerrymandered class from a legitimate one.

The debtor may create multiple classes of claims for a quite different reason. Once claims are placed in a separate classes, the plan no longer must pay them in the same coin. If separate classification were permitted, the debtor might give claims in one class cash and those in another long-term notes. To be sure, a class could vote against the plan and assert that the plan "discriminated unfairly" under §1129(b), but the debtor might have to do little more than show that the notes had the same principal amount as the cash and a plausible interest rate. In any event, a class that feels discriminated against may be able to oppose a plan only by forcing the opponents to invoke the court's cramdown power, a process that can be costly to all. When creditors are in the same class, they receive the same treatment automatically. Thus mandatory common treatment of claims with the same legal entitlement would prevent this sort of mischief before it could be proposed.

These issues along with other aspects of classification are explored in the exercises below together with the case that follows, *Woodbrook Associates*, as well as in the related notes and problem. Before reading the case, you should be aware of the way in which §1111(b)(1) treats nonrecourse loans. Like many classification cases, *Woodbrook* involves a debtor that owns real property and that is subject to the claim of one creditor who dominates all others. This creditor is the one that financed the purchase of real property and that holds a mortgage on the land. As is often the case, the loan is "nonrecourse." If the debtor defaults outside of bankruptcy, the creditor can look only to the real property to satisfy the obligation. Even if the property proves to be worth much less than the amount of the loan, the creditor cannot go against the debtor's other assets for the deficiency. Section 1111(b)(1) of the Bankruptcy Code, however, permits an undersecured creditor with a nonrecourse loan to treat the loan as if it were recourse in Chapter 11. Thus, a creditor holds both a secured claim equal to the value of the collateral and an unsecured claim for the balance of its loan. The court in *Woodbrook* asks whether this fact alone—that the unsecured claim exists only in Chapter 11 and no where else—keeps it from being "substantially similar" to ordinary unsecured claims, claims that exist outside of bankruptcy and in Chapter 7 as well.

As you work through this material, including the related exercises, notes, and problems, keep in mind the Chapter 11 priority scheme and be aware that strategic behavior is usually just below the surface of most classification disputes.

Key Provisions: Bankruptcy Code §§1122; 1123

EXERCISES

13A(1) Debtor has filed a plan of reorganization. The plan divides unsecured creditors into three classes. The first class comprises attorneys and accountants. The second class consists of Bank, which holds an unsecured claim against Debtor that is guaranteed by Debtor's president. The third class is made up of all other unsecured creditors. The plan of reorganization proposes to pay the first two classes 25 percent of their claims, in cash, and proposes to give the third class common stock of a value equal to 10 percent of their claims. Is this plan eligible for confirmation assuming no defects in the terms not presented here?

13A(2) Debtor Corporation's plan of reorganization specifies three classes of unsecured claims: those under $20,000, those over $20,000, and disputed claims. The plan proposes to treat the over- and under- $20,000 classes identically. The plan fails to state how it would treat the disputed-claims class. Is this plan eligible for confirmation assuming no defects in the terms not presented here? Would your answer change if the first two classes were separated at a threshold of $2,000 rather than $20,000? Of $200? Would it matter to your answer that the class of claims below the threshold amount was to be paid in full in cash on the effective date of the reorganization while the other claims were to be paid less? Assume instead that the plan's proponents modified the plan by combining the first two classes and by providing for the treatment of the disputed-claims class. Would your answer then depend on whether the disputed-claims class was to be paid more as opposed to less than the other class?

13A(3) Debtor Corporation is a restaurant-supply wholesaler that has lost money for years and files for bankruptcy under Chapter 11. Shortly after the bankruptcy case begins, the creditors committee discovers that Debtor's managers have stolen money from the corporate treasury. The court appoints a trustee, and Bank, Debtor's largest creditor, files a reorganization plan. The plan includes administrative expense and tax classes. Bank's claim is put in its own class. All unsecured claims are in a single class. Preferred shareholder interests are in one class while common shareholder interests are in another. The plan would pay all administrative expenses and taxes in cash in full as of the effective date of reorganization. Bank's loan, which is oversecured and on terms favorable to Bank, would be reinstated on its original terms, with any default cured. The unsecured creditors would receive 90 percent of the reorganized Debtor's common shares. The preferred shareholders—who under state corporate law hold a preference in a fixed amount to be paid before any distribution to common shareholders—would receive the remaining 10 percent of new common shares. The prebankruptcy common shareholders would receive nothing. Bank and the entire preferred class support the plan. All others oppose. Is this plan eligible for confirmation, assuming no defects in the terms not presented here?

CASE

IN RE WOODBROOK ASSOCIATES

United States Court of Appeals, Seventh Circuit, 1994
19 F.3d 312

ZAGEL, DISTRICT JUDGE.

Woodbrook Associates ("Woodbrook"), is an Indiana real estate limited partnership whose sole asset is the Woodbrook Apartments constructed in 1980 in Indianapolis. The apartment complex was primarily funded by a first mortgage loan of $5,559,700, at 7.5%, insured by the United States Department of Housing and Urban Development (HUD). Woodbrook Apartments failed to generate the expected income levels, the partnership defaulted, and the original mortgage holder assigned the mortgage in 1988 to HUD.

In July 1990, HUD advertised Woodbrook Apartments for sale by private bid on September 5, 1990, stating that it would not bid over $3.4 million. On August 21, 1990, Woodbrook filed a voluntary Chapter 11 petition, and the advertised foreclosure sale was stayed.

Deci-Ma Management Corporation ("Deci-Ma Management") continued to serve as project manager of the apartments during the bankruptcy, as it had since the inception of the project. Woodbrook then ceased paying net operating revenues to HUD, which had been less than the stipulated debt service.

Woodbrook filed a proposed Plan of Reorganization on April 19, 1991, eight months after the bankruptcy petition, and a substantially similar amended plan on June 14, 1991, by which time Woodbrook had possession of a net operating surplus of about $225,000 which it would otherwise have paid to HUD. The plan creates eight classes of claims and interests. Classes 1 and 2, as is typical, are reserved for expenses incurred by professionals and other administrative costs. Payments to creditors are structured as follows: HUD's secured claim (Class 3), valued at $3.6 million, is to be paid over 30 years at the mortgage interest rate of 7.5%; HUD will also be paid 5% of its unsecured deficiency claim (Class 4), plus all funds on hand at confirmation excluding $100,000 (reserved for repairs, working capital and bankruptcy fees, and expenses); Deci-Ma Management's unsecured claim (Class 5) will be paid in full over one year; Deci-Ma Corporation's unsecured claim (Class 6) will be paid monthly from any remaining cash flow from the debtor's operations until paid in full; other unsecured creditors (Class 7) will be paid in full 30 days after confirmation; and the general and limited partners of the debtor (Class 8) will retain their ownership interests in return for new capital contributions. * * *

Woodbrook argues that separate classification of HUD's §1111(b) unsecured deficiency claim was proper because the amount and character of HUD's claim rendered it different from the unsecured claims of other creditors. HUD maintains that dismissal for cause was proper because Woodbrook engaged in "abusive" classification aimed at gerrymandering an affirmative vote. We review de novo the propriety of classification.

Woodbrook possesses considerable, but not complete, discretion to classify claims and interests in its Chapter 11 plan of reorganization. Some limits are necessary to offset a debtor's incentive to manipulate a classification scheme and ensure the affirmative vote of at least one impaired class, which is what the debtor needs to gain confirmation of the plan. What these limits may be is subject to debate. Section 1122(a) says: "a plan may place a claim or interest in a particular class only if such claim or interest is substantially similar to the other claims or interest of such class." §1122(a). Section 1122 does not expressly forbid the separate classification of similar claims. Yet, the Fifth Circuit has coined a phrase referred to as the "one clear rule": "thou shalt not classify similar claims differently in order to gerrymander an affirmative vote on reorganization." In re Greystone III Joint Venture, 995 F.2d 1274, 1279 (5th Cir. 1991). *Greystone* condones separate classification "for reasons independent of the debtor's motivation to secure the vote of an impaired, assenting class of claims."

The "one clear rule" is not easy to apply since it is not about "classifying similar claims"; it is about the debtor's purpose. Similarity is not a precise relationship, and the elements by which we judge similarity or resemblance shifts from time to time in bankruptcy. Some courts had permitted separate classification based simply on a readily perceived legal distinction between unsecured deficiency claims created by §1111(b) and general unsecured claims. These courts noted that general unsecured claims are recourse claims cognizable under state law while §1111(b) claims exist only within a Chapter 11 bankruptcy case and are not cognizable under state law. This legal distinction has been eliminated by the Code (because a §1111(b) deficiency claim is an unsecured claim in Chapter 11), and it has been rejected as the sole basis for separate classification by a majority of circuits. Other courts have permitted separate classification on the grounds that the vote of §1111(b) claims "will be uniquely affected by the plan's proposed treatment of the secured claim held by the creditor"; a §1111(b) claimant may vote its large deficiency claim to defeat any plan, obtain relief from the automatic stay and foreclose, while the general unsecured claimant has a strong incentive to vote to accept the plan because it may receive nothing from liquidating the debtor if the automatic stay is lifted. The voting incentive theory is worthy of careful study, but we need not reach the question of whether the voting incentive rationale supports the separate classification of HUD's claim.

Significant disparities do exist between the legal rights of the holder of a §1111(b) claim and the holder of a general unsecured claim which render the two claims not substantially similar and which preclude the two from being classified together under §1122(a). Thus, we cannot accept the proposition implicit in *Greystone* that separate classification of a §1111(b) claim is nearly conclusive evidence of a debtor's intent to gerrymander an affirmative vote for confirmation. These disparities in rights stem from the most obvious difference between the two claims: a general unsecured claim exists in all chapters of the Code, while a §1111(b) claim exists only as long as the case remains in Chapter 11 and, once converted to a Chapter 7 case, recovery is limited to its collateral. This difference is amplified when the debtor is a partnership (as in this case) and the creditors face possible failure of its Chapter 11 case. Under such circumstances, the general unsecured creditors can seek equitable relief to prevent dissipation of the assets of the general partners, who upon conversion to Chapter 7, are liable for the debts of the partnership. Such equitable relief is not likely to be available to a §1111(b) claimant, whose recovery is confined to its collateral.

This legal difference between the two claims also can lead to anomalous results when applying other sections of the Code to a class containing both §1111(b) claimants and general unsecured claimants. First, §1129(a)(7) requires that, for confirmation of a plan where a holder of a claim or interest in an impaired class rejects the plan, each claimant must "receive or retain ... property of a value, as of the effective date of the plan, that is not less than the amount ... receive[d] or retain[ed] if the debtor were liquidated under [C]hapter 7." §1129(a)(7). A §1111(b) claimant is not entitled to payment under Chapter 7. Yet, because the §1111(b) claimant has been classified with other general unsecured creditors and because §1123(a)(4) mandates the same treatment of all claims in the class, the §1111(b) claimant can block confirmation unless it receives payment of an amount equal to that of the general unsecured creditors. More importantly, there are anomalies in the application of §1111(b) itself. Section 1111(b)(a)(A)(i), which requires that a §1111(b)(2) election be made by "the class of which such [§1111(b)] claim is a part," means the general unsecured creditors, included in the class, must vote on whether the §1111(b) claimants should make the §1111(b)(2) election. The general unsecured creditors, consequently, can block approval of the election by a majority of votes. Finally, general unsecured creditors, who have no lien claims, can participate in the election process because the class comprised of the §1111(b) claimants holds collateral that is not of inconsequential value. * * *

The drafters of the Bankruptcy Code did not intend these results. We find that, at least where the debtor is a partnership comprised of a fully encumbered single asset, the legal rights of a §1111(b) claimant are substantially different from those of a general unsecured claimant. Accordingly, we hold that §§1111(b) and 1122(a) not only permit but require separate classification of HUD's §1111(b) unsecured deficiency claim in Class 4. Woodbrook's separate classification of HUD's §1111(b) claim neither prevents confirmation of Woodbrook's plan nor serves as conclusive evidence in this case that Woodbrook manipulated the plan to obtain an affirmative vote. * * *

[The court went on to hold, however, that because a class rejected the plan, the plan had to comply with the fair and equitable test of §1129(b) and it failed to do so.]

Notes

13A.1. In *Woodbrook*, HUD's deficiency claim was so large that it would control any class in which it was placed. (HUD's deficiency was for far more than a third of all the unsecured claims. Hence, no class of unsecured claims in which HUD was placed could ever muster approval of two-thirds of the claims by amount, as §1126 requires, without HUD's vote.) Hence, the debtor could confirm a plan over HUD's objection only if the plan could be crammed down HUD under §1129(b). Section 1129(b), in theory, ensures that HUD is paid in full before the old equity receives anything on account of its old interest. As we have noted, however, Chapter 11's cramdown procedures are expensive and time-consuming. HUD would enjoy far more power in a reorganization if it could block a plan of reorganization without having to go through the time and expense of a cramdown hearing. It could do this if it could insist on being classified with the other general creditors. If it were, no impaired class would under the plan would approve the plan, and such approval is a requirement of confirmation under 1129(a)(10).

13A.2. The court in *Woodbrook* did not reject the plan *on classification* grounds merely because the plan treated HUD's claim and those in the other class of unsecured claims differently. An individual creditor cannot object on the ground that its claim is treated worse than claims entitled to the same priority but in a different class. Only when a class rejects the plan can the issue be raised. (Section §1129(b)'s requirement that a plan not unfairly discriminate ensures parity, even if not identical treatment, across different classes of claims with the same priority.) Nevertheless, courts will take into account an illicit purpose for classification. Any strategic classification has as its goal a distribution that plan proponents favor and opponents disfavor. Thus, it is not possible to separate classification issues from treatment issues in a dispute over whether a plan's classification scheme is appropriate. Consider this as you work through Problem 13A-1.

Problem

13A-1. Debtor is one of the largest retailers of ski equipment in a small mountain town. Bank holds Debtor's $250,000 full recourse obligation secured by Debtor's retail building and warehouse, both in need of repair. Under the terms of this loan, Debtor pays only interest until maturity, then the principal. After several bad winters, and near the maturity date of Bank's loan, Debtor files for bankruptcy under Chapter 11. At that time, in addition to the Bank loan, Debtor owes $400,000 to various Suppliers, all on an unsecured basis. Debtor's assets include its real estate, then worth less than $50,000, and little else other than some goodwill among customers. Debtor's reorganization plan places the secured portion of Bank's loan in one class, Bank's deficiency claim in another, and Suppliers' claims in a third. The plan proposes that Debtor retain its real estate and provide Bank with a new secured loan of extended maturity with a slightly higher interest rate. The plan would compensate each class of unsecured claims with common shares in the reorganized company. Debtor's shareholders would also receive some of these new shares, though a trivially small number, to encourage their continued participation.

Bank opposes the plan. It believes that Debtor's prospects are so grim that the interest rate on the proposed new loan is insufficient. Bank wants to foreclose. Suppliers look forward to doing future business with Debtor, and all of them favor the plan. Debtor requests a hearing so that the court may consider a cramdown against Bank. Bank wishes to avoid this costly and time-consuming process. What is Bank's argument? What is Debtor's defense? Would Bank's position likely change if its collateral were worth more than $50,000 and the plan placed its deficiency claim in a separate class, otherwise offering the same rate of compensation for Bank's claims?

2) VOTING

We now look at the process of plan confirmation. After a plan is drafted, its proponents must prepare a disclosure statement for distribution to eligible holders of claims and interests. §1125. The disclosure statement resembles a securities prospectus. Section 1125(b) provides that proponents may not solicit acceptances until a court determines, after notice and a hearing, that the disclosure statement contains adequate information.

The procedural burden is lessened somewhat if the debtor is a small business. In that case, the debtor may obtain conditional approval of a disclosure statement, solicit acceptances, and combine the hearing on the disclosure statement with a hearing on confirmation of the plan. See §1125(f). Even outside of small business, bankruptcy judges may adopt a similar practice in straightforward cases, such as when the plan calls for liquidating the assets and distributing the proceeds to the creditors. Moreover, many bankruptcy judges expedite the process informally through their power to hold status conferences under §105(d). These most often prove useful when the United States Trustee takes an active role in small cases and is able to flag problems for the bankruptcy judge. These procedures tend to work best when everyone cooperates. In a contested or complex case, efforts to expedite matters and combine procedures often misfire.

The hearing on the disclosure statement replaces the scrutiny that the securities laws require outside of bankruptcy. See §1145. The court hearing over the disclosure statement is an important event in the life of the reorganization. Many issues, such as whether another plan of reorganization should be proposed, are effectively resolved in the hearing over the disclosure statement.

The information in the disclosure statement itself will not always be useful. Section 1125(b) allows the court to approve a disclosure statement without a valuation of the debtor or an appraisal of the debtor's assets. Plans typically ask holders of claims and interests to accept new claims against or interests in the debtor in exchange for old ones. Unless the disclosure statement puts forward valuations that have been vetted by the bankruptcy judge, holders of claims and interests may not be able to assess the plan.

After the preparation of a disclosure statement, the next step is the solicitation of votes. There are two key exceptions to the general rule that creditors and shareholders vote on whether to approve a plan. First, any holder of a claim or interest not impaired by the plan, as defined by §1124, is deemed to have accepted the plan. No solicitation of such holder is required. See §1126(f). The core notion is that the reorganization plan would not affect such holders, so their approval of the plan is irrelevant. Second, a class that receives nothing under the plan is deemed to have rejected the plan. See §1126(g). There is no reason to ask holders of claims or interests in such a class what they think of the plan. In many situations, these claims and interests are so far from being in the money that the holders will not insist upon an elaborate cramdown proceeding or even invoke the best-interests test.

For classes that do vote, approval is determined by §1126. That provision requires positive votes by those who hold two-thirds in amount and a majority by number of the allowed claims duly voted in a class. In the case of equity interests, actual approval requires positive votes by those who hold two-thirds in amount of the shares duly voted. Whether a claim or interest is duly voted depends on §1126(e), which allows the court to disqualify votes that are not procured and exercised in good faith. The exercises below ask you to consider some general aspects of the class approval process, and the case that follows, *Figter*, along with the related note and problem address the good-faith requirement.

Key Provisions: Bankruptcy Code §§1125; 1126

EXERCISES

13A(4) Debtor Corporation files for bankruptcy under Chapter 11, and Debtor soon proposes a reorganization plan. Bank is Debtor's largest creditor and opposes the plan. Bank's opposition has met with moderate success. A month before the Debtor's §1121 exclusivity period is about to expire, Debtor's plan remains just short of confirmation in the unsecured creditors class. Supplier is the pivotal creditor in that class. Supplier is not enthusiastic about Debtor's plan, but believes that the plan is better than nothing. Bank outlines for Supplier the alternative plan Bank will propose if Debtor's plan fails to obtain acceptance and the exclusivity period expires. Supplier likes what it hears from Bank and votes against Debtor's plan. Debtor learns about Bank's conversations with Supplier and asks the court to sanction Bank for unlawfully soliciting votes for that plan during Debtor's exclusivity period and without an approved disclosure statement. Bank argues that it did nothing of the kind. Who will prevail? See Century Glove, Inc. v. First American Bank, 860 F.2d 94 (3d Cir. 1988); In re Clamp-All Corp., 233 Bankr. 198 (Bankr. D. Mass. 1999); Apex Oil Co., 111 Bankr. 245 (Bankr. E.D. Mo. 1990).

13A(5) Ten years ago, at a time when Debtor Corporation had many assets and few debts, Bank lent Debtor $1 million, principal payable in twenty years, interest payable quarterly at a rate of 5 percent per annum. Since that time, Debtor's value has declined steadily and its debts have increased. Debtor has not yet missed an interest payment. Debtor's weak financial condition, however, gives Bank the right under the loan agreement to declare Debtor in default and to accelerate the principal obligation. Before Bank can do so, Debtor files for bankruptcy under Chapter 11. Debtor proposes a reorganization plan that would reinstate Bank's loan according to its original terms, with maturity still ten years in the future. Bank's claim is the only one in its class. The plan otherwise provides that creditors will receive a mixture of new debt and new equity such that the Debtor would emerge from bankruptcy solvent but highly leveraged.

The court considers it more probable than not that Debtor will thrive under its new capital structure. All parties in interest favor the plan except Bank, which vehemently objects and asks the court not to confirm. Is this plan eligible for confirmation assuming no defects in the terms not presented here? In answering this question consider, among other provisions, §§1124 and 1129(a)(7), (11).

CASE

FIGTER, LTD. v. TEACHERS INSURANCE & ANNUITY ASSOCIATION

United States Court of Appeals, Ninth Circuit, 1997
118 F.3d 635

Fernandez, Circuit Judge.

* * * Figter filed a voluntary petition under Chapter 11 of the Bankruptcy Code. It owns Skyline Terrace, a 198-unit residential apartment complex located in Los Angeles. Teachers is a creditor. It holds a $15,600,000 promissory note executed by Figter. The note is secured by a first deed of trust on Skyline Terrace and by $1,400,000 of cash on hand. In fact, Teachers is Figter's only secured creditor and is the only member of Class 2 in a reorganization plan proposed by Figter. The plan contemplates full payment of Teachers' secured claim, but at a disputed rate of interest. ... The plan calls for the impairment of Class 3 unsecured claims by payment at only 80% of their face value.

Teachers has opposed Figter's reorganization plan from its inception because, among other things, that plan contemplates the conversion of Skyline Terrace Apartments into condominiums, with payment to and partial releases by Teachers as the units sell. That could easily result in a property that was part condominium and part rentals, if the plan ultimately fails in operation.

Teachers proposed a plan of its own, which provided for the transfer of Skyline Terrace and the cash collateral to Teachers in satisfaction of its secured claim, as well as a payment of Class 3 unsecured claims at 90%. Teachers' plan was premised on the assumption that its claim was partly unsecured. However, on May 31, 1994, before the purchases of other claims took place, the bankruptcy court determined that Skyline Terrace had a value of $19,300,000. Thus, Teachers' claim in the amount of $17,960,000 was fully secured. It did not thereafter pursue its plan. From October 27, 1994 until October 31, 1994, Teachers purchased twenty-one of the thirty-four unsecured claims in Class 3 at one hundred cents on the dollar, for a total purchase price of $14,589. Teachers had made the same offer to all of the Class 3 claim holders, but not all accepted it. The offer remained open. Teachers then filed notices of transfer of claims with the court, as is required under Bankruptcy Rule 3001(e)(2). Those notices were served on all affected parties, including Figter. No objections were filed by the unsecured creditors. The district court upheld the bankruptcy court's determination regarding Teachers' purchase of the unsecured claims. As a result, Figter's plan is unconfirmable because it is unable to meet the requirements of §1129(a)(10); there will not be an impaired, consenting class of claims. That will preclude a "cram down" of Teachers' secured claim under §1129(b). Figter has appealed in an attempt to avoid that result. * * *

Figter asserts that Teachers should be precluded from voting its purchased Class 3 claims because it did not buy them in good faith. Figter also asserts that even if the claims were purchased in good faith, Teachers cannot vote them separately, but is limited to one total vote as a Class 3 creditor. If Figter were correct in either of its assertions, it could obtain Class 3 approval of its plan and enhance its chances of cramming down Teachers' Class 2 claims. But Figter is not correct.

The Bankruptcy Code provides that "[o]n request of a party in interest, and after notice and a hearing, the court may designate any entity whose acceptance or rejection of [a] plan was not in good faith, or was not solicited or procured in good faith or in accordance with the provisions of this title." §1126(e). In this context, designate means disqualify from voting. The Bankruptcy Code does not further define the rather murky term "good faith." That job has been left to the courts.

The Supreme Court brought some clarity to this area when it decided Young v. Higbee Co., 324 U.S. 204 (1945). In *Young*, the Court was discussing the predecessor to §1126(e) when it declared that if certain persons "had declined to accept [the] plan in bad faith, the court, under §203 could have denied them the right to vote on the plan at all." Id. at 210-11. It went on to explain that the provision was intended to apply to those "whose selfish purpose was to obstruct a fair and feasible reorganization in the hope that someone would pay them more than the ratable equivalent of their proportionate part of the bankrupt assets." Id. at 211. In other words, the section was intended to apply to those who were not attempting to protect their own proper interests, but who were, instead, attempting to obtain some benefit to which they were not entitled. While helpful, those reflections by the Court do not fully answer the question before us. Other courts have further illuminated the area.

If a person seeks to secure some untoward advantage over other creditors for some ulterior motive, that will indicate bad faith. But that does not mean that creditors are expected to approach reorganization plan votes with a high degree of altruism and with the desire to help the debtor and their fellow creditors. Far from it.

> If a selfish motive were sufficient to condemn reorganization policies of interested parties, very few, if any, would pass muster. On the other hand, pure malice, "strikes" and blackmail, and the purpose to destroy an enterprise in order to advance the interests of a competing business, all plainly constituting bad faith, are motives which may be accurately described as ulterior.

In re Pine Hill Collieries Co., 46 F. Supp. 669, 671 (E.D. Pa. 1942). That is to say, we do not condemn mere enlightened self interest, even if it appears selfish to those who do not benefit from it.

Thus, if Teachers acted out of enlightened self interest, it is not to be condemned simply because it frustrated Figter's desires. That is true, even if Teachers purchased Class 3 claims for the very purpose of blocking confirmation of Figter's proposed plan. That self interest can extend even further without being an ulterior motive. It has been held that a creditor commits no wrong when he votes against a plan of a debtor who has a lawsuit pending against the creditor, for that will not, by itself, show bad faith. It has also been held that no bad faith is shown when a creditor chooses to benefit his interest as a creditor as opposed to some unrelated interest. And the mere fact that a creditor has purchased additional claims for the purpose of protecting his own existing claim does not demonstrate bad faith or an ulterior motive. "As long as a creditor acts to preserve what he reasonably perceives as his fair share of the debtor's estate, bad faith will not be attributed to his purchase of claims to control a class vote." In re Gilbert, 104 Bankr. 206, 217 (Bankr. W.D. Mo. 1989).

Courts, on the other hand, have been sensitive to situations where a company, which was not a preexisting creditor, has purchased a claim for the purpose of blocking an action against it. They have seen that as an indication of bad faith. The same has been true where creditors were associated with a competing business and desired to destroy the debtor's business in order to further their own. And when the debtor had claims against itself purchased by an insider or affiliate for the purpose of blocking a plan, or fostering one, that was seen as a badge of bad faith. Figter would have us add that in a single-asset bankruptcy, claim purchasing activities, like those of Teachers, are in bad faith. It cites no authority for that, and we see no basis for establishing *that* as a per se rule.

In short, the concept of good faith is a fluid one, and no single factor can be said to inexorably demand an ultimate result, nor must a single set of factors be considered. It is always necessary to keep in mind the difference between a creditor's self interest as a creditor and a motive which is ulterior to the purpose of protecting a creditor's interest. Prior cases can offer guidance, but, when all is said and done, the bankruptcy court must simply approach each good faith determination with a perspicacity derived from the data of its informed practical experience in dealing with bankrupts and their creditors.

Here, the bankruptcy court did exactly that. It decided that Teachers was not, for practical purposes, the proponent of an alternate plan when it sought to purchase the Class 3 claims. Nor, it found, did Teachers seek to purchase a small number of claims for the purpose of blocking Figter's plan, while injuring other creditors, even if it could do that in some circumstances. Rather, Teachers offered to purchase all Class 3 claims, and only some of those claimants' refusals to sell precluded it from doing so. Moreover, Teachers was a lender, not a competing apartment owner. It acted to protect its interests as Figter's major creditor. It reasonably feared that it could be left with a very complex lien situation, if Figter went forward with its plan. Instead of holding a lien covering the whole of the property, it could have wound up with separate fractured liens on various parts of the property, while other parts were owned by others. That could create a very undesirable mix of owners and renters and of debtors and non-debtors. Added to that was the actual use of cash, which was collateral for the debt owed to Teachers. It cannot be said that Teachers' concerns were irrational.

Based on all that was before it, the bankruptcy court decided that in this case Teachers was a creditor which acted in a good faith attempt to protect its interests and not with some ulterior motive. We cannot say that it erred in making that ultimate determination.

Figter's fallback position is that even if Teachers did act in good faith, it must be limited to one vote for its twenty-one claims. That assertion is answered by the language of the Bankruptcy Code, which provides that:

> A class of claims has accepted a plan if such plan has been accepted by creditors ... that hold at least two-thirds in amount and *more than one-half in number of the allowed claims* of such class held by creditors ... that have accepted or rejected such plan.

§1126(c) (emphasis added). That language was interpreted in *Gilbert*, 104 Bankr. at 211, where the court reasoned:

> The formula contained in §1126(c) speaks in terms of the number of claims, not the number of creditors, that actually vote for or against the plan. ... Each claim arose out of a separate transaction, evidencing separate obligations for which separate proofs of claim were filed. Votes of acceptance ... are to be computed only on the basis of filed and allowed proofs of claim. [The creditor] is entitled to one vote for each of his unsecured Class X claims.

That same view was iterated in Concord Square Apartments of Wood Cty., Ltd. v. Ottawa Properties, Inc., 174 Bankr. 71, 74 (Bankr. S.D. Ohio 1994), where the court held that a creditor with "multiple claims, has a voting right for each claim it holds." We agree. It would not make much sense to require a vote by creditors who held "more than one-half in number of the allowed claims" while at the same time limiting a creditor who held two or more of those claims to only one vote. If allowed claims are to be counted, they must be counted regardless of whose hands they happen to be in. * * *

Of course, that is not to say that a creditor can get away with splitting one claim into many, but that is not what happened here. Teachers purchased a number of separately incurred and separately approved claims (each of which carried one vote) from different creditors. There simply is no reason to hold that those separate votes suddenly became one vote, a result which would be exactly the opposite of claim splitting.

Therefore, the bankruptcy court did not err. * * *

NOTES

13A.3. Not every court would necessarily have the *Figter* court's benevolent view of Teachers' actions. Although it does not seem that Teachers intended to collect more than its due on any claim, one might still classify its objective as an ulterior motive. Teachers purchased Class 3 claims and voted against the plan for reasons that had nothing to do with the way the plan treated Class 3 claims. Teachers objected only to the way the plan treated its *Class 2* claims, treatment to which it could otherwise have objected only by invoking its rights in a cramdown hearing under §1129(b). At such a hearing, the debtor might still have been able to confirm the plan over Teachers' objection. Thus, one might characterize Teachers' maneuver as a subversion of the rule that permits cramdown against an impaired class if another impaired class accepts the plan. Another court might consider such a maneuver a lack of good faith.

13A.4. Even under the *Figter* court's interpretation of good faith, hard questions can arise. Imagine that a debtor proposes a reorganization plan within the exclusivity period and solicits acceptance of such plan. In the meantime, a prebankruptcy creditor, or an outsider, purchases claims in all classes, not for one hundred cents on the dollar, as in *Figter*, but at a discount. The purchaser hopes to gain complete control of the debtor and substitute its own plan for the debtor's plan. The purchaser also hopes to replace current managers with the purchaser's own management team. Like any other corporate acquirer, the purchaser hopes ultimately to profit from its acquisitions. One might argue that this anticipated profit is not a legitimate creditor's attempt to benefit its interest as a creditor but is instead an illegitimate unrelated interest. This was the view of the court, for example, in the well-known claims-trading case of In re Allegheny International, Inc., 118 Bankr. 282, 289-90 (Bankr. W.D. Pa. 1990). In that case, a would-be acquirer was designated under §1126(e) as a bad-faith actor and was not permitted to vote its purchased claims.

Under one view, those who buy up claims of firms in Chapter 11 disrupt the bargaining process that is at the core of Chapter 11. It is hard to gain acceptance of a reorganization plan if the owners of the claims shift constantly. But one can take a more generous view of these "vulture" investors, as they are sometimes called. They assemble dispersed claims and thus mitigate a central problem that makes bankruptcy necessary in the first instance. The negotiation and conflict inherent in the reorganization process would vanish or greatly diminish if a single entity owned all or most of the claims against a debtor. A sole or majority owner of claims has a strong incentive to maximize the value of the debtor's assets. Moreover, the other creditors are protected in bankruptcy by the best-interests test of §1129(a)(7). Finally, there is not only one vulture. By creating a market for claims in distressed firms, these investors create competition for the claims. This competition may tend to increase the amount that prebankruptcy creditors can realize on their claims.

While the structured negotiation inherent in the reorganization process may be desirable when markets do not function properly, one might well argue that the process itself should not keep a market from coming into being. From this perspective, the prospect of profiting by trading in claims should not without more be considered an illicit ulterior motive and should not constitute lack of good faith or disqualify votes of purchased claims. Problem 13A-2 asks you to consider a related fact pattern and to determine whether votes there are cast in good faith.

13A.5. *Figter* is a single-asset case with a single dominant creditor. The case is, in essence, merely a dispute between a debtor's equity investors and its major lender. In this context, it is not surprising that the court was unsympathetic to the debtor's assertion that Teachers was acting in bad faith. Consider whether, if the debtor were instead a manufacturing concern with many employees and multiple creditors, the court might have looked on Teachers' actions differently.

PROBLEM

13A-2. Debtor is a large, insolvent corporation in Chapter 11. Investor holds 15 percent of the common stock (the largest single block) and controls one of the five seats on the board. As a result of her equity position, Investor received significant information regarding the reorganization process, but she had little control over the process because of her minority position on the board. As of the bankruptcy petition date, Investor held no claims against the estate.

Under Debtor's proposed plan of reorganization, unsecured creditors will receive cash and freely tradable stock with a present value of approximately sixty-five cents on the dollar. Existing equity will be canceled as valueless.

During the case, Investor purchased 40 percent of the outstanding debentures at an average price of about thirty cents on the dollar. Investor's stated purpose was to protect her equity investment. Immediate profit was not Investor's principal goal.

The creditors' committee discovers Investor's trading in claims just prior to the confirmation hearing and is seeking to:

1. designate Investor's votes on the plan;

2. equitably subordinate the entirety of Investor's claims; and

3. in the event Investor's claim is not subordinated, limit either Investor's claims or Investor's distribution under the plan to the amount Investor paid for the claims.

How should the court resolve this matter as it relates to each of the transactions in question? What actions should the parties have taken before any trading took place? See Citicorp Venture Capital, Ltd. v. Committee of Creditors, 160 F.3d 982 (3d Cir. 1998).

3) ABSOLUTE PRIORITY RULE

To confirm a plan over the objection of an impaired class, the court must find that the plan does not discriminate unfairly and is fair and equitable with respect to each impaired class that has not accepted the plan. §1129(b)(1). These terms were used in judicial decisions long before the current Bankruptcy Code and over time have become synonymous with the absolute priority rule. The prohibition against unfair discrimination ensures that claims that enjoy the same priority outside of bankruptcy are treated comparably inside of bankruptcy as well. The fair and equitable test ensures that a claim that enjoys priority outside of Chapter 11 enjoys priority inside of Chapter 11 as well.

Section 1129(b) is invoked when a reorganization plan fails to garner the acceptance of all impaired classes of claims and interests and thus fails to satisfy §1129(a)(8). The requirement that a plan not discriminate unfairly is relatively straightforward. If two classes contain claims or interests of identical priority, absent some special circumstance that would justify subordination of one class, a plan cannot provide less to one class on a pro rata basis unless that class consents. This requirement, however, stops short of mandating identical treatment for classes at the same priority level. A plan does not discriminate unfairly merely because it gives cash to one class of general creditors and long-term notes to another. The plan will pass muster if there is a reason for the different treatment and if the cash payments and the notes give claims in each class the same pro rata share of the debtor's assets.

Section 1129(b) implements the absolute priority rule first by a general requirement that each class that rejects the plan be treated in a way that is fair and equitable. The section then goes on to add specific requirements for secured claims, unsecured claims, and equity interests that are included within the concept of fair and equitable. These requirements have the effect of ensuring that the core ideas of the judicially created fair and equitable doctrine remain fixed even if the outer edges of the judge-made doctrine continue to evolve.

With respect to a class of allowed secured claims, the fair and equitable principle requires, at a minimum, that each holder of a secured claim receive a stream of payments with a discounted present value equal to the value of the collateral. See §1129(b)(2)(A). Moreover, this stream of payments must be secured by a lien on the creditor's collateral. If the collateral is sold, the creditor's lien attaches to the proceeds. In the alternative, the plan can propose a different treatment that provides for the realization of the indubitable equivalent of the secured claim. The "indubitable equivalent" language is taken from Learned Hand's opinion in In re Murel Holding, 75 F.2d 941 (2d Cir. 1935). The test is sufficiently stringent that it is likely to be of use to the debtor only under narrow circumstances.

There is one additional requirement that a plan must meet to be confirmed over the objection of a class of secured claims. The plan must also provide a stream of payments equal to the face amount of the secured claims. In most cases, this requirement is redundant. Because discount rates are positive, a stream of payments over time equal in value to a given amount must total more than the face amount owed. Hence, this requirement matters only if the secured claim is for more than the value of the collateral despite the operation of §506(a), which generally equates the two. A mismatch can occur if a secured creditor makes what is called the §1111(b)(2) election. Under this provision, a secured creditor can elect to have its entire claim treated as secured regardless of the collateral's value. As a result, the stream of a plan's payments must not only be equal in value to the collateral, as determined by the judge, but the face amount of the stream of payments in the aggregate must equal the total amount of the claim that the collateral supports. The election is a way in which the secured creditor gives up its deficiency claim and in return prevents its lien from being stripped down. We explore the §1111(b)(2) election in Problem 13A-6.

Section 1129(b)(2)(B) fleshes out the fair and equitable standard with respect to a class of unsecured claims that rejects the plan. If the plan awards any property to old equity (or to a junior class of claims) on account of the old equity's interest (or junior claim), the plan must provide each holder of an unsecured claim with property that is at least equal in value to the amount of such claim. In other words, unless the plan proposes to pay unsecured claims in full, those junior to them must be wiped out if the plan is to be crammed down over objection by the holders of unsecured claims. This provision seems straightforward enough. But as we shall see in *LaSalle Street* below, complications arise when holders of old equity wish to remain and are contributing new value. They can argue that they receive new equity on account of the new capital, not "on account of" their old interests. Hence, holders of old equity argue that notwithstanding §1129(b), the plan does not have to pay the unsecured claims in full.

Section 1129(b)(2)(C) applies to a class of preferred stock interests. Under corporate law, preferred stock, though classified as equity and thus as an interest, is a hybrid between debt and equity, inferior to the former but superior to the latter. The "preference" is typically a right to insist that neither dividends nor any other payments go to the firm's common shares unless and until the firm pays the preferred shareholders specified amounts analogous to interest and principal on a debt. The fair and equitable standard requires that a reorganization plan honor these preferences—called liquidation preferences or sometimes redemption prices—with provision of full payment, though not necessarily in cash. If the plan fails to do this, then the holders of more junior interests, those who hold common stock, may not receive any property on account of their old interests.

For its part, common equity too is protected by the fair and equitable standard of §1129(b)(2)(C), though in a more limited way befitting common equity's status of lowest priority. A plan is not fair and equitable to a class of common equity interests unless the plan provides property of a value at least equal to the value of those interests. This is simply a requirement that creditors may not capture the entire value of a solvent debtor. Thus, this requirement is only as important as solvent debtors in bankruptcy are common.

As you consider these provisions, keep in mind that the fair and equitable standard is a *class-based* right. The holder of an individual claim or interest can demand at least that which it would have received in a Chapter 7 liquidation. If, however, a class votes to make a sacrifice of its priority, a dissenter within the approving class cannot block the plan on the basis of that sacrifice.

In interpreting §1129(b), it is important to understand that the specific tests it sets out form only part of the fair and equitable principle. To understand all the contours of that principle, one must know the sequence of cases out of which the principle emerged. The most important of these is Northern Pacific Railway Co. v. Boyd, 228 U.S. 482 (1913).

In 1886, a man named Spaulding had supplied $25,000 worth of materials and labor to the Coeur D'Alene Railroad for which he was never paid. The assets of the Coeur D'Alene, after several restructurings, ultimately became part of the Northern Pacific Railroad. Spaulding believed he could hold the Northern Pacific Railroad liable for this debt. Before he acquired a judgment against it, however, the Northern Pacific Railroad became insolvent and went through a common law reorganization—an equity receivership—out of which emerged a new entity called the Northern Pacific Rail*way*.

Spaulding's successor, a man named Boyd, did not participate in the reorganization of the Northern Pacific Railroad and instead sued the new entity. The dispute finally reached the United States Supreme Court in 1913. The Court found first that the old Northern Pacific had indeed been responsible for the obligations of Coeur D'Alene. Hence, the Court had to determine whether the new Northern Pacific was responsible for the debts of the old.

Boyd argued that the court-supervised sale could not extinguish his rights because the old shareholders remained the shareholders of the new entity. He invoked the common law rule, based on fraudulent conveyance doctrine, that a landowner who purchases back his property at a foreclosure sale takes it subject to the claims of junior creditors, even though a third party buying at arm's length would not. Boyd had not participated in the reorganization or relinquished his claims. Hence, he could hold the Northern Pacific Rail*way* answerable for the obligations of the Northern Pacific Rail*road*.

Lawyers for the Railway argued that the sale had to be respected. The real estate analogy was inapt, they asserted. The Rail*way* was an entity that was distinct from the Rail*road*. One should respect the formal differences, even though the shareholders of the two were the same. The judicial sale was regular in form and free from fraud. The assets had been sold for a fair price and that price was for less than what the secured creditors were owed. Had Boyd participated in the reorganization, he would have received nothing. Recharacterizing the transaction would only foster strike suits and make reorganizations of insolvent railroads impracticable. The Railway lost below and appealed to the Supreme Court.

In *Boyd*, a divided court found that the common law principle that limited the effect of debtor purchases at a foreclosure sale existed in the law of corporate reorganizations as well:

> As against creditors, [the sale] was a mere form. Though the Northern Pacific Railroad was divested of the legal title, the old stockholders were still owners of the same railroad, encumbered by the same debts. The circumlocution did not better their title against Boyd as a nonassenting creditor. They had changed the name but not the relation.

228 U.S. at 506-7. Nor did it matter that the assets were worth less than what creditors senior to Boyd were owed:

> [T]he question must be decided according to a fixed principle, not leaving the rights of the creditors to depend upon the balancing of evidence as to whether, on the day of sale the property was insufficient to pay prior encumbrances. * * *

> If the value of the road justified the issuance of stock in exchange for old shares, the creditors were entitled to the benefit of that value, whether it was present or prospective, for dividends or only for purposes of control. In either event it was a right of property out of which the creditors were entitled to be paid before the stockholders could retain it for any purpose whatever.

Id. at 507-8.

The Court did not go so far as to say that all of real estate foreclosure law should be mechanically transplanted to the law of corporate reorganizations. The Court held only that a complete freezeout of an intervening creditor was not permitted. Indeed, the Court itself was quick to note that its holding was narrow:

> [We do not] require the impossible and make it necessary to pay an unsecured creditor in cash as a condition of stockholders retaining an interest in the reorganized company. His interest can be preserved by the issuance, on equitable terms, of income bonds or preferred stock. If he declines a fair offer he is left to protect himself as any other creditor of a judgment debtor, and, having refused to come into a just reorganization, could not thereafter be heard in a court of equity to attack it.

Id. at 508. In contrast to real estate foreclosures, a plan of reorganization could include shareholders if the creditor were given a "fair offer" in a "just reorganization." Exactly what this meant, the Court did not explain. Lower courts had to identify on their own the contours of the "fixed principle" that should be at work.

After *Boyd*, a plan could not bypass junior creditors unless such creditors consented or had their day in court. Ex post assertions of fairness by a coalition of senior creditors and shareholders would not suffice. The question remained, however, whether or under what conditions a nonconsensual bypass of junior creditors was permissible *even given* their day in court. The Court ultimately confronted this question in Case v. Los Angeles Lumber Products, 308 U.S. 106 (1939).

In *Case*, the debtor was a holding company whose principal asset was the Los Angeles Shipbuilding & Drydock Corporation. This shipyard had built ships for the Navy during World War I, but had languished during the isolationism of the 1920s and 1930s. It sought to reorganize itself in 1937. The only creditors were holders of twenty-year bonds due in 1944. More than 90 percent of the face amount of the bondholders voted in favor of the plan. The plan of reorganization gave 23 percent of the stock in the new corporation to the old shareholders. These shareholders planned to continue to play a managerial role in operating the business, but they were not contributing any new cash.

The district court had held that the plan was fair and equitable. It noted that only two bondholders had objected to the plan, and the court did not want to give a few dissenters the ability to hold up a reorganization approved by a substantial majority of the bondholders. The court justified the continued participation of the old equity on the grounds that the shareholders were willing to assume managerial responsibilities in the company and that they were "the only persons who [were] familiar with the company's operations and who [had] experience in shipbuilding." In addition, the court noted:

> Most of the present bondholders are widely scattered with small holdings, and their position would be benefited by being associated with old stockholders of financial influence and stability who might be able to assist in proper financing.

The reorganization was brought about, it seems, from the need for additional capital, and not from the threat of foreclosure by existing creditors. Due to a previous workout, interest payments were owed only if earned, and the creditors lacked the power to foreclose until 1944.

When *Case* reached the Supreme Court on appeal, the Court had a vehicle to confront the different interpretations of the fair and equitable principle that had been debated in the wake of *Boyd*. Under one view, the approval of the plan by 90 percent of the creditors was enough. Requiring unanimity was unreasonable, and the old shareholders had to be given some of the going-concern value or they would not cooperate in reorganizing the firm. A court should confirm a plan if a class of diverse investors approved the plan, if each of them received what they would receive in a liquidation, and if the overall process was regular.

The competing view was altogether different. Under this view, allowing the old equity to continue was a source of mischief. Rather than making it possible to obtain their help after the reorganization, it gave old shareholders an opportunity to hold up other investors. In a firm such as a shipyard, shareholders do not control the day-to-day operations. Professionals can be brought in to do the job. On this account, only in the narrowest of circumstances should old equity be permitted to continue in the face of any dissent.

Speaking through Justice William O. Douglas, the Court in *Case* squarely sided with the second view. The Court first rejected the idea that dissenters are entitled only to their share of a debtor's liquidation value, leaving others to decide how any surplus would be divided. The Court held instead that the fair and equitable standard afforded each creditor its full right of priority in the firm as a going concern. Id. at 121. *Case* thus forged a link between the terms "fair and equitable" and "absolute priority," a link accepted by lawyers, judges, and Congress ever since.

Once Justice Douglas established the link between fair and equitable and absolute priority, he cut back sharply on shareholders' ability to participate in the reorganization of an insolvent firm over a creditor's objection. The absolute priority rule required first that shareholders could participate in the new venture, if at all, only if they paid fair value for their continuing interest in a reorganized debtor. Moreover, to ensure that the shareholders in fact paid fair value, the Court required that any payments be easy to value. If a creditor objected to a reorganization plan of an insolvent debtor, the plan could not include a distribution to equity unless equity participation was based "on a contribution in money or in money's worth, reasonably equivalent in view of all the circumstances to the participation of the stockholder." Id. at 122.

Under pre-Code law, a single dissenting creditor could insist that a plan be fair and equitable. This gave one creditor considerable holdup power. Indeed, in *Case* itself, one of the dissenting creditors had a long history of buying claims at a deep discount and holding up reorganizations until he was paid in full. As we have seen, under the Bankruptcy Code, the full right of absolute priority Justice Douglas identified now comes into play only if a class as a whole opposes the plan. But once absolute priority comes into play, the question arises again, central to both *Boyd* and *Case*, whether or under what conditions may old equity participate over the objection of a creditor class.

After the exercises below touch on some basics of §1129(b), the first case that follows, *LaSalle Street*, is the Supreme Court's most recent effort to come to grips with the fair and equitable standard, there in the context of a new-value contribution, where equity holders attempted to purchase a continuing interest in the debtor over creditor objection. The second case, *Armstrong*, revisits the precise question addressed by *Boyd* and by *Case*. The related notes and problems ask you to consider more broadly the questions presented by these cases. As you do, keep in mind the principle that underlies the doctrine. That is, you might ask yourself why it matters that bankruptcy law honors nonbankruptcy priority. One answer, an important one, is that if the law honors the terms of a loan ex post, those terms may be favorable to the debtor ex ante. See Alan Schwartz, A Normative Theory of Business Bankruptcy, 91 Va. L. Rev. 1199 (2005).

Key Provision: Bankruptcy Code §1129(b)

EXERCISES

13A(6) At the close of Debtor Corporation's Chapter 11 case, Bank holds a claim of $1 million secured by equipment worth $900,000. The equipment depreciates quickly and steadily over time. Because of such depreciation, and because Bank is not optimistic about Debtor's prospect for success even after reorganization, Bank moves to reject Debtor's reorganization plan, which would replace the secured portion of Bank's claim with a new obligation, secured by the same collateral, to pay $990,000 a year hence. Can Bank effectively veto this plan? Would your answer change if the plan provided instead for Bank to receive for its secured claim $1,089,000 two years later?

13A(7) Debtor Corporation files for bankruptcy under Chapter 11. Because Debtor's managers have engaged in misconduct, a trustee is soon appointed. Bank files a reorganization plan that includes only two creditor classes. Bank's oversecured claim is in one class. All unsecured claims are in another class. The plan proposes to have Debtor retain all assets other than cash that will be used to pay administrative expenses and tax liabilities as of the effective date of the plan. The only other distribution under the plan is of common equity shares, all to Bank on its secured claim. Is this plan eligible for confirmation? Does your answer derive support from the fact that conditions for a plan to be fair and equitable merely include the requirements specified in §1129(b)(2)?

13A(8) Debtor Corporation is a high-profile motion picture talent agency with large offices in New York, Los Angeles, and Toronto, and with smaller offices throughout the United States. Debtor's value is in the combination of its name, its client list, and the relationships among its employees. Debtor would be worth next to nothing if its assets were liquidated piecemeal. Consequently, Debtor chooses Chapter 11 when it is forced into bankruptcy by cash flow problems from the loss as a defendant, and subsequent appeal, of a large lawsuit. After three years in Chapter 11, the Debtor locates an investor that offers to pay all administrative expenses and all claims in cash in full as of the effective date of the bankruptcy. The only other distribution under the plan is of common equity shares, all to either Debtor's prebankruptcy shareholders or the new investor. The plaintiff in the lawsuit, in its own class, accepts the plan as settlement of its case. The unsecured claims are in a separate class. The holders of these claims neither dispute the amount of that settlement nor challenge the proposed distribution to the plaintiff, yet they reject the plan. What is the source of their objection? Is the plan eligible for confirmation?

13A(9) Debtor Corporation owns six assets of value, each a chemical process patent complementary to the others. Each patent is subject to a security interest on a loan to each of six different creditors. Debtor becomes insolvent and defaults on its loans. Each secured creditor threatens to foreclose on and sell its collateral to one or another of Debtor's competitors. Before this can happen, Debtor files for bankruptcy under Chapter 11. At that time, Debtor owes each secured creditor $2 million and owes $6 million to various unsecured creditors. Each patent is worth $1 million if sold in isolation. The patents together are worth $12 million. Debtor proposes a reorganization plan that would have Debtor sell each of the six patents to Purchaser Corporation for an amount just over $2 million in cash. The plan would pay administrative expenses and taxes, then distribute the remaining cash, $2 million, to each of the secured creditors. Is this plan eligible for confirmation assuming no defects in the terms not presented here? Is it relevant to your answer that the shareholders and managers of Purchaser Corporation are Debtor's six secured creditors and Debtor's managers, respectively? Would it affect your answer if no secured creditor had made a foreclosure threat prior to bankruptcy but instead formed Purchaser before Debtor's bankruptcy petition?

CASES

BANK OF AMERICA v. 203 NORTH LASALLE STREET PARTNERSHIP

United States Supreme Court, 1999
526 U.S. 434

JUSTICE SOUTER DELIVERED THE OPINION OF THE COURT.

* * * Petitioner, Bank of America National Trust & Savings Association (Bank), is the major creditor of respondent, 203 North LaSalle Street Partnership, an Illinois real estate limited partnership. The Bank lent the Debtor some $93 million, secured by a nonrecourse first mortgage on the Debtor's principal asset, 15 floors of an office building in downtown Chicago. In January 1995, the Debtor defaulted, and the Bank began foreclosure in a state court.

In March, the Debtor responded with a voluntary petition for relief under Chapter 11 of the Bankruptcy Code . . . The Debtor's principal objective was to ensure that its partners retained title to the property so as to avoid roughly $20 million in personal tax liabilities, which would fall due if the Bank foreclosed. . . .

The value of the mortgaged property was less than the balance due the Bank, which elected to divide its undersecured claim into secured and unsecured deficiency claims under §506(a) and §1111(b). Under the plan, the Debtor separately classified the Bank's secured claim, its unsecured deficiency claim, and unsecured trade debt owed to other creditors. The Bankruptcy Court found that the Debtor's available assets were prepetition rents in a cash account of $3.1 million and the 15 floors of rental property worth $54.5 million. The secured claim was valued at the latter figure, leaving the Bank with an unsecured deficiency of $38.5 million.

So far as we need be concerned here, the Debtor's plan had these further features:

The Bank's $54.5 million secured claim would be paid in full between 7 and 10 years after the original 1995 repayment date.

The Bank's $38.5 million unsecured deficiency claim would be discharged for an estimated 16% of its present value.

The remaining unsecured claims of $90,000, held by the outside trade creditors, would be paid in full, without interest, on the effective date of the plan.

Certain former partners of the Debtor would contribute $6.125 million in new capital over the course of five years (the contribution being worth some $4.1 million in present value), in exchange for the Partnership's entire ownership of the reorganized debtor.

The last condition was an exclusive eligibility provision: the old equity holders were the only ones who could contribute new capital.

The Bank objected and, being the sole member of an impaired class of creditors, thereby blocked confirmation of the plan on a consensual basis. The Debtor, however, took the alternate route to confirmation of a reorganization plan, forthrightly known as the judicial "cramdown" process for imposing a plan on a dissenting class. * * *

The absolute priority rule was the basis for the Bank's position that the plan could not be confirmed as a cramdown. As the Bank read the rule, the plan was open to objection simply because certain old equity holders in the Debtor Partnership would receive property even though the Bank's unsecured deficiency claim would not be paid in full [in apparent violation of the requirement in §1129(b)(2)(B)(ii) that old equity holders not receive any property "on account of" their old interests.] * * *

Three basic interpretations have been suggested for the "on account of" modifier. The first reading is proposed by the Partnership, that "on account of" harks back to accounting practice and means something like "in exchange for," or "in satisfaction of." On this view, a plan would not violate the absolute priority rule unless the old equity holders received or retained property in exchange for the prior interest, without any significant new contribution; if substantial money passed from them as part of the deal, the prohibition of subsection (b)(2)(B)(ii) would not stand in the way, and whatever issues of fairness and equity there might otherwise be would not implicate the "on account of" modifier.

This position is beset with troubles, the first one being textual. Subsection (b)(2)(B)(ii) forbids not only receipt of property on account of the prior interest but its retention as well. A common instance of the latter would be a debtor's retention of an interest in the insolvent business reorganized under the plan. Yet it would be exceedingly odd to speak of "retain[ing]" property in exchange for the same property interest, and the eccentricity of such a reading is underscored by the fact that elsewhere in the Code the drafters chose to use the very phrase "in exchange for," §1123(a)(5)(J) (a plan shall provide adequate means for implementation, including "issuance of securities of the debtor ... for cash, for property, for existing securities, or in exchange for claims or interests"). It is unlikely that the drafters of legislation so long and minutely contemplated as the 1978 Bankruptcy Code would have used two distinctly different forms of words for the same purpose.

The second difficulty is practical: the unlikelihood that Congress meant to impose a condition as manipulable as subsection (b)(2)(B)(ii) would be if "on account of" meant to prohibit merely an exchange unaccompanied by a substantial infusion of new funds but permit one whenever substantial funds changed hands. "Substantial" or "significant" or "considerable" or like characterizations of a monetary contribution would measure it by the Lord Chancellor's foot, and an absolute priority rule so variable would not be much of an absolute. Of course it is true (as already noted) that, even if old equity holders could displace the rule by adding some significant amount of cash to the deal, it would not follow that their plan would be entitled to adoption; a contested plan would still need to satisfy the overriding condition of fairness and equity. But that general fairness and equity criterion would apply in any event, and one comes back to the question why Congress would have bothered to add a separate priority rule without a sharper edge.

Since the "in exchange for" reading merits rejection, the way is open to recognize the more common understanding of "on account of" to mean "because of." This is certainly the usage meant for the phrase at other places in the statute, see §1111(b)(1)(A) (treating certain claims as if the holder of the claim "had recourse against the debtor on account of such claim"); §522(d)(10)(E) (permitting debtors to exempt payments under certain benefit plans and contracts "on account of illness, disability, death, age, or length of service"); §547(b)(2) (authorizing trustee to avoid a transfer of an interest of the debtor in property "for or on account of an antecedent debt owed by the debtor"); §547(c)(4)(B) (barring trustee from avoiding a transfer when a creditor gives new value to the debtor "on account of which new value the debtor did not make an otherwise unavoidable transfer to ... such creditor"). So, under the commonsense rule that a given phrase is meant to carry a given concept in a single statute, the better reading of subsection (b)(2)(B)(ii) recognizes that a causal relationship between holding the prior claim or interest and receiving or retaining property is what activates the absolute priority rule.

The degree of causation is the final bone of contention. We understand the Government, as amicus curiae, to take the starchy position not only that any degree of causation between earlier interests and retained property will activate the bar to a plan providing for later property, but also that whenever the holders of equity in the Debtor end up with some property there will be some causation; when old equity, and not someone on the street, gets property the reason is res ipsa loquitur. An old equity holder simply cannot take property under a plan if creditors are not paid in full.

There are, however, reasons counting against such a reading. If, as is likely, the drafters were treating junior claimants or interest holders as a class at this point, then the simple way to have prohibited the old interest holders from receiving anything over objection would have been to omit the "on account of" phrase entirely from subsection (b)(2)(B)(ii). On this assumption, reading the provision as a blanket prohibition would leave "on account of" as a redundancy, contrary to the interpretive obligation to try to give meaning to all the statutory language. One would also have to ask why Congress would have desired to exclude prior equity categorically from the class of potential owners following a cramdown. Although we have some doubt about the Court of Appeal's assumption that prior equity is often the only source of significant capital for reorganizations, old equity may well be in the best position to make a go of the reorganized enterprise and so may be the party most likely to work out an equity-for-value reorganization.

A less absolute statutory prohibition would follow from reading the "on account of" language as intended to reconcile the two recognized policies underlying Chapter 11, of preserving going concerns and maximizing property available to satisfy creditors. Causation between the old equity's holdings and subsequent property substantial enough to disqualify a plan would presumably occur on this view of things whenever old equity's later property would come at a price that failed to provide the greatest possible addition to the bankruptcy estate, and it would always come at a price too low when the equity holders obtained or preserved an ownership interest for less than someone else would have paid. A truly full value transaction, on the other hand, would pose no threat to the bankruptcy estate not posed by any reorganization, provided of course that the contribution be in cash or be realizable money's worth. * * *

Which of these positions is ultimately entitled to prevail is not to be decided here, however, for even on the latter view the Bank's objection would require rejection of the plan at issue in this case. It is doomed, we can say without necessarily exhausting its flaws, by its provision for vesting equity in the reorganized business in the Debtor's partners without extending an opportunity to anyone else either to compete for that equity or to propose a competing reorganization plan. Although the Debtor's exclusive opportunity to propose a plan under §1121(b) is not itself "property" within the meaning of subsection (b)(2)(B)(ii), the respondent partnership in this case has taken advantage of this opportunity by proposing a plan under which the benefit of equity ownership may be obtained by no one but old equity partners. Upon the court's approval of that plan, the partners were in the same position that they would have enjoyed had they exercised an exclusive option under the plan to buy the equity in the reorganized entity, or contracted to purchase it from a seller who had first agreed to deal with no one else. It is quite true that the escrow of the partners' proposed investment eliminated any formal need to set out an express option or exclusive dealing provision in the plan itself, since the court's approval that created the opportunity and the partners' action to obtain its advantage were simultaneous. But before the Debtor's plan was accepted no one else could propose an alternative one, and after its acceptance no one else could obtain equity in the reorganized entity. At the moment of the plan's approval the Debtor's partners necessarily enjoyed an exclusive opportunity that was in no economic sense distinguishable from the advantage of the exclusively entitled offeror or option holder. This opportunity should, first of all, be treated as an item of property in its own right. While it may be argued that the opportunity has no market value, being significant only to old equity holders owing to their potential tax liability, such an argument avails the Debtor nothing, for several reasons. It is to avoid just such arguments that the law is settled that any otherwise cognizable property interest must be treated as sufficiently valuable to be recognized under the Bankruptcy Code. Even aside from that rule, the assumption that no one but the Debtor's partners might pay for such an opportunity would obviously support no inference that it is valueless, let alone that it should not be treated as property. And, finally, the source in the tax law of the opportunity's value to the partners implies in no way that it lacks value to others. It might, indeed, be valuable to another precisely as a way to keep the Debtor from implementing a plan that would avoid a Chapter 7 liquidation.

Given that the opportunity is property of some value, the question arises why old equity alone should obtain it, not to mention at no cost whatever. The closest thing to an answer favorable to the Debtor is that the old equity partners would be given the opportunity in the expectation that in taking advantage of it they would add the stated purchase price to the estate. But this just begs the question why the opportunity should be exclusive to the old equity holders. If the price to be paid for the equity interest is the best obtainable, old equity does not need the protection of exclusiveness (unless to trump an equal offer from someone else); if it is not the best, there is no apparent reason for giving old equity a bargain. There is no reason, that is, unless the very purpose of the whole transaction is, at least in part, to do old equity a favor. And that, of course, is to say that old equity would obtain its opportunity, and the resulting benefit, because of old equity's prior interest within the meaning of subsection (b)(2)(B)(ii). Hence it is that the exclusiveness of the opportunity, with its protection against the market's scrutiny of the purchase price by means of competing bids or even competing plan proposals, renders the partners' right a property interest extended "on account of" the old equity position and therefore subject to an unpaid senior creditor class's objection.

It is no answer to this to say that the exclusive opportunity should be treated merely as a detail of the broader transaction that would follow its exercise, and that in this wider perspective no favoritism may be inferred, since the old equity partners would pay something, whereas no one else would pay anything. If this argument were to carry the day, of course, old equity could obtain a new property interest for a dime without being seen to receive anything on account of its old position. But even if we assume that old equity's plan would not be confirmed without satisfying the judge that the purchase price was top dollar, there is a further reason here not to treat property consisting of an exclusive opportunity as subsumed within the total transaction proposed. On the interpretation assumed here, it would, of course, be a fatal flaw if old equity acquired or retained the property interest without paying full value. It would thus be necessary for old equity to demonstrate its payment of top dollar, but this it could not satisfactorily do when it would receive or retain its property under a plan giving it exclusive rights and in the absence of a competing plan of any sort. Under a plan granting an exclusive right, making no provision for competing bids or competing plans, any determination that the price was top dollar would necessarily be made by a judge in bankruptcy court, whereas the best way to determine value is exposure to a market. This is a point of some significance, since it was, after all, one of the Code's innovations to narrow the occasions for courts to make valuation judgments, as shown by its preference for the super-majoritarian class creditor voting scheme in §1126(c). In the interest of statutory coherence, a like disfavor for decisions untested by competitive choice ought to extend to valuations in administering subsection (b)(2)(B)(ii) when some form of market valuation may be available to test the adequacy of an old equity holder's proposed contribution.

Whether a market test would require an opportunity to offer competing plans or would be satisfied by a right to bid for the same interest sought by old equity, is a question we do not decide here. It is enough to say, assuming a new value corollary, that plans providing junior interest holders with exclusive opportunities free from competition and without benefit of market valuation fall within the prohibition of §1129(b)(2)(B)(ii).

The judgment of the Court of Appeals is accordingly reversed, and the case is remanded for further proceedings consistent with this opinion. It is so ordered.

IN RE ARMSTRONG WORLD INDUSTRIES, INC.

United States District Court, D. Delaware, 2005
320 Bankr. 523

ROBRENO, DISTRICT JUDGE.

This case involves the Chapter 11 bankruptcy of Armstrong World Industries, Inc. and two of its subsidiaries. The Court must determine whether the Fourth Amended Plan of Reorganization, which the Bankruptcy Court endorsed in its Proposed Findings of Fact and Conclusions of Law, should be confirmed. * * *

After extensive negotiations with the Committees and other interested parties, Debtor filed its Fourth Amended Plan of Reorganization and Amended Disclosure Statement. Under the Plan, eleven classes of claims and one class of equity interests were created. The proposed distributions of Debtor's property to three of these classes—the Unsecured Creditors, the Asbestos PI Claimants, and the Equity Interest

Holders—are particularly relevant to the issues before the Court. Debtor estimates that the Unsecured Creditors, Class 6, have claims amounting to approximately $1.651 billion. Under the Plan, the Unsecured Creditors would recover about 59.5% of their claims. The Asbestos PI Claimants, Class 7, have claims estimated at $3.146 billion and would recover approximately 20% of their claims under the Plan. The Equity Interest Holders, Class 12, would be issued New Warrants valued at approximately $35 million to $40 million.

A key to the Plan lies in the consent by the class of Asbestos PI Claimants to share a portion of its proposed distribution with the Equity Interest Holders. [I]f the Unsecured Creditors reject the Plan, the Asbestos PI Claimants will receive the New Warrants, but then will automatically waive the distribution, causing the Equity Interest Holders to secure the New Warrants. The net result of the Asbestos PI Claimants' waiver is that the Equity Interest Holders (i.e., the old AWI shareholders) receive Debtor's property (i.e., the New Warrants) on account of their equity interests, although a senior class (i.e., the Unsecured Creditors) would not have full satisfaction of its allowed claims. It is the lawfulness of this arrangement that forms the central issue in the case.

The Court concludes that the distribution of New Warrants to the class of Equity Interest Holders over the objection of the class of Unsecured Creditors violates the "fair and equitable" requirement of §1129(b)(2)(B)(ii), a codification of the absolute priority rule. Thus, the Court must deny confirmation of the Plan. * * *

Confirmation of a reorganization plan breathes new life into a debtor. This significant step affords the debtor a "fresh start" by relieving the debtor of certain pre-petition obligations and altering its financial and legal relationships with its creditors. Given the substantial consequences these rearrangements will have on the debtor, the creditors, and other parties in interest, Congress—not surprisingly—has provided explicit requirements that a proposed plan must meet for confirmation. The congressional calculus embodied in the Bankruptcy Code for confirmation of a Chapter 11 reorganization plan is the product of long experience with reorganization legislation and hard-fought battles over policy judgments. Therefore, unless these congressionally mandated requirements are satisfied, a court may not place its imprimatur on a reorganization plan.

A plan may be confirmed under either of two scenarios. One is consensually, provided all classes have accepted the plan or are not impaired. The other is non-consensually, over the non-acceptance of an impaired class if all the requirements of §1129(a), except paragraph (8), have been met and the plan "does not discriminate unfairly" and is "fair and equitable." This latter approach, typically referred to as a "cramdown," is sometimes necessary in order to allow the debtor to override certain objections under appropriate circumstances, which might otherwise allow a small minority to prevent confirmation of the plan. * * *

The principles underpinning §1129's "fair and equitable" requirement are rooted in the judicially created absolute priority rule. The Supreme Court first articulated and applied the absolute priority rule, originally referred to as the "fixed principle," in Northern Pacific Railway Co. v. Boyd, 228 U.S. 482 (1913), which involved a corporate reorganization in an equity receivership. In *Boyd*, a general unsecured creditor in a railway company's reorganization was not fully compensated, but the "old" stockholders received property in the reorganized entity. The Supreme Court stated:

> [I]f purposely or unintentionally a single creditor was not paid, or provided for in the reorganization, [that creditor] could assert [its] superior rights against the subordinate interests of the old stockholders in the property transferred to the new company ... . Any device, whether by private contract or judicial sale under consent decree, whereby stockholders were preferred before the creditor, [is] invalid. Id. at 504.

In what would lead to the coining of the expression "fixed principle," the Supreme Court wrote: "[I]n cases like this, the question must be decided according to a *fixed principle,* not leaving the rights of the creditors to depend upon the balancing of evidence as to whether, on the day of sale, the property was insufficient to pay prior encumbrances." Id. at 507 (emphasis added). And with that, the "fixed principle"—now known as the absolute priority rule—was established. Through the early 1900s, the Supreme Court continued to apply this principle in equity receivership cases. Moreover, the Supreme Court reinforced the importance of the "fixed principle," recognizing that this basic tenet should be strictly applied. * * *

[A] a plan is not "fair and equitable" if a class of creditors that is junior to the class of unsecured creditors receives debtor's property because of its ownership interest in the debtor while the allowed claims of the class of unsecured creditors have not been paid in full. Applying these plain requirements to the instant case, it is clear that (1) the Equity Interest Holders hold a claim junior to the Unsecured

Creditors; (2) under the Plan, the Equity Interest Holders will receive property of Debtor (by way of New Warrants) because of their ownership interest in Debtor; and (3) the Unsecured Creditors' allowed claims will not be satisfied in full. Under these circumstances, the Plan violates §1129(b)(2)(B)(ii) and is not "fair and equitable" with respect to the Unsecured Creditors. * * *

Even if the plain meaning of §1129(B)(2)(B)(ii) were not evident, the available legislative history demonstrates that Congress did not intend for the Bankruptcy Code to allow a senior class to sacrifice its distribution to a junior class when a dissenting intervening class had not been fully compensated. Congress anticipated, but ultimately rejected, this possibility.

The Senate Report written prior to the Bankruptcy Code's enactment proposed that a senior creditor be permitted to alter its distribution for the benefit of stockholders under the "fair and equitable" doctrine. Later, Representative Don Edwards and Senator Dennis DeConcini-key legislators of the Bankruptcy Code-explicitly rejected this example. Both Representative Edwards and Senator DeConcini stated that "[c]ontrary to the example contained in the Senate report, a senior class will not be able to give up value to a junior class over the dissent of an intervening class unless the intervening class receives the full amount, as opposed to value, of its claims or interests." 124 Cong. Rec. S. 34007 (Oct. 5, 1978) (remarks of Sen. DeConcini); 124 Cong. Rec. H. 32408 (Sept. 28, 1978) (remarks of Rep. Edwards).

Reliance upon statements made by Representative Edwards and Senator DeConcini for a determination of congressional intent is particularly appropriate given the recognition by the Supreme Court that "[b]ecause of the absence of a conference and the key roles played by Representative Edwards and his counterpart floor manager Senator DeConcini, we have treated [Representative Edwards's and Senator DeConcini's] floor statements on the Bankruptcy Reform Act of 1978 as persuasive evidence of congressional intent." Begier v. I.R.S., 496 U.S. 53, 64 n.5 (1990). * * *

Debtor contends that, notwithstanding the text of §1129(b)(2)(B)(ii), the Asbestos PI Claimants may share their proposed distribution with the Equity Interest Holders without violating the absolute priority rule. To support this contention, Debtor relies on Official Unsecured Creditors Committee v. Stern (In re SPM Manufacturing Co.), 984 F.2d 1305 (1st Cir. 1993). Because *SPM* and its progeny have been misread, a full recitation of *SPM's* facts and the First Circuit's rationale is in order.

In *SPM,* a secured lender entered into a "sharing agreement" with general unsecured creditors to share in the proceeds that would result from a debtor's reorganization. The apparent purpose of the agreement was to obtain the cooperation of the unsecured creditors in the debtor's reorganization which, given that the secured lender had a perfected, first security interest in the debtor's assets, would not have inured to the benefit of the unsecured creditors. The reorganization did not work. Instead, the case was converted to a Chapter 7 proceeding, and the debtor's assets were liquidated.

The secured lender and the unsecured creditors then sought to compel the Chapter 7 trustee to distribute proceeds from the sale of debtor's assets in accordance with the sharing agreement. The sharing agreement provided for the distribution of proceeds from the sale of the debtor's assets to the unsecured creditors, ahead of the priority tax creditors in apparent contravention of the Bankruptcy Code's statutory scheme for distribution. The bankruptcy court disagreed and, relying upon its equitable powers under §105(a), ordered the trustee to distribute the portion of the proceeds due to the unsecured creditors under the sharing agreement in accordance with the distribution scheme embodied by the Bankruptcy Code, i.e., priority tax creditors should be paid ahead of the unsecured creditors. After the district court affirmed the bankruptcy court's decision, the Court of Appeals reversed.

The question before the First Circuit, which is relevant here, was "whether an order compelling [the secured lender] to pay [to the trustee] from monies realized under its secured interest the amount required by the [Sharing] Agreement to be paid to [the unsecured creditors] is within the equitable powers of the bankruptcy court." Id. at 1311. The Court answered this question in the negative.

First, the Court recognized that the secured lender was entitled to the entire proceeds of the debtor's assets under its lien, whether or not there was a sharing agreement. "Because [the secured lender's] claim absorbed all of [the company's] assets, there was nothing left for any other creditor in this case." "The 'siphoning' of the money to general, unsecured creditors came entirely from the [distribution] belonging to the [secured lender], to which no one else had any claim of right under the Bankruptcy Code."

Second, the secured lender only shared its proceeds *after* the estate property had been distributed. Hence, the sharing agreement had no effect on distributions to other creditors. Even without the agreement between the secured lender and the unsecured creditors, the secured lender would have received the entire allotted distribution under the reorganization plan while the tax creditors would have received nothing. "While the debtor and the trustee are not allowed to pay non-priority creditors ahead of priority creditors [from property of the estate], creditors are generally free to do whatever they wish with the bankruptcy dividends they receive, including to share them with other creditors." Id. at 1313. (internal citation omitted).

SPM is inapposite to the instant case for several reasons. First, the distribution in *SPM* occurred in a Chapter 7 proceeding, where the sweep of §1129(b)(B)(ii) does not reach. Moreover, the unsecured creditors in *SPM,* rather than being deprived of a distribution, were receiving a distribution ahead of priority. Therefore, the teachings of the absolute priority rule-which prevents a junior class from receiving a distribution ahead of the unsecured creditor class-are not applicable.

Second, the secured lender in *SPM* held a perfected, first security interest in all of the debtor's assets, with the exception of certain real estate. Although the agreement between the secured lender and the unsecured creditors implicated property of the estate, the property was not subject to distribution under the Bankruptcy Code's priority scheme. In fact, as the First Circuit recognized, the distribution scheme under the Bankruptcy Code, is not implicated "until all valid liens on the property are satisfied." Id. at 1312.

Third, rather than viewing a distribution of the debtor's property in contravention to the Bankruptcy Code's distribution scheme, the sharing agreement approved in *SPM* may be more properly construed as an ordinary "carve out." . . . Unlike the Debtor in the instant case, the secured lender in *SPM* had a substantive right to dispose of its property, including the right to share the proceeds subject to its lien with other classes.*.*.*

Bluntly put, no amount of legal creativity or counsel's incantation to general notions of equity or to any supposed policy favoring reorganizations over liquidation supports judicial rewriting of the Bankruptcy Code. Accordingly, the New Warrants distribution to the Equity Interest Holders under the Fourth Amended Reorganization Plan violates §1129(b)(2)(B)(ii). The Plan, therefore, cannot be confirmed.

NOTES

13A.6. In *LaSalle Street*, the Court found that the failure to use market mechanisms doomed the debtor's plan of reorganization. The Court did not actually reach the question whether equity can participate by contributing new value even in satisfaction of a market test. This question will arise, presumably, if a court is asked to confirm a plan with a new-value contribution and, despite an open process, no one has topped old equity's offer for the new equity but a creditor class objects nonetheless and moves for the debtor's liquidation.

13A.7. In his dissent to the majority opinion in *LaSalle Street*, Justice John Paul Stevens stresses the fact that the creditor did not challenge the court's valuation. If the valuations are accurate, the creditor is already receiving more than the debtor's assets are worth. In this case it would seem that the creditor is holding up debtor's equity investors. Such a holdup is possible in this case because of the tax benefit the equity holders enjoy if they remain as owners. Problems 13A-3 through 13A-6 ask you to consider more generally potential holdup strategies after *LaSalle Street*.

13A.8. *Armtrong* distinguished *SPM* by noting that the sharing agreement in the latter case was to be executed after the bankruptcy distribution. This seems a thin reed on which to hang a decision, even in part. The sharing agreement in *SPM*, like that in *Armstrong*, was designed to purchase the consent of a junior class that might otherwise block a reorganization plan. If the rule that prohibits class skipping has any justification, at least where valuation is not disputed, it must be to prevent just that sort of bargain. The objective is not to protect the bypassed class ex post, but the senior class ex ante, which under such rule might not be coerced into the arrangement in the first place.

13A.9. Although not addressed directly in *Armstrong*, the objection to distributions that skip a class may simply be an objection to the determination that the share for the junior class comes out of the distribution properly owed to the senior, rather than the intermediate, class. Problem 13A-7 asks you to contemplate this possibility. As you do, consider what tools a court could employ to prevent in the first instance the holdup power that the class skipping distribution is purported to remedy and consider too whether it will be commonly the case that a class skipping distribution will truly buy peace for the reorganization plan rather than substitute one objecting class for another.

PROBLEMS

13A-3. Debtor Corporation is a dinner theater in the suburbs of a large city. Manager is the sole shareholder. He had only a modest career in Hollywood, but his gregarious good nature has allowed him to develop many contacts with famous entertainers. He is able to persuade many of them to appear at the dinner theater, but construction cost overruns and lackluster ticket sales lead Debtor to file for bankruptcy under Chapter 11. Bank has a security interest in all of Debtor's assets, both tangible and intangible. It is owed $10 million. A number of trade creditors are owed a total of $4 million. During the reorganization, Debtor's assets are appraised at $5-$6 million. Debtor has no long-term contract with Manager, who has made it clear that he will continue to run the dinner theater only if he owns the equity.

Manager proposes a plan of reorganization. Manager has found Investor, who is willing to invest $6 million cash in the business. Manager will put up $2 million of his own money, also in cash. Under the plan, Bank will receive a one-time cash payment of $7 million. The remaining $1 million will be reinvested in the business. The general creditors will receive a $1 million note, secured by all of Debtor's assets. Investor will take an unsecured $6 million note, and Manager will retain the equity.

The bankruptcy judge terminates the exclusivity period and Bank files a plan in which it proposes that the assets be sold at auction. Bank tells the court that at the auction Bank will make a cash bid of $10 million. Under this plan, the proceeds will be distributed first to pay administrative expenses and the like, which are negligible, then according to the dictates of absolute priority.

Can the bankruptcy judge confirm the first plan over Bank's objection? Can the court confirm the second plan over the objection of Manager and the general creditors? Assume in each case that there are no defects in terms not presented here. If both plans can be confirmed, how does the bankruptcy judge choose between them? See Kham & Nate's Shoes No. 2, Inc. v. First Bank, 908 F.2d 1351, 1360 (7th Cir. 1990).

13A-4. Computers Corporation is the parent company of two wholly owned subsidiaries, Software Corporation and Hardware Corporation. Entrepreneur is the sole shareholder of the parent. Software steadily loses money and Bank becomes worried about its $100,000 unsecured loan to Software. Bank's concern stems from the fact that Software leases its space and equipment, all from Hardware, and owns only a single valuable asset, a software program. After an extensive search, Bank has located a buyer who will pay $50,000 for the program. Bank encourages Software to sell before the software becomes obsolete and worthless. Bank, who is at this time Software's sole significant creditor, would take most of the $50,000 proceeds and then move to gain the unpaid remainder from Hardware, which has guaranteed Bank's loan to Software. Entrepreneur replies that she believes the program can be tweaked and thus will be worth much more despite recent setbacks. She says that she believes Software can be saved and declines Bank's request on behalf of her corporate affiliate.

As Bank prepares to declare its loan in default, Entrepreneur orchestrates the following set of simultaneous transactions. Hardware sells Software the formerly leased equipment for $200,000, the fair market value. Software pays $10,000 down on this equipment with cash newly borrowed on an unsecured basis from Finance Company, which is also a lender to Hardware. After receiving the cash, Hardware accepts Software's unsecured obligation for the remainder of the purchase price. Software files for bankruptcy under Chapter 11 and immediately files a reorganization plan. The plan places Bank, Hardware, and Finance Company into the same class. Each is to receive a new ten-year note with a principal amount equal to its claim and an interest rate barely above the market rate for the industry's lowest risk borrowers. Entrepreneur is to contribute $10,000 in cash in exchange for all the equity in the reorganized debtor. The cash will go immediately upon confirmation to pay administrative expenses in full and all the claims in a small administrative-convenience class at ninety cents on the dollar. Everyone but Bank will vote for the plan. Assuming the plan has no defect in terms not presented here, can court confirm the plan over Bank's objection? Why do you suppose Bank objects, particularly given Hardware's guarantee of Bank's loan?

13A-5. Debtor Corporation is subject to $10 million of Debt, $100,000 to the holder of a claim secured by collateral worth $95,000, and $9.9 million to an unsecured creditor. Debtor files for bankruptcy under Chapter 11. Debtor's managers assess that Debtor's business as a going concern is worth $9.9 million. Within Debtor's exclusivity period, the managers file a plan that calls for them to contribute $100,000 in cash for the reorganized Debtor's new equity. Under the plan, the secured creditor would receive $95,000 in cash and would relinquish its deficiency claim. The unsecured creditor would receive a new promissory note with a slightly reduced principal, an extended maturity, and a higher interest rate, each as compared to its claim. The managers seek confirmation of Debtor's plan before the exclusivity period expires, without an open market test for their contribution. The secured creditor accepts this plan. The unsecured creditor does not. Can the court confirm this plan assuming that the court accepts the managers' valuation? Might your answer change if the managers assessed Debtor's value at $10.1 million instead of at $9.9 million, raised the principal on the new note to the amount of the unsecured creditor's claim, and withdrew their $100,000 contribution? Assume that the plan is otherwise the same and assume again that the secured creditor accepts while the unsecured creditor objects.

In connection with this problem, consider Barry E. Adler, The Emergence of Markets in Chapter 11: A Small Step on *North LaSalle Street*, 8 S. Ct. Econ. Rev. 1 (2000); Douglas G. Baird and Robert K. Rasmussen, *Boyd*'s Legacy and Blackstone's Ghost, 1999 S. Ct. Rev. 393.

13A-6. Debtor is a limited partnership whose only asset consists of a single parcel of real estate. Bank is owed $100 million and holds a nonrecourse mortgage on the real estate. Various unsecured creditors are owed $1 million. The bankruptcy judge has found that the parcel is worth $60 million. The debtor contemplates a plan that gives Bank a ten-year note for $60 million secured by a lien on the real estate. Bank's deficiency claim is put in a class by itself and paid $4 million on plan confirmation. The claims of the general creditors are put in a separate class. They are to be paid $100,000 in cash on plan confirmation. The general creditors, suppliers with an ongoing relationship with Debtor, will vote in favor of the plan. The old equity retains its equity interest in return for a cash contribution of $4.1 million. The case is filed in a jurisdiction that follows *Woodbrook*, which appears earlier in this section of the book.

Bank is convinced that the judge has underestimated the value of the real estate and that within a few year Debtor will turn around and sell the parcel for $100 million or even more. Bank knows that Debtor's plan is vulnerable under *LaSalle Street*, but does not want to spend a year in Chapter 11 given the volatility of the real estate market. What other options does Bank have? Consider §1111(b)(2).

13A-7. Debtor Corp., a heavy-equipment manufacturing concern, is a wholly owned subsidiary of Holding Inc. Debtor owes Holding $100 million, an obligation secured by all of Debtor's assets, including inventory, receivables, and intangibles. Debtor is also subject to debt of $100 million on senior but unsecured bonds and of $100 million on junior unsecured bonds. Deeply insolvent, Debtor files for bankruptcy under Chapter 11, where it initially seeks to distribute all its assets to Holding. Shortly thereafter, Equipment Acquisition Corp. purchases on the open market (for a nominal sum) virtually all of Debtor's junior bonds and seeks to block the distribution. After some negotiating with Acquisition, Debtor files a bankruptcy plan under which Debtor and Holding would merge into Newco, a wholly owned subsidiary of Acquisition, "to achieve a unique synergy" between Debtor's assets and those of Acquisition. In exchange, Holding share-holders would receive $105 million, $10 million of which will be paid by a "carve out" of the return on Holding's claim, which the plan describes as "undersecured by any measure." As a class, holders of the senior bonds object. They argue that Debtor's assets are worth more than $100 million in liquidation and that there is no synergy between Debtor and Acquisition, just a scheme to deprive the senior bondhold-ers of their just return. What result? What reaction should the senior bondholders have to an argument by Holding that without the carve out Acquisition could hold up the reorganization process and any attempt to preserve Debtor's going concern value?

(4) BEST-INTERESTS TEST

There is one more hurdle a plan must overcome after it has satis-fied the class-based and other miscellaneous requirements for confir-mation. Section 1129(a)(7) allows each holder of a claim or interest in an impaired class to insist on receiving "property of a value, as of the effective date of the plan, that is not less than the amount that such holder would so receive or retain if the debtor were liquidated" under Chapter 7. This requirement is known as the best-interests test.

As we have seen, the absolute priority rule of §1129(b) generally provides a class its priority not only in the debtor's liquidation value but in its going-concern value as well. Hence, §1129(a)(7) protects the individual claimholder when the class as a whole favors the plan. Even in the typical case, not every member of a class has the same objectives. When individual holders of claims or interests dissent from their class, the best-interests test provides access to a judicial determination of a bedrock entitlement, the amount (though not nec-essarily in cash) each holder would have received in liquidation.

The liquidation entitlement is not arbitrary. It roughly reflects what each creditor or interest holder would have expected to receive had bankruptcy not intervened and prevented individual creditors from using their nonbankruptcy remedies of foreclosure or levy. Chapter 11 is justified largely by its capacity to preserve a debtor's going-concern surplus, the amount by which the firm's value as a whole exceeds the sum of its parts. The best-interests test can be seen as recognition that achievement of this goal need not and should not require any creditor or equity holder to accept less than the return it would have enjoyed absent reorganization.

The exercises below explore whether and to what extent the best-interests test works as designed. Consider both whether the test is sufficient to protect every member of a class and whether the test sometimes serves the class as a whole as opposed to merely a dissenter. The case that follows, *Crowthers McCall*, along with the related note and problem touch on issues that arise in practice.

Key Provision: Bankruptcy Code §1129(a)(7)

EXERCISES

13A(10) Just before Debtor Corporation filed for bankruptcy under Chapter 11, it defaulted on three identical obligations to three unsecured creditors. Each obligation carries a prepayment fee, which entitles the holder not only to the principal plus accrued interest upon default but also to an additional sum measured by the difference between the obligation's contractual interest rate and the prevailing market interest rate upon default. Debtor's reorganization plan places each of the three obligations in the same class and proposes to compensate each creditor with new shares in the reorganized Debtor. These shares are worth approximately the amount of each claim's principal and accrued interest.

Two of the creditors, tired of the reorganization process, agree to such a plan. The third believes that Debtor is worth about as much liquidated as reorganized and considers raising an objection. It wants to obtain compensation as well for the prepayment fee. This amount would be substantial given the current low interest rates. Is the third creditor's objection well advised?

13A(11) For many years, Debtor Corporation had many assets and few debts. During this period, Debtor borrowed substantial sums from various creditors on an unsecured basis at a low interest rate. In recent years, Debtor's value has declined steadily and its debts increased. While still solvent but under cash-flow pressures, Debtor files for bankruptcy under Chapter 11. After a little more than a year in bankruptcy, Debtor raises new funds and proposes a reorganization plan. All claims are placed in a single class. The plan provides for curing all defaults, reinstating the original maturity dates, and otherwise honoring all their terms. Debtor would emerge from bankruptcy still solvent but highly leveraged. The court considers it more probable than not that Debtor will thrive under its new capital structure.

Almost all of the creditors are happy that the bankruptcy case is nearing an end. One creditor, with a single small claim, however, would like to fight on and demand better terms or liquidation of the Debtor, which the creditor believes would provide a higher return than the plan. Can the plan be confirmed over the sole objection of this creditor? Assume, for the purposes of this question, that classification is proper. In answering the question compare Exercise 13A(5) and consider, among other provisions, §1124.

13A(12) Debtor Corporation files for bankruptcy under Chapter 11 and proposes a reorganization plan. Under the plan, Debtor would issue new equity interests to Debtor's secured creditors and would pay every allowed unsecured claim twenty-five cents on the dollar in cash as of the reorganization's effective date. No holder of a prebankruptcy equity interest would receive any property under the plan. The secured creditors accept the plan but the unsecured creditors do not. The unsecured creditors argue not that the plan overcompensates the secured creditors but that Debtor is worth more in liquidation than reorganized as a going concern. Can the unsecured creditors succeed in their objection? If so, on what basis?

CASE

IN RE CROWTHERS McCALL PATTERN, INC.

United States Bankruptcy Court, S.D. New York, 1990
120 Bankr. 279

BUSCHMAN, BANKRUPTCY JUDGE.

* * * The Debtor manufactures and sells, largely through dealer-distributors, home sewing patterns for women's, men's, and children's garments and "soft" crafts. Although the market has declined somewhat since 1976, the Debtor's share has grown to 35.7%. It has two principal competitors in the United States and limited competition from abroad. * * *

Section 1129(a)(7)(A)(ii) speaks of a comparison between plan values on the effective date and those to be hypothetically received were the Debtor liquidated "on such date." An overly literal reading of these words would indicate that Congress intended comparison with a fire sale taking only one day. We strongly doubt that this is what Congress intended. Section 704, in setting forth the duties of a Chapter 7 trustee, contains no such intimation. Rather it permits a trustee with court approval to continue to operate a business for a limited time, and speaks in terms of flexibility requiring a trustee to "collect and reduce to money the property of the estate ... and close such estate as expeditiously as is compatible with the best interests of parties in interest." [§704(a)(1)]. * * *

Here, it would appear that an orderly liquidation, through retaining a small staff to ship out, as ordered, the inventory remaining at the Debtor's premises, to order, perhaps, the printing of additional copies of catalogues necessary to sell that inventory, and to take care of the myriad of other tasks necessary to winding down the business would be the path a prudent trustee would take in satisfying his duty of maximizing a distribution to creditors.

The industry in which the Debtor operates is fairly oligarchic in nature. The Debtor has a 35.7% market share and only two principal competitors. This is not a case where a restaurant has closed and a trustee needs to immediately sell furniture in order to avoid an additional month's rent or where the supply of goods in established stores outstrips whatever demand may remain for the debtor's product. To be sure, the patterns are seasonal in nature because the garments that can be made from them are seasonal in nature. And to be sure, styles do change and some patterns are discarded in recognition of changing styles. But there is no indication that competition could step in immediately to service the demand for the Debtor's patterns evidenced by its market share or that those patterns cannot be liquidated in an orderly fashion rather than in a fire sale. It is with these notions in mind that the Debtor's assets are to be evaluated.

In calculating an estimated realizable value of the Debtor's assets in a Chapter 7 liquidation, the Disclosure Statement itemizes various assets and calculates a liquidation value of $35.46 million on the basis of various assumptions. Two mistakes are admitted: cash should be reduced by $168,000, and trade receivables should be reduced by $669,000 because of the erroneous inclusion of a receivable from shareholders which is separately listed. In other respects, the valuation of trade receivables at $14,667,000 ($15.33 million stated in the Liquidation Analysis less $669,000), or roughly 75% of book value, appears to be reasonable even though the Debtor has a bad debt reserve of 0.5%, in light of the general difficulties bankruptcy trustees have in collecting receivables.

1. Inventory

More material is the dispute concerning the value of the Debtor's inventory. Of its book value of net inventory of $9.504 million, the Debtor's books reflect a book value of raw materials of $1.178 million, reduced by 50% in liquidation. This appears to be reasonable; perhaps a buyer might pay 60% of book value. For its $501,000 book value of work in process, the Debtor assigns no value in liquidation. This also appears to be reasonable. Generally, a trustee might realize 10-15% of work-in-process, or $50,100 to $75,150. Partially completed patterns for specific designs would not appear to have any market.

It is in valuing the Debtor's finished goods inventory that the parties sharply clash. That inventory consists of 6.3 million patterns located at the Debtor's facilities in Manhattan, Kansas and about 20 million patterns held by dealers on behalf of the Debtor on "standing debit" or a consignment basis.

These finished goods have a book value of $8,280,000. In the Liquidation Analysis, it is estimated that in a Chapter 7 liquidation, $3.6 million would be realizable from the finished pattern inventory held by McCall's dealers at 15 cents per pattern or 45% of cost. No value was given to the completed patterns located at the Manhattan, Kansas facility, although the only difference between the field inventory and the retained inventory is location.

In justifying a value of 15 cents per pattern for patterns held by dealers and a "best case" value of 20% of wholesale, the author of the Liquidation Analysis stated that he assumed that liquidation entailed flooding the market with patterns, and asserts that the "best deal" the Debtor could make with respect to inventory held by dealers leaving the pattern business was 20% of wholesale, He added that chain stores have sometimes discounted patterns up to 80%, or to less than wholesale. In justifying no value for patterns held on its own premises, he stated that these patterns may not be covered by the current catalogue and cannot be sold otherwise.

As noted above, the first of these assertions does not appear to be plausible with respect to this Debtor and the market in which it holds a 35.7% share. Nor does the absence of catalogues appear to justify a zero value for some 6.3 million patterns located on the Debtor's premises. Since the Debtor does not retain dated or discarded patterns, these patterns are current. The Debtor's current catalogue consists primarily of pages from former catalogues with new pages concerning new patterns inserted. On this record, it would appear that the retained patterns are largely reflected in the current catalogue. No reason has been advanced why additional copies could not be printed if needed or why dealers would not continue to obtain patterns, albeit at a discount.

That stores have sometimes discounted patterns is also of little significance. This is a Debtor which projects $2.7 million of net after tax income for 1991. That projection is totally inconsistent with any notion of widespread discounting by retailers to a price below wholesale.

Nor can it be said that prior instances of dealer liquidation provide much assistance in evaluating the Debtor's inventory. Prior liquidation history is a strong indication of liquidation value. But the liquidations referred to here are of dealers discontinuing their pattern lines presumably because of lack of success. In such instances, a lower value is to be expected. Under consideration here, however, is the orderly liquidation of the Debtor, a successful entity whose patterns command a significant market share and could be liquidated through successful dealers or direct sales to stores. That history does not appear to be of much weight here.

Of greater weight is that in liquidation, a significant amount of merchandise might be returned, demand for the Debtor's patterns will likely diminish, and that discounts will be given. John Erickson, an accountant having great familiarity with liquidations in Chapter 7, testified that an orderly liquidation usually results in receipt of 25% to 70% of wholesale value. At a $3 per pattern wholesale price, these values translate into a range of $19,725,000 to $55,230,000 for all of the Debtor's pattern inventory.

On the basis of the entire record it appears that the most probable orderly liquidation value of this inventory lies between 45% and 55% of wholesale. The factors noted above, and added shipping, packing and possible additional catalogue costs relating to the Kansas inventory, indicate that higher amounts are likely not achievable. The nature of this industry and the Debtor's role in it indicate that lower amounts are inappropriate. We thus find the orderly liquidation value of the Debtor's finished goods inventory ranges between $35.505 million and $43.395 million.

2. Cabinets

To store its inventory with dealers, the Debtor owns approximately 20,000 (or perhaps 24,000) cabinets. The Liquidation Analysis gives them no value. The Debtor has, however, sold some cabinets to dealers at $5 to $10 each. With this history, a zero value is inappropriate. Instead, they should be valued at $100,000 to $200,000.

3. Machinery and Equipment

According to the Disclosure Statement, these items are carried at $5.153 million net on the Debtor's books, and valued at $0.87 million on the Liquidation Analysis. This figure concerns only an envelope press, guide press and shelving. The other machinery and equipment, i.e., tissue presses and folding machines, were believed to be scrap upon liquidation and valued at zero. Most of the machinery and equipment is described as highly specialized, as very old and having an original basis of $7 million, and of value only on a going concern basis. * * *.

In light of the special competitive posture of this industry, however, valuation of this machinery and equipment should reflect a value for the specialized tissue presses and folding machines notwithstanding their age. Were the Debtor liquidated, it would appear that competitors will desire this equipment in order to increase their own market share. The age of the equipment may reduce the price, but not to scrap value. The higher value of 20% of book value, or $1.4 million, testified to is more reasonable and accepted here.

4. Leasehold Improvements and Building

Having a book value of $3.056 million, the Debtor assigns a liquidation value of $926,000 to its leasehold improvements at its New York offices (book value $1.4 million) and Manhattan, Kansas premises. It justifies this 30% valuation on the basis of the specialized nature of the improvements and their consequent lack of significant value to a new tenant. Erickson testified that receipt of 30% to 40% of book value for leasehold improvements is acceptable. There is no factual basis on this record to differ with the Debtor's assessment.

Nor is there any basis to criticize the Debtor's valuation of its leases for its Manhattan, Kansas, plant and its New York offices at nil. Although these leases have several years to run, particularly the

Kansas plant lease which can be extended to 2005, there is no dispute that the rent is at or above market value for long-term leases. Thus, there would be little incentive for a prospective assignee to pay a premium when it would pay the same, or perhaps less, rent if it dealt with the landlords.

5. "Construction in Progress"

Carried, according to the Disclosure Statement, at $1.207 million on the Debtor's books and evaluated as $0.525 million (or 43% of the book value) in the Debtor's Liquidation Analysis, this item consists of various partially completed asset projects that are located mostly in Kansas and partly in New York. That figure was chosen, presuming a semi-completed state that would not be completed, and relying on prior consultation with counsel. Erickson viewed a 50% realization as possibly a bit high with regard to the Kansas project but assumed the estate would receive some proceeds from the New York project.

Although the 43% of book value employed in the Liquidation Analysis is arbitrary, it is not unreasonably low and may in fact be overstated. These projects apparently relate to the leased premises in New York and Kansas. Unless packaged with the leases or, at least, with sale of the leasehold improvements, the opportunity for realizing value would appear to be low. Since the leases themselves are at market value, there does not appear to be significant opportunity to sell these projects.

6. Goodwill and Intangibles

The Debtor's books and records carry goodwill and intangibles at $48,297,000. Of this amount, $45 million is attributed to goodwill. No value was attributed to goodwill and intangibles in the Debtor's Liquidation Analysis.

The principal assets falling in this category are (a) the Debtor's perpetual rights, pursuant to contract, to use the trademark "McCall" in connection with the sewing pattern industry, (b) license agreements with certain well-known fashion design houses enabling the Debtor to sell garment designs, (c) distribution contracts relating to the sale of the Debtor's products in certain foreign markets, (d) computer software, (e) the Debtor's greeting division and other items such as a fashion magazine and subscription and customer lists.

At the confirmation hearing, the author of the Liquidation Analysis changed his testimony to state that in the best case, some $4 to $5 million might be received in liquidation on the sale of the limited right to use the trademark. He had earlier testified that the name had no value, not even to the Debtor's competitors.

The name "McCall" is long established in the home sewing industry. The "target market" of individuals making garments at home "is difficult to reach through standard, mass-media advertising." Thus, the name has a value.

One of the difficulties in establishing value on the basis of the hypothetical liquidation referred to in §1129(a)(7)(A)(ii) is that the liquidation is just that—hypothetical. The exercise assumes a state of facts inconsistent with a debtor's present prospects as a going concern.

[The opponent of the plan], in contending that the value of the name "McCall" can be calculated on the basis that a competitor would purchase the name, assumes that the buyer would pick up the Debtor's market share through using the name, and attempts to value the name, calculated at $33.5 to $37.7 million, on the basis of the present value of the resulting hypothetical income stream to each of the Debtor's two principal competitors. This set of assumptions shows the danger in selective valuation of intangible assets. The valuation ignores that other intangibles such as marketing skills, quality, consistency, and advertising programs in combination with a recognized name, may account for market share. Legion are the instances where a company having a well-recognized name tinkered with its product to the detriment of market share and product acceptability. It simply cannot be said that, were the Debtor liquidated and the name purchased, the purchaser would ipso facto obtain the Debtor's market share. Moreover, new entrants may emerge and other competition may increase their market shares.

The name "McCall" has value but its value in isolation of other nonsaleable factors such as those mentioned above is limited. In that light, a range of $4 to $5 million is reasonable.

The author of the Disclosure Statement also changed his testimony to value its license agreements "in the best case" at $900,000 but believes that that amount will not be obtained in liquidation. These two-year agreements with Laura Ashley, CP Shades, The GAP, Raggedy Ann and other recognized names have an average remaining term of one year. They are automatically renewable unless cancelled by either party. Products sold under those agreements generated $8.4 million net sales in 1989.

[G]iven that they have only one year remaining subject to renewal rights, if any, a valuation of $700,000 to $900,000 appears appropriate. * * *

The Debtor's greeting card division appears to have some value. Revenues are $400,000 to $500,000 per year. After a loss in 1989, it may break even in 1990. Perhaps someone who wanted to take the risk of growing the business in these recessionary times would pay $100,000 to $200,000 at most. Perhaps not. The sum is not material. For purposes of this analysis we assign it a value of $100,000.

In total, . . . these amounts indicate that the value of the Debtor's assets for purposes of §1129(a)(7)(A)(ii) ranges between $71,600,000 and $81,500,000.

Valuation, however, is not an exact science, nor is it a product of mere calculation. It is an imprecise tool, perhaps the best we currently have, designed to reach a calculated decision on the basis of the hypotheses and assumptions in light of a set of facts. To be sure, the command of §1129(a)(7)(A)(ii) is perhaps the strongest protection creditors have in Chapter 11. Nonassenting creditors are to be given in a plan not less than they would receive in a Chapter 7 liquidation. The judgment is to be made on the basis of "evidence, not assumptions." In re Northeast Dairy Co-op. Fed'n, Inc., 73 Bankr. 239, 253 (Bankr. N.D.N.Y. 1987). But the exercise is hypothetical and valuation evidence is often replete with assumptions and judgments. For example, a simple appraisal of a house is based on the assumption that the real estate market will not shift in the period that it will take to sell the house and the judgment that comparable properties are truly comparable. The judgments made here are on the basis of assumptions regarding the desirability of various assets principally to the Debtor's main competitors in a fairly oligarchic but declining market of which the Debtor commands a 35.7% share in light of the evidence pertaining to those assets.

[The opponent of the plan] contends that the Debtor has not met its burden of proof in that it did not contact those competitors and its customers in order to learn of the price they would pay for various assets in a hypothetical liquidation and asserts that the Debtor should have produced appraisal evidence. Expressions of hypothetical offers might be of interest but it is readily apparent that no such evidence should be required. It is hard to envision anything more inimical to a plan based on a debtor's continuance as a going concern or, as here, a plan grounded on the sale of the debtor as a going concern. To inject into the marketplace the notion that a debtor might liquidate, even hypothetically, may sow the seed of its own destruction. Customers may consider alternatives, competitors may pounce, employees might seek more secure positions. Section 1129(a)(7)(A)(ii), in charging the Court with making the determination that nonassenting creditors will receive the same or more under a plan than they would in a Chapter 7 liquidation, does not require the hypothesis to become a possible reality.

Nor should appraisal testimony be the sine qua non of compliance with the best interests of creditors test codified in §1129(a)(7)(A)(ii) in a case such as this. Albeit, generally such evidence should be presented, but the market for this Debtor's assets is narrow, consisting of (i) its principal competition who may desire its machinery and equipment, its trademark and its agreements with fashion design houses, (ii) its dealers and their customers who may desire its completed patterns; and (iii) a few others who might desire its leasehold improvements and construction in progress. It is highly doubtful that a general appraiser could testify meaningfully as to at least the first two of these topics. This case is not the ordinary case involving a debtor having assets that are commonly liquidated and with which an appraiser would have familiarity.

More persuasive than the absence of an appraisal in this case is that this Debtor has been shopped extensively. * * *

[The bid that the Debtor ultimately received for the firm as a going concern] strongly supports, given the hypothetical nature of the exercise, the liquidation value range of $71,600,000 to $81,500,000 that we have found through independent analysis of each material category of assets. * * * [Although this amount is greater than that given in the Disclosure Statement, it is not so much that the plan opponents would receive more in liquidation than under the plan.]

For all the foregoing reasons, we hold the §1129(a)(7)(A)(ii) has been satisfied. * * *

NOTE

13A.10. The opinion in *Crowthers McCall* clearly sets out the nature of a hypothetical liquidation for the purposes of §1129(a)(7). The standard is a piecemeal liquidation where a trustee on behalf of each creditor that would foreclose or levy on an item of property takes reasonable efforts to obtain a high sales price. As the case illustrates, this standard is not easy to apply in practice. In principle, however, it approximately matches the best-interests entitlement to the return that the creditor (or interest holder) would have expected, on average, had liquidation resulted from a creditors race outside of bankruptcy (with any sale proceeds in excess of a claim returned to the debtor). In Problem 13A-8, we pursue the question whether a creditor can argue that it should be entitled to any portion of a firm's going-concern value under §1129(a)(7).

PROBLEM

13A-8. After years of economic decline, Debtor Corporation has largely, though not completely, righted itself and is now a viable enterprise. The managers are Debtor's largest shareholders and have relationships with Debtor's clients that are crucial to the business. Debtor would lose much of its value as a going concern if they left. The past has taken its toll, however, and Debtor finds itself insolvent.

Debtor's managers seek to renegotiate the debt. With the help of major creditors, a workout would be either privately executed or proposed as a prepackaged reorganization plan. If necessary, the plan could be run quickly through Chapter 11 to deal with any holdouts. The managers first approach Bank, Debtor's biggest creditor. Bank holds one quarter by amount of Debtor's outstanding obligations, all of which are unsecured. The managers suggest a plan in which the creditors scale back their debt and take in return 80 percent of the equity. The managers insist, however, on retaining day-to-day control of Debtor's operations.

Bank puts forward a counteroffer. Under Bank's proposal Debtor's creditors would ratably divide 95 percent of Debtor's equity. Debtor's current shareholders would receive the remaining 5 percent. The managers would also commit to specified changes in Debtor's business. Bank believes that these changes would improve productivity. These negotiations eventually collapse. Bank declines the managers' counteroffer, citing its well-cultivated reputation as a fair lender but one not to be taken lightly by a greedy borrower.

Debtor files for bankruptcy under Chapter 11 and promptly proposes a reorganization plan that would provide the unsecured creditor class with 80 percent of the reorganized Debtor's new equity. The managers would retain the rest. The managers then seek acceptance from Debtor's varied creditors, who, unlike Bank, are unconcerned about any effect the outcome in the case may have on their reputation. The managers convey their intent to engage in a scorched-earth policy, under which they will work tirelessly for confirmation of this plan, during and after the exclusivity period, regardless of the direct or indirect costs to Debtor. What is the likely outcome of the case? Would your answer change if the best-interests test allowed each individual creditor to insist on its full measure of absolute priority? Would your answer change if, under the plan, the entire firm were sold as a going concern to third party for cash?

B. TRANSNATIONAL BANKRUPTCY

The United States Constitution entrusts the federal government with the power to establish "uniform laws on the subject of bankruptcies throughout the United States." Article I, Section 8. The Constitution also takes away from states the corresponding power to impair "the obligation of contracts." Article I, Section 10. Even in the eighteenth century, debtors held assets and had creditors in several jurisdictions. The framers recognized the usefulness of a single forum in which a debtor's rights and obligations could be sorted out under one set of uniform rules. The same problem arises today for firms having assets and creditors both in this country and abroad, but no treaties exist to ensure that transnational bankruptcies are resolved coherently.

In the United States, Chapter 15 of the Bankruptcy Code, created by the 2005 Bankruptcy Act , replaces §304 and provides for the administration of cases ancillary to foreign proceedings. This Chapter, based on the Model Law on Cross Border Insolvency, permits an American bankruptcy court to recede and serve as an adjunct to a foreign case, enjoining actions in the United States and relinquishing control of the debtor's assets to the foreign proceeding. But Chapter 15, like §304 before it, fails to offer clear direction to an American court on when to step aside. There is a presumption of validity for a petition by a foreign representative in a duly initiated foreign proceeding. See §1516. And recognition of the foreign proceeding under that presumption invokes the automatic stay against creditor collection. See §1520. But §1507 states that the bankruptcy court should offer "additional assistance" to the foreign proceeding only after considering a number of factors such as whether the foreign distribution scheme is "substantially in accordance" with that in the United States, whether the foreign proceeding is fair and convenient to claim holders in the United States, and, where applicable, whether the foreign law affords an individual debtor a fresh start. See also §1522. There is no algorithm for the court to follow in combining these factors. Nothing in United States law, moreover, can affect the treatment of American interests in other countries, not all of which will have laws that similarly respect United States process.

Even seemingly straightforward conflicts over priority alone may be difficult to resolve, regardless of a court's good intentions. In Russia, for example, workers are ordinarily entitled to be paid all their back wages before secured creditors receive anything. In the United States, back wages are afforded a limited priority among unsecured claims but are inferior to secured claims. See §§725, 726, and 507. Imagine that a debtor firm has plants in both countries and nationals of each country work at both plants. If a bankruptcy petition is filed in both jurisdictions, there is no easy way to decide how to treat the workers. A court in either country could find that all the workers at the plant in the United States lack priority for unpaid wages, regardless of nationality. Alternatively, a court could find that only Russian nationals are entitled to priority, regardless of where they work. Or the bankruptcy court in Russia might give all the workers priority with respect to all the assets under the court's control, regardless of the workers' nationality or where they worked. The bankruptcy court in the United States might forbid any workers over whom it has jurisdiction from asserting priority in a Russian court. It is even possible that the bankruptcy court in one of the countries might find that the bankruptcy laws of the other should apply in their entirety on the ground that the other country was the true "home" of the debtor.

Difficulties only increase when a multinational debtor attempts to reorganize and the issues go beyond mere priority. Consider the absolute priority rule and best-interests test discussed earlier in this chapter. While some countries have similar rules, few, if any, have adopted or will adopt laws that match precisely. Thus, whether a plan can be *effectively* confirmed in a United States or a foreign court may depend both on the highly specific confirmation rules in each country and on whether the conflict of law rules in each country apply the substantive laws of the same jurisdiction. This last determination, moreover, may depend on whether the priority scheme established in bankruptcy law alone, as opposed to general commercial law, is considered a procedural or a substantive rule.

The material below offers a sense of the problems that multinational debtors face as they attempt to reorganize. The exercise asks you to consider basic plan-confirmation questions under the laws of different jurisdictions. The case that follows, *Maxwell Communications*, arose from the Maxwell Communication reorganization. In that case the court grapples with the problem of deciding whether to entertain a preference action in the United States. The assets in question were located in the United States, but the debtor's principal place of business and the creditors were located in Great Britain. In reading the opinion, as well as the related notes and problem, you should consider both how well the court confronts the issues before it and whether the court's methodology is likely to work well when applied to other controversies. Consider too, whether the analysis in the case would be different under new Chapter 15 of the Bankruptcy Code.

Key Provisions: Bankruptcy Code §§1501 et seq.

EXERCISES

13B(1) Debtor is a Canadian corporation that manufactures appliances mainly in Canada, financed for the most part by Canadian shareholders and creditors. Debtor does produce a key component in the United States, where Debtor employs numerous United States nationals. Debtor becomes insolvent and files for bankruptcy under Chapter 11. Canadian Bank is Debtor's largest creditor and hopes to reorganize Debtor quickly or seek its liquidation. Because Canadian law does not permit quite the extended reorganization process common in Chapter 11, Bank files an involuntary petition against Debtor in Canada. A representative of the Canadian court asks that the United States bankruptcy court administer the case as one merely ancillary to the Canadian process. Will the American court comply? What are the likely consequences if it does not?

13B(2) Debtor is a Delaware corporation that manufactures automobiles and automobile components in both Russia and the United States. Substantial assets and the holders of significant claims are located in each country. Debtor is cash starved and insolvent. It files for bankruptcy under Chapter 11. Debtor also files the case in the Russian courts. Debtor files a reorganization plan in the United States. The plan separately classifies the claims of Russian workers and provides for those claims with shares in the reorganized Debtor. Given the opportunity, more than three-fourths of the Russian workers would accept the reorganization plan, which qualifies for confirmation under United States law. Russian law, however, would require that such a plan pay all wage claims in cash in full. As a result, were this plan under Russian law alone, a court there would require a sale of Debtor's assets. The sale would likely lead to a piecemeal liquidation.

Will the United States bankruptcy court defer to Russian law if asked? Would a Russian court defer to United States law if Russia followed American comity principles? Would your answer depend on whether the shares the Russian workers are to receive reflect an interest in Debtor worth at least the amount of the workers' claims? Would it affect your answer that the shares are to be traded on the New York Stock Exchange? What would be the consequences if the American and Russian courts reached different substantive determinations on confirmation?

CASE

MAXWELL COMMUNICATION CORP. v. SOCIÈTÈ GÈNÈRALE

United States Court of Appeals, Second Circuit, 1996
93 F.3d 1036

CARDAMONE, CIRCUIT JUDGE.

The demise of the late British media magnate Robert Maxwell and that of the corporation bearing his name, the Maxwell Communication Corporation, followed a similar and scandalous path, spawning civil and criminal litigation in England and around the world. This case illustrates that some positive consequences have resulted from these parallel demises. From Maxwell's mysterious death, which forced his international corporation into bankruptcy, was born a unique judicial administration of the debtor corporation by parallel and cooperative proceedings in the courts of the United States and England aimed at harmonizing the laws of both countries and also aimed at maximizing the benefits to creditors and the prospects of rehabilitation. * * *

The debtor was originally incorporated in England over 60 years ago as a limited company. Robert Maxwell acquired control of this limited company 15 years ago. The following year, the company was re-registered under English law as a public limited company and, in 1987, it became Maxwell Communication Corporation (hereafter Maxwell or the debtor). Before filing for bankruptcy protection, Maxwell functioned as a holding company for Robert Maxwell's "public side" holdings—as distinguished from Maxwell's private holdings, which at one time included the New York Daily News—and controlled a variety of media-related companies. Although Maxwell was headquartered and managed in England and incurred most of its debt there, approximately 80% of its assets were located in the United States, most notably its subsidiaries Macmillan, Inc. and Official Airlines Guide, Inc.

Maxwell alleges that in the fall of 1991, less than 90 days before its Chapter 11 filing, it made several transfers—transfers it now seeks to avoid—to three European banks (collectively, the banks) with whom it had credit arrangements. Two of these banks are Barclays Bank plc (Barclays) and National Westminster Bank plc (National Westminster), both of which have their headquarters in London and maintain an international presence, with branches in New York and elsewhere. The other bank is Société Générale, a French Bank headquartered in Paris with offices, among other places, in London and New York.

From 1985 until 1991 Maxwell obtained credit from Barclays under the terms of a credit arrangement known in England as an "overdraft facility." This written agreement, negotiated in London, stated that any disputes arising under it would be governed by English law. Maxwell drew $30 million under the overdraft facility, none of which had been repaid on November 24, 1991, the agreed-upon maturity date. Two days later, under pressure from Barclays' banking director in London, Maxwell repaid the $30 million from the proceeds of the sale of Que Computer Books, Inc. (Que), a subsidiary of Macmillan in New York. The Que proceeds had originally been deposited in a Maxwell account at the New York branch of National Westminster and subsequently credited to Maxwell's U.S. dollar account with National Westminster in London. On November 26, 1991 repayment was effected by transferring $30 million from Maxwell's dollar account in London to Barclays' New York branch, which was then credited the following day against the balance in the appropriate Maxwell overdraft account at Barclays in London. In addition to this transfer from the Que proceeds, Maxwell alleged in its amended complaint that 11 other transfers of funds were made to Barclays during the 90 days preceding Maxwell's bankruptcy filing, amounting to a total of £2,110,970 (net of various payments by Barclays to or on behalf of Maxwell during the same period). No connection between these other transfers and the United States was alleged in the complaint.

National Westminster's relationship with the debtor began in the 1930s and continued through the bankruptcy filing. As of late 1991 Maxwell maintained several accounts with National Westminster, with overdraft facilities to help it meet its cash needs. These arrangements were similar to those it had with Barclays in that they were negotiated in England and provided for the governance of English law. In October 1991 Maxwell received $145 million from the sale of Macmillan Directories, Inc. (another Macmillan subsidiary in the United States) and used the proceeds—which had been paid into a Maxwell account at Citibank in New York and thereafter credited to an account at Citibank in London—to purchase British pounds. Maxwell then applied the £15 million from these proceeds to an account it maintained at National Westminster's London branch. Maxwell then applied the £15 million to satisfy an overdraft balance with National Westminster.

In November 1991 Maxwell converted a portion of the $157.5 million of Que proceeds (originally deposited in National Westminster's New York branch but then transferred to its London branch) into £27.5 million. It used this sum to cover its overdraft balances in National Westminster's London branch. The purchase of pounds sterling and subsequent credits to the National Westminster overdraft accounts occurred in London. Maxwell also alleges it made eight other transfers to National Westminster from accounts at Midland Bank in London shortly before Maxwell's bankruptcy filing, payments which amounted £29,046,738 (net of payments by National Westminster to Maxwell during the same period).

Société Générale also extended credit to Maxwell under an agreement negotiated and administered in England. On October 7, 1991, in satisfaction of principal and interest on a $10 million loan extended under that credit arrangement, Maxwell made a payment of roughly £5.765 million to Société Générale. The funds were transferred from an account Maxwell maintained at Marine Midland Bank in London to Société Générale's London branch. Although the debtor did not allege that the transfer was connected to the United States, the district court assumed for purposes of its decision that the funds came from the sale of Macmillan Directories because that sale also occurred on October 7, 1991.

On December 16, 1991 Maxwell filed a petition for reorganization under Chapter 11 in the Bankruptcy Court for the Southern District of New York. The next day, it petitioned the High Court of Justice in London for an administration order. Administration, introduced by the Insolvency Act 1986, is the closest equivalent in British law to Chapter 11 relief. Acting under the terms of the Insolvency Act, Justice Hoffman, then of the High Court (now a member of the House of Lords), appointed members of the London office of the accounting firm of Price Waterhouse as administrators to manage the affairs and property of the corporation.

Simultaneous proceedings in different countries, especially in multi-party cases like bankruptcies, can naturally lead to inconsistencies and conflicts. To minimize such problems, Judge Brozman appointed Richard A. Gitlin, Esq. as examiner, pursuant to §1104(c), in the Chapter 11 proceedings. The order of appointment required the examiner, inter alia, to investigate the debtor's financial condition, to function as a mediator among the various parties, and to "act to harmonize, for the benefit of all of [Maxwell's] creditors and stockholders and other parties in interest, [Maxwell's] United States Chapter 11 case and [Maxwell's] United Kingdom administration case so as to maximize [the] prospects for rehabilitation and reorganization."

Judge Brozman and Justice Hoffman subsequently authorized the examiner and the administrators to coordinate their efforts pursuant to a so-called Protocol, an agreement between the examiner and the administrators. In approving the Protocol, Judge Brozman recognized the English administrators as the corporate governance of the debtor-in-possession. As the bankruptcy judge later explained, this recognition was motivated not only by the need for coordination but also because Maxwell was "incorporated in England and run ... by [Maxwell] executives out of Maxwell House in London subject to the direction of an English board of directors." Justice Hoffman reciprocated, granting the examiner leave to appear before the High Court in England. * * *

The administrators, the examiner, and other interested parties worked together to produce a common system for reorganizing Maxwell by disposing of assets as going concerns and distributing the proceeds to creditors. The mechanism for accomplishing this is embodied in a plan of reorganization and a scheme of arrangement, which are interdependent documents and were filed by the administrators in the United States and English courts respectively.

The reorganization plan incorporates the scheme and makes it binding on Maxwell and its creditors. The plan and scheme thus constitute a single and integrated system for realizing the value of Maxwell's assets and paying its creditors. As was set forth in a letter from the administrators to Maxwell's creditors, the proposal was to pay in full all holders of secured claims and of claims enjoying preferential status under United States or English law. The plan and scheme treat all of Maxwell's assets as a single pool and leave them under Maxwell's control for distribution to claimants. They allow any creditor to submit a claim in either jurisdiction. And, in addition to overcoming many of the substantive differences in the insolvency laws of the two jurisdictions, the plan and scheme resolve many procedural differences, such as the time limits for submitting claims.

Following the requisite creditor voting in the United States and England, the plan was approved in the United States and the scheme was approved in England. Judge Brozman entered an order confirming the plan—and, by implication, the scheme incorporated therein—on July 14, 1993. Justice Hoffman thereafter entered an order sanctioning the scheme under §425 of the Companies Act 1985 on July 21, 1993. Barclays, National Westminster, and Société Générale each filed a notice of claim with the administrators, seeking pro rata distributions on various unsecured claims against Maxwell.

Despite the unusual degree of cooperation and reconciliation of the laws of the two forums, the plan and scheme predictably did not resolve all the problems that might arise from the concurrent proceedings. For example, these documents did not specify which substantive law would govern the resolution of disputed claims by creditors. More importantly, they did not address the instant dispute regarding the debtor's ability to set aside prepetition transfers to certain creditors.

In July 1992 Barclays faced the possibility that the administrators would institute litigation in the bankruptcy court to recover the $30 million it had received from Maxwell on November 26, 1991. Barclays therefore obtained an ex parte order in the High Court (not from Justice Hoffman) barring the commencement of such an action. In seeking to prevent litigation in the bankruptcy court, Barclays was apparently motivated by a difference in the American and British "avoidance" rules. Rules governing avoidance generally allow the estate to recover certain prepetition transfers of property to creditors occurring within a defined period of time. Such rules are sometimes referred to as the law of preferences because such transfers, left unchecked, may put transferees in a better position than other creditors if the debtor becomes insolvent.

Thus, under §547(b), a trustee may avoid certain transfers to outside creditors made within 90 days before the filing of the petition.

The corresponding provision in English law is §239 of the Insolvency Act 1986. That section is in many respects similar to the American law, but the British law imposes an additional condition—it limits avoidance to those situations where placing the transferee in a better position was something the debtor intended. This seemingly innocuous subjective intent requirement in English law apparently would be a significant or insurmountable obstacle for the administrators were they to litigate the preferences question in London under English law. For obvious reasons, they opposed the anti-suit injunction sought by Barclays, that is, they wanted this issue litigated in the Southern District bankruptcy court.

Following a hearing, Justice Hoffman vacated the ex parte order Barclays had obtained. The British judge declined to interfere with the American court's determination of the reach of our avoidance law. He cited the British presumption that in such a situation the foreign judge is normally in the best position to decide whether proceedings are to go forward in the foreign court, and the rule that anti-suit injunctions will issue only where an assertion of jurisdiction in the foreign court would be "unconscionable."

In so doing, Justice Hoffman noted the cooperative course of the parallel insolvency proceedings. He distinguished recent cases involving the extraterritorial application of American antitrust law, reasoning that injunctive relief is available only if it appears that a foreign court is likely to assert jurisdiction in a manner "contrary to accepted principles of international law." The High Court's decision did not pass judgment on the merits of whether the application of American law would violate such norms. It did assume, however, that the bankruptcy court would dismiss the anticipated suit if it found that there was an insufficient connection with the United States. This ruling was affirmed by the Court of Appeal, and leave for further review by the House of Lords was denied.

Freed from the constraints of an anti-suit injunction, the administrators commenced adversary proceedings in the bankruptcy court against Barclays, National Westminster, and Société Générale. The complaints sought the recovery of the above-described transfers to the banks on the theory that they were avoidable preferences under §547(b) and therefore recoverable under §550(a)(1). * * *

Defendants filed motions for dismissal. . . . The bankruptcy court granted the motions, holding that the transfers were extraterritorial and that the Bankruptcy Code does not apply to these transfers, whose "center of gravity" lies outside the United States and, in the alternative, that international comity precluded the application of the Code in this instance.

Treating comity as a "canon of statutory construction," the bankruptcy court emphasized choice-of-law principles and asked "which jurisdiction's laws and policies are implicated to the greatest extent." The answer, the court found, was England. It also noted Maxwell's insolvency did not jeopardize United States interests because its holdings were sold as going businesses, because most of its creditors were not residents of the United States, and because the two countries' preference laws in any event serve similar ends, and that England had a greater interest in applying its own laws. * * *.

The district court affirmed on both the extraterritoriality and comity grounds. * * *

Maxwell and the examiner appealed. * * *

Analysis of comity often begins with the definition proffered by Justice Gray in Hilton v. Guyot, 159 U.S. 113, 163-64 (1895):

> "Comity," in the legal sense, is neither a matter of absolute obligation, on the one hand, nor of mere courtesy and good will, upon the other. But it is the recognition which one nation allows within its territory to the legislative, executive or judicial acts of another nation, having due regard both to international duty and convenience, and to the rights of its own citizens or of other persons who are under the protection of its laws.

Although *Hilton* addressed the degree to which a foreign judgment is conclusive in a court of the United States, the principle expressed is one of broad application.

Whether a court is applying the common law, as in *Hilton*, or applying a statute enacted by Congress, as in the present case, "[i]nternational law, [including] questions arising under what is usually called private international law, or the conflict of laws, and concerning the rights of persons within the territory and dominion of one nation, by reason of acts, private or public, done within the dominions of another nation—is part of our law." *Hilton*, 159 U.S. at 163. The doctrine does not impose a limitation on the sovereign power to enact laws applicable to conduct occurring abroad. Instead, it guides our interpretation of statutes that might otherwise be read to apply to such conduct. When construing a statute, the doctrine of international comity is best understood as a guide where the issues to be resolved are entangled in international relations.

In Murray v. The Charming Betsy, 6 U.S. (2 Cranch) 64 (1804), Chief Justice Marshall said that a statute "ought never to be construed to violate the law of nations, if any other possible construction remains." And, as Judge Learned Hand observed in United States v. Aluminum Co. (Alcoa), 148 F.2d 416, 443 (2d Cir. 1945), "we are not to read general words ... without regard to the limitations customarily observed by nations upon the exercise of their powers; limitations which generally correspond to those fixed by the 'Conflict of Laws.' " * * *

Because Congress legislates against a backdrop that includes those international norms that guide comity analysis, absent a contrary legislative direction the doctrine may properly be used to interpret any statute. * * *

The examiner contends the doctrine is inapplicable to the present case because Congress has "conclusively resolved" whether the preference law applies "by legislative direction." Although such a direction would obviously make it easier to decide this case, the examiner has not pointed us to a statutory section that supports his contention. Instead, he relies on §103(a), which simply states that the provisions of Chapter 5 of the Bankruptcy Code, including §547 and §502(d), "apply in a case under [Chapter 11]." But §103(a) contains only "general words," which we have held must be read with regard to the traditional limitations states impose on the exercise of their power to prescribe laws. * * *

We move next to plaintiffs' argument that the use of the doctrine is improper because there is no conflict between the Bankruptcy Code and English law. International comity comes into play only when there is a true conflict between American law and that of a foreign jurisdiction. Plaintiffs maintain there is no true conflict between American and English avoidance rules because English law does not require conduct that violates American law. They insist, in addition, that the English courts' decision not to enjoin the debtor's estate from bringing the instant avoidance action against Barclays suggests there is no conflict between the two countries' laws. These propositions are unpersuasive. We believe there is a true conflict necessitating the application of comity principles to ascertain the compass of the Code. * * *

[A] conflict between two avoidance rules exists if it is impossible to distribute the debtor's assets in a manner consistent with both rules. Second, although our allusions to English law should not be understood as an attempt to prejudice the outcome of any future litigation on that subject in British courts, the parties in the present actions have assumed that the "intent" requirement in the English law would dictate a different distributional outcome than would United States law. Consequently, it is not possible to comply with the rules of both forums and the threshold requirement of a true conflict exists for purposes of comity analysis. * * *

England has a much closer connection to these disputes than does the United States. The debtor and most of its creditors—not only the beneficiaries of the prepetition transfers—are British. Maxwell was incorporated under the laws of England, largely controlled by British nationals, governed by a British board of directors, and managed in London by British executives. These connecting factors indicated what the bankruptcy judge called the "Englishness" of the debtor, which was one reason for recognizing the administrators—who are officers of the High Court—as Maxwell's corporate governance. These same factors, particularly the fact that most of Maxwell's debt was incurred in England, show that England has the strongest connection to the present litigation.

Although an avoidance action concededly affects creditors other than the transferee, because scrutiny of the transfer is at the heart of such a suit it is assuredly most relevant that the transfers in this case related primarily to England. The $30 million received by Barclays came from an account at National Westminster in London and, while it was routed through Barclays' New York branch like all payments received in U.S. dollars, it was immediately credited to an overdraft account maintained in England. Plaintiffs claim no particular United States connection to the other alleged transfers to Barclays, all of which were denominated in the amended complaint in pounds sterling. Similarly, the transfers to National Westminster and Société Générale were made to and from accounts maintained in Great Britain.

Further, the overdraft facilities and other credit transactions between the transferee banks and the debtor resulted from negotiations that took place in England and were administered primarily there. English law applied to the resolution of disputes arising under such agreements. We recognize that some of the money transferred to the banks came from the proceeds of the sale of Maxwell subsidiaries in the United States, which is a subject we discuss in a moment. In almost all other respects, however, the credit transactions were centered in London and the fund transfers occurred there. * * *

Virtually the only factor linking the transfers to the United States—that the sale of certain Maxwell subsidiaries in the United States provided the source of some of the funds—is not particularly weighty because those companies were sold as going concerns. Hence, the potential effect that such sales might have had on local economies is not here implicated.

The examiner warns that dire consequences would result from a failure to enforce the Code's avoidance provision. The first one he mentions is that such a course ignores §103(a). This contention is one we have already addressed and rejected. The examiner next urges that the purposes underlying §547 and §502(d) would be thwarted unless both of these provisions were applied in all Chapter 11 proceedings. Although the non-application of these or other Bankruptcy Code provisions certainly might detract from the Code's policies in other cases, here the negative effects are insubstantial. The principal policies underlying the Code's avoidance provisions are equal distribution to creditors and preserving the value of the estate through the discouragement of aggressive prepetition tactics causing dismemberment of the debtor. These policies are effectuated, although in a somewhat different way, by the provisions' British counterpart.

In the present case, in which there is a parallel insolvency proceeding taking place in another country, failure to apply §547 and §502(d) does not free creditors from the constraints of avoidance law, nor does it severely undercut the policy of equal distribution. All avoidance laws are necessarily limited in scope because time limits and other conditions are imposed on the voidability of transactions. Although a different result might be warranted were there no parallel proceeding in England—and, hence, no alternative mechanism for voiding preferences—we cannot say the United States has a significant interest in applying its avoidance law. Moreover, as noted, international comity is a policy that Congress expressly made part of the Bankruptcy Code, and a decision consistent with comity therefore furthers the Code's policy.

Because of the strong British connection to the present dispute, it follows that England has a stronger interest than the United States in applying its own avoidance law to these actions. Its law implicates that country's interest in promoting what Parliament apparently viewed as the appropriate compromise between equality of distribution and other important commercial interests, for instance, ensuring potentially insolvent debtors' ability to secure essential ongoing financing. In addition, although complexity in the conduct of transnational insolvencies makes choice-of-law prognostication imprecise, we agree with the lower courts that English law could have been expected to apply. * * *

In addition to the relative strength of the respective jurisdictional interests of England and the United States, there is a compelling systemic interest pointing in this instance against the application of the Bankruptcy Code. These parallel proceedings in the English and American courts have resulted in a high level of international cooperation and a significant degree of harmonization of the laws of the two countries. The affected parties agreed to the plan and scheme despite differences in the two nations' bankruptcy laws. The distribution mechanism established by them—beyond addressing some of the most obvious substantive and procedural incongruities—allowed Maxwell's assets to be pooled together and sold as going concerns, maximizing the return to creditors. And, by not requiring a creditor to file its claim in both forums, the arrangement eliminated many of the inefficiencies usually attendant in multi-jurisdiction proceedings.

Taken together, these accomplishments—which, we think, are attributable in large measure to the cooperation between the two courts overseeing the dual proceedings—are well worth preserving and advancing. . . . Where a dispute involving conflicting avoidance laws arises in the context of parallel bankruptcy proceedings that have already achieved substantial reconciliation between the two sets of laws, comity argues decidedly against the risk of derailing that cooperation by the selfish application of our law to circumstances touching more directly upon the interests of another forum. * * *

Although comity analysis admittedly does not yield the commercial predictability that might eventually be achieved through uniform rules, it permits the courts to reach workable solutions and to overcome some of the problems of a disordered international system. Given that the scheme and plan in this case did not clearly address the choice-of-law and choice-of-forum questions that have generated this litigation, resort to comity and choice-of-law principles should naturally have been foreseen. Consequently, the interests of the affected forums and the mutual interest of all nations in smoothly functioning international law counsel against the application of United States law in the present case. * * *

NOTES

13B.1. When a legal dispute spans two jurisdictions, a court faces two distinct questions. First, it must decide whether to hear the case at all. If it decides to hear the case, it must then decide whether to apply its law or the law of the other jurisdiction. When presented with a two-party contract, a court can simply defer to the wishes of the parties as expressed in the contract with respect to both questions. One might imagine that the matter could be as simple in a bankruptcy case, at least for a corporate debtor. Each jurisdiction might treat the jurisdiction of incorporation as dispositive on choice of law, just as courts in the United States treat the jurisdiction of incorporation as dispositive over questions of a corporation's internal affairs. Bankruptcy law, however, is not limited merely to a corporation's internal affairs. Instead, bankruptcy law in the United States and elsewhere contains explicit and implicit regulations of a debtor's activity. Indeed, the very structure of a bankruptcy reorganization process, as in the United States, can be seen as a regulation designed to maximize the opportunity of a debtor's continued operation despite the objection of creditors or any prior promise by the debtor to comply with creditor wishes. Thus, any bankruptcy court must ask what interests it is charged with protecting as well as whether there is a coherent way to implement its charge across many cases. As *Maxwell* illustrates, this is not easy.

13B.2. The court in *Maxwell* recognizes the connection between a jurisdiction's bankruptcy law and the effects of corporate insolvency on the communities governed within that jurisdiction. But the court rejects the notion that this connection supported application of United States preference law in the case:

> Virtually the only factor linking the transfers to the United States—that the sale of certain Maxwell subsidiaries in the United States provided the source of some of the funds—is not particularly weighty because those companies were sold as going concerns. Hence, the potential effect that such sales might have had on local economies is not here implicated.

This conclusion, however, neglects the potentially detrimental incentives that lax preference laws might create in advance of a sale. Problem 13B asks you to consider such incentives.

13B.3. Although, with the adoption of Chapter 15 of the Bankruptcy Code, the law on transnational bankruptcy has changed in the United States, the issues discussed in *Maxwell* remain constant. Considerations of comity, central to the decision of *Maxwell*, extend beyond specific statutory language.

PROBLEM

13B. Designer is the sole shareholder and chief officer of Debtor Corporation, which produces and sells designer clothes in the United States and in England. Debtor is insolvent and owes substantial funds both to English Bank and to American Suppliers. Bank actively monitors all its borrowers. It examines each of its debtors' books every quarter. If a payment from a debtor is late, Bank immediately scrutinizes the debtor and, frequently, calls its entire loan. Such a call in Debtor's case would force Debtor into bankruptcy. After an ordinary quarterly inspection, Bank becomes concerned about Debtor's affairs and, as permitted by the loan agreement, requests repayment of a portion of the loan within two months. As this deadline approaches, Designer has Debtor cut corners on its fall line, damaging Debtor's goodwill with its customers but allowing Debtor to pay Bank. A few weeks after the failure of the fall line, Suppliers cut off credit to Debtor. Debtor then files for bankruptcy in England. Suppliers file an involuntary case against Debtor in the United States. As the cases progress, all involved, and both bankruptcy courts, agree to sell Debtor's business as a going concern. The purchaser will continue operations in both countries, though substantially scaled back because dissatisfaction with Debtor's fall line has eliminated its market in high-end merchandise.

Debtor's bankruptcy trustee seeks to recover as a preferential transfer money Debtor paid Bank within ninety days of Debtor's bankruptcy petition. Bank argues that English law should apply and that it should not have to repay the money because Debtor was unaware that its payment to Bank would ultimately prove preferential. Designer testifies to this effect, noting that he simply "paid the bills as they came due" and had assumed that Debtor would "weather the storm and pay all bills." Should United States or English law apply? How might events have unfolded had Bank at all relevant times assumed application of United States law? Compare Problems 8D-3 and 8D-4. In connection with this problem and its general topic, see Robert K. Rasmussen, Resolving Transnational Insolvencies through Private Ordering, 98 Mich. L. Rev. 2252 (2000); Lucian A. Bebchuk and Andrew T. Guzman, An Economic Analysis of Transnational Bankruptcies, 42 J. L. & Econ. 775 (1999).

C. RESPONSIBILITIES OF PROFESSIONALS

Issues of professional responsibility in Chapter 11 are often similar to those outside, but in bankruptcy the issues can become more difficult and less tractable. First, every lawyer must ensure that the client is aware of the risks in every legal proceeding. A Chapter 11 lawyer should also make sure the debtor is aware of its chances if only to ensure that the remaining assets are not swallowed up by legal fees. This concern arises frequently when family-run businesses use Chapter 11. Second, even when it is clear that the attempt to reorganize is worthwhile, the lawyer must decide whose interests she represents among the varied corporate constituents. The potential for conflicts of interest is great, especially when the lawyer works for a large firm and the debtor is a large corporation.

On the issue of feasibility, quite apart from the difficulties inherent in justifying the law as it exists, the grim record of all but large firms in Chapter 11 should sound a note of caution. The debtor's lawyer must assess to some extent the debtor's chances of reorganizing successfully. If nothing else, the lawyer should be certain that the benefits of attempting to reorganize (or the benefits from delaying debt collection efforts) are at least worth the fees thereby incurred. Even in the case of a small, family-run business such as a restaurant, the lawyer's fee usually exacted up front, will run at least five figures. If a debtor's business is almost certain to fail anyway, creditors will be unhappy with this fee and will object. Even if the family equity owners are willing to pay the bill, the lawyer should advise them that the debtor's most valuable asset may be the family's own expertise, an asset that the family can take away whether the corporate debtor reorganizes or liquidates. The money needed in any effort to keep the existing business afloat may be better used starting a new one. In any event, the debtor should be made aware of what the future is likely to hold.

For a small-business reorganization to succeed, the debtor's business venture itself must be fundamentally sound. If the firm is not at least generating a positive cash flow—if it is not able to meet its day-to-day operating expenses—then the lawyer should ask whether it will ever be able to do so. Even if the debtor is able to meet its operating expenses, those in control of the firm must be willing and able to make the changes that will allow it to survive over the long term. These changes frequently include getting rid of an ineffective manager. Sometimes, this manager is one of the firm's shareholders. This person may be the son or daughter of the firm's founder who has none of the energy or business sense that made the company succeed in the first instance. More to the point, this manager may be the very person who hired the lawyer to represent the debtor. Sometimes ownership of the firm can remain in the family only if this person steps aside and lets someone else run the firm.

Most small firms in Chapter 11 need new cash to reorganize successfully. In many cases, the old shareholders are the only plausible source. The cash is needed to pay not only the lawyer's fee but also the other costs of the bankruptcy. In most cases, cash is also needed to pay the general creditors a large enough part of their claim so that they are willing to vote in favor of a reorganization plan. Moreover, many businesses in financial distress need to overhaul their operations or buy new equipment or, as just noted, bring in new managers. These, too, require capital. If the firm needs new capital to survive Chapter 11, the shareholders should confront the problem early. Again, too many owners of small businesses learn too late that one of the marks of successful entrepreneurs is knowing when to cut their losses.

The small businesses that succeed after a Chapter 11 reorganization are typically those in which the major creditors are cooperating (save perhaps for a lone holdout). To survive after bankruptcy, a business will typically need someone to finance the accounts receivable and sell it new supplies. The old creditors have no obligation to extend new credit or sell new supplies to the firm after it leaves bankruptcy, yet their willingness to do so may be essential if the firm is to succeed. Reaching an accord with the major creditors is especially important to the individuals involved if the debtor's equity owners have personally guaranteed the loan to the firm and put up the family home as collateral.

In some cases, especially when the firm is small, the lawyer will come on the scene too late. For example, those who run small firms sometimes postpone the inevitable with money the debtor was obligated to withhold for the Internal Revenue Service or to pay as state sales tax. These obligations, even in the case of small firms, often amount to tens or hundreds of thousands of dollars. These taxes typically must be paid in full in any plan of reorganization and, even though the debtor may have done business in corporate form, the government often will be able to collect the tax from, and perhaps criminally prosecute, the firm's owners.

When a debtor is larger, a lawyer's role as a business advisor may diminish somewhat. Sophisticated managers of sizeable enterprises tend to understand what it will take to keep a concern afloat. Still, there is a second set of obligations with which counsel must contend: duties of loyalty. A corporate lawyer faces special challenges representing an insolvent firm. When a publicly traded firm is healthy, the shareholders are the residual owners. They are the ones who stand to gain or lose from any particular decision. For this reason, the duties and responsibilities of professionals, such as lawyers, accountants, and investment bankers, ultimately relate back to the interests of the shareholders. Professionals take direction from the managers and directors of a firm. The managers and directors in turn enjoy a large measure of discretion under corporate law. Nevertheless, there are always problems identifying the "client" because of this tension between those who own the firm (the shareholders) and those who speak for it (the directors and managers).

When a firm is insolvent, matters become even more clouded. The residual owner is often hard to identify, and there is support in the case law for the proposition that fiduciary loyalties in an insolvent firm shift to the creditors. The professional continues to take direction from the managers and directors, but creditors occupy the position formerly occupied by shareholders. The managers and directors may not internalize the creditors' concerns in the same way they internalized the shareholders' concerns when the firm was solvent. Nevertheless, the lawyer still takes direction from them in much the same way.

The Bankruptcy Code itself requires that the lawyer's behavior be scrutinized. Bankruptcy judges regularly deny fees to lawyers who fail to cut square corners. The fees of such lawyers, like those of all professionals in a bankruptcy case, are subject to scrutiny under §328. The debtor's lawyer must disclose the amount and source of her fee, generally even when the estate is not going pay the bill. See §329. Fees must be reasonable, regardless of who pays. Moreover, in general, the estate won't pay a debtor's lawyer or a committee's lawyer unless the lawyer is disinterested and neither holds nor represents an interest adverse to the interest of the estate. §328(c).

In many cases, lawyers have had previous relationships with the firm, its principals, or its creditors. Whether these create conflicts is often not clear. Sunlight is the best disinfectant, and disclosure solves many problems. Disclosure is often easier said than done, however, and is not a panacea for all conflicts. When a large law firm represents the debtor in possession, sorting out the relationships among all the members of the firm and all the players in a case may be hard to do, especially on short notice.

The material below requires that you further consider a lawyer's ethical responsibilities. The exercises ask you to work through some of the language in the Bankruptcy Code, while the following case, *Everett*, as well as the related note and problem explore more fully the difficulties inherent in representing a Chapter 11 debtor.

Key Provisions: Bankruptcy Code §§327; 328; 329

EXERCISES

13C(1) After Debtor Corporation files for bankruptcy under Chapter 11, a duly appointed creditors committee hires counsel. The lawyer retained also represents the largest creditor on the committee. At the committee's behest, the lawyer works tirelessly to seek Debtor's liquidation. Debtor is reorganized anyway, and the lawyer submits her request for fees. Will the fees be approved if reasonable in amount? In answering this question consider, among other provisions, §1103(b).

13C(2) Debtor was a small, closely held manufacturer owned by various members of a single family and named after its founder. Lawyer represented Debtor in its unsuccessful effort to reorganize. Just as Lawyer was about to submit her fee application, she discovered that one of her partners once represented a family member, the founder's oldest daughter. The partner helped the daughter set up some routine trusts. Moreover, one of the new associates in the firm guided a college friend, the founder's grandson, through a tax audit. Debtor paid Lawyer's firm directly for the tax work because the audit related to the grandson's ownership interest in Debtor. The $1,500 payment for the tax work came to the firm several months after the tax work was done, two months before Debtor's bankruptcy petition. Before Lawyer took on representation in the bankruptcy reorganization, she ran a routine conflicts check but missed the relationship among the founder and his relatives because the client's last name in each case was not the same as that of the founder. The individual lawyers who did the trusts and tax work, however, did know that their clients were the daughter and grandson of the founder, respectively. Will Lawyer's firm have trouble collecting its fee for the reorganization work?

CASE

EVERETT v. PEREZ

United States Court of Appeals, Ninth Circuit, 1994
30 F.3d 1209

KOZINSKI, CIRCUIT JUDGE.

[This] case arises out of a personal Chapter 11 petition filed by the debtor, Gary Ronald Perez. The estate is not large, and neither is the claim of the objecting creditor, Frank Everett. Nevertheless, the case has generated a fair number of difficult legal issues and more than a little acrimony. Perhaps both consequences are endemic to a legal process so complex and malleable that, as happened here, even experts are led astray.

Perez makes his living buying, renovating and selling income property, and owning and managing two Jimboy's Tacos franchises. He hired Frank Everett to supervise the remodeling of one of the franchises. After the work was completed, the two had a falling out and Everett sued to get paid. Everett won but Perez parried by filing a Chapter 11 petition.

Perez proposed two successive plans of reorganization which the bankruptcy court rejected, the first because it unfairly discriminated against Everett and the second because it did not justify Perez's retained interest. Before us now is Perez's third plan ("Plan III"). As required in Chapter 11 reorganizations, Perez's plan divided the creditors into classes based on the nature of their claim. Perez put governmental units claiming back-taxes in Class I, officers of the estate seeking administrative expenses in Class II and secured creditors in Class III. He then put Everett, along with the six other general unsecured creditors, in Class IV. Because Everett's claim was listed as $30,000, while the sum of the other unsecured claims was $20,400, Everett was the controlling member of the class. As to creditors in Everett's class, Plan III called for a payment of the full amount of their claims over the course of 67 months.

Anxious, no doubt, to put the bankruptcy process behind them, all but one of Perez's creditors—including all the other creditors in Everett's class—voted to approve the plan. Only Everett voted against it, but this was enough to cause his class to reject the plan.

Even so, the bankruptcy court approved Plan III, invoking the Code's cram-down provisions which empower it, in certain closely-defined circumstances, to approve a plan over the objection of a class of creditors. Everett appealed and the Bankruptcy Appellate Panel ("BAP") affirmed in an unpublished disposition.

Undaunted, Everett appeals again, raising several objections to the bankruptcy court's order approving Plan III ...

We conclude that under Plan III Everett was to be paid the face amount of his debt over 67 months without interest. . . . [W]e hold that this renders the plan fatally defective and that the bankruptcy court erred in approving the plan under these circumstances . . .

This case and others like it raise troubling doubts about the efficacy and fairness of our bankruptcy process. Almost five years ago, Everett secured a judgment against Perez for a trade debt. Having hired a lawyer to enforce his rights in state court, he found himself blocked from collecting on the judgment because of federal bankruptcy proceedings. This was no coincidence. Perez's disclosure statement reveals that "the major contributing factor" causing him to file was "the financial difficulties incurred as a result of" Everett's lawsuit and judgment. The bankruptcy then led to more delay, more attorney's fees, more aggravation, while Perez continued operating his business unmolested. Rather than using the opportunity provided by the bankruptcy process to work out a plan for paying his just debts fairly, Perez has now proposed three plans, all of which have proved inadequate for failing to secure Everett's rights. With each step, the day on which Everett will see his money recedes into the distance, while he has had to keep paying a lawyer to represent his interests. The natural reluctance of most creditors to do just that is an incentive for many a debtor to prolong and complicate bankruptcy proceedings. The heavy scent of manipulation is in the air; vigilance on the part of the courts and, most especially, of the lawyers and other professionals hired by the estate, is imperative if the process is to operate fairly.

None of the repeat players in the bankruptcy system have covered themselves with glory in this case. The bankruptcy court and then the BAP approved a plan that violated §1129(b)'s absolute priority rule, delaying final resolution of the case by three years, perhaps more. We are disappointed by the BAP's failure to even address the absolute priority issue and its cursory handling of the other issues presented to it. But we are most disappointed in the estate's counsel, who is responsible for proposing and seeking confirmation of the three failed plans. How to deal with a dissenting creditor who holds the controlling interest in his class is not, after all, that difficult or complicated a matter: The creditor must be bought off, by giving him (and those similarly situated) a sufficient stake in the proposed plan so that they'll be induced to vote yes; or, failing that, the dissenting class must be crammed down—a somewhat complicated procedure but hardly beyond the competence of someone appointed to serve as debtor's counsel.

Counsel for the estate, nevertheless, has now proposed three plans that do not comply with the Code's requirements. He has defended Plan III on appeal before the BAP and before us despite what appears to have been his clear understanding that §1129(b)(2) was not satisfied.[1] This conduct may well have helped Perez as an individual,

---

[1] That counsel was well aware of the statutory requirements for a cram-down is clear from his colloquy with us:

> *Court:* How about a finding pursuant to §1129(b)(2)(B)—that no creditor in a lower class can receive anything until there's been a 100% payment to every creditor in a higher class? . . .
>
> *Counsel:* There is no finding [on that issue].
>
> *Court:* Why isn't that here? . . . Why isn't that in and of itself a basis for reversal? What was the bankruptcy judge doing here?
>
> *Counsel:* You mean because there's no finding?
>
> *Court:* Yes, because there's no finding. I mean, don't we have a statute to work with? I don't understand. You're a bankruptcy practitioner. You knew full well about this problem. I mean you weren't surprised by this? Why wasn't this raised in the bankruptcy court? . . .
>
> *Counsel:* The finding of the bankruptcy court was that the debtor was entitled to a living allowance out of the plan.
>
> *Court:* And he retains the property. When all is said and paid, he will keep the property. And under §1129(b)(2)(B) he is entitled to nothing until everyone in a higher class that's an objecting class gets paid 100 cents on the dollar.
>
> *Counsel:* That's true.
>
> *Court:* And there's no finding to that effect.
>
> *Counsel:* No. There is no finding to that effect.
>
> *Court:* Can you explain that? I mean, these things [the findings of fact and conclusions of law] were prepared by you. The debtor presents the plan. . . .
>
> *Counsel:* Yes, and I omitted the finding with respect to that because it wasn't at issue at any point in the proceedings.

but it's not clear why this benefited the estate or how it satisfied Perez's fiduciary responsibilities.

Counsel for the estate must keep firmly in mind that his client is the estate and not the debtor individually. Counsel has an independent responsibility to determine whether a proposed course of action is likely to benefit the estate or will merely cause delay or produce some other procedural advantage to the debtor. While he must always take his directions from his client, where counsel for the estate develops material doubts about whether a proposed course of action in fact serves the estate's interests, he must seek to persuade his client to take a different course or, failing that, resign. Under no circumstances, however, may the lawyer for a bankruptcy estate pursue a course of action, unless he has determined in good faith and as an exercise of his professional judgment that the course complies with the Bankruptcy Code and serves the best interests of the estate.

We make no finding of wrongdoing here. We simply remind counsel that his responsibility is to help lead the estate on a just, speedy, inexpensive and lawful path out of bankruptcy. Failure to live up to this responsibility may result in a reduction in allowable fees and other sanctions.

NOTE

13C. The debtor in *Everett* was an individual. But the message of the case is clear to any lawyer who represents a debtor in bankruptcy. The lawyer must represent the interest *of the estate*, not of the debtor individually or of a corporate debtor's managers. This principle is easy to state but difficult for a lawyer to follow in practice. Imagine the reaction of a debtor's chief executive after the debtor's lawyer refuses to work on a reorganization plan because, in the lawyer's view, the value of the estate would be maximized under an alternative plan or by liquidation of the debtor. Cases such as *Everett* should make lawyers reluctant to represent debtors when their reorganization has little chance of succeeding and when the principal goal of its managers is to play for time. But as Problem 13C illustrates, the limits of *Everett* are hard to specify.

Court: But isn't it the debtor's responsibility to comply with the statute?

Counsel: Yes.

PROBLEM

13C. Debtor Corporation is a manufacturer of compact disc recorders in a small rural town. Although only recently formed and not as large as its principal competitors, it has quickly become the largest employer in this town. Debtor's business plan called for moderate operating losses for a period of years, followed by substantial profits later as consumers turn more heavily to home digital recording. The direction of technology changes, however. While home digital recording is experiencing significant growth, it is with servers and other computer hard drives, not compact discs.

Debtor files for Chapter 11. Debtor's management wants Debtor to continue in business with an altered manufacturing process and a reorganized capital structure. Debtor's creditors want to liquidate. Debtor's management hires Lawyer to represent Debtor in the bankruptcy case. Lawyer believes that Debtor's assets are worth slightly more sold off to other manufacturers than kept under current management, despite the proposed changes. (Other manufacturers are in a better position to sell Debtor's products in the limited markets where it is likely to have an edge over the dominant technologies.) Lawyer is also aware, however, that the community in which Debtor operates will suffer substantially if Debtor closes down. May Lawyer push vigorously for reorganization? What is likely to happen to Lawyer if she does not?

TABLE OF CASES

Principal cases are in bold type. Non-principal cases are in roman type. References are to Pages.

769

TABLE OF KEY BANKRUPTCY CODE PROVISIONS

---

*

INDEX

ABANDONMENT OF ASSETS
Generally, 36, 467 et seq.
CERCLA compliance, 474
Environmental liabilities, 468, 469
Law compliance requirement, 469
Lien stripping and abandoned property, 580

ABSOLUTE PRIORITY
Generally, 520, 675, 707 et seq.
Corporate reorganizations, 675, 707 et seq.

ABSTENTION
Generally, 79 et seq.
Corporate debtors, 92
Definition, 84
Discretion of court, 84
Involuntary bankruptcies, 95
Workouts, policy favoring, 93

ABUSE PREVENTION
See also Fraud, this index
Bankruptcy planning discharge denial, 610, 612
Credit card debt abuse, 79
Deadbeat jumping, 620
Frequent filers, 57
Presumptive abuse, 80, 81
Successive filings, 127

ACCOUNTS RECEIVABLE
Security interests, 377

ADEQUATE PROTECTION
Automatic stay tension, 35, 418, 428
Definition, 414
Financing the estate, tension, 476
Interest owed secured creditor, 418
Management of estate tension
    Generally, 401, 411 et seq.
    Collateral, necessary, 411, 413
    Nominal values, adequate protection of, 415, 418
Property of estate, 411 et seq.

ADJUSTMENT OF INDIVIDUAL DEBT
See also Chapter 13, this index
Automobile retention, 647, 658
Bifurcation of secured and unsecured claims, 649, 658
Collateral retention, 644 et seq.

ADJUSTMENT OF INDIVIDUAL DEBT—Cont'd
Cramdown, 654, 655
Cramdown, this index
Disposable income projections, 626, 628, 637
Eligibility, 621
Expenses and disposable income projections, 626, 637
General creditors, 625 et seq.
Hanging paragraph, 658
Home mortgages, 644 et seq.
Length of plan, 642
Liens stripping. See Strip Down of Liens, this index
Means test, 642
Projections of income, 642
Reasonably necessary expenses, 642
Secured claims, 644 et seq.
Strip Down of Liens, this index
2005 Act, 626, 628
Unsecured claims, 625 et seq.

ADMINISTRATION OF ESTATE
See Management of Estate, this index

ADMINISTRATIVE EXPENSES
Generally, 494
CERCLA compliance, 502, 513
Costs and expenses, 500
Credit, postpetition, 477, 494
Credit extensions as, 494
Distribution priorities, 36, 523
Environmental regulation compliance, 502, 513
Executory contract assumptions, 506
Insurance policies, 498
Lease payments, postpetition, 506, 514
License royalties, 506, 514
Loans to bankruptcy estate, 477, 494
Periodic license payments, postpetition, 506, 514
Priorities, 36, 523
Royalties, license, 506, 514
Tort claims against estate, 495, 513

ADMINISTRATORS, BANKRUPTCY
Generally, 34

ALIMONY
See Domestic Support Obligations, this index

779

†